FUGITIVE
DEMOCRACY

FUGITIVE
DEMOCRACY

and

OTHER ESSAYS

Sheldon S. Wolin

Edited by
Nicholas Xenos

PRINCETON UNIVERSITY PRESS

PRINCETON AND OXFORD

Published by Princeton University Press, 41 William Street, Princeton, New Jersey 08540

In the United Kingdom: Princeton University Press, 6 Oxford Street, Woodstock, Oxfordshire OX20 1TR

press.princeton.edu

Jacket art courtesy of Shutterstock

"The Destructive Sixties and Postmodern Conservatism" by Sheldon Wolin, from *Reassessing The Sixties: Debating the Political and Cultural Legacy*, edited by Stephen Macedo. Copyright © 1997 by W. W. Norton & Company, Inc. Used by permission of W. W. Norton & Company, Inc.

Library of Congress Cataloging-in-Publication Data

Names: Wolin, Sheldon S., author. | Xenos, Nicholas, 1948- editor.
Title: Fugitive democracy : and other essays / Sheldon S. Wolin ; edited by Nicholas Xenos.
Description: Princeton, New Jersey : Princeton University Press, 2016. | Includes
    bibliographical references and index.
Identifiers: LCCN 2016007796 | ISBN 9780691133645 (hardback)
Subjects: LCSH: Democracy—Philosophy. | Political science—Philosophy. | BISAC:
    POLITICAL SCIENCE / History & Theory. | POLITICAL SCIENCE / Essays. |
    POLITICAL SCIENCE / Civics & Citizenship.
Classification: LCC JC423 .W57 2016 | DDC 321.8—dc23
LC record available at https://lccn.loc.gov/2016007796

British Library Cataloging-in-Publication Data is available

This book has been composed in Minion Pro and News Gothic Std

Printed on acid-free paper. ∞

Printed in the United States of America

10 9 8 7 6 5 4 3 2 1

CONTENTS

PART FOUR ▪ POSTMODERNS

PART FIVE ▪ REVISIONING DEMOCRACY

FOREWORD

IN REVISITING THESE ESSAYS I was struck by the contrast between, on the one hand, the individual theorists singled out for extended discussion and, on the other, my preoccupation with democracy. All of these writers are widely recognized as possessing exceptional, superior minds, able to illuminate the concrete by the abstract, the particular by the systematic. In the extraordinary abilities that set them apart they might be said to constitute an elite. Not coincidentally, their views are in varying degrees either critical of democracy (e.g., Hobbes, Weber), or suspicious (Horkheimer and Adorno), wary (Arendt), or qualified (Marx, Rawls). And, with the exception of Rawls, all were in varying degrees sympathetic to some form of elitism.

Is there an inherent antagonism between the individualism of theory and the commonality of democracy? Should the democrat be suspicious of the theorist, especially when the latter professes to be a "democratic theorist"? A self-described democratic theorist who set out to prescribe the proper form of a democracy; or the essential democratic institutions; or the policies, foreign and domestic, which ought properly to follow might be said to be practicing a version of Rousseau's Great Lawgiver, the inspired one who makes a gift of a comprehensive set of prescriptions for setting the "fundamental" principles and practices which the society and its members ought to "follow." While such a conception of theory contradicts the point of self-government, it also replicates the historical experience of the so-called founding of the American political system. Although Americans are taught that unlike socialist or communist societies, our politics is pragmatic and antitheoretical (= nonideological) the historical actuality is that American politics has been shaped primarily by a constitution that was intended by its framers to embody a theory, an abstract formula for creating a new reality, a certain type of government, a republic, by which the Few could govern the Many while allowing the latter a degree of inclusion (e.g., male whites could vote for the House of Representatives). Perhaps the vaunted "American exceptionalism" might be a reflection of the triumph of theory rather than the beginnings of a democracy.

The principal reason for the bias against democracy, and for the presence of elitist tendencies among the twentieth-century thinkers represented here, was the threat believed to be posed by the modern phenomenon of "mass society" and its alleged complicity to the rise of totalitarian dictatorships. The mass was perceived as irrational, resentful, credulous, manipulable, suspicious of all forms of superiority and difference, and highly susceptible to demagoguery. It was not unusual for intellectuals to characterize the mass as "unthinking," hence their natural enemy, the intellect's "other."

Arguably mass tendencies do exist today in the United States: in the culture of consumption, in the media conglomerates producing popular entertainment and slanted news, and in an increasingly manipulative electoral politics where "hot button issues" (e.g., anti-abortion, anti-immigration) are programmed to elicit the desired reflexes from voters. Above all and especially at election time or in moments of national crisis, a mass is fashioned that is responsive to uncritical forms of patriotism, nationalism, and religiosity.

Considered in the abstract, certain ideas conventionally associated with democracy, such as majority rule, popular sovereignty, and equality, might seem to share a kinship with "massiness" and its connotation of mere undifferentiated numbers and its menace of aggregated power. But thanks to the strategies that have shaped mass consumption and its culture, as well as the electoral and lobbying systems, massiness is now less a menace than a domesticated subject. Long before modern sociologists discovered the mass, our Founding Fathers had anticipated the problem and designed a governmental system to filter, check, and balance any tendencies toward expressing "the industrious and uninformed mass of the people" (James Madison).[1] Thus the constitution's guarded view of democracy was not only a theoretical and a political achievement, but the perpetuation of the antagonism between theory and democracy that is as old as Plato's *Republic*.

Paradoxically, despite the successful construction and marketing of "sameness," ours is also a society driven by growing and increasingly sharp differences reflective of inequalities of wealth, education, and life prospects. These inequalities are not celebrated, for that would be an affront to democratic sentimentalism. However, other types of inequality have been both celebrated and deplored: various and intense allegiances to race, or gender, or ethnicity or sexual orientation, or religious beliefs, each united by difference and protest against the corresponding forms of discriminatory treatment. The consequence is that in arousing and organizing these separate and distinct forms of group-consciousness, elites have made it politically more difficult to form majorities that are both effective and legitimating.

The fact that the "politics of difference" is primarily the achievement of elites, many of whose members are academics, has contributed to the growing tendency in public discussions by both liberals and conservatives to accept elitism as normal in all areas of society and tacitly to legitimate it. This despite the fact that historically, more often than not, apologists for elitism have consistently rejected democracy and depicted elitism as its natural opponent. The ultimate irony was that the administration of George W. Bush, arguably the most anti-democratic and openly elitist since the pre–Civil War era, proclaimed the United States the world's foremost exemplar of democracy and proceeded to prove the point by imposing democracy in Iraq.

Elitism is the claim that special skills are required to operate the major institutions of society and to articulate and represent coherent diversities. These skills are described as demanding and uncommon, hence unattainable except by the few. The production of elites is the business of various institutions whose hallmark is certification through competitiveness and proper grooming. These include law, business, journalism, and graduate schools; the marketplace for competing goods, ideas, and investment; corporate institutions; and the apparatuses of the major parties (internships). The fact that the politics of difference has been primarily the achievement of ideological elites has contributed to the growing tendency in public discourse both in the popular media and more elevated journals of opinion, liberal as well as conservative, to accept elitism as normal in all areas of society and tacitly to legitimate it, even though, historically, elitism has, more often than not, been a persistent opponent of democracy. Hence the incongruity of a public ideology that proclaims the United States is the exemplar of democracy and an actual politics and governance dominated by elites.

As a consequence, equality remains the most contested of all democratic claims. Opponents tend to view it as a euphemism for leveling, for denying the claims of merit, contribution, and achievement. In reality today's democrats often find themselves having to defend differences rather than sameness: for example, to defend university admission programs that reserve a specified number of places for minorities. Most defenders of equality argue that far from championing sameness or denying the existence of differing abilities and contributions, equality acknowledges their presence and contributions while questioning some glaring forms of unfairness. Just how democratic is a system of rewards whereby corporate executives who are being fired are nonetheless given several million dollars in severance pay while workers in highly skilled and socially essential jobs (public school teachers, firefighters, nurses, etc.) barely manage to scratch along? Egalitarians believe, therefore, that the effects of a free enterprise system need to be moderated. This is especially urgent in a society dominated by contemporary capitalism in its corporate and globalizing forms. In the reward system of these versions of competitive society the expectation is that achievement brings power. In a market society this comes down to money—and the resources and influence it is able to command.

It is relevant in this connection to recall that in the midst of all the dire warnings about the demand which global competition would necessarily require of the American worker—hard work, longer hours, weak trade unions— American pundits wrote scornfully of the French and German "welfare" states where workers enjoyed a shorter work week, longer vacations, and relatively easy access to health care. The same pundits did not take note that those societies also registered higher levels of political participation than the United States.

The containment of political democracy is, I believe, intimately connected with the animus against social democracy. The programs launched during the New Deal—minimum wage laws, limits on the hourly work week, social security, empowerment of trade unions, government programs for employing the unemployed—combined with vigorous government regulation of business practices and of financial markets, marked the realization that the egalitarian potential of political democracy had to be complemented by social democracy, that programs of social democracy are necessary to counter the inherent structure of a capitalist economy to produce growing inequalities, not as an unintended consequence but as essential to capital's modus operandi. Perhaps opponents of social democracy should welcome it for its conservative effects. Social democracy brings to society generally and to the political system contributions that serve to soften the potential radicalism of political democracy. All contribute, all benefit, and all have a stake. By promoting public education, social security, and expanded health care, social democracy helps to mitigate the divisiveness of wealth, race, ethnicity, and other potentially explosive identities. It promotes a commonality of shared contributions and benefits that encourages a moderate, rather than an enraged, form of majority rule. While democratic political groups operate within the constraints of a constitutional structure designed to constrain democratizing movements and of a center-to-right politics defined by the major political parties, social democracy likewise must operate within and against a hostile and unwelcoming environment, the reward structure of corporate capital.

Democratization became, perforce, a struggle for acceptance as an essential element of the system. It was not a primary factor in the formation of the constitution. Even today the political status of democracy is akin to that of perennial opposition, of against the grain. Even when it appears to be "in" power it has simply entered into structures organized according to principles of elitism, command, secrecy, and the legitimating of a process whereby economic power (e.g., virtually unlimited corporate contributions) is translated (e.g., by corporate lobbyists) into political power. These are at odds with democratic principles of participation, transparency, and equality.

Modern governance, like that of feudalism and of classical republicanism, reflects the perennial character of societies driven by inequalities of wealth, cultural opportunities, education, and life circumstances. It is also a reflection of the necessarily episodic character and limitations of democratic action. The "fugitive" character of democracy is partly the reflection of the increasingly anachronistic plight of democracy due to the seemingly irreversible trends toward social and economic inequalities coupled with the predominant favoritism of governmental organizations toward the Few, but partly it is also necessarily episodic. It is based on those whose modest economic circumstances prevent them from engaging in politics full time, or of hiring proxies. I have often called attention to Aristotle's dictum that democracy is the form of government exercised by those who work—in other words, by those who do not enjoy much, if any, leisure time. Recall that under Athenian democracy citizens were paid to participate, which suggests that is not solely the so-called small scale of Athenian democracy that makes it irrelevant to the sprawling nation-state, as Madison gleefully pointed out. On the contrary, what makes Athens suggestive beyond the question of scale was the notion that the practice of participatory democracy on the part of the citizen-body could be meaningful only if their economic circumstances were alleviated so that political participation did not entail sacrifice by those classes that could least afford it. Under contemporary conditions, this means social democracy.

Sheldon S. Wolin

EDITOR'S INTRODUCTION

SHELDON S. WOLIN'S STATURE as one of the preeminent political theorists of his generation was established with the 1960 publication of *Politics and Vision: Continuity and Innovation in Western Political Thought.*[1] At a time when university courses in political theory relied mainly upon secondary sources, Wolin's text represented a radical departure from the prevailing practice of treating the history of political theory as a succession of ideas leading up to the present moment, however conceived. George H. Sabine's *A History of Political Theory*, originally published in 1937, with a third edition in 1961, exemplified that approach and was widely used in courses at the time *Politics and Vision* appeared. Sabine's text presupposed the very history it delineated, surveying a succession of one form of political organization to the next along with the ideas said to correspond to it. Thus the Greek city-state (Plato and Aristotle) is succeeded by the Hellenistic universal state (from the Stoics to Christian thinkers) and then the national state (Machiavelli to liberalism, fascism, and communism). At once learned and linear, Sabine attempted to include every important writer conventionally supposed to constitute the history of political theory, and then some.[2] By contrast, *Politics and Vision*, as the subtitle implied, was organized according to an altogether different purpose, which dictated an altogether different substantive approach.

While Sabine assumed that a "theory of politics" would continue to exist as long as "politics itself,"[3] Wolin's text appeared at a point in time when political theory had been thrown into question. Whereas Sabine treated political theory essentially, and unproblematically, as the ideological accompaniment to institutional forms of government, Wolin understood it to constitute a particular tradition with a distinct set of problems and languages. "My hope," he wrote in the preface, "is that this volume, if it does not give pause to those who are eager to jettison what remains of the tradition of political philosophy, may at least succeed in making clear what it is we shall have discarded." Wolin chose a historical approach to his subject not only to make possible "understanding the preoccupations of political philosophy and its character as an intellectual enterprise," but also because "an historical perspective is more effective than any other in exposing the nature of our present predicaments; if it is not the source of political wisdom, it is at least the precondition."[4] Thus what set Wolin's work apart from those exemplified by Sabine is a twofold distinction: *Politics and Vision* was a self-consciously interpretive effort to delineate a tradition of political theory, which accounts for the selectivity of authors and texts chosen for inclusion (as opposed to Sabine's encyclopedic approach); secondly, it was intended to provide some perspective on "our present predicaments." Wolin did not explicitly state what those predicaments were in his preface, but they become clear when considering the book as a whole and enable us to see the trajectory of the life's work that issued from *Politics and Vision*, and that is represented in the texts collected in this volume.

Wolin's conceptualization of the tradition of political theory as constituted by the continuities of language and problems does not imply a similar continuity in what is thus understood as "political" at specific historical moments. He noted that "the difficulties of preserving a clear notion of what is political form the basic theme of this book." Thus one of the fundamental problems confronting the political theorist is the question, "what is political?"[5] In conceptualizing the work of political theory in this way, Wolin effectively takes on the task of constructing its tradition in the process of articulating it.

To appreciate Wolin's approach to tradition, it is helpful to consider it in relation to other prominent approaches. In an important respect, Wolin's text bears a similarity to Georg Gadamer's *Truth and Method*, also published in 1960. Indeed, Wolin later noted the similarity, "both in spirit and substance," in interpretive positions he and Gadamer had independently taken when elucidating Gadamer's concept of historicity. "One of Gadamer's main points," he observed, "concerns the reflexivity of the inquiring subject who is not only trying to understand some aspect of the historical past but is also conscious of the historical character and locus of his own understanding. Historicity has to do with the convergence of the two, and the inquirer's contribution of his present is crucial."[6] What this meant in Wolin's case is that the tradition of political theory is more properly understood as a plurality. As the historical situation of the theorist alters, so does the understanding of past theories, and thus the tradition in which individual theorists situate themselves alters too. What gives the various traditions that political theory had taken within the history of Western political thought coherence is a cumulative or recurring political vocabulary, including such terms and concepts as authority, obligation, power, security, the common good, and the city or state. However, the precise meaning of these terms is never firmly fixed but is determined within a particular, situated practice of theorizing. Reflecting on *Politics and Vision* more than two decades after its original publication, Wolin observed that rather than a comprehensive history of political thought, as Sabine had attempted, his "approach and perspective were directed toward the meaning of theory and of the political. It was, in other words, a historical approach to the practice of political theory."[7] This is an approach that can also be distinguished from those historians of political theory, such as Quentin Skinner or J.G.A. Pocock, who delineate different traditions of political theory according to conceptual or linguistic trajectories over time.[8]

After *Politics and Vision*, Wolin's work continued to focus primarily on two intricately interwoven themes: the elaboration of what is meant by "theory" and its modifier "political," and how the political issues of the day can be adequately theorized. If *Politics and Vision* laid the initial foundation for the first focus, it was the Berkeley Free Speech Movement that ignited the second. Wolin and his collaborator John H. Schaar, both faculty participants in the events that engulfed the Berkeley campus, wrote a series of articles on it for the *New York Review of Books*, later published as *The Berkeley Rebellion and Beyond*.[9] These articles articulated a critique of the university as a political institution and indirectly led the pair to leave Berkeley in 1970 for the University of California Santa Cruz, Schaar permanently and Wolin until his move to Princeton University in 1973. But they also marked a new direction for Wolin's practice of political theory. From 1974 until 1980, Wolin wrote regularly for the *New York Review* on such subjects as Jimmy Carter, Henry Kissinger, Ronald Reagan, and conservatism in America. In an essay titled "Political Theory and Political Commentary," Wolin distinguished between different forms of political commentary. Citing such writers as Plato and Aristotle, Machiavelli and Marx, he noted that their theoretical works all contained commentary on contemporary institutions, personalities, and events. These represent "the element of commentary within a political theory."[10] But then there is a form of political commentary that is not presented within "the symbolic form of a theory," but is presented rather as direct commentary on current issues in newspapers, pamphlets, or other forms of public media. Wolin adduces John Locke, John Stuart Mill, Edmund Burke, G.W.F. Hegel, Max Weber, and once again Marx as classical examples of theorists who assumed the role at one time or another of political commentator. The purpose of political theory in the form of commentary is to change the perception of the public's view of politics. The problem such a practice encounters, particularly today, is that most commentary is untheoretical and takes the form of delimiting the political world through a focus on choices relating to problems that are conceived entirely within the existing political order. A properly theoretical commentary requires distance in space and time from the daily, taken-for-granted political arrangements that form the context for untheoretical commentary. In other words, what is at stake is the perspective on politics, "seeing familiar phenomena differently," that only theory can provide.[11] Such was the nature of Wolin's political commentary in the *Review*, but it is even more evident in the editorials and other contributions he made to the quarterly political journal *democracy*, which he edited from its founding in 1980, coinciding with the election of Ronald Reagan. Several of those contributions are collected in this volume.

After the demise of *democracy* in 1984, the events surrounding the Bicentennial of the US Constitution presented Wolin with the opportunity to reflect more closely on American political and economic structures in a series of essays and public lectures, resulting in *The Presence of the Past: Essays on the State and the Constitution*. In the introduction to that book, Wolin wrote that "political theory might be defined in general terms as a tradition of discourse concerned about the present being and well-being of collectives. It is primarily a civic and secondarily an academic activity. In my understanding this means that political theory is a critical engagement with collective existence and with the political experiences of power to which it gives rise."[12] One of the governing concepts in his analysis of American power in *The Presence of the Past* was the "economic polity," which captured his conviction that this form of intermingled public and private power incorporates capitalism and applied science to generate an endless expansion of totalizing power while simultaneously depoliticizing the citizenry. Though the lineaments of this power formation go back to Alexander Hamilton, it was the administration of Ronald Reagan that cemented its ideology, in Wolin's view. In subsequent works, while retaining the concept of the economic polity, Wolin also began to refer to "managed democracy" as another element of this new power formation, as in his *Democracy Incorporated: Managed Democracy and the Specter of Inverted Totalitarianism*, aimed at a broad public audience.[13] It was the notion of "inverted totalitarianism" that garnered the most attention, however. In the book's original preface, Wolin emphasized that in distinction from the totalitarianisms of Hitler, Mussolini, and Stalin, which captured the state in order to get control of the economy, the inverted form "is only partly a state-centered phenomenon. Primarily it represents the *political* coming of age of corporate power and the *political* demobilization of the citizenry."[14] In the conditions described and analyzed in *Democracy Incorporated*, managed democracy could be contested only by a "fugitive democracy," meaning that democracy can only be realized today in episodic irruptions of collective power rather than as institutionalized in the state.

Wolin's practice of political theorizing developed in symbiosis with his reflections on theory and the political. Following on *Politics and Vision*, three essays either written or published in 1968 structured Wolin's approach to these reflections. Chief among them was his most famous essay, "Political Theory as a Vocation," originally published in the *American Political Science Review* and reprinted here.[15] A common element of these essays is the influence of Thomas Kuhn's *The Structure of Scientific Revolutions*. Wolin delineated what he terms the paradigm of classical political theory, deriving from Plato and Aristotle, as being constituted by three features: 1) the "political" understood as things of public concern; 2) theory as the observation of collective practices and experience, gaining a perspective on one's own society, and appraisal of the importance of what had been observed; and 3) philosophy as the establishment of grounds for reliable knowledge and the pursuit of wisdom with regard to common affairs.[16] While Wolin accepted the notion that the behavioral revolution in political science did constitute a paradigm shift, he argued in his "Vocation" essay that this was not a shift in a theoretical paradigm. Rather, the behavioral revolution was based on considerations of method that substituted for political theory. Insofar as a paradigm lay behind behaviorism it is one that structures contemporary society as a whole, the main feature of which is a routinization of life effected by institutions and mechanisms of order and control. The obsession with method unreflectively presupposes and reinforces this social structure by valorizing techniques for measuring increasingly predictable behavior. Add to this the American tradition of pragmatism and the behavioral revolution amounts to a reflection of the status quo, thus surrendering the critical standpoint of classical theory as well as its philosophical foundations. Under such circumstances, Wolin stressed that the teaching of the history of political theory is a form of political education. At the same time, he extended Kuhn's distinction between "normal" and "extraordinary" science and argued that while the practice of behavioral political science can be classified as belonging to the former, the practice of political theory closely resembles the latter, insofar as that practice, while part of a tradition, entails periodic efforts to see the political world in a new way. Wolin calls those who perform such shifts "epic theorists." Epic theorists wish not only to change perceptions, but also to change their societies. While he deployed the term in the "Vocation" essay to characterize a long list of "great" theorists from Plato to Marx, and later developed it further by focusing on Thomas Hobbes in "Hobbes and the Epic Tradition of Political Theory," reprinted here, Wolin clearly believed that the contemporary times called for such a new vision.

These investigations into the nature of political theory were not only a continuation of *Politics and Vision* but also part of a project that Wolin saw as correcting some perceived shortcomings of his pathbreaking book. "I failed to grasp fully the radical changes that have taken place, especially during the last century, in the understanding and practice of philosophy," he admitted.[17] While that project appears to have been forecast as another book, it resulted instead in a never completed series of discrete essays and articles engaging such figures as Max Weber, Hannah Arendt, Richard Rorty, John Rawls, Max Horkheimer, Theodor Adorno, and Michel Foucault, all included here, as well as in the seven chapters added to the expanded edition of *Politics and Vision*, with extended discussions of Marx and Nietzsche. In part, the fragmented effort to think through the meaning of political theory in the years since the late 1960s was a result of the rapid changes taking place in the US academy, producing an ever-expanding field to be comprehended and interpreted. The scientization of political science that had been an important impetus and foil for his thinking continued apace, but along with it came a flourishing of new theoretical schools and approaches that cut across the social sciences and humanities. In a reflective essay included here titled "Political Theory: From Vocation to Invocation," written to mark the thirtieth anniversary of "Political Theory as a Vocation," Wolin once again had recourse to Kuhn in order to make sense of what he saw as a new "overtheorization" represented in a plethora of discourses claiming to find politics everywhere. Noting that when he wrote his original essay, in the context of the Cold War, the Vietnam War, and the civil rights movement, "critical" was associated with crisis, and he charged political science with being unable to acknowledge that society was in crisis and was therefore uncritical, while political theory was charged with intervening into the world in response to crisis. Now, he claimed, "critical" is "related more to 'critic' than to 'crisis'—

that is, it carries a more contemplative, Kantian spectatorial connotation of a 'judgment' in search of distance rather than an intervention driven by urgency. It is theoretic theory rather than political theory." Theory has itself become fragmented in the face of what is perceived to be a fragmented, decentralized power. Absent a "plane of generality" there can be no paradigmatic theory, and so "critical theorists are normal scientists for a society without a paradigm."[18]

A central defining element of inverted totalitarianism in Wolin's view is programmed change that is the result of the wedding of capitalism, technology, and the state. He indicted much contemporary theory for mirroring that element and insisted that the work of political theory requires a slowing down of time and, increasingly, an attention to what is being left behind. In this context, Wolin's book on Alexis de Tocqueville, *Tocqueville between Two Worlds: The Making of a Political and Theoretical Life*, may be seen as an expression of his own struggles to realize political theory as "primarily a civic and secondarily an academic activity." Given his career-long effort to keep alive a tradition of political theory as a practice, and given his analysis of inverted totalitarianism, his remark concerning his book's eponymous subject takes on added significance: "There is an important sense in which Tocqueville was engaged in a lifelong task of retrieving a receding aristocratic past in order to counteract the new forms of despotism. One possible task for today's theorist is to ponder his example and to undertake the task of retrieving a receding democratic present in order to counteract even more novel forms of despotism."[19]

Note: This selection of essays was made in collaboration with Prof. Wolin. The last conversation regarding the contents of the volume occurred in August 2015, two months before his death.

PART ONE

THE POLITICAL AND THEORETICAL

CHAPTER 1

POLITICAL THEORY AS A VOCATION

THE PURPOSE OF THIS PAPER is to sketch some of the implications, prospective and retrospective, of the primacy of method in the present study of politics and to do it by way of a contrast, which is deliberately heightened, but hopefully not caricatured, between the vocation of the "methodist"[1] and the vocation of the theorist. My discussion will be centered around the kinds of activity involved in the two vocations. During the course of the discussion various questions will be raised, primarily the following: What is the idea which underlies method and how does it compare with the older understanding of theory? What is involved in choosing one rather than the other as the way to political knowledge? What are the human or educational consequences of the choice, that is, what is demanded of the person who commits himself to one or the other? What is the typical stance toward the political world of the methodist and how does it compare to the theorist's?

The discussion which follows will seek, first, to locate the idea of method in the context of the "behavioral revolution," and, second, to examine the idea itself in terms of some historical and analytical considerations. Then, proceeding on the assumption that the idea of method, like all important intellectual choices, carries a price, the discussion will concentrate on some of the personal, educational, vocational, and political consequences of this particular choice. Finally, I shall attempt to relate the idea of the vocation of political theory to these same matters.

I. THE IDEA OF "METHOD" IN THE BEHAVIORAL REVOLUTION

In compiling its recent *Biographical Directory*, the American Political Science Association distributed a questionnaire which in its own way helped raise the present question, "What is the vocation of the political theorist?" Political Theorists were invited to identify themselves by choosing among "Political Theory and Philosophy (Empirical)," "Political Theory and Philosophy (Historical)," and "Political Theory and Philosophy (Normative)." Although the choices offered may signify vitality and diversity, they may also testify to considerable confusion about the nature of political theory. For their part, political theorists may think of it as an identity crisis induced by finding themselves officially assigned a classification which others have defined, a classification traceable to a set of assumptions about the nature of the theoretical life perhaps uncongenial to many theorists.

Beyond the matter of professional identity there are far more compelling reasons for raising the question of vocation. Whatever one's assessment of the "behavioral revolution," it clearly has succeeded in transforming political science. What is less clear is the precise nature of that revolution. Among leading spokesmen of the profession it has become stylish to interpret that revolution as a close facsimile of the sorts of scientific changes discussed by Thomas Kuhn in *The Structure of Scientific Revolutions*.[2] Accordingly, the behavioral revolution is described as the inauguration of a new theoretical paradigm. Such a view, I think, is mistaken. It blurs the significance of the change. A more accurate account is suggested by the following: "One of the most significant recent developments in the social sciences is the revolution in data gathering and data evaluation. This revolution depends upon the developments in techniques by which data can be collected and analyzed."[3]

Assuming that this statement reflects a widespread sentiment which guides the actual practice of the profession, it provides a clue to the nature of the changes, what they are and what they are not, and what they signify for the vocations of political scientists and theorists. Despite claims to the contrary, political science has not undergone a revolution of the type described by Kuhn in which a new and dominant theory is installed. Although an abundance of new "theories" is available to the political scientist, it should be remembered that, by Kuhn's canon, the mere existence of new theories, or even the fact that some theories have attracted a following, are not conclusive evidence of a revolution. What counts is the enforcement by the scientific community of one theory to the exclusion of its rivals.

Although it is sometimes contended that "systems theory" constitutes the paradigmatic theory of the revolution, it is doubtful that this claim is tenable. Not only is there confusion about which of the several versions of the theory is the preferred one, or even whether any version is useful, but, above all, the popularity of systems theory followed rather than produced the behavioral revolution.

Whatever else it may be, a revolution without an initiating theory cannot qualify as a revolution by Kuhn's criterion. It may be, rather, a typically American revolution in which theories play a minor role. American political scientists, for the most part, have not only generally supported the traditional American diffidence toward theories, but they have elevated it to scientific status. The suspicion of theories is alleged to be a powerful contributor to the political stability of America and to its genius for pragmatic rather than ideological politics. In making this assertion I am not unmindful that there is hardly to be found a journal of political science in which some contemporary has not noted that "the mere accumulation of data without a guiding theory is, etc." Nor has it escaped my attention that a wide variety of theories exists for the political scientist to choose among. To call them political theories is, in the language of philosophy, to commit something like a category mistake. Systems theories, communication theories, and structural-functional theories are unpolitical theories shaped by the desire to explain certain forms of nonpolitical phenomena. They offer no significant choice or critical analysis of the quality, direction, or fate of public life. Where they are not alien intrusions, they share the same uncritical—and therefore untheoretical—assumptions of the prevailing political ideology which justifies the present "authoritative allocation of values" in our society.

Nonetheless, to say that there has been no political theory which has inspired the revolution in political science is not to say either that there has been no revolution or that no intellectual patterns are being widely promoted throughout the discipline. There has in fact been a certain revolution in political science, one that reflects a tradition of politics which has prided itself on being pragmatic and concerned mainly with workable techniques. Like all technique-oriented activity, the behavioral movement presupposes that the fundamental purposes and arrangements served by its techniques have been settled and that, accordingly, it reenforces, tacitly or explicitly, those purposes and arrangements and operates according to a notion of alternatives tightly restricted by these same purposes and arrangements. The emphasis upon methods does not signify simply the acquisition of a "kit" of new "tools," but presupposes a viewpoint which has profound implications for the empirical world, the vocation and the education of political scientists, and the resources which nourish the theoretical imagination.

To contend that the idea of method is the central fact of the behavioral revolution is merely to repeat what the revolutionaries themselves have stated. "Most important, perhaps, the criteria by which one accepts or rejects statements about social life are of a special nature. The ultimate criterion is the method by which they are gathered."[4] If it should be the case that a widespread set of assumptions is commonly held among those committed to the primacy of method, it is of little consequence that the techniques are diverse and changing. What matters are the common assumptions and consequences which accompany the emphasis on technique. The extent of this transformation is such as to suggest that the study of politics is now dominated by the belief that the main objective—acquiring scientific knowledge about politics—depends upon the adoption and refinement of specific techniques and that to be qualified or certified as a political scientist is tantamount to possessing prescribed techniques. Concurrent with this development there has been an effort to imbue political scientists with what is understood to be the ethic of science: objectivity, detachment, fidelity to fact, and deference to intersubjective verification by a community of practitioners. These changes add up to a vocation, a *vita methodica*, which includes a specified set of skills, a mode of practice, and an informing ethic. This vocation, and the education which it requires, may mark the significance of the behavioral revolution.

At this point a protest might be made that too much is being read into the idea of method. Methods per se do not presuppose a philosophical view of things, but are neutral or instrumental, analogous to the technician in being indifferent to the purposes of their master. Such an argument is not only wrong but superficial. In the first place, the elevation of techniques has important curricular consequences. The requirement that students become proficient in an assortment of technical skills preempts a substantial portion of their time and energy. But more important, training in techniques has educational consequences, for it affects the way in which the initiates will look upon the world and especially the political portion of it. "Methodism" is ultimately a proposal for shaping the mind. Social scientists have sensed this when they have noted that research methods are "tools" which "can become a way of looking at the world, of judging everyday experience."[5]

In the second place, the alleged neutrality of a methodist's training overlooks significant philosophical assumptions admittedly incorporated into the outlook of those who advocate scientific inquiry into politics. These assumptions are such as to reenforce an uncritical view of existing political structures and all that they imply. For the employment of method assumes, even requires, that the world be of one kind rather than another if techniques are to be effective. Method is not a thing for all worlds. It presupposes a certain answer to a Kantian type of question, What must the world be like for the methodist's knowledge to be possible? This presupposition is illustrated by a recent example which listed the major assumptions alleged to underlie the "movement" of political behavior. The first item was: "*Regularities*. These are discoverable uniformities in political behavior. These can be expressed in generalizations or theories with explanatory and predictive value."[6] It follows that the methodist is in trouble when the world exhibits "deformities" or emergent irregularities. As the unhappy state of theories of "development" or "modernization" suggests, similar trouble appears when the world manifests "multiformities."[7]

This is but to say that there are inherent limits to the kinds of questions which the methodist deems appropriate. The kind of world hospitable to method invites a search for those regularities that reflect the main patterns of behavior which society is seeking to promote and maintain. Predictable behavior is what societies live by, hence their structures of coercion, of rewards and penalties, of subsidies and discouragements are shaped toward producing and maintaining certain regularities in behavior and attitudes. Further, every society is a structure bent in a particular and persistent way so that it constitutes not only an arrangement of power but also of powerlessness, of poverty as well as wealth, injustice and justice, suppression and encouragement.

It is symptomatic in this connection that political scientists have increasingly taken to describing themselves as "normal scientists."[8] The phrase is Kuhn's and he used it to designate a type of scientist whose vocation is not to create theories or even to criticize them but to accept the dominant theory approved by the scientific community and to put it to work. But if we ask, what is the dominant theoretical paradigm of our normal (political) scientists, the answer is that, in Kuhn's sense, there is none. Yet, surely, although there is no paradigm derived from what Kuhn calls "an extraordinary theory," such as Galileo or Newton produced, there must still be some guiding assumptions or framework which the methodist follows. The answer, I have suggested, is that there is such a framework of assumptions. It is the ideological paradigm reflective of the same political community which the normal scientists are investigating.[9] Thus when a researcher takes "the normal flow of events in American politics" as his starting point, it is not surprising to find him concluding that "the long-run stability of the system depends on the underlying division of party loyalties."[10]

These considerations become even more compelling if we concentrate for a moment upon the "systems" theorist. If society is conceived to be a system of decision-making, and if the recurrence of unjust decisions is commonly acknowledged, it follows that the system is, to some persistent degree, a structure of systematic injustice, otherwise the idea of a system is an inadequate account. The built-in embarrassments of a particular system have sometimes been recognized, as when it is asserted that a supposedly democratic system requires a certain measure of indifference or apathy, especially on the part of the poor and the uneducated. This reservation about systems which purport to be democratic, and hence participatory, is sometimes stated more bluntly when the system in question is non-Western:

> In the Congo, in Vietnam, in the Dominican Republic, it is clear that order depends on *somehow compelling* newly mobilized strata to return to a measure of passivity and defeatism from which they have recently been aroused by the process of modernization.[11]

For the most part, however, the systems theorist prefers to emphasize more formal regularities. Thus, for example, the political system is defined as a special form of "social interactions . . . that are predominantly oriented toward the authoritative allocation of values for a society."[12] What is most revealing about this definition is the location of the word "predominantly": it is placed so as to qualify the "interactions" and thereby to enable subsequent research to distinguish political from social interactions. If the same word had been used, instead, to qualify the "allocations," a substantially different view of a system would have emerged, one in which the allocations would be seen to favor some interactions rather than others. It is acknowledged in the work cited that the favored theory may "inadvertently" exclude "some elements of major importance,"[13] but not that a system may require deliberate and systematic exclusion of major elements. Rather, it is agreed that "a systems approach draws us away from a discussion of the way in which the political pie is cut up and how it happens to get cut up in one way rather than another." The remedy for this "status quo bias" is to fall back upon "partial theories" which deal with selected aspects of the *same* system, e.g., theories of "decision-making, coalition strategies, game theories, power, and group analysis."[14] What is conveniently overlooked by this recipe is that it merely reaffirms in different form, the same culinary assumptions about the common pie, for each partial theory claims to be a plausible account of the same whole.

That a discussion of method should naturally lead to considering some prominent theories current among political scientists is not surprising. Most contemporary theories are dependent upon the behavioral revolution, not only in the methodological sense that the theories in question look to behavioral techniques for confirmation or disconfirmation, but in the more important sense of sharing the same outlook regarding education, philosophical assumptions, and political ideology. The close linkage between contemporary ideas of theory and of methods justifies treating them as members of the same family, forming a community of common features which I have labeled "methodism." As the earlier pages have tried to suggest, the idea of method has come to mean far more than was implied by Bentham, for example, when he called it "the order of investigation."[15] It can be better understood as constituting an alternative to the *bios theoretikos*, and, as such, is one of the major achievements of the behavioral revolution. To grasp the nature of the *vita methodica* is not only important for its own sake, but should help in distinguishing it from the activity and vocation of theory.

II. HISTORY OF THE IDEA OF "METHOD"

One way to get at the idea of method is to recognize that it has a history reaching back to ancient Greek philosophy. Like *philosophia*, *methodus* was often used in association with the notion of a "way" (*aporie*) to truth.[16] Before long, *methodus* and *philosophia* began to diverge. Generally speaking, while *philosophia* and its sister, *theoria*, tended to stress the arduous difficulties awaiting those who sought truth, the devotees of *methodus* began to emphasize the economy of being methodical, that is, of faithfully following a prescribed sequence of mental steps, a "straight road" in Descartes's phrase.[17] The old metaphor of the "way" was subtly altered and became associated with the advantages of adhering to a beaten path rather than "blazing" a trail. A premonition of this change appeared in the Middle Ages when *methodus* tended to acquire the connotation of a "short-cut." It found popular expression in numerous attempts to compose *compendia* on various subjects.[18]

During the Middle Ages and well into the sixteenth century the idea of method remained encumbered by Aristotelian and scholastic logic. As a result, method was tightly bound by logical procedures whose main aim was to sift and order inherited knowledge and experience rather than to discover new things. Thus the two main procedures of scholastic logic were "invention" (*inventio*), or the methods by which contestable propositions could be analyzed pro and con, and "judgment" or "disposition" (*iudicium*), which comprised the methods of arranging words into propositions, then into syllogisms or inductions, and finally into whole discourses. The conservatory quality of method was illustrated in a sixteenth-century work, *The Rule of Reason*, written by Thomas Wilson and published in 1551. Declaring that "a reason [is] easier found than fashioned," he compared the logic of "invention" with the sort of traditional lore acquired by huntsmen, saying that "he that will take profite in this parte of logique, must be like a hunter, and learne by labour to knowe the boroughes. For these places [i.e., a marke whiche gieuth warnyng to our memory what we maie speake probablie] be nothyng els but couertes or boroughes, wherein if any one searche diligentlie, he maie fynd game at pleasure." In his definition of "method," Wilson clearly expressed the view of one who saw it primarily as an ordering and clarifying procedure, "the maner of handeling a single Question, and the readie waie howe to teache and sette forth any thyng plainlie, and in order, as it should be, in latine *Methodus*."[19]

Throughout the sixteenth century method continued to be thought of mainly in organizational terms. Petrus Ramus, the most influential writer of the period, reflected this tendency. "Method," according to his definition, "is of arrangement, by which among many things the first in respect to conspicuousness is put in the first place, the second in the second, the third in the third, and so on. This term refers to every discipline and every dispute. Yet it commonly is taken in the sense of a direction sign and of a shortening of the highway."[20] Despite the static nature of Ramus's conception, there was some anxiety about "the new devised aid." With his customary irony, Richard Hooker entered some reservations:

> Of marvellous quick despatch it is, and doth shew them that have it as much almost in three days, as if it dwell threescore years with them ... Because the curiosity of man's wit doth many times with peril wade farther in the search of things than were convenient; the same is thereby restrained unto such generalities as every where offering themselves are apparent unto men of the weakest conceit that need be. So as following the rules and precepts thereof, we may define it to be, an Art which teacheth the way of speedy discourse, and restraineth the mind of man that it may not wax over-wise.[21]

Scarcely a generation later the restraints were rejected and Descartes introduced a new "way of speedy discourse" that promised to make men "the lords and possessors of nature."[22] The crucial step between Hooker and Descartes had been taken by Bacon who developed a distinction between two kinds of *inventio*, one a technique for the discovery of things not previously known, the other for the rediscovery of something previously known but temporarily forgotten.[23] Rightly understood, method promised not only "the use of knowledge" but, above all, "the *progression* of knowledge."[24]

With the gradual development of the idea of method, its significance soon extended beyond the simple advantages of economy and efficiency of mental effort. In following a shortcut, the mind was literally "conducting" inquiry, that is, comporting itself in a special way, following a code of intellectual conduct which, while it might not automatically lead to new truths, would for the most part prevent the methodist from wandering into grievous errors. Thus method came to mean, among other things, a form of discipline designed to compensate for unfortunate proclivities of the mind. "I am indeed amazed," Descartes exclaimed, "when I consider how weak my mind is and how prone to error."[25]

Descartes was among the first to realize that the adoption of the methodical point of view was at least as important as the acquisition of specified techniques. To adopt a method was not equivalent to buying a new suit, to a transaction in which only the external appearance of the purchaser was altered. It was, instead, a profound personal choice, perhaps the closest functional equivalent to conversionary experience that the modern mind can achieve. At the very least, it was intended as a form of reeducation, as one of Descartes's works, *Regulae ad directionem ingenii,* implied. The educational force of the title has been partially lost in translation, *Rules for the Direction of the Mind. Ingenium* carries the meaning of "nature, character, temperament," rather than the more narrowly intellectualistic connotations of "mind." That work described the specific steps for conditioning and disciplining the *ingenium* of the novice, for "rendering [it] more apt in the discovery of yet other truths." The human tendency "to guess unmethodically, at random," not only produced error but mental flabbiness as well. "In so proceeding we are bound to weaken the mind's powers of insight" and, therefore, a strict program was required. "We ought to train ourselves first in those easier matters, but methodically. Thereby we shall accustom ourselves to proceed always by easy and familiar paths, and so, as easily as though we were at play, to penetrate ever more deeply into the truth of things."[26]

The celebrated Cartesian principle of doubt formed a vital part of the new regimen for the mind. Doubt was the means of preparing the mind for *regulae* by first depriving it of the major forms of resistance. Bacon, anticipating the difficulty, had noted that "a new method must be found for quiet entry into minds so choked and overgrown" that only an *expurgatio intellectus* would suffice.[27] Radical doubt was Descartes's version of the purge. Before the mind could proceed methodically, it must be turned upon itself, stripping off acquired habits, beliefs, and values until compelled to face the primordial truth of the *cogito* whose *sum* now stood divested of its cultural heritage in an ahistorical silence. "Those who have learned the least of all that has hitherto been distinguished by the name of philosophy are the most fitted for the apprehension of truth."[28] What Bacon had exultingly proclaimed earlier, "I have purged and swept and levelled the floor of the mind,"[29] had now been programmed by Descartes.

Descartes attached certain self-denying ordinances to his program that are not without interest in the light of the recent evolution of political science. He singled out some subjects, God among them, as privileged and, therefore, protected from the destructive effects of doubt and methodical probing. He cautioned especially against bringing the new method to bear upon questions of morality and practical action. He himself had decided to accept existing moral values as a "provisional code" before submitting all else to doubt, "lest," as he explained, "I should remain irresolute in my actions." More tellingly, since conflicting opinions often existed about what was right, he would regulate "[his] conduct in conformity with the most moderate opinions, those furthest removed from extremes."[30] On political matters he was equally cautious, but more am-

bivalent. On the one hand, he expressed great admiration for those political societies which exhibited the rational symmetry legislated by a single intelligence;
on the other, he abstained from drawing practical conclusions from this, saying
only that most societies manage to work tolerably well over the long run.[31]

Although these political remarks underscore Descartes's preference for rational method over inherited knowledge, they are mainly significant for revealing
the reason for his support of the status quo: fear of disorder. He was convinced
that upheaval invariably followed fundamental reform and that innovators
should be warned away:

> Great public institutions, if once overthrown, are excessively difficult to re-establish,
> or even to maintain erect if once seriously shaken; and their fall cannot but be
> very violent.[32]

From a preference for the existing scheme of institutions and for "the most
moderate" morals it was easy to pass to an identification of the two so that
existing arrangements were taken to be the expression of what was reasonable
and "furthest removed from extremes." Such a political world snugly fits the
methodist's need, not only for the security it provides for his investigations, but
also for the assured regularities it gives him to investigate.

What sort of political commitment is likely from a self which has been purged
of inherited notions, pledged to the support of existing political and moral
schemes, yet inhibited by the belief that they are "provisional"? A self of this type
is likely to treat politics and morals in a way that avoids fundamental criticism as
well as fundamental commitment. This lack of commitment is connected with
the special form which the fear of fundamental change takes with the political
methodist. He will boldly renounce any belief in a natural structure of political societies, and declare that "any set of variables selected for description and
explanation may be considered a system of behavior. At the outset, whether it is
a system given in nature or simply an arbitrary construct of the human mind, is
operationally a pointless and needless dichotomy."[33]

Once doubt has abolished all privileged beginnings, there is no compelling
reason why *this* rather than *that* should constitute the point of departure or the
way of conceiving the problem, just as there is no logical or scientific reason for
siding with the status quo. And yet the astonishing culmination of these arbitrary choices is not a truly skeptical temper but, as Descartes frankly admitted,
rigidity and single-mindedness.

> My second maxim was to be as unwavering and as resolute in my actions as pos-
> sible, and having once adopted opinions to adhere to them, however in them-
> selves open to doubt, no less steadfastly than if they had been amply confirmed.

Descartes embellished the point by a contrast between the person who
clings steadfastly to a chosen belief and the confused traveler who constantly
changes directions. "Even though at the start it may have been chance alone

which determined . . . [the] choice of direction," and even though what the resolute person takes to be "very certain and true" may be very doubtful, he is still likely to get *somewhere*, and, at the same time, he most certainly will be relieved from "all the repentings and feelings of remorse which are wont to disturb the consciences" of those who vacillate.[34]

How does the state of contemporary political science compare with the Cartesian philosophy of method? Despite occasional deference paid to "the tradition of political theory," there is a widely shared belief that that tradition was largely unscientific where it was not antiscientific and that the defining characteristic of a scientific revolution is to break with the past.[35] This animus against tradition will be considered at greater length when we try to assess its significance for the study of politics. Here we are concerned with Descartes's view of politics and especially with his counsels about political change. It is easier and safer, he declared, to reconstitute the foundations of knowledge than to attempt "the slightest reformation in public affairs."[36] An echo in contemporary political science is the following:

> A political system is an accident. It is an accumulation of habits, customs, prej
> udices, and principles that have survived a long process of trial and error and
> of ceaseless response to changing circumstance. If the system works well on the
> whole, it is a lucky accident—the luckiest, indeed, that can befall a society . . . To
> meddle with the structure and operation of a successful political system is there
> fore the greatest foolishness that men are capable of. Because the system is intri
> cate beyond comprehension, the chance of improving it in the ways intended is
> slight, whereas the danger of disturbing its workings and setting off a succession
> of unwarranted effects that will extend throughout the whole society is great.[37]

It might be objected that many contemporary political scientists would disavow this formulation as extreme and would draw attention to their repeated efforts at reform. Without wishing to deprecate these efforts, the contention remains that most proposals for reform on the part of political scientists represent a narrow range of alternatives founded on the assumption that the system has no inherent defects, or if it has, that these are acceptable "costs." The result is to foreclose a genuinely theoretical discussion which would seriously question and reflect upon the qualities of the system as a whole. Accordingly, the political scientist tends to follow the Cartesian path of extolling the existing as "the most moderate" or "further removed from extremes," and then defending it as though it were "very certain and true." This has taken the by now familiar form of identifying the American political system with "normal politics" and then seeking to establish by empirical methods the factors which produce it. There then follows the general explanation that the system has functioned normally, i.e., in a stable way, because it has avoided immoderation, i.e., "extremism" or "intensity." America has been spared these evils, it is alleged, not because of the excellence of her institutions or her citizens, but because of such factors as: the absence of ideologi cal conflicts and political passions, a healthy amount of voter apathy, a measure of voter ignorance, political parties whose genius is to abstain from presenting clearly defined alternatives, the influence of cross-pressures which fragment the citizen's loyalties and reduce his commitments to the consistency of Jell-O, a strategy of decision-making which favors "small or incremental change" because it is not disruptive,[38] and a system where the access to power succeeds in keeping at bay the poor, ignorant, deviant, and deprived.

III. CONSEQUENCES OF "METHODISM" IN CONTEMPORARY POLITICAL SCIENCE

It would be easy, especially at the present time when attacks upon liberal pluralism are increasing, to dismiss as an unfortunate lapse the way in which contemporary political science has come to such good terms with American politics. To accuse political science of an ideological bias is not to explain why it succumbed to the bias, or whether the nature of political science in America is or has always been such that identification with the going scheme of things is a recurrent temptation. Only a superficial view would hold that the condition of American political science can be remedied merely by substituting an opposing ideology. Perhaps the problem is far more deeply rooted in the past of American political science and American political society itself. If this should be the case, it would be mere *ante bellum* nostalgia to attempt to return to the state of political science before the behavioral revolution. If such an attempt were made, it is likely that both political science and political theory would be found similarly tainted.

To expose the common root of a problem as vast as this is patently beyond our present scope, but a suggestion as to its nature is perhaps possible. Two assertions by Tocqueville supply the starting point. The first is: "Hardly anyone in the United States devotes himself to the essentially theoretical and abstract portion of human knowledge." The second is: "Among democratic nations . . . the woof of time is every instant broken and the track of generations effaced."[39] These may be characterized as a diffidence toward theory and history. Rather than attempt to trace the course of this diffidence, let us try to suggest how it is manifested in contemporary political science, but remembering that today's political science is remarkable for its Cartesian methodism and for its protestations about the importance of theory as a guide for empirical research. The possibility to be explored is whether the age-old problem of America, its suspicion of theory and of the human past, has not been worsened by the behavioral revolution, especially in the domain of education.

The first methodistic act for the Cartesian was to purge the self of the opinions acquired by upbringing, education, and common experience. The contemporary methodist performs the same act of divestment, except that he will use the language of social science in order to explain that he must, as far as possible, rid the mind of biases and preconceptions, such as those produced by class, status, occupation, family, religious upbringing, or political attachments. In so doing, he is performing a true ritual, the reenactment of the archetypal American experience of breaking with the past. Or, if this seems too esoteric, perhaps the purged methodist is merely a footnote to Tocqueville's remark that "America is one of the countries where the precepts of Descartes are least studied and are best applied."[40]

This antitraditionalist bias, cultivated in the name of the elimination of bias, has manifested itself on numerous occasions during the past decades as the effort to diminish the significance of "traditional political theory," as it has revealingly been called. Some have wished to have it eliminated entirely from the education of political scientists, while others have been mainly concerned to substitute a more scientific version of theory, and still others have wished to rescue individual "propositions" from the corpus of the ancient literature and submit them to operational testing. Leaving aside the criticisms which are antitheoretical in principle, the other responses are interesting because what they are objecting to is not "theory" but a tradition of theory. Stated differently, what is bothersome about the history of theory is that it displays the working out of an inherited form, which is what a tradition is all about. Political theory has been perhaps the only field of study in all of American political science to exhibit this peculiar feature. Moreover, since the vast bulk of the literature which composes the tradition is European, as well as ancient, it is not difficult to see why it should be an object of suspicion.

This same bias is also manifested against the traditional forms of knowledge to which the methodist falls heir when he chooses to become a student of politics. As an ancient field of study, political science has acquired considerable knowledge about laws, constitutions, institutions, and unwritten practices. This inherited knowledge evokes a typically Cartesian and American response:

> Traditional methods [of political science]—i.e., history writing, the description of institutions, and legal analysis—have been thoroughly exploited in the last two generations and now it seems to many (including myself) that they can produce only wisdom and neither science nor knowledge. And while wisdom is certainly useful in the affairs of men, such a result is a failure to live up to the promise in the name of political *science*.[41]

Although one might be troubled by the kind of human concern which would provoke a confrontation between "political wisdom" and "political *science*," the antithesis has the merit of opening the question, What is political wisdom? Put in this vague form, the question is unanswerable, but it may be reformulated so as to be fruitful. The antithesis between political wisdom and political science basically concerns two different forms of knowledge. The scientific form represents the search for rigorous formulations which are logically consistent and empirically testable. As a form, it has the qualities of compactness, manipulability, and relative independence of context. Political wisdom is an unfortunate phrase, for, as the quotation suggested, the question is not *what* it is but *in what* does it inhere. History, knowledge of institutions, and legal analysis were mentioned. Without violating the spirit of the quotation, knowledge of past political theories might also be added. Taken as a whole, this composite type of knowledge presents a contrast with the scientific type. Its mode of activity is not so much the style of the search as of reflection. It is mindful of logic, but more so of the incoherence and contradictoriness of experience. And for the same reason, it is distrustful of rigor. Political life does not yield its significance to terse hypotheses, but is elusive and hence meaningful statements about it often have to be allusive and intimative. Context becomes supremely important, for actions and events occur in no other setting. Knowledge of this type tends, therefore, to be suggestive and illuminative rather than explicit and determinate. Borrowing from Polanyi, we shall call it "tacit political knowledge."[42]

The acquisition of tacit political knowledge is preeminently a matter of education of a particular kind and it is on this ground that the issue needs to be joined with the political methodist. The mentality which is impatient of the past and of traditional political theory is equally curt with the requirements of tacit political knowledge which is rooted in knowledge of the past and of the tradition of theory. The knowledge which the methodist seeks is fairly characterized in his own language as composing a "kit of tools" or a "bag of tricks." To acquire knowledge of techniques is no small matter, for they are often difficult and require considerable "retooling," which is to say that they imply a particular kind of program of instruction in specific methods.

Tacit political knowledge, on the other hand, accrues over time and never by means of a specified program in which particular subjects are chosen in order to produce specific results. Whatever may be the truth of the adage that he who travels lightest travels farthest, diverse, even ill-assorted baggage, is needed because the life of inquiry preeminently demands reflectiveness, that is, an indwelling or rumination in which the mind draws on the complex framework of sensibilities built up unpremeditatedly and calls upon the diverse resources of civilized knowledge. But if the life of inquiry is narrowly conceived as the methodical "pursuit" of knowledge, it is likely to become not a pursuit but an escape from the spare and shabby dwelling which Descartes literally and symbolically occupied when he composed his *Meditations*. Even those who would wish to address their minds to "data" are aware that data are constituted by abstractions, and that usually what has been culled from the phenomena are the subtle traces of past practices and meanings which form the connotative context of actions and events.

To recognize the connotative context of a subject matter is to know its supporting lore; and to know the supporting lore is to know how to make one's way about the subject field. Such knowledge is not propositional, much less formulary. It stands for the knowledge which tells us what is appropriate to a subject and when a subject matter is being violated or respected by a particular theory or hypothesis. Although appropriateness takes many forms, and we shall return to some of them, it is impossible to reduce its contents to a checklist of items. For example, can we say with exactness what is the precise knowledge which makes us uneasy with statements like the following?

> The interesting issues in normative political theory are in the end generally empirical ones . . . There does exist, however, *one interesting problem in political theory* which is strictly normative. That is the problem of evaluating mixes of desiderata. . . . It may be called the "utility problem" or in still more modern terminology, the "dynamic-programming problem." . . . On this strictly normative problem of program packages more progress has been made in the past half century than in all the previous 2,000 years of political theory put together.[43]

Although these assertions may appear absurd, it is not easy to say why, except that some important political and theoretical questions are being rendered unrecognizable. Behind the assertions, however, lie some revealing attitudes toward knowledge. These bear upon the contrast between methodistic knowledge and the forms of theory congenial to it, and, on the other hand, the kind of knowledge characteristic of tacit political knowledge and the forms of theory built upon it. The methodistic assumption holds that the truth of statements yielded by scientific methods has certain features, such as rigor, precision, and quantifiability. The connection between the statements and their features is intimate so that one is encouraged to believe that when he is offered statements rigorous, precise, and quantifiable, he is in the presence of truth. On the other hand, an approach to the "facts" consisting of statements which palpably lack precision, quantifiability, or operational value is said to be false, vague, unreliable, or even "mystical." In actuality, the contrast is not between the true and the false, the reliable and the unreliable, but between truth which is economical, replicable, and easily packaged, and truth which is not. Methodistic truth can be all these things because it is relatively indifferent to context; theoretical truth cannot, because its foundation in tacit political knowledge shapes it toward what is politically appropriate rather than toward what is scientifically operational.

Questions concerning appropriateness, context, and respect for a subject do not concern effete matters, but very practical ones. They involve the resources, or the lack thereof, which we draw upon when the decision concerns matters for which there can be no certitude. What "belongs" to a given inquiry is one such matter, and how to decide between one theory and another, or between rival methods, are others. Yet the kind of knowledge necessary to these decisions, tacit political knowledge, is being jeopardized by the education increasingly being instituted among political scientists. To illustrate the problem, we might consider the implications for tacit political knowledge of a typical proposal for increasing the student's mastery of methods. Our example is a recent volume on survey research methods for undergraduates and graduates in political science. In the spirit of Descartes's *regulae*, the authors describe it as a "handbook" or "manual," "a checklist" or inventory of "dos and don'ts," whose aim is to encourage the "empirical emphasis" in political science. Not content with offering a manual of technical instruction, the authors claim advantages of an educational and vocational kind will be promoted if survey research is made part of the curriculum. Thus the instructor, impaled by the twin demands of teaching and research, is reassured that the two can be reconciled if students are put to work learning survey methods while conducting his research. Further, the method is extolled as a way of overcoming the shortcomings of "the lone scholar" whose skills are inadequate for dealing with the size and range of problems confronting empirical political science. The imperative, "resources must be increased," decrees that the lone scholar be replaced by "group activity and teamwork." In the same vein, it is claimed that "the educational advantages for students are impressive" and among the putative advantages are the acquisition of an *ingenium* with traits congenial to the new emphasis:

> Students gain the opportunity to learn more about themselves . . . Too few students get the experience of fighting to remain neutral while carefully probing attitudes hostile to their own. Such instruction in self-control is valuable for the headstrong and overprotected.

Despite the tenor and direction of this conception of education, it is insisted that the new generation of students will be able to do "what was not expected of the previous generation of college students—i.e., to discover new knowledge as well as to acquire old."[44]

But will they? As for acquiring "the old," the authors bemoan the fact that political science departments have been hampered by the "lack of knowledge of research skills" and that the conventional academic calendar does not afford sufficient time for students to learn "sampling, interviewing, coding, analysis, etc." Exactly how the student will "acquire the old" when the demands of the "new" are so great is not discussed. In this connection it is relevant to recall Kuhn's description of the way scientific education has been affected by this determination to consolidate scientific advances and insure cumulative knowledge. He characterized scientific education as "narrow and rigid . . . probably more so than any other except perhaps in orthodox theology." It is not well designed "to produce the man who will easily discover a fresh approach," but it is admirably suited for preparing "normal scientists" and for enabling the community to readapt itself when a fundamental change occurs in theoretical orientations. "Individual rigidity is compatible with a community that can switch from paradigm to paradigm when the occasion demands."[45] To the best of my knowledge, political scientists who otherwise approvingly cite Kuhn have consistently declined to take up the implications of his analysis of scientific education.

Although the invention of methods, like the invention of theories, demands a high order of creativity and is entitled to the highest praise something important, perhaps ironical, occurs when that discovery is institutionalized in a training program. The requirements for those who are to use the theory or method are very different from the talent which discovered them, although, paradoxically, the technical skills may be the same. Descartes noted that a child might become as proficient as the genius in following the rules of arithmetic, but he never argued that the child could discover the rules. This is so, not simply because of the chance element in discovery, but because of the more baffling questions of the personal and intellectual qualities of the discoverer and of the cultural conditions of discovery.[46]

In this context the contemporary methodist's notion of training becomes significant. The idea of training presupposes several premeditated decisions: about the specific techniques needed and how they will be used; about what is peripheral or irrelevant to a particular form of training; and about the desired behavior of the trainee after he has been released from his apprenticeship. The idea of theorizing, on the other hand, while it presupposes skills, cannot specify briefly and simply the skills needed, their degree, or combinations. Kepler's followers could be contemptuous of their master's Platonism and astrology, as Newton's admirers were of his religious fascinations; but it would be risky to discount the influence of these extrascientific considerations upon the formation of the respective theories.

The impoverishment of education by the demands of methodism poses a threat not only to so-called normative or traditional political theory, but to the scientific imagination as well. It threatens the meditative culture which nourishes all creativity. That culture is the source of the qualities crucial to theorizing: playfulness, concern, the juxtaposition of contraries, and astonishment at the variety and subtle interconnection of things. These same qualities are not confined to the creation of theories, but are at work when the mind is playing over the factual world as well. An impoverished mind, no matter how resolutely empirical in spirit, sees an impoverished world. Such a mind is not disabled from theorizing, but it is tempted into remote abstractions which, when applied to the factual world, end by torturing it. Think of what must be ignored in, or done to, the factual world before an assertion like the following can be made: "Theoretical models should be tested primarily by the accuracy of their prediction rather than the reality of their assumptions."[47] No doubt one might object by pointing out that all theorizing does some violence to the empirical world. To which one might reply, that while amputations are necessary, it is still better to have surgeons rather than butchers.

It is not enough, therefore, to repeat commonplaces, viz., that facts are senseless without theoretical concepts, or that the meaning which facts acquire from a theory is purchased at the price of shaping the facts by the theoretical perspective employed. It is not enough because so much depends upon the kind of theory being used and the personal and cultural resources of the user. Perhaps it is some debilitating legacy of Puritanism that causes us to admire "parsimony" in our theories when we should be concerned that the constitution of the factual world depends upon the richness of our theories which, in turn, depends upon the richness of the inquiring mind. This concern may well be what fundamentally unites the scientific theorist and the so-called traditional theorist.

When a scientist observes a fact, he "sees" it through concepts which are usually derived from a theory. Facts are, as one philosopher has neatly put it, "theory-laden." Kepler, for example, observed many of the same facts as his predecessors, but because he viewed them differently a new era of science was ushered in.[48] The same might be said of Machiavelli, as well as of every major theorist from Plato to Marx. Some theorists, as Tocqueville suggested, see differently, others see farther. All would probably have agreed with Tocqueville that, for the theorist, nothing is more difficult to appreciate than a fact,[49] and nothing, it might be added, is more necessary as a condition for theorizing than that facts not be univocal. If they were, creativity and imagination would play a small role and it would be appropriate to speak of theorizing as a banal activity, as "theory-construction." If facts were simply "there" to be collected, classified, and then matched with a theory (or with the observation-statements derived from it), the political scientist might well declare, "Whether [a] proposition is true or false depends on the degree to which the proposition and the real world correspond."[50] But although everyone is ready to acknowledge that facts depend upon some criteria of selection or of significance, what is less frequently acknowledged is that such criteria usually turn out to be fragments of some almost-forgotten "normative" or "traditional" theory.

Because facts are more multifaceted than a rigid conception of empirical theory would allow, they are more likely to yield to the observer whose mental capacities enable him to appreciate a known fact in an unconventional way. As one philosopher has said, "Given the *same* world it might have been construed differently. We might have spoken of it, thought of it, perceived it differently. Perhaps facts are somehow moulded by the logical forms of the fact-stating language. Perhaps these provide a 'mould' in terms of which the world coagulates for us in definite ways."[51] Once again we are confronted by the warning that the richness of the factual world depends upon the richness of our theories: "The paradigm observer is not the man who sees and reports what all normal observers see and report, but the man who sees in familiar objects what no one else has seen before."[52] Thus the world must be supplemented before it can be understood and reflected upon.

Vision, as I have tried to emphasize, depends for its richness on the resources from which it can draw. These extrascientific considerations may be identified more explicitly as the stock of ideas which an intellectually curious and broadly educated person accumulates and which come to govern his intuitions, feelings, and perceptions. They constitute the sources of his creativity, yet rarely find explicit expression in formal theory. Lying beyond the boundaries circumscribed by method, technique, and the official definition of a discipline, they can be summarized as cultural resources and itemized as metaphysics, faith, historical sensibility, or, more broadly, as tacit knowledge. Because these matters bear a family resemblance to "bias," they become sacrificial victim to the quest for objectivity in the social sciences. If scientists have freely acknowledged the importance of many of these items,[53] how much more significant are these human creations for the form of knowledge, political science, which centers on the perplexities of collective life, on objects which are all too animate in expressing their needs, hopes, and fears?

Doubtless the objection will be raised that if a discipline is to be empirical its practitioners must be equipped to "handle" data in ways approximative of the sciences which have been more successful, and that to suggest otherwise is to consort with the heresy of saying that philosophical and moral knowledge may lead to a better empiricism. Yet we might consider the following.

Throughout the history of political theory a student will find a preoccupation with the phenomenon of "corruption." Today, however, we scarcely know how to talk about it,[54] except when it flourishes in non-Western societies. Yet it is a common and documented fact that "organized crime" exerts significant power and influence, controls enormous wealth, and exhibits many of the same features which ordinarily arouse the interest of political scientists, e.g., organization, authority, power, kinship ties, rules, and strong consensus. Despite the promising research possibilities, no textbook on American government provides a place for organized crime in "the system," no study of "polyarchy" or community-power has taken cognizance of it. It is not far-fetched to suggest that this empirical oversight is connected with the belief that moral knowledge is empirically irrelevant.

Or, to take another example, one can think of many fine empirical studies which have never been conducted because contemporary political science has substituted the bland, status quo–oriented concept of "political socialization" for the ancient idea of "political education." If, instead of blinkering the inquiring eye with a postulate that "conduct is *politicized* in the degree that it is determined by considerations of power indulgence or deprivation of the self by others,"[55] we took seriously an old-fashioned hypothesis, such as that advanced by J. S. Mill, that "the first element of good government . . . being the virtue and intelligence of the human beings composing the community, the most important point of excellence which any form of government can possess is to promote the virtue and intelligence of the people themselves,"[56] we might be better sensitized to the importance of genuinely empirical studies of truly fundamental political concern. For example, think of the empirical richness of an inquiry into the current structure of income taxes, especially in terms of the moral and political implications it holds for civic education. The structure of income taxes is a registry of the power and powerlessness of our social, economic, and ethnic groups; of the official way we rate the value of various social activities by the one standard generally accepted. It is also a system of incentives for behavior that define what is virtuous, unvirtuous, and morally indifferent; and, by tacitly encouraging behavior otherwise deemed blameworthy, encourages the gradual legitimation of that behavior, and thereby shapes what used to be called "the virtue of the citizenry." It would be difficult to imagine a richer field for behavioral inquiry, or one more likely to yield important knowledge about the quality of life in this republic. Yet it remains unharvested because our impoverished understanding of civic virtue and education has caused us to neglect the field.

Finally, one cannot help wondering whether political science, having jettisoned "metaphysical" and "normative" preoccupations about justice in favor of research into "judicial behavior" and the "judicial process," are not reaping the results: an inability to address a major phenomenon like the dangerous rash of *political* trials in America today and to reflect upon what these trials signify for the future of the authority and legitimacy of the state.

If the presence or absence of the moral and philosophical element affects the process by which theories constitute the empirical world, the choice among theories would seem to be a serious matter. But again, the contemporary mood trivializes what is involved in a theory's formulation and thereby obfuscates the importance of the choice among rival ways of constituting the world. The following quotation may be extreme but it does disclose the fantasies of the behavioral scientist about theories:

> In a report entitled *Communication Systems and Resources in the Behavioral Sciences*, the Committee on Information in the Behavioral Sciences outlines an ideal system that would in effect provide researchers with a computer analogue of the intelligent, all-informed colleague. Such a colleague would read widely, have total recall, synthesize new ideas, always be accessible, and be sensitive to each researcher's needs . . . The computer based system could respond to an individual's direct request for facts, data, and documentation; it could take the initiative and stimulate the researcher by suggesting new ideas, facts, or literature of interest; it could react intelligently to a scientist's work (analyze its logic, trace implications, suggest tests); and it could help disseminate ideas and provide feedback from the scientific community.[57]

If we can safely assume that choosing a theory or a method is not quite the same as choosing a helpful friend who, as Nietzsche taught, must be worthy of being your enemy, we might want to press the question further. When we choose a theory or a method, are we choosing something momentous, like a self, or something innocuous, like an "intellectual construct" or "conceptual scheme," or something depersonalized, like "a series of logically consistent, interconnected, and empirically verifiable propositions," or like "a generalized statement of the interrelationships of a set of variables"?

Undoubtedly these characterizations tell us something about the formal features of a theory, but they are deceptive in their parsimony. If the question is slightly reformulated to read, What is the human significance of choosing a theory?, then it becomes evident that much more is involved. Choosing a theory is significant for two conflicting reasons: it initiates new ways of thinking, evaluating, intuiting, and feeling; and it demands a substantial sacrifice in the existing forms of these same human processes. The first point is obvious, the second less so. This is because, like the law of treason, history books tend to be written by the victors and hence the sacrifices which accompany the triumph of a new theory are apt to be overlooked or bathed in a kind of Jacobite nostalgia.

The history of political theory is instructive on this score, for many of the great innovative theorists were highly self-conscious about choosing among theoretical alternatives. They knew that the true drama of theorizing involved offering a theory which could not be accommodated within prevailing values and perceptions of the world. When Hobbes allowed that his readers would be "staggered" by his theory,[58] he was not merely stating the obvious fact that his views concerning religion, authority, rights, and human nature were incompatible with traditional religious and political notions, but the more profound point that unless his readers were prepared to revise or discard those notions, they would not be able to grasp the full meaning of the theory and the theory itself could not become an effective force in the world. The same general assumptions had been made by Plato in his challenge to traditional Greek values and to the democratic ethos of Athens, and by Augustine in his effort to demolish classical notions of history, politics, virtue, and religion. Among more recent writers, none has been as sensitive as Max Weber to the emotional and cultural losses attendant upon the commitment to scientific rationalism.

Where our contemporary way of talking has not obscured the drama and demands of theorizing, it has trivialized them. Theories are likened to appliances which are "plugged into" political life and, since it is the nature of appliances to be under sentence of built-in obsolescence, "theories are for burning," leaving only a brief funereal glow which lights the way to "more scientific theories and more efficient research procedures."[59] If adopting a theory were equivalent to "trying out an idea," testing an hypothesis, or selecting a technique, there would be little reason to object to treating it casually.

At the very least, a theory makes demands upon our time, attention, energy, and skills. More fundamentally, the adoption of a theory signifies a form of submission with serious consequences both for the adopter and for those who imitate him, as well as for the corner of the world which the theory seeks to change our mind about. A certain sensibility is needed, qualities of thinking and feeling which are not readily formulable but pertain to a capacity for discriminative judgment. Why is this so? To compress the answer severely, in political and social matters we tend to think in one of two ways: in trying to explain, understand, or appraise we may ask, What is it like?; or we may ask, What is appropriate? The first way invites us to think metaphorically, e.g., Hobbes's argument that a representative is like an agent, or the contemporary notion of a political society as a system of communications. Ever since Plato, theorists have recognized the fruitfulness of metaphorical thinking, but they have also come to realize that at certain crucial points a metaphor may become misleading, primarily because the metaphor has a thrust of its own which leads to grotesque implications for the object or events which it is supposed to illuminate. A recent example of this pitfall is provided by Professor Deutsch's *Nerves of Government*, which argues for the concept of a communications system as a useful and proper model for political theory. The argument rests on a combination of metaphors and the success of the argument depends upon a confusion of the two. The first metaphor consists in likening the nature of human thinking and purposive action to the operation of a communications system, e.g., the "problem of value" is like a "switchboard problem," or "consciousness" is "analogous" to the process of feedback.[60] The second metaphor involves the reverse procedure: a communications system may be treated like a person. Human qualities, such as "spontaneity," "freedom of the will," and "creativity," can be "built into" a machine, and then it becomes possible to propose empirical propositions about society derived from the operations of the machine. But the whole argument depends upon, first, mechanizing human behavior and, second, humanizing mechanical processes. Once this is accomplished, grotesque results follow, e.g., internal rearrangements in a system, or in a person, which reduce goal-seeking effectiveness are described as "pathological" and resemble "what some moralists call 'sin.'"[61]

A second way of judging asks, What is appropriate? Appropriateness of judgment cannot be encapsulated into a formula. This is because it depends upon varied forms of knowledge for which there is no natural limit. This dependence is rooted in the basic quest of political and social theory for theoretical knowledge about "wholes" made up of interrelated and interpenetrating provinces of human activity. Whether the primary theoretical task be one of explanation or critical appraisal, the theorist will want to locate "divisions" in the human world and embody them in theoretical form. For example, what aspects of that division which we call "religion" have a significant bearing on the activity called "economic"? Perforce, a political theory is, among many other things, a sum of judgments, shaped by the theorist's notion of what matters, and embodying a series of discriminations about where one province begins and another leaves off. The discriminations may have to do with what is private and what is public, or they may be about what will be endangered or encouraged if affairs move one way rather than another, or about what practices, occurrences, and conditions are likely to produce what states of affairs. The difficulty is the same regardless of whether the theoretical intention is to provide a descriptive explanation, a critical appraisal, or a prescriptive solution. By virtue of their location in a whole, one province shades off from and merges into others: Where, for example, does the cure of souls end and the authority of the political order over religion begin? Where do the effects of technical education merge into questions about ethics and character? Where does the autonomy of administrative and judicial practices start and the "mysteries of state" stop? How much of the impetus for the Crusades is to be assigned to religious motives and how much to political or economic considerations?

If, as Plato suggested long ago, the task of theory is to locate "the real cleavages" in things and to "avoid chopping reality up into small parts" or drawing false boundaries,[62] then the sense of what is appropriate is critical. Given the theorist's preoccupation with wholes, the interconnectedness of human provinces, the values and expectations with which men have invested each of their provinces, and the ultimate bewildering fact that man is single but his provinces are multiple, a theoretical judgment which, by definition, must discriminate can only be restrained from rendering inappropriate determinations if it is civilized by a meditative culture. To be civilized is not only the quality of being sensitive to the claims and characters of many provinces, but, according to an older definition, rendering what is proper to a civil community.

IV. THE VOCATION OF THE POLITICAL THEORIST

If the preceding analysis has any merit it will have suggested that the triumph of methodism constitutes a crisis in political education and that the main victim is the tacit political knowledge which is so vital to making judgments, not only judgments about the adequacy and value of theories and methods, but about the nature and perplexities of politics as well. Here lies the vocation of these who preserve our understanding of past theories, who sharpen our sense of the subtle, complex interplay between political experience and thought, and who preserve our memory of the agonizing efforts of intellect to restate the possibilities and threats posed by political dilemmas of the past. In teaching about past theories, the historically minded theorist is engaged in the task of political initiation; that is, of introducing new generations of students to the complexities of politics and to the efforts of theorists to confront its predicaments; of developing the capacity for discriminating judgments discussed earlier; and of cultivating that sense of "significance" which, as Weber understood so well, is vital to scientific inquiry but cannot be furnished by scientific methods; and of exploring the ways in which new theoretical vistas are opened.

For those who are concerned with the history of political theories, the vocation has become a demanding one at the present time. How demanding it is can be seen by glancing at Kuhn's account of the manner in which scientific invention treats its own past.[63] In the formative period of their education students are required to master textbooks rather than to familiarize themselves with the creative writings of the great scientists of the past. The characteristic teaching of scientific textbooks, according to Kuhn, is to show how the great achievements of the past have prepared the way for the present stage of knowledge and theory. As a result, discontinuities are smoothed over, discarded, or unsuccessful theories are assumed to have been inferior, and the idea of methodical progress dominates the entire account.

How easy it is to impoverish the past by making it appear like the present is suggested by the way in which social scientists have lapsed into the same idiom as Kuhn's scientific textbooks. "As Aristotle, the first great behavioral scientist, pointed out a long time ago,"[64] or, again, "the behavioral persuasion in politics represents an attempt, by modern modes of analysis, to fulfill the quest for political knowledge begun by the classical political theorists," although it is admitted that classical theory is "predominantly prescriptive rather than descriptive."[65] What seems to have been forgotten is that one reads past theories, not because they are familiar and therefore confirmative, but because they are strange and therefore provocative. If Aristotle is read as the first behavioralist, what he has to say is only of antiquarian interest and it would be far more profitable to read our contemporaries.

What we should expect from a reading of Aristotle is an increase in political understanding. What we should expect from the study of the history of political theories is an appreciation of the historical dimension of politics. The cultivation of political understanding means that one becomes sensitized to the enormous complexities and drama of saying that the political order is the most comprehensive association and ultimately responsible as no other grouping is for sustaining the physical, material, cultural, and moral life of its members. Political understanding also teaches that the political order is articulated through its history; the past weighs on the present, shaping alternatives and pressing with a force of its own. At the present time the historical mode is largely ignored in favor of modes of understanding which are inherently incapable of building upon historical knowledge. One of the most striking features of game theory, communications models, and mechanical systems is that in each case the organizing notion is essentially history-less.

The threat to political understanding is not to be denied by arguing that we can substitute more precise functional equivalents for older language or that we can translate older notions into more empirical terms. From time immemorial writers have talked of the "burdens" of ruling, the "anguish" of choosing, and the "guilt" of actors who must employ coercion. To assimilate these actions to the calculations of gamesters or to describe them as "decision-making" or "outputs" is to distort both sides of the analogy. If in game-playing, for example, anguish, burdens, and guilt were recurrent features, the whole connotative context surrounding the idea of a game would be lost and nobody would "play." The ancient writer Philostratus once remarked of painting that no one could understand the imitative techniques of the painter without prior knowledge of the objects being represented. But when the attempt is being made to convey knowledge, not by imitative techniques, but by abstract signs and symbols which stand for objects commonly understood, everything depends on whether one truly understands what the symbol means. Does he understand, for example, the kinds of discriminative judgments which have been suspended when the symbol of an "input" is made to stand equally for a civil rights protest, a deputation from the National Rifle Association, and a strike by the U.A.W.? Does he understand that what allows him to discriminate between these "inputs" is a tacit knowledge derived from sources other than systems theory? Again, will he be able to compensate for the fact that systems theory makes it possible to talk about an entire political society without ever mentioning the idea of justice, except in the distorting form of its contribution to "system maintenance"? Is he aware that if one can focus on the American political order as a *system*, he does not have to confront the unpleasant possibility of it as an *imperium* of unsurpassed power? If, in rebuttal, the political scientist claims that the sort of studies referred to above really do presuppose the knowledge which would make political sense out of formal methods, then it is necessary to reply that the contemporary political scientist threatens to chalk around himself a vicious circle: his methods of study presuppose a depth of political culture which his methods of education destroy.

But what of the vocation by which political theories are created rather than transmitted? Testimony that such a vocation has existed is to be found in the ancient notion of the *bios theoretikos* as well as in the actual achievements of the long line of writers extending from Plato to Marx. How shall we understand this tradition as containing an idea of vocation which is relevant both to the challenge raised by the prestige of science and to the contemporary state of political life?

V. NATURE AND ROLE OF EPIC POLITICAL THEORISTS

In what follows I shall develop the thesis that the traditional idea of political theory displays some features which resemble forms of scientific theory, but which, by virtue of their political bearing, are uniquely the properties of political theory. As a way of bringing out the distinctive nature of this vocation, I shall call it the vocation of "epic theorist," a characterization which probably seems pretentious or precious, but which has been selected in order to call attention both to the unusual "magnitudes" of this form of theorizing, and to its distinguishing purpose and style.

Perhaps the pretentiousness of the phrase may be lessened by briefly recalling a comparable conception of theory in Kuhn's work. He employs the phrase "extraordinary" science to describe the contributions of the great scientific innovators. Kuhn's main point is that these theories mark a break with previous ones; that is, they inaugurate a new way of looking at the world, which includes a new set of concepts, as well as new cognitive *and* normative standards. Taking this as a suggestion of how to think about great theories, the first feature shared by epic theorists has to do with magnitudes. By an act of thought, the theorist seeks to reassemble the whole political world. He aims to grasp present structures and interrelationships, and to re-present them in a new way. Like the extraordinary scientific theory, such efforts involve a new way of looking at the familiar world, a new way with its own cognitive and normative standards.[66]

The second aspect of epic theory can be brought out if we look upon a theory not only as a structure of formal features, but also as a *structure of intentions*. The structure of intentions refers to the controlling purposes of the theorist, the considerations which determine how the formal features of concept, fact, logic, and interconnection are to be deployed so as to heighten the effect of the whole. In using the word "purposes" I mean to acknowledge that the structures exhibit considerable variety, and yet I also mean to maintain that there has been a persistent feature in all of them, one which may perhaps seem naive to our age of unmasking where all emperors are naked. All of the major theories of the past were informed by "public concern," a quality which was not incidental to the activity, but fundamental to the very notion of being engaged in *political theory*. The cynical "realist," Machiavelli, professed, "I love my country more than my soul."[67] In his dialogue *Utopia* Thomas More wrote emphatically about the theorist's commitment: "If you cannot pluck up wrongheaded opinions by the root, if you cannot cure according to your heart's desire vices of long standing," he declares to the pure political philosopher, represented by Hythloday, "yet you must not on that account desert the commonwealth."[68] Hobbes, who was never one to romanticize men's motives, represented himself as "one whose just grief for the present calamities of his country" had driven him to theorize.[69] Similar sentiments abound in the writings of Plato, Augustine, Locke, Rousseau, Bentham, Tocqueville, and Marx, among others. This unanimity suggests that if a Plato or a Marx had said what the modern scientist says repeatedly, and some social scientists come perilously close to saying, namely, that they are not responsible for the political and social consequences of their inquiries, it would appear more foolish than blameworthy. Concern for *res publicae* and *res gestae* are as irreducible and natural to the vocation of theorist as a concern for health is to the physician. This quality of caring for public things contrasts sharply with the mental set which believes that "the formulation of the topic into a research problem is the first step in scientific inquiry and, as such, should be influenced primarily by the requirements of scientific procedure."[70]

Because history suggests that all political societies have both endured and employed violence, cruelty, injustice, and known the defeat of human aspirations, it is not surprising that the theorist's concern for *res publicae* and the commonweal has issued in theories which, for the most part, have been critical and, in the literal sense, radical. Why this is the case and the import of it for the contemporary vocation of theorist can be shown by referring once more to Kuhn. He has argued that scientific revolutions tend to occur when research begins to turn up persistent "anomalies," i.e., when phenomena are encountered that cannot be squared with the theory. To qualify as an anomaly, the phenomena should, in principle, be explicable by the theory; or, stated differently, the anomaly must be relevant to the kinds of problems for which the theory purports to furnish an explanation. It does not count as an anomaly if it raises a question which the theory cannot be said to recognize as important and hence be expected to answer.

The concept of anomaly suggests that a scientific crisis occurs because something is wrong "in" the theory. When nature does not conform to the scientist's expectations, he reacts by reexamining his techniques and theories. He assumes that the "mistake" lies with one or the other, not with nature. The bearing of this upon political science becomes clearer when we consider some frequent criticisms directed at traditional political theories by contemporary political scientists. It is charged that such theories are useless in explaining voting behavior, political apathy, the formation of politically relevant attitudes, and the precise degree of actual control exercised by the electorate. "If someone were to ask, 'How can I learn about what sorts of people participate most in politics, and why?,' I would urge him to start with the most recent studies and work backwards. I seriously doubt whether he would get much help from Aristotle, Rousseau, or the *Federalist Papers*."[71] From such criticisms one would conclude that traditional political theories are valueless because they cannot explain why the political world is as it is. There is, in other words, something "wrong" in the theories. Whether this type of criticism will stand depends upon a prior understanding of the intentions of epical theorists: To what were their theories a response? As we have noted earlier, when it is believed that something is "wrong," scientists look for the error in the theory, not in the world. The same assumption is echoed by a contemporary behaviorist when he writes, "If there is a crisis, then, it is a crisis in the theory of representation and not in the institution of representation."[72] The assumption of the epic theorist has been of a different and contrasting kind. He has been preoccupied with a particular magnitude of problems created by actual events or states of affairs in the world rather than with problems related to deficiencies in theoretical knowledge. To be sure, problems-in-the-world and problems-in-a-theory are often interconnected, but the former has taken precedence among epic theorists and has been determinative of the latter. The shaping experience has been the recurrently problematic state of the political world, not the problematic state of theories about that world. What is problematic emerges when political life is experienced either as a threat or as a promise. Most of the important theories were a response to crisis; they have reflected a conviction either that political action might destroy certain civilized values and practices, or that it might be the means for deliverance from evils, such as injustice or oppression. These polarities can be illustrated by the contrasting responses of Burke and Paine to the French Revolution, or of Tocqueville and Marx to the events of 1848. The point is not that theories come in pairs, or that the "same" events can be viewed very differently and equally persuasively; but rather that epic theories issue not from crises in techniques of inquiry, but from crises in the world.

In the language of theory, crisis denotes derangement. One form of derangement is the result of forces or conditions beyond control, e.g., the plague which hit Athens during its struggle against Sparta and, according to Thucydides, weakened the vital conventions governing Athenian political life. Other kinds of derangement are closer to what Aristotle called contingent matters, that is, matters about which men can meaningfully deliberate and choose. These kinds of derangements are the result of certain types of "errors" or "mistakes": errors in *arrangements*, in *decisions*, and in *beliefs*. Obviously the three types are often interrelated and combined: mistaken beliefs may produce faulty arrangements and foolish decisions; an unwise decision, e.g., one which overextends the resources of a society, may encourage mistaken beliefs, such as the illusion of omnipotence. Despite their obviousness, these three types may help in clarifying the defining, specific problems of traditional political theory. It is too vague to leave it that theorists are stimulated by problems-in-the-world, and it is misleading to say simply that they are drawn to a class of problems about which something can and should be done. What is all-important is that a problem be a truly theoretical one. A problem such as that presented by the inefficiency of postal services or the ineffectuality of legislative committees may be traceable to errors in arrangement (such as faulty delegations of administrative authority), or to mistaken beliefs (such as that seniority is the most expedient principle for determining committee chairmanships), or to a combination of erroneous arrangements and mistaken beliefs. Without denying the practical importance of these problems, they are not theoretical but technical in nature: they concern the most expeditious means of achieving goals which are, for the most part, agreed on beforehand. Likewise, the question of what decision is proper under particular circumstances is a matter for practical reason or judgment, not for theory.

There is one setting, however, in which specific arrangements, decisions, and beliefs become theoretically interesting. That is when they are "systematically mistaken": when arrangements or decisions appear not as random consequences of a system which otherwise works tolerably well or as the result of the personal foibles of a particular office-holder but as the necessary result of a more extensive set of evils which can confidently be expected to continue producing similar results. Such a system would be systematically deranged. An illustration of what is being argued here is provided by Plato's criticism of Athenian democracy. The main thrust of his criticism was not directed against certain policies which he opposed, or even against the democracy's condemnation of Socrates.[73] Rather, the main thrust was toward arguing that the bad policies and actions were bound to occur in one form or another, because the entire polity was systematically ordered in a mistaken way. Another example is provided by Marx. His case against capitalism did not rest on the charges that it chained the workers to a subsistence level, produced wastefully, and unfairly enriched those who owned the instruments of production. It was aimed, instead, at exposing the logic of capitalism which made injustice, alienation, and exploitation inevitabilities rather than contingencies.

This concept of the *systematically* mistaken explains why most political theories contain radical critiques. Their authors have tried to get at the basic principles (in the sense of starting points) which produce mistaken arrangements and wrong actions. This same impulse determines why a political theory takes the form of a symbolic picture of an ordered whole. That it is a whole is dictated by its function, which is to be complementary to, or a substitute for, the systematically disordered whole which the theory seeks to displace. The possibility that the factual world is the outcome of a systematically disordered whole produces still another major difference between the epic political theorist and the scientific theorist. Although each attempts to change men's views of the world, only the former attempts to change the world itself. Although the scientist surely may claim for his theories the daring, beauty, and imaginativeness that are claimed for other forms of endeavor, he will concede that at some point his theory must submit to confirmation by the world. T. H. Huxley spoke sadly of "beautiful" theories tragically murdered by "an ugly little fact." Plato, in contrast, had asked defiantly, "Is our theory any the worse, if we cannot prove it possible that a state so organized should be actually founded?" Epic theory, if it has not strictly attempted to use theory to murder the ugly facts of the world, has taken a very different view of them, refusing to yield to facts the role of arbiter. Facts could never prove the validity of a true theory, because facts, in the form of practices or actions, were "less close to truth than [is] thought."[74] Thus for Plato the political facts of Athenian democracy were perfectly consistent with the theory of democracy, but the theory itself was systematically mistaken in its organizing principles, that is, deranged.

When we turn our attention to political life in the modern states, its appearance seems more suitable to methodical inquiry and mechanical models or theories. Our political and social landscape is dominated by large structures whose premeditated design embodies many of the presuppositions and principles of methodism. They are deliberately fabricated, their processes are composed of defined "steps," and their work is accomplished by a division of specialized labor whose aggregate effect seems marvelously disproportionate to the modest talents which are combined. Not only do these organizations impart regularity and predictability to the major realms of our existence, thereby furnishing the conditions whereby methodical inquiry can pursue its goal of scientifically verifiable knowledge with reasonable hopes of success—for what could be more hopeful than to know that the political and social world is deliberately fashioned to produce regular and predictable behavior?—but also, since these organizations are uniquely the product of mind, rather than of mysterious historical forces, we are able to say with far greater confidence than Hobbes and Vico, who first announced the principle, "we can know it, because we made it."

Yet this is the state of affairs which the greatest modern philosopher of method, Max Weber, foresaw and despaired of, a world of bleak, forbidding, almost sterile reality, dominated by large and impersonal bureaucratic structures which nullified the strivings of those political heroes evoked in "Politics as a Vocation." "A polar night of icy darkness and hardness" was his description of the world to come.[75] In a fundamental sense, our world has become as perhaps no previous world has, the product of design, the product of theories about human structures deliberately created rather than historically articulated. But in another sense, the embodiment of theory in the world has resulted in a world impervious to theory. The giant, routinized structures defy fundamental alteration and, at the same time, display an unchallengeable legitimacy, for the rational, scientific, and technological principles on which they are based seem in perfect accord with an age committed to science, rationalism, and technology. Above all, it is a world which appears to have rendered epic theory superfluous. Theory, as Hegel had foreseen, must take the form of "explanation." Truly it seems to be the age where Minerva's owl has taken flight.

It would seem, then, that the world affirms what the leaders of the behavioral revolution claim, the irrelevance of epic theory. The only trouble is that the world shows increasing signs of coming apart; our political systems are sputtering, our communication networks invaded by cacophony. American society has reached a point where its cities are uninhabitable, its youth disaffected, its races at war with each other, and its hope, its treasure, and the lives of its young men dribbled away in interminable foreign ventures. Our whole world threatens to become anomalous.

Yet amidst this chaos official political science exudes a complacency which almost beggars description. It is excusable that a decade ago a political scientist could contend that only a "fanatic" would want to "maximize" political equality and popular sovereignty at the expense of other values, such as leisure, privacy, consensus, stability, and status. But it is less excusable to find the following in a recent collection of papers delivered before the APSA and subsequently published under its imprimatur: "Our discipline is enjoying a new coherence, a pleasant sense of unity, and self-confident identity that fits its rapid growth and healthy mien."[76] Polanyi has remarked that "it is the normal practice of scientists to ignore evidence which appears incompatible with the accepted system of scientific knowledge, in the hope that it will prove false or irrelevant."[77] In this spirit American political scientists continue to devote great energy to explaining how various agencies ingeniously work at the political socialization of our citizens and future citizens while mobs burn parts of our cities, students defy campus rules and authorities, and a new generation questions the whole range of civic obligations. And while American political scientists have laboriously erected "incrementalism" into a dogma and extolled its merits as a style of decision-making that is "realistic," it is apparent to all that the society suffers from maladies—the decay of the cities, the increasing cultural and economic gap between our minorities and our majority, crisis in the educational system, destruction of our natural environment—which call for the most precedent-shattering and radical measures.

Amidst all this, a political scientist approvingly quotes the following from a social scientist: "To argue that an existing order is 'imperfect' in comparison with an alternative order of affairs that turns out upon careful inspection to be unobtainable may not be different from saying that the existing order is 'perfect.'"[78]

This assertion poses squarely the issue between political theory on the one side and the alliance between the methodist and the empirical theorist on the other. The issue is not between theories which are normative and those which are not; nor is it between those political scientists who are theoretical and those who are not. Rather it is between those who would restrict the "reach" of theory by dwelling on facts which are selected by what are assumed to be the functional requisites of the existing paradigm, and those who believe that because facts are richer than theories, it is the task of the theoretical imagination to restate new possibilities. In terms of theory, the basic thrust of contemporary political science is not antitheoretical so much as it is deflationary of theory. This is most frequently expressed in the anxiety of the behaviorist who discovers that the philosophy of democracy places excessive demands on the "real world" and hence it is the task of political science to suggest a more realistic version of democratic theory. Thus the authors of *The Civic Culture* admit that it would be possible to "explain" the low degree of political involvement on the part of citizens by "the malfunctioning of democracy." But, they caution, this kind of explanation rests on a belief "that the realities of political life should be molded to fit one's theories of politics." A "somewhat easier and probably more useful task," they contend, is suggested by "the view that theories of politics should be drawn from the realities of political life." Because "the standards have been set unreasonably high," the theory should be changed.[79]

Is it possible that in this genial, Panglossian twilight Minerva's owl is beginning to falter as it speeds over a real world that is increasingly discordant and is beginning to voice demands and hopes that are "unreasonably high"? Perhaps it is possible, especially if we remember that according to Greek statuary, Minerva's pet was a screech-owl, for a screech is the noise both of warning and of pain.

CHAPTER 2

POLITICAL THEORY

FROM VOCATION TO INVOCATION

I

The occasion for the following essay was a conference devoted to the future—to future political theorists and their future and to the future of political theory. No millennial justifications were needed for those choices. A perennial uncertainty and controversy have accompanied political theory: about its relationship to political and social science, to philosophy, and to history, as well as its relationship, if any, to the "real" political world. In my case any invitation to contribute to a volume concerning the future is no simple matter. If that is not sufficient warning about the temporal divide between us, be prepared for a confessional note.

My formative experiences are: a child during the Great Depression, a flier in World War II, a Jew during the era of the Holocaust, and an activist during the sixties—all, except the last, experiences dominated by loss. Although cultural conservatives might count the sixties as a disaster, it was, instead, the loss of liberal innocence. I have asked myself many times how to think about loss—perhaps as the attempts of ordinary men and women to gain a modest purchase on the world, to make a living, only to find it all gone smash by forces over which they have no control? Or as the fate of ordinary youths, barely out of high school, their lives suddenly over in the twisting, helpless spiral of a plane out of control, its black smoke tracing a blasphemous trail against a brilliant Pacific sky, most of the doomed having little idea of making a living, only of outwitting death? In a culture that measures life by notions such as progress, development, innovation, and modernization, loss tends to be an experience we are advised to "get past." Loss belongs to history, while politics and life are about what is still to be done. But maybe loss is related to power and powerlessness and hence has a claim upon theory.

How to memorialize loss theoretically? Shall we memorialize it as contingency, the ill-luck of the draw, as mis(sed)fortune, a mere shortening of our allotted span, another footnote to the Book of Job? Among conservative political theorists of the past—Burke, Tocqueville, and Hegel, for example—loss figured importantly in their responses to the French Revolution, and it is no exaggeration to count political loss as what qualifies them as moderate counterrevolutionaries rather than as reactionaries. Let me try to place the stakes in a more contemporary context by quoting from Adorno:

Knowledge must indeed present the fatally rectilinear succession of victory and defeat, but should also address itself to those things which were not embraced by this dynamic, which fell by the wayside—what might be called the waste products and blind spots that have escaped the dialectic. It is in the nature of the defeated to appear, in their impotence, irrelevant, eccentric, derisory. What transcends the ruling society is not only the potentiality which it develops but also that which did not fit properly into the laws of historical movement. Theory must needs deal with cross-grained, opaque, unassimilated material, which as such admittedly has from the start an anachronistic quality, but is not wholly obsolete since it has outwitted the historical dynamic.[1]

I have chosen that text because it dramatizes a familiar theme in the history of political theory—and in much else—about triumph and defeat. It pictures the triumphant movement as shoving aside, ignoring, the "defeated"—the defeated as that which even the "dialectic" has refused to appropriate, that which is not merely superseded, but surpassed, "anachronistic." What survives of the defeated, the indigestible, the unassimilated, the "cross-grained," the "not wholly obsolete" is what should interest the theorist.

I propose a gloss on that passage of Adorno's: Supposing the thesis has defeated but not obliterated the antithesis, even though potentially it could; the thesis does not choose to destroy the antithesis nor to ingest it, because, paradoxically, the peculiarity of this particular thesis is the condition attached to its perpetuation: if it is to continue as the triumphant thesis, it cannot eliminate, though it has neutralized, the antithesis; indeed, it must see to it that the antithesis remains just healthy enough, even though anachronistic or cross-grained and oppositional. The relationship is symbiotic in the biological sense rather than the dialectical: Symbiosis exists when two different organisms live attached to each other, or one as a tenant of the other, and contribute to each other's support. The antithesis is not lost but subsidized; or perhaps its representatives do not know whether they are lost or even subsidized; they may believe the symbiosis represents just deserts.

I want to pursue these glosses with reference to my original essay, "Political Theory as a Vocation," but now complemented by the notion of invocation.

II

Vocation and invocation produce contrasting resonances. While vocation is associated with "calling" and—thanks to Max Weber and Martin Luther—is freighted with a rich genealogy, invocation is associated with "recalling," and its genealogy or theoretical relevance seems, at first glance, unpromising, since it is apt to be associated with defect, as in the recall of faulty cars. But defect suggests that something is missing, and invocation does have that association.

In ancient Rome an invocation was an appeal to a departed deity. While vocation implies action, a practice, invocation may be said to imply memory and to enjoin recovery. Vocation predicates a certain commitment, "ideal" though not disinterested, to the particular practice in question. Invocation is a response to a certain kind of loss.

A few centuries ago there was a ready answer to the obvious question raised by referring to a practice as a calling, "Who does the calling?" Who authorizes it? Secularism has long since rendered the old answer quaint, but it may not follow that the question itself is irrelevant or necessarily obscurantist.

Consider, for example, the formulation "X is a democratic theorist" or "Y does democratic theory." Are X and Y "called" to "do" democratic theory? By whom? And should theory then become institutionalized, programmatic, and the theorist someone who is certified as a qualified democratic theorist? Or is being a democratic theorist simply a matter of self-selection, a contingent choice of a specialty? Or is the idea of a democratic theorist or of democratic theory an oxymoron and the idea of a calling superfluous in that context? Or is the concept of a calling still plausible, even urgent, in the context of pseudo-democracy, not as a personal choice or as institutional certification but as a public commitment for a time when the idea of publics has pretty much been superseded by that of constituencies or dissolved into various identities based on race, gender, or sexual preference?

For Weber it was precisely the threat to calling in an age of disenchantment that prompted him to distinguish the person called both from the merely technically accomplished and from the enthusiast and to assert at the same time that a person with a true sense of vocation was a rarity because of the demanding combination of exceptional intellectual talents and a moral commitment to the standards prevailing in a particular intellectual "discipline."

Something else is set in motion by the concept of an intellectual calling. The substance of what it is the committed practitioner intends to practice, what he or she is called to, is elevated because deemed worthy of dedication and selflessness, thereby justifying the aura of authority claimed by the practitioner. The paradox that Weber begins to explore is that at the same time that the modern practice of knowledge was attaining unequaled rigor such that the phrase "the search for truth" could be uttered without embarrassment, and the idea of authority taken for granted, that conception of practice was being threatened by two equally modern, well-entrenched subversions, one the cultivation of subjective individualism and the other of objective or rational self-interest. The one causes vocation to lapse into dilettantism, the other to harden into professionalism. To survive, the idea of vocation might have to be revoked and replaced by the sobrieties of method or invoked: Invocation as vocation's conscience recalling it to the cross-grained.

In Luther's formulation there was an aspect of vocation that got lost when Weber attempted to adapt *Beruf* to the age of bureaucratization, the nation-state, and capitalism. For Luther a calling presupposed a certain structure to the community, including a "place" into which the practice fit. In extending hospitality to the holder of a vocational office, the community, in turn, presumed that in pursuing his/her calling the practitioner would, ipso facto, be acting in the interests of the community, and that the community stood in need, not merely in want, of what the practitioner provided. The identity of the community was not problematic: the community was a "historical settlement," either local or provincial, but not yet nationalized. Not "the" community but a noncommunity of communities and of communities within communities. Significantly, for Weber the master theorist of organizational rationalism, vocation rested on an inner decision of the individual, with the inner signifying the passion, devotion, and conviction denied by the structures among which the called had to find a place. Vocation was thus historically out of place and necessarily cross-grained.

III

But what of invocation, of that which signified that something irreplaceable has gone, perhaps fled or been rendered ineffectual, with the result that the world has been diminished? What is at stake is not mere recognition of loss but how one works through it. To invoke presupposes that one has a grasp of how things have been, perhaps how something came to be, how some practice, expectation, or value became sufficiently powerful to gain a foothold and become established in the world. Certainly earlier centuries were no strangers to loss. Thucydides declared that one of the aims of his *History* was to prevent the actions and events of a great war from being forgotten. Loss as the result of a lapse of memory was thus understood to be a historical rather than a theoretical problem. The historian's task was one of recovery and the reconstruction of "true" memory, especially the memory of extraordinary actions, rather than assessment of the effects on the political of the passing or demise of some practice, expectation, or value. The historian's invocation is properly addressed to Mnemosyne, the goddess of memory and Muse of history. Appropriately, Thucydides leaves his *History* unfinished at the point where the contemporary political consequences of the Peloponnesian War press for consideration.[2] Wars have always been among the major instigators of change; yet wars are "over," even though their consequences may not be evident until long afterward. The distinctiveness of modern forms of power is captured by the phrase "the process of modernization," the institutionalization of continuous change so that everything—how, where, and even whether we live, how we relate and communicate—assumes the character of an advance toward incompleteness. But the advance of modernization is made possible by the *displacement* and *replacement* that accompany it. Loss is as often a prerequisite as a side effect. When the casualties involved have figured importantly not only in personal lives but in the fabric of common concerns and, at the same time, the rate at which casualties are produced radically exceeds the limits of ordinary expectancy, with the result that there is not enough time to mourn, to absorb the loss and make sense of it, then there is the political equivalent of blocked grief. For example, the loss may be acted out by erecting a memorial—to the Confederate dead, to the Holocaust, to those who died in the Vietnam War—yet the resentments remain and the questions are unresolved. Blocked grief can take many political forms, some of them twisted: the politics of religious fundamentalism, the religion of patriotic fundamentalism (invoking a mythical common law or original constitution).

In response, a postmodern sensibility might interject that when change is normal, then there are only two constants, appearance and disappearance, both of which reduce to one, change. So why invoke? Why grieve, especially when functional equivalents can be designed? That solution, however, need not foreclose some questions. Who or what has departed? To focus on our present concerns, Is it theory that has departed? Or the theorist? To suggest that theory or theorists are absent and require invocation because they have ceased to be a presence seems only slightly less perverse than the implicit suggestion that they were once objects of veneration. So, what sort of presence are they now? And are they being welcomed into a community, a *Gemeinschaft*, or, instead, into a *Gesellschaft*? Are they a vocation or a profession or dilettantism?

IV

To begin with the most obvious: the number of theorists is, depending on one's view of quantities, impressive or alarming. Although there may be comparatively fewer academic positions in political theory, there are, undeniably, more academics with incomparably more diverse identities claiming to be theorists, more journals devoted to theory, and more theoretical books and articles than in the entire previous history of the world. And the number is not appreciably diminished if one restricts theory to mean "political" theory. Perhaps the strongest testimony to the attraction of theory is that even political scientists, who used to pride themselves on being a collective of hard-nosed empiricists and quantifiers poised to pounce at the slightest scent of theory, now invest their hopes for survival in rational choice, the in-house version of theory. One is tempted to say that the choice of rational choice itself may qualify as rational because there exist hospitable communities with well-defined hierarchical structures that respond to that same language, the business corporation and the public bureaucracy. Does this signify that the supremely practical world has become theory-dependent, and that as a consequence theory-power has become a social or political reality? What kind of world might it be that would welcome not only rational, economics-inspired theories but also theories that rational theorists view as irrational, Adorno's cross-grained representatives? Has, then, an imagined unity of vocation dissolved into various professional forms with different constituencies? And are these multiple possibilities reflective of a new condition in which politics is finally freed of the constraints of an overarching political and becomes a politics of multiplicity?

Certainly it is new politics when, in a constitutional democracy, politics is widely presumed to be merely a synonym for power relationships[3] and at the same time is alleged to be so ubiquitous that one is hard-pressed to identify what is nonpolitics. Moreover, the proliferation of politics is not a simple quantitative phenomenon involving more and more of the same elements but instead is hailed as the discovery or invention of diverse forms of politics, of heterogeneity.

The profusion of politics created by academics is paralleled by the "real-world" industry that produces politics similar to the way that conventional industries produce material goods. The production of politics is made possible by think tanks, pollsters and survey researchers, and pundits. Who owns the means of political production? And is the heavily subsidized research university merely a way of describing a division of labor and a different plant location? What can it mean that a society that produces unparalleled material abundance also produces more politics than any previous society?

Let us call this situation, where no one is called but virtually anyone can come, and where an invocation seems superfluous, "overtheoretization," and let us describe the objects of theories as composing a world profuse with politics, a world of political plenty where the supply of manufactured politics is sufficient to allow political action and power to be perceived in virtually every relationship, presumably no monopolies. In this world both theory and politics are ubiquitous and indeterminate. It might seem then that invocation is in a condition worse than anachronistic; it is emeritus, senile. The conception of political theory as vocationless practice is threatened by incoherence or, alternatively, it is enjoying a healthy disjointedness—which is the literal synonym for incoherence. But if we have a situation of disjointed theorists, overtheoretization, and a surplus of politics—that is, a large amount of political activity that goes nowhere—and possibly even an abundance of power, why haven't the laws of supply and demand driven down the price of politics, power, and theorists instead of making them more expensive? Why, if not a monopoly, at least a political oligopoly? Perhaps because of a disconnection. . . . Which brings me to the next question:

What of the political, of that conception of commonality and shared fate? One could say that it is a casualty of the essentialism of antiessentialism and let the matter drop. Instead think of its departure as marking the crumbling of the language of commonality. What remains of commonality is the experience of feeling embarrassed by references to "the common good" or even to its corrupt form, "the public interest." Politics takes advantage and promotes privatization, attacking what has been left exposed by a weakened commonality, erasing affirmative action, affirming a punitive welfarism, loosening the connection between public education and democracy while strengthening the influence of business interests over educational policy. Thus the answer to an earlier question of how to memorialize loss is: as a voucher; how to theorize it: as the privatization of commonalities, as reversing what had been achieved only after intense *political* struggles.

The sentence of archaism that has been passed on the language of commonality is reflective of something more serious than a move in a Lyotardian language game. Consider the profound change in the nature and status of public administration. It used to be described as "public service" to distinguish it from business practices and to demarcate the difference between serving the common good and working for private profit. Now government work is publicly stigmatized as bureaucracy, privately sneered at as the last refuge for minority preferences, and practiced as managerialism and as a prep school for admission to the private sector. Perhaps diversity, with its simultaneous advocacy of hyperpluralism and its demands for inclusiveness, has placed too great a strain on the political, causing it to lose whatever coherence it may have had.

Despite or rather because of disenchantments, Weber balked at embracing reflexivity and clung to the notion of vocation. Was this because he did not doubt that in the practices of the natural sciences the ideal form of true knowledge was now realized, and that in the process the idea of vocation had been preserved? And this even though Weber recognized that science was subverting the communal structures and belief systems that originally had made the idea of vocation meaningful—so much so that when Weber tried to defend "politics as a vocation" he appealed not to truth but to conviction, citing Luther's "Ich kann nichts anders" as the appropriate motto of political man.

For a post-Weberian generation—and I include myself—that found inspiration in alternative, antipositivist philosophies of science, the theoretic primacy of science remained largely unchallenged. On the contrary. The work of Kuhn and others in the history and philosophy of science was invigorating not only because it offered a counterparadigm of science to the positivist paradigm popular among political and social scientists but because it seemed to locate science in a context much like that being traced by some political theorists: a context charged with political contingencies and elements of subjectivity, presided over by an obtuse scientific establishment reluctant to recognize a growing gap between a regnant theory and the purported reality it explained.

V

Yesterday's animosities, as well its areas of mutual concern, are today's indifferences. Assuming that indifference on matters of importance ought not necessarily be viewed indifferently, allow some reflections on that dramatic change and the contrast that it presents to the situation three decades ago, when theory seemed older because its critics categorized it as "traditional" or "normative" and political science seemed younger thanks to the rejuvenating effects of the alleged revolution of behavioralism. My original essay was in part a protest against what might be termed the "undertheoretization of the world" by political scientists and behavioralists, and in part an attempt to indicate the *political* consequences of undertheoretization. Undertheoretization characterizes an uncritical *mentalité* of which many variations are possible. One was described in my original essay: the obsession with perfecting methods of inquiry and relying upon empirical analysis to yield testable propositions and, ultimately, valid laws covering the phenomena under investigation. In general this variation— call it positivism—was driven by a need to find out how the world works and sustained by the faith that there was "a" way to find out, the way of scientific method. It was also driven by a fear that a world left underexplained would fall victim to a riotous subjectivism of which academic political theory was one ideological expression. And so, instead of theory, the search was for "laws" and "regularities," in part because the investigators were suspicious of deviance and in part because they feared chaos. The actual consequence of undertheoretization was not chaos but conformism. What were—and are—the theoretical implications and political consequences of "undertheoretization"? I shall return to that question shortly. First its opposite.

Why "overtheoretization"? And what, if any, are its consequences? If it is being subsidized, what social or political function or contribution is being performed? And whence the urge to theorize even though the idea of theory is ridiculed and condemned by some of the most influential "theorists" of postmodernism? Is it related to the change in the status of politics?

Among the populace politics used to be, and still is, redolent of corruption; now among the cognoscenti it is associated with domination, even though a plausible case might be made for corruption being as prevalent as domination and its necessary condition. Yet the very generality of corruption, the lack of a focused victim, seems to disqualify it as a theoretical object, a casualty of the declining importance of the language of commonality. Domination and its variants (oppression, subjugation, rape, patriarchy, etc.), on the other hand, are the subjects of highly sophisticated theorizing, sensitive to gradations of wrong, to the variety of contexts, different victims, insistent that their subject be theorized. Perhaps overtheoretization is representative of a new and refined theoretic sensibility that has come into being, expressed in the normalization of "heavy" terms, such as domination, violence, oppression, terror—terms that once were reserved for the exceptional or abnormal. Is overtheoretization a response to rampant wrong, and hence fully warranted as a description of both private worlds and the official world, and not at all superfluous or hyperbolic? Or is it trapped in a symbiotic relationship, and if so, to what?

But if overtheoretization is the response to rampant wrong, how to explain a housing situation in which the most notorious theorists of wrong are not only extended hospitality by a certain community, the academy, and even honored as they are being "called"? Where, despite the rage of self-styled "cultural conservatives" for cultural wars to purge the academy of alleged radicalisms, the most subversive, dangerous, and deliberately outrageous among them find that, despite their best efforts, their market value rises in synch with the Dow Jones Index as the most affluent institutions, those most integrated into the same power structures responsible for the wrongs exposed by critics and ever hospitable to the powerful elites that man them, bid for the most celebrated subversives? And how is it that subversion flourishes alongside class divisions within the academy—between "regular" appointees and "gypsies" or contract laborers, not to mention union-busted teaching assistants?

How might we try to understand this peculiar condition where undertheoretization has mutated into overtheoretization, where academic discourse is overloaded with discourses speaking on behalf of those whose lives have been deeply damaged by the official structures of power? In a fragmented academy, where the plane of generality, once represented by ideals of a liberal or humanistic education, has been displaced by particularities, to whom are the theoretical discourses being addressed, and what is the theoretical status of the addressee? Is it as hapless as that of the "citizen" in the public rhetoric? How to characterize and account for an ongoing system of wrongs and for the various discourses specializing in wrongs? I want the emphasis here to fall on "ongoing."

An insight into the "ongoing" is provided by a recent story in the *New York Times*. It described the emergence and popularity of publications that deal solely with the reporting of "the juicy inside stuff" of politics, the tactics, intrigues, and strategies, but not the substantive issues, much less the stakes for those affected by the outcomes and decisions. It depicted a politics deprived of substance, a hermetic politics without a public, the political as pure tactics. Inside politics with no "outside." The story also reported how politicians and their staffs were such avid consumers that work stopped when the periodicals appeared. As an afterthought the story mentioned that the subscription price of these publications was well over two hundred dollars, and that profit margins ran as high as 40 percent, thanks to corporate advertising.[4]

One question suggested by the account might be, what sort of condition, other than narcissism, has been created by accepting as politics actions and actors severed from the concerns that traditionally were their raison d'être? How is it possible for a society to sustain this disembodied, supremely tactical version of politics? Would it be analogous to having *The Prince* unqualified by *The Discourses*? Perhaps a contrast might illuminate what is striking, even unique, about this condition.

Whatever the shortcomings of my original essay, its reference point was plainly to a widely acknowledged crisis in American politics centered in the Vietnam War. Although at the time the war was understood to be connected to other conflicts, such as those over civil rights and racism, and to the revolts taking place in the inner cities, the fact that there was a center lent an intensity to politics as well as to theorizing. The essay accused political science of complicity by its uncritical, accommodative relationship to power, and of being so focused on methodological applications as to be unaware that it was merely producing a simulacrum of the existing political order. Like that of classical paradigm-workers, the ordinary reflex of political scientists was to dismiss any anomalies that might imply that the system was violating its own norms or falling seriously short of them. In the eyes of critics, anomalies were symptomatic of crisis, and crises seemed to be everywhere, not only in the political and constitutional crisis associated with the war, with race relationships, and later with Watergate, but also in the emerging concerns about ecology, the status of the family, sexual mores, and the claims of women. While domestically the political seemed too narrow, too inelastic, in terms of the license it granted to presidential power and to the reach of the national security state, the political was too elastic, too expansive, too inclusive.

In this setting the idea of crisis was pointed and deeply invested with its etymology from the ancient Greek, where *krisis* referred to a condition so grave as to force a turning point. Crisis signified a pathological condition with three essential aspects. First, it represented a decisive moment, either recovery (that is, political renewal) or death (that is, the continuing transfiguration of the state into a megapower justified in demanding the unlimited sacrifices celebrated in John Kennedy's inaugural address and, necessarily, requiring new political and economic structures appropriate to that scale). Second, it was a general condition of politics involving serious constitutional questions as well as questions that transcended the law: about the effects of imperial ambitions upon free institutions at home, and about whether democracy was possible within the present political framework, and about the connections between injustices being visited on a weak minority and what Marx called "wrong in general." And third, it was a moment of suspense and urgency in which things could go one way or the other: Kennedy might attack Cuba; the war might be extended to Cambodia; the police violence against nonviolent African Americans might also be turned against antiwar demonstrators. Theory had, therefore, to adopt a broadly conceived form of intervention sufficient to encompass the scope of the problem yet sufficiently concrete and pointed so as to be able to interpret swiftly changing events to a broad but deeply divided public.

Now in that context "critical" meant something very different from what it tends to mean today, when it is related more to "critic" than to "crisis"—that is, it carries a more contemplative, Kantian, spectatorial connotation of a "judgment" in search of distance rather than an intervention driven by urgency. It is theoretic theory rather than political theory. And even though it makes references to real-world controversies, its engagement is with the conditions, or the politics, of the theoretical that it seeks to settle rather than with the political that is being contested over who gets what and who gets included. It is postpolitical.

But what if society, like theory, is in retreat from general norms and is converging instead toward theory by preferring to be decentered? To whom or what is the claim of wrong being addressed? How can one dissolve the public into differences, that is, privatize the public as the personal, and then launch an appeal that seems to presuppose a public of shared values traditionally represented by the idea of the citizen? Conservatives and postmodernists alike are antistatist, except that conservatives know what some postmodernists have forgotten, that multiple centers mean multiple masters: witness feudalism, the great Western experience of decentered societies, and then consider the baronial claims of Ted Turner (with or without Lady Jane) or of George Soros or of Bill Gates.

If the plane of generality is proscribed to the contemporary theoretical vocabulary and, as a consequence, no paradigmatic theory is possible, nor any concept of anomalies, at least not in the sense previously understood, then the paradox: critical theorists are normal scientists for a society without a paradigm; the new paradigm is the nonparadigmatic, and critical theory is the revolt of the normal scientists, or is normal theory for a world that has apparently transcended anomalies, crises, and turning points.

Perhaps, however, there is something paradigmatic left: the domination of the world by change, by changes that are, to a significant degree, premeditated, however imperfect the grasp of unintended consequences. Change as the euphemism for the systematic gain and loss of power,[5] which is helped along as the prevalence of change undercuts the fact/norm distinction: the fact of change, the particular form that it assumes in a technology-driven culture (say, a computer or genetic cloning), is simultaneously an assertion of power-as-value, as the embodiment of a demonstrable superiority. That means, among other things, that the standpoint of criticism is undercut: power erases the disjunction between fact and value; fact has become value and value inseparable from the fact of its embodiment. The connecting element is power made possible by the loss, by that power which has been eliminated or cast off to allow full rein to fact.

To say that critical theory is normal suggests that it has taken or usurped the place of description and that this accounts for why, in the absence of crisis, criticism flourishes, and why it has assumed the forms that it has—that is, forms that are adapted to a world without crises, anomalies, or turning points.

VI

What is the shape of the present political world such that it is either immune to crisis or capable of postponing it indefinitely, but at the same time acknowledges that misfortune, intolerance, inequalities, and injustice are present, yet is so self-assured as to be broadly tolerant to theories that proclaim themselves to be subversive, transgressive, even outrageous—and that are viewed as such by conservative commentators? Here is a not unrepresentative pronouncement about the condition of the world:

> Has there ever been a moment quite like this? In the United States high yield re-tirement accounts are making near-millionaires of thousands of salaried workers and hourly wage earners. In India resort towns are crammed. . . . No major inter-national wars are being fought. The world has its ugly regional conflicts . . . but no Stalin, no Hitler, no Mao. . . . Democracies flourish. The end of the cold war has removed ideological chains and with them distortions of economies rooted in big-power rivalries.[6]

Or as a writer put it in the *Wall Street Journal*, the present state of the nation's economy is "utopia." Or as an economic advisor to the president put it, "This is the best of all possible worlds."

The importance of such pronouncements is not that their authors make no allowance for the possibility of, say, a lapse into a recession; or that no one seems upset by the hyperbole. Rather what is significant is that there is no notion of a turning point. A setback perhaps, even a downturn. Instead a system seem-ingly crisis-proof. It is as though the sole motor of change is the one embodied in the dynamics of the system itself; that the system sets the terms or limits of change so that setbacks do not disrupt the perpetual motion machine. The ap-propriation of change means control over the definition of acceptable risks or consequences, injuries, damages: e.g., downsizing, worker obsolescence, safety standards in the workplace, income gaps, health care, etc. I shall call this the "systematization of loss." In the official rhetoric, however, loss is integrated into a system that is represented as too complex, too universal and interconnected—in short, so overpowering (literally) yet exquisitely sensitive as to forbid actions any more challenging than those enveloped in the Delphic soporifics of the chairman of the Federal Reserve Board. Certainly the conviction that we live in utopia is not wholly groundless, given the opportunities of the educated or trained for achieving wealth and status, the low levels of unemployment (leaving aside the quality of the jobs), scientific progress, technological innovations, and the unchallenged status of the world's only super- and potentially interstellar power.

Yet there is the dark and seemingly inseparable side: the horrendously harsh system of criminal justice, the persistent racism, the hostility toward the aspira-tions of women, the widening chasms between classes, the epic levels of politi-cal and corporate corruption, the reluctance of political and corporate leaders to confront ecological dangers except by proposing a system whereby indus-trialists who pollute less than their assigned quota may sell that differential to those who pollute more: which provokes the question, which is the nightmare, the problem or the solution? But the answer is "both and simultaneously." Or, stated differently, the answer is that we live in a utopia in which loss has been systematized, a utopia whose existence depends symbiotically on the perpetuation of dystopia.

Perhaps, then, it is the combination of utopia and dystopia that is the peculiarity of our time. To be sure, every epoch embodies some elements of that combination, and Dickens did characterize a certain epoch as "the best of times" and "the worst of times." To cite such examples, however, only obscures the peculiar relationship between the contemporary utopia and its dystopia. Dystopia is not the name for a political condition where injustice is frequent, or officials act arbitrarily, or the populace is systematically misled—although these actions may, in fact, recur regularly. Rather, dystopia represents a political condition in which injustice, arbitrariness, and deception literally contradict the core principles that form the identity of the utopia. Racism is dystopia's antithesis to utopia's equal protection of the laws. Thus the two, though antithetical, are connected: we might think of utopia as the positive pole, dystopia as the negative.

For the most part, although not always, past theories of utopia were unambiguous: their realization did not depend upon the misery, insecurity, and dependency of many but was supposed to preclude those evils. So the peculiarity of this utopia is that unlike previous utopias, where the blessed land was depicted as the antithesis of the wicked and unjust world "outside," the realized utopia incorporates dystopia. Its opposite is "inside" because this particular utopia cannot be realized without dystopia, without reproducing it; hence utopia never promises to eliminate dystopia, merely to be allowed to recruit from its meritocratic escapees. The very language used, "the *persistence* of racism," "*generations* of those on welfare," is not meant to call the utopia into question but to state some of its conditions while offering object lessons. Similarly the periodic calls for cleaning up political and corporate corruption. A few sacrificial bulls may be offered up but, as every Poli Sci 1 student learns, the system could not work without corruption or with republican civic virtue. Since the eighteenth century, it has promoted, instead, the policy sciences for containing and, if necessary, ameliorating dystopia manifestations, though never eliminating them altogether.

The inherency of dystopia within utopia was understood early on when the ideological representation of the utopia, of its allegedly lawlike character, was first adumbrated by Adam Smith and then confirmed by the so-called gloomy science of the Manchester School of economics.

What does the persistence of dystopia signify? If it does not represent a crisis because of its inherency, then where, if anywhere, is crisis located? If crisis has lost its salience in the "real" world because the real has annexed the symptoms of crisis to the "ideal," made evil integral to the process, that would suggest either that the concept of crisis should simply be abandoned or, alternatively, that it should be sought in a different location.

The first alternative is a counsel of surrender to precisely that form of technological determinism advocated daily by the pundits, but perhaps at least one concession has to be entered into the classical conception of crisis: the notion of a crucial turning point may have to be discarded, defeated by the combination of utopian and dystopian elements.

A historian of an earlier generation once remarked that "1848 was the turning-point of the 19th century on which the century forgot to turn." One hundred and fifty years after that revolutionary moment went uncelebrated, one is tempted to say that ours is a century unable to turn, except linguistically. This would confirm Marx's worst fear, conceived in the *Grundrisse*, of a capitalism that would experience ups and downs yet be sufficiently crisis-proof to avoid an apocalypse. Marx's gloom would be deepened had he witnessed the institutions developed by later capitalism to ameliorate crises: the IMF, the World Bank, the European Union, and the Federal Reserve system. To which we might also add the political counterpart, the politics of centrism. Thus we are left with the two remaining criteria of crisis: urgency and generality. What in our present condition might satisfy those criteria? It would not be difficult to show that social, economic, political, and cultural inequalities—all those dystopian phenomena—are running deep and wide in our society, and that, given the present concentration of power in the society, there is no evidence of a will to reverse them or of the oppositional culture committed to nurturing that will.

Marx's utopia envisioned not only the liberation of productive power, the power that formed the necessary condition of all the other forms of power, but that the material and cultural fruits of power's liberation would be shared as equally as possible and, just as important, shared synchronistically—that is, the benefits would not be confined to some while others would have to postpone their gratifications. To state it differently, Marx might be said to have envisioned a society in which every member was contemporaneous with every other member, dwelling in the same material and cultural temporality and enjoying its advantages.

But what if our utopia is peculiar, not only because it depends on dystopic elements, or because it systematically excludes many of its members from the advantages of utopia, but because it forces many of its members to remain in a different epoch or epochs than that being experienced or exploited by those who occupy various levels of power and reward in the utopia? The first group remains mired in history—and, parenthetically, makes cultural studies possible—while the second has evolved into some ahistorical stage, that is, a stage in which the traditional idea of history has been transcended. The posthistorical stage is characterized by the rapid changes associated with technological innovation—so rapid that while innovation may be temporarily experienced, its relentlessly protean character means that it cannot be *lived*. It cannot be preserved, held in trust, or inherited. The most spectacular form of continuous change is, of course, in communications, especially in computer technology.

To illustrate our point that change is the euphemism for a new constitution of power relationships: Consider Silicon Valley; consider further those, mostly of poor Hispanic extraction, who patiently assemble the chips crucial to the technology: one knows for certain that when the workday is over the chip assemblers do not go home and click on Windows 2000.

The difference in epochs also marks contrasts in wealth, power, education, and life-chances. The difference in epochs and the contrasts in power have their political counterpart; that brings me to the second criterion of crisis, the criterion of generality. The political is the most revealing of these differences because it is there that the manipulation of epochs is most evident or blatant. The mass of the population is periodically doused with the rhetoric of democracy and assured that it lives in a democratic society and that democracy is the condition to which all progressive-minded societies should aspire. Yet that democracy is not meant to realize the demos but to constrain and neutralize it by the arts of electoral engineering and opinion management. It is, necessarily, regressive. Democracy is embalmed in public rhetoric precisely in order to memorialize its loss of substance. Substantive democracy—equalizing, participatory, commonalizing—is antithetical to everything that a high-reward, meritocratic society stands for. At the same moment that advanced societies have identified their progressive character with perpetual technological innovation they have defined themselves through policies that are regressive in many of their effects. Democracy is where those effects are registered. By virtually every important official norm—efficiency, incentives to unequal rewards, hierarchical principles of authority, expertise—it appears anachronistic, dysynchronous. The crux of the problem is that high-technology, globalized capitalism is radically incongruent with democracy. Politics, society, and individual modes of existence are being defined in ways that empirically falsify democracy as untrue of the powerful utopian side and therefore suitable for the powerless dystopian side.

But are the surviving forms of democracy sufficiently cross-grained to form the stuff of a continuing opposition to the technological thesis of corporate, global capitalism, or is democracy doomed to become merely an archaic deposit in the archaeology of power? The answer depends importantly on the vocation chosen by a "class," that is, by the standards of technological capitalism, as anachronistic as the idea and practice of democracy.

The crisis of democracy is also a crisis for the intellectual, especially for the academic intellectual in most of the social sciences and humanities. A climate of opinion is being developed in which tenure, academic freedom, and faculty roles in university governance are likely to be changed in favor of even more managerial control. At the same time, the idea of the "virtual university" tailored to the needs of a technologically driven society is gaining support, not least because it offers the hope, mainly illusory, that by a severely practical curriculum its students can climb the wall separating the dystopian from the utopian side. When scrutinized according to such measures as cost-effectiveness, the bottom line, and productivity, the ideals of the humanistic liberal arts education cannot survive, except as an appendage to the culture industry or as a Potemkin village where the sons and daughters of the rich and infamous receive a polish unobtainable elsewhere. Otherwise, from the point of view of our utopia managers, there is no justification for the remainder of traditional scholarly and intellectual activities.

It would be nice to end on an uplifting note and invoke political theory to come to the aid of democracy, but besides being fatuous that call may be too late in the day. During the few decades that have elapsed since my original essay the academic intellectual has undergone a dizzying series of intellectual permutations—Marxism, critical theory, poststructuralism, deconstructionism, neopragmatism, etc. The theorist, in other words, has replicated the pace of technological change: he and she are synchronous with the utopia. That means, among other things, that they have aligned themselves with a future that is identified not with the elevation of the brawny, but with the care and feeding of the brainy classes. While the brainy classes live lives of permanent revolution, the masses, who represent the stuff of democracy, live lives of quiet desperation at the opposite end of that revolutionary pole, which Gramsci described as "detached from their traditional ideologies."

Gramsci also defined crisis: "The old is dying and the new cannot be born."[7] Perhaps our invocation might revise this definition to read, "The new is killing us and the old, as yet, is not required to be reborn, but revitalized." Revitalized, that is, as an element in the unborn theory that will recognize democracy as the dystopia of our time and understand that the opposite is condemned to be oppositional.

PART TWO

HISTORICAL

ANCIENT AND MODERN DEMOCRACY

CHAPTER 3

TRANSGRESSION, EQUALITY, AND VOICE

I

Thanks to the influence of ancient writers and of Aristotle in particular, it was long believed that the practices of governance and politics naturally grouped themselves into forms or constitutions, such as kingship or aristocracy, and that each form provided the norms that its type of regime should strive to realize.

That belief is reflected in contemporary liberal versions of democracy. According to one of the most influential theorists of liberal democracy, the "coercive political power which citizens exercise over one another when fundamental questions are at stake" is legitimate "only when it is exercised in accordance with a constitution the essentials of which all citizens may reasonably be expected to endorse in the light of principles and ideals acceptable to them as reasonable and rational."[1] This way of thinking eliminates the possibility that democracy may have been, and still is, a phenomenon that can be housed, but may not be realized, within a form.

The notion of "transgression" will be my way of representing a different location of democracy, while the notion of "voice" is meant to call attention to what ancient democracy most notably lacked, discursive traditions that emphasized, as the core of democracy, its demotic and participatory elements.

In discussing democracy, it is almost irresistible for students of ancient political theory to adopt Aristotle's starting point and to treat equality as the decisive mark of democracy and to assume that the meaning of democracy is exhausted in a description of the constitutional form given to equality. Democratic equality is usually conceived within, rarely apart from, a constitutional structure. This is not to suggest that ideas of equality have not been an important part of the ideology of democracy or that the role of constitutional forms is insignificant. My point is exactly the opposite: a constitution can be a potent means of shaping a particular kind of democracy by subjecting the demos to institutional constraints in the hope of preventing certain kinds of outcomes, such as the confiscation of the property of the rich. Similarly, the idea of equality can be articulated in a set of practices designed to delimit its possibilities, e.g., all citizens regardless of property may vote but only those with a certain amount of property may hold the higher state offices. Without resorting to legal disqualifications, constitutional practices may favor certain modes of action (e.g., formal eloquence) and privilege certain acting abilities (mastery of legislative strategies) that disadvantage those with no formal education or legal background.[2]

Notwithstanding the efforts of constitutionalists to shape actors, to domesticate them to accord with the practices of a particular *politeia* (constitution), there have been certain spectacular types of action that have broken with constitutional modes. The agonistic impulse of heroic actors is a familiar theme in Greek literature and philosophy. The uneasy relationship of a demonic Alcibiades to Athenian democracy belongs to that same genre. Modern liberal constitutions have frequently been troubled, sometimes subverted, by men bred in military modes of action, and have even more frequently been corrupted by those schooled in the rule-bending ways of financial speculators. The nineteenth-century American *politeia* managed to elect a heroic but hapless general (Grant), who managed to surround himself with clever and unscrupulous speculators, representatives of those great transgressors and heroes, the Robber Barons of nineteenth-century capitalism.

Because the heroic has been claimed as an individualistic category, the idea of an agonistic demos seems not only unfamiliar but oxymoronic. Why should it seem intuitively absurd that an agonistic demos, like an agonistic Alcibiades, might be driven by the needs of its nature to strain at constitutional restraints? Or that the relationship of Alcibiades to Athenian democracy was vexing because two overreachers were confronting each other? The problem that democratic action poses for sensibilities bred to notions of heroic or individual actors is its anonymity.

From this perspective one can easily identify the modes of action, both in antiquity and modern times, by which one can say that a democratic agon has been performed: revolution or popular uprising, collective disobedience, and mass protest. These are typically regarded as destructive or disruptive of established order and as either anticonstitutional or threatening to become such. Democratic action, or the demos as autonomous agent, might be defined as collective action that initially gathers its power from outside the system. It begins with the demos constructing/collecting itself from scattered experiences and fusing these into a self-consciousness about common powerlessness and its causes. The demos is created from a shared realization that powerlessness comes from being shut out of the councils where power's authority is located. The demos becomes political, not simply when it seeks to make a system of governance more responsive to its needs, but when it attempts to shape the political system in order to enable itself to emerge, to make possible a new actor, collective in nature.

Among the ancient writers most often consulted by political theorists today—Thucydides, Plato, Aristotle, and Cicero—equality, like democracy, was typically discussed in relation, first, to a ranked order of virtues or disabilities attributed to each social class, and, second, to the social or political contribution possible to each class in the performance of the various offices that formed the constitutional structure.[3] The common assumption of the ancient commentators was that equality had to be qualified by the "objective" requirements of office in a system.

The most striking feature of political controversies in the contemporary United States is that while philosophers and social scientists have produced a vast literature on equality, the word itself is virtually taboo among practical politicians and in the rhetoric of politics. Talk about "discrimination," while widespread, works to confine public discussion of equality rather than to promote a conception of an egalitarian society. Discrimination is assumed, whether rightly or wrongly, to be a limited phenomenon, referring to discrete practices and specific groups (identified by race, gender, religion, etc.) and hence requiring only pragmatic adjustments such as equal pay for equal work. Equality, on the other hand, implies a general condition and hence is more threatening. In a competitive society with a volatile economy, members do not typically strive for equality but for differential rewards. Accordingly, today no politician dares run on a platform of equality and this despite the well-known fact that inequality, both social and political, is on the increase.[4]

When equality is invoked, it is most often associated with the denial of some status, right, or opportunity, which in turn diminishes the physical, material, and intellectual well-being of persons, their dignity, and their chances of living fulfilling lives. Neither the original American Constitution nor its Bill of Rights mentioned equality. However, Article I, section 2, establishing the basis for representation and direct taxation, sanctioned inequality by distinguishing "free persons" from Indians and "other persons," meaning slaves, and excluding those two categories from incorporation into the civic body. Although later amendments outlawed slavery, affirmed the right to vote regardless of race or "sex," and guaranteed "equal protection" of the laws, a century of struggle was required after the Civil War before African American voting rights were assured, although that did not make equal protection under law a practical reality.

Unequal treatment is less a consequence of unequal rights than of unequal power. Unequal power is often, although not always, related to an inability to act effectively or at all. The question then arises, what kind of democracy is it where equal rights are formally guaranteed but where wealth and power are no less concentrated than poverty and powerlessness?

I propose to explore that question by way of a contrast between Athenian democracy, in which the demos was the major actor, and a democracy I shall call "electoral democracy," or a democracy without the demos.[5]

II

Aristotle's assertion that man is by nature a *politikon zōion* is so familiar that it is easy to overlook the extraordinary element in that characterization (*Pol.* 1253a1–6). To an antidemocratic writer as careful as Aristotle, a notion so sweeping could only make sense if there had been a powerful, undeniable experience of political-ness, an actual practice sufficiently widespread to justify claiming it not simply as a human possibility but as the teleological principle of human nature itself. What was captured, a posteriori, by Aristotle's formula was the revolution in the political accomplished by Athenian citizen democracy of the fifth century.

If space permitted, it would be possible to show that the *politikon zōion* formula was merely one of several instances in which the vocabulary of ancient Greek political theory implicitly accepted the broadening effects of the egalitarian, participatory politics pioneered by Athenian democracy. Plato's efforts to devise a conception of a polity that would promote the good of all social classes (*Rep.* 420b–421c); Aristotle's admission that justice had to respect the claims of equality, that a polity had to accommodate diverse claims, not merely those of birth or wealth, and that the common good should be the criterion for any form of governance (*Pol.* 1283a29–42), were all acknowledgments of the broadened understanding of the political which the achievements of Athenian democracy forced on the intellectualized consciousness.

But if these are the compliments antidemocratic theorists paid to democracy, they are also the source of tensions within theories that strove to preserve various forms of elitism or political exclusivism while simultaneously celebrating the comprehensive or inclusive character of the polis: only beasts or gods, according to Aristotle, had no need of the polis, though manual workers, women, metics, and slaves could never be full members (*Pol.* 1262a1–6; 1277b33–1278a13). He thus denied that the political community (*politikē koinonia*) was coextensive with the polis.[6]

If critics like Tocqueville may be believed, the ongoing crisis of postrevolutionary French politics was principally due to the failure of the bourgeoisie to become precisely what the Athenian demos did become, a politically committed class. That achievement, the self-transformation of the demos into the citizen body (*politeuma*), of the subject into the citizen (*politēs*), is given indirect confirmation by an antidemocrat, such as Aristotle, who acknowledged that whatever the shortcomings of individuals, the demos was better at deliberating public policies than were the few.[7] Or put slightly differently, deliberative politics was the crucial element in the experience by which a demos constructed itself as a political actor. Deliberative politics was for the demos a mode of political development, and by the same token certain other types of politics—bureaucratic, charismatic, or even representative government—arrest that development. A participatory and egalitarian politics that is deliberative serves the political education of the demos. It is the nurturing ground of a democratic *paideia* to which Plato's Academy was the self-consciously radical alternative.

III

The claim, then, is that Athenian democracy was not simply about the extension of something old but the creation of something new that enlarged the conception of the political, expanded the boundaries of political space, and transformed the practices of politics. It involved, above all, the construction of a new actor, autonomous, able to choose and to deliberate collectively. But for the demos to occupy a stage hitherto reserved for heroes, kings, and nobles, it had to overcome or destroy barriers of class, status, wealth, and expertise.

In attempting to establish the idea of the demos as actor, one runs up against certain difficulties created by the dramaturgical models that have strongly influenced conventions governing the understanding of action.[8] This was especially true at Athens, where theatricality was a powerful element in the culture, including the theoretical culture,[9] and where epic standards of action persisted.[10] Accordingly, a "true" political actor was portrayed as an individual who performs a notable individual deed or who utters something memorable.[11] It was as tempting to a Thucydides as it is to modern scholars to fix upon a Pericles and pronounce him to be the paradigm of the praiseworthy democratic actor and, from the same dramatizing impulses, to pounce upon a Cleon and portray him as the counterparadigm, the actor who embodies the violence, passion, and crudity of the demos when it is unrestrained by "moderate" leadership. And later, when there is no Pericles, the rhetors stand in.[12]

Thus the formula of actor-action, with its clear-cut notion of agency, excludes the demos, always a somewhat shadowy, inchoate identity, always in need of the crystallizing energy of a "leader." But if the Athenian demos could not simply be dismissed, it might be reconceptualized as "audience," or spectators who shout their approval or disapproval, or as the buffoon in *The Clouds*.[13] As a result the novelty of the phenomenon of collective force tends to remain conceptually undeveloped. Dramaturgical categories, even those that have been "philosophized," have trouble dealing with a power that does not "act" as a discrete subject, that lacks an identifying genealogy such as birth or wealth or wisdom and the claims to power that accompany them. And it lacks the celebratory voice of the poet, philosopher, or historian that can lend dignity and awe to the bearers of those genealogies. The genealogy of lesser folk presents an exact contrast to genealogies of power: it is a tale of abuse and exploitation, not of great deeds; of powerlessness, not power; of inarticulateness, not voice. A fragment from Antiphanes preserves their protest: "'not democratic' = 'unfair.'"[14] When they manage to exert power, it is only by inventing forms that pool individual weakness.

Accordingly the tendency of historians to link the expansion of equality to changes in the structure of the Athenian military forces seems to me too narrow and to fit more properly under Weber's category of "passive democratization."[15] Recall that during the English civil wars of the 1640s and the wars that followed shortly after the French Revolution of 1789 there were mass armies mobilized and their members exposed to radical political ideologies. Nonetheless, in the immediate postrevolutionary decades there was no significant expansion of popular participation in the major decision-making institutions of those societies. In the case of Athens, doubtless the military contributions of hoplites and thetes lent a certain logic to the extension of civic equality, but something more was needed to explain the hegemony of the demos. In a comparable case Aristotle conceded that slaves and manual workers were "necessary" conditions for the existence of the polis, yet he denied that this constituted grounds for including them in the *politeia*. In American history the descendants of African slaves served in every war fought by the United States but, though emancipated and legally citizens, they have yet to be admitted fully to the equivalent of the *politeuma*. Instead their formal status as voters is subject to the kind of parody that would have delighted Aristophanes: allegedly, during the 1993 gubernatorial election in New Jersey, efforts were made to pay Afro-Americans not to vote—and this by the party of Lincoln.

The tenuous character of modern democratic participation underlined in that incident helps to underscore as well the magnitude of the Athenian achievement of inventing a demos that would be a continuous political subject, one that took part in the operation of the major decision-making institutions of its society. Its presence meant the transformation of politics, from an activity monopolized by those whose property and status allowed them leisure time, to an occupation for those who had little property or leisure. Consequently, instead of the political being the private property of the few, it was broadened and became the property of a new subject, the public.

Historically, democratization has had an energizing effect on social strata whose previous political activity has been sporadic, such as protests, "murmurings," local uprisings, and acts of collective disobedience.[16] At Athens democratization was concentrated in political institutions. Citizens took part in assemblies, law courts, and a range of offices; the sheer volume of their activity has amazed later scholars, who found it incredible that citizens of little means would travel great distances and spend considerable time away from their own concerns to deal with public matters. But with the outbreak of the Peloponnesian War in 431 B.C., that energy would be directed outward and expressed in new ways. Athenian democracy was admired or feared by contemporaries for its innovativeness, boldness, and *periousia*, or "superabundance" of energy, "adventurous beyond their power and daring beyond their judgment," and forever hopeful (1.13, 70). That energy and daring, according to Thucydides, remained focused singlemindedly on winning the war so long as Pericles could restrain the impetuosity of the citizens and persuade them to place the public good of winning the war above their private interests (1.74; 2.40, 61, 65).

Yet the public/private dichotomy that Thucydides has Pericles praise in the Funeral Oration was a standing threat to the leadership principle that Pericles allegedly embodied. In a democracy public concern might legitimately lead to pressures for greater involvement and thus encroach on that "government by the first citizen" admired by Thucydides (2.65). On the other hand, if citizens grew more preoccupied with private concerns, leadership might become more autonomous and democracy more attenuated, an eventuality not unwelcome to modern elites frustrated at the "ungovernability" of democracy.[17]

Following the death of Pericles, Athenian democracy—according to Thucydides—exhibited the excesses that Pericles had managed to contain. It squandered the resources he had carefully husbanded; its whims became the decisive element in public decisions; and its political predominance encouraged a politics of cabals among politicians vying for favor (2.65). Yet Thucydides unintentionally provides the most telling example of post-Periclean popular participation as intelligent, ultimately able to control its passions, and interacting with leaders who offered genuine alternative policies in the context of an illuminating debate concerning the necessary conditions for democratic deliberations—an example, in short, of what Pericles had called the singular achievement of Athenians, combining "daring and deliberation, each carried to its highest power, and both united in the same persons" (2.40).

IV

The episode of the revolt at Mytilene recounted by Thucydides best reveals the demos learning how to be an actor and, at the same time, the kind of experience by which the political was being democratized. It provides, I believe, a more revealing description of Athenian democracy than does Pericles's manipulative Funeral Oration.

When the Mytilineans revolted, the Athenians' first response was to order the killing of the whole male adult population and the enslavement of the women and children. Then, Thucydides relates, "the morrow brought repentance with it and reflexion on the horrid cruelty of a decree, which condemned a whole city to the fate merited only by the guilty" (3.36). A new discussion was begun as "most of the citizens" wanted a chance "to reconsider the matter." Cleon, whom Thucydides despised as "the most violent man at Athens" and "by far the most powerful with the commons," advocated enforcement of the original decree. Despite his alleged influence, he loses the debate and despite his alleged appetite for violence, his speeches contain numerous passages that aim to instruct the citizens on how they ought to deliberate, how grave matters should be pondered, and the situations in which democracy and empire conflict.

His speech begins by daring to pose the possibility Pericles had avoided, of whether "a democracy is incapable of empire" (3.37). Then, provocatively, he tells the Assembly that their empire is a tyranny—the form of political rule that democrats considered their exact opposite—and hence sentimentality has no place in deliberations about imperial rule because it produces confusion about policies. He reassures them that ordinary men are more capable of holding to a steady course than the orators who fit their policies to the prevailing popular mood (3.38). The issue, Cleon insists, is that Mytilene rebelled without cause and by that action challenged the very principle of empire. "For if they were right in rebelling, you must be wrong in ruling." Ruling requires a clear-eyed view of one's interests, "or else you must give up your empire and cultivate honesty without danger" (3.40).

Thucydides's portrait of Cleon was clearly intended as a contrast to Pericles, a judgment modern historians, repelled by the cruelty of the decree, tend to embrace. Yet Cleon's defense of the decree not only echoed a warning made by Pericles but one that was a standard criticism of democracy, now as well as then, that democracies are by nature fickle.[18] In advice that borders on self-subversion, Cleon urges the Athenians to display the steady virtues they have, to ignore the blandishments of orators, and to resist allowing politics to become primarily a contest between leaders (3.37). Like his opponent in the debate, Diodotus, Cleon attempts to instruct the citizenry about the political by emphasizing the distinctive character of the proceedings and the gravity of a setting that requires that they behave not like "the audience of a rhetorician" but like "the council of a city" (3.38).

Cleon's adversary, Diodotus, opposed the decree, but as his argument develops it becomes an analysis of the conditions necessary to genuine deliberation and encompasses a conception both of the democratic citizen and of the democratic, though not Periclean, leader. For Diodotus the issue of the decree does concern Athenian interest, but the context of empire requires that interest be considered on a long-run, enlarged basis rather than an immediate interest, such as punishing a rebellion. How, then, should a democracy go about consulting its long-run interests, and what are they?

As framed by Diodotus, the broad context is political education in democratic responsibility, not only for the assembled citizens but for the rhetor who is engaged in arguing the merits of one policy over another. Those who would serve the citizenry must impose on themselves a certain discipline if democracy is to act wisely. They should avoid calumnizing their rivals, for otherwise citizens will hesitate to stand forward and serve the polis. "The good citizen ought to triumph not by frightening his opponents but by besting them fairly in argument."[19] The crucial obligation is that the speaker ought not to encourage suspicions of the idea of speech (*logos*) or language itself, for that would be to deprive the actor of that which speech makes possible, namely, action informed by forethought (3.42).

Diodotus's rhetor may be said to serve the demos as Plato would later have his Socrates serve the nobility: by raising the particular problem to a more general level, a level, however, that was comprehensible to the Many rather than just the Few and that tried to teach them about the nature of the demands of democratic ruling.[20] The virtue with which Diodotus was concerned was that of the citizen, not, as for Plato, that of the good man. The citizen of Diodotus was man in his corporate capacity.

For their part the citizens should not punish a speaker who offers his best advice but proves unsuccessful in persuading them. (3.42) The relationship between the speakers, who should "make it their business to look a little further," and the citizenry who perforce "judges offhand" is depicted as delicate. It requires, when the counsels of the speakers turn out badly, that the citizenry not absolve themselves of complicity by blaming the speakers alone (III.43). The citizen should understand what the demands of the political are and what it means to think in a political context. "We are not in a court of justice, but in a political assembly; and the question is not justice, but how to make the Mytilineans useful to Athens" (3.44). Citizenship is a deliberative activity, a mode of thinking that deals in considerations and categories different from those used in one's own affairs or when one is a juror judging someone's guilt or innocence. Unlike a law court, a political deliberation means that "we are deliberating for the future more than for the present" (3.44).[21] Adopting the long view not only requires taking into account a wider range of considerations and forces than when a personal matter is involved or when a legal judgment is reached; it demands certain virtues just as surely as Plato's insistence that the search for truth is as much a matter of character as of intellect. At a minimum it requires repressing immediate gratifications, such as the desire for revenge, while recognizing the values of taking care of arrangements so that they will endure.

Diodotus's emphasis on the future as the necessary perspective for the political act of deliberation signals that he is entering that treacherous domain of imperial politics where Thucydides's Pericles had excelled. A modern critic has represented that entrance by Diodotus as an attempt "to break out of the careful rational limits" of politics as taught by Thucydides. Diodotus's speech is said to depict "a world of shadowy powers . . . of pure physis, of nature without limitations or restraint."[22]

The passages in the speech of Diodotus that seem to reflect a deep irrationalism are accompanied by some broad generalizations about the inefficacy of legal restraints that suggest a more analytical bent than he is credited with. There are, Diodotus held, certain driving forces in human nature that take different forms with different social classes. "As long as poverty gives men the courage of necessity," they will defy the laws. That reference is clearly to the poorer classes, and it anticipates the notion of later writers, from Aristotle to Marx to Hannah Arendt, that those classes live in a "realm of necessity."[23] Diodotus does not exempt the upper classes: equally dangerous are those to whom "power gives . . . the ambition natural to the confident and the proud" (3.45).[24] The futile attempts to control those drives Diodotus named "legal terror." A city such as Mytilene will rebel because it refuses to believe that it can fail. Men and cities break the law or exceed their own capabilities because hope and cupidity feed on each other while fortune (tuchē) tempts them on:

> This is especially the case with communities because the stakes played for are the highest, freedom or empire, and, when all are acting together, each man irrationally magnifies his own capacity. 3.45

Diodotus has been charged with "imposing a rigid antithesis between the right and the expedient," and this despite the fact that his policy spared more lives.[25] In emphasizing the moral deficiencies of Diodotus's policy, an accompanying concern is overlooked: not only what is to be done but what is to be taught. Diodotus draws on familiar proverbial wisdom about man's temptation to overreach, but he uses it to orient the listeners to the unfamiliar, to give them some means of understanding the magnitudes of power and human emotions involved in empire, the most massive form of human power known to the times. Imperial power was at least as awe-inspiring to that age as science-based technological power is to our own. Hence, when Diodotus and others appeal to *expediency* and *interest*, those terms strike a certain deflationary, demythologizing note, humanizing what is otherwise inhuman, delimiting the effects of concentrated power without claiming to control it perfectly, much less being able to abandon it.

> It is far more useful [Diodotus says] for the preservation of our empire voluntarily to put up with injustice [i.e., the revolt] than to put to death, however justly, those whom it is our interest to keep alive. 3.47

Diodotus's appeal to interest against justice, although it offends the modern sensibility, is a more complex argument than is usually conceded. It can be construed as a claim on behalf of freedom against the coercive necessity now embodied in justice, a justice that leaves no room for political considerations but insists on enforcing what is justified, even if it results in horrendous human suffering. Diodotus makes plain what those political considerations should be. "In all the cities the people is your friend." To butcher "the people of Mytilene . . . will play directly into the hands of the higher classes" (3.47). What matters is the policy proper to a democratic imperium:

> The right course with freemen [who have revolted to protect their independence] is not to chastize them rigorously when they do rise, but rigorously to watch them before they rise, to prevent their even entertaining the idea, and, the insurrection suppressed, to make as few responsible for it as possible. 3.46

V

> To discover the complete horizon of a society's symbolic values, it is
> necessary to map out its transgressions.
> —Marcel Detienne[26]

Spinoza aside for the moment, throughout the history of what might be called formal political theory, it is difficult to find a theorist who devoted much care to developing a conception of the "people" as actor. Save for some comments about a limited right of the people to revolt, as in the *Vindiciae contra tyrannos* (1579), or in some of the pamphlet literature of the English Civil War and Locke's *Second Treatise*, it was not until Rousseau's *Social Contract* and its concept of the "general will" that collective action was located at the center of politics. However, Rousseau's "general will" was constructed so as to be "right" rather than populist.[27] Rousseau could not conceive of a self-fashioning people and so he invents, literally, a deus ex machina, a Great Legislator who is to transform human nature by giving it a collective cast and then prescribe the framework of beliefs and practice that ensures the proper operation of the *volonté général*.[28] Except for rare elections, the idea of a democratic practice, of how ordinary people might actually cultivate political skills, remained undeveloped by Rousseau.

Given the traditional silence on the matter, if we are to theorize about Athenian democracy and the emergence of a new conception of political practice, it is necessary to find appropriate ways of representing a new collective actor. A conception of the demos as an actor requires a theoretical equivalent to Hobbes's account of an actor whose passions and power drives, uncertainties and anxieties, fancies and hopes provide an account of a new and complex presence, and to a transformation in the terms of the political. Such a conception would have to allow, as Hobbes had, that the dynamic that leads to great achievements may also be its undoing.

I want to sketch an alternative, drawn from a contemporary of Hobbes, that would do for the democratic collective actor what Hobbes had done for the bourgeois individual. Then I want to show, first, how that alternative was prefigured in ancient Greek theory but given a negative formulation; second, how Athenian democratic practices helped to transform the democratic actor; and third, what the implications of that transformation were.

My alternative starting point is Spinoza.[29] My concern here is not with the qualifications he placed on democracy but with his delineation of a new kind of actor and its raw power. Specifically, his concept of *conatus*, which Spinoza was especially concerned to relate to his notion of "the multitude" (*multitudo*), identifies the Many with a certain elemental force. A similar characterization had been made by ancient critics of democracy and would be repeated by modern ones.[30] Everything, Spinoza declared, endeavors to persist in its own being; it opposes any other thing that would take away its existence. Accordingly, the essence of any thing is its power, "whereby, either alone or with other things, it acts or endeavors to act."[31] The multitude collectively embodies a *conatus*, but because its psychology is limited to what Spinoza called the realm of imagination (*imaginatio*) and unable to ascend to the level of reason, it remains ignorant, superstitious, prone to crude and fantastic religious beliefs. The *imaginatio* of the multitude leaves it vulnerable to violent emotions that breed conflict, violence, and other forms of social disorder. Even when it is not violent, the multitude is gripped by wildly fluctuating opinions that oscillate between fear and hope.[32]

Spinoza believed the multitude was incapable of achieving rationality, but he hoped that by establishing proper institutions, including a religion purified of superstition, the mentality of the multitude could be elevated to an imitation of rational thought. Without endorsing Spinoza's conclusion, which leads to a system of dual truth, one for the masses and the other for the rational few, we need to ask what was the dynamic that Spinoza perceived in the multitude and its *conatus* that led him beyond the ancient critics to a rare defense of democracy?

The dynamics of *conatus* are such as to require an external cause for a thing to come into existence: resistance brings with it a heightened sense of self-awareness, of distinctive identity. Nietzsche, who had a critical admiration for Spinoza, described it this way:

> The wish to preserve oneself is the symptom of a condition of distress, of a limitation of the really fundamental instinct of life which aims at the expansion of power and wishing for that, frequently risks and even sacrifices self-preservation.[33]

Applying these notions to ancient Athens, we might say that while the demos represents the existence and vitality of a natural entity, its *conatus* may also be the source of a problematic. The demos exists as striving, but that drive may be directed not at assuring duration to its existence but at challenging its own finitude. The tangible expression of that problematic would be the leap from polis to empire.

Spinoza's multitude, absent Spinoza's sympathies and hopes, is prefigured in Plato's "beast" and belongs to a chain of similar images: of Muentzerites, Luther's "murdering, thieving peasants," Shakespeare's Jack Cade, the "mob" or revolutionary sansculottes, and Alexander Hamilton's "great beast." The resort to physical or animalistic imagery to describe the multitude, or hoi polloi, recognizes, *malgré lui*, the actual condition of most people in premodern societies.

Farmers and craftsmen, Socrates tells Alcibiades, "know but the things of the body" (*Alc.* 1.131a–b). They lived and worked close to the earth; they were often the victims of scavenging armies; and they were the evidence for claims that some beings were not fully human. That their psychology should be typically described as "passionate" confirms Spinoza's ontology in which existence follows essence: they threaten because their existence is continuously threatened.

Although it is possible to catch anticipations of Spinoza's *multitudo* and its *conatus* in unfriendly comments by ancient critics of Athenian democracy, the Athenian demos seems to have evolved into a different being whose essence is civic: a full-fledged citizenry whose being is validated through the numerous institutions in which it takes an active part. The beast has somehow become a deliberating citizen.

VI

How to understand the transformation? A starting point is provided by one of the great modern Hellenists who was also a great antidemocrat and, perhaps coincidentally or not, a great icon among postmodernists.

I want to recall Nietzsche's contrast between "slave morality" and "aristocratic morality." Nietzsche's aristocrat is pictured as a vigorous warrior-type, a man who takes risks, provokes strife, overflows with vitality, in short, a natural transgressor of conventions.[34] In contrast, slave morality, the morality of the masses, is leveling, resentful of aristocratic superiority, artful in contriving meshes of law and morality by which to trap their superior and to devitalize him, and aspires only to secure small pleasures.[35]

If, in the context of Athenian politics of the fifth century, we were to turn the perspectivist trick against Nietzsche and reverse his account of the two moralities, a case might be made that transgression was crucial to the making of a democratic actor. The signs of a presence, transgressive but anonymous, have to be sought in those who were its foes, in those who looked on the demos as the embodiment of the antipolitical and the antitheoretical.

Recall Plato's portrait of Callicles in *Gorgias*: a transgressive actor,[36] a figure of primal energy and demonic will, who delights in images of "smashing" the restraints imposed by the masses in the name of "equal shares" and "trampling" on all of the cultural restraints designed to repress the worthy few. Yet Callicles is not proposing to imitate the Homeric hero who seeks to best another solitary champion; rather he is matching himself against the demos, tacitly acknowledging that they have defied the norms of nature to set up their own standards.

> Those who lay down the rules are the weak men, the many. And so they lay down the rules and assign their praise and blame with their eye on themselves and their own advantage. They terrorize the stronger men capable of having more. *Gorg.* 483b–c.[37]

The identification of the Many with a natural power that is said, paradoxically, to transmute itself into artificial conventions, which equally paradoxically are described as the triumph of the weak, resurfaced in Plato's *Republic*. There the demos is likened to "a great strong beast" (493a–b) but its qualities are again embodied in its enemy, Thrasymachus, the sophist who panders to the many while exploiting their elemental power (336b). Thrasymachus is pictured by Plato as a crude man, physically threatening and verbally aggressive, and likened to a wolf. The position that Thrasymachus attempts to defend is equally crude and physical. The strong rule in their own interest and adopt injustice as their guiding principle. This leads initially to the claim that all forms of government operate according to those same principles and that democracy is the power of sheer numbers (338d6–339a4). Later in the dialogue, however, Socrates refines that characterization of democracy while at the same time retaining the elemental, physical quality of democratic power, but now condensed and institutionalized. In a passage where Socrates depicts the plight of the exceptional man in a democracy, the physical power of the Many has undergone a transformation without losing its coercive quality:

> Whenever the populace crowds together at any public gathering, in the Assembly, the law-courts, the theater, or the camp, and sits there clamoring its approval or disapproval, both alike excessive, of whatever is being said or done; booing and clapping till the rocks ring and the whole place redoubles the noise of their applause and outcries. . . . What sort of private instruction will have given him the

strength to hold out against the force of such a torrent, or will save him from being swept away down the stream, until he accepts all their notions of right and wrong, does as they do, and comes to be just such a man as they are?[38]

In such hostile representations of democracy as the embodiment of a barely civilized, almost raw force—the demos as Id and crude Superego—there was the suggestion of a new political presence that had succeeded in developing its own political culture. The strength of that achievement can be measured by the nature of its threat. Plato conjures up horrific imagery as he contemplates the deformed Many invading "the shrine of philosophy": "a multitude of stunted natures, whose souls a life of drudgery has warped and maimed no less surely than their sedentary crafts has disfigured their bodies" (*Rep.* 495d–e). As perceived by Plato, democracy was an invasion of the psyche, contesting for nothing less than the "soul" of all citizens. Plato's political philosophy and moral psychology were shaped as much by the cultural challenge of democracy as by its political claims, so much so that Plato felt compelled to defend the soul in political terms:

> And for the structures and orderings of the soul the name is "lawful" and "law," from which people become lawful and orderly; and these are justice and temperance. *Gorg.* 504d

Behind the achievement by which the beast became a political animal with its own *paideia* lay a long and dim history. It included institutions and practices of self-help by which ordinary people came to the assistance of their neighbors: interceding for those threatened with slavery; responding to the call for witnesses to crimes; shouldering communal responsibility for actions by its members; relying on violence, not for revenge or simple brutality but to redress wrong; and, not least, rebelling against unpopular authorities.[39] There is a long political anthropology by which the demos is prepared for the politics of the city. Corporate solidarity and self-consciousness are its responses to oppression. "The harshest and most resented aspect" of the pre-Solonian constitution, according to Aristotle, was the enslavement by the rich of the debt-ridden poor, who "had virtually no share in any aspect of government." When Solon later intervenes to mediate the "severe strife" between classes, it is apparent that the Many have acquired a measure of cohesion; they are one "side" to the struggle, and they "oppose the leaders of the state."[40] Thus the "essence" of the Many acquires more complexity as it invents itself in collective action and becomes— save for military formations—the principal collective actor.[41]

VII

The complexity of the collective actor is displayed not only in its adaptation to the institutions of the polis, such as the assembly and law courts, and by the adaptation of those institutions to demotic needs, but in its greatest monument, the empire dominated by the democratic polis of Athens and defended in a war that eventually resulted in its loss. The empire was testimony to both the transgressive and aggressive impulses of the Many and to an epical hero whose agon goes mostly uncelebrated by poets and philosophers and only ambivalently by ancient historians. The Many display a willingness to sacrifice and a seemingly inexhaustible energy that enables them to perform prodigies, to succumb to hubris, to rebound from defeats, even to continue to fight after abandoning their city. The beast has become the citizen without losing its vitality, truly a *politikon zōion*.

That actor is portrayed in one of Thucydides's most striking episodes, the so-called Melian dialogue that is commonly interpreted as a brutal, excessive display of the natural right of the stronger. Melos, a colony of Sparta, refused to capitulate to Athens and in the end its adult male population was slaughtered and its women and children enslaved. Because the doomed Melians, with an attractive naiveté, choose to die rather than surrender, the Athenian part of the dialogue is rarely discussed as an example of political sophistication strikingly at odds with the dismissive treatment of democratic capabilities by the philosophers. At the first discussions the Athenians display a confidence in their own abilities to conduct political negotiations: they accept the Melian proposal to discuss matters in private with "the few," thus waiving the advantage of a public setting where the democrat was most at home. The Athenians go a step further and propose that both sides abstain from set speeches, a format familiar to a rhetorical democracy, and proceed, instead, to deal with practical matters one at a time (5.85, 89). In the exchanges that follow, the Athenians instruct the Melians in how one should go about reasoning in public matters. They should attend to the facts and not allow hope to cloud reality and, above all, bear in mind always that the paramount consideration is the survival of the state (5.87). They should not attempt to plead principles of right so long as they are the weaker party (5.89) and expect that the stronger will risk the danger that its rivals might see that generosity as a sign of vulnerability. The world of gods and of mortals is a place, the Athenians explain, where those who can rule others do so. But that does not at all mean that power politics is devoid of principles. "It is certain that those who do not yield to their equals, who keep terms with their superiors, and are moderate towards their inferiors, on the whole succeed best" (5.111). At the end of the exchange, it is the representatives of the demos who urge their enemies to "think over the matter and reflect once and again that it is for your country you are consulting" (5.111). If we recall that the Melians were the representatives of a ruling aristocracy, the episode has the piquancy of a role reversal not unlike Sancho Panza lecturing Don Quixote.

The so-called radical democracy of the fifth century, the democracy of unparalleled popular participation, created an equally extraordinary release of energy that was sublimated into the political. This meant, among other things, a conception of the political sufficient to absorb the energies of a high proportion of the members of the polis, or, more precisely, a straining toward such a conception by extending its limits outward while destroying certain internal social boundaries erected in the name of birth or wealth or virtue.

Perhaps the most striking confirmation of this are the words that Thucydides attributes to a Corinthian who is part of a delegation sent to gain Sparta's support against the Athenians:

> The Athenians are addicted to innovation, and their designs are characterized by swiftness alike in conception and execution. . . . They are adventurous beyond their power, and daring beyond their judgment, and in danger they are sanguine. . . . They are never at home . . . for they hope by their absence to extend their acquisitions. Their bodies they spend ungrudgingly in their country's cause; their intellect they jealously husband to be employed in her service. . . . They were born into the world to take no rest themselves and to give none to others.[42]

The Aristotelian author of *The Constitution of Athens*, after describing the overthrow of The Thirty, asserts that that was the eleventh change of constitution for the Athenians (41.2). Not all of the changes, perhaps none, were the equivalent of a revolutionary overthrow of an entire social order. Yet most of them enlarged the power of the demos until, in this author's words:

> They have made themselves supreme in all fields: they run everything by decrees of the Ekklesia and by decisions of the dikasteria in which the people are supreme. 41.2

What is more remarkable is the language that Aristotle, no fan of democracy, uses in an immediately preceding passage to characterize the overthrow of The Thirty, the punishment exacted of them and their followers, and the restoration of democracy. "The Athenians appear to have handled their affairs, both private and public, as well and with as much statesmanship as any people have ever shown in a similar situation" (40.3). He goes on to praise the demos for their moderation and their scrupulous insistence on repaying the State debts incurred by The Thirty. He concludes that "it was just that the people should take control because they had secured their return by their own efforts" (41.1–2). It is not too much to say that what is being described is an unusual level of political maturity and self-confidence that had been acquired by the demos during the previous century.[43] That is, its political skills were "refined" by the constitutional conflicts of the period. Two things about those struggles should be emphasized, since they tend to be true of comparable events later on.

One is that there is always more politics involved than concrete results might suggest.[44] A new statute, a change in the powers of an institution, the abolition of certain established practices are all pitifully small testimony to the enormous amount of human activity, interaction, changes in consciousness, and acquisition of skills that brought about the changes in question. Significant political changes are the product of transgressive actions. They disturb the power relations, interests, expectations, and taboos that typically cluster around all laws and institutions. This leads into the second point.

No ruling group voluntarily cedes its power. "The only way in which oligarchy could be transformed into democracy," de Ste. Croix has written, "was by revolution. I know of no single case in the whole of Greek history in which a ruling oligarchy introduced democracy without compulsion and by a single vote."[45] Transgression provokes contestation because it is, in effect, a social invasion of a preserve from which the invaders had been previously excluded. Hobbes would later claim that something accessible to all is not by nature valuable—except, the democrat would demur, the status of citizen.[46] The triumph of the latter means the democratization of political values, because it entails a rejection of the fundamental aristocratic or oligarchic value of exclusivity.

The invention of a new actor was accompanied by a new conception of politics. Its radicalism can be best appreciated by recalling Aristotle's account of how the tyrant Peisistratus went about destroying the public realm and its demotic politics. While speaking to the people, he had his men collect the people's weapons.

> When he had concluded his speech, he told the crowd not to be surprised or alarmed by what had happened to their weapons; they should go home and look after their private affairs—he would take care of the state. . . . [Peisistratus also offered financial assistance to encourage farming.] He did not want them in the city but scattered in the country, and if they had enough to live on, and were busy with their own affairs, they would neither want to meddle with affairs of state nor have the time to do so. *Ath. Pol.* 15.5–16.5

The new ideal involved not only reclaiming public space but rendering politics transparent. It would be a politics in which discussion and decision were open; where all citizens might speak freely without suffering the humiliation of a Thersites; where power was visible, audible, countable, accountable, and above all, accessible to those without leisure. Transparent politics was the corollary of the revolutionary principle of full popular participation or, more precisely, of freedom understood as truly popular participation.

That politics also posited a contrast between the demotic politics of the Assembly (Ekklesia) and the selective politics of aristocratic factions (*hetaireia*). The central point of the contrast was captured by Aristotle's famous definition of the ideal citizen as one who knows how to rule and be ruled in turn.[47] That definition, though it seems democratic, is not. For it rests on the assumption that the good man, like the aristocrat and oligarch, not only wants to rule and would accept rule by others of his kind, but he would object to being ruled by inferiors. Now while it is true that the demos refused to extend democratic citizenship to women, metics, and slaves, that refusal, unlike the refusal of the aristocrat to admit the demos to high office, would contradict the idea of democratic equality. Or, stated differently, democracy was and is the only political ideal that condemns its own denial of equality and inclusion. This was recognized long ago, for example, in the speech Thucydides has a Syracusan democrat make:

> The demos includes the whole State, oligarchy only a part. . . . None can hear and decide as well as the many: those talents receive their due in a democracy. 6.39[48]

VIII

The identification of democracy with "the whole State" was an effective trope because it drew attention to the paradox at the center of alternative systems. Monarchy, aristocracy, and oligarchy each claimed that ruling and citizenship should be restricted to a narrow social stratum; thus exclusion of the Many from politics was declared to be a necessary condition for ruling in the interests of all. The resulting idea of the political was of a good benefiting all and to which all should contribute without, however, sharing in power. Athenian democracy challenged the coherence of that formula by greatly broadening the base of power so as to identify the good of the whole with the benefits or advantages of those whose aggregated wealth, skills, and lives formed the greater part of the whole.

The demos might be said to be the carrier of an ideal political that was more inclusive than the class promoting it.[49] To counter that claim, without denying it or reasserting the claims of status or wealth, critics of democracy adopted a new, postdemocratic argument, that democracy could function effectively only when combined with strong leadership.[50] Pericles was the favored paradigm of the wise leader whose political genius lay in his ability to restrain the excesses/transgressions of democracy while rekindling hope when, in the face of reverses, the demos became disheartened.[51] That paradigm recurs in modern times, in, for example, Max Weber's notion of "leadership democracy."[52]

The idea of an "outstanding" leader involves a strategy of establishing "distance" between the demos and the individual who owes his position to popular choice or support. Distance was not meant as an idle metaphor but as the symbol of practices that might range from special education to indirect elections. The development of these notions owed much to the philosophers. Although Plato's *Republic* and *Laws* are familiar examples of the genre, one of the most striking is the neglected Platonic dialogue *Alcibiades I* or (*Alcibiades*) *Major*.[53] There virtue and knowledge are asserted to be the marks that set off leaders from the mob: You will be "deformed," Socrates tells the young Alcibiades, if you become a "lover of the people." Knowledge is likened to weapons that will protect the leader against the mob (132b).

Although in the dialogue Socrates uses the value of knowledge to establish distance between leader and led, he exploits that distance by introducing a strong manipulative element that assumes the demos has become an object in the thinking of the few. He describes an "eye" that sees into the eye of another but sees itself. This knowledge of self, which is declared to be beyond the powers of most humans, enables its possessor to understand not only the things that "belong" to himself but those of others (133a–c). The run of mankind, Socrates declares, does not even know its own "belongings"—a carpenter may know how to build houses but he does not know the nature of a construction or the meaning of tools—and so there can be no doubt that they have no knowledge of "affairs of state" (133d–e). At one point in the dialogue, Alcibiades responds to Socrates's argument that the noble and just should rule by saying that would mean that rule would be by "men who do business with each other and make use of one another, as is our way of life in our cities." Alcibiades's reference to the factious politics of the *hetaireiai* is then reformulated by Socrates by superimposing the true leader on top of the faction that is able to control the people. "Then," he says, "you speak of ruling over men who make use of men" and so rule over men who are fellow citizens (125c–d).

But perhaps the most complex stratagem for loosening the hold of the demos over the political—and one that has hardly been noted—was to separate democracy from the state. I am not referring here to the problem posed by Aristotle, of whether a change of constitution necessarily means a change in the identity of the polis (*Pol.* 3.1276b 1–10). Rather, I want to call attention to a development in the thinking of critics of democracy that argued for, or appealed to, a meta-political plane, higher and more enduring, which democracy had entered upon but could not democratize. A good example is provided by Pericles's speech following the second invasion, when the mood of the Athenian citizens was defeatist. Pericles appeals to them to place the safety of the polis above their personal misfortunes (Thuc. 2.61). Then he asks them to consider a new way of thinking about power, one so bold that he had not dared to pose it previously. It was: that while their city has been lost, their power is not tied solely to that place.[54] Sea power, which Pericles describes as "widely different," remains intact and Athenian vessels are free to go where they please (2.62). The power they had inherited from their fathers, who had defeated the Persians, and was now their responsibility to pass on, was constituted by their empire, not by their polis. That power was different in kind, tyrannical not democratic, and in magnitude, "a power greater than any hitherto known" (2.63–64).

In that formulation Pericles never once refers to democracy; he is representing the empire as the apotheosis of a power that has shattered its connection to the polis, to power structured by a constitution. Once that meta-plane has been charted, an Alcibiades can appeal to it at the same moment that he is betraying the city:

> I do not consider that I am now attacking a country that is still mine; I am rather trying to recover one that is mine no longer. 6.92

The culminating moment of this development occurs when the Athenians debate whether to allow Alcibiades to return. The question is put by Pisander in a form that reveals how much had been abandoned while cultivating power independent of a city or a constitution: "The safety of the state" is superior to the question of "the form of its government" (8.53).

Aristotle had asserted that the two essential elements of a polis were its citizen body and its territory (*Pol.* 7.1325b40). In Ehrenburg's phrase, a polis was a "community of place."[55] The Long Wall built to protect Athens from the land forces of Sparta was a reflection of the importance to political identity of a "ground," as were the public architecture and layout of Athens. We might say that all of the elements of the political—the citizen-body, the main institutions of political and judicial deliberation, public festivals and rituals, in short, the constitution of state power—were associated with a place wherein the powers of the state were generated because confined, "a law and order," as Plato put it, "marked by limit" (*Phlb.* 26b).

But the growth of naval power and reliance on it by Athens during the Peloponnesian War attenuated the connection between power and place. Instead of the city representing the place where power was constituted, it served more as a naval base, that is a launching point for a form of power that was to be projected abroad rather than embodied primarily in internal deliberations, policy decisions, or decrees.[56]

A democracy whose power is imperial and naval and described as continually "grasping at more" (Thuc. 4.41) is in symbiosis with, rather than the antithesis to, the Alcibiades who would, according to Socrates, prefer to die at once if he were prevented from pursuing ambitions that would take him beyond Pericles and anyone else who had ever existed, Greek or barbarian, and who ultimately aimed to "fill the whole world with (his) name and power" (*Alc.* 1.105a–c).

The symbiosis between democratic Athens and Alcibiades included a common element of deracination. When Alcibiades went over to the Spartan side and sought their support, he referred to democracy as a contingent fact, distinct from the identity of Athens. He explained that he had once served that democracy but only because "it was necessary in most things to conform to established conditions" (Thuc. 6.89). For Athenian democracy it was Athens that had become contingent. The apotheosis of power independent of place and political identity attained a certain pathos toward the end of the Syracusan debacle when Nicias tried to rally the Athenian forces by saying,

> Reflect that you are at once a city wherever you sit down . . . the one thought of each man [on a march] being that the spot on which he may be forced to fight must be conquered and held as his country and stronghold. Thuc. 7.77

IX

Plato and Aristotle both emphasize freedom as the basic principle of democracy, but, interestingly, both tend to characterize democratic freedom in social rather than political terms. For Plato democratic freedom is license to speak, dress, and behave in ways that violated traditional norms of deference. Aristotle simply absorbs democratic freedom into the demand for equality in matters that properly require deference to qualitative differences.[57]

The democratic conception of freedom is perhaps best preserved in an unexpected place, Cicero's *De Republica*. There freedom is identified with participation on a continuous basis. It is insufficient, the exponent of democracy declares, if the people merely vote, elect officials, and have bills proposed to them: "They are really granting only what they would have to grant even if they were unwilling to do so and are asked to give to others what they do not possess themselves" (1.31.47; tr. C. W. Keyes, Loeb). The case for democracy is about a partnership among political equals; it is not, the speaker emphasizes, about denying unequal talents or confiscating the fortunes of the wealthy (1.32.48–49).

This last point finds confirmation among historians today. Athenian democracy was guilty of few, if any, excesses against the wealthy.[58] The importance of this point is that the demos was not so much concerned with gaining forms of social recognition as creating a distinct political place where power was equally shared. In short, the ideal was political, not social. To my mind the best account of that kind of politics and of the essence of Athenian democracy is provided by the critic of Athenian democracy known as the Old Oligarch or Pseudo-Xenophon. He begins with the question of why instead of following the leadership of "the ablest" and "best," the demos insists upon heeding one of their own, even though he is uneducated and unvirtuous. The answer is masterful in conveying the flavor of Athenian democracy: The demos will prefer the unvirtuous man because he is better disposed to protecting their interests than the man of "virtue and wisdom."

> Such practices do not produce the best city, but they are the best way of preserving democracy. For the common people do not wish to be deprived of their rights in an admirably governed city, but to be free and to rule the city: they are not disturbed by inferior laws, for the common people get their strength and freedom from what you define as inferior laws. If you are looking for an admirable code of laws you will find that the ablest draw them up in their own interest. . . . As a result of this excellent system the common people would very soon lose all their political rights.[59]

The passage is notable for its juxtaposition of a democratic theory of rule over against the conceptions that are more familiar to us from the political and constitutional theories of Plato and Aristotle. It is no exaggeration to say that modern prejudices against democracy still bear the imprint of those theories. Democracy never produced its own "word-smiths," but beginning with the intervention of Solon—the man who formulates the terms for understanding the first recorded contest between inchoate democratic stirrings and oligarchic power—and continuing down to Aristotle, it was the antidemocratic critics who developed conceptions of politics, constitutionalism, and governance that were intended to eliminate democracy, as in the case of Plato, or to qualify and contain it, as in the case of Thucydides and Aristotle.

Among the many achievements of Greek theory, one of particular consequence remains so much a part of our own thinking today as to be virtually
an unconscious reflex rather than a considered choice. I am referring to what
might be called "the intellectualization of the political and the relocation of
politics from the assembly to the academy." By that I mean not only the reshaping of politics into a theoretical object and the power that technique makes
available to those who can manipulate it, but the association of a higher political understanding with a higher education and a permanent dissociation of democracy from theory and intellect. The crucial figure in this development was
Aristotle—although, here as usual, Plato cast a long shadow. Aristotle's achievement was to redefine aristocracy as meritocracy, downplaying the elements of
birth and wealth and emphasizing the qualities of education, culture, and ability. To bring out further what the stakes were in this development, we might
contrast two different pictures of politics, one sketched by the Old Oligarch, the
second taken from Aristotle's *Rhetoric*.

> It is right that the poor and the ordinary people should have more power than the
> noble and the rich, because it is the ordinary people who man the fleet and bring
> the city her power.[60]

In this formulation politics has a directness and immediacy: the power of
the polis is, literally, the power of the people. That power runs, as it were, in
a direct line from them to the major institutions. In the *Rhetoric*, however, a
certain "distance" is evident between those who aim to play a leading part in
politics, that is, those who now find themselves in the position the demos had
previously been of seeking entry into politics, and the intellectualized form of
the politics that is presented to them by the theorist who makes a virtue of remaining outside politics:

> But the most important and effective of all the means of persuasion and good
> counsel is to know all the forms of government and to distinguish the manners and
> customs, institutions, and interests of each.[61]

Aristotle concludes with a description of the political point of this education.
Each form of government has "a character," and hence the political man will be
most effective when he displays the characteristics appropriate to the political
system in which he is vying for influence.[62] Here politics consists of manipulable beliefs and practices, with the self-manipulating actor standing to one side
and surveying its possibilities. Clearly intellectualization promotes a community of understanding between the actor and the theorist: one manipulates concrete things abstractly, the other manipulates abstract ideas concretely.[63] But
above all it is a community that is trying to generate a form of power different
from the power of mere numbers represented by the demos.[64] To the theorist
democracy represents the power/threat of the undifferentiated.[65] Aristotle attempts to deal with it, not as Plato's *Republic* had, by suppressing it, but by

short-circuiting the power of the demos and by refusing to recognize democracy as other than quantitative. In his versions of acceptable constitutions, such as "polity" or a "law-abiding democracy," he acknowledges a simple numbers principle that allots to the demos the right to elect but not to hold office.

The evolution of theory from Solon to Aristotle might be summarized this way: Solon was not only, as Vlastos put it, "a man of the center" but a man at the center who actively intervened to redress injustice in order to forestall civil strife.[66] He is the man of words, the poet-theorist as mediator. Aristotle is the theory-man, standing outside but taking sides, prepared to assert that it is the virtuous few, not the many, who should rule and, moreover, the few are really justified in revolting when they are denied—although he hastens to add that they never do.[67]

X

The *conatus*-driven character of Athenian democracy achieved a democracy in which ordinary human beings overcame the barriers to power represented by wealth, status, education, and tradition and succeeded in inventing the practice of collective action on a continuing basis. Taking that achievement as a background, we can now address the question raised earlier, of the kind of democracy where equal rights are formally guaranteed but social and political inequalities are widespread and the demos is a negligible political actor. That system might be called electoral democracy.[68]

Electoral democracy is almost universally held to be the best form of government for the contemporary world. Its basic elements are formal provisions for equal civil liberties of all citizens: freely contested and periodic elections; mass political parties competing for the support of voters; elected officials who are accountable and removable by the electorate; a politics largely financed by powerful economic interests; and a constitution that specifies the authority and powers of the main governmental organs and stipulates the rules controlling politics and policymaking. To this list should be added the "free market." In a recent speech before the United Nations, President Clinton coupled "democracy and the free market" as the principal objectives of American foreign policy, a pronouncement that was meant to reaffirm this country's position toward the new societies emerging in Central and Eastern Europe and in the former Soviet Union.

The virtually unchallengeable status of the free market and capitalism in general in the contemporary public rhetoric of democracy is important to the theme of this volume, ancient and modern democracy. For whatever else one may want to say about free market capitalism, it is definitely not an arrangement for producing equality. Its principal motor force comes from the differentials in reward, status, and power that it makes available. In the United States evidence is substantial that various inequalities are increasing, especially along racial lines. It follows that contemporary democracy contradicts Aristotle's fundamental principle for identifying the distinctive character of a democratic *politeia*, that each citizen should be on an equality with the rest (*Pol.* 6.1317b5–7).

The contradiction between ancient and modern democracy is, however, only part of the picture. Contemporary democracies are in contradiction with modern conceptions of democracy, not simply with ancient ones. To take only the most striking instance, modern democracy adopted popular sovereignty as its first or defining principle. Power was supposed to be derived from the people, the people were supposed to exercise continuing vigilance over those using their powers, and the powers were supposed to "return" to the people at stated intervals. No one would take seriously such a conception as even remotely approximating the political realities of contemporary democracy.

Early modern doctrines of popular sovereignty are commonly interpreted by later commentators as posing a question of "will" and hence the political problem was conceived to be one of finding the constitutional or institutional means not of expressing, but of sublimating, the popular will, beginning with elections but reemerging as the legitimation of legislative, executive, or bureaucratic policymaking. What remained stillborn was the possibility of popular sovereignty as a will to power on the part of an actor struggling to be both collective and autonomous.

For "the people" to become an actor, not simply an elector, more than will was needed; a voice was also required. In the early gropings toward democracy during the English civil wars of the seventeenth century, one finds numerous references to "vox populi, vox Dei."[69] The remarkable idea was not so much the claim that the voice of the people was the voice of God but rather that the people had a voice at all. That notion implied a citizenry that expressed itself corporatively, that is, was able to frame its own understanding of its needs and, equally important, its own estimate of its situation. Three of the most important popular revolutions of modern times—of the 1640s in England, 1776 in America, and 1789 in France—were accompanied by an extraordinary outpouring of popular pamphlet and newspaper literature, a good part of it devoted to giving voice to the people.[70]

It is obvious that today—in the age of communication conglomerates, media pundits, television, public opinion surveys, and political consultants—the exercise of popular will, the expression of its voice, and the framing of its needs have been emptied of all promise of autonomy. Periodically American politicians and publicists claim that theirs is the world's greatest democracy. The reality is a democracy without the demos as actor. The voice is that of a ventriloquous democracy.

CHAPTER 4

NORM AND FORM

THE CONSTITUTIONALIZING OF DEMOCRACY

> A constitution [is] an organization of offices in a state, by which the method of their distribution is fixed, the sovereign authority is determined, and the nature of the end to be pursued by the association and all its members is prescribed.
> —Aristotle, *Politics*

MY CONCERN IN THIS ESSAY is with the political uses of "democracy" in relation to two diametrically opposed notions that symbolize two equally opposed states of affairs. One is the settled structure of politics and governmental authority typically called a constitution, and the other is the unsettling political movement typically called revolution. Stated somewhat starkly: constitution signifies the suppression of revolution; revolution, the destruction of constitution. The two notions, though opposed, are connected by democracy. The English revolution of 1688, the American one of 1776, and the French of 1789 are generally considered major milestones on the road to modern democracy. The first two have long been interpreted as culminating in constitutional settlements that, in effect, justified and fulfilled the prior revolutions. In France the most common criticism of the Great Revolution was that it failed to produce a lasting constitution, with the result that France suffered a series of revolutions throughout much of the nineteenth century, and the French continue to look back on their revolutionary past with far more ambivalence than either the British or Americans.[1]

While preparing *Democracy in America*, Tocqueville complained that he found it difficult "to distinguish what is democratic from what is revolutionary . . . because examples are lacking."[2] The question is, If democracy is rooted in revolution, what of democracy is suppressed by a constitution? Violence? Or is revolution politically richer than that, especially when contrasted with coups and putsches, the alternative methods of overthrow favored by oligarchs and would-be dictators? When a democratic revolution leads to a constitution, does that mark the fulfillment of democracy, or the beginning of its attenuation?

Lest this seem solely a question of terminology, recall the two different associations of democracy during the "revolutions" that led to the overthrow of communist tyrannies in the Soviet Union and in central and Eastern Europe.

When the revolutions were under way in Poland, Czechoslovakia, Hungary, East Germany, and the Soviet Union, they were described as "democratic." When they succeeded, most of the constitutions subsequently adopted were characterized as "democratic." Yet a vast change had taken place in the character of politics from the revolutionary to the constitutional moment.[3]

During the revolutions, politics was primarily the affair of "civil society," not of conventional political parties or parliamentary processes. Various extralegal groups of workers, teachers, intellectuals, artists, students, religious dissidents, and ordinary citizens energized and sustained revolutionary movements whose internal politics was remarkably participatory and egalitarian. After the success of those movements, a different politics began to take shape, a politics of organized parties, professional politicians, and economic interest groups. Above all, it was a politics in which the overriding problems were declared to be economic. Suddenly Solidarity was rendered anachronistic by the faceless representatives of the International Monetary Fund. Solidarity-style democracy had become a burden. The sea change was captured in a contemporary headline in the *New York Times*, which a short time earlier had hailed the "triumph" of democracy: "East Europe's Next Test: To Survive Democracy." And so too in Asia, where immediately after the electoral victory of Thailand "prodemocratic forces" over the military, their leader remarked, "The Cold War is over. Now is the era of the economic leading the political."[4]

Nonetheless, it is probably true that insofar as the modern political consciousness favors any universal political form, it is constitutional democracy; and insofar as it has an image of "normal" democracy, it is of democracy housed within a constitution.

I

> We must, I think, regard it as fairly certain that the other institutions as
> well [as class distinctions] have been in the course of the ages discovered
> many times over, or rather infinitely often. . . . So we should accept it as
> fact that the same process takes place in the case of constitutional features
> too. . . . Thus we ought to make full use of what has already been discovered while endeavoring to find what has not.
> —Aristotle, *Politics*

In the estimation of virtually all the canonical political theorists from Plato to Jean Bodin, democracy was rated either the worst of all forms of government, save for tyranny, or the least objectionable of the worst forms.[5] As most of these writers had Athenian democracy in mind, it is hardly surprising that it stood in equally bad odor. The recurrent charge has been that, by nature, democracy is prone to bouts of extreme lawlessness. "The vice engendered by it and inseparable from it," according to Polybius, was "the savage rule of violence."[6] The impression left by these accounts was of a natural incompatibility, a lack of proper fit between democracy and the sort of law-defined, institutionally constrained political structure represented by a constitution.

In contrast, American democracy appears to have succeeded precisely where Athenian democracy failed. When Tocqueville asserted that in nineteenth-century New England he had discovered "a democracy more perfect than antiquity had dared to dream of," he meant that Americans had resolved the tension between democracy and constitutionalism, between liberty and law, majority rule and legal limitations on power. Not coincidentally, Tocqueville also attributed the stability of American democracy to the fact that democracy was not the product of a great revolutionary upheaval.[7] Tocqueville's judgment seems thrice vindicated: the United States is the world's oldest democracy combined with the world's oldest continuous written constitution and the beneficiary of a revolution whose genius was its nonrevolutionary character.

That facile formula leaves unanswered, however, a question that, curiously, is rarely raised: How is it that a political society that had been deliberately constituted as an antidote to democracy is able to identify its collective self with the type of system that its founders set out to check? My purpose in this essay is to explore the political implications of understanding democracy in constitutional and institutional terms. I attempt to show that "constitutional democracy" is not a seamless web of two complementary notions but an ideological construction designed not to realize democracy but to reconstitute it and, as a consequence, repress it. I also want to show that the ancient theory of democracy as well as the practices of Athenian democracy have figured importantly in the texts constructed by modern and contemporary theorists in their efforts to set democracy within a constitutional frame.

James Madison's contribution to the *Federalist Papers* is the crucial link connecting ancient democracy to the democracy of his day and both of them to the democracy of ours. Madison's essays are significant both for what they defend, a theory of national government as yet untested by practice, and for what he chose to attack, the theory and practice of democracy. An essential part of Madison's strategy was to deflect the criticism that the proposed constitution was insufficiently democratic in comparison with democracy being practiced by the American states and localities. It would have been impolitic for him to attack local democracy, so he did the next best thing. He attacked the ancient democracy of Athens, hoping that by indicting the weaknesses of the latter, he would be indirectly exposing those of the former. His critique was summed up in a single sentence: "Had every Athenian citizen been a Socrates every Athenian assembly would still have been a mob."[8]

The ghost of Athenian democracy still haunts the thinking of Madison's heirs and none more than the doyen of American political scientists, Robert Dahl. "The theory and practice of democracy," he writes, "had to burst the narrow bounds of the polis."[9] Dahl's life work has been to join the theory of American democracy with its practice, and that has meant explicitly building a political science upon "Madisonian democracy" and critically engaging the meaning of Athenian democracy.

Why should a rupture between ancient and modern conceptions of democracy be considered a necessary condition for modern democracy to come into being? The familiar answer, and one that Dahl develops at length, is that the huge physical dimensions, large populations, and social complexity of modern societies render the politics of a tiny polis anachronistic. Accordingly, modern democracy is said to consist of two principal elements: a constitution that establishes representative government and so enables a large, scattered citizenry to "participate"; and a pluralistic politics that is generated by free competition between highly organized economic and social interests. These are the means by which democracy is adapted to modern conditions.

If the stakes involved merely quantitative differences, it is difficult to see why the memory of Athens should continue to nag, unless Athenian democracy stands as a judgment. If representative government constitutes the form of modern democracy and interest group politics its content, these may not be merely the means by which democracy has been enlarged; they may also be the means by which it has been diminished in order to smooth the way for a third element, the effective organization of the power to govern. The third element was clearly uppermost in the minds of the framers of the American Constitution, and it is taken for granted by Dahl. A central government that stands as the culminating point of national power and which includes not only a representative legislature but such nonrepresentative institutions as bureaucracy, the courts, and the armed forces, reveals how democracy has been suppressed: at its height, Athenian democracy extended to all institutions, not only those now designated "representative" but those that clearly are not and one, the presidency, which is representative only in the most tortuous sense. The exclusion of the practice of democracy from the center suggests other stakes than practical necessities.

II

Is it that the moderns have broken with the ancient practice of democracy while preserving continuity with both the ancient theory critical of democracy and its project of constitutionalizing democracy? If it is the persistence of ancient suspicions rather than their disappearance that is defining of modern democracies, then the reason may be the persistence of certain "dangerous" tendencies of democracy which ancient theory could name but modern constitutional theory and practice represses.

The attacks on Athenian democracy have owed much to the consistently hostile portrait of democracy drawn by Greek political theorists, such as Plato,

Aristotle, Thucydides, and Polybius. Although it has become commonplace to-day to write of the Greek invention of the idea of political theory, of democracy, and of politics,[10] it is rarely noted that the Greeks also invented the theory of constitutionalism.[11] Over the centuries, that theory has furnished a large part of the basic grammar of political theorists discussing constitutions. The no-tions that a constitution enshrines certain ideals (see the Preamble to the US Constitution); that it is the "foundation" of government; that it represents the rule of law rather than caprice; and that it expresses "a way of life" are examples of Greek influences. Before the nineteenth century, a politically well-read per-son would have been familiar with the typology invented by Greek theorists to classify and distinguish three good or rightly ordered constitutions (monarchy, aristocracy, and some "mixed" system) from three bad or perverted ones (tyr-anny, oligarchy, and democracy). The underlying assumption of the scheme was that politics occurred only within a determinate form and that the func-tion of a form was to order politics so that it served the "ends" distinctive to that form.

Ancient Greek theorists were the first to conceive the idea of codifying both the practices of ruling and the competing claims to rule while, at the same time, enclosing the dynamics of politics within a determinate structure and desig-nated political space. Their achievement was to create nothing less than a the-ory of structure by conceptualizing various institutions, such as kingship or assemblies, *norm*alizing their operation,[12] diagnosing their maladies, and relat-ing different institutions in space and projecting them over time. The purpose they all inscribed in structure was the establishment of stability through the containment of the demos.[13] Greek theorists developed a critique of democracy and then constructed a conception of a constitution as a means of demonstrat-ing how democracy might be domesticated, rendered stable, orderly, and just. Constitutionalism might be defined as the theory of how best to restrain the politics of democracy while ensuring the predominance of the social groups and classes represented by the "best men."

Athenian democracy was not founded or established by a singular act. A long string of events, which included reverses as well as gains, brought a new political way of life into existence. Traditionally, its beginnings are identified with the archonship of Solon (594 or 593 B.C.). Modern historians continue to dispute the significance, even the substance, of such Solonian reforms as the cancellation of debts, the elimination of debt bondage for citizens, the di-vision of citizens into four distinct classes according to wealth, allowing the least wealthy of the four access to the Assembly, and establishing a people's court. Most historians agree that Solon was no democrat and his reforms did not establish a democratic constitution. Yet, as an incident related by Plutarch reveals, there were moments when democracy was created by citizens in a way that overflowed the institutions introduced by Solon. After enacting his reforms, Solon was besieged by citizens who sought him out to deliver their opinions of his laws, to ask for detailed explanations and clarifications, and to urge revisions. Plutarch recounts Solon's reaction: "He saw that to do this was out of the question, and that not to do it would bring odium upon him, and wishing to be wholly rid of these perplexities and to escape from the captiousness and censoriousness of the citizens . . . [he] set sail after obtaining from the Athenians leave of absence for ten years." Plutarch concludes by recording the firm faith of the institutionalizer: Solon hoped that during his absence the citizens "would be accustomed to his laws."[14]

Athenian democracy of the fifth century was shaped by class conflicts, rivalries between the rich and the well-born, the ambitions of politicians, and the struggle for empire. It developed as the demos became a self-conscious actor. Democracy began as a demand for a "share" of power in the institutions for making and interpreting the laws and deciding questions of diplomacy and warfare. It culminated in popular control over most of the main political institutions at Athens. Democracy's triumphal occupation of those institutions was, however, the beginning of its transformation.

Institutionalization brings not only settled practices regarding such matters as authority, jurisdiction, accountability, procedures, and processes but routinization, professionalization, and the loss of spontaneity and of those improvisatory skills that Thucydides singled out as an Athenian trademark.[15] Institutionalization depends on the ritualization of the behavior of both rulers and ruled to enable the formal functions of the state—coercion, revenue collection, policy, mobilization of the population for war, law making, punishment, and enforcement of the laws—to be conducted on a continuing basis. It tends to produce internal hierarchies, to restrict experience, to associate political experience with institutional experience, and to inject an esoteric element into politics.

III

Modern political discourse, especially in its social science version, has largely abandoned the ancient vocabulary of "form" but not the idea. The modern variant is the concept of "organization" or its equivalents "bureaucracy," "administration," or "management."[16] The idea of organization is comparable to the idea of form in specifying a set of integrated conditions for the production of power. Among the conditions are a hierarchical system of authority; centralization of decision-making; division of labor and specialization, especially in the form of professional politicians; and increasing reliance on expert knowledge.

The institutionalization I associate with the transformation of democracy into a constitution is viewed differently in the writings of some classical scholars, who see it as the stabilization of democracy.[17] One striking feature of this scholarship is the self-conscious attempt to draw on the methods and concepts of twentieth-century sociology; another is an unselfconscious acceptance of organizational values. Thus one historian describes his work as concerned with "how the evolving relationship between mass and elite was institutionalized and how constitutional development in turn contributed to changes or encouraged stability in the political sociology of Athens."[18] A main concern here is to defend Athenian democracy against the charges of lawlessness, incompetence, and leveling by showing that during the fourth century B.C., Athenian democracy did not discriminate unduly against the wealthy, nor expropriate their wealth, nor show disrespect for law but, rather, that the demos imposed limitations on its own powers. Thus one scholar says of restrictions on the Assembly that these "protected democracy, but an orderly and constitutional democracy, not an undisciplined one."[19] In arguing that Athenian democracy eventually purged itself of the tendencies toward excess which ancient critics had insisted were natural to democracy, modern revisionists are tacitly claiming the same curative properties for constitutionalism as the ancient writers.

Instead of a conception of democracy as indistinguishable from its constitution, I propose accepting the familiar charges that democracy is inherently unstable, inclined toward anarchy, and identified with revolution and using these traits as the basis for a different, aconstitutional conception of democracy. Instead of assuming that the "natural" direction, the telos, of the democratic encounter with the political is toward greater institutional organization and that the problem is to adapt democracy to the requirements of organization, we might think of democracy as resistant to the rationalizing conceptions of power and its organization which for centuries have dominated Western thinking and have developed constitutionalism and their legitimating rationale. This democracy might be summed up as the idea and practice of rational disorganization. The claims of the demos and its kind of power appear to ancient critics and modern democrats as both inefficient and disruptive because the demos has been keyed to values other than the economy of power suggested by Max Weber and Robert Michels and championed by a long succession of priests, philosophers, warrior chiefs, and kings who have presented variations on the same theme: that ruling should be organized by some representatives of "the best," of those who truly know how to organize, exercise, sacralize, and exploit power.

One of the shrewdest analyses of why the demos should be distrustful of the best was written by an enemy of Athenian democracy who is known to us only as the "Old Oligarch." In his *Constitution of the Athenians* (ca. 412 B.C.), he imagines a situation in which some disreputable demagogue persuades the Assembly to adopt a proposal that is to the advantage of the common people as well as to himself. Then the Old Oligarch asks the question that the "better" sort of citizen would raise: Why would the people prefer to follow the advice of a bad man rather than "a respectable man of virtue and wisdom"? The answer is that the people know that the bad man is well disposed toward the people whereas the good man is not. The demos thus has a very different understanding of what is politically best, one that is not comprehended by ruling elites and philosophers: "Such practices do not produce the best city, but they are the best way of preserving democracy. For the common people do not wish to be deprived of their rights in an admirably governed city, but to be free and to rule the city. . . . The common people get their strength and freedom from what you define as inferior laws."[20]

IV

A hint of the antagonism between democracy and institutionalized politics is in the paradoxical status democracy occupies in contemporary political discourse. Democracy is, on the one hand, widely acclaimed to be the universal criterion of legitimacy for political systems and, on the other, almost universally dismissed as an impractical scheme of government and condemned as a bad one. The contemporary euphemism for "bad" or "perverted" democracy is "populism."

Perhaps the most compelling testimony to the paradox is that although very few publicly deny the claims of democratic legitimacy periodically made by the official spokesmen for each of the so-called advanced, industrialized democracies, fewer still dare to argue that "the people" actually rule in any of them. What is being measured by their claim to democratic legitimacy is, therefore, not the vitality of democracy in those nations but the degree to which democracy is attenuated so that it may serve other ends. The most fundamental of these ends— which more than any other could be safely called "the original intent of the framers of the American Constitution"—is the establishment of political conditions favorable to the development of the modernizing state. This suggests that the contemporary "problem of democracy" is not, as Dahl and others have asserted, that the ancient conception of democracy is incompatible with the size and scale of modern political societies. Rather, it is that any conception of democracy centered on the citizen-as-actor and politics-as-episodic-activity is incompatible with the modern choice of the state as the fixed center of political life and the corollary conception of politics as organizational activity aimed at a single, dominating objective, control of the state apparatus.

In what follows I use "constitutional democracy" and "democratic constitutionalism" to signify alternatives rather than similars. The first term refers to a situation in which constitutionalization has priority over democracy; the second, to a situation in which democratization has dictated the form of constitution. The first involves the selective addition of democratic elements to a constitution that previously was not democratic and, despite the addition, remains such. Thus we might claim that the Reform Act of 1832 was a first small step in the democratizing of the British constitution, but it was absorbed into a political system in which all the other major political institutions—the monarchy, the two houses of Parliament, administration, courts, and the military—remained highly undemocratic in recruitment, structure, and operation. Democracy was incorporated on terms set by the constitution, that is, by the social and political powers that had shaped the constitution to their needs and preferences. A broader social and political constitution or hegemony was defined which conceded a measure of democracy while simultaneously marginalizing and repressing the larger movement. At the same time, and often reluctantly and without fully appreciating the consequences, the dominant groups redefined themselves.

The second term, *democratic constitutionalism*, can mean the domination of democracy over constitution: that has been, historically and contemporaneously, the view of critics of democracy. In the words of Apollodorus, "the Athenian demos has supreme authority over all things in the polis and it is in its power to do whatever it wishes" (*Against Neaera* 88). I try here to account for the mostly abortive efforts at democratic constitutionalism and for the stubborn reemergence of democratic movements by proposing a theory in which democratic constitutionalism is representative of a moment rather than a teleologically completed form.

V

Solon realized that the city was often split by factional disputes but some citizens were content because of idleness to accept whatever the outcome might be; he therefore produced a specific law against them, laying down that anyone who did not choose one side or the other in such a dispute should lose his citizen rights.

—Constitution of Athens

The common assumption of both defenders and critics of democracy is that the extent and degree of democratization, present or absent, in any given society, whether "real" or "ideal," corresponds to, or is a function of, the extent to which democracy has been embodied in the "core" political institutions of that society.[21] That assumption encourages the view that the history of democracy is a search for its proper form, as suggested, for example, in the very Aristotelian title of Martin Ostwald's magistral study of Athenian democracy, *From Popular Sovereignty to the Sovereignty of Law*. Ostwald writes, "The end of the fifth century B.C." was "the time [when] the principle of the sovereignty of law was given official primacy over the principle of popular sovereignty."[22]

Ostwald's formulation suggests that before the end of the fifth century, Athenian democracy was defined by popular sovereignty rather than the rule of law—that, in effect, there were two Athenian democracies. In my formulation, first there was Athenian democratic constitutionalism, and then there was Athenian constitutional democracy, or what Ostwald describes as "a new kind of democracy, which subordinated the will of the people to the regulating hand of the law."[23] A hypothetical line separating the two democracies might be located in two counterrevolutions—one by the Four Hundred in 411 B.C. and the other by the Thirty in 404—which overthrew democracy and attempted to replace it by oligarchy. In 403, democracy was restored and continued until the Macedonian conquest of 322.

Concerning the restoration of 403, the Aristotelian author of the *Constitution of Athens* wrote, "It was just that the people should take control because they had secured their return by their own efforts. This was the eleventh change of constitution."[24] Thus 403 might be taken as the dividing line between what one historian has called "the radical democracy" of the fifth century and what another has called "the constitutional democracy" of the fourth.[25]

What makes this division suggestive for the problem of the institutionalization of democracy and for the distinction between constitutional democracy and democratic constitutionalism is that, by and large, the same political institutions of "radical democracy" were revived and continued to function down to 322. The demos was not disenfranchised, nor were its powers formally curtailed. Yet the political life of the two democracies presented a contrast between the active democratization of political life and the virtually total institutionalization of it.

VI

The fifth-century democratization of the Athenian constitution was the work of the demos. It was not established by a single document or one heroic act of founding but by a series of struggles that ended (ca. 403–399) with the provision that those who attended the Assembly were to be paid. The politics of the demos was disorderly and often rebellious, defined by its opposition to existing arrangements rather than by them. Its hegemony was achieved by repeatedly challenging regimes dominated by the men of wealth and noble birth. To be sure, many of the democratic reforms of the century were associated with notable leaders, such as Solon, Cleisthenes, Ephialtes, and Pericles, but the evidence suggests that the demos was an active force in all the reforms, exerting pressure, siding with one leader rather than another, and gradually extending its power by gaining access to existing institutions or by establishing new ones. Often its leaders were demagogues and tyrants, that is, men who owed their legitimacy not to institutional authority but to popular support and who became the means of breaking through existing forms to extend the power of the demos.[26]

The author of the *Constitution of Athens* summarized the results by saying that the demos "had made themselves supreme in all fields" (41.2). By any standard of civism, the intensity and varieties of participation, as well as the sheer number of participants, was impressive. Concretely, by 400, there ceased to be property qualifications for citizenship; the Assembly of citizens was the principal legislative body; the boards of lawmakers (*nomothetai*) and the juries were chosen by lot from the citizen body; the Council, which prepared the agenda for the Assembly, was chosen annually by lot from the citizenry; the decisions of the Assembly were subject to review only by the people's courts; most of the offices were open to all citizens and were filled annually by lot; the magistrates' actions were subject to legal audits by the people's courts.[27] Citizens deliberated and took decisions in the Assembly, the Council, and the courts. They chose leaders, made decisions about foreign policy and war, judged the credentials of officeholders, issued decrees, and much more.[28] Nor was the political culture limited to the central institutions of Athens. There was a flourishing system of local institutions in the demes, where citizens acquired experience and joined in nominating local men to serve in the central institutions.[29] Athens was, in effect, a complete democracy insofar as that democracy defined its identity against an alternative of antidemocratic regimes.

The great achievement of self-government was to transform politics in sight and speech; power was made visible; decision-making was opened so that citizens could see its workings; ordinary men personified power, spoke to it unservilely, and held themselves answerable. The most crucial and revealing element in Athenian democracy was the system of annual rotation in office, the lot, and the public subsidization of citizen participation.

Rotation and lot both function to limit the effects of institutionalization: they are, paradoxically, institutions that subvert institutionalization. When a legislature, a council, or an administrator enjoys secure and lengthy tenure, the tendency is to develop the traits associated with the ideology of organization: offices tend to become the permanent property of a political class; distance is quickly established between knowledgeable professionals and ignorant citizens; and that distance becomes real rather than symbolic. The contrast is between experience based on continuous practice and reactive impressions grounded in passivity. Rotation and lot, together with pay for the citizen, sharply reduce the contrast. The disruption in continuity of personnel injected an element of rational disorganization.

Before its fourth-century institutionalization, Athenian democracy was less a constitution in the Aristotelian sense of a fixed form than a dynamic and developing political culture, a culture not only of participation but of frequent rebellion. For Athenian democracy to continue to democratize, it would have had to confront itself rather than its enemies. The crucial moment occurred in 403 or 402 b.c. when the restored democracy rejected a proposal to limit the franchise to property owners, thereby preserving its egalitarian conception of citizenship. At the same time, however, it refused to extend citizenship to those slaves who had assisted in the revolution against the Thirty.[30] Each of the proposals, from opposite directions, struck at the Athenian conception of democracy; one would contract it, the other enlarge it. The double rejection was symptomatic not simply of a determination to defend democracy against oligarchy—which it was—but of a conservative temper indicating that democracy had "settled down" and found its constitutional form, its ne plus ultra.

In the fourth century, however, subtle changes took place. In the words of one scholar sympathetic to those changes, certain restrictions placed on the Assembly "protected democracy" and produced "an orderly and constitutional democracy, not an undisciplined one." He goes on to note that "other developments . . . did restrict the direct and immediate power of the people" and that "Athens took a number of steps in the direction of governmental efficiency and specialization, sometimes at the expense of democracy." This "constitutional democracy" was one in which "the wealthy were overrepresented."[31] The phenomenon of institutionalization, none of it offensively antidemocratic to twentieth-century sensitivities, become pronounced. A distinction emerged between what one scholar has called the "expert politician" and the ordinary citizen.[32] At the same time, certain inhibiting devices assumed greater importance in the fourth century: the *graphē paranomōn* (indictment for proposing a law contrary to existing law) and *eisanglia* (political impeachment) posed grave risks for a citizen (not holding an official position) if found guilty of having proposed an unlawful decree to the Assembly or, among other things, of having been bribed to speak against the public interest.[33]

Modern scholars who have defended fourth-century democracy against Aristotle's criticism of it as "extreme democracy" have been less concerned to defend fifth-century democracy, thus tacitly implying that Aristotle may have been correct about fifth-century democracy but wrong about fourth.[34] It is argued that experts became "necessary" because of the inhibitions of the *graphē paranomōn* and *eisanglia*; that without the experts "there would be few bold and original policy initiatives";[35] that "consensus" had been "lost" in the polarization of the fifth century, and "the question" for fourth-century Athens "was how effective leadership and decision-making could be achieved within the context of egalitarian direct democracy."[36] The twentieth-century image of the "constitutional democracy" of the fourth century bears a striking resemblance to Madisonian democracy.

VII

> It is curious that in the abundant literature produced in the greatest democracy in Greece there survives no statement of democratic political theory.
> —A.H.M. Jones, *Athenian Democracy*

Greek political theory developed a political science that was notable for its rule-centeredness.[37] Its preoccupations were with who should rule and how rule by the best or better sort might be assured. In defining and working out those concerns, Greek writers succeeded in establishing a stable vocabulary in which constructs such as "the many" or the "few," "the people" and "the best" were assigned attributes and behavioral regularities that were then connected to what was asserted to be the nature of "rule" so that what would or should be done was made in accord with the "nature" of some social groups (e.g., the highest military offices require certain skills or experience that only aristocrats are likely to possess) and to be incongruous with the nature of others (the demos was said to lack the experience, knowledge, and temperament necessary to command). According to the Old Oligarch, "Throughout the world the aristocrats are opposed to democracy, for they are naturally least liable to loss of self control and injustice and most meticulous in their regard for what is respectable, whereas the masses display extreme ignorance, indiscipline and wickedness, for poverty gives them a tendency towards the ignoble, and in some cases lack of money leads to their being uneducated and ignorant."[38]

Generally speaking, Greek political theory understood "rule" to mean the exercise of power by some over others. Its major thinkers mostly recognized this relationship as potentially, possibly inherently, debasing. Plato and Aristotle, for example, tried repeatedly to distinguish right rule from forms of rule which were not right, but the distinction kept breaking down, as in Aristotle's attempt to moderate tyranny without transforming it or in Plato's attempt to etherealize oligarchic rule by denying his guardians money or property yet subsidizing their lives by the labors of workers, farmers, and slaves.[39] Rule was understood to be inherently exploitative. In Aristotle's words: "But whenever one thing is a means and another an end, there can be no other thing in common between them than this—that the one acts, the other is acted upon."[40]

Aristotle did seek to modify the harshness of this principle by stipulating that in a politeia in which citizenship was restricted to true equals, the citizen should know how to rule and be ruled.[41] But that dictum applied primarily to oligarchies, aristocracies, and the "polity" of middle-class property owners and did not significantly qualify his belief that the virtue or function of a ruler lay in knowing how to use others. The virtue of the ruled, he noted, is "like a flute-maker while the ruler is like the flute player, the user [of what the other makes]."[42]

Theoretical justifications, such as appeals to a principle of "natural" hierarchy (higher and lower) or to a right of the superior to rule over inferiors, merely restated the exploitative relationship without altering it. The movement toward democracy in fifth-century Athens, and its ideology of equality (*isonomia*), can be seen as a protest by the demos against that conception of rule. The democratic practices of rotation, lot, and ostracism, by emphasizing "taking turns" in office or banishing those whose power or prestige seemed to threaten democracy, struck directly at the debasing effects of rule conceived as a superior-inferior relationship. Perhaps nothing symbolizes more strikingly the divergence between the politics legitimated by constitutional theory and the assertive politics of democracy than the mute silence of the demos—the lack of its own voice—in the pages of Plato and Aristotle and the contrasting explosion of demotic speech once the people won *isēgoria*, the right of speaking freely in the Assembly.[43]

The push toward democracy during the fifth century was not, as it was and still is represented to be, a simple demand for "equality before the law."[44] It was an attempt to redefine the terms of ruling and being ruled by insisting on a share of power. That demand issued not from a leveling impulse but from a realization by the demos that the power of the polis was, in large measure, their power. No one recognized that brute fact more squarely than the Old Oligarch: "It is right that the poor and ordinary people [in Athens] should have more power than the noble and rich, because it is the ordinary people who man the fleet and bring the city her power; they provide the helmsmen, the boatswains, the junior officers, the lookouts and the shipwrights; it is these people who make the city powerful much more than the hoplites and the noble and respectable citizens."[45]

In response, the theorists of constitutionalism qualified the questions of who should rule and how they should rule, by inventing the question of *what* should rule. That led to treating a constitution as the means of stabilizing a way of life according to certain principles, such as justice, goodness, and manly action, whose function was to serve as meta-principles, superior to other principles. They were ruling principles, a (syn)*tactical* representation of the axiom of Greek constitutional theory that a constitution was essentially about ruling and being ruled.

The objective status of those principles was contrasted with the flux, uncertainty, and subjectivism attributed to politics and, most important, to the forced entry into politics of social strata previously excluded. The essence of the contrast, which became, as well, the essence of constitutionalism, was between depersonalized principles and partisan politics. The freer, more accessible politics came to be, the more threatening it appeared. The principal means for ensuring and representing depersonalization, and for containing the perpetual challenge to established power potentially present in politics, was the law. Aristotle's famous characterization of law distilled all these elements of depersonalization and objectivism: "He who commands that law should rule may thus be regarded as commanding that God and reason alone should rule; he who commands that a man should rule adds the character of the beast. . . . Law may thus be defined as 'Reason free from all passion.' "[46]

It was but a small theoretical step to compare democracy's transgressive disrespect for limits and boundaries with tyranny and to claim that both displayed an innate impulse toward lawlessness.[47] This step prepared the way for the project, first undertaken by Aristotle, of devising mechanisms that would force the politics of democracy to be law abiding or, more precisely, to express itself structurally. Together with objective normativity and depersonalization, legalism formed the center of a project that I call "the constitutionalizing of surplus democracy." What is the nature of the surplus in democracy such that it is seen to require confinement within a constitution?

A clue to an answer is in the contrast Aristotle constructed between the unchanging character of law and the changing character of political practice. He explains that, as one of the arts, politics share in the claim made on behalf of other arts, such as medicine, that beneficial changes have resulted from abandoning traditional notions. But, Aristotle then insists, "To change the practice of an art is not the same as to change the operation of a law." Law depends on the habits of obedience which have been fostered over time. A disposition to change the laws, which is one of the most persistent charges leveled against democracy from ancient to modern times, allegedly undermines the power of law and the habits of obedience to government.[48]

The reified status Aristotle wanted to assign law in theory appears as special pleading in the context of the continuous struggle of the demos to equalize its economic and social condition by changing the practice of the political art. That struggle was to redefine politics from being a "civilized" version of warrior politics in which elites compete for honors and office to being the means of reversing the universal tendency of institutionalized systems of power to advantage the few and exploit the many. The political challenge of the demos inevitably overflowed the customary and institutional boundaries within which elites were attempting to fix politics. Consequently, democratic politics appeared as revolutionary and excessive, irregular and spasmodic. The response of Greek constitutional theory was to attempt to suppress the eruptive character of demotic politics but, if necessary, to incorporate it selectively as a preliminary to reconceptualizing the "problem" of politics as a contest involving competing claims to rule and conflicting views of equality. The solution was "contained" in the pivotal notion of "form."[49]

VIII

> Determinatio negatio est.
> —Benedict Spinoza, *Correspondence*

Since antiquity the idea of a form has often served as a metaphor of control signifying mastery, hence superiority, over "content." Implicit in the metaphor were political questions such as, Who designed the form? Who had knowledge of the design? What or who was destined to be content, and were they naturally receptive to the impress of that form? How were the limits of a form established, and what was excluded in the process?

Adapted by Plato and Aristotle to political discourse, form was made into a justification for various distinctions, each of which implied subordination: the distinctions between ruling (applying the form) and being ruled (accepting the form), between acting and being acted upon, between authority and submission, and inevitably, between the best or better men and the common or base people, such as workers, women, and slaves. Accordingly, a form symbolized a structure that contained the distinctions allowing the actions of the few to direct the activities of the many.

From there it was but another short step to employing form as a synonym for "constitution" and for constitution to mean a "preform," and a priori shape, the articulation prior to content and defining of it. The form was assigned a monopoly over the political and became the locus of legitimate politics. It reconstitutes politics as identity. A form supplied a distinctive character, structure, order, and boundaries, and a mode of ruling in which power was sublimated into presiding over and preserving the identity of that form. A constitutional form signified a structure to which politics should con*form* and become the kind of politics expressive of that constitution. Whatever did not conform was extra-constitutional, improper, illegal, and non- or antipolitical. Form might be described as constitutional theory's answer to ostracism.

That conception of form allowed an Aristotle to assert that a democracy manipulated by demagogues (i.e., leaders of the demos) who bring all matters before the people and persuade them to rule by decree was not a constitution at all.[50] To exist, democracy had to satisfy or to contradict the criteria that would qualify it as a form. Those requirements were merely another way of asserting the primacy of a philosophically based political science, of saying that democracy must be in*formed* or mis*informed*, that is, so constituted that it could be treated discursively as a theoretical object.[51]

IX

Democracy's political surplus, the unwillingness of the demos to remain contented with a simple "share" in the major political institutions, produced perplexities about how to account for democracy as a form, a politeia. This was true even for Plato, the master theorist of forms. Beneath his sardonic descriptions of democracy in the *Republic* (whose Greek title was *Politeia*, or "constitution") was an uncertainty about what democracy "is." He did not describe it as rule by the people, nor did he dwell on democracy's scandal of equality (although he did mention it).[52] Instead he produces a paradox of a distinct life-form that he associates—significantly for our notion of democracy's surplus politics—with absolute freedom, that is, with a total disrespect for form. Democracy is not primarily a set of political institutions but a cultural practice that extends to striking changes in the behavior of women, children, and slaves. Democratic freedom and equality signify the radical denial that social deference and hierarchy are "natural." Democracy permits all manner of dress, behavior, and belief: it is in*formal*, indifferent to *form*alities. Democracy is as careless about obeying the law as it is about respecting distinctions of age or social status. Its citizens, according to Plato, do not observe any constitution in the strict sense (8.557e–558a). They finally pay no heed even to the laws "written or unwritten so resolved are they to have no master over them" (563d–e). Thus democracy is wayward, inchoate, unable to rule yet unwilling to be ruled. It does not naturally *conform*. It is inherently formless.

But Plato then makes a remark about democracy and constitutions which introduces a somewhat different note. Because of the diverse human types it breeds, democracy is worth examining if one is looking for any sort of constitution: "Anyone who wishes to organize a state . . . must find his way to a democratic city and select the model that pleases him, as if in a bazaar of constitutions" (8.557d). Although its intention was satiric, the passage preserves a suggestive point that democracy, far from evoking images intimative of monochromatic, mass society, is diverse and colorful. Democracy is unique in being related to all constitutions; it is not so much amorphous as polymorphous.[53]

In the *Laws*, Plato appears more appreciative of democracy, even borrowing, with suitable modifications, many of the practices of Athenian democracy.[54] He describes it, along with monarchy, as one of the two generative principles of all constitutions (3.693d). Its distinctive quality is the friendly feeling that liberty and equality promote among citizens. Yet when Plato lists seven distinct claims to rule, democracy is not among them (690a–c).[55]

These theoretical gyrations were the consequence of the dilemma emerging from a growing recognition that the demos was the necessary basis of any constitution, that to exclude the masses was not only, as Aristotle put it, to place a constitution under siege but to contradict the kind of comprehensiveness which distinguished a polity from other groupings.[56] Aristotle could recommend a constitution as one that allows most men to participate and as suitable to most cities; yet it would exclude the poor and the skilled craftsmen because they were akin to slaves in their lack of autonomy and consequent deficiency in reasoning ability.[57]

As Greek thinkers came to conceive of a constitution as an object requiring a "ground," or a "base," they began to realize that exclusion of the demos was not so much morally wrong as politically incoherent.[58] If, as Aristotle argued, a constitution should serve the common good, how can that good be common when it is identified with virtues whose excellence is that they are uncommon? How could an exclusionary conception of the political, one that explicitly withholds citizenship from those whose labors are acknowledged to be "necessary" to the existence of the polis, be reconciled with a vision of the polis as an association of shared advantages?[59]

The incoherence attending political theory's vision of the political produced the guilty knowledge that all political forms are prone to favor some group. Again, the Old Oligarch, whose commentary was not remarkable for its subtlety, testifies to the point. After noting that the people prefer a faulty constitution that

preserves their power to a better one that does not, he remarks, "If you are looking for an admirable code of laws, first you will find that the ablest draw them up
in their own interest; secondly, the respectable will punish the masses and will
plan the city's affairs and will not allow men who are mad to take part in planning or discussion or even sit in the Ekklesia. As a result of this excellent system
the common people would very soon lose all their political rights."[60]

Aristotle virtually conceded that point by acknowledging that a *politeuma*, or
ruling group, whether one, few, or many, was the politeia, or constitution.[61] The
admission that all constitutions were one-sided made the realization of distributive justice—equal rewards, honors, and offices for the equal, unequal ones for
the unequal—appear as a confession that built-in political tendencies toward partiality could be overcome only under ideal conditions. "It so happens," Aristotle
remarks in the course of arguing that happiness is the end of the state, "that some
can get a share of happiness while others can get little or none" (1328a38–40).[62]
Accordingly, Aristotle's rightly ordered constitutions seem less the realization of
justice than a balancing act intended to enable one set of biases to "correct" another (e.g., democracy should allocate some offices to the wealthy). Although
Aristotle also suggested that nondemocratic regimes could achieve stability by
granting some political concessions to the demos, his political science was not
evenhanded. Monarchy and aristocracy, even tyranny—but not democracy—
were treated as capable of surmounting their biases if rulers and elites were properly educated. Not so for the demos. Democracy and education were viewed as
contradictory notions. Instead of offering to teach the demos how to rule in the
interests of all, Greek theorists showed how democracy could be controlled by
constitutional reforms that would reserve offices for the other social classes.

It is revealing of the perplexities of Greek theory when confronting the political abundance of Greek democracy that the two forms of acceptable democracy proposed by Aristotle, one agrarian and the other pastoral, both separate
democracy from the city and thereby deny the heterogeneity of the political
and identify its value with its scarcity. Aristotle's best democracy consisted of
farmers who would, of necessity, be so busy tending their land that they would
have "no time for attending the assembly." Such people, Aristotle observed, prefer work to politics, money to honor—except of course when some profit was
to be made from office (1318b9–16).

X

The tensions were compounded by a further admission that nagged virtually
all constitutional thinking: that while all forms were biased, not all were biased
to the same degree or in the same way. Although a democracy might be biased
in favor of the people, that "perversion" appeared to be a closer approximation
to the ideal of a polis than the perverted constitutions that favored one or the

few. In Herodotus's famous "Persian" debate about political forms, the defense of democracy closes with the claim that in a democracy, polity and people are the same.[63] This view was echoed by Thucydides, who, however, was careful not to put the sentiment in the mouth of an Athenian: "The word demos, or people, includes the whole state, oligarchy only a part."[64] Precisely because the demos was a fuller representation of the polis and its different kinds of ordinariness, democracy appeared to be closer in spirit to the principle that most theorists insisted on, that the distinctive mark of all "right" constitutions was that rule served the well-being of all. In other words, the more general or inclusive the criterion of the political, the more persuasive the case for democracy as being the most political of constitutions.[65]

Greek constitutional theorists tried to ward off the claims of democracy to be the true representation of the political by a strategy of transforming political practices into fixed structures or "arrangements." The theoretization of structure depended on the ability to envision discrete institutions as forming a whole—a constitution—made up of interrelated parts or functions and then to combine this imaginary with the logically separate notion that the interrelationship provides a nexus wherein the meaning of the whole constitution allegedly inheres.[66] At the same time, theoretization of structure also included another principle that seemed to contradict the emphasis on the wholeness of a constitution by suggesting that the parts of a constitution need not be homogeneous. Both Plato and Aristotle adopt the notion that though a constitution consists of interconnected parts, those parts are potentially replaceable by a part or parts from an entirely different, even "opposed" constitution; or, stated the other way round, that a part of one constitution, or, more precisely, the idea represented by that part's place in another form, could be transplanted along with the part to an entirely different constitution, where it would modify the "natural" tendencies of that constitution. Thus the requirement of a property qualification for office, which was the normal practice of an oligarchical constitution, could be inserted into an otherwise democratic constitution and thereby not only modify democracy but institutionalize within it the political claims of wealth.

XI

> If any democracy has ever flourished, it has been at its peak for only a
> brief period, so long as the people were neither numerous enough nor
> strong enough to cause insolence because of their good fortune, or jeal-
> ousy because of their ambition.
> —Dio Cassius, *History of Rome*

I have been attempting to retrieve aspects of democracy that are in tension with the organizational impulses of ancient and modern constitutionalism. A reflection of that tension is the fact that democracy has no continuous history after the absorption of Athens into the Macedonian empire. From 322 B.C. to the political experiments launched by the American and French revolutions of the eighteenth century, there were examples of city-state republics in which the "people" sometimes had a small share, but the evidence overwhelmingly indicates that these were oligarchies dominated by the rich and wellborn. That hiatus ends in the destruction of democratic hopes by the failure of modern revolutions and in the creation, instead, of the modern misrepresentation of democracy, the nation-state organization.

As I have noted, ancient democratic politics never possessed its own voice. From the fifth century B.C. to the end of the eighteenth century, democratic theory's sole spokesmen were the English Levellers of the seventeenth century and Tom Paine in the eighteenth. The idea of democracy comes to us, therefore, primarily through hostile interpreters. But because of the meaning of the "people" overlaps that of "the political," making it virtually impossible to discuss the latter without including the former, the politics of the demos has not been lost to memory but is preserved though half-buried in the political theories of democracy's critics.

The idea of the political and the democratic experience of its loss can be found in the myth recounted in Plato's *Protagoras* (320c–323a). The notions are also preserved by Polybius, in his theory of cycles, and in early modern times by Locke in particular. In a few paragraphs largely overlooked by commentators who have concentrated on Locke's myth of the state of nature, is another myth that serves to explain why there *was* a state of nature, not in the first place but in the second. Locke's "original myth" describes a golden age that came to an end when the people "forgot" what men might do when naïvely entrusted with absolute power.[67]

The lesson embedded in Polybius's cyclic myth and in Locke's myth of an original contract and right of revolution, is that, historically, it falls to democracy to have to reinvent the political periodically, perhaps even continually. Democracy does not complete its task by establishing a form and then being fitted into it. A political constitution is not the fulfillment of democracy but its transfiguration into a "regime" and hence a stultified and partial reification. Democracy, Polybius remarks, lapses "in the course of time."[68] Democracy is a political moment, perhaps *the* political moment, when the political is remembered and recreated.

Here we might recall that in the classical theories of cycles of political forms, democracy typically followed after aristocracy or oligarchy or monarchy.[69] According to most cyclic accounts, democracy emerged from the trauma of misgovernment and the exhaustion of alternatives represented by the other forms. In most of the classical versions, each form, whether monarchy or aristocracy, begins by being "political"; that is, those who rule are, for the moment, public spirited, genuinely concerned with the common good. Each is supported by the people. Yet each, according to its own nature, betrays that trust and perverts the political.

Polybius, no friend of democracy, describes a situation in which rule by aristocracy has degenerated into a corrupt and rapacious oligarchy:

> When the common people have killed some of the oligarchs and driven the rest into exile, they neither dare to make a king their ruler, since they still think with terror of the wickedness of the kings of former times, nor do they have the courage to entrust the state to a selected group, since they have the results of their former mistakes before their eyes. Thus they naturally turn to the only hope that has not yet been disappointed, namely the hope that they place in themselves. This is why the people turn from oligarchy to democracy and take the administration and the trust of public affairs upon themselves.[70]

Democracy, historically, has not just been about oppositions, however. It has been about the abuse and misuse of one's powers by others. As the Polybian passage suggests, democracy is a rebellious moment. It involves the taking back of one's powers, not just the re-vocation of legitimacy. When powers are taken back, when the "flow" of power from people to ruler (or "trust") is interrupted, what was being depicted by political theorists was a kind of cautionary fable about political consciousness. Among modern political theorists, Locke recorded just such a fable when he tried to explain why monarchy seemed to be the oldest and most natural form of government. He attributed its origins to "the Innocence and Sincerity of that poor but vertuous Age" when, in addition to their powers, men naively transferred to one man the natural affection they felt toward their fathers.[71]

Such fables register a moment when the people realize that all forms of governance have built into them a principle of partiality that promotes the exploitation of the powers of the many by the few. Aristocracy confines rule to those of noble birth and uses power for purposes associated with aristocracy, most notably, for war. Hereditary monarchy does the same, whereas nonhereditary monarchy wants to rest its case on sheer ability or virtue. Oligarchy elevates wealth as the principle governing access to public offices and wants to organize society into a machine for the production of wealth, to make wealth the measure of achievements as well as the principle governing access to public office (this can be done indirectly by allowing wealth to dominate formally democratic elections). Tyranny proclaims the intention of the stronger to use the powers of others to satisfy the tyrant's ambitions or desires.

The taking back of one's powers is the crucial move. In the history of political theory, it was expressed through the concept of the state of nature. State-of-nature theorists who were not themselves democrats nonetheless preserved an archaic remnant of a democratic experience. When governments fail or, in Locke's formulation, when they violate the principles according to which they were constituted, power reverts either to a natural "community" or to individuals.

Then follows the truly "democratic moment" and the crucial political moment, the moment when power is to be renewed democratically (2.243). Locke's theory stipulates that each individual must consent to the terms on which power is to be reconstituted and a political condition resumed. Underlying Locke's thinking was the assumption that the political is a condition subject to failure and hence requiring healing and renewal. The sole source of renewal is democracy (2.132, 149, 155).

XII

> But were the whole frame here,
> It is of such a spacious, lofty pitch,
> Your roof were not sufficient to contain it.
> —Shakespeare, *Henry VI*

It is no longer fashionable to appeal to cycles of government or to states of nature. Yet it might be argued that a belief in the restorative power of democracy is still part of the American political consciousness. Certain events illustrate that belief: the recurrent experience of constituting political societies and political practices, beginning with colonial times and extending through the Revolution and beyond to the westward migrations, where new settlements and towns were founded by the hundreds; the movement to abolish slavery and the abortive effort at reconstructing American life on the basis of racial equality; the populist and agrarian revolts of the nineteenth century; the struggle for autonomous trade unions and for women's rights; the civil rights movement of the 1960s and the antiwar, antinuclear, and ecological movements.

Just what constitutes a restorative moment is a matter for contestation. Ancient historians claimed that the hegemony Athens established over Greece as a result of her leadership in the war against Persia was due to the energies and talents encouraged by democracy. In the most recent "Persian War," American leaders hailed the triumph of American arms as a new restorative moment. "Desert Storm" was represented not as the restoration of democracy, nor as the taking back of power by the people, but as a certain kind of healing, one that meant "kicking the Vietnam syndrome" and thus restoring the national unity deemed essential to remaining the world's only superpower. That understanding of the restorative moment represents a perfect inversion in which the state of war, rather than the state of nature, serves as the condition of renewal.

Desert Storm, or postmodern democracy's "Persian War," demonstrates the futility of seeking democratic renewal by relying on the powers of the modern state. The possibility of renewal draws on a simple fact: that ordinary individuals are capable of creating new cultural patterns of commonality at any moment. Individuals who concert their powers for low-income housing, worker ownership of factories, better schools, better health care, safer water, controls over toxic waste disposals, and a thousand other common concerns of ordinary lives are experiencing a democratic moment and contributing to the discovery, care, and tending of a commonality of shared concerns. Without necessarily intending it, they are renewing the political by contesting the forms of unequal power which democratic liberty and equality have made possible.

CHAPTER 5

FUGITIVE DEMOCRACY

I

"... beyond all civil bounds."
—Shakespeare, *Twelfth Night*, I.4.21

By way of preliminaries I want to set out my own understanding of some basic notions so that the reader may have some notion of the orientation that guides my discussion.

I shall take the *political* to be an expression of the idea that a free society composed of diversities can nonetheless enjoy moments of commonality when, through public deliberations, collective power is used to promote or protect the well-being of the collectivity. *Politics* refers to the legitimized and public contestation, primarily by organized and unequal social powers, over access to the resources available to the public authorities of the collectivity. Politics is continuous, ceaseless, and endless. In contrast, the political is episodic, rare.

Democracy is one among many versions of the political but it is peculiar in being the one idea that most other versions pay lip service to. I am reluctant, for reasons to be discussed later, to describe democracy as a "form" of government or as a type of politics distinguished by its "experimentalism."[1] In my understanding, democracy is a project concerned with the political potentialities of ordinary citizens, that is with their possibilities for becoming political beings through the self-discovery of common concerns and of modes of action for realizing them.

II

The notion of boundaries is a rich and complex one. Boundaries proclaim identity and stand ready to repel difference. They may signify exclusion, "keep out!," or containment, "keep inside!" Those who guarded the Berlin Wall were as much concerned to keep their citizens in as to keep foreigners out. In most modern political discourse, boundaries are commonly identified with frontiers, frontiers with nation-States, and the State with the bearer of the political.

This cluster of notions can be illustrated by Hobbes's striking metaphor of sovereign authorities that are "in the state and posture of gladiators" standing guard at "the frontiers of their kingdoms." In Hobbes's formulation, the frontier protected by "forts, garrisons and guns" separates the antipolitical state of nature from political society and from "the industry of their subjects," from, that is, a private condition which the power of the sovereign is constructed to secure and which Hobbes fondly hoped would serve to sublimate the political passions that might otherwise challenge the sovereign's monopoly upon the political.[2] There is no public or legitimized politics in Hobbes's scheme; each has been squeezed between the absolute political in the form of the sovereign on the one hand and, on the other, the private domain of absolute, competitive self-interested men protected by it.

Both as container and excluder, boundaries work to foster the impression of a circumscribed space in which likeness dwells, the likeness of natives, of an autochthonous people, or of a nationality, or of citizens with equal rights. Likeness is prized because it appears as the prime ingredient of unity. Unity, in turn, is thought to be the sine qua non of collective power. During the nineteenth century, however, boundaries were associated with collective identity defined in historical and cultural terms and identified with a nation. Nationalism was, and is today, an avid proliferator of boundaries. Nationalism absorbs the political into the pursuit of an homogenous identity that is sometimes quickened through such purgatives as ethnic cleansing or the imposition of religious orthodoxy.

As the twentieth century winds to a close, the preoccupation with boundaries has not diminished. If anything it has become intensified. Postmodern cultural politics follows in the footsteps of nationalism in insisting upon boundaries that establish differences (as in gender or racial politics) but proclaims identities as well. Here, too, the political becomes associated with purification or, more precisely, a reversal in which the stigma of impurity as well as the badge of purity are switched so that the pariah or victimized group is now pure, even innocent, while the dominant group is impure.[3] Politics centers around the unmasking of the various disguises of oppression regardless of whether the alleged act has occurred yesterday, or in the distant past, or in an ancient text of philosophy, a nursery fable, a textbook, a modern novel, or a Senate confirmation hearing. Here the quest for boundaries has been closely linked with a myth of homogeneity that seeks to establish cultural perimeters within which oppression disappears. Dwelling amidst similars, human beings will now be free at last to enjoy a good that is truly common. The vision is of a political in which similarities are treated as commonalities and purity/innocence is adopted as a prophylactic against the politics of mere power.[4]

III

Boundaries are the outlines of a context; or, more precisely, boundaries signify the will to contextualize. Politically, contextualization signifies the domestication of politics in a double sense. A domestic politics is established with its distinctive practices and forms and distinguished from those of similarly bounded societies and from international or intercontextual politics. But the domestication of politics also corresponds to one dictionary definition of domestication, "to tame, bring under control." The "native country" (*domus*) is the site of *domitus* or "taming."

What do boundaries bound? How is the space circumscribed by boundaries filled in or structured? And how does that "fill" or structure relate to democracy and, most importantly, to its prospects? Boundaries are a metaphor of containment. I shall try and show that the reality cloaked in the metaphor of boundaries is the containment of democracy and that the crucial boundary is a constitution.

For some of the familiar exemplars of modern theory, Hobbes, Hegel, Weber, their answer to the question of what is bounded by boundaries was: the constitution that founded the authority and power of the State. The political in this reading is the active element, concentrated in those who lead. Political leadership is both the management of collective desires, resentments, anger, fantasies, fears, and hopes as well as the curatorship of the simulacra of democracy.[5] The political is focused upon an organization of power that guarantees domestic peace and security, including the security of the State; that promotes, guards, oversees, and interlocks with the corporate powers upon which the citizenry is dependent for their material well-being; that adjudicates social conflicts, punishes lawbreakers, and keeps the whole of society under a watchful eye; and that is continually trying to reconcile or conceal the contradiction between the State as the symbol of justice, impartiality, and the guardian of the general welfare—the steady State—with a dynamic politics that registers the intense competition that pervades not only the economy but cultural formations as well.[6] To contain that contradiction, the State cultivates the political education of its citizens to instill the virtues of loyalty, obedience, law-abidingness, patriotism, and sacrifice in wartime. Through the practice of those virtues, the State encourages identification of the self with the power of the State, the surrogate of participation and the sublimate of self-interest.

It is easy to think of democracy and constitution as "naturally" belonging together and each as incomplete without the other; to refer unselfconsciously to a "constitutional democracy"; and to assume that democracy is the sort of political phenomenon whose teleological or even ideological destination is a constitutional form.

What this means, literally, is that democracy as we know it in the self-styled "advanced industrial democracies" has been constituted, that is, given forms, structure, and boundaries. Constitutional democracy is democracy fitted to a constitution. It is not democratic or democratized constitutionalism because it is democracy without the demos as actor. Its politics is based, not as its defenders allege, upon "representative democracy" but on various representations of democracy: democracy as represented in public opinion polls, electronic town meetings and phone-ins, and as votes. In sum, a constitution regulates the amount of democratic politics that is let in.

The crucial institution is the Presidency. As chief executive he symbolizes the modern hope that politics may be regularized as policy and rationalized as administration; at the same time he is, as the textbooks constantly remind, the one politician elected by the whole body of the people. Thus he is the tribune who administers; he is democracy *and* rationality. He is also the cruelest symbol of the impotence of the demos and, fittingly, the highest office of constitutional democracy. The demos has no effective voice in what the president does, yet once the election is over their mythical act is carefully preserved as ritual and invoked whenever a president feels the need of courting public support. Voting merges into a fluent process whose illusory connection with the demos is prolonged by the periodic election of senators and representatives and by the continuous commentary manufactured by the media. The result is an illusion of perpetual political motion launched initially by democratic elections. Meanwhile a parallel politics of process—legislative, administrative, judicial, and military—flows continuously of its own accord. Electoral campaigns are preserved as the lessons which consultants huckster. For the demos they are soon forgotten. It must now get its politics vicariously and passively through the pronouncements of television oracles, talk-show babble, and the political burlesque hustled by the pundits.

Thus a constitution in setting limits to politics sets limits as well to democracy, constituting it in ways compatible with and legitimating of the dominant power groups in the society. Constitutions are not only about what is legal and what illegal political activity, but they regulate the amount of politics, the temporal rhythms or periodicity of politics, and they give it ritualistic forms, e.g., every four years the "voice of the people" is given the opportunity to "speak" by entering an appropriate mark beside the name of one or another presidential candidate. In the political economy, elections are "free" in the double sense that no one coerces the citizen into voting and the voter does not pay directly for the privilege of voting; that expense is footed by the dominant powers that organize, operate, and finance campaigns. For them elections are investment opportunities from which they hope to reap a return.

IV

But for reasons diametrically opposed to Hobbes, the idea of boundaries as frontiers is anathema to some postmodern writers. Boundaries signify that the State has predetermined that the primary locus of the individual's concerns and commitments should be within the boundaries presided over by the State when, in fact, the contemporary individual may consider that her deepest concerns are with certain groups of foreign women rather than with her fellow citizens. The Hobbesian notion of "frontiers" has also been disputed on other grounds: as anachronistic by those who claim that all mankind now inhabits an electronic "Global Village"; or as obstructionist by those who point to the grave problems whose causes and solutions defy political boundaries; pollution, famine, abuses of human rights, nuclear weapons, and epidemics. Thus while boundaries signified to the early modern the limits of the political, to the postmodern they are a sign of its limitations.[7] In the attempt to transcend boundaries these views strain to enlarge the political by retaining the core notion of shared concerns and values while extending them to include humanity. But that conception of the political reproduces the conception associated with representative government, a trustee or stewardship notion of acting on behalf or in the interests of others with the tacit assumption—also held by modern champions of representative government—that the vast majority of the "others" had an "interest" but not a coherent, that is, well-informed opinion about how to protect or promote it. The highest political expression of the postmodern ideal is of a Rio Conference where the representatives of boundary-transcending human interests meet face-to-face with representatives of sovereign States.

V

The modern State as the guardian of boundaries has been rendered paradoxical, if not anachronistic, because of the problematical status of boundaries. The many phenomena that seem to escape or transcend boundaries, e.g., electronic communications, are often cited as confirmation of the real existence of the postmodern. If such is the case, then that development may not only shed some light on the future of the State, and its conception of the political, but also on the democratic or nondemocratic tendency of the postmodern.

Postmoderns are not alone in being indifferent to boundaries. The forms of power upon which the modern State has come to depend are notoriously cavalier about boundaries. Thus modern State-power is inseparable from modern science and technologies; both are boundary-leapers and, to an important extent, both carry their own contexts. Further, modern State-power is deeply dependent upon the market. Market activity too has its share of indifference to national boundaries and its own ethos-creating context. Then, too, from its beginnings the modern State was indelibly shaped by those who claimed to possess systematic forms of knowledge that would advance the power of the State and place it on firmer foundations. Lawyers, financiers, administrators, and then economists shaped State bureaucracies; but as their skills became more systematic, even scientific, they too assumed a universalist character. Like the ancient royal courts, the modern State also aspires to intellectual and artistic embellishment to its power. It subsidizes and honors writers, artists, actors, musicians, and scholars who then respond with contributions. The Kennedy Center is as much the symbol of State power as the Bell Laboratories. But the contemporary artist, scholar, and intellectual is also a multinational operative, at home in any performance center.

Finally, the State itself, though the boundary-keeper par excellence, is also a great boundary-defier that seeks to project its power abroad, carrying with it the contributions of the components just described. In passing, we might note that each of the components of State power—scientific, technological, economic, and cultural—is a representation and perpetuation of elitism.

The domus has thus become the equivalent of a home base of operations, a launching pad for projecting the modern forms of power. The constitution of the domus provides a stable foundation that guarantees to the State a steady supply of human and material resources. The democratization of "advanced industrial democracies" comes down to this: the labor, wealth and psyches of the citizenry are simultaneously defended and exploited, protected and extracted, nurtured and fleeced, rewarded and commanded, flattered and threatened.

VI

The democracy we are familiar with is constitutionalized democracy, democracy indistinguishable from its constitutional form. Its modern ideological justification can be found in Harrington, the English republicans, the *Federalist Papers*, and Tocqueville. Each was a critic of democracy. Each records a reaction to revolution, although not a reactionary reaction. Each of their constitutions is constructed against democracy; while each seeks to repress democracy none seeks to suppress it. It is to be given a "place," as the American framers did in the House of Representatives, otherwise the legitimacy allegedly bestowed by "the sovereign people" would lack all credibility.

The representation of democracy which the theorists of modern constitutionalized democracy have sought to counteract is as old as the classical theories of Plato and Aristotle and was a staple of early modern political thought. It is the specter of democracy as lawless and prone to fits of violence. "A popular state," according to Jean Bodin, "is always the refuge of all disorderly spirits, rebels, traitors, outcasts who encourage and help the lower orders to ruin the great. The laws they hold in no esteem."[8] Madison warned that

> [pure] democracies have ever been spectacles of turbulence and contention; have ever been found incompatible with personal security, or the rights of property; and have in general been as short in their lives, as they have been violent in their deaths.[9]

Tocqueville once complained of there being no example of a democracy introduced without revolutions; and he proceeded to invent one, claiming that the reason for the stability of American democracy was that, unlike France, democracy in America was not the creature of revolution.[10] Tocqueville's eagerness to

dissociate democracy from revolution and his concern over not finding supporting examples invite the question of how the two phenomena became associated in the first place and what that association reveals about democracy.

The truth contained in those images of democratic disorder is that historically modern democracy and ancient Athenian democracy all emerged in combination with revolution. In each case (the fifth century B.C.E., the 1640s, 1776,
and 1989) revolution inspired the creation of democratic ideas and radically
enlarged the circle of political participants to include the active involvement of
social classes hitherto excluded or marginal.

Revolution might be defined for our purpose as the wholesale transgression
of inherited forms. It is the extreme antithesis to a settled constitution, whether
that constitution is represented by documents ("basic laws") or by recognized
systems or practice. Democracy was born in transgressive acts, for the demos
could not participate in power without shattering the class, status, and value
systems by which it was excluded.

VII

What we tend to think of as systematic political philosophy is conventionally said
to have begun with Plato and Aristotle in fourth-century Athens. The modern
tendency for philosophy to set the terms for interpreting Plato and Aristotle has
obscured another achievement of the ancient thinkers. They also invented constitutionalism, the theory and political science of constitutions. They intended it
to be a measured, antidotal response to the democratic revolutions of the fifth
century B.C.E. and the consequent democratization of the Athenian constitution.
Constitutional theory was distinctive for its urge to use the political to synthesize
the entire life of the polis, to encapsulate it within a form, and then to distribute/
enclose the varieties of political life within a classificatory scheme of constitutions. Yet that enterprise harbored an inner tension that was evident even in the
ideal form of Plato's *Republic*. At one juncture of the dialogue Socrates declaims:

> The object on which we fixed our eyes in the establishment of our state was not the
> exceptional happiness of any one class but the greatest possible happiness of the
> city as a whole. [420 C]

But having posited that ideal of solidarity, Socrates then proceeds to sketch an
ideal society in which class divisions are etched in the sharpest possible lines of
superiority/inferiority. The same problem of combining commonality with exclusivity crops up in Aristotle's three well-ordered constitutions. The identity of
each form was dependent upon excluding some distinct social elements from
political citizenship.[11] In the end Aristotle concedes that each constitutional form
embodies the values and interests of a ruling class and hence in one way or another each is deficient in commonality.[12]

These tensions were strikingly preserved in some passages in Cicero's *De Republica*. Cicero has his own Socrates in Scipio Africanus who recites the arguments for each of the conventional forms of rule, monarchy, aristocracy, and democracy. In the surviving manuscripts, the longest and most systematic discussion is devoted to that *civitas* "in which the power of the people is the greatest" (I.xxxi.47). In presenting the case for democracy, Scipio declares that only the *res populi* deserves to be called a *res publica* (I.xxxii.48). *Res publica* was not only the phrase designating the political identity of the Romans of Cicero's day, it was also the quintessential rendering of what Romans understood as the political: that which was of common concern and belonged to all. Those connotations linked it more closely to the Latin for democracy, *res populi*, than to the exclusivist language associated with aristocracy, oligarchy, or monarchy.

Centuries later, Karl Marx remarked that democracy was the basis of every constitution in the sense that each pays its respects to the principle of commonality but without allowing the people to rule.[13] But throughout history it is not difficult to identify the social groups whose interests have been consistently exploited so as to render commonality a mockery; it has been the same groups that have been excluded from active participation in the political.[14]

Democracy is not about where the political is located but how it is experienced. Revolutions activate the demos and destroy boundaries that bar access to political experience. Individuals from the excluded social strata take on responsibilities, deliberate about goals and choices, and share in decisions that have broad consequences and affect unknown and distant others. Thus revolutionary transgression is the means by which the demos makes itself political. It is by *stasis* not *physis* that the demos acquires a civic nature.

For the very idea of equality is transgressive of the social and political boundaries that have formed the precondition for political exclusion which, in turn, is the precondition for legitimizing economic exploitation. Those boundaries have been formed around highly prized scarce values, such as noble birth, wealth, military prowess, and certain forms of arcane knowledge, the possession of which forms the basis of a claim to power, i.e., to office. The excluded—farmers, artisans, mechanics, resident foreigners, women, slaves—represent values and virtues that are, at best, minimally valued even though, as Aristotle recognized in the case of manual workers and slaves, their activities were "necessary" to the being if not the excellence of a society.

The story of Athenian democracy was of a succession of popular uprisings that succeeded in transforming the so-called ancestral constitution and its various boundaries so that eventually, in the words of Apollodorus, "the Athenian demos has supreme authority over all things in the polis and it is in its power to do whatever it wishes" (59.88).

But the democracy carried along by revolution comes to appear as surplus democracy when revolutions are ended and the permanent institutionalization of politics is begun. Consider the narrowing of the political that is represented in the contrast in Locke's *Second Treatise* between, on the one hand, the state of nature where each individual has to use his own judgment in executing the law of nature—where, in other words, participation is universal, obligatory but fluent—and, on the other, the three prerequisites of a political society postulated by Locke: "an establish'd, settled, known Law," "a known and indifferent Judge," and an effective executive.[15] The political has become specialized, regularized, and administrative in character and quality. Institutionalization marks the attenuation of democracy: leaders begin to appear; hierarchies develop; experts of one kind or another cluster around the centers of decision; order, procedure, and precedent displace a more spontaneous politics: in retrospect the latter appears as disorganized, inefficient.[16] Democracy thus seems destined to be a moment rather than a form. Throughout the history of political thought virtually all writers emphasize the unstable and temporary character of democracy.[17] Why is it that democracy is reduced, even devitalized by form? Why is its presence occasional and fugitive?

VIII

In an attempt to throw some light on those questions I want to turn to that workhorse of modern political theory, the state of nature, especially in its Lockean formulation. Although the Hobbesian state of nature is clearly one where the idea of boundaries does not operate and where a prepolitical condition reigns, for Locke it is a condition that is "bounded" by the law of nature. What that law "bounds" is a condition of commonality and "Equality . . . without Subordination or Subjection." We might call Locke's construct a democracy without form. In that "one community of nature," each is under an obligation "to preserve the rest of Mankind" by enforcing the law of nature (II.4,6). Originally, too, all men hold the earth in common, including its natural "fruits" and "the Beasts it feeds" (II.26). Thus, insofar as these elements of commonality exist and each man performs the public role of guardian of the law of nature, the condition could be described as political and democratic.

But the "natural" commonality of Locke's state of nature seems artificial because of its near absolute homogeneity. To the modern, Madisonian eye it appears as a condition lacking that most modern of phenomena, conflicts between different interests. Notwithstanding the suggestion of heterogeneous elements in Locke's description of the origins of private property and money in the state of nature, once his argument begins to crystallize around the main event, the contract, heterogeneity is suspended and plays no part in the consensus—with one exception, as we shall see shortly. When contract time approaches, distinctions of property, class, religion, gender, race, ethnicity, or language are blacked out; or, more precisely, the distinctions previously acknowledged, as between husband and wife, parents and child, master and servant, are treated by Locke as special cases because they are nonpolitical (II.80–86). Those differentia are ignored by Locke when he prepares his argument for the contract because without a postulate consisting of the homogeneity of democratic commonality Locke would have lacked the mechanism needed to operationalize an agreement among similar individuals.

What homogeneity makes possible is a species of power based upon nondifferentiation. The power of homogeneity is most strikingly evident in the language which Locke used to introduce the idea of a majority constructed from the consent of single but unsingular men:

> For when any number of Men have by the consent of every individual, made a "community," they have thereby made that Community one Body, with a Power to Act as one Body, which is only by the will and determination of the "majority" (II.96).

The assumption behind Locke's claim that a community has "a Power to Act as one Body" is that it was composed of equal and undifferentiated units, each of whose act of consent was a registry of similar units of power. When added together their sum enabled the community to act as one body:

> "The Body should move whither the greater force carries it" which was "the will and determination of the majority" (II.96).

Yet when Locke attempted to meet the argument that "one body" seemed to imply unanimity rather than a majority and that the mere notion of a majority was a confession that heterogeneity rather than homogeneity—inequality/difference rather than equality/similarity—had prevailed in the state of nature, he fell back on a commonsense rationale that casts doubt upon the homogeneity of interests in the state of nature. Unanimity is an impossible basis of action because

> the Infirmities of Health and Avocations of Business, which a number, though much less than that of a Commonwealth, will necessarily keep many away from the publick Assembly (II.96).

But Locke then continues his retreat from the homogeneity of the state of nature: "To which if we add the variety of Opinions and contrariety of Interests which unavoidably happens in all Collections of Men," then "insistence upon unanimity can only end in the dissolution of the community" (II.96). Thus, the homogeneity of the state of nature turns out to have been the suspension of heterogeneity.

Yet the state of nature is not so much a fiction as a metaphor of lost commonality, an exceptional moment that keeps returning in moments of revolutionary crisis when power returns to "the Community" and agency to "the People." The democratic moments in revolutions have been the carriers of commonality, the perduring conscience of the political:

The Power that every individual gave the Society, when he entered it, can never revert to the Individuals again, as long as the Society lasts, but will always remain in the Community (11.243).

Homogeneity might then be reinterpreted. When Locke's individuals place themselves under an obligation to observe the law of nature and to treat others as free and equal beings, they create homogeneity, not as a description but as a norm.

IX

If any democracy has ever flourished, it has been at its peak for only a brief period, so long as the people were neither numerous enough nor strong enough to cause insolence because of their good fortune, or jealousy because of their ambition.
—Dio Cassius, 44.2

That heterogeneity should emerge in Locke's state of nature is not a tribute to its universality or naturalness. Rather heterogeneity is a consequence of liberty and equality, the two values which since antiquity have been associated solely with democracy.[18] As Tocqueville observed of Jacksonian America, democratic equality results in an extraordinary release of human energies, the net result of which is social inequalities arising from individual differences of natural endowment, luck, and circumstance.[19] Add the peculiarity of democratic liberty that it shields antidemocratic forms of power—corporations are "persons" that enjoy some of the same rights as individuals while its officers acquire immunities denied to ordinary citizens—and the fugitive character of democracy is no mystery. For while democratic freedom encourages the expression of diversity and its attendant fragmentation of the homogeneity signified by "the people," some fragments are less fragmented than others. Multiculturalism and multinational corporations are not equivalences.

The surrogate of lost homogeneity and of the power of the demos is majority rule; but constitutionalism, especially in its Madisonian version, is designed to strew as many barriers as possible to demotic power.

X

I have been attempting to retrieve aspects of democracy that suggest a tension with the organizational impulses of ancient and modern constitutionism. A reflection of that tension is the fact that democracy has no continuous history following the absorption of Athens into the Macedonian empire. From 322 b.c. to the political experiments launched by the American and French revolutions of the eighteenth century, there were examples of city-state republics in which the "people" sometimes had a small share but the evidence overwhelmingly indicates that these were oligarchies dominated by the rich and well-born. That hiatus ends in the destruction of democratic hopes by the failure of modern revolutions and in the creation, instead, of the modern representation of democracy, the nation-state organization. Today democracy is universally acclaimed as the only true criterion of legitimacy for political systems and its real presence is said to consist of free elections, free political parties, and free press. And, of course, the free market. The specifications are so precise that the United States periodically dispatches experts to Central America to determine whether those requirements have been met.

Paradoxically, while hardly anyone questions that the self-styled "advanced industrialized democracies" really are democracies, fewer still care to argue that "the people" actually rules in any one of them, or that it would be a good idea if it did. For in societies where managerial rule is widely practiced, democracy appears as inherently crude and hence unsuited for the task of governing complex and rapidly changing societies. At the same time in those same quarters, it is often declared that democracy demands such a high level of political sophistication from citizens as to make it doubtful that it can be mastered by Third World peoples. Thus democracy is too simple for complex societies and too complex for simple ones.

What is actually being measured by the claim of democratic legitimacy is not the vitality of democracy in those nations but the degree to which democracy is attenuated so as to serve other ends. The most fundamental of these is the establishment and development of the modernizing State. The so-called problem of contemporary democracy is not, as is often alleged, that the ancient conception of democracy is incompatible with the size and scale of modern political societies. Rather it is that any conception of democracy grounded in the citizen-as-actor and politics-as-episodic is incompatible with the modern choice of the State as the fixed center of political life and the corollary conception of politics as continuous activity organized around a single dominating objective, control of or influence over the State apparatus.

Democracy in the late modern world cannot be a complete political system, and given the awesome potentialities of modern forms of power and what they exact of the social and natural world, it ought not to be hoped or striven for. Democracy needs to be reconceived as something other than a form of government: as a mode of being which is conditioned by bitter experience, doomed to succeed only temporarily, but is a recurrent possibility as long as the memory of the political survives. The experience of which democracy is the witness is the realization that the political mode of existence is such that it can be, and is, periodically lost. Democracy, Polybius remarks, lapses "in the course of time" (VI.39). Democracy is a political moment, perhaps the political moment, when the political is remembered and recreated. Democracy is a rebellious moment that may assume revolutionary, destructive proportions, or may not.

Today it is no longer fashionable to appeal to cycles of government or to states of nature. Yet it might be argued that a belief in the restorative power of democracy is still part of the American political consciousness. Certain events support that belief: the recurrent experience of constituting political societies and political practices, beginning with colonial times and extending through the Revolution and beyond to the westward migrations where new settlements and towns were founded by the hundreds; the movement to abolish slavery and the abortive effort at reconstructing American life on the basis of racial equality; the Populist and agrarian revolts of the nineteenth century; the struggle for autonomous trade unions and for women's rights; the civil rights movement of the '60s and the antiwar, antinuclear, and ecological movements of recent decades.

Just what constitutes a restorative moment is a matter of contestation. Ancient historians claimed that the hegemony which Athens established over Greece as a result of her leadership in the war against Persia was due to the energies and talents encouraged by democracy. In the most recent Persian war, American leaders hailed the triumph of American arms as a new restorative moment. "Desert Storm" was represented not as the restoration of democracy, nor as the taking back of power by the people, but as a certain kind of healing, one that meant "kicking the Vietnam syndrome" and thus restoring America's unity and its status as Number One. That understanding of the restorative moment represents a perfect inversion in which the state of war, rather than the state of nature, serves as the condition of renewal.[20]

"Desert Storm," or constitutional democracy's Persian War, demonstrates the futility of seeking democratic renewal by relying on the powers of the modern State. The possibility of renewal draws on a simple fact: that ordinary individuals are capable of creating new cultural patterns of commonality at any moment. Individuals who concert their powers for low-income housing, worker ownership of factories, better schools, better health care, safer water, controls over toxic waste disposals, and a thousand other common concerns of ordinary lives are experiencing a democratic moment and contributing to the discovery, care, and tending of a commonality of shared concerns. Without necessarily intending it, they are renewing the political by contesting the forms of unequal power which democratic liberty and equality have made possible and which democracy can eliminate only by betraying its own values.

But renewal also must draw on a less simple fact, that a range of problems and of atrocities exists that a locally confined democracy cannot resolve. Like pluralism, interest group politics, and multicultural politics, localism cannot surmount its limitations except by seeking out the evanescent homogeneity of a broader political. Recall the remarkable phenomenon of Polish Solidarity, a movement composed of highly disparate elements—socialists, artists, teachers, priests, believers, atheists, nationalists, etc. Yet one of the literal meanings of solidarity is: "community or perfect coincidence of (or between) interests."[21] Clearly homogeneity was not then and need not now be equated with dreary uniformity, any more than equality need be mere leveling. What it does require is understanding what is truly at stake politically: heterogeneity, diversity, multiple selves are no match for modern forms of power.

HOBBES

CHAPTER 6

HOBBES AND THE EPIC TRADITION OF POLITICAL THEORY

LESSING ONCE REMARKED ABOUT a contemporary book that what was important in it was not new and that what was new in it was not important. A like judgment awaits anyone who would undertake another commentary upon Hobbes, not merely with the purpose of saying something new—which is not difficult—but saying something that is both new and important. The political theory of Hobbes has been subjected to close and continuing examination for about three centuries. What is more, he belongs to that select company of political theorists—which includes Plato, Machiavelli, and Marx—whose ideas have excited intense controversy long after the authors have died.[1]

In our own day interest in Hobbes has quickened rather than diminished. Philosophers of language have heeded Hobbes's injunction that "the light of human minds is perspicuous words, but by exact definitions first snuffed, and purged from ambiguity," and they have produced a formidable and ever-growing number of publications analyzing and dissecting Hobbes's assertions. Yet, as Hobbes himself had warned, something is lost when a writer of unusual range and versatility is treated with Procrustean hospitality by his critics:

> For it is not the bare words, but the scope of the writer, that giveth the true light, by which any writing is to be interpreted; and they that insist upon single texts, without considering the main design, can derive nothing from them clearly.[2]

Fortunately, the broader ethical and political themes of Hobbes's theory, as well as its spirit, have been admirably discussed by recent writers such as Strauss, Oakeshott, Polin, and Macpherson.[3] Mindful of the great debt owed by all students of Hobbes to these writers, I shall venture a somewhat different approach, concentrating upon the informing intention which governed Hobbes's political thought. I shall be concerned with the way in which intention and style affect substance. No claim is being offered that this approach is the only, or the best, way of coming to grips with the theoretical issues posed by Hobbes. It is simply a suggestion for recapturing what tends to be lost in an age of analysis: the human excitement which moves the theorist. If there is a leading theme to what follows it is the activity which the ancients called the *bios theoretikos*.

Briefly, my argument will be that the intentions which inform Hobbes's political theory were epical in nature and that his theory can be understood as having an epical aim. I shall also suggest, without supplying exhaustive proof, that from Plato to modern times an epic tradition in political theory has existed and that Hobbes is one of its ornaments. The phrase "epic tradition" refers to a type of political theory which is inspired mainly by the hope of achieving a great and memorable deed through the medium of thought. Other aims that it may have, such as contributing to the existing state of knowledge, formulating a system of logically consistent propositions, or establishing a set of hypotheses for scientific investigation, are distinctly secondary.

As a preliminary to considering Hobbes as a theorist in the epic tradition, an attempt must first be made to sketch some of the identifying marks of that tradition. In the Homeric epic Achilles is described as "a doer of great deeds and a speaker of great words." For the heroes of political theory, the great deed *is* the great word. Thucydides prefaced his *History* by saying that he had recorded the grounds of the quarrel between Athens and the Peloponnesians "in order that no one may ever have to ask from what origins so great a war arose among the Hellenes."[4] In an ultimate sense the great words of Plato, Machiavelli, Rousseau, or Marx were not invitations to other men to pronounce upon the logical or factual merits of the words, but an attempt to compel admiration and awe for the magnitude of the achievement. If the great words failed to be translated into reality, if society could not be made into the image of the word, the word might endure nonetheless as a memorial to the aspirations of thought.

Plato was the paradigmatic figure of this tradition. The *Republic* was the heroic issue of his political frustrations. It was intended as an alternative to the dilemma posed for the philosopher by the prevailing structure of society. The state of politics was such, he believed, that if a philosopher accepted a political role, he would be corrupted by the pursuit of power and the necessity of flattering the masses. If he chose to remain aloof, he might "keep his hands clean from iniquity" but at the price of surrendering all hope of "accomplishing some great thing."[5]

In his own life Plato had failed to achieve a "great thing" in politics, although he had tried at Syracuse. The *Republic* was a redemptive act, redeeming in thought what had been denied in practice. Yet this was but one element in a structure of intentions and not the most revealing of its heroic claims. The latter were expressed in a theoretical vision whose sweep included the transformation of man, the recasting of all social relationships, a revolutionary conception of knowledge, and a new version of the destiny of the human soul. These awesome accomplishments were fused into one supreme, agonistic assertion: that the theory had traced the pattern of the best society. It surpassed any mere deed, for it could not be erased by forgetfulness or destroyed by history. Although his polity was a "commonwealth founded in the realm of discourse," its duration might yet exceed that of any rival commonwealth. It stood open forever to all men living or yet unborn who longed "to take part in politics":

> There is a pattern set up in the heavens for one who desires to see it and, seeing it, to found one in himself. But whether it exists anywhere or ever will exist is no

matter; for this is the only commonwealth in whose politics [the true philosopher] can ever take part.[6]

What Plato thought to be a heroic achievement leaves us unmoved, conditioned as we are to suspicions of a theoretical claim which, in principle, cannot be substantiated by facts. That the ideal state was never put to the test of practice proves that it belongs properly to the realm of fantasy rather than theory. Yet it is precisely on this point that Plato was most infuriating about his achievement, teasing us with the suggestion that in some absurd way practical failure proved the truth of his theory. "Is our theory any the worse," he asked, "if we cannot prove it possible that a state so organized should be actually founded? . . . Is it not in the nature of things that action should come less close to truth than thought? People may not think so; but don't you agree?"[7]

Late in life, long after his failure at Syracuse, the heroic urge compelled him to make one last epical statement. In *The Laws* he achieved a more perfect realization of the idea that theory might serve as a form for expressing action in thought. Accordingly, theory became an imaginative imitation of the highest form of political action known to the Greeks, the action of the great lawgiver who lays the foundations of a new political order. The simple but dramatic rendition of this combination of thought and action, which, incidentally, restated from the theorist's viewpoint the dual prowess of Achilles, was contained in the casual remark of the Athenian Stranger: "Let us proceed to found the state by word."[8]

The heroic impulse reappears many times during the later history of political theory. In the *Discorsi* Machiavelli likened himself to the great explorers of his day and suggested that the dangers surrounding his "new route" in politics were comparable to those which threatened anyone bold enough to seek a new world.[9] Even the practical-minded Jeremy Bentham was not immune to these feelings. A legislator who had grasped the fundamental principles of legislation, he asserted, "might lay claim to the attributes of universality and eternity." One who had raised "his contemplation to that elevated point from which the whole map of human interests and situations lies expanded to his view" would have grasped principles which "will be so everywhere, and to the end of time."[10] In the correspondence of Alexis de Tocqueville the heroic impulse is evident, almost painfully. "I have on most occasions," he confessed, "the ambition to be first . . . Pride may be at the bottom of it." Before departing for America, he voiced the fear that France might establish a republic before he returned; he hoped that his projected volume on America would gain public attention and cause the political parties to notice him. The letters which he wrote while he was hard at work on *Democracy in America* reveal a passionate intensity which seems strange, mainly because his motives for writing a book are so alien to the scholarly community which now claims his writings as its property. "How I long for an opportunity, if Heaven would only grant it, of directing the fire that burns within me without object, to the achievement of great and noble ends, no matter through what dangers I might have to pass."[11]

Statements such as these express no purity of motive, either toward "pure" theory or action. They are the product of mixed motives whose aim is a "thought-deed." Theories of this mold are forms of action and the actions at which they aim are expressions of a theory. For Plato, Marsilius, More, Machiavelli, Hobbes, Rousseau, and Marx, theory is the means for making a great political gesture, and action is looked upon as a vehicle for rendering a great theoretical statement. In this they stand at the opposite pole from our contemporaries, whether it be the philosopher who believes that "philosophy leaves everything as it was," or the empirical political scientist who hesitates to cross the mythical line between fact and value. According to the empirical political theorist, the truth of a theory is determined by whether or not it produces empirical propositions "about the world we experience." The world itself, so we are told, is left unchanged by the theoretical act: "Whether the proposition is true or false depends on the degree to which the proposition and real world correspond."[12]

The epical theorist has ignored the formal protocols which, in every age, thought has decreed for its own sanity and certitude. If anything, he has resembled the bisected lover of Plato's *Symposium*, who was forever searching for his other half. The theorist's wholeness awaited that deed which would unite idea and act, *theoria* and *praxis*. His aim has been to make the world reflect a theory, not as the empirical theorist would have it, to make the theory correspond to the world, and not as the philosopher would have it, to make the theory an elucidation of meanings extracted from words about the world. In the structure of epical theory, concepts, symbols, and language are fused into a great political gesture *toward* the world, a thought-deed inspired by the hope that now or someday action will be joined to theory and become the means for making a great theoretical statement *in* the world.

Throughout the centuries, epical theory has carried the stamp of its origins in a particular kind of contest over intellectual and cultural mastery. The terms of the contest were such that the type of thinker who came to be known as a theorist had to adopt the epical mode if he hoped to compete for recognition. The competition took place in the fifth century B.C. and the protagonists were Greek philosophy and poetry.[13] The dispute was over rival claims to knowledge in matters of individual conduct, political action, and collective goals. The pre-Socratics, the followers of Socrates, as well as the historian-theorist Thucydides, made common cause against Homer, Hesiod, and the Greek dramatists. "When Homer undertakes to tell us about matters of the highest importance, such as the conduct of war, statesmanship, or education," Plato insisted, "we have a right to inquire into his competence."[14] As Plato's criticism implies, philosophy and political theory had to contest ground already preempted by poetry and drama. Poetry and drama provided much of the content of education. As public arts, publicly performed and supported, they did much to shape Greek ideas about religion, society, politics, and ethics. Above all, they were the special guardians and interpreters of that agonal, heroic conception of action which dominates the Homeric epics and much of Greek tragedy and is personified in kings, warriors, and founders. By their choice of subject, epic and tragedy were committed to a scale appropriate to heroic actions and to a standard of poetic achievement which was itself heroic. In retrospect, then, the crucial decision of philosophers and political theorists was to enter the lists against poetry and drama, and to enter while accepting poetic standards of scale and achievement.

Although poetry did much to shape the stylistics of early theory, its gestural content was shaped by the effort to outdo the political actor. "A private man," Plato asserted, "who knows the royal or political science . . . must be called a king [for] he is just as much a king when he is not in power as when he is."[15] Plato's claim went far beyond what is usually attributed to it. He was not saying merely that the theorist possesses knowledge and therefore should rule, but that theorizing is a thought-deed, a series of mental acts which pre-form in thought precisely what actors, when they are acting rightly, perform in fact.[16]

Contemporary fashions being what they are, the conception of a theory as a thought-deed seems not only wrong-headed but embarrassing. The guardians of contemporary orthodoxy, especially in the social sciences, find it more persuasive to believe that theories are the product of plodding, cumulative efforts. They prefer to picture it as a form of manual labor and, accordingly, describe the activity as "theory-construction."[17] It is ironical that the activity which has been esteemed by its practitioners—from Plato to Tocqueville—as the ultimate civic commitment should now be identified as banausic in nature: ironic because banausic activity was considered by the founders of political theory as inherently incompatible with the requirements of citizenship.[18]

If we are to understand the intentions which prompted epical theories, we must temporarily suspend today's familiar notions and try to recapture the excitement of those who first took self-consciously to inventing political theories. If we are successful in this act of imaginative recovery, we shall find that early theorists were not only striving to persuade their audiences of a truth, but, above all, to astonish them by a deed.

One step in recapturing the drama surrounding the early theories is to recall that the ancients felt it natural to express astonishment about a memorable act of thought. Here are the awestruck words of an ancient Greek historian who tried to record the first great achievement in cartography:

> Anaximander the Milesian, a disciple of Thales, first dared to draw the inhabited world on a tablet; after him Hecataeus the Milesian, a much travelled man, made the map more accurate, so that it became a source of wonder.[19]

A similar boldness and daring inspired the great classical theorists, such as Thucydides, Plato, and Aristotle. If we recall what they tried to accomplish by theory, it may not be bathetic to suggest that their deeds were worthy of comparison to those of Anaximander and Hecataeus. In theory they achieved nothing less than the reduction of the political world, with all of its buzzing confusion, its mysterious forces, and its sacral overtones, to a rational, manageable, intellectual order. As surely as the cartographer, they had charted a world by an act of thought, re-presented it in the form of a coherent theory, and thereby rendered it intelligible. The sense of astonishment, which all epics seek to arouse in their audiences, was artfully suggested in Plato's *Republic*, where the participants in the dialogue gasp in awe as Socrates unleashes, one after the other, "waves" of novel proposals.[20]

The epic, god-rivaling qualities of Greek theory were also expressed in the gradual extension of its spatial dimensions until the whole known political world was claimed as the province of theory. Thucydides had taken the Peloponnesian War as his theme, "the greatest movement yet known in history," one which had tested to the utmost the political resources of an entire civilization and had stretched them beyond their breaking point. Plato, too, drew on the totality of Greek city-state experience and wove much of it into the fabric of the city established in *The Laws*; he even made a tentative effort to go beyond the boundaries of Greece and to borrow from the political lore of Egypt. It was Aristotle who consolidated the spatial domain of theory. He assembled what was known of political societies, Greek and non-Greek alike, classified the various forms of political life, and analyzed their possibilities as well as their limitations. More than a matter of scale was at stake in the rivalry between epic and theory. A genuine difference in intention emerged from the theorist's concern with action. Plato had stated it in the form of a challenge to Homer and the poets. "If a man were able actually to do the things he represents as well as to produce poetic images of them do you believe he would seriously give himself up to making these images and take that as a completely satisfying object in life? I should imagine that, if he had a real understanding of the actions he represents, he would far sooner devote himself to performing them in fact. The memorials he would try to leave after him would be noble deeds, and he would be more eager to be the hero whose praises are sung than the poet who sings them." "Yes, I agree; he would do more good in that way and win a greater name."[21]

The truly novel element in Plato's conclusion was not that the theorist should become a political actor, but that action should become the means of realizing theory. This meant, among other things, claiming that the theorist could succeed where the epic writer had failed. Theoretical knowledge might provide that competence in "matters of the highest importance, such as the conduct of war, statesmanship, or education" which poetry could not.

These more ambitious objectives entangled the early theorists in another form of competition, this time with the rhetoricians and sophists. In the Platonic dialogues the rhetoricians and sophists were portrayed as rival claimants to political knowledge. The attention which Plato devoted to them implies that their case appeared plausible and powerful to the same audience sought by

Plato. Their knowledge might lack epical pretensions and theoretical rigor, but it more than compensated by promising practical knowledge of how to succeed in politics, especially by the arts of popular persuasion. This form of knowledge has always had an inherent appeal to those who must cope with the daily problems of politics in a setting where political support must be constantly mobilized and retained in the face of jealous political rivals. This pragmatic knowledge, which Machiavelli later called *effetuale verità*, was intended to teach men how to "do" politics. It stood in sharp contrast to the abstract philosophy of Plato and its world of immaterial forms, its complex dialectic, and its thinly disguised contempt for the "real" world of politicians. Because of its close alliance with experience, practical knowledge exhibited a "feel" for the immediate context of political decisions, a quality which helps to explain why the tradition of practical knowledge persisted into later centuries, sometimes turning up in the form of "advice to princes," or "public counsel," or, more recently, "expert knowledge." In order to establish his superiority over exponents of practical political knowledge, the theorist had to demonstrate that theoretical knowledge was more important in the realm of action.

In the centuries which followed the classical age, theory appeared to have established its title as the guardian of political knowledge, despite some powerful dissenting voices. Polybius among the ancients and Machiavelli among the moderns denied that philosophy was the way to political knowledge and maintained instead that history and practical experience provided the correct combination. During the age of Hobbes the hegemony of philosophy was directly attacked. The burden of most criticism was that political philosophy had failed to unite epic and *praxis* and had succeeded, instead, in perpetuating the effete vices of the poets with none of the practical benefits of the sophists. Political philosophy had been turned into a medium for the poetic fancy, useless to the statesman. One such critic was Lord Bacon, Hobbes's one-time employer, whose wide experience in law and politics, together with his philosophical learning, lent a special authority to the charge. Political philosophers, he declared, "make imaginary laws for imaginary commonwealths, and their discourses are as the stars, which give little light because they are so high."[22] Spinoza, a younger contemporary of Hobbes, was more emphatic:

> Philosophers have never conceived a political system which can be applied in practice, but have produced either obvious fantasies, or schemes that could only have been put into effect in Utopia, or the poet's golden age, where, of course, there was no need of them at all.[23]

The first step toward locating Hobbes in the epic tradition is to recall that by education and outlook he was not primarily a product of the scientific revolution of the early seventeenth century but of the humanistic renaissance of the sixteenth century.[24] "He was 40 yeares old," according to Aubrey, before he discovered geometry; over forty-five before he met Galileo; and nearly fifty before he became deeply immersed in philosophy.[25] Until his middle years he cultivated mainly classical languages and literature, the writings of grammarians and historians, and Aristotelian and scholastic philosophy. These subjects were supplemented by precisely the kind of reading which would encourage a taste for heroics. He was an avid reader of plays and romances and wholly fascinated by maps and geography, as befitted one born in the age of great explorers.

Before embarking upon seemingly different intellectual orientations, he had published his famous translation of Thucydides in 1629. The *History of the Peloponnesian War* is, if not epical,[26] deeply preoccupied with great actions, such as those of Pericles, Brasidas, and Alcibiades, as well as with great events, such as the revolution at Corcyra or the devastation wrought by the Great Plague. The parallels which modern scholars have established between Thucydides and the Greek tragedians[27] were implicit in Hobbes's Epistle Dedicatory to the *History*. Hobbes noted that "in history, actions of honour and dishonour do appear plainly and distinctly" and he recommended Thucydides "as having . . . profitable instructions for noblemen, and such as may come to have the managing of great and weighty actions."[28] Later, when he came to write *Leviathan*, Hobbes changed his mind about the value of history, contrasting the fallibility of prudence and experience derived from the knowledge of past events with the "infallible rules" and "prospective glasses" of political philosophy. Yet he did not forsake the Thucydidean example but replaced the political heroes by a single figure, the heroic theorist.

Even after his shift in intellectual emphases Hobbes retained his affiliation with humanistic concerns.[29] He numbered among his friends and acquaintances several poets and dramatists, such as Ben Jonson, Aytoun, Cowley, and Waller.[30] He was the subject of one of Cowley's odes and a significant influence upon Dryden. In 1651, while Hobbes was still in exile in Paris, Davenant's unfinished epic, *Gondibert*, appeared accompanied by a preface in which the poet acknowledged his debt to Hobbes; there was also included *Answer to Davenant*, in which Hobbes appended his views of the nature of epic poetry. Toward the very end of his life Hobbes turned to the greatest of all epics, the *Iliad* and the *Odyssey*, and produced translations which included a "Preface concerning the Vertues of an Heroic Poem." The closing lines of the "Preface," written when Hobbes was eighty-six, showed the old warrior to be as peppery as ever:

> Why then did I write it: Because I had nothing else to do. Why publish it: Because I thought it might take off my adversaries from showing their folly upon my more serious writings, and set them upon my verses to show their wisdom. But why without annotations? Because I had no hope to do it better than it is already done by Mr. Ogilby.[31]

Hobbes's reference to his "more serious writings" can be misleading if it is taken to mean that the works of his middle period constitute a sharp contrast to the epic-inspired writings of his "pre-Euclidean period" and the Homeric

translations of the last years. The epic impulse infected all of his writings, causing him to venture into such widely varied fields as philosophy, political theory,
mathematics, science, and theology, and to go forth in the temper of one who
seeks glory by a memorable deed. In each of these areas, Hobbes's writing was
not primarily governed by the solemn intention of making a "contribution," but
by the focused intensity of one who strives for mastery. Excepting his deference
for the obscure Mr. Ogilby, Hobbes never entered a field without seeking to dis-
lodge the reigning "heroes" and to establish his own supremacy. Sometimes, of
course, he succeeded only in falling flat on his face, as in his belligerent efforts to
prove to the Oxford mathematicians that a circle could indeed be squared. There
was not a little of the Don Quixote in the sage of Malmesbury.

At the age of eighty-four Hobbes composed an *Autobiography* in Latin ele-
giacs. The work is remarkable, not only for the way in which Hobbes compares his intellectual achievements to heroic deeds, but also for the manner in
which he treats intellectual disputation as a form of physical combat. Midway
in the verses he begins jousting, first with the mathematician Wallis, the "deadly
enemy of geometry," then with Wallis's followers, who, despite some "rough
handling," proved "too strong for my medicine." He then dismisses his controversy with Bishop Bramhall by the devastating remark: "He follows the schools;
I think for myself." A brief pause follows while Hobbes commends one of his
works as "a fountainhead of pure physics" which, "I think, will stand the test of
time." Then back to the wars: "[I] returned to my beloved mathematics, for my
adversary had at last withdrawn from the field."

> I brought out another little book on Principles . . . Here my victory was acknowl-
> edged by all. In other fields my opponents were doing their best to hide their
> grievous wounds. Their spirits were flagging and I pressed home the assault on
> my flagging foes, and scaled the topmost pinnacles of geometry . . . [Hobbes then
> recalls what happened after he wrote another book on geometry.] Wallis enters
> the fray against me, and in the eyes of the algebraists and theologians I am wor-
> sted. And now the whole host of Wallisians, confident of victory, was led out of
> their camp. But when I saw them deploying on treacherous ground, encumbered
> with roots thick-set, troublesome and tenacious, I resolved on fight, and in one
> moment scattered, slaughtered, routed countless foes.[32]

Despite the mock-heroic tone and the abundant fantasies, it is easy to see an
impulse to mastery which could not be satisfied with small triumphs but hun-
gered for a measure of immortality. This suggests the possibility that his conception of theory had been formed by heroic intentions and that, sensitive as
he was to the structure and nature of literary epics, strong traces of and resemblances to epic poetry might be found in his political theory.

At the outset, one glaring contrast appears between epic poetry and the epic
theory of Hobbes, but it enhances rather than detracts from the parallels. In
keeping with the objective purpose of narrative the authorship of many ancient

epics is anonymous. The personality of the narrator is rigorously suppressed so that the exploits and person of the hero may stand in bolder outline.[33] In contrast, theorists are constantly intruding themselves: one feels the presence of Plato in all of his dialogues, even though he is at great pains to conceal it; Machiavelli, when he is not writing prefaces and dedications which call attention to the author, makes liberal use of the first person singular; Sir Thomas More inserts himself into the dialogue of *Utopia*; Rousseau is perhaps the most extreme example, for he compels his readers to confront the man as well as the theory. Hobbes, too, was concerned that the deed not overshadow the identity of the doer. He described his work *De Corpore* in this way: "I was forging the shackles of reason in which I could bind Proteus to force him to confess the art by which he cloaks his tricks."[34] Of *De Cive* he declared, "I know of no book more magnified than this is beyond the seas."[35]

What seems like self-advertisement in Hobbes and the others is inherent in the claim of originality and novelty which every major theorist makes. The nature of novelty is to call attention to the maker. The heroic poet is more self-effacing because he wants to celebrate the novel and extraordinary actions of his hero, not to distract the readers by making them conscious of his own virtuosity. Heroic poetry celebrates the hero, but epic theory celebrates the theorist.

If the hero of epic theory is the theorist, it is natural to ask about the qualities which heroes are expected to display. Turning first to the epic, it concentrates upon actors whose exploits surpass those of most other men, including other heroes who challenge the epic figure. The epic hero, then, is an agonal figure who is pictured as seeking immortality by going beyond the highest mark set by others. We have already had occasion to note this competitive quality in Hobbes's *Autobiography*; it was equally evident in his political theory. In *Leviathan* we are told that the task of "great minds" is "to help and free others from scorn; and to compare themselves only with the most able." Virtue, as Hobbes notes repeatedly, has to do with "comparison" and "eminence."[36] True to the heroic code of disdaining trivial victories or combat with inferior minds, Hobbes made a special point of singling out only the most notable opponents. His readers of later centuries were never set to wondering, as they were in the case of Locke, why all the fuss about Filmer? Hobbes attacked "the vain and erroneous philosophy of the Greeks, especially of Aristotle," Cicero, the medieval schoolmen, and Bellarmine; he was scornful of famous ancient books whose false opinions had remained unchallenged until "a discreet master," namely, himself, had emerged to explode them.[37]

These ordeals of battle with dead giants who survive only in books might easily become the stuff of Swiftian parody; but there was a special urgency to Hobbes's combativeness. The "vain philosophy" of the ancients had helped "to fright men from obeying the laws of their country" and "to lessen the dependence of subjects on the sovereign power of their country."[38] Hobbes was concerned not just to win intellectual victories, but to win them because they might serve to better the human political condition in fundamental respects.

This point needs to be underscored because it is connected to the question of what kind of hero Hobbes aspired to be. Hobbes's indictment of the classical heroes of theory was not meant to refute old errors, but rather to undo a far more complex achievement, and one far harder to rectify. He insisted that the theories and ideas of the ancients and of the schoolmen had shaped the cultural tradition "of these western parts"; they were deeply embedded in the whole civilization. To rid society of this kind of legacy was not a simple matter of exploding a false or pernicious theory, but more like trying to extricate mankind from a vat of soft marshmallow. It required an effort which would liberate and transform the most vital thoughts and feelings that men had about the world and their place within it.

Hobbes believed that a cultural revolution was possible because his own age had demonstrated that, for the first time in history, men could produce theories which would transform the world in thought and practice. His epoch had witnessed the emergence of the scientist as a hero-figure. The new paradigm of the hero, incarnated in Galileo and Kepler, had shown what marvels the human mind might achieve if it dared to renounce the past and rely on no authority save human reason.

Hobbes was the first in a long line of political theorists to sense the excitement surrounding those whom Locke later called "master-builders," and the first to judge political philosophy to be in a backward state in comparison with mathematics and the sciences.[39] In more personal terms, the scientist-hero not only furnished the model for what Hobbes hoped to accomplish by way of transforming political and moral philosophy, but served also as a standard of theoretical action with which he strove to compete.

What, then, was the standard by which Hobbes wished to have his achievement judged? In part it consisted of the labor of destroying the dominant worldview through which his contemporaries surveyed man and political society: "I am not ignorant how hard a thing it is to weed out of men's minds such inveterate opinions as have taken root there."[40] But beyond the requirement of laying fresh foundations of thought, the scientific achievement stipulated the test of results. Science had produced "the greatest commodities of mankind," such as navigation, engineering, architecture, and the like.[41] Thus, to compete with the scientific hero required that the political theorist create a theory which embodied the power to produce tangible benefits. This was the challenge which Hobbes proposed for himself: to have his thought-deed measured by the scientific achievement. For, as he wrote, "to honour is to value highly the power of any person; and . . . such value is measured by comparing him with others."[42] The next step was to translate the quest for honor into theoretical terms which would enable the political hero to be compared with the scientific hero. Accordingly,

Hobbes proclaimed, "The end of knowledge is power; and the use of theories . . . is for the construction of problems; and, lastly the scope of all speculation is the performing of some action, or thing to be done."[43]

To adopt science as a model would seem to require that the theorist accept a picture of the world far different from the fancy-ridden, supernatural world of the epic. Epic heroes move in a world of dark and occult forces; they encounter great perils and horrors, sometimes at the hands of nature, sometimes by the machinations of malevolent powers; they are constantly in the midst of violent death and widespread destruction; and yet by a superhuman effort, which stretches the human will to its limits, they succeed nonetheless.

We moderns, however, have been taught a different view. Our world is, as Weber put it, "disenchanted," without "mysterious and incalculable forces," and it is we who, by science, rationalism, technique, and calculation, have disenchanted it.[44] If we turn once more to Hobbes's *Autobiography*, however, we seem to be in an older premodern world where heroes are still possible:

> It was now one thousand six hundred and forty years since the birth of the Virgin's son, when a wonderful distemper seized my native land whereby innumerable learned men afterwards perished. . . . Now the Civil War had raged for four years and had ground down the English, Irish, and Scotch. Treacherous Fortune remained in the criminal camp; honest men fled by whatever route they could . . . I could not endure that so many monstrous crimes should be put down to the command of God . . . Then for six months I was prostrated by illness; I was preparing myself for the approach of Death. But *I* stood my ground and *she* fled. Then I finished a book in my native idiom, so that it could be read and re-read by my English fellow country-men to their advantage. From the press in London it sped to neighbour regions. Its name was *Leviathan*. That book now fights for all kings and for all those who exercise the rights of kings.[45]

The language of *Leviathan* itself paints a world that is not wholly disenchanted. Neither is it completely demon-free. It is a world ringed by hostile powers of great subtlety and tenacity. Hobbes attacked the powers with the weapons of jest and irony, and yet he cannot quite deny that beneath the flummery there is a malevolent substance which must be taken seriously. The world may be populated by "ghostly powers"; part of it may be likened to a "kingdom of fairies"; and the monster of "mixed government" may prowl about[46]—and yet these apparitions exert a profound influence over men and society. Hence the hero is driven to a mighty effort, for he is not just combatting beliefs but great powers. Accordingly, the whole of Part Four of *Leviathan* takes the form of a frontal assault on "the kingdom of darkness," which is in reality "a confederacy of deceivers, [who] to obtain dominion over men in this present world, endeavor by dark and erroneous doctrines to extinguish in them the light, both of nature, and of the gospel."[47] Warning that "we are . . . yet in the dark," the hero-theorist vows to dispel that "darkness of mind," "enchantment," and "mist" which the deceivers have cast on mankind.[48]

If heroes are to perform extraordinary deeds, they must be endowed with gifts of a special order. By these gifts they are set off from other men and armed with unusual powers. In heroic poetry, for example, the hero often possesses some remarkable piece of equipment, such as a mighty sword, a shield, or an amazing horse. The epic poet will frequently take special care to describe how the hero has forged some fabulous weapon or acquired it. In Bowra's summary, "The hero's weapon is both an instrument and an emblem of his power. It rounds off his nature and helps him to fulfill his potentialities."[49]

We have already had occasion to quote Hobbes's dictum that knowledge is a form of power, but it remains to show in what sense that power was due to a special kind of equipment, one which Hobbes had forged himself. In the Preface to De Cive, he says to the reader, "I promise thee here such things, which ordinarily promised, do seem to challenge the greatest attention, and I lay them here before thine eyes." Foremost among these was "the right method of handling" the subject matter.[50] This phrase, "right method," identifies the new hero's weapon. Knowledge, by being systematized, was transformed into power. The effect of systematization was to render knowledge wieldy. Although "some general truths" were as old as language itself, "they were at first but few in number; men lived upon gross experience; there was no method."[51] The "want of method" signifies weakness. Without it, men err and are deceived, and while experience, prudence, and natural wit may help by supplying bits of knowledge, they afford no guarantee of certainty, no assurance that they will serve well when they are most needed. All is changed by the advent of method, for it magnifies human power and certitude. Reason is rendered infallible: "Nothing is produced by reasoning aright, but general, eternal, and immutable truth."[52]

Rational method is not a weapon easily fashioned or easily mastered, especially in political matters. The prolonged preparation, constant practice, and pure dedication which it demands are analogous to the long apprenticeship and severe trials which a knight had to undergo before he was declared fit for chivalric tests. To be able to "read" all mankind, which according to Hobbes was required of those who governed, was far more difficult "than to learn any language or science."[53] "Industrious meditation" and prolonged study were necessary.[54] Practical political experience, by itself, was an inadequate substitute. "Infallible rules" were needed and only reason, guided by method, could produce them. To be infallible meant being not merely correct, but invincible, as the following example suggests. To mark the difference between "science" and "prudence,"

> let us suppose one man endued with an excellent natural use and dexterity in handling his arms; and another to have added to that dexterity, an acquired science, of where he can offend, or be offended by his adversary, in every possible

posture or guard: the ability of the former would be to the ability of the latter, as prudence to sapience [i.e., science]; both useful; but the latter infallible.[55]

Hobbes had tempered and tested the weapon of "method" in *Elements of Law* and *De Cive*. Now, in *Leviathan*, it was ready for the supreme achievement.

Leviathan was an epical work both in its fullness of scope and boldness of execution. The grandness of its theme was struck in the opening sentences: God governs the world by the art of nature, but it is possible by human art to rival what had been thought to be a unique act, to create an "artificial animal." The challenge goes further: by art man can surpass nature, for he can create "that great Leviathan" which "is of greater stature and strength" than natural man. This artificial animal will have its own "soul" in the form of sovereignty which gives "life" to the body; its own joints, nerves, memory, reason, and will.[56]

But this is only a promise of what is to be achieved. Before his task has been completed, Hobbes will have created a new image of man, outfitted with a specific nature, powered by the dynamics of fear and pride, and instructed how he must move in a perilous world. Hobbes, too, did not rest after this first day's labor, but proceeded to construct society, arrange its parts, arm it with the power to defend itself, and then turn it loose on a world where all states are in the "posture of gladiators." When he has finished, Hobbes will have ranged from man to society, from earth to heaven, rearranging and reducing all that was therein to laws: laws of human behavior, laws of nature, laws of God. He will tell man what is necessary for his political as well as his spiritual salvation. When the labor is finally over, he will stand back so that we may marvel at the magnitude of his challenge: his "artificial man" has become a "mortal god," wielding "awesome power," frightening men by the "terror of great punishment," and worthy of comparison with the great beast described in the Book of Job: "There is nothing on earth to be compared with him. He is made so as not to be afraid. He seeth every high thing below him; and is king of all the children of pride."[57] Save for the ultimate threat of foreign invasion, against which there can be no absolute protection, the mortal god is "designed to live as long as mankind, or as the laws of nature, or as justice itself, which gives [it] life."[58]

The deed which is symbolized by the theory is performed against the kind of stylized background common to most epics. This background was, in many ways, Hobbes's supreme literary achievement, combining the pictorial vividness of the epic with the relentless precision of logic. The background was titled "the state of nature," a condition which had the same universal significance and dramatic intensity for the Hobbesian myth as man's fall from grace has for the Christian myth. There was horror, destruction, and violence, real and impending; for the background, which accentuates the extraordinary quality of the theory-deed, described what human life was like when the authority of the political order is dissolved or fatally weakened. In the absence of effective authority, men move fearfully and warily through a state of nature, a condition of war between every man, where the human animal sheds his humanity and becomes as a wolf to other men, and life is "solitary, poor, nasty, brutish, and short."[59]

Hobbes invites us to measure the magnitude of his deed both by the enormous difference between the chaotic state of nature and civil society and by the unpromising materials with which the hero must work. Hobbesian men are not heroes sprung from dragon's teeth. They are, instead, timid but highly competitive; insecure but ambitious; always self-interested, sometimes vain, and frequently aggressive. In contrast to the carefully sorted human types which were fed into Plato's *Republic, Statesman*, and the *Laws*, Hobbesian man is poor stuff. Although he is capable of thinking and of constructing trains of thought, he is all too prone to fantasy, illusion, and absurdity, all too ready to make "private appetite . . . the measure of good and evil."[60]

To compound *Leviathan* from such material is to create power from human insufficiency and weakness. This fabulous achievement is made possible by the weapon of deliverance which Hobbes alone has fashioned. By "speech and method" man can learn to reason from causes and effects; and if he proceeds with "study and industry," "instruction and discipline," he will come to understand the causes of his miserable condition and to hit upon the means of his salvation.[61] Method will enable him to hunt out the sources of conflict and to discover what he must do if there is to be an end to the war of each against all. Despite the weakness of each individual, it is possible to generate "an unlimited power" which, potentially, "is as great as possibly men can be imagined to make it."[62]

The covenant is the means of man's deliverance. The details need not be considered here, except to call attention to one aspect. The condition of "mere nature" which the compact is designed to overcome is a condition of approximate equality. Hobbes took special care to emphasize this point and, consequently, it must have had an important bearing, not only for the logic of his theory, but for its epic purpose. In terms of the theoretical argument, natural equality results in a kind of "stand-off." Where there is no law or authority, the strong are as vulnerable as the weak, provided the latter are cunning enough; where there are no "general and infallible rules called science," each can acquire the same amount of experience as another, and hence there is no unassailable superiority based on knowledge. The force of this description is not only to emphasize equality in a physical sense, but to nullify any notion of natural preeminence. As Hobbes puts it, "the question who is the better man has no place in the condition of mere nature."[63] The reduction of differences reaches its climax in the covenant when men agree to join together on equal terms and to surrender all power and natural rights (save that of self-defense).

There is a close connection between this insistence on leveling and the epic ambitions of the theorist. It is made evident by the following:

> For men, as they became at last weary of irregular jostling, and hewing one another, and desire with all their hearts, to conform themselves into one firm and

lasting edifice; so for want, both of the art of making fit laws to square their actions by, and also of humility, and patience, to suffer the rude and cumbersome
points of their present greatness to be taken off, they cannot without the help
of a very able architect, be compiled into any other than a crazy building, such
as hardly lasting out their own time, must assuredly fall upon the heads of their
posterity.[64]

The objective of removing "the rude and cumbrous points of their present
greatness" was part of an overall strategy aimed at diminishing all forms of
superiority, especially the form of superiority most likely to compete with the
theorist-hero. For more than a century political adventurers had exploited the
instabilities of English politics and the personalized government of Tudors and
Stuarts. From Cromwell, Cecil, and Raleigh to Buckingham and "King Pym"
there was a line of political men for whom pride and arrogance were second
nature. Beckoned by "a world of profit and delight," they scrambled for power,
office, and preeminence. To contain and devitalize this form of politics was a
fundamental purpose of Hobbes.

The instrument which he fashioned for this end consisted of a new code of
conduct. He called his code the "Laws of Nature." Although he could not resist
l'esprit de géométrie in calling the provisions "theorems . . . immutable and eternal," their purpose was to legislate human "manners" into conformity to the
requirements of order. "By manners," he explained, "I mean not here, decency
of behaviour; as how one should salute another, or how a man should wash his
mouth, or pick his teeth before company, and such other points of *small morals*;
but those qualities of mankind that concern their living together in peace and
unity."[65] If "small morals" were not the solution to the political problem, small
passions were not its cause. Great disorder, such as sedition or rebellion, was
rooted in the great passions which inclined men toward "injustice, ingratitude,
arrogance, iniquity, acception [i.e., exception] of persons, and the rest."[66]

The attack on the great passions was pressed home in Hobbes's fifth law of
nature. It exalted the quiet virtue of "complaisance, that is to say, that every man
strive to accommodate himself to the rest." Hobbes compared this requirement of
social accommodation, or conformity, to the task of fitting irregular stones into
a structure. Some men possess natures whose "asperity and irregularity" cause
them to take "more room from others" than they need. A wise social architect
will cast away such stones, because "a man that by asperity of nature will strive to
retain those things which to himself are superfluous, and to others necessary; and
for the stubbornness of his passions, cannot be corrected, is to be left, or cast out
of society, as cumbersome thereunto."[67]

Elsewhere Hobbes was more sardonic about those who lived by a "higher"
morality and restlessly searched for new heights of preeminence. Madness, he
suggested, dwelt in these heights and depths of spirit to which the overreachers
were invariably drawn; it was to be found in "great vain-glory which is com-

monly called pride and self-conceit, or [in] great dejection of mind."[68] Hobbes's society was not intended to be, like Lloyd-George's Britain, a land fit for heroes. Accordingly, the social code consisted of quiet virtues, such as modesty, equity, mercy, gratitude, and justice.[69] It defined the kind of civil decorum which society needs if everyday routines were to be carried on and if the conditions of peace and order were to be sustained. These virtues, Hobbes thought, were comfortably within the reach of most men.

Beyond the fundamental principles laid down in the Laws of Nature, the remainder of the political landscape of Leviathan-land had been rendered inhospitable to heroic achievement. The aristocracy, which in the past had produced many a wayward spirit to torment political conventions, was deprived of its favorite indoor sport of palace politics: the security of sovereign authority required that "the power and honor of subjects vanisheth in the presence of the power sovereign."[70]

At first glance it might seem that the sovereign himself, armed with complete authority to command all members of society, was the foremost candidate for greatness. Despite the fact that sovereignty was what *Leviathan* was all about, Hobbes consistently ignored all the obvious questions about the character of the person who was to wield the awesome power. No extended discussion is to be found concerning the education or moral qualities necessary to the exercise of sovereignty.

What we find instead is that Hobbes has employed philosophy in a way most revealing of his intentions vis-à-vis the sovereign. He has resorted to abstract concepts, such as "sovereignty," "office," and the like, to depersonalize the sovereign. Only rarely did he mention, and in minor connections, the name of any modern ruler. He said the truth when he wrote, "I speak not of the men, but, in the abstract, of the seat of power."[71] Hobbes had grasped the central tenet of epic theory: when politics is treated as the medium whereby theory is translated into reality, political rulers are reduced to being members of a supporting cast in a play where the dominant figure is the playwright.

Having disposed of the rivalry of kings and aristocrats, Hobbes could look with equanimity upon the men of middling degree for whom his society was intended. These busy and industrious men presented no challenge, for, in Hobbes's view, they longed for the peace and security of Leviathan-land. Further, their lifestyle differed significantly from the hero's. It was formed by an endless chase after "continual prospering," and epitomized in the basic value of "felicity," "a continual progress of the desire from one object to another, the attaining of the former being still but the way to the latter."[72] Endless striving, without rest or repose, might seem to resemble in intensity the style of heroes; but it lacked the crucial notion of a terminal achievement, of a climactic moment when the weary hero could point to his triumph. One can only wonder whether Hobbes would have revised his belief about the unheroic temper of the middle class had he been allowed to witness the astonishing ways in which nineteenth-century "captains of industry" and "robber barons" defied the commands of sovereign lawmakers and exploited the quiet virtues of their workers.

Once aristocrat, prince, and bourgeois man have been assigned their niches, the identity of the one remaining hero is evident to all—the theorist-creator of a new political cosmos. To have ordered an entire society and the lives of all of its members is an achievement dazzling in its scale and truly heroic in its reach, even if—or perhaps because—it is only a deed enacted in thought. Once more we are led to wonder about the secret power of the theorist-hero: what are the unique means which have set him to boasting that he has succeeded where all of his great predecessors, such as Plato and Aristotle, had failed? Earlier I have suggested that "method" served Hobbes as the "functional equivalent" of the hero's sword or other piece of exceptional equipment. I shall now elaborate this point in order to bring out the special quality of that Hobbesian weapon.

The peculiarity of the Hobbesian conception of method is that it unites two elements which many of his philosophical predecessors had separated. The two elements which he combined were reason and passion. In the thinking of many earlier philosophers reason had stood for the possibility of objective, disinterested, and detached knowledge. Reason's natural enemy was passion and/ or interest, for they undermined the selflessness which was thought to be essential for right reasoning. Some of Hobbes's predecessors, Plato for example, had sought to sublimate passion into the quest for truth; but Hobbes took the different course of harnessing passion to reason rather than fusing the two. In this way he was able to enlist in the cause of reason the driving energy of the heroic passions which he had repressed in his political actors. At the same time he used reason to rescue the passions from their usual fate of "wandering amongst innumerable absurdities."[73] The conjoining of reason and passion was of fundamental importance to Hobbes's entire scheme, because the conjunction converted knowledge into power. The simple coupling device was method.

In today's social science the idea of method has a distinctly unheroic ring. It sets us to thinking in terms of step-by-step procedures, doggedly sequential activity, unimaginative and passionless plodding; in short, the methodical way of doing things. Hobbes sometimes wrote in this vein, as when he suggests that correct reasoning is "attained by industry" and by following "a good and orderly method in proceeding."[74] If we look more closely at his account, however, this first impression is dispelled and it becomes evident that method is not only rooted in passion but dependent on great passion for its driving force.

The main discussion occurs in Chapter Eight of *Leviathan* where the intellectual virtues are analyzed. Virtue, according to Hobbes, is something which is "valued for [its] eminence and consisteth in comparison." The intellectual virtues are associated with "good wit," of which there are two types, "natural" and "acquired." The first is derived from experience and is "without method, culture, or instruction." Its principal characteristics are "*celerity of imagining*, that is swift succession of one thought to another; and *steady direction* to some approved end."[75] Acquired wit, on the other hand, is achieved by "method and instruction" and its end product is "science," which Hobbes associates with "infallible" knowledge.[76] Both forms of wit appear in different proportions among men, but the cause of the difference is "in the passions." The different degrees of quickness in wit are also due to the same cause. Differences in passion, in turn, are traceable to differences in physical make-up, education, and upbringing.[77] The most crucial consideration, however, is that the driving force behind wit is "the desire of power" which directs wit toward worldly goods and honor, and also toward knowledge. "A man who has no great passion for any of these things cannot possibly have either a great fancy or much judgment." The two psychological extremes are to be without any passion for power ("to have no desire is to be dead") or, more likely, to have uncontrolled passions, which leads to madness.[78]

In Hobbes's view, the restraints of method serve to channel passion into the quest for knowledge and power and to prevent it from wandering into absurdity and insanity. Men will submit to its discipline because of the promise of greater and surer gratifications. The process begins when desire, which is rooted in the passions, prompts man to seek to reproduce some effect which he finds pleasurable. Reason, in the form of "regulated thoughts," methodically hunts out the causes of the effect, or it may reverse the procedure and seek the effects of some cause. To know these causes and effects means that we have the knowledge which, potentially, enables us to reproduce them, possibly at will. It means, in brief, that we have power.[79]

The emphasis upon the power of knowledge is wholly predictable in one who eagerly sought to identify himself with the forces of light, the scientists and mathematicians, against the forces of darkness and obscurantism, the "dogmatici" who "take up maxims from their education, and from the authority of men, or of custom, and take the habitual discourse of the tongue for ratiocination."[80] Although Hobbes continued to proclaim the epical quality of his achievement, the epical style would seem jeopardized by the rigor and sobriety, the doggedness, and "the absence of controversies and dispute" which, Hobbes insisted, accompany the style of science and mathematics.[81] The *"mathematici,"* he noted, "proceed from most low and humble principles, evident even to the meanest capacity; going on slowly, and with most scrupulous ratiocination (viz.) from the imposition of names they infer the truth of their first propositions; and from two of the first, a third . . . and so on, according to the steps of science."[82] The very language of the *stile nuovo* seems most unheroic—"low and humble principles," "evident even to the meanest capacity," "going on slowly," etc.—even if the end result, "infallibility," is extraordinary. But when these notions are placed alongside those which, for example, pervade the *Autobiography*, one cannot help wondering whether Hobbes was a faithful Hobbist or, more precisely, whether Hobbes the theorist and Hobbes the methodist followed the same precepts.

One suspects that an uneasy tension existed in Hobbes's thought between an heroic impulse which required for its fulfillment a hostile world defined in epical terms and a scientific impulse which required that mystery and romance be dropped out of the world so that ratiocination and utility could be made the main business. Thus, reasoning is described as the "addition of parcels" or the "subtraction of one sum from another."[83] Similarly, in his account of scientific activity Hobbes appeared determined to expunge any suggestion of epic action. Science "is the knowledge of consequences, and dependence of one fact upon another." It is "attained by industry; first in apt imposing of names; and secondly by getting good and orderly method." Any temptation to depict truth-seeking as a drama is repressed in favor of making it appear as a matter of routine and technique: "Truth consisteth in the right ordering of names in our affirmations, [and] a man that seeketh precise truth had need to remember what every name he uses stands for, or else he will find himself entangled in words."[84]

Hobbes's gusto for attacking the absurdities and pernicious effects of classical and scholastic philosophies and Christian theologies creates the expectation that a radically new version of truth and truth-seeking is about to be unveiled. Yet the Hobbesian conception of truth and method furnishes a rather unremarkable life-style for the mind. Some of his predecessors and contemporaries had injected a powerful heroic quality into science by emphasizing the venturesome nature of experimental inquiry or by appealing to the example of selflessness on the part of those who labored tirelessly to add their tiny contribution to the cumulation of scientific knowledge. But Hobbes gave little attention either to experimentalism or to the notion of organized, collaborative research.

What are missing from his account of theoretical activity are just the qualities usually accompanying an heroic thought-deed, the qualities which suggest the novel, the unexpected, the extraordinary, and the venturesome. Their absence is all the more striking in view of the genuinely radical positions which Hobbes took on basic questions concerning the nature of man, authority, law, justice, church-state relationships, and many more. We are left with a profound incongruity between a rather prosaic conception of theoretical activity and the devastating consequences which, Hobbes would like to have us believe, followed from its use. In reality, the logical dress with which he outfits his arguments serves rather as a form of authority intended to command our assent than as a symbol of the genius which produced the distinctive and often shocking assertions of *Leviathan*. Consider some of the characteristic definitions set out in that work: The curiosity to know the causes of things is defined as "a lust of the mind." Or, "The value or worth of man is, as of all other things, his price."[85] There are scores of such assertions in all of his writings and, although they are logically extended and formed into a rigorous system, or what passes for one, their "bite" comes not from logic but from the novel and daring view of man, society, and the world which inspired them.

That there should be a strongly imaginative element in Hobbes's thought is not surprising. It is commonly recognized today that imagination has played a vital role in many great scientific theories and philosophical systems. But what does it mean to say that a political theory exhibits imagination? A contemporary political scientist might answer by suggesting that a theorist displays imagination by the ingenuity of his explanation. Older political theories embodied imagination in a different way. Among writers like Plato and Machiavelli political imagination took the form of conceiving the political world to be other than it was. This required that the existing world be looked at in new ways so that the path to a new state of affairs could be plotted and that new state itself visualized. To conceive of new interconnections and possibilities, the theoretical mind must be free to use words and concepts in unorthodox ways and to range widely over its chosen province, inspecting it from new angles, disclosing hitherto unsuspected relations, and imagining it arranged differently. Political imagination, then, requires an inventive mind, playing upon a world which, in mental terms at least, possesses some measure of plasticity.

Imagination has a special significance in the present context beyond the role it plays in theory. Imagination has always been recognized to be one of the main characteristics of great poetry and drama, and never more so than in the age of Hobbes.[86] More important, imagination constitutes, perhaps, the most fundamental trait which unites science, theory, literature, and music, a consideration which is particularly suggestive when dealing with epic forms of political theory. Epic theory is likely to display imaginative elements more clearly than theories which concentrate upon description or explanation. The fascinating problem which Hobbes presented was that, while practicing the epic mode with consummate mastery and imagination, he experienced great difficulty in reconciling the claims of imagination with those of "orderly method." As a close analyst of the nature of human thought, he might be expected to give some attention to the psychology of imagination, but, in fact, he was far more concerned with the knowledge-claims than the psychology of imagination. The defenders of poetry and drama had argued that imagination enabled the poet to discover and create truths about man and his world. They defined imagination in terms of mental abilities such as "fancy," playfulness, and free-ranging, abilities which Hobbes was to consider under the heading of "virtues of the mind."

In keeping with his admiration for the step-by-step style of inquiry of the *mathematici*, Hobbes wrote disparagingly of imagination as but a "conception" which lingers in the mind, and "by little and little decaying from and after the act of sense." Of that ranging quality of the mind he was equally unflattering: "We proceed from anything to anything," stimulated by our senses "like hounds casting about" while hunting.[87] Yet when Hobbes leaves the psychological plane and examines fancy, imagination, and ranging in relation to knowledge, they are, as it were, rehabilitated and outfitted so splendidly that, in contrast, the *mathematici* appear drab and dull. In *The Elements of Law*, from which we have been quoting his eulogies of the *mathematici*, there is a long but significant passage devoted to "that quick ranging of mind . . . which is joined with curiosity of comparing the things that come into his mind with one another." As the passage proceeds, it becomes evident that Hobbes is talking about what we have called the theoretical imagination and that he is prepared to enlarge the conception of truth and permit poetry to enjoy access:

> In which comparison, man delighteth himself with finding unexpected similitude in things, otherwise much unlike, in which men place the excellency of FANCY: and from thence proceed those grateful similies, metaphors, and other tropes, by which both poets and orators have it in their power to make things please or displease . . . or else in discerning suddenly dissimilitude in things that otherwise appear the same. And this vertue of the mind is that by which men attain to exact and perfect knowledge; and the pleasure thereof consisteth in continual instruction, and in distinction of persons, places, and seasons; it is commonly termed by the name of JUDGMENT: for, to judge is nothing else, but to distinguish or discern; and both fancy and judgment are commonly comprehended under the name of WIT, which seemeth a tenuity and agility of spirits, contrary to that restiveness of the spirits supposed in those that are dull.[88]

The Elements of Law is believed to have circulated in manuscript form as early as 1640, although it was not until 1650 that the two parts of it were published separately. In 1651 his *Answer to Davenant* appeared. There Hobbes was concerned to analyze the nature of an heroic poem, and in the course of his analysis he expanded upon his notions of fancy and judgment and upon the responsibilities of the poet and the philosopher. Fancy and judgment were singled out as the two main elements of an heroic poem. Fancy is the mind as free spirit, playful and imaginative, choosing as it pleases from its memories of sense experience, and ranging with a marvelous swiftness and abandon wherever it pleases, sometimes at the price of extravagance.

> So that when she seemeth to fly from one Indies to the other, and from heaven to earth, and to penetrate into the hardest matter and obscurest places, into the future, and into herself, and all this in a point of time, the voyage is not very great, herself being all she seeks. And her wonderful celerity, consisteth not so much in motion, as in copious imagery discreetly ordered, and perfectly registered in the memory; which most men under the name of philosophy have a glimpse of, and is pretended to by many, that grossly mistaking her, embrace contention in her place. But so far forth as the fancy of man has traced the ways of true philosophy, so far it hath produced very marvellous effects to the benefit of mankind.[89]

Despite the obscurity of parts of this passage, this much seems clear: just as philosophy, in its way, may approximate the ability of fancy to control its imagery and remember it perfectly, so fancy in its way may follow the same path as true philosophy. Elsewhere in the *Answer* Hobbes applauds the occasions when philosophy and fancy come together to produce the imaginative "workmanship of fancy." But when the problem concerns moral virtue, he finds that no union has been achieved. Philosophy has pursued an independent course and, accordingly, has failed. "The architect Fancy," Hobbes declared, "must take the philosopher's part on herself." The heroic poet, therefore, should furnish "a venerable and amiable image of heroic virtue." To do so, however, the poet must be part philosopher.

One might conjecture that a civil philosopher, if he was part poet and possessed of the right proportions of reason and fancy, might be tempted to trace the ways of the true philosophy in the hope of producing "very marvellous effects to the benefit of mankind." If, on the other hand, such a philosopher became convinced that reason had found new and unexpected resources, he might dispense with fancy and rely solely on reason.

The case for demoting fancy was strengthened by the nature of the second element which Hobbes found in heroic poems. This was the element of "judgment." It was of crucial significance, not only for identifying the intellectual weakness of fancy, but for providing an intellectual virtue which was simultaneously useful for theoretical inquiry *and* practical political decisions. In the preliminary formulation given in the *Answer to Davenant*, judgment was described as "the severer sister" of fancy and "begotten" also by memory. Judgment was said to proceed by "a grave and rigid examination of all the parts of nature . . . [to] register the order, causes, uses, differences, and resemblances" found therein. Thus judgment represents analytical ability, the power to discriminate and identify principles of structure and causal sequence. Of necessity it operates as a restraint upon fancy, preventing the latter from flying beyond "the conceived possibility of nature." Because of its repressive function, Hobbes noted, judgment finds little favor among the connoisseurs of poetry who tend to rank it beneath fancy.[90]

The relative merits of fancy and judgment were taken up once more in *Leviathan*, which appeared in 1651, shortly after the *Answer*. In the more pronouncedly political context of *Leviathan*, fancy was given some hard knocks and, apparently, reduced to being a mere embellishment of truth. For example, in the *Answer* fancy was said to be able to detect differences and similarities of the sort which escape the average eye, but in *Leviathan* it is strictly confined to detecting nonobvious similarities. The role of judgment, at first, is stated rather modestly. It is to identify differences not ordinarily noted. In practical matters this ability is called "good judgment" or "discretion." Hobbes's hostility to fancy begins to take shape when he asserts that fancy divorced from judgment does not even rate as a virtue. Judgment, on the other hand, "is commended for itself without the help of fancy." Great fancy may even end in madness. More important, to the extent that any intellectual activity aims at truth or deals with political policies it should renounce fancy. Accordingly, fancy's proper place is in poetry, oratory, and special pleading where "disguise" of truth "serveth best to the design in hand." Although an element of judgment is necessary to "a good poem, whether it be epic or dramatic . . . fancy must be more eminent, because they please for the extravagancy." Fancy has no part, except as ornament, in writing history and very little in "demonstration, counsel, and all rigorous search of truth."[91]

With the exclusion of fancy from philosophical inquiry and political deliberation, it might seem that epical theory had impoverished its own resources and committed itself to the "grave and rigid" style of judgment. Fortunately, Hobbes practiced poorly what he preached. If *Leviathan* was meant, as it surely was, to be an example of the "rigorous search for truth," it requires no unusual aesthetic sensibility to point out that, despite Hobbes's admiration for the austerity of geometry, the imprint of fancy was everywhere to be seen. The discrepancy between preachment and practice is so glaring as to be comical. Thus Hobbes denounced the use of metaphor, the favorite device of fancy, and demanded that it be "utterly excluded [from] counsel of reasoning."[92] This from a writer who delights in stringing one metaphor after another, including "the appetite of the state," the law as "public conscience," "the soul of the commonwealth," and "the mortal god" which is the state. The title of his work gives everything away. *Leviathan* itself is a metaphor, while the argument supporting it is but an extended metaphor, a superb and sustained display of imagination and fancy and not always restrained by "judgment." Recall the vivid imagery of the state of nature; or the extravagant discussion of the human passions; or the translation of the state into the language of mechanism; or the fanciful act whereby men covenant themselves into society; or the mock-heroic assault on the Kingdom of Fairies. No further comment is needed except that Hobbes had been more honest in his *Autobiography*, where he had written that his life had been spent serving peace *and* "her companions, the Muses."[93]

If the author of *Leviathan* does not suppress fancy, but uses it to "trace the ways of true philosophy," one might expect him to claim political results comparable to those achieved by the heroes of science. Before asking how these results were to be achieved, we must first ask what they were. "The utility of moral and civil philosophy," Hobbes states, "is to be estimated, not so much by the commodities we have by knowing these sciences, as by the calamities we receive from not knowing them."[94] This seems a modest claim when compared with the list of benefits produced by "natural philosophy and geometry." The latter have to their credit "the greatest commodities of mankind," such as "measuring matter and motion; moving ponderous bodies; architecture; navigation; making instruments for all uses; calculating the celestial motions, the aspects of the stars, and the great parts of time; geography, etc." Yet without peace and security none of these arts can flourish. The justification of civil philosophy, then, is its ability to state the conditions which make possible the pursuit of science and the arts. "Commodious living," which is the promise contained in science, presupposes that men know and practice "the rules of civil life."[95] Just as practical arts and techniques serve as the middle term which translates science and geometry into "the greatest commodities," so "civil rules" are the means for translating civil philosophy into civil order.

Once the point is reached where it is proper to ask how and by what means the promise of political theory is to be realized, the hero, for the first time, falters. The nature of the task is such that he is no longer self-sufficient, for he must rely on others to give practical substance to his "infallible rules." In the history of political theory, Hobbes was not the first uncertain hero. From Plato onward, theorists had recognized the need for some kind of alliance between theory and power. The difficulty was not to persuade theorists that by some means they must gain control of power; this was obvious, and most theorists devised stratagems for the purpose. The main stumbling-block was to persuade rulers that their business was to effect theories and then, having persuaded them, to insure that the practice of the ruler would remain in accord with the teachings of the theory. Plato's solution had been the most thoroughgoing and demanding. He had proposed the complete reeducation of rulers, including the requirement that they become proficient in philosophy, the most difficult type of knowledge. Hobbes, however, believed that Plato had demanded too much of rulers and that the virtue of his own method was to have simplified a difficult subject so as to make it comprehensible and useful to rulers. In place of the "depth of moral philosophy," he put "theorems of moral doctrine." In place of the abstruse and difficult political philosophies of the past and the endless disquisitions on civility, he was prepared to offer in handy and convenient form "the true rules of politics":[96]

> Considering how different this doctrine is, from the practice of the greatest part of the world, especially of these western parts, that have received their moral learning from Rome and Athens; and how much depth of moral philosophy is required, in them that have the administration of the sovereign power; I am at the point of believing this my labour, as useless, as the commonwealth of Plato. For he also is of the opinion that it is impossible for the disorders of state, and change of governments by civil war, ever to be taken away, till sovereigns be philosophers. But when I consider again, that the science of natural justice, is the only science necessary for sovereigns and their principal ministers; and that they need not be charged with the sciences mathematical, as by Plato they are, farther than by good laws to encourage men to the study of them; and that neither Plato, nor any other philosopher hitherto, hath put into order, and sufficiently or probably proved all the theorems of moral doctrine, that men may learn thereby, both how to govern, and how to obey; I recover some hope, that, one time or other, this writing of mine may fall into the hands of a sovereign who will consider it himself (for it is short, and I think clear,) without the help of any interested, or envious interpreter; and by the exercise of entire sovereignty, in protecting the public teaching of it, convert this truth of speculation, into the utility of practice.[97]

To have succeeded in making political knowledge useful and accessible was no mean achievement, but it raised another kind of difficulty, one that Hobbes seemed totally unaware of and that, in his unawareness, affirmed his modernity.

Hobbes overlooked the difficulty which Plato had never forgotten: if political knowledge were available in digest form, rulers might be armed without being educated. If rulers were simply handed the power of knowledge without prolonged exposure to the moralizing and civilizing influence of the philosophical way of life, they would naturally use that knowledge for the ends of *Machtpolitik*. Unless men have a countervision of a better way of life, one that transcends politics, they will destroy society and themselves. "All goes wrong," Plato had declared, "when starved for lack of anything good in their own lives, men turn to public affairs hoping to snatch from thence the happiness they hunger for. They set about fighting for power, and this internecine conflict ruins them and their country. The life of true philosophy is the only one that looks down upon offices of state; and access to power must be confined to men who are not in love with it."[98]

Plato's full formula provided not only that philosophers should become kings and kings philosophers, but also that access to power should be denied to the lovers of power, just as access to knowledge should be opened to those who loved it. In contrast, Hobbes had sought to detach "rules" from the broader, civilizing context of philosophical education, because only in that form would political knowledge make a difference to human life.

Hobbes was thus the first to practice the "technical fallacy" in its truly modern form, the fallacy of concentrating exclusively upon knowledge that will work immediately and leaving moral culture to take care of itself. In this he was being perfectly consistent: if knowledge is only another form of power, then it behooves us to seek its most compact, efficient form, trusting either that men will somehow acquire the tacit moral understandings needed if rules are to be adapted to life, or that men will develop a mode of life in which those understandings are no longer important.

A further dimension of the problem was suggested by the closing lines of the important passage in which Hobbes boasted that he had reduced political knowledge to convenient rules.

> I recover some hope, that one time or other, this writing of mine may fall into the hands of a sovereign, who will consider it himself, (for it is short, and I think clear,) without the help of any interested, or envious interpreter.[99]

The reference to interested or envious interpreters was aimed at the royal counselors. By the time that Hobbes wrote, it was common practice for kings to surround themselves with all manner of expert and experienced advisers and to rely on them to propose major policies. The career of Bacon, despite its humiliating conclusion, suggested that if kings were not to be philosophers or philosophers kings, it might be possible for philosophers as counselors to gain the ear of kings. But this was not the form which the issue took. Rather it centered around the question of whether the kind of knowledge needed by counselors was acquired by political experience or supplied by political theory.

Certainly Bacon believed that political theory was too speculative to be useful to the statesman. Even more pointedly, Hobbes's great contemporary, Edward Hyde, Earl of Clarendon, the most important and experienced of royal advisers during the period, devoted a lengthy critique to *Leviathan* and pronounced its author politically naive and ignorant.[100] Behind Clarendon's attack lay a view of political knowledge shaped by the concept of expertise. Counselors would be expected to offer expert judgments on highly specialized matters, such as finance, diplomacy, administration, ecclesiastical policy, and judicial administration.

Strictly interpreted, this idea of counselor's knowledge left no place for the theorist in the very activity for which he was prescribing. Hobbes took up the challenge and attempted to redefine the nature of the counselor's knowledge in terms compatible with theoretical knowledge, and with the mental abilities distinctive to the theorist. Counselors, he noted, have "not only to deliberate what is to be done hereafter, but also to judge of facts past, and of law for the present."[101] The idea of judgment, which he had used against fancy, is now introduced to defend theory. Judgment is proclaimed to be the primary virtue of counselors. It represents the ability to settle thoughts in due order and to deduce consequences, both of which are necessary to making wise choices concerning policies and future actions, and both of which happen also to be the mark of good theorizing.[102]

Despite this stout defense of the theorist and an outright attack upon counselors for their tendency to promote their own interests in the guise of advice to the ruler, Hobbes had to admit that judgment was not simply a matter of logical rigor and that it included also the ability to know what was appropriate in a concrete situation. Appropriateness suggested a quality derived from experience rather than study.[103] But if experience was what counted, the claims of the counselor could once more be raised and Hobbes's argument about the superiority of "sapience" over "prudence" would seem jeopardized. At first Hobbes tried to wriggle out by a verbal solution, declaring that a good counselor would combine "experience" and "long study":

> No man is presumed to be a good counsellor, but in such business, as he hath not only been much versed in, but hath also much meditated on, and considered.[104]

At the end of the argument he returns to the point, obviously dissatisfied with his own cliché, and insists defiantly that "infallible rules" exist and that the man who knows them will be superior to "all the experience of the world."[105] This claim, which intimates that counselors should be theorists, is then stated more explicitly:

> Good counsel comes not by lot, nor by inheritance; and therefore there is no more reason to expect good advice from the rich or noble, in matter of state, than in delineating the dimensions of a fortress; unless we shall think there needs no

method in the study of politics, as there does in the study of geometry, but only
to be lookers on; which is not so. For the politics is the harder study of the two.[106]

Although Hobbes's spirited defense of theoretical knowledge supported the
claim of the theorist to participate in high councils and thereby help shape the
course of politics according to theory, it was obvious even to Hobbes that the claim
was limited. A qualified counselor needed knowledge of a vast range of specialized
subjects, "of which things, not only the whole sum, but every one of the particulars
requires the age and observation of a man in years, and of more than ordinary
study." Moreover, as Hobbes admitted, it may be the case that in certain matters
theory had produced no "infallible rules," "and when there is no such rule, he that
hath most experience in that particular kind of business, has therein the best judgment, and is the best counsellor."[107]

Compelled to retreat on this front, Hobbes took his stand on different and
more traditional ground. If theory could not compete with a combination of
experience and specialized knowledge, it could lay claim to a more fundamental kind of knowledge having to do with the basic arrangements of a political
system rather than with its day-to-day decisions. "There may principles of reason be found out, by industrious meditation" which will enable men "to make
their constitution, excepting by external violence, everlasting." Knowledge of
constitutional principles occupies a different status than the expert knowledge
of the counselors. The former represents the ancient notion of the theorist-
legislator who prescribes political foundations. At the time *Leviathan* appeared,
Englishmen were squabbling over the basic form of their political system. It was
not wholly absurd for Hobbes, therefore, to believe that circumstances were
such as to favor a new beginning and that his principles supplied precisely the
kind of knowledge relevant to such a situation. There is strong support for this
reading, because at this point Hobbes, suddenly remembering his own cynical
and oft-repeated dictum that most claims to truth are suspect because men "are
apt to look asquint towards their private benefit," has to disclaim any personal
interest:

> Such [principles of reason] are those which I have in this discourse set forth:
> which whether they come not into the sight of those that have power to make use
> of them, or be neglected by them, or not, concerneth my particular interests, at
> this day, very little.[108]

Thus Hobbes's hope of effecting some great change in the world required
that his theory be translated into fundamental political arrangements. But this
raised two great difficulties: who was to preside over that translation and, assuming that the proper institutions and practices for effecting the theory were
established, what guarantee was there that the system would be supported over
the long run? The second difficulty pointed to the requirement of every political
system for some kind of broadly diffused and shared beliefs among the citizens

which would furnish continuing support and legitimacy to the ruling authority. Popular political knowledge, as we may call it, has always been recognized by political theorists as a crucial element in sustaining a system. Burke likened it to "prejudice," Hume called it "sentiments," and Tocqueville dealt with it under the concept of "*mores.*" Today we tend to talk about the same subject in terms of "political culture" and about the process of acquiring it as "political socialization" or "the internalization of social norms."

Although theorists have long recognized that to make a theory work in the world more is needed than a pretty scheme of institutions or even the good will of a ruler or ruling class, what has not been squarely faced is the difficulty posed by the fact that existing political arrangements, which the theorist proposes to replace, form a piece with an existing body of popular beliefs, attitudes, values, and expectations. Consequently, a new set of arrangements cannot be piled upon a body of beliefs shaped to support the old one. Moreover, the attempt to replace one body of popular political beliefs by another inevitably encounters difficulties of an unusual magnitude. By nature, popular political knowledge is not easily located and, by form, it is not refutable in the way that an argument or a theory is. It tends to be amorphous, vague, and unsystematic. Its shape tends to evolve slowly over time and to seep deeply into the unconscious recesses of the mind where it is being constantly reenforced by the influence of many agencies, most of them unpolitical. The family, local community, church, school, theater and music hall, all contribute in some measure to reenforcing and diffusing this kind of rudimentary political understanding. To change it would be a staggering task, one that would necessarily exceed the lifetime of one man, no matter how astonishing his genius; and one that, by comparison, makes the task of placing *Leviathan* in the hands of princes or counselors seem like child's play. Yet if a theory is to be embodied in a society's arrangements, it must acquire a supporting political culture and it must, at the same time, eradicate those aspects of the existing culture which would subvert the new theory. The question involves nothing less than the question of what is required to get a society to exchange one political culture for another.

Hobbes's solution to the two problems, by what agent is the theory to be translated into practice and by what means is popular political culture to be changed, was sketched at the end of a passage already quoted: "that one time or other, this writing of mine may fall into the hands of a sovereign, who will . . . by the exercise of entire sovereignty, in protecting the public teaching of it, convert this truth of speculation, into the utility of practice."[109] In formulating the program of "public teaching," Hobbes set out his notion of political education. One part of it was aimed at a popular audience and hence the teaching was to be adjusted accordingly. He proposed a program of "public instruction both of doctrine and example," designed to indoctrinate the populace with beliefs conducive to strict obedience. The specific principles of the new belief system formed a new political decalogue deliberately modeled after the Ten Commandments. Its first commandment may serve as an illustration of the work of the new Moses: "The people are to be taught . . . that they ought not to be in love with any form of government they see in their neighbour nations, more than with their own." This is then compared by Hobbes with the original first commandment, which he smoothly rendered as "Thou shalt not have the Gods of other nations." He followed this same technique in the remaining commandments, first stating his own, then relating it to the sacred model.

Hobbes was undaunted by the objection that his principles were too abstruse for the common understanding. He insisted that if these principles were preached and continually repeated in the way that the Christian teaching was, the people would learn. "The common people's minds, unless they be tainted with dependence on the potent, or scribbled over with the opinions of their doctors, are like clean paper, fit to receive whatsoever by public authority shall be imprinted in them." If the people can be successfully taught the "great mysteries" of Christianity, how much easier is the task with a teaching "so consonant to reason that any unprejudicated man, needs no more to learn it than to hear it."[110]

In the second half of his program, Hobbes turned his attention to the educated élite. He was especially bitter about the role of the educated classes in the revolutionary struggle and charged them with the responsibility for scribbling seditious *graffiti* on the minds of the commoners. The source of the evil was the education received by the upper and middle classes at the universities, where all manner of false and dangerous doctrines were taught, especially "Aristotelity," classical literature with its bias toward democracy and tyrannicide, and religious convictions about "private judgment" and conscience.[111] The strategic importance of the universities was evident as soon as Hobbes asked about "the means and conduits by which the people may receive instruction" in political and religious matters. Hobbes's answer was that popular attitudes and beliefs were largely formed by the influentials, the opinion-makers, to whom the lower classes were apt to defer. "The greatest part of mankind," he declared, was composed of two groups: "they whom necessity or covetousness keepeth intent on their trades and labour," and "they whom superfluity or sloth carrieth after their sensual pleasures." Unable or unwilling to undertake the "deep meditation" needed to learn about "truth," "natural justice," and the "sciences,"

> [both groups] receive the notions of their duty chiefly from divines in the pulpit, and partly from such of their neighbours or familiar acquaintance, as having the faculty of discoursing readily, and plausibly, seem wiser, better learned in cases of law and conscience, than themselves. And divines, and such others as make show of learning, derive their knowledge from the universities, and from the schools of law, or from the books, which by men eminent in those schools and universities, have been published. It is therefore manifest, that the instruction of the people, dependeth wholly, on the right teaching of youth in the universities.[112]

The natural response to this tirade was anticipated by Hobbes:

> But are not, may some man say, the universities of England learned enough already to do that? or is it you, will undertake to teach the universities?

Acknowledging that these were "hard questions," he then proceeded to answer them. First, he recounted the many false doctrines, particularly those which upheld the pope's authority against kings or denied the king's sovereignty over law, circulated by those who had been educated at the universities. To the second question, "is it you [who] will undertake to teach the universities?" Hobbes also had a frank reply: "It is not fit, nor needful for me to say either aye, or no: for any man that sees what I am doing, may easily perceive what I think."[113]

With this prescription for transforming the political culture of his society, Hobbes may be allowed to cease his labors. There seems nothing left to conquer. The theory which he created was truly borne on the wings of fancy, seeming "to fly from one Indies to another, and from heaven to earth, and to penetrate into the hardest matter and obscurest places, into the future and into herself." The epical dimensions of the Hobbesian achievement are probably beyond dispute, however much one may disagree with its parts. Yet there is something missing from our portrait of Hobbes as hero, and because it is missing there may be some important aspect still hidden in the achievement. The clue to what is missing lies in a remark by Bowra concerning the hero in poetry: "Once a society conceives of the hero as a human being who possesses to a notable degree gifts of body and mind, the poets tell how he makes his career from the cradle to the grave. He is a marked man from the start, and it is only natural to connect his superiority with unusual birth and breeding."[114]

We are fortunate in the case of Hobbes to have a hero who was his own poet. In the *Autobiography* he described his progress from "cradle to grave," including a vivid account of his "unusual birth":

> Our Saviour, the Man-God, had been born one thousand five hundred, and eighty-eight years, and the famous enemy fleet, the Armada, soon destined to perish in our sea, was standing at anchor in the Spanish ports, and the fifth day of April was beginning, when, in early spring, the little worm that is myself was born in Malmesbury.
>
> I have no reason to be ashamed of my birthplace, but of the evils of the time I do complain, and of all the troubles that came to birth along with me. For the rumour ran, spreading alarm through our towns, that the Armada was bringing the day of doom to our race. Thus my mother was big with such fear that she brought twins to birth, myself and fear at the same time.[115]

The suspicion that we are being invited to celebrate an antihero increases when Hobbes recalls his reaction at the outbreak of the civil war: "I shuddered at what I beheld, and betook myself to my beloved Paris."[116] We may also remember that Hobbes tucked tail and returned to England, making his submission to the Council of State, as he was to do again when the royalists finally returned. When this prudential behavior is placed alongside the heroic dimensions of this theory, instead of being puzzled by the discrepancy, we may instead be startled by the complementarity. The society of *Leviathan* is the antihero's utopia: a society of formal equality, where all subjects have been humbled and made dependent upon the sovereign for the security of their lives, goods, rights, and status. It is a utopia for those who wish to be rid of the anxieties produced by political instability so that they may concentrate upon "industry" and "culture of the earth" and all of the other goods of "commodious living," which "natural philosophy" and mathematics make possible. The political epic of the antihero proves, in the end, to be an attempted epitaph to politics, another denial of the ancient hope of a public setting where men may act nobly in the furtherance of the common good, another way of absolving men of complicity and guilt for their common predicaments.

CHAPTER 7

HOBBES AND THE CULTURE OF DESPOTISM

> Unless either philosophers become kings or those who are now called
> kings come to be sufficiently inspired with a genuine desire for wisdom;
> unless power and philosophy meet together.
> —Plato *Republic* 473c–d

> And my own social theory which favors gradual and piecemeal reform
> strongly contrasts with my theory of method, which happens to be a
> theory of scientific and intellectual revolution.
> —Karl Popper

SHORTLY AFTER THE END of the war against totalitarianism, Karl Popper launched a famous criticism of Plato. He charged Plato with advocating a totalitarian regime in which philosophers would have absolute power because they alone possessed absolute or true knowledge. Such claims, Popper argued, were based upon a metaphysical conception of absolute truth that was logically false as well as politically pernicious. Thus Plato's system stood condemned as a double absolutism, epistemological and political.

Ironically, the relationship that Popper detected in Plato's thinking between knowledge-claims and forms of rule, between the structure of truth and the structure of power, was unintentionally reproduced when Popper set out his alternative conceptions of truth and politics. Popper, too, relied upon a homology between politics and knowledge that modeled the former upon the latter and would have political practice emulate the "free" methods of science. The result, while not totalitarian as Plato's combination was alleged to be, displays some strikingly authoritarian elements. That such a result should occur in a thinker whose intentions were antiauthoritarian might be explained by suggesting that his scheme disguised the presence of power from the author, not just in the political domain but in the scientific as well. The disguise was provided by reducing politics to a series of technical problems with the result that power, especially in its coercive aspects, virtually disappears. Concurrent with his scientization of politics, Popper's description of scientific method contained authoritarian and intolerant elements, although he believed that his description of science portrayed an "open society."

Popper was concerned primarily to justify a new form of politics—social engineering—by appealing to scientific methods; that is, a politics in which social policies would be treated experimentally was recommended because it was "like" the logic of science. The methods of science represented the rational grounds for demonstrating the truth of a given statement. "The only [sic] course open to the social sciences is . . . to tackle the practical problems of our time with the help of the theoretical methods which are fundamentally the same in *all* sciences."[1] What Popper labeled the "logic of discovery" involved a so-called crucial experiment designed to falsify statements submitted to it. Only statements that passed the test of falsification qualified as "acceptable." Popper looked upon the notion of "the falsifying experiment" as a liberating advance over views of science that demanded "ultimate grounds" for statements rather than probable ones. The falsifying experiment, he asserted, "has opened up new vistas into a world of new experiences."[2]

"Piecemeal social engineering" was presented by Popper as the political correlative of falsification procedures. Like the latter, piecemeal engineering was based upon a negative criterion: to attack "the greatest and most urgent evils of society rather than searching for, fighting for, its greatest ultimate good." It involved "the alteration of one social institution at a time . . . without revolutionizing the whole society."[3]

Popper's defense of social engineering was strongly criticized at the time by advocates of central economic planning, a notion then much in favor among democratic socialists and liberal exponents of the interventionist/welfare state. That criticism had the effect of obscuring the strong technological impulse in Popper's political thinking and the similarity between Popper's scientist/social engineer and Plato's philosopher king. Against the "total ideologies" of Plato, Hegel, and Marx, he called for "a social technology . . . whose results can be tested by social engineering."[4] Popper's formulation, in principle, provided no limit to the application of the engineering mentality to society nor to the number of "problems" society might appear to produce. The only limit would be the scale of discrete projects. Unfortunately, incrementalism is no barrier to totality or to what Popper deprecated as "revolutionizing the whole society."

At the same time Popper reproduced a comparable form of elitism based on a faith that institutions of knowledge—in his case, the community of scientists—could produce "objective" truth in spite of the frailties of individual scientists or social engineers. The "objectivity" of science, Popper argued, was assured by the "public character" of the experience to which science appealed. From the claim about public experience, Popper slid easily into an unargued implication that Everyman, if he felt dubious about a scientific claim, could simply proceed to test it. Yet as soon as Popper formulated that principle, it became clear that the nature of testing rendered it the preserve of the few: "Everyone who has learned the technique of understanding and testing scientific theories can repeat the experiment and judge for himself."[5] The selfless rule that Plato had hoped to produce by the education of his guardians Popper discovered in the "impartiality" produced in the "institutionally organized objectivity of science."[6] For Plato's rule by mind Popper offered rule by method; for a vision of a virtuous society Popper presented a technological society. Technological society, *technē* + *logos* = technical reason, was the perfect combination of a structure of theoretical reasoning: the *logos* represented by scientific reason, "the one method of all rational discussion,"[7] and a structure of rule, the *techne*-represented by "that rational method of piecemeal engineering."[8]

Scarcely two decades after Popper's attack on Plato and radicalism generally, the main target of social criticism in "advanced, developing nations" was "technological society." The terms of the attack were almost identical with those that Popper had used against Plato: critics wrote of "the domination" of nature and the "exploitation" of man, of dehumanization, the arrogance of social engineers, the prevalence of elitism, and, above all, the relentless extension of technology to every corner of existence, from probing the fetus to probing the universe.

Now, nearly a quarter-century after the debates of the sixties, the conception of the technological society has ceased to be in vogue, although its ghost still prowls among environmental groups. However, its reality persists, exalted into "high-tech societies." Social engineers have fallen from favor while genetic engineers have been elevated. At the present moment in the history of most so-called industrial democracies, Plato's formula for rule-by-knowledge appears in a less offensive light and triggers a less negative reaction, not because of the triumph of Platonism but because of the widespread acceptance of Popperism. Knowledge, particularly scientific knowledge useful to high-tech(ne) societies, is assumed to be the *arche*, or ruling principle, of such societies, and in that sense, Plato's formula has been translated into practice. Similarly, the assertion that high-tech societies are necessarily elitist goes virtually uncontested either as a description or as a norm.

What kind of reasoning concludes that a high-tech society requires rule by elites? The commonest answer is that for "advanced societies," science represents the most valued kind of social knowledge. It happens to be the most difficult to comprehend and is most likely, therefore, to be possessed by the few who are technically qualified or scientifically educated. Although this conclusion seems sensible, it dilutes the original question. That question is not solely about "who" should rule but what "principle" rule should be "based" upon. The crux concerns the kind of knowledge that should rule. Those who worry over the economic "threat" of Japan and the other "tigers" of the Far East seldom spend their energies defending elitism. This is because the problems of a high-tech society do not appear to them in a form that requires such a defense. Rather, the "challenge" is usually portrayed as the need to increase scientific research or to hasten the practical application of scientific knowledge or to reform American education at all levels so as to make the United States competitive in the international economy. Such discussions abound with antidemocratic implications and assumptions, but this may owe more to certain political views embedded in conceptions of technical knowledge than to a consciously elitist conception of politics.

What goes unnoticed is the peculiarity of the assumption that "principles of knowledge" should "rule," that the nature of the one is fitted to the nature of the other, that truth and power have not only complementary structures but mimetic ones, that there is a power-structure to truth and a truth-structure to power. The sense in which elitism is a "necessary" feature of advanced societies may have less to do with a theory of politics than with an imperative whose political character is no longer recognized. The imperative is to organize political power in order to best exploit the structural character of truth while concealing from exploiters and especially the exploited the political elements that have helped to constitute the understanding of truth and shaped its structure.

Accordingly, an advanced society might ideally be defined as one whose decision-making structure is so arranged as to present qualified individuals with the opportunity to make the necessary decisions.[9] With only slight exaggeration, one might say that in an ideal high-tech society, the right knowledge would "possess" people while decision-making structures would construct "problems" so as to apply them to the construction which goes under the name of the decision-maker!

II

Virtually every thinker who accepted [early seventeenth-century] mechanistic physics claimed that material bodies followed laws imposed on the world much as good citizens followed laws imposed on society.[10]

When Condorcet referred to the "tyranny of reason," does that apparent oxymoron hint at a correspondence between political structure and forms of theoretical discourse? Is it sufficiently pronounced that we might say that the political structure of a theory intimates/imitates a corresponding form of political rule? If the relationship holds, we might expect, for example, that a theory which argues that absolute authority is a legitimate political form, because it is a necessary condition for peaceful relationships among the particular persons and groups of a society, will have incorporated a prior commitment to absolutism in the theoretization of its formal structure. Such a theory would not only have proposed absolutism as a political system but represented it in the theorizing of the proposal. One might hypothesize that it would have stipulated certain absolutist conditions in its methodology; for example, that relations between empirical particulars, facts, or definitions, on the one hand, and theoretical generalizations or propositions, on the other, must scrupulously obey certain unappealable notions of rigorous reasoning if the theory is to be authorized.

Perhaps we might secure a better grip on what is being proposed here by repeating the earlier way of posing the question. What is it about, say, scientific, mathematical, or technical knowledge that favors an elitist or antidemocratic regime? The obvious answer is that these forms of knowledge are so complex, abstruse, and difficult that they are beyond the reach of ordinary people. Moreover, the growing political power of elites corresponds to the fact that only a relatively small number of people are capable of grasping the implications of the highly technical character which public policies inevitably assume in "an advanced industrial society."

This seemingly obvious answer is not, however, an answer at all. The question is not whether nonscientific people can master astrophysics or any other body of scientific knowledge. It does not concern the substantive knowledge by which experts communicate with one another. It involves, instead, how highly technical knowledge is (re)presented to a more general public; in what sense such representations are knowledge; and to what genres they belong. Leaving aside such potent considerations as the powers available to those who produce social representations of socially valued knowledge of a highly technical character, is there a political element embedded in the social representation of scientific knowledge, such that to think in certain representational terms is to redescribe certain political postures, depending on the political character of the representations?

In putting the question in this way, no claim is being made that always and everywhere the contents of scientific statements have been "contaminated" by political elements. Rather, as I phrased it above, political elements become "attached," say, as interpretative categories. Such categories need not be, and among twentieth-century scientists rarely are, in use in the scientific community. But it is not primarily scientists who interpret science to general audiences or even to the nonscientific academy. Science, like the gods, needs intermediaries. The common practice is for those who hold credentials bearing the title "of science"—as in philosopher of science, sociologist, historian, or popularizer of science—to mediate, or interpret, science to the rest of us. They endeavor to make science accessible to nonscientists by describing its epistemic importance or "contribution" while embedding that description in a context that gives it social and political meaning as well.[11] The title "of science" lends to the mediator a modest reflection of the aura of power that surrounds "real" science. The philosopher of science or the historian of science is slightly elevated above, say, the philosopher of language or the historian of bourgeois culture, because the mediators are presumed to be in closer proximity to those whose arcane knowledge actually "unlocks" the "powers of nature."

To return to Plato's *Republic*: unlike our high-tech society, Plato made no provision for mediating agencies to interpret the meaning of the Forms to the most numerous class of "bronze" members. The latter were deemed incapable of the higher knowledge. Their understandings were to be the product of the institutional practices which Plato carefully sketched in to control family, sexual relations, labor, and property. In addition, and more striking, the inhabitants of Plato's imaginary society were to be treated to certain so-called noble falsehoods, such as "the myth of the metals" concerning the origins of social distinctions.[12] That the falsehoods were presented by Plato as fabrications is a signal that their discursive structure is discontinuous with that of philosophical knowledge—politically discontinuous, that is, in both their substance and their modes.

Knowledge of the Forms, according to Plato's various accounts, could never be imposed. It yielded only to a combination of dialectical inquiry and the intuitions of a purified mind. In contrast, Plato's "citizens" were to be indoctrinated into the "truth" of the falsehoods. Thus the "true" falsehoods embodied the political element, which Plato's authoritarian mind identified with unthinking submission. Philosophical truths were, ironically, antipolitical because they arose from uncoerced conviction—indeed, so uncoerced that as the mind ascended, Plato had it abandon even its dependence upon hypotheses. Hence the peculiar formulation: the true falsehood is political = imposed while the truly true or philosophic is antipolitical = persuasion.

Thus there is no homology existing between Plato's theory of knowledge and his theory of rule. The structure of truth for Plato does not result from mental activity modeled after political action but from activity modeled after religious rites of purification. It is true that the Platonic dialogue is heavily laden with political motifs. In the encounters, for example, between Socrates and Thrasymachus or between Socrates and Callicles in *Gorgias*, the atmosphere is politically charged and the action is politically symbolic in the extreme. But the dialogues, as most readers recognize, never end in a claim to truth, only to having dispelled errors and glimpsed the shadow of truth. Truth and politics were structurally antithetical for Plato, and so the only way that Platonic truth can rule is through imposition and falsehood; that is, by a nontruth that requires the elimination of politics and other forms of public contestation. The structure of rule is discontinuous with the structure of truth. This is confirmed by arrangements in the *Republic*, requiring that when the guardians take their turn at governing, they cease temporarily to engage in philosophical activity.

But what if the structure of truth were to exhibit features similar to those associated with despotic rule? What if the despotic mind were to emerge as an ideal of theoretical activity and, at the same time, as the subject of a new version of Plato's formula concerning philosophers and kings? These possibilities began to crystallize in the eighteenth century when despotism acquired what it had rarely enjoyed in the ancient world, namely, a theory about its nature. Montesquieu wrote a famous critique of it; the fact that it figures so prominently in his writings suggests that his contemporaries were fascinated by the subject.[13] It is also well known that the idea of "enlightened despotism," while not as ubiquitous as some modern scholars once believed, was nonetheless a theme that surfaced in a number of philosophies and among the early founders of Physiocracy.[14] Despotism can also be detected as a latent element in Bentham's writings, notably those-dealing with prison reform (the Panopticon) and the administration of the poor laws.[15]

Prior to the eighteenth century, despotism had appeared mainly in association with tyranny and had signified a particular mode of exercising power that was absolute, willful, and illegitimate, either because the despot had seized power from its rightful owner or because in the course of ruling he would predictably violate the laws, customs, or accepted norms of the society.[16] The legitimation of despotism was made possible by more than two millennia of monotheism and monarchism; and by theological justifications of omnipotence, omniscience, and what might be called omnilegalism, or the corsetting of the world and of man in a totalistic framework of laws divine, natural, and human. In the seventeenth century, the religious bond to that matrix of totality was challenged by philosophers and publicists in the name of science, but the paradigm of power formally represented by science was inspired by the political theology under attack by scientizing theorists.[17]

Ever since antiquity, despotism has exercised a fascination as a potential liberating force, but with modern times, that emancipatory hope has become linked to the theorizing mind and a theorizable world. Accordingly, what is striking about the interest in despotism is that it emerged among thinkers whose modernizing credentials were, save for Montesquieu, impeccable and whose commitment to the advancement of scientific knowledge and to a culture of rationality was strong and steady. This development appears as the intellectualization of despotism. It involves dissolving the person of the despot and reconstituting him as an abstraction—absolute reason, a combination of power and reason that disguises power as rational legislation. This picture found support in common notions about the rationality of physical laws of nature. A law of nature pre(de) scribed regularities and uniformities among natural phenomena, that is, "necessary" relationships that phenomena "obeyed."

These notions are conveniently assembled in a famous document of the Enlightenment, d'Alembert's "Preliminary Discourse" to Diderot's *Encyclopedia*. D'Alembert's statements reveal the extent to which the attempt to explain scientific methods was permeated with bureaucratic and monarchical modes of thought, with themes of superior-inferior, of power, and of domination and submission. Explanation becomes a political metaphor—explanatory power. Describing the "systematic spirit" by which scientists apply mathematical methods to the study of terrestrial bodies, d'Alembert wrote that we come to know about the relationship among such bodies "by the comparisons we make among them, by the art of reducing, as much as that may be possible, a large number of phenomena to a single one that can be regarded as their principle. . . . The more one reduces the number of principles of a science, the more one gives them scope." D'Alembert's account culminates in a vision in which all that is in the world has been reduced to a single center of understanding: "The universe, if we may be permitted to say so, would only be one fact and one great truth for whoever knew how to embrace it from a single point of view."[18]

Eighteenth-century French conceptions of the laws of nature were, one might say, undialogical. Such laws were as arguably "compelling" to the phenomena "obeying" them as they were "irresistible" to the minds being instructed about the "necessary truths" contained in these laws. The laws of nature were the decrees of a rational despot—God—or of a rational despotism—Nature. The science of despotism was the despotism of science, and each had a common opposite: not freedom, because freedom became associated with accepting rational necessity, but prejudice. Thus modernity takes shape as the struggle not simply between scientific rationality and nescience/ignorance but between despotism/science and inherited prejudice.

The political implications of this version of science emerged in a conception of social science which found favor in the 1760s among the members of the so-called Turgot Circle. It was refined by various philosophies and Encyclopedists and kept alive during the French Revolution by former Turgotians such as Condorcet.[19] It was taken up in the first quarter of the nineteenth century by Comte and incorporated into his new science of sociology. The project can be described as the attempt to create a culture of despotism; i.e., a social mentality and practice that enable power to operate unhindered.

III

> Geometry is therefore demonstrable, for the lines and figures from which we reason are drawn and described by ourselves; and civil philosophy is demonstrable because we make the commonwealth ourselves.
> Wherefore Man is made fit for Society not by Nature, but by Education.
> —Hobbes[20]

These preliminaries are germane to our main discussion because of the strong influence that Hobbes and his former employer Francis Bacon exercised over many of the philosophes, particularly those who helped to produce the great *Encyclopédie*. I am concentrating on Hobbes because his theory unites several of the themes alluded to in my previous discussion. Hobbes was one of the first, after Bacon, to interpret the radical political and social implications of modern science and one of the first moderns to undertake the role of political mediator between science and society. Hobbes called simultaneously for the reconstitution of theoretical knowledge and for the reconstitution of society on the new basis of scientific modes of thought. What connects the two is a common thread of despotism.

For Hobbes to achieve both theoretical and political despotism, he had to overcome the bad odor that had trailed despotism since antiquity. His achievement was to help fashion a mindset in which the despotic eventually would assume the status of an unacknowledged cultural icon. Obviously such an achievement was not solely the work of one man. The mentality celebrated by Hobbes was described in the language of a new form of despotism in which truth and power were released from theological language but not from its presuppositions of monotheistic absolutism.

> If any man . . . by most firm reasons demonstrate that there are no authenticall doctrines concerning right and wrong, good and evil, besides the constituted lawes in each Realme and government; and that the question whether any future action will prove just or unjust, good or ill, is to be demanded of none but those to whom the supreme hath committed the interpretation of his Lawes: surely he will not only shew us the high way to peace, but will also teach us how to avoid the close, darke, and dangerous bypaths of faction and sedition.[21]

Leviathan would become Deuteronomy outfitted as political geometry.

As interpreted by Hobbes, the scientific revolution would both displace as well as replace the absolutist modes nurtured by theological thinking. The most striking features of that revolution were the appropriation of the most available model of omnipotence and omniscience, the creator-god of the Old Testament, and the reversal of his order: instead of God creating man as his subject, man creates a collective being of incomparable power to whom he is perfectly subject (*non est potestas super terram quae comparebur*). Although "the Art whereby God hath made and governes the World is by the *Art* of man . . . imitated,"[22] man's creation is accomplished in full view—a transparent prodigy, as it were. It rests on a simple and open fiction: "as if every man should say to every man."[23] Man could become the self-conscious maker of his own myth, for by a simple exchange of oaths, men would create a "Mortall God" by "conferr(ing) all their power and strength upon one Man," a miracle only slightly less staggering than that in the Book of Genesis—although perhaps less credible, since Hobbes's act of creation involves no exhausting labors such as had compelled a weary god to rest on the seventh day. On the contrary, Hobbesian subjects are receptive to the "architect" of Leviathan because they are "weary" from the fears and anxieties inherent in a society that attempts to reduce or limit its ruling powers or to divide them polytheistically into competing centers of legitimacy, e.g., parliamentary versus royal authority.

IV

Thomas Hobbes is said to have been the first modern "to show an interest in adding the word [despotic] to the stock of terms used in the political discussions of Europe."[24] I further suggest that he was the first modern in whom a despotic mentality was at work. He perpetuated Bacon's political reading of science, and he fully appreciated the political structure implicit in Bacon's conception of scientific knowledge. Bacon's credo "knowledge is power" was transcribed to read "knowledge is for the sake of power" (*scientia propter potentiam*).[25]

Hobbes's despotic mentality is revealed in the several departments of his theory, not just in his political writings: in his thinking about human nature, physical nature, knowledge, scientific inquiry, and thinking itself. He fashioned images of man and mind as subjects fit for despotic rule: the one for the rule or rules of a sovereign lawgiver, the other for the rules of method decreed by a sovereign science. The homogeneity attributed to human nature and the mind was inspired by the success which a comparable assumption concerning matter had had in the construction of scientific laws.

Hobbesian science promised not merely truth but "infallible" knowledge focused on the supreme end of power. The vision of power that science promised went far beyond simple governance to an unlimited capability of producing any desired result at "another time." The necessary condition for the realization of that vision of power was succinctly stated by Hobbes: "For whoso is freed from all bonds is lord over all those that still continue bound."[26] Laws represent the conditions of power decreed by an unconditioned sovereign. They are norms of social behavior that should be designed to enlarge the opportunities for the powers of individuals to be exerted while controlling the harmful social and political consequences of conflict among the aggressive individuals who constitute Hobbesian society. The sovereign tells his subjects what right consists in, what is justice, and what salvation.

Although absolutism is the necessary condition for the maximization of power, it is not sufficient by itself. When legislating, the sovereign must observe the basic requirement of all scientific thinking—logical consistency. The absolute lawmaking authority of the sovereign means that he is the master of meaning in the social world or, more precisely, its monopolist. Hobbes extended the despotic into the very terms of discourse and sought to expel the forms of communication which threatened his monological ideal. The despotic is expressed in his insistence that scientific progress and man's happiness depend upon "exact definitions, first snuffed and purged from ambiguity." What lies behind his obsession for linguistic purity is a concern to constrain the possibilities of interpretation while extending those of undeniable, logically necessary demonstration. The danger, as Hobbes saw it, is represented by "Metaphors and senselesse and ambiguous words" which, instead of falling into the orderly progression promised when reason works with "exact definitions," produces "wandering amongst innumerable absurdities; and their end, contention, and sedition, or contempt."[27] Clearly "Metaphors, Tropes, and other Rhetoricall figures"[28] invite interpretation, prolong controversy, and frequently fail to produce agreement. A metaphor is open-ended: it has no correct meaning.

Hobbes's sovereign is never portrayed as listening, because his function is to reduce the "different tempers, customes, and doctrines of men,"[29] the analogue to the Babel deliberately introduced by the jealous God of the Old Testament in order to halt the dangerous growth of human power and presumption. The monologic of despotism is perfectly conveyed in Hobbes's great metaphor about the law: "Men . . . have made an Artificiall Man, which we call a Commonwealth; so also have they made Artificiall Chains, called Civill Laws, which they themselves, by mutuall covenants, have fastned at one end, to the lips of that Man, or Assembly, to whom they have given the Soveraigne Power; and at the other end to their own Ears."[30]

What is the model for a discourse that produces silence among those addressed? In the passage just cited, as well as in numerous others, there is the visible outline of the Old Testament god who commands, who gives his decalogue to a chosen intermediary, and who demands obedience. That outline has now been overlain by a discourse which promises scientific rather than revealed truth—overlain but not superseded.

Hobbes's guiding assumption is that the structure of scientific truth and the structure of political order are interchangeable, an assumption that, significantly, had its parallel among those who argued for true religion as the structural correlate of political order. His assumption emerges in the remarkable argument introduced to support the claim that the sovereign had the right to determine "what Opinions and Doctrines are averse, and what conducing to Peace." In addressing the obvious objection that this would allow a sovereign to suppress scientific truths, Hobbes acknowledged that "in matter of Doctrine nothing ought to be regarded but the Truth," but he added that "Doctrine repugnant to Peace can no more be true than Peace and Concord can be against the Law of Nature." If a commonwealth was presently enforcing "false Doctrines," it is possible that "contrary Truths may be generally offensive." But even under such circumstances, peace would not be disturbed but rather a latent condition of war stirred. Thus the structure of pseudo-doctrines corresponds to the structure of pseudo-peace: "Yet the most sudden, and rough busling in of a new Truth, that can be, does never breake the Peace, but only somtimes awake the Warre."[31]

In Hobbes's vision, scientific knowledge parallels the structure of despotic rule: it is knowledge of the power that is guaranteed by a chain of dependency which reason constructs as it links one of its definitions to another while pursuing the connections between cause and effect. The structure of connections is taken as representing the structure of all things in which "cause" signifies power. When scientific reasoning establishes logical connections, it is reproducing a system of power: "*Science* is the knowledge of Consequences, and dependance of one fact upon another. . . . Because when we see how any thing comes about, upon what causes, and by what manner; when the like causes come into our power, wee see how to make it produce the like effects."[32]

The despotic element in Hobbes's vision of science is most fully realized when the objects represent an order of reality that is completely open to human fabrication and manipulation. Geometry is demonstrable in its absolute character because "the generation of the figures depends on our will."[33] The same possibility of truth lies open to politics. Because "neither public good nor public evil was natural among men any more than it was among beasts," politics is like mathematics but unlike physics where "the causes of natural things are not in our power but in the divine will." In politics, too, "we ourselves make the principles . . . whereby it is known what justice and equity and their opposites, injustice and inequity, are."[34]

The "making" of principles has a direct bearing upon politics, for it contains the Hobbesian conception of action: man knows what he can make. Hobbesian political science is the science of political construction in which absolute and arbitrary elements are combined and presuppose one another. It teaches men what they can make, but what they make is arbitrary. If they wish, they can establish a parliamentary sovereign or a monarchical one. Similarly, when once authorized, the sovereign is equally free to establish whatever kind of system of rules he prefers. Thus absolutism in politics parallels absolutism in thought. Each begins from an arbitrary act of definition or identification, and then both proceed to "work out" the dependence of one definition upon another; i.e., fit them into a power relationship with each other. It is a purely mentalized conception of power. Hobbesian political science is indifferent to external facts of geography, economics, and culture that had played such a large role in Aristotelian political science, had been revived by Hobbes's contemporary Jean Bodin, and subsequently would be a crucial factor in Montesquieu's argument against despotism.

V

> The most perfect organization of the universe can be called God.
> —Nietzsche[35]

Hobbes accomplished the legitimation of despotism through a multiple revolution that challenged several traditional conceptions concerning the scope and meaning of that form of rule. Hobbes denied that despotism was anomalous, a pariah form of political rule; that its mode of arbitrariness was inconsistent with the rule of law; that it furthered only the interests of the despot or that the interests of the despot and society were irreconcilably opposed; and, finally, that the necessarily repressive policies needed to produce political submissiveness would discourage industriousness and thereby impoverish society and weaken the despot as well.[36] When Hobbes completed his revolution, the appearance of despotism was transformed and its substance reproduced as lawfulness and rule-governed behavior, as well as a promise of "commodious living."

The core notion of the Hobbesian revolution was "organization." It was the equivalent of a meta-constitution, the *politeia* of the *despotikos*. It can be thought of as the equivalent of a formal theory of politics in the sense that it specified abstractly what was universally necessary for all "independent political systems."[37] Although the word "organization" was available, Hobbes did not use it. Instead he developed the idea of political society as a rational-scientific construction by transforming older political language. He introduced radically new, even opposing, meanings into two traditional terms—"commonwealth" and "body politic." There could be no sharper contrast than that between the sixteenth-century image of the commonwealth as an organic, natural body and Hobbes's profoundly constructivist conception of "the Pacts and Covenants by which the parts of this Body Politique were at first made, set together, and united."[38] The distinctively organizational character of the Hobbesian commonwealth is manifested most strikingly in two ideas: sovereign authority and covenant. The former embodies the central feature of organization: a sovereign whose arbitrary will expresses itself as rule-rationality. The latter embodies both the trauma that necessitates the institution of sovereign authority and the statement of the conditions that will make it possible.

Constructivism subjects passion to conformity, as mathematical reasoning displaces sense by abstraction. Just as natural phenomena are inherently lawful and only await discovery by the scientific lawgiver, so men exhausted by the anxieties and perils of an insecure existence want to be constructed into order. They need a maker who constructs by instructing.

> For men, as they become at last weary of irregular justling, and hewing one another, and desire with all their hearts, to conforme themselves into one firme and lasting edifice; so for want, both of the art of making fit Lawes, to square their actions by, and also of humility, and patience, to suffer the rude and combersome points of their present greatnesse to be taken off, they cannot without the help of a very able Architect be compiled into any other than a crasie building.[39]

Unlike older conceptions of political constitutions, commonwealth/organization signified a premeditated structure, not a perversion of another form, as oligarchy was of aristocracy, or tyranny of monarchy. Nor was it one of the so-called good regimes. It transcended the categories of good and bad, normal and perverted. Thus it did not grow out of anything or derive from it. Instead it "resemble(s) that Fiat, or the Let us make man pronounced by God in the Creation"; that is, it comes from nowhere, *ex nihilo*, and for that reason it is potentially universal, as unconditioned by time or place as scientific truth itself or God. Any type of constitution, normal or perverted, could be rightly organized. Right organization did not imply a pledge to promote justice or any other moral or religious good. Indeed, the quality of relations established by the Hobbesian organization appeared remarkably analogous to the absolute unconditionality of God postulated by theologians. The organization was endowed with a quality which had previously been considered to be the peculiar property of God: it was the defining source of justice, hence it could not be unjust. At the same time, the subjects of the organization were like God's believers, capable of injustice when they violated their covenantal obligations to the sovereign.

Organization represented a departure from all previous forms. It renounced all of the personalizing categories that had characterized the classical types. The sovereign, it should be emphasized, was not identical with the organization but was the supreme "office" of its structure.[40] "I speak not of the men but (in the Abstract) of the Seat of Power."[41] The *politeia*, or constitution, was thus dehumanized. It did not represent a class principle, such as rule by the wealthy, or an ethical principle, such as rule by the best (*aristoi*). Instead, organization represented the convergence of necessity in its two most irresistible forms: the undeniable fact of death and the necessity inherent in logical demonstration of the requirements of peace and prosperity, or what Hobbes called "commodious living." Thus despotism stands for an absolutism of the undeniable. The rudiments of that order were worked out by Hobbes in his conceptions of covenant, sovereign representative, subject, and law.

VI

Fabian: I will prove it legitimate, sir, upon the oaths of judgment and
reason.
    —Shakespeare, *Twelfth Night*, III. ii. 13

In *Leviathan*, Hobbes attacked the pariah status of despotism by two distinctive claims: that despotic power was entitled to the same rights of authority as any other form of political rule; and that all forms of political authority, whether democratic, aristocratic, or monarchic, had of necessity to incorporate the same despotic principle of a final and uncontrollable rule-making power if they were to survive. "The Rights and Consequences of both *Paternall* and *Despoticall* Dominion are the very same with those of a Soveraign by Institution [i.e., by formal consent]."[42] Tyranny, Hobbes declared, was not a form of government but merely an expression of dislike by those "that are discontented under *Monarchy*."[43] Thus the traditional division between "good" polities and perverted ones is dismissed, and the distinction collapsed. "*Tyranny* and *Oligarchy* . . . are not the names of other Formes of Government, but of the same Formes misliked."[44]

The legitimation of despotism and the destruction of the traditional distinctions between it and all other political life-forms reveals an antipathy toward difference that pervades Hobbes's attitude toward diversity of opinions, of social rank, and of truth-claims. His world is a bare place of abstract space and time, and his man a dehistoricized bit of matter-in-motion. For Aristotle, despotism had been the reflection of natural differences; for Hobbes, it was justified by a common denominator to all men, a "similitude of *Passions*" and natural equality.[45]

It was directed at those who strove for preeminence or were obsessed by comparisons of worth, and it threatened the rest who were content with equality.[46]

The reduction of difference signifies that an organization is a creature of conditions rather than grounds. So Hobbes abstracted the sociological, historical, and normative elements from the various political forms and presented them as a choice between "conveniences" and "inconveniences." Those criteria prove to involve essentially matters of efficiency and effectiveness, and they lead to a strikingly new conclusion: since the power is the same in all forms, the choice comes down to which is more likely to produce better "administration of its affairs." Hobbes concluded that absolute monarchy had the fewest inconveniences.[47]

VII

A despotic mentality pervades the structure of Hobbes's arguments. It appears in a coercive quality attaching to Hobbes's demand that all forms of authority must incorporate an absolutist principle, even if the ideology of the regime abhors that principle. He depicted those who would contrive to establish a rational governance as no freer to resist a provision for absolute power than matter-in-motion is able to resist the laws of physics. Whether the government is monarchic, popular, or aristocratic, "the Soveraign Power . . . is as great as possibly men can be imagined to make it." Men may "fancy many evill consequences" of "so unlimited a Power," but the consequences of its lack are the direst possible: "perpetual warre of every man against his neighbour."[48] Hobbes was not trying to persuade his readers but to compel them. The logical structure of his argument is a sequence of stark compulsions forcing on his reader-citizen the choice between controlled violence and violent oblivion: if men are to survive they must establish a sovereign power; if power is less than sovereign, men are condemned to an endless *bellum omnium contra omnes*.[49]

The symbol of the despotic mentality is in its chosen icon, the irresistible force of a geometric proof. "A necessary act is that, the production whereof it is impossible to hinder."[50] Geometry means, first, "Universall rule," which relieves the mind from having to adjust its assertions to local peculiarities. A universal rule "discharges our mentall reckoning, of time and place . . . and makes that which was found true *here* and *now*, to be true in *all times* and *places*."[51] Geometry also means "necessary truths," and the "necessary" signifies power whose unchallengeability simply reduces all talk of legal limits or restraints to irrelevancy. What is necessary already embodies the idea of following a law and of renouncing what is arbitrary or capricious. It is the route whereby *despotikos* is legalized. The origins of the route are crucial, for they not only confirm the despotic character of geometry's necessary truths but also foreshadow the despotic nature of the Hobbesian sovereign.

The necessary truths of geometry originate in the arbitrary—the contradictory opposite of the necessary. They begin with "definitions" (e.g., of a circle) that cannot themselves be proven, that is, legitimated. The fascination with geometrical reasoning is its incredible combination of the undeniability of its proofs, along with the fact that man, the most subjective of all creatures, has nonetheless willed the existence of geometry and freely chosen its starting point. An arbitrary will that reasons consistently/relentlessly can produce perfect "laws" that legitimate the otherwise despotic starting point: "The generation of the figures depends on our will; nothing more is required to know the phenomenon peculiar to any figure whatsoever, than that we consider everything that follows from the construction that we ourselves make in the figure to be described."[52] Cryptically stated, Hobbes's sequence is perfect truth as the product of will; free will as the creator of necessary truths; the necessary as the irresistible. "*Liberty* and *Necessity* are Consistent" because all acts proceed from "causes in a continuall chaine" of "necessity."[53]

Thus logical reasoning functions as the microcosm of despotism, and despotism as the macrocosm of logic. Logical reasoning shares the characteristic that is present absolutely in all men and that will reemerge in the absolute power of the sovereign. Logical reasoning is undeniable; death as the fate of all men and their deepest fear is undeniable; and the power of the sovereign must be as undeniable as the fact of death and the proofs of reason.

VIII

In terms evocative of the slavemaster's authority, Hobbes attributed "the Soveraign Power of life and death" to his creature. In the Hobbesian commonwealth, however, life is secured by the fear of death, by the fear of that which represents the absolute (because unavoidable) coercion. The *despotes* of death, the great leveler to which all men are enslaved, becomes transmuted into the despotism of sovereign authority—the magic solvent before which "The Power and Honour of Subjects vanisheth."[54] Death, in the form of a "Mortall God" or sovereign, authorizes the terms for life: "The Liberty of a Subject, lyeth therefore only in those things, which in regulating their actions the Soveraign hath prætermitted."[55] Despotism exists to institute and maintain a nonpolitical lifespace where "men have the Liberty, of doing what their own reasons shall suggest for the most profitable to themselves."[56]

"Fear and Liberty are consistent."[57] Because Hobbes depicted man as timid and fearful by nature, it appears in keeping with that character that Hobbesian man should submit himself to absolute power. Yet the nature with which Hobbes actually endowed man is completely contrary to the picture of timidity, although perhaps its psychological complement. The anatomy of human nature embodies a despotic potential, for its quintessence is power. "Man's nature is the sum of his natural faculties and powers." The faculties of the body are classified as "power nutritive, power motive, and power generative." The "powers of the mind" are "power cognitive" and "power imaginative."[58] Accordingly, the life of such a being can be compared to a race for domination: "But this race we must suppose to have no other goal, nor other garland, but being foremost."[59]

Hobbesian liberty is designed to channel and legitimate the dynamics of domination implanted in every individual. Man is being in continuous motion, for "Life it selfe is but Motion, and can never be without Desire, nor without Feare."[60] Human motion is power, but it is under the same "laws" that control the motions of "Inanimate creatures." This assimilation of man to natural objects—and like them, subject to the necessity of laws—puts the meaning of liberty in a special light.

"*Liberty* and *Necessity* are Consistent."[61] Liberty is not a unique property of man, and it does not signify freedom to choose but "the absence of externall Impediments" that block his power, i.e., his motion according to law.[62] Liberty is the despot's dream of opposition-free rule now held out as the ideal of freedom, of unobstructed individual motion/desire. For just as the despot brooks no opposition or rival, Hobbesian liberty "signifieth (properly) the absence of Opposition; (by Opposition, I mean externall Impediments of motion)." And like the despot who disdains to be constrained by law or by political rivals, the Hobbesian man cannot be "so tyed, or environed, as it cannot move, but within a certain space, which space is determined by the opposition of some externall body."[63]

IX

> For life is perpetual motion that, when it cannot progress in a straight
> line, is converted into circular motion.
> —Hobbes[64]

> For the use of Lawes . . . is not to bind the People from all Voluntary
> actions; but to direct and keep them in such a motion, as not to hurt
> themselves by their own impetuous desires, rashnesse, or indiscretion,
> as Hedges are set, not to stop Travellers, but to keep them in the way.
> —Hobbes[65]

The space left by the silence of the law was not conceived by Hobbes as bounded like a geometric figure but as an unobstructed path capable of accommodating indefinitely the despotic compulsions reflected in the Hobbesian description of human happiness. Men seek more than "a bare Preservation, but also all other Contentments of life."[66] Their happiness is in "proceeding" rather than in contentment. It "consisteth not in having prospered but in prospering."[67]

Hobbesian despotism thus must accommodate the driving motions of men in search of prosperity, as well as the uncertain needs of sovereign power that must defend itself in an international state of nature. "And Law was brought into the world for nothing else, but to limit the naturall liberty of particular men, in such manner, as they might not hurt, but assist one another and joyn together against a common Enemy."[68] Theoretically, a despot could use his absolute power to stifle the energy of society and discourage individual initiatives, but such a course would plainly be self-defeating. Yet man, the relentless pursuer of his own interests and opinions, must be contained. Despotism cannot rule society oppressively in the literal sense of weighing it "down." It must repress but not suppress the vital motions of its members. It must manipulate fear while maintaining anxiety.

Hobbes's resolution of these difficulties is more clearly set out in chapter 10 of *De Corpore*, titled "Of Power and Act." There he developed a schema in which the fullness of power depends crucially upon the character of the "patient" or object (sc., citizen), not upon the agent alone (sc., sovereign). "Power," Hobbes noted, "and Cause are the same thing," and "power and act" correspond to "cause and effect." To exercise power or "produce" an effect, the agent must have "all those accidents which are necessarily requisite for the production of some effect in the patient." The power of the patient consists of the "accidents" of his which produce a given effect. The power of the patient is "passive." "The power of the agent and patient together" corresponds to "plenary power"; it is the "sum or aggregate of all the accidents" in both parties that produce an effect. Power differs from a cause in that it applies to the future. Power is ineffectual or "impossible" when some of the requisites are lacking in either agent or patient. When the two are closely matched, so that the attributes of the patient mesh with those of the agent, the potential for power is maximized. Then, "every act which is not impossible is possible."[69] The attributes Hobbes assigned to sovereign authority corresponded to the "requisites" of an agent. Given that Hobbes wanted his sovereign authority to be absolute, it follows that a "patient" or subject needs to have or be given the "requisites" for a role that, while passive, is still contributory.

Hobbes turned immediately in part 1 of *Leviathan* to endowing man with a nature whose drives make him a creature fit for despotic rule. The first image of despotism accompanies the basic description of human nature in its natural condition. His right to self-preservation is a statement of despotism in the extreme: "THE RIGHT OF NATURE . . . is the Liberty each man hath, to use his own power, as he will himselfe, for the preservation of his own Nature . . . of doing any thing, which in his own Judgement, and Reason, hee shall conceive to be the aptest means thereunto. . . . in such a condition [of Nature] every man has a Right to every thing; even to one anothers body."[70] In the state of nature, then, the first despot is man himself, and despotism is the original and universal condition.

The despotic nature of man is defined by the fact that he is an endangered and a self-endangering species. His deepest driving force is the fear of death, and the whole of his mechanism of motion is bent toward fleeing death and preserving the self. Man certifies that he is alive by responding to his desires—

the Hobbesian definition of death is the cessation of desire—and he acts out his escape from death by the unending pursuit of his desires.[71] He cannot stop without dying: "The object of mans desire is not to enjoy once onely, and for one instant of time; but to assure for ever the way of his future desire. . . . he cannot be content with a moderate power . . . because he cannot assure the power and means to live well . . . without the acquisition of more."[72] "Felicity is a continuall progresse of the desire from one object to another." Man is not so much a seeker of happiness as its victim. Happiness seeks him out and drives him in "a perpetuall and restlesse desire of Power after power that ceaseth onely in Death."[73]

X

And as to the faculties of the mind, (setting aside the arts grounded upon words, and especially that skill of proceeding upon generall, and infallible rules, called Science; which very few have, and but in few things . . .) I find yet a greater equality amongst men, than that of strength.
—Hobbes[74]

Hobbes's attempt to impose laws of behavior upon man prefigured the creation of a sovereign authority who would shape men to obedience. The despotism of theory and the despotism of sovereignty are both produced from the realization that man, the object of their power, is inherently refractory, both in his natural as well as his civil capacity. "The constitution of a mans Body is in continuall mutation; it is impossible that all the same things should alwayes cause in him the same Appetites and Aversions." This damning admission is followed by another that threatens to subvert the basic premise of a sovereign authority created by covenant: "Much lesse can all men consent in the Desire of almost any one and the same Object."[75] An inexpungeable subjectivity that manifests itself in a wide range of human differences, from opinion to types of madness, threatens the basic assumption of the covenant—that all men can agree on the need for an absolute sovereign authority because all fear death and all possess reason.

This difficulty puts Hobbesian science in a certain light. It is a science that resorts to fictions about human nature that, in reality, are lies. Men are not in fact what the requirements of the theory demand that they must be if its theoretical power is to be realized. Before Hobbesian citizens can be the object of absolute sovereignty, they must first be transformed into the abstract subject of a despotic theory. The laws of motion thus turn out to be constructions of the god-theorist who had declared his intention of legislating an "Artificiall Man" who would exceed in power the natural man first created by the theorist-god of the Old Testament.[76] The laws are prescriptive of an ideal form of motion that is "true" of human behavior in the sense that it can serve as a reference point for legislating "real" laws for human conduct. The political problem set for the sovereign is to shape men into law-abiding citizens. "Man is made fit for Society not by Nature, but by Education."[77] Man is taught to be "bound" by the "laws of nature." These laws are "generall rule(s) of Reason" whose observance is necessary if there is to be social peace. Thus they are the analogues to the laws of nature which dictate "order" to physical bodies.[78]

Hobbes's confession—that for all of the analogies between human behavior and physical motion and between cause-and-effect relations in nature and human desires and aversions, there remained a stubbornly subjective core, a "constitution individuall"—defined the tasks of political culture. In order to make man into an animal fit for society, he had to be made into a being who would approximate the "behavior" of natural phenomena. While "terror" was not an insignificant means, it ran the risk of provoking resentment or, worse, paralyzing activity. The solution was indoctrination/education. It begins with Hobbes's legislating "a fifth Law of Nature" by which "every man strive to accommodate himselfe to the rest." This law aims at nothing less than to overcome "a diversity of Nature, rising from the diversity of Affections" among men. Men are compared to "stones" assembled for a building, but their "asperity, and irregularity . . . takes more room from others." So some will have to be "cast away" as "unprofitable, and troublesome."[79]

The next step in rendering man's nature lawful is to reform education, beginning with the universities where the nation's teachers are produced. Reform would aim at insuring that "true" political and religious doctrines were taught.[80] More ambitiously, Hobbes proposed a new political cult that would instruct the common people in opinions that would dispose them to submissiveness. "The Common-peoples minds, unless they be tainted with dependance on the Potent, or scribbled over with the opinions of their Doctors, are like clean paper, fit to receive whatsoever by Publique Authority shall be imprinted in them."[81] The ideal of a truly "lawfull" subject is caught in Hobbes's despotic image of "rooting out of the consciences of men all those opinions" that potentially might lead to rebellion.[82]

The political and theoretical problem for Hobbes was to find a notion which could render plausible the analogy between the social and the physicalist meanings of the laws of nature. How would man have to be conceived to make him seem as much the "natural" subject of civil laws as natural phenomena were of natural laws? The solution was the notion of natural equality—the analogue to the operation whereby geometers posit abstract triangles divested of the "irregularities" that are present in "actual" triangles. "And therefore for the ninth law of Nature, I put this, That every man acknowledge other for his Equall by Nature."[83]

Nature is thus introduced to legitimate equality, but "nature" really functions as a metaphor for methodological requirements transferred to politics. When Hobbes stated that "the question who is the better man, has no place in the condition of meer Nature,"[84] the statement was equivalent to saying that for purposes of demonstration all objects having certain specified traits will be considered to be the same, regardless of individual variations in other respects. Equality is the consequence of a methodological need rather than a normative claim. Its function is to promote power through equal treatment. "Nature" is identified with abstraction rather than with the "natural" differences apparent to common observation. It is not that men are equal; Hobbes acknowledged that some men are stronger and others of "quicker mind." Yet the differences, Hobbes insisted, are "not so considerable" that the strong cannot be killed by the weak or that experience, which is available to all men, has not made them all roughly equal in wisdom. Thus the needs of a political science of nature coincide with the necessary condition for society: politics cannot become a science if it starts from the differences which exist among men, and diverse particulars cannot make a society if those differences are treated as primary. "Men . . . will not enter into conditions of Peace, but upon Equall termes."[85] Absolutism comes into the picture because, according to Hobbes, men want to flee the consequences of natural equality. The rough equality among men leaves each insecure. A man can never become sufficiently powerful in nature to prevent others from harming him. Thus the natural equality which allows for the covenant that makes society possible also makes absolutism necessary.

The extent to which the authority of the Hobbesian sovereign complements the despotic nature of Hobbesian man was not accidental. It rests upon a vision whose unique power lies, not in its defense of absolutism, but in its conception of a culture of despotism that reproduces a conception of mind: it is at one and the same time a conception of mind and an ideal of collective mentalité.

MODERN THEORISTS

CHAPTER 8

ON READING MARX POLITICALLY

> Instead of collapsing as Marx predicted that it would, capitalism has emerged stronger than ever.
>
> In advanced capitalist societies, the material condition of the working class has improved rather than worsened.
>
> Working-class movements have become less rather than more revolutionary.

FOR THE BETTER PART OF A CENTURY, critics of Karl Marx have pointed to unfulfilled predictions of the sort represented above as evidence of the falsity of Marx's theory. Typically, their criticism rests on a view that a theory which claims to be scientific is seriously defective if its predictions fail to materialize. The main point of much of this criticism is not the predictions themselves as the discredit that their failure casts upon Marx's analysis of capitalism. If the predictions can be shown to be false, the analysis becomes suspect; if Marx's self-proclaimed science fails as prediction, how can it succeed as scientific analysis?

I. MARX'S INTENTIONS

When Marx is judged by scientific standards, whatever the standards may be and whatever conception of science they may reflect, a certain intention is attributed to him. Marx, we would want to say, aimed to produce a theory that would qualify as scientific. To support this view of his intentions we could point to statements by him such as: "Every opinion based on scientific criticism I welcome."[1] If Marx were judged to have conscientiously pursued his aim, the resulting theory could be said to be shaped by a scientific purpose. The theory's structure of statements—its descriptions, explanations, analyses, and predictions—would expectably be governed by the intention to be scientific, however successful it should turn out to be. For our purposes it is not crucial that we identify precisely Marx's conception of science, but rather that we treat "science" as a metaphor indicative of a commitment to the search for truth. When Marx declared that his theoretical conclusions were "the outcome of conscientious research carried on over many years,"[2] the statement can be read as an intention to be a truth-teller.

While the ideal of science was undeniably important in shaping Marx's theoretical intentions, there were other and conflicting determinants as well. One was a highly developed notion of theoretical *activity* or, more precisely, of theorizing as action. Its basis was laid before Marx became immersed in the study of economics. His intensive research into ancient philosophy while preparing his doctoral dissertation and his close association with the Young Hegelians helped to produce a pronouncedly "political" view of theoretical activity. There were, he believed, distinct philosophical epochs in the history of philosophy that represented the founding of a dominant "total system" by a "master," "a philosophical giant." These periods were frequently followed by times of "gigantic discord" that Marx likened to the wars of the Titans in Greek mythology, where the sons of Uranus depose the father as king of the gods, install Kronos, and then war against Zeus after he successfully challenges Kronos. For would-be philosophers, born as it were in the shadow of a Plato, an Aristotle, or a Hegel, the choice is either to live an Alexandrian existence and be content to refine the all-encompassing system of the master; or to challenge it and to seek its overthrow.[3] Then theory abandons the contemplative mode and becomes action rather than activity. Marx described it as "critical" and "destructive," but its intentions are plainly revolutionary and political: theory aims at overthrowing a philosophical "order" and reconstituting it.[4]

II. THOUGHT AND ACTION

The third element in the structure of Marx's intentions is action itself. Marx's earliest thoughts on that subject were not primarily concerned with the proletariat but with the theorist-as-actor. Throughout most of his life Marx was a passionate political actor: the test of that passion was not so much his involvements in the revolutionary events of 1848, when his theoretical vision was primarily political rather than economic—the *18th Brumaire* (1852) rather than the *Contribution to the Critique of Political Economy* (1859)—as his continued action after many failures and setbacks for the proletarian cause, as though individual commitments still mattered. What made the test so demanding was that Marx did not think of action as merely "doing." Beginning with some of his earliest notations on the nature of theory and action, Marx envisioned action as an extension of thought and theory as a political mode of activity. "It is a psychological law," Marx noted while preparing his doctoral dissertation, "that the theoretical mind, having become free in itself, turns into practical energy . . . The practice (*praxis*) of philosophy, however, is itself *theoretical*. It is *criticism* which measures individual existence against essences, particular actuality against the Idea."[5]

If these early formulations found Marx straining to convert theory into action, to *act*ualize thought, they also suggest that he was seeking to impregnate action with thought, with theory. This latter impulse was expressed in the phrase "'revolutionary', 'practical-critical' activity" (*praktisch-kritischen Tätigkeit*) and in his criticism of Feuerbach for having exalted theory while denigrating practice as mere "appearance."[6] Action would no longer be confined to the pragmatic and to the fluctuating realm of appearance and opinion: it would become "revolutionary," action that would self-consciously transform a whole society, realizing in fact what the theoretical mind could envision only as idea.

Thus Marx's theoretical intentions were not purely theoretical. Their most extreme formulation was in the second of his theses on Feuerbach. There Marx inverted the Aristotelian principle of the superiority of theoretical contemplation over political action by switching predicates so that theory would be judged by its power, action by its truth: "The question whether human thinking can arrive at objective truth—is not a question of theory but a *practical* question. In practice man must prove the truth, that is, actuality and power, this-sidedness of his thinking."[7]

Aristotle had formulated his conception of *theoria* as a contrast between two lives which ought not to be combined, the political life and the theoretical life.[8] In rejecting that formulation, Marx seems closer to Plato's ideal of the philosopher who alternates between contemplation and action. But while Plato had been concerned to render the two lives compatible while preserving the superiority of the *bios theoretikos*, Marx wanted to make them complementary modes of activity. This aim was evident in his early critiques of Hegel and Feuerbach. In his famous preface to the *Philosophy of Right* Hegel had argued a version of Aristotle's separation of the two modes of activity. Theory "comes on the scene too late" to be of any practical importance because theoretical truth about the world is only possible when the world's actuality is "cut and dried after its process of formation has been completed."[9]

While theory's vision for Hegel was necessarily interpretative and retrospective, a lineal descendant of an ancient tradition of the theorist-as-spectator,[10] for Marx it was to be constitutive and prospective, inspired not by the image of a divine unmoved Mover, but by "the same spirit that constructs railways with the hands of workers."[11] and so drawn toward the dynamics of life-in-becoming rather than its cut-and-dried maturity. As he stated, "the time must come when philosophy not only internally by its content but also externally through its form, comes into contact and interaction with the real world of its day."[12]

III. PREDICTION AND TRUTH

In these early writings Marx's notion of theoretical activity was radically different from Plato's archetype of the *demiurgos* who "took over all that is visible . . .

and brought it from disorder into order,"[13] Marx was both the antidemiurgos, committed to disordering the world—"Worlds I would destroy forever/Since I can create no world"—and the Young Hegelian philosopher whose thought has been nuanced by the "interventionist" Aristotle of the *Politics* rather than the contemplator of the *Ethics* and so is sustained by the belief that not only is "philosophy becoming worldly" but "the world is becoming philosophical."[14] Marx's intention of making philosophy political while making action philosophical presupposed that the quest for truth would remain the decisive mark of philosophy. Philosophy, he insisted, "asks what is true" and makes no compromises with opinion, or with political or parochial loyalties.[15] Commitment to truth was not a mere rhetorical flourish for Marx. Few theorists in the entire history of political theory have been so steadfast in their devotion to the theoretical calling, have made so many personal sacrifices and taken so many risks on its behalf, or have dared to rethink basic presuppositions and begin anew when evidence or argument had cast doubts on years of their previous work.

The commitment to truth, to action, to the symbiosis of theory and action made for a highly complex structure of intentions with numerous possibilities for inner tensions and contrary tugs. The major condition for preserving the structure and preventing its disintegration was that theoretical inquiry would not turn up results that would undermine the aims or project of action. A commitment to truth always carried that possibility and with it the possibility that theory and action might be compelled along divergent paths.

That possibility will be explored in this paper. The form that it took for Marx was theoretic failure. The meaning of theoretic failure was not in Marx's unfulfilled predictions but in the complex fact that faces every interpreter of Marx, that Marx failed to complete his theory. This fact, I shall suggest, is the expression of a conflict that develops between Marx's theoretical findings and his political commitments.

I shall approach this conflict by posing a question that is prompted by the common criticism which attempts to discredit Marx's theory by claiming that history has failed to confirm Marx's prediction about the demise of capitalism. Could Marx's theory be "true" in an important sense despite the patent falsity of the prediction? Conceding for the moment that it might be both possible and illuminating to isolate a theory from its predictions, we would want to know what the remaining theory was a theory of. Would we find an implicit, incompletely articulated theory that was inconsistent with the prediction that capitalism was doomed? Would we have the outlines of a social system with the potentiality to survive periodic crises? If such a system can be detected, then the theory describes a successful rather than a doomed system, a *perpetuum mobile*, as Marx called it, that could endlessly reproduce new conditions for its own perpetuation.

Clearly, if it can be shown that Marx developed a theory that furnished strong grounds for the perpetuation rather than the revolutionary overthrow of capitalism, the implications would be severe. It would cast into doubt the central role assigned the proletariat. It would alter the tenor of the theory, from hopeful to problematic. In addition, it would present Marx's theoretical activity in a different light, having to take account of the possibility that as his inquiries into capitalism were extended, they turned up increasing evidence of the system's unrivalled capability for adaptation and innovation. Thus a conflict internal to the theory was generated, between the results of inquiry and the political intentions of the inquirer. One consequence of the conflict would be registered in the predictions attached to the theory. They would serve as the medium by which Marx would strive to reinstate the political intentions that he had invested in the revolutionary role of the proletariat. Prediction would be the means of recovering what analysis had rendered problematic, of averting rather than confirming the analysis. It was a way of theory being false to itself in order to be true to action.

One further preliminary. I depart from the conventional assumption that what Marx was intent upon describing as "capital" was an historically specific economic formation. Rather, the view I take is that the great economic writings of Marx's later years—*Grundrisse*, *Capital*, and *Theories of Surplus Value*—represent a continuation of the project that had preoccupied him from the beginning of his theoretical career, to find the right way of describing a system of power. He would discover that the system could not be adequately comprehended by relying exclusively upon categories drawn from either philosophy, political theory, or economics, although each was essential to identifying different dimensions of power.

IV. THEORETICAL INCOMPLETENESS

I turn first to the matter of theoretical incompleteness. As is well known, the bulk of Marx's writings is mostly unfinished. Much of it has become available only within the last half-century, and then only after heavy editing.[16] The writings that are most discussed today were unknown to his contemporaries, while the work that was most widely read in his day, *The Manifesto of the Communist Party*, is frequently downgraded by today's commentators. Marx is the only major writer in the history of theory whose reputation rests substantially on what he chose not to publish.

No theorist of comparable stature has left so many loose ends, so many unfinished themes. It is not merely that the writings are unfinished; the theory is incomplete. Yet no thinker was ever more conscious that the purpose of theory was to pull together "the whole thing in its totality."[17]

"There is no royal road to science," he remarked toward the end, "and only those who do not dread the fatiguing climb of its steep paths have a chance of gaining its luminous summits." Yet unlike others who had struggled to the heights, Marx claimed no full vision of the city below, only a "method of analysis . . . which had not previously been applied to economic subjects."[18] At one time he was persuaded that the completion of the theory was close at hand, that "the system of bourgeois economy" was now within his grasp. "The entire material lies before me in the form of monographs, which were written not for publication but for self-clarification at widely separated periods; their remolding into an integrated whole . . . will depend upon circumstances."[19] Circumstances decreed instead that Marx would leave a vision scattered among numerous "critiques"—no rounded and complete view of the whole, no *Republic*, or *Discorsi*, or *Leviathan*. Even if Marx had succeeded in "remolding" his material, the "system of bourgeois economy" would not have fulfilled the promise of what Engels had called "the famous Positive, what you 'really' want."[20] There was only the unredeemed promise "to present the interconnected whole, to show the relationship between the parts."[21] When Kautsky once asked the elderly Marx if the time had not come to publish his complete works, Marx replied, "They would first have to be completed."

In accounting for the incompleteness of Marx's theory our task is not to expose theoretical shortcomings, but to interpret the meaning of theoretical defeat. It means asking, what is the contribution failure makes to a great theory? Another and closely related question, or problem, needs some elaboration at this point, because it haunts the whole of Marx's mature vision. Stated simply, there was something troubling about the world and the special way in which Marx perceived it that caused the theory to falter, and hence to be incomplete. One is unprepared for this in a theory whose vision was magnificent in its sweep, sure in its grasp of concreteness, remarkable for its penetration of complex interrelationships, and memorable for its language. Although Marx is typically described as dogmatic, optimistic, and apocalyptic, his later thought sounded an uneasy note as he mused on the "insanity" that "determines the economic and practical life of nations."[22] It was most evident in the pessimism that tinged certain expressions; they are familiar to any reader of Marx, but their enigmatic quality is usually overlooked. The two expressions are "the forces of production" and "the order of things." Marx perceived the world in a special way, as an enormous structure of cumulating power generated by the "process" of production. These processes, ever changing, ever more efficient and voluminous, were genuine "forces." They appeared benign because of their evident capability of satisfying man's most expansive material dreams. But if their potential was benign, their power was staggering and could only be described in hyperbole: "The bourgeoisie, during its rule of scarce one hundred years, has created more massive and more colossal productive forces than have all preceding generations together."[23] As Marx was perhaps the first to show, the development of these forces had exacted a price, appallingly in the case of the workers whose humanity was threatened with extinction, more subtly among those responsible for tending and perfecting a system founded on innovation, and more ominously in the case of the world in which, as Marx was among the first to recognize, the modern economy had fulfilled the Baconian dream of dominating nature and was now bent on consuming her. The highest price of all, and the source of Marx's deepest disquiet, was that this magnificent apparatus of power, constructed by man's labor and ingenuity and requiring centuries of painful evolution, had become an uncontrollable order of things, increasingly less needful of its human operatives and more contemptuous in its treatment of them. At the center of the palace of production reigned a kind of Miltonic chaos:

> The commercial crises by their periodic return put on trial, each time more threateningly, the existence of the entire bourgeois society. . . . A great part not only of the existing products but also of the previously created productive forces are periodically destroyed . . . [in] the epidemic of overproduction . . . and why? Because there is too much civilization, too much means of subsistence, too much industry, too much commerce.[24]

V. DISCORDANT THEMES AND DISQUIET

The disturbing paradox of the system was that it was man-made, yet mysterious; it operated by rational methods, yet it issued in irrational, unpredictable results; it had been contrived for the most prosaic purposes of producing goods, services, and livelihoods, and yet, suddenly, it would veer out of control or break down altogether. Although Marx prophesied that eventually men would master the forces of production and humanize the order of things, he never completed the argument to support it. The system was too protean to remain caught for long. As he wrote to Lassalle:

> The job is making very slow progress because things which one has for many years made the chief object of one's investigations constantly exhibit new aspects and call forth new doubts whenever they are to be put in final shape.[25]

The last three decades of Marx's life were spent not in prescribing solutions or itemizing the future of man, but spinning out in tireless detail the inner complexities of the greatest productive system in history. He left behind three massive volumes which we know as *Capital*, three more collected under the title *Theories of Surplus Values*, and a bulging manuscript later designated as the *Grundrisse*.[26] Scattered throughout all of these works were substantial clues about the shape of the future, but these have mostly to be ferreted out from beneath the mass of detail relating to the mechanisms of capitalism.

What is troublesome about these unconsolidated heaps is the latent discord among some of the major themes. In the *Grundrisse* and in *Capital* he was concerned to show that the growing use of technology had already produced a state of affairs in which workers were increasingly superfluous and human labor, in its modern form, was becoming anachronistic. Some revision seemed called for, because Marx's ideas on revolution had been formulated in a period when he had conceived of the identity of the worker and the formative experience of work in significantly different terms. The worker who dominates Marx's writing before 1850 is a pretechnological figure; the system of capital that dominates Marx's writings during the 1850s and beyond is in the throes of technological change. In the pages of the *Grundrisse* Marx affords a glimpse of a new kind of worker, one that might be called the versatile technician, but the discussion sheds no light on the question of whether the new worker will exhibit a new form of revolutionary consciousness, or whether he can be expected to act in a revolutionary manner at all. One feels cheated by the silence of a theorist who, more than any modern, had done so much to revive the ancient word *praxis* and to bind it to theory.

What was the source of Marx's disquietude, the obstacle to completing his theory? The explanation falls into two parts. The first has to do with the peculiarities of Marx's thought processes and the way in which they developed; the second with a crucial disproportion that began to emerge between his theory of society and his theory of revolution, between the power of the system and the power to be mobilized against it.

VI. A GENERAL THEORY OF SOCIETY AND POWER

Beginning in 1843 with his critique of Hegel's *Philosophy of Right*, Marx set out on a search for a general theory of society. The two most striking aspects of a search that was to occupy him for the rest of his life were, first, the astonishing number and variety of philosophical and political theories that he consumed in the process, and, second, the persistence with which he judged each theory according to the standard of power, that is, whether the theory in question had an adequate grasp of the real powers in the world and whether the possession of it significantly empowered the theorist in his efforts to change the world. The search, then, was not for an intellectually satisfying theory but for a power-laden theory.

Marx's quest took him from one theoretical position to another. At the outset, he understood theory to be philosophy, and philosophy to be the system of Hegel. Once within the Hegelian system, which he never wholly escaped, he gravitated toward the "critical" philosophy of the Hegelian Left. Upon discovering Feuerbach, he turned against his former position, and before long, against Feuerbach as well. For each renunciation he gave the same explanation: the theory had failed to grasp the nature of power in the world and, as a consequence, it left the theorist impotent. In the end Marx renounced philosophy itself, and in savage terms: "Philosophy and the study of the actual world have the same relation to one another as onanism and sexual love."[27]

From philosophy Marx turned to the study of economics and theories of communism and socialism. After mastering most of the extant literature of political economy, he pronounced it "shit," saying that no progress had been made in the subject since Smith and Ricardo.[28] He had only a slightly higher opinion of the communist and socialist writings of his time. Increasingly, each of these bodies of thought served Marx as symptoms rather than as theoretical aids. Political economy revealed the assumptions upon which capitalism operated and the delusions that prevented the economist from perceiving the problematic status of bourgeois society as an historical entity. Socialist and communist theories, on the other hand, showed what it meant for thought to be immature. These theories suffered either from an excessive reliance upon moral criticism to the detriment of any serious analysis of the structure and processes of capitalism, or, when serious analysis was attempted, it was conducted with little understanding of the rigorous requirements of truly scientific work. For his own part, Marx's eventual understanding of capitalism as a massive structure of power, "stupendous" in size and global in scope,[29] while it owed something to all of these other theories, was the product of his own unique conception of what had to be known in order to understand the theory and practice of capitalism. The question of the origins and genesis of this "world-historical power" sent Marx rummaging into the remote past,[30] reading not only history but anthropology in the hope of discovering how, from the simple need to sustain existence, men had produced a system of matchless promise and actual destitution. Then to unlock its inner secret, he drove himself to examine the actual conditions of life that, historically, capitalism had created in the cities and rural areas, as well as in the domains of politics, culture, and ideas. Finally, there was an imperative need to master the new science of economics, for capitalist society was unique in having produced a body of theory concurrent with producing an economic revolution.[31] Never before had an undertaking of this magnitude been attempted by any theorist, but then, no theorist had ever confronted the massive powers Marx found ranged against humanity.

VII. CAPITALIST CIVILIZATION

Marx's genius was to expose the contemporary structure of capitalism in all of its historicity. The crucial significance of this achievement was not the trite discovery that capitalism had a history but that it constituted a civilization.[32] The structure of capitalist civilization comprised what is ordinarily distinguished as society, politics, the economy, and culture. This totality became the focus of Marx's theory. Although he did not complete the theory, the reason had as much to do with his mode of vision as with the scope of the undertaking. That mode of vision is familiarly described as dialectical and misleadingly analyzed as Marx's "method." In truth, the dialectic served Marx not only as a method of inquiry but also as a way of seeing the world. His vision of capitalism bears this out. In laying bare its structure, he draws attention to more than the processes and relations of production and exchange. He analyzes techniques, instruments, and knowledge, as well as the forms of behavior and values enforced by the system. In each of these elements, whether techniques, relations, or behavior, Marx saw a "congealment" of the whole history of capitalism, as well as traces of previous modes of production. In the accumulation of capital he saw the accumulation of history.[33] The rhythm of accumulation was dialectical: capitalism had evolved through various stages in which new developments superseded existing forms and relations without totally annihilating them. Elements of the old were caught up in the new and perpetuated. The weight of things that capitalism carried forward included not only its own history, but the historical deposits of the systems preceding it.

VIII. TRADITION

The massive proportions of the capitalist system had a telling influence both upon Marx's theory and his estimate of revolutionary prospects. "The tradition of all dead generations," Marx once wrote,

> weighs like a nightmare on the brain of the living. And just when they seem engaged in revolutionizing themselves and things, in creating something entirely new, precisely in such epochs of revolutionary crisis they anxiously conjure up the spirits of the past to their service and borrow from them names, battle slogans and costumes in order to present the new scene of world history in this time-honored disguise and this borrowed language.[34]

In the undertones of this passage one can detect something of Marx's despair at the cumulated massiveness of the modern world, which disposes men to cling to the past even while they are engaged in changing the present. But the passage also suggests something more autobiographical, a hint of a common malady afflicting the theorist as well as the world.

The malady is tradition. Earlier we had pointed out that Marx looked upon capitalism as a system that combined innovation along with perpetuation of elements of the past. Capitalism would eventually topple, according to Marx, because it could no longer support the weight of its accumulated contradictions. Yet the collapse of capitalism would not signify the beginning of an absolutely fresh state of affairs. Just as the capitalist revolution had brought forward the past, so would the postcapitalist era.[35]

IX. REVOLUTION AND CONTINUITY

Marx's conception of social change reveals him to be a revolutionary with an acute awareness of continuity. It is as though he combined Burke's sensitivity to tradition with Saint-Simon's insight into the destructive dynamics of technological change. The combination produces an almost painful sense of the overwhelming odds against anyone bent on "creating something entirely new." It is reflected in the way that Marx's practice of theory strikingly reproduces the processes at work in history. Theorizing becomes a mimetic rendering in thought of the ultimate powers whose rhythms dictate the course and contours of the world; a symbolic reenactment of the processes of history: "All that exists . . . exists and lives only by some kind of movement. . . . There is a continual movement, of growth in productive forces, of destruction in social relations, of formation in ideas; the only immutable thing is the abstraction of movement—*mors immortalis*."[36]

Like the world, Marx's theory took shape as movement, growth, destruction, and perpetuation. Like the world, it was an unfinished process; in this sense Marx never "produced" a completed theory, only a series of approximations, each more inclusive than the last. The way in which Marx practiced theory insured that his theory could never be located in space, as, for example, Hobbes's *Leviathan* could in England's Interregnum, but only observed over time. He used the methods of "critical" theory to force "contradictions" between what he had affirmed and what he was coming to believe; his theory progressed by a dialectical rhythm of discovery and reintegration of the new and the old; and, in imitation of the history of social formations, the theory grew bulkier as it added new concepts, insights, and empirical illustrations to its expanding structure—and more desperate. Its crisis, too, was a crisis of overproduction as it struggled to assimilate into its scheme of interconnections the profuse and intricate relations that its own insights had uncovered. The incompleteness should be read as theoretic failure occasioned by the defeat of heroic intentions. *Mors immortalis.*

Although Marx's revolutionary temper and his passion for theoretic supremacy goaded him into practicing theory as a form of combat, a way of destroying rivals and enemies, his practice was equally distinguished by its remarkable concern for existing intellectual traditions, and for treating truly great theorists with utmost seriousness. He always felt under an obligation to take careful account both of the reigning ideas and their antecedents. Because Marx's search for a theory took him into areas of thought that had long been well-cultivated, the search resembled a succession of forced entries into occupied domains.[37] Typically, it took the form of a critique, either of some writer, such as Feuerbach or Ricardo, or of some problem, such as the nature of revolution. Marx's first move would be to locate the writer or problem in the appropriate tradition. Thus, behind Ricardo stood James Mill, the Physiocrats, and Adam Smith; before Ricardo's concept of value could be understood critically, it was necessary to examine all of the strands of economic thinking that had led to it.[38] Or, to take another example, before Marx would commit himself to "materialism," he first had to compose its history so as to locate Feuerbach's version, which had helped to stimulate his own interest in the doctrine; only then was Marx prepared to describe his own position.[39] Similarly, he hesitated to declare himself a communist until he had thoroughly digested the history of its ideas and of related theories.[40]

In Marx's practice it was as though no theory, concept, or problem could be understood apart from its location in a well-defined and cumulative tradition, and as though Marx's own achievement depended upon its being correctly situated in relation to previous achievements. At the same time, this practice proved to be a formidable obstacle to the completion of his own theory. In addition to the labor of mastering large and complex bodies of theory, there was the task of selecting relevant notions from the various theories, and of integrating them into one's own theory or of relating the appropriate parts of one's own theory to previous writings. "As long as there is an unread book which you think important," Engels complained, "you do not get down to writing."[41] In a sense, however, Marx was always engaged in writing his theory. The world's difficulty was his: of carrying forward more than he destroyed.

X. THE TRANSFORMATION OF CAPITALISM

In Marx's introduction to his *Contribution to the Critique of Political Economy* (1859), he recounted how the 1848 revolutions had interrupted his "economic studies" and that when he was able to resume them in London in 1850, the "enormous amount of material relating to the history of political economy assembled in the British Museum," the advantages that London afforded "for the observation of bourgeois society," and "the new stage of development which the society seemed to have entered with the discovery of gold in California and Australia" caused him "to start again from the very beginning" of his theoretical labors.[42] These remarks underscore once more that Marx was intent upon portraying a system that was constantly undergoing significant change. The changes have a triple character: they are harbingers of the social formation that is to succeed capitalism; they are also changes within capitalism, transformations of it; and they are the source of opposing tendencies that "are so many mines to explode" the capitalist system and "can never be abolished through quiet metamorphosis." He wrote "if we did not find concealed in society *as it is* the material conditions of production and the corresponding relations of exchange prerequisite for a classless society, then all attempts to explode it would be quixotic."[43]

The phrase "as it is" points to the fact that capitalism has been undergoing modifications that eliminated some of its earlier features, transforming it into a formation that is somewhere between classical capitalism and early communism. The status of the worker changes dramatically under the impact of technological innovations; the capitalist as bold entrepreneur and tireless innovator will have been replaced by functionaries; and the pervasively social character of production and increasing "material dependence" of all members of society will have all helped to diminish some of the hierarchical features of society and to replace them by more universalistic relations appropriate to a "system of general social interchange."[44] In its latest phase the system can be described in terms that dwell lingeringly upon the enormous power compacted into the structures of production and into the tremendous "velocity" generated by exchange relations, but the description makes virtually no reference at all to the actors caught up in the system of power. Capital is represented as the "endless and limitless drive to go beyond its existing barrier," "the infinite urge to wealth [that] strives consistently towards infinite increase of the productive forces of labor."[45] Even wealth itself is treated less as a symbol of avarice and exploitation than as the summary expression of the power already in evidence under capitalism:

> When the limited bourgeois form is stripped away, what is wealth other than the universality of individual needs, capacities, pleasures, productive forces, etc., created through universal exchange? The full development of human mastery over the forces of nature, those of so-called nature as well as of humanity's own nature? The absolute working-out of his creative potentialities . . . i.e. the development of all human powers as such the end in itself, not as measured on a *pre-determined* yardstick?[46]

XI. REVOLUTION, PROLETARIAT, AND POWER

It was only after 1850 that Marx came to appreciate fully the system of power that capitalism had amassed and that he was able to work out the complex and tortuous relations and transactions that composed it. That achievement clearly represented a considerable redirection of Marx's political impulses and their absorption into the "politics" being played out in a domain seemingly (if only temporarily) beyond human control and the common understanding. Before 1850, roughly speaking, Marx's political impulses had been fixed upon the two concepts of "revolution" and "proletariat." These concepts were formulated in his preindustrial and preeconomics period and they served as the main vehicles by which traditional political concerns were being carried forward by Marx. That they were formulated before Marx's thinking was profoundly shaped by economics enables one to see how they perpetuated certain traditional themes of political theory.

Revolution and proletariat embody the constitutive or founding element, the beginning of a new order, that classical and early modern political theory had associated with the art of the legislator and especially with a legislator who would be guided by the counsels of those who had acquired political knowledge. They also express a notion of action that is preliberal as well as preindustrial: action of heroic proportions, waged against powerful adversaries, and undertaken to save humanity ("the total redemption of humanity").[47] Not surprisingly, in these early discussions of the working class and revolutionary action Marx introduced traditional themes regarding the importance of political education and political virtue: "What we say to the workers is: 'You will have 15, 20, 50 years of civil war and national struggle and this not merely to bring about a change in society but also to change yourselves and prepare yourselves for the exercise of political power.'"[48]

The crucial political importance of the concepts of revolution and proletariat is that they formed the core of Marx's conception of power. He embraced and developed them before he had begun his intensive studies of the literature of political economy in 1844 and hence before he had incorporated the language of economics into his theoretical outlook. When Marx wrote that "Germany . . . can only make a revolution which upsets the whole order of things" and that the proletariat is the appointed instrument for "the emancipation of man,"[49] his concepts of revolution, proletariat, and power correspond to what Hobsbawm and others have dubbed "precapitalist formations." They were formulated before he had grasped the nature of capitalism as a system of power. His conception of a revolutionary movement, for example, was primarily inspired by reading about the French Revolution of 1789 and composed of images of an aroused mass, goaded into fury by privation, moving against a visible enemy that flaunted its status from atop the social and political pyramid. The most vivid expression of this understanding of revolution was the essay of 1844, *A Contribution to the Critique of Hegel's "Philosophy of Right" Introduction*. There he invests the German workers with a revolutionary potential that will produce a general European contagion, even though, as he specifically noted, Germany's political and economic development lagged behind that of France and Britain.[50]

When Marx (in collaboration with Engels) came to write *The German Ideology* (1845–46), he had begun to acquire a firmer grasp of economics, not least because of his association with Engels, and with it the first appreciation of the power embodied in the system whose overthrow he was advocating. Capitalism, he realized, was a worldwide phenomenon that demanded a revolutionary response commensurate with this new scale. This realization produced the beginning of a crisis in Marx's thinking, for he now saw the futility of investing revolutionary hopes in a precapitalist society such as Germany. A revolution in Germany would necessarily be a revolution against feudalism, a repeat of 1789; but everywhere, including Germany, industrialism was rapidly eradicating the vestiges of feudalism and hence revolution had to be reconsidered.

"The organisation of revolutionary elements as a class supposes the existence of all the productive forces which could be engendered in the bosom of the old society."[51] This formulation crucially determines the nature of revolution. Given the extraordinary magnitude of power consolidated in the modern world, only a massive power can overcome it, a violent "driving force," a "total revolution."[52] The revolution must be worldwide in scope if it is to be commensurate with the universal power of capitalism, "the act of the dominant peoples 'all at once' and simultaneously."[53] Similarly, if the revolutionary force is to succeed it must be the expression of the most modern and hence most powerful phase of productive forces. Revolution under backward conditions merely generalizes a condition of want "and with destitution the struggle for necessities and all the old filthy business would necessarily be reproduced."[54]

The nature of the force that alone can overthrow the monolith of capitalism is summarized in the word "movement," to denote that it, too, is a power equally rooted in the nature of *things* and not in the realm of wishes. "Communism is for us not a *state of affairs* to be established, an *ideal* to which reality [will] have to adjust itself. We call communism the *real* movement that abolishes the present state of things. The conditions of this movement result from the premises now in existence."[55] The power of the "movement" must then be commensurate with those dynamic laws of motion that governed the development of historical forces.[56] Only movement could overcome movement.

It is significant that in the *Communist Manifesto*, where some effort is made to depict the developing crisis of capitalism and to indicate its signs, there is also a different emphasis on revolution. The *Manifesto*, in general, meets the question of how the revolutionary dynamic is generated by borrowing one of Hegel's famous metaphors, *die List der Vernunft*. In place of the cunning of reason, Marx introduces the cunning of necessity. The bourgeoisie, he declared, are *compelled* to create the agents of their own destruction. By exposing the proletariat to the advanced culture of industrial society, the "political and general education" of the bourgeoisie is unintentionally transmitted to the workers; by inveigling the proletariat to help in the bourgeois struggle against remnants of the old regime, the workers are "dragged into the political arena," rendered more politically conscious; and by associating workers in the social activity of production, their sense of common association is stimulated. Thus the bourgeoisie "is compelled to set the proletariat in motion."[57] This view in the *Manifesto* represented a highly subtle shift of emphasis, an accenting of one of the two sides of the "antinomy" that Marx had first elaborated in *The Holy Family*. In that earlier work he had described them as the antinomies of "proletariat and wealth"—the latter usage being a significant sign that Marx had not as yet enlarged the notion of wealth or, as he also called it, private property, into a concept of a dynamic system of productive forces. To the extent that the antinomy of wealth, or the later notion of the bourgeois economy, is emphasized, the task of the proletariat is greatly aided by the impersonal forces of history.

XII. THE PROBLEM OF ORGANIZATION

The result of this emphasis is not, as critics have often claimed, to advise the proletariat that they need only passively await their triumph, but rather something more subtle: it is to shift attention from the personal or moral characteristics of the proletariat to the problem of their organization. It is, in other words, to seek ways of generating an impersonal unity of forces to overcome the total-ity of forces represented by the bourgeois organization of productive forces. On the other hand, if, without ignoring the great power of "wealth," emphasis is placed on the effects of alienation upon the consciousness of the proletar-iat, then the natural human reaction to oppression and suffering comes to the fore and the qualities of the oppressed become the key consideration. To put it boldly, the question then is what the workers can make of themselves and of their cruel experiences, rather than the wounds that the system inflicts upon it-self. It is the difference between emphasizing the self-destruction of the system and emphasizing the self-creation of the proletariat.

This difference, it must be reiterated, was not an absolute contrast in Marx's mind, but a shifting emphasis on elements that "form a whole" and are dialecti-cally related.[58] Thus in *The Holy Family* the emphasis falls on the reactions of the proletariat to their condition and their growing awareness of their plight, which makes revolution appear a *human* necessity. Thus the proletariat "feels annihilated . . . sees its own powerlessness." When inevitably private property advances "towards its own dissolution" this occurs solely because "it produces the proletariat *as* proletariat, poverty which is conscious of its spiritual and physical poverty, dehumanization which is conscious of its dehumanization, and for this reason trying to abolish its dehumanized self."[59] It is "absolutely im-perative need," "the practical expression of necessity" that causes the proletariat "to revolt against this inhumanity." It "can and must emancipate itself."[60] But this theme that the proletariat is driven to revolt in protest against their inhu-man lot ends on an equivocal note. In *The Holy Family* Marx feels compelled to deny that he is elevating the proletariat to the status of "gods" and he ends in a kind of uneasy ambivalence that combines the experience of the proletariat and its suggestion of strengthened character with an ordained historical destiny:

> Not in vain does [the proletariat] go through the stern but steeling school of *la-bor*. It is not a question of what this or that proletarian, or even the whole prole-tariat, at the moment *regards* as its aim. It is a question of *what the proletariat is*, and what, in accordance with this being, it will historically be compelled to do. Its aim and historical action is visibly and irrevocably foreshadowed in its own life situation as well as in the whole organization of bourgeois society today.[61]

XIII. THE REVOLUTIONARY TASK

In *The German Ideology* the emphasis on the qualities of the proletariat was heightened as a result of Marx's growing appreciation of the enormous power of the opposing system. The expression of this concern takes the form of con-ceiving revolution as more than a matter of political overthrow: it becomes the basic medium of political education that will enable the proletariat to rid itself of its brutalized past and prepare for the unprecedented task of controlling ag-gregates of power such as no ruling class has ever had to contend with. The proletariat will now be measured by the difference between what it has been and what it must become. Here again Marx began from the system's effects on the proletariat: the "contradictions" between the productive system and its relations produces unprecedented "antagonisms" that are humanly registered:[62] they are "unbearable."[63] At one level the struggle is not merely to wrest control over forces which deny men the freedom of "self-activity" but to defend life itself, "to safeguard [men's] very existence."[64] In this account revolution resem-bles a raw Hobbesian response to the threat of extinction. But this threat is ex-perienced by human beings whose condition, in a sense, has become not only inhuman but dangerously so. Never before has mankind faced such an enor-mous power that rules in systematic disregard of the ruled. Accordingly human subjects are reduced to an unprecedented condition, "robbed of all life-content," "abstract individuals," "stunted," denied all "self-activity."[65]

The magnitude of the revolutionary task is extraordinary because of the yawn-ing gap between the universal significance of the productive forces potentially available to man and the shriveled stature of the vast majority of individuals. To hand over the former to the latter would be a disaster, for the economy is not a mechanical device, so simplified that the unskilled working man can take it over. The forces to be appropriated "have been developed to a totality." They are uni-versal in scope. Hence they lay a demand on the proletariat of measuring up to their inheritance: men to match the machines.

> This appropriation [by the proletariat] must have a universal character corre-sponding to the productive forces and the intercourse. The appropriation of these forces is itself nothing more than the development of the individual capacities corresponding to the material instruments of production. The appropriation is, for this very reason, the development of a totality of capacities in the individuals themselves.[66]

How, then, are the proletarians to prepare themselves for this staggering task? How is the mass of mankind, wholly without experience in controlling power, to be made competent to do what no class has ever done and has never been called upon to do?[67] How to develop "the universal character and energy of the proletariat, without which the revolution cannot be accomplished; and in which, further, the proletariat rids itself of everything that still clings to it from its previous position in society?"[68]

Marx's answer was that revolution itself could produce the necessary trans-formation in men:

> Both for the production on a mass scale of this communist consciousness, and for the success of the cause itself, the alteration of men on mass scale is necessary, an alteration which can only take place in a practical movement, a *revolution*;

this revolution is necessary, therefore, not only because the *ruling* class cannot be overthrown in any other way, but also because the class *overthrowing* it can only in a revolution succeed in ridding itself of all the muck of ages and become fitted to found society anew.[69]

XIV. META-POLITICS OF AN INDUSTRIAL COSMOGONY

Thus in *The German Ideology* revolutionary struggle appears as the political means of preparing the workers for accession to power. Indeed, the political element assumes a particular importance at this stage of Marx's thinking because, as yet, he has not developed a clear notion of a "crisis" within capitalism, a condition in which the system begins to founder because of the consequences of its own "logic." As we shall see, the idea of crisis will imply the presence of a second layer of politics over and beyond (although related to) the politics of class confrontation. It will involve the collision of impersonal forces generated by the laws of capitalist production and exchange, and often occurring unperceived by the human actors ("behind their backs," in a favorite phrase of Marx's). This meta-politics would eventually become a dominant theme in Marx's theory.

The shift of significant politics to the level of meta-politics was not the result of the reification of economic processes but was rather the culmination of a line of thought in Marx that had begun as early as the *1844 Manuscripts* to locate politics in economic relations. "Wages," he wrote, "are determined by the bitter struggle between capitalist and worker." "Capital," he declared, "is the *power of command* over labor and its products."[70] These notions were given a sharper focus when Marx identified the crucial element in the power of capitalists, the ability to buy labor. It is "merely the appearance," Marx wrote in *Wage, Labor and Capital*, that capitalists are buying "labor with money" or that laborers are selling their labor. "In reality what they sell to the capitalist for money is their labor *power*."[71] The power the laborer sells becomes the source of his servitude—"he belongs not to this or that capitalist but to the capitalist class"[72]—and of the enormous productive power of the system. "Capital is concentrated social force."[73]

As Marx's understanding of the power of capitalism was deepened by his intensive reading in economic theory and history, his undisguised fascination for, even admiration of, the achievement of the system grew. Nonetheless, he remained steadfast in his belief that the workers could gain power. "To conquer political power has become the great duty of the working classes," he declared in his inaugural address to the first International. But at the same time he was clear that only an international movement, characterized by "numbers," "combination," and "led by knowledge," could prevail against the power of capital.[74] It becomes all the more revealing of the growing disproportion in power between "the concentrated social force" of capitalism, "entirely beyond the control of the actors,"[75] and the revolutionary organization of labor that Marx himself should have participated in, some would say encouraged, the liquidation of the first International at the Hague conference of 1872. For in his major theoretical undertakings of the 1850s and 1860s, *Grundrisse* and *Capital*, it is the meta-political plane that preoccupies him, evoking an imagery of power drawn in almost equal parts from industry and classical mythology:

> A system of machinery . . . constitutes in itself a huge automaton, whenever it is driven by a self-actuating prime mover. We have in place of the isolated machine a mechanical monster whose body fills whole factories, and whose demon power, at first veiled under the slow and measured motions of his giant limbs, at length breaks out into the fast and furious whirl of his countless working organs.[76]

Elsewhere he describes "Modern Industry" as chafing under the "unbearable trammels" of existing means of communication and transportation and releasing its frustrations by "its feverish haste of production, its enormous extent, its constant flinging of capital and labor from one sphere of production into another, and its newly created connections with the markets of the whole world." Modern Industry constructs machinery "on a cyclopean scale," including machines for the production of other machines that embody the secret of "a prime mover capable of exerting any amount of force, and yet under perfect control."[77]

XV. CRISES AND IMPERSONAL FORCES

It is in this context of the meta-politics of an industrial cosmogony that the idea of "crisis" acquires significations that differ from its usual associations with impending collapse. Crisis is not necessarily a fatal condition, but rather an ordeal in which the subject reemerges, its powers strengthened but infected with new susceptibilities, "contradictions which are constantly overcome but just as constantly posited." In other words, crisis may imply repeated transformations rather than final catastrophe. As Marx phrased it in *Grundrisse*, crises are "the general intimation which points beyond" the present state of a social formation and they are "the urge which drives towards the adoption of a new historic form."[78] They emerge in the natural course of capitalism's "constant revolution," which dwarfs the existential politics of ordinary beings as it "tears down all the barriers which hem in the development of the forces of production, the expansion of needs, the all-sided development of production, and the exploitation and exchange of natural and mental forces."[79] These barriers, Marx insisted, will never really be overcome, but far from signifying the readmission of human politics, they merely reenforce the self-absorbed character of the meta-politics of the system: "The universality towards which it irresistibly strives encounters barriers in its own nature, which will, at a certain stage of its development, allow it to be recognized as being itself the greatest barrier to this tendency, and hence will drive towards its own suspension."[80]

The transfer of politics to the plane of impersonal forces signified that Marx's theoretical inquiries into capitalism were making it increasingly difficult for him to locate the revolutionary force that would overthrow the system other than in "the immanent laws of capitalistic production itself,"[81] laws that work "with iron necessity towards inevitable results."[82] To be sure, Marx preserves an element of revolutionary efficacy as when he describes the Last Days of capitalism: there "grows the mass of misery, oppression, slavery, degradation, exploitation; but with this too grows the revolt of the working class, a class always increasing in numbers, and disciplined, united, organized by the very mechanism of the process of capitalist production itself."[83]

XVI. DISAPPEARANCE OF THE PROLETARIAT

Yet the curious quality of the last encounter between proletariat and capitalist is that the protagonists are both, in an historical sense, vestigial. The capitalist class has not only been decimated by the cannibalism of the law of monopolistic concentration, but it has also all but disappeared as a human category. "The capitalist is merely capital personified and functions in the process of production solely as the agent of capital."[84] The disappearance of the capitalist, *while capitalism is still operative*, appears as an instance of a more general systematization of economic relations. "Characters who appear on the economic stage," Marx notes, "are but the personifications of the economic relations that exist between them."[85] The laborer, too, is an impersonation, in his case of "labor-power."[86] But, equally important, the protagonists have each been steadily displaced by technology, so that both in numbers and in contribution the proletariat will have surrendered much of the symbolism that Marx had used to interpret capitalism. As large industry advances, Marx wrote in *Grundrisse*, the creation of real wealth depends less and less upon the laborer's production than upon "the power of those agencies" whose significance "is itself out of all proportion to the direct labor time spent on their production but depends rather on the general state of science and the progress of technology." The laborer ceases to be "chief actor" and so he "steps to the side."[87]

It is not unimportant to note in this connection that while the lengthy analysis in *Capital*—and the same holds of *Grundrisse*—shows in detail the etiology of the crisis of capitalism, it does not demonstrate or describe the course of proletarian rebellion. No such work can be found among Marx's writings from the period after the *18th Brumaire* (1852) until *The Civil War in France* (1871), occasioned by the Paris Commune. The proletariat thus is left in a curious position: Marx's economic researches have produced results that steadily relieve the proletariat of a revolutionary burden that it lacks the power to carry, yet its name is invoked ("dictatorship of the proletariat") to summarize a course of development that led to its extinction—which is to say that the theory has overcome its original intention.

The fate of the proletariat was sealed when Marx insisted in *The German Ideology* that the proletariat, like Odysseus, must never look backward out of nostalgia for a simpler economy. It must accept the foundations laid by "Big Industry" as the equivalent of the new *logos*, the ultimate reality that dictates the disappearance rather than the triumph of the proletariat. What is being legitimated in its name is a unique system of power that had, prior to the revolution, rendered exploiter and exploited alike superfluous: "This organic system itself, as a totality, has its presuppositions, and its development to its totality consists precisely in subordinating all elements of society to itself, or in creating out of it the organs which it still lacks."[88]

XVII. SCIENCE AND TECHNOLOGY

The proletariat has to be abolished because it is unlike any victorious group imagined by previous political theorists: it lacks the *virtù* to constitute the new society. The future belongs to the practitioners of science and the technological innovators, because the future takes off from the point attained by the "stupendous productivity" of capitalism: "There is a limit, not inherent to production generally, but to production founded on capitalism." Capitalism is not "the absolute form for the development of the forces of production."[89]

Thus in the end Marx had found the truly revolutionary force, the permanent revolution in the powers that capitalism had organized into what appeared to be an autonomous system. "Modern Industry has a productive organism that is purely objective."[90] The contributions of science and technology have worked to establish a system that seems close to being separable from the fate of capitalism, reducing the latter to an incident in the evolution of power:

> Modern Industry rent the veil that concealed from men their own social process of production. . . . The principle which it pursued, of resolving each process into its constituent movements . . . by the hand of man, created by the new modern science of technology. . . . Technology also discovered the few main fundamental forms of motion which, despite the diversity of instruments used, are necessarily taken by every productive action of the human body.[91]

By their ability to develop byproducts and to discover unsuspected uses of existing materials, science and technology have opened the prospect of a system that renews itself:

> Like the increased exploitation of natural wealth by the mere increase in the tension of labor-power, science and technology give capital a power of expansion

independent of the given magnitude of the capital actually functioning. They react at the same time on that part of the original capital which has entered upon its stage of renewal. This, in passing into its new shape, incorporates gratis the social advance made while its old shape was being used up.[92]

XVIII. REVOLUTION AS SOLACE

Thus the revolution has been institutionalized before the proletarian revolution has taken place. The prediction of revolution appears not as a failed prophecy, but as solace, a memorial to an older faith in the power of human action. In this, as in practically everything he wrote, Marx was his own best analyst. In 1867, half in irony, he prepared some guidelines that would serve as a model for future reviews of *Capital*. His work, he suggested, embodied two lines of thought. One was the treatment of economic relations; it represented a "fundamental enrichment of science" comparable to Darwin's achievement. The other was "the tendentious conclusions" of the author, which "imagines or presents the end result of the present movement" of history when it has no demonstrated connection "with his [theoretical] development of the economic relations proper." As one of Marx's most sympathetic interpreters concludes, "If one were to take the trouble, one could perhaps show that his 'objective' analysis refutes his own 'subjective' fantasies."[93]

CHAPTER 9

MAX WEBER

LEGITIMATION, METHOD, AND THE POLITICS OF THEORY

MAX WEBER IS WIDELY REGARDED as one of the founders of twentieth-century social science and probably its greatest practitioner. Modern and ancient theorists commonly believed that founding—or giving a form or constitution to collective life—was reckoned to be the most notable action of which political man is capable. It is superior to other types of political acts because it aims to shape the lives of citizens by designing the structure or "dwelling" which they and their posterity will inhabit. In describing this extraordinary action, political theorists often had recourse to architectural metaphors: the founder "lays foundations." No such images were invoked to explain the routine acts that occur in the daily life of a polity. Ordinary action is commonly described as "doing," "effecting," or "bringing something about." If political actors are to bring something about, they presuppose conditions that make possible the action in question and the means for doing it. They also presuppose a context that permits the action to be understood and interpreted. The founder is quintessentially an author of political presuppositions.

By analogy, to found a form of social science entails an act of demarcation that indicates the subject matter peculiar to the science, the kind of activities that are appropriate (e.g., empirical inquiry), and the norms that are to be invoked in judging the value of the results produced by the activities. These demarcations become presuppositions of subsequent practice. Weber was engaged in founding when he wrote the following:

> The historical and cultural sciences teach us how to understand and interpret political, artistic, literary, and social phenomena in terms of their origins. But they give us no answer to the question, whether the existence of these cultural phenomena have been and are *worth while*. To take a political stand is one thing, and to analyze political structures and party positions is another.[1]

As this passage indicates, founding attempts to prescribe what shall be considered legitimate activity in a particular field.

But how does the founder acquire his authority to grant or withhold legitimation: who legitimates the legitimator? That question cannot be posed in isolation from the context in which, typically, it arises. The founders of a new science are not in the fortunate position of some of the legendary legislators of antiquity who were able to establish constitutions where none had previously existed. Empty space may be a geographical and even a political reality, but it seems not to be a theoretical possibility. Theories are not like explorations where a flag is planted for the first time. They are, in the revealing language frequently employed, "attacks" upon another theory. They contest ground that is already held and so they must not only establish their own legitimacy but delegitimate the prevailing theory and its practitioners.

I

Theoretical founding has both a *political* dimension and a *politics*. The former is the constitutive activity of laying down basic and general principles which, when legitimated, become the presuppositions of practice, the ethos of practitioners. This definition is modeled upon the Aristotelian conception of "the political" (*he politike*) as the "master science" that legislates for the good of the whole, that is, for the purpose of shaping the whole to the concept of the good relevant to it. Founding is thus *political* theorizing.

The politics of founding, or theory destruction, refers to the critical activity of defeating rival theoretical claims. It is Socrates against Thrasymachus. This politics is conducted by means of strategies (e.g., "the Socratic method," Locke's "clearing Ground a little, and removing some of the Rubbish") and intellectual weapons (various logics, conceptions of "facts"). The politics of theory was recognized as early as Plato:

> ELEATIC. And when combat takes the form of a conflict of body with body, our
>   natural appropriate name for it will be *force* . . . .
> THEAETETUS. Yes.
> ELEATIC. But when it is a conflict of argument with argument, can we call it any-
>   thing but controversy?[2]

We may call this "profane politics" in order to distinguish it from a "higher," ontological politics. The latter is illustrated by Aristotle's assertion that the theoretical life is "more than human. . We must not follow those who advise us to have human thoughts, since we are (only) men . . . On the contrary, we should try to become immortal."[3] Ontological politics is preoccupied with gaining access to the highest kind of truth, which is about the nature of ultimate being. The political theorist seeks that truth because he believes that it is the truth about power, the power that holds together the entire structure of things and beings, and holds them together in a perfectly right or just way. The reason why ultimate reality was ultimate was that it contained the solution to the fundamental political riddle, how to combine vast power with perfect right. Holding to this conception of reality, political theorists over many centuries sought to find the way of ordering the life of the collectivity into a right relationship with reality, connecting collective being with ultimate being and thereby assuring that the power and rightness of the one would translate into the safety and well-being of the other. "For all the laws of men are nourished by one law, the divine law; for it has as much power as it wishes and is sufficient for all and is still left over."[4] Politics at the ontological level is different from profane politics and more intense. Recall Moses's arguments with Yahweh, Plato's *Phaedrus*, or Augustine's tortuous efforts to find even a small place for the *civitas terrena* in the divine scheme of things. The echoes of ontological politics can still be heard as late as Max Weber's famous essay "Science as a Vocation":

> So long as life remains immanent and is interpreted in its own terms, it knows only of an unceasing struggle of these gods with one another. . . . The ultimately possible attitudes toward life are irreconcilable, and hence their struggle can never be brought to a final conclusion. Thus it is necessary to make a decisive choice.[5]

The point of engaging in the politics of theory is to demonstrate the superiority of one set of constitutive principles over another so that in the future these will be recognized as the basis of theoretical inquiry. Thus the founder's *action* prepares the *way* for *inquiry*, that is, for activity which can proceed uninterruptedly because its presuppositions are not in dispute. Inquiry is both a tribute to the triumph of a particular theory and its routinization. Or, to say the same thing differently, inquiry signals that the legitimation struggle is over; it is depoliticized theory. This explains why inquirers are usually quick to deplore as "political" (or "ideological") those who challenge the dominant presuppositions and who seek to refound the activity.

As a mode of activity, theorizing has been conceived as a *performance* whose political significance extends beyond the circle of theorists. It is intended as a model for a new form of politics, not only in the manifest sense of presenting a new political vision, but in the examplary sense of showing how political action should be conducted extramurally To refer to a previous example, Socrates and Thrasymachus not only represented opposing conceptions of theory, one philosophical and the other rhetorical, and contrasting modes of theoretical action (Socratic *elenchus* or cross-examination versus Thrasymachus's set speeches), but also opposing prescriptions of governance. Socrates not only maintains that the true ruler is one who rules for the betterment of the members of the political community, but in the actual course of the dialogue Socrates can be observed at work improving the mental and moral qualities of the participants, including his opponent Thrasymachus. On the other hand, Thrasymachus both maintains that ruling is and should be in the interest of the stronger and he himself seeks to overpower the listeners by the force of his rhetorical style, to diminish them as tyrants diminish their subjects.

It is within this political conception of theory and of theoretical activity that I want to reconsider Max Weber. The appropriate context for analyzing the political nature of his activity as a founder is provided by the triumph of modern science. Laying the foundations of social science was a possible action only because of the prestige of the natural sciences. Modern science was a new form of theory that rapidly became paradigmatic for all claims to theoretical knowledge. It achieved that position by defeating rival claimants, such as philosophy, theology, and history, and, in the course of more than three centuries of controversy, by delegitimating their respective reality-principles (reason, God, and experience). The spectacular theoretical and practical achievements of science served to obscure the legitimation crisis that was in the making. For centuries science was admired because men thought it provided a true picture of the nature of reality. This had to be so, men reasoned, because of the enormous, godlike power which science was increasingly making accessible to humankind. As long as men continued to believe that science was merely deciphering the laws of nature decreed by a beneficent god, they could preserve sufficient traces of the ancient belief that theoretical knowledge continued to embody the solution to the riddle of power and right. Very few doubted that science had demonstrated its superior ability to generate power. Bacon had compared ancient philosophy to boyish puberty: "It can talk, but cannot generate."[6]

This illusion began to dissolve in the nineteenth century. Science appeared to be power without right, an appearance that became all the more unsettling with the realization that science was acknowledging that, by nature, it was incapable of supplying the missing component of rightness, and yet the powers made available by scientific discoveries and technological inventions were increasingly becoming the main influences upon daily life. Equally serious, unlike the discredited forms of theory, such as philosophy, history, and theology, science *qua* science could not even provide a justification of its own activity. This produced a legitimation crisis within theory, or more precisely, within social science. The triumph of modern science had discredited all of the earlier forms of political theory (philosophy, theology, and history) as well as their reality-principles (reason, revelation, and experience). By dint of this discreditation, social science became the natural successor of political theory.

Max Weber was the ideal-type to deal with the developing crisis of the political nature of theory and the politics of theorizing. The title of a book written by his friend Karl Jaspers suggests why: *Max Weber. Politiker. Forscher* [inquirer]. *Philosoph.*

Weber was a profoundly political man. At several points in his life he gave serious consideration to abandoning academic life: "I am born for the pen and the speaker's tribune, not for the academic chair," he once wrote.[7] He was deeply involved in politics before and during the first World War and in the brief period from the armistice to his death in 1920. Max Weber also wrote a great deal about politics, much of it in newspapers, and his formal sociology was laced with political themes. Yet Weber never set down a coherent political theory comparable to the great theories of the tradition of political theory. That inability may well be the meaning of social science.

Although Weber's formal sociology is not much read outside departments of sociology and his studies of the great religions have been largely superseded, the so-called methodological essays continue to attract attention, especially from philosophers interested in the topic of explanation. Virtually all discussions of Weber's methodology assume that his essays on that subject can be strictly separated from his political writings proper, a distinction that was observed by Weber's German editors who collected his *Politische Schriften* in one volume, his *Aufsätze zur Wissenschaftslehre* in another. Following this principle, two of his best-known essays, "Politics as a Vocation" and "Science as a Vocation," were assigned to different volumes on the assumption, no doubt, that each represented a radically different conception of vocation, one political, the other scientific. I shall suggest, in contrast, that they are companion-pieces, united by common themes, all of them profoundly political. I shall suggest further that methodology, as conceived by Weber, was a type of political theory transferred to the only plane of action available to the theorist at a time when science, bureaucracy, and capitalism had clamped the world with the tightening grid of rationality. Methodology is mind engaged in the legitimation of its own political activity.

II

In the Prefatory Note to *Wirtschaft und Gesellschaft*, Weber acknowledged what most readers have keenly felt, that the discussion is "unavoidably abstract and hence gives the impression of remoteness from reality." He explained that the "pedantic" air of the work was due to its objective, to supply a "more exact terminology" for "what all empirical sociology really means when it deals with the same problems."[8] When readers first encounter his famous threefold classification of ideal types of legitimation, for example, they are apt to be puzzled because of the absence of any apparent context. Weber simply stipulates that "there are three pure types of legitimate domination. The validity of the claims may be based on":

(1) Rational grounds.
(2) Traditional grounds.
(3) Charismatic grounds.[9]

The service being rendered "empirical sociology" was not as innocent as it was made to appear, either in content or form. The bestowing of names is, as any reader of the Book of Genesis will recall, an act of power, an ordering of the world by specifying the place of things. Establishing the basic terms of sociology is a constitutive act that brings order to a distinct realm, especially if that realm has been disturbed by controversy, by a *Methodenstreit*. Weber's definition of the charismatic grounds of authority become relevant at this point:

"resting on devotion to the exceptional sanctity, heroism or exemplary character of an individual person, and of the normative patterns or order revealed or
ordained by him."[10] In keeping with this note of the extraordinary nature of the
pattern represented by basic sociological terms, Weber, in a phrase that echoes
temple prophets and early philosophers, remarked that

> the most precise formulation cannot always be reconciled with a form which can
> readily be popularized. In such cases the latter had to be sacrificed.[11]

The context for reading Weber's abstract terms is political, and for the reading of his methodological essays it is political and theoretical. We can begin to
construct the context for his terminology by noting the peculiarities of translation surrounding *Herrschaft*. It is often translated as "authority," but it is not
an exact equivalent of *die Autorität*; and the meaning of *Herrschaft* is only ob-
fuscated when translated as "imperative coordination" by Henderson and Parsons.[12] Although *Herrschaft* may refer specifically to the estate of a noble,[13] a
reference which was taken up by Weber in his distinctions between patriar-
chal and patrimonial dominions, *Herrschaft* typically connotes "mastery" and
domination." Thus Weber would write about the "domination (*Herrschaft*) of
man over man." This means that while in some contexts it may be perfectly
appropriate to translate *Herrschaft* as "authority" or "imperative control" and
to emphasize the element of "legitimacy," it is also important to attend to the
harsher overtones of *Herrschaft* as domination because these signify its connection to a more universal plane: "The decisive means for politics is violence . . .
who lets himself in for politics, that is, for power and force as means, contracts with diabolical powers."[14] Conflict and struggle were endemic in society
as well as between societies. " 'Peace' is nothing more than a change in the form
of conflict."[15] Even when Weber addressed what seemed on its face a purely
methodological question, he transformed it into a political engagement, stark,
dramatic, and, above all, theological. Thus in the context of "a non-empirical
approach oriented to the interpretation of meaning," he wrote:

> It is really a question not only of alternatives between values but of an irreconcil-
> able death-struggle like that between "God" and the "Devil."[16]

Even a casual reader of Weber must be struck by the prominence of "power-
words" in his vocabulary; struggle, competition, violence, domination, *Machtstaat*,
imperialism. The words indicate the presence of a powerful political sensibility
seeking a way to thematize its politicalness but finding itself blocked by a paradox of scientific inquiry. Science stipulates that political expression is prohibited
in scientific work, but the stipulation is plainly of a normative status and hence its
"Validity" (to use Weber's word) cannot be warranted by scientific procedures and
is, therefore, lacking in legitimacy. The same would hold true of all prescriptions
for correct scientific procedure. As a consequence, instead of a politics of social
scientific theory, there was the possibility of anarchy.

At the same time, the modern theoretical mind had come to regard the political and the scientific as mutually exclusive: the political stood for partisanship, the scientific for objectivity. Since science reigned as the paradigmatic form of theory and the political impulse could not be directly expressed in the form of theory, it had to seek its outlet elsewhere, through the circuitous route of ideal-type constructions and more transparently, as we shall see shortly, in the meta-theoretical form of "methodology." This meant, however, that social science *qua* science was unable to externalize a political theory and that Weber's political views, which were strongly held and unhesitatingly expressed publicly, could not be legitimated by his science. Accordingly, in 1917 when he published his remarkable essay on the postwar reconstruction of German political institutions, he felt obliged to preface it with the disclaimer that "it does not claim the authority of any science."[17]

Although Weber published his political views, his efforts took the form of occasional pieces. He never created a political theory even though the manifest breakdown of German politics and society cried out for one. His political-theoretical impulse was turned inward upon social science where he replicated the problems, dilemmas, and demands which he perceived in the "real" political world. For that impulse to be released, Weber had to find a way of modifying the scientific prohibition against the injection of politics into scientific inquiry and locate a domain within science where he could theorize both the profane politics of theory and the ontology of theory. The strategy which he followed required that he attack the positivist ideal of a presuppositionless and hence "value-free" social science but that, at the same time, he defend the scientific character of social science against subjectivist conceptions of social inquiry that emphasized personal intuitions and moral-political concerns. The positivist position called for the elimination of "values" from scientific work so that "objectivity" could be preserved; Weber accepted that formulation as the terrain of controversy and proceeded to invest "values" with political meaning so that, in the end, values functioned as the symbolic equivalent of politics. At the same time, he adopted from the subjectivist argument its starting point of the "subject," that is, the inquiring self whose passions the positivists had hoped to overcome by the rigors of scientific method. As the price of admitting the morally passionate subject, Weber was willing to concede to the positivists that this would introduce an element of arbitrariness into scientific investigations, but he preferred to gamble that he could revitalize the conception of vocation and make it into a prophylactic that would prevent subjectivity from degenerating into subjectivism.

The initial move that allowed for the political penetration of scientific work was in Weber's definition of social science as one of the "cultural sciences." This enabled him to exploit what he saw as the difference between science and culture. The latter was concerned with "meaning" or "patterns" rather than with predictions and the closely associated notion of regularities in phenomena.[18]

Weberian social science would be devoted to analyzing "the phenomena of life in terms of their cultural significance." The social scientist, according to Weber, derives his ideas of what is significant and worthy of investigation from the "value" element accompanying all human actions and historical events. "The concept of culture is a *value-concept*."[19] Significance is grasped as well as expressed by the constructs which Weber designated as "ideal types." These are based, he noted, on "subjective presuppositions" and they are "formed by the one-sided accentuation of one or more points of view and by the synthesis" of numerous "concrete individual phenomena." He likened them to "a *utopia* which has been arrived at by the analytical accentuation of certain elements of reality" although they "cannot be found empirically anywhere in reality."[20]

The subjective element in these one-sided constructs formed part of Weber's conception of human life: "Every single important activity and ultimately life as a whole is a series of ultimate decisions through which the soul—as in Plato—chooses its own fate."[21] That conception, first advanced in the context of a methodological discussion, later reappears to color the whole of Weber's essay on the political "hero" in *Politics as Vocation*.[22] Choice is the essence of true science as it is of true politics:

> The *objective* validity of all empirical knowledge rests exclusively upon the ordering of the given reality according to categories which are *subjective*.[23]

Scientific activity, Weber argued, represents a series of decisions; it is "always" from "particular points of view."[24]

The effect of these formulations is to politicalize social science, not in the vulgar sense of corrupting it by ideology, but in an allegorical sense. The highest form of available politics is a politics of the soul. In the passage cited earlier, it is revealing that Weber should have referred to Plato's conception of the soul. Classical political theory was remarkable for its profoundly political conception of the soul. Most readers are familiar with Plato's threefold division of the soul (reason, appetite, and passion) and his comparison of it to the "three orders" that were to "hold together" his ideal state.[25] For Weber, the politics of the soul appears in the identical virtues which he ascribed to scientific and political man: "objectivity" or "distance," "passion," and "responsibility" for the consequences of one's choices.

The complexity that the politics of theory took in Weber's case is all the more interesting when we realize that in the early stages of his career, long before he had become embroiled in methodological controversies, he had championed a radically different view of the relation between social science and politics, a view in which the political nature of theoretical activity was frankly espoused. It was set out in the inaugural lecture which he gave at Freiburg in 1895 under the title, "The Nation State and Political Economy." The theme of the lecture was political and deliberately provocative. As Weber remarked shortly afterward, he decided to publish the lecture because of the disagreement it had aroused among his listeners ("nicht die Zustimmung, sondern Widerspruch").[26] Midway through the lecture he announced, "I am a member of the bourgeois class and feel myself to be such, and I have been educated in its outlook and ideals. But it is precisely the vocation of our science to say what will be heard with displeasure."[27]

A reader who chances upon the Freiburg lecture and who had associated Weber with a strict view of the fact-value distinction, a rigid commitment to "ethical neutrality" (*Wertfreiheit*) and "objectivity," and disdain for professors who assumed the role of political prophets, would be startled to find Weber declaring roundly that "the science of political economy is a *political* science" and that it ought to be "the servant" of politics; that the nation-state is the ultimate value and political economy should be shaped to its needs.[28] In his prescription for the politicalization of this theoretical science, Weber broke with common belief that political economy should be exploited to promote the material happiness of society; and he rejected the sentiment of liberal free traders that economics should serve the cause of international peace by promoting the ideal of free trade and an international division of labor. "For the dream of peace and humanity's happiness there stands over the portals of the future of human history, *lasciate ogni speranza* (abandon all hope)."[29] The nature and purpose of political economy, he argued, was dicated by "Machtkämpfe," the power struggles in a Darwinian world where nations "were locked in an endless struggle for existence and domination."[30] "The economic policy of a German state," he warned his academic audience, "like the norm for German economic theoreticians, can only be German."[31]

The lecture gave not the slightest hint of a possible tension between the conditions needed for scientific inquiry and the requirements of "die weltliche Machtorganisation der Nation."[32] Equally notable in the light of Weber's later pessimism, there was no suggestion that political struggle might be meaningless. Rather there was an air of exaltation at the prospect of participating in "the eternal struggle for the preservation and improvement of our national type," as though in serving the *Machtstaat* in its quest for "elbow-room"[33] the political economist placed himself in contact with the most elemental force in the political world, the mustering of national power in the fight for survival.

The explicitly political conception of a social science was, however, abandoned over the next decade. Weber suffered a devastating nervous disorder in 1898 and it was not until 1902 that he began to resume his scholarly activity. Beginning in 1903 and continuing over the next several years, he published a series of essays on the methodology of the social sciences. As we have already noted, in the eyes of later commentators and critics, the essays constitute a self-contained series of texts which can be interpreted independently of Weber's sociological and political writings. They are described as the "philosophy of social science" which Weber worked out in the context of the famous *Methodenstreit*, initiated in 1883 by Schmoller's attack upon Menger over the fundamental nature of the social sciences.[34]

This is, as I have suggested earlier, a far too restrictive context for interpreting the methodological essays and for grasping the meaning of methodology.

That context needs to be enlarged to accommodate its author's political concerns. The expression of these concerns was powerfully evident in Weber's substantive, as opposed to his methodological, writings of the same period. Almost simultaneously with the publication (1903–1906) of Weber's first methodological essays, those dealing with Roscher and Knies, Weber published what is perhaps his most famous work, *The Protestant Ethic and the Spirit of Capitalism* (1904–1905). So much scholarly ink has been expended on the question of whether and in what sense Weber "explained" the rise of capitalism that the political importance of the work has been almost totally neglected. Yet it contains the most extensive formulation of Weber's ideal conception of the political actor and the most polemical, for it is directed squarely at Marxism. Weber wanted not only to counter the Marxist explanation of the origins of capitalism, but to celebrate the moral and political superiority of the capitalist hero of the past over the proletarian hero of the present and future. In these respects, the *Protestant Ethic* is a complex work concerned with the historical legitimation of capitalism. It is complex because that work also marks the first sustained discussion of a theme that was to preoccupy Weber for the remainder of his life, the meaninglessness of human existence. This intimation of a posttheological theme has been overlooked in most discussions of Weber's methodology, yet it figures prominently in his later essay on " 'Objectivity' in Social Science." Meaninglessness was less a concept than a theme. In the *Protestant Ethic* the context for interpreting it was supplied by another crucial theme, "rationalization." Rationalization refers to a world shaped by what Weber called "the special and peculiar rationalism of Western culture." Rationalization is expressed in the mastery of modern science over nature and of bureaucratic organization over society. It signified the status of human action in a world whose structures encased action in routines and required it to be calculating, instrumentalist, and predictable. Weber attacked that conception of action as its most basic assumption that "self-interest" is the main motive for action in "capitalistic culture."[35] His attack was paradoxical because it was conducted through the figure of a fanatical capitalist who brought an intensity to capital accumulation that would convert it into an epic deed, a spiritual triumph. Puritan zeal would also be brought to bear on human activity and to order it so systematically that it would generate structures of power that would transform the world. The Puritan would be, however, a capitalist without "purely eudaemonistic self-interest." He represented, instead, an alternative form of action, the action of a man defined by his "calling" or vocation, a man who submits to the requirements of a discipline without moderating his passion and who displays "a certain ascetic tendency" for "he gets nothing out of his wealth for himself, except the irrational sense of having done his job well."[36]

The Puritan actor of the *Protestant Ethic* was the prototype for Weber's most famous ideal-types, Political Man and Scientific Man and their respective vocations. His two essays, *Politics as a Vocation* and *Science as a Vocation*, appeared in 1919, during which he was at work preparing a revised version of the *Protestant Ethic*.[37] But the model had not only been developed much earlier, it had exercised a decisive influence upon Weber's conception of scientific activity at the time when he was writing the methodological essays. The exacting, even obsessive, demands which Weber imposed on the social scientist form a counterpart to the Calvinist's adherence to the letter of Scripture and to the rules of piety prescribed by Puritan divines. The Calvinist is, as we have noted, ascetic, but he accumulates material goods with a controlled frenzy. "The God of Calvinism demanded of his believers not simple good works, but a life of good works combined into a unified system." The Puritan made no appeal to "magical sacraments" or confessions; he relied, instead, on "rational planning" and proceeded "methodically" to supervise his own conduct and, in the process, to objectify the self.[38] Scientific man is likewise to be a model of rational self-discipline, not only in his scrupulous adherence to scientific protocols, but in controlling his values and biases, and in suppressing the special vice of modern man, his fondness for "self-expression." Like the Calvinist, scientific man accumulates, only his activity takes the form of knowledge; yet what he amasses has no more lasting value than other things of the world. Scientific knowledge is always being superseded. Finally, scientific man is also a renunciatory hero. His form of renunciation is dictated by the demands of specialization that require him to abandon the delights of the Renaissance and Goethean ideal of the universal man who seeks to develop as many facets of his personality and as many different fields of knowledge as possible: "Renunciation of the Faustian universality of man . . . is a condition of valuable work in the modern world."[39]

The extent to which Weber shaped his social scientist in the image of the Calvinist went beyond the attempt to emulate the precision of Calvinism. It extended to Calvinist doctrine, which proved to be an extraordinary move for it meant adopting the demands without being able to presuppose a comparable faith. In Weber's portrait, the most striking feature of the Calvinist's furious dedication to ascetic labor is that, during his unending labors, he can never know whether he has been chosen for election and he can never win it by his own efforts, regardless of how strenuously he tries. The dogma of predestination decrees that the Calvinist will labor amidst unrelieved uncertainty. Scientific man is in a comparable predicament. "Our highest values" are "a matter of faith." Although they are crucial in orienting us toward our scientific work, there is no way that we, as scientists, can be assured that these values are "true." Knowledge of values, like the knowledge of secret election by God, is inaccessible.[40] Appropriately, when Weber argued this point in the essay on "objectivity," he drew upon the oldest theological parallel:

> The fate of an epoch which has eaten of the tree of knowledge is that it must know that we cannot learn the *meaning* of the world from the results of its analysis, be it ever so perfect.[41]

The fundamental premise from which Weber argued for the fact-value distinction, which occupied such an important place in the "discipline" of Weberian social science, was that values had to be preserved in their unscientific state so that human beings would have to choose.[42] The existence of the fact/ value distinction was nothing less than the fundamental article of faith on which rested the entire decisionist framework of Weber's politics of the soul. As long as science could not, in principle, determine choice, men were forced to be free to choose. In that formulation one can see the secular equivalent of the age-old religious controversy over human free will versus divine predestination, only now scientific "laws" take the place of the providential plan.

Weber laid special emphasis on the transforming effects of Puritan zeal when it was transferred to business activity. It converted money-making into a moral *praxis*, characterized by selflessness and competence. When Weber took the next step of transferring the Calvinist spirit to the domain of social science, he formulated the idea of methodology to serve, not simply as a guide to investigation but as a moral practice and a mode of political action. The Calvinist, Weber wrote,

> strode into the market-place of life, slammed the door of the monastery behind it, and took to penetrate just the daily routine of life, with its methodicalness, to fashion it into a life in the world, but neither of nor for this world.[43]

But as a model for the *bios theoretikos* the Calvinist was worlds removed from the classical idea of theory as contemplative and reflective. "Scientific work is chained to the course of progress . . . this progress goes on *ad infinitum*."[44]

As Weber sketched the Calvinist, he injected into his portrait the political themes of struggle which had so sharply defined his own view of politics and especially of international politics as evidenced by the Freiburg lecture. The "heroism" of the Calvinist was displayed in the "fight" for "supremacy against a whole world of hostile forces." In the end he shattered the powers of church, society, and state, ushering in a new era of "universal history."[45] "Bourgeois classes as such have seldom before and never since displayed heroism."[46]

The bourgeois actor of Weber's epic is a political hero in the classical sense. He is a founder of a new order, the order of capitalism which has transformed the world. He can stand comparison with another hero, the world-conquering proletariat, a comparison that pits a Protestant hero against a classically inspired one. Marx, particularly in his writings of the early 1840s, likened the proletariat to Prometheus, the rebellious god who saved mankind from destruction by bringing it the techniques of material production. While the proletarian hero signifies material and cultural deprivation and hence implies the promise of gratification, the Protestant is a renunciative hero who disdains the material sensuous pleasures eagerly sought by the materially deprived and sensuously starved man of the *Paris Manuscripts*. A major difference between the two epics is that, unlike Marx, Weber knew that he was composing a portrait of the last hero before the age of rationalization set in and rendered both heroes, Marx's and his own, anachronisms. Henceforth, the possibilities of significant action will be determined and limited by the constraints of rationalization. In the closing pages of the *Protestant Ethic* the fate of action is described in the imagery of the "iron cage."

The iron cage is a symbol with many meanings. It symbolizes the transformation of vocation from a religious and moral choice to an economic necessity. It also signifies our helplessness before "the tremendous cosmos of the modern economic order . . . which today determine[s] the lives of all who are born into this mechanism." And the iron cage stands for the stage of "victorious capitalism" when the social order no longer needs the spiritual devotion of the ascetic for "it rests on mechanical foundations."[47]

The rationalization of existence foreshadowed by the iron cage became a *leitmotif* in all of Weber's subsequent writings. The cage is iron because the main forces of modern life, science, capitalism, and bureaucratic organization are triumphs of rationality and so the mind has no purchase point to attack them. They *are* mind incarnated into legal codes and administrative organizations that promise order, predictable decisions, regularity of procedures, and responsible, objective, and qualified officials; into economies that operate according to principles of calculated advantage, efficiency, and means-ends strategies; and into technologies that promote standardization, mechanical behavior, and uniform tastes. The advantages of rationalization in terms of power and material satisfaction are so overwhelming that the historical process which has brought that system is "irreversible." But, finally, the cage is iron because "the fulfillment of the calling cannot directly be related to the highest spiritual and cultural values." Instead of being fired by religious, ethical, and political ideals, action has become simply a response to "economic compulsion" or to "purely mundane passions."[48]

Action without the passions that Weber associated with spiritual and moral ideals was "meaningless," a category that became a major one in Weber's thinking henceforth. Meaninglessness was of special concern in the methodological essays because of the central part which modern science had played in destroying the sources of meaning. Capitalism and bureaucratization may have produced the social and political structures of rationalization but the equation of rationalization with meaninglessness was the special responsibility of modern science. Science had attacked religious, moral, and metaphysical beliefs and had insisted that everything could, in principle, be reduced to rational explanation. Such explanations had no need of gods, spirits, revelations, and metaphysical principles. The result was a bare world, denuded and drained of meaning, which science makes no pretense to replenishing. Science deals with fact, material reality, and rational demonstration. It is so helpless to restore what it has destroyed that, *qua* science, it cannot even justify its own value. Its own activity comes perilously close to being the definition of meaninglessness: "Chained to the course of progress," its "fate" is that "it asks to be 'surpassed' and outdated."[49]

The inherent limitations of science, its inability to make good the deficiencies of the world's meaning, provide the backdrop to the political role of the methodologist. His task is not to undertake scientific investigations or even to instruct his coworkers on how best to conduct research, much less to offer a special field of study. Rather it is to show them that significant action in their chosen realm is possible. It is, therefore, a form of political education in the meaning of vocation. Its politicalness comes from the seriousness, even urgency, of the relationship between vocational action and the world.

In order to bring out the unusual nature of Weberian methodology, a slight excursion is necessary, but it will be one that will reestablish direct contact with our original concern: social science as the postmodern form of political theory. Previously we had noted that Weber frequently asserts that science cannot validate the legitimacy of its own authority This assertion calls attention to the interesting consideration that Weber never attempted in any systematic fashion to apply his concepts of *legitime Herrschaft* to science, even though the significance of science for the major conceptions of legitimate authority is clear. For example, given Weber's definition of "traditional authority" as "resting on an established belief in the sanctity of immemorial traditions and the legitimacy of the status of those exercising authority under them,"[50] it is clear that science, which strives to be "outdated," is hostile to that form of authority. Further, *pace* Kuhn, science as an institutionalized activity appears to be consistent with the "rational–legal" type of authority which rests on "a belief in the 'legality' of patterns of normative rules and the right of those elevated to authority under such rules to issue commands."[51] But the most interesting question concerns the possible relations between science and charisma, the form of authority which appears, on its face, to be the least hospitable to science. Charismatic authority, as we have already noted, rests on "devotion to the specific sanctity, heroism, or exemplary character of an individual person, and of the normative patterns or order revealed or ordained by him."[52] Now, although Weber never explicitly connected science and charisma, there is a sufficient number of scattered clues to suggest that the connection was in his mind. Science is charisma "in a godless and prophetless time" and it is displayed by the person "with an inward calling" who can endure that "the world is disenchanted."[53] It is for the chosen few, "the affair of an intellectual aristocracy."[54] It is, above all, charisma because science requires "inspiration" (*Eingebung*). "It has nothing to do with any cold calculation."[55] Weber's discussion of inspiration is compressed but highly suggestive. "Psychologically," he declared, inspiration was related to "frenzy" or "Plato's 'mania' "—a reference to the discussion of "divine madness" in the dialogue *Ion*. "Whether we have scientific inspiration," he continued, "depends upon destinies that are hidden from us, and besides upon 'gifts.'"[56] "Gifts" (*Gabe*) clearly refers to a charismatic quality for elsewhere Weber defined charisma as "the gift of grace," a phrase which he took the pains to associate with "the vocabulary of early Christianity."[57] Although the significance of "grace" (Gr. *caris*) was not explicitly connected by Weber to his discussion of science, a brief account of that term should immediately establish its relevance in the highly decisionistic framework of Weberian social science.

In the New Testament, "grace" refers to the idea of God's redemptive love which is always actively at work to save sinners and maintain them in the right relationship to Him. Grace is God's free gift, and while it is not the result of man having earned it, there is still an element of choice, though an ambiguous one: "Work out your own salvation," Paul exhorted his followers, "with fear and trembling; for God is at work in you" (*Phil.* 2.12–13).

From these considerations we can distill three elements in the idea of charisma: a "gifted" exceptional person of heroic or risk-taking qualities; a normative pattern that he ordains and that gives him authority; and the element of choice, both for the charismatic figure who commits himself to the revelation entrusted to him and for the others who must decide whether to follow him. Throughout, the decisionist element ("work out your own salvation") rests uneasily with a necessitarian one ("God is at work in you"). All of these elements reappear in Weber's methodological discussions.

But what is the meaning of methodology? What is its connection with the disenchanted world and its meaninglessness? How does it compare as a form of action with political theory?

The word "methodology" did not come into use until the nineteenth century and it was mostly employed in scientific discussions, at least during the first half of the century. Its etymology is revealing. It is derived from two Greek words, *méthodus* and *logos*. *Méthodus* is itself an interesting compound of *meta* and *hodos*. *Meta*, which is characteristically used as a prefix, had some meanings that bristle with political overtones. They include: sharing, action in common, pursuit or quest. *Hodos*, on the other hand, means "way." It is one of the oldest words in the historical lexicon of Greek philosophy. The pre-Socratics, for example, typically described philosophy as a "way" to the truth or even as a "way" to ultimate Being. Ancient philosophy, we should recall, deliberately challenged religion, myth, and tradition; its "way" often provoked opposition, even danger. Thus Parmenides described his "way" as "strife-encompassed."[58]

Logos ís probably the richest word in the entire vocabulary of ancient philosophy and theology. It has meant: account, explanation, truth, theory, reason, and, more simply, word. Among several of its usages there is a recurrent element: *logos* as signifying the truth that resides in the deepest layer of Being and that the *logos* has succeeded in embodying. It is represented by a phrase from Parmenides: "The same thing exists for thinking and for being."[59]

Methodology might then be rendered as the political action (*meta*) which thought takes on the route (*hodos*) to being (*logos*). Weber referred to it as "metatheoretical."[60] The reason for this designation had to do with the political nature of the crisis which gives methodology its raison d'être, the kind of crisis experienced by Weber and his contemporaries in the course of the *Methodenstreit* when the nature of the social sciences *qua* science was being contested. Weber took special pains to define the meaning of crisis so that the function of methodology could be made clear. Methodology, he insisted, does not legislate methods; these are "established and developed" by practicing social scientists in the course of dealing with "*substantive problems.*" "Purely epistemological and methodological reflections have never played the crucial role in such developments."[61] Crises come about because of the dependence of social scientists upon "evaluative ideas" which give "significance" to their work. The "foundation" for empirical inquiry comes not from empirical data but from "the meta-empirical validity of ultimate final values in which the meaning of our existence is rooted." These foundations, however, tend to shift and even crumble because life itself is "perpetually in flux. . . . The light which emanates from these highest evaluative ideas falls on an ever changing finite segment of the vast chaotic stream of events which flows away through time."[62] Meanwhile, researchers gradually lose their immediate awareness of the "ultimate rootedness" in values of their own research. The result is that research falters. "The significance of the unreflectively utilized viewpoints becomes uncertain" in the mind of the researcher. "The road is lost in the twilight." This crisis creates the opportunity for the type of intervention associated with methodology:

> Science prepares to change its standpoint and its analytical apparatus and to view the stream of events from the heights of thought.[63]

The methodologist seizes the opportunity to show the researcher that science cannot flourish without "evaluative ideas" for it is these that nourish notions of what is "significant" and hence worthy of inquiry. "Significance" becomes the crucial concept in Weber's politics of knowledge. It symbolizes the moment of freedom for the social scientist when he registers his affirmations, when he exchanges the settled routines of inquiry for the risks of action. It is akin to a form of momentary and secular salvation for it creates meaning in an otherwise meaningless world. " 'Culture,' " Weber declared, "is a finite segment of the meaningless infinity of the world process, a segment on which *human beings* confer meaning and significance." Humans impart significance by taking up "a deliberate posture (*Stellung*) towards the world."[64]

The politics of mind in its struggles against meaninglessness finds its most powerful expression in Weber's conception of "ideal types." These are the most crucial instruments of social scientific inquiry and hence their nature becomes all-important. Ideal types are constructs created by the social scientist to render a particular historical reality intelligible and coherent. They are constructed by abstracting features of a phenomenon (e.g., capitalism or bureaucracy) and reconstructing them to form an internally consistent whole. Ideal types are, Weber emphasized, deliberately constructed to be "one-sided"; they are meant not only to accentuate the phenomena under study and thereby leave the investigator's mark on a portion of the world, but to accentuate as well the value-orientations of the investigator. Ideal types "illuminate reality" although they cannot "exhaust its infinite richness":

They are all attempts to bring order into the chaos of those facts which we have drawn into the field circumscribed by our *interest*.[65]

The investigator does not usually face a situation where no prior constructs exist. Rather he is faced with the challenge of overcoming the constructs of the past. It is not surprising, therefore, to find Weber's description of the use of ideal-types reminiscent of descriptions of the *agon* of classical politics. Inherited constructs are "in constant tension with the new knowledge which we can and *desire* to wrest from reality. The progress of cultural science occurs through this conflict."[66]

Weber looked upon the ideal-type as a means of provoking a "confrontation with empirical reality."[67] This somewhat curious formulation reflects the larger problem of political action in a world dominated by huge structures. Where theorists of earlier times were haunted by the fragility of order and by the difficulties of maintaining it, postmodern theory appears to suffer from a surfeit of order. Order is the empirical reality of postmodern theory. And ultimately, of course, the heroic meta-theorist will suffer the same fate as the political hero and all charismatics: his *agon* will be routinized. The meta-theorist is replaced by the normal social scientist, the meta-politician by the technician.

The fate of the meta-theorist is not, perhaps, a great loss. He has turned out to be a theorist *manqué*, his methodology a displaced form of political theory confined within the walls of the academy but serving a legitimating function once removed. As practiced by Weber, methodology provides a rationale for social science, while social science tacitly bestows the peculiar form of legitimacy that is within its power to grant, the legitimacy of fact. Against the *Herrschaft* of facticity, ideal-type constructions afford only a small purchase-point for criticism. Ideal-types cannot serve as substitutes for a theoretical counterparadigm, an alternative vision to what is too often the case. Weber's own views about bureaucracy confirm that while an ideal-type construction may highlight how bureaucracy trivializes politics and reduces human beings to classifications, the only rational choice is resignation before its massive facticity: "The needs of mass administration make [bureaucracy] completely indispensable."[68]

Weber's torment was that while he prophesied "a polar night of icy darkness and hardness" and a totally bureaucratized condition wherein mankind would be "as powerless as the fellahs of ancient Egypt,"[69] he could neither turn theory against science—for science *was* theory—nor venture upon the quest for an ontology. His torment was expressed, paradoxically, at the ontological level which science had completely destroyed:

There are no mysterious incalculable forces. One can, in principle, master all things by calculation. This means the world is disenchanted. [In antiquity] everybody sacrificed to the gods of his city, so do we still nowadays, only the bearing of man has been disenchanted and denuded of its mystical but inwardly genuine plasticity. Fate, and certainly not "science" holds sway over these gods and their struggles. One can only understand what the godhead is for the one order or the other, or better, what godhead is in the one or the other order. With this understanding, however, the matter has reached its limits so far as it can be discussed in a lecture-room and by a professor.[70]

Weber's ontological politics, populated with the furious struggles of gods and demons, and seemingly so incongruous in the thought of a founder of the scientific study of society and politics, issues from the frustration of a consciousness that knows that its deepest values are owed to religion but that its vocational commitments are to the enemy. Science has caused the meaning of the universe to "die out at its very root." Science is "specifically [an] irreligious power."[71] The tension left Weber ambivalent toward science: "I personally by my very work . . . affirm the value of science . . . and I also do so from precisely the standpoint that hates intellectualism as the worst devil."[72]

The dramatic rendition of this ontological politics where science destroys the possibility of political renewal is in a figure that reappears frequently in Weber's writings, the prophet. The personal significance of the prophet is obscured because, as was his custom, Weber would frequently throw out sarcastic references about professors playing prophet, or about those who "cannot bear the fate of the times like a man" and for whom "the arms of the old church are opened widely and compassionately."[73] But, of course, it was Weber's prophecies that have made his writings enduring; not so much because they see into the future but because they reveal him deeply engaged with the powers that dominate the soul of modern man: bureaucracy, science, violence, and the "intellectualism" that has destroyed the spiritual resources on which humankind has fed for three thousand years or more. Prophecy, like religion, was a political symbol for Weber, as evidenced by his treatment of the Old Testament prophets. They were, in his eyes, supremely political figures who "stood in the midst of their people and were concerned with the fate of the political community."[74] They practiced a "prophetic politics" while exhorting their people in the midst of "political disaster."[75] Prophecy, we might say, is closet-theory in the age of science. It achieved pathos in *The Protestant Ethic and the Spirit of Capitalism*, not in the closing pages where Weber pronounced his famous jeremiad about the "iron cage," but in the introduction which he wrote shortly before his death. They are powerful pages and can only be described as akin to a secular crucifixion. This was because the book, and the prophecy about the future and the myths of the Protestant hero of the past, was considered to be an invasion of special fields or preserves of scholarly experts, "trespassing" as Weber called it. Acknowledging that he had violated the scientific division of labor, he was prepared to offer himself up for trial. "The specialist is entitled to a final judgment" and "one must take the consequences." To do otherwise would be to "degrade" the specialist below the "seer." "Whoever wants a sermon," Weber wrote contemptuously, "should go to a conventicle."[76] He then ends on an equivocal note that gives a glimpse of his own agony:

> It is true that the path of human destiny cannot but appall him who surveys a section of it. But he will do well to keep his small personal commentaries to himself, as one does at the sight of the sea or of majestic mountains, unless he knows himself to be called and gifted to give them expression in artistic or prophetic form.[77]

The feebleness of Weber's equivocation corresponded to the powerlessness of the prophet in a "prophetless and godless" world. Meaninglessness was no longer an aesthetic experience of the few, but a contagion. Having undermined religious, moral, and political beliefs, the forces of rationalization had finally exposed the meaning of meaninglessness to be power without right.

PART THREE

RECENT THEORISTS

CHAPTER 10

REASON IN EXILE

CRITICAL THEORY AND TECHNOLOGICAL SOCIETY

I

The present age is continually being reminded that, like late nineteenth-century Vienna or pre–World War I Europe, it is experiencing its own fin de siècle. Thoughtful writers tell us that we are living through a time of endings—of American hegemony, of history, of Marxism, of philosophy, and of modernity.

Although in each of these examples the meaning of "end" is significantly different, there is a common element of anxiety hinting that some distinctively modern enterprises are in extremis. One tempting interpretation, prompted by the collapse of communism abroad and the triumph of American conservatism at home, is that we are witnessing the end of deep crisis; that the last major turning point has occurred; that the old formula of "crisis = opportunity" has been fulfilled so that opportunity, released from its dependence upon crisis, now points toward infinity. With ends no longer a matter of contestation, human beings can dwell forever in a kingdom of pure means.

Marxian political theory was the last representation of the ancient theme that deep crisis is theory's opportunity to change the world. Many of its earlier critics had claimed that this belief was the spawning ground for the "totalitarian temptation" to shape society as though it were potter's clay. Ironically, the theme appears to have reemerged among the apologists for capitalism. Opportunity's new formula, touted as the universal panacea for Asia, Central Europe, the Soviet Union, as well as the rest of the world, is "high technology + the free market." Thus at the very moment when theory in the form of a Marxist "utopia" is pronounced dead, theory in an equally doctrinaire, but more economistic, form is being thrust upon those societies struggling for relief from theory. The Utopia of opportunity, like the workers' utopia it has replaced, eerily repeats the same demand: present generations must sacrifice themselves for a future society whose assurance lies in the power of technology.

Assuming that a more skeptical interpretation is still credible, one might appropriately consider two writers, Max Horkheimer and Theodor Adorno, who nearly a half-century ago set down a very different version of Endgame in which the opportunity created by crisis produced a bad infinity whose formula was "total domination through technology." The crisis involved the destruction in Germany, Italy, Spain, and France of the type of liberal societies being promoted today in Central Europe and Russia and the establishment of societies of varying degrees of totalitarianism. Although Horkheimer and Adorno were deeply critical of all dictatorships, including Stalin's, they believed that the crisis could not be understood as the breakdown of parliamentary structures or the triumph of mass parties organized around a charismatic leader. The crisis centered, instead, in the culture of the intellect and involved the core notions in the heritage of the Enlightenment: faith in progress and its major driving forces, reason and science. The tangible expression of that faith and of its power was modern technology in its various forms of mass-production techniques, a vast array of consumer goods, rapid transportation of goods, services, and people, and, last but not least, mass communications, including unprecedented technologies for disseminating education and culture. The faith in technology was especially strong among Marxists, whose hopes for human emancipation had been pinned to the productive potential of new technologies.

Confronting a world in which cruel dictatorships had come to power in some of the world's most "advanced" countries, Horkheimer and Adorno argued that the brute facts of the twentieth century—totalitarianism, racism, death camps, genocide, cultural barbarism, and the celebration of military aggression—made it no longer possible to believe in the inevitability of progress or the neutral character of modern technology. "The basis on which technology acquires power over society is the power of those whose economic hold over society is greatest. A technological rationale is the rationale of domination itself. It is the coercive nature of society alienated from itself."[1]

By itself that conclusion was not particularly original. What was striking was the claim accompanying it: that reason and science, the fundamental principles of "the party of humanity," were complicit in the horror of a "relapse into darkest barbarism."[2] Reason and science were not simply instruments exploited by totalitarian regimes but symptoms of a mindset that was continuous with such regimes and set mind against itself. "Enlightenment is totalitarian": that, *in mice*, was the thesis propounded by Horkheimer and Adorno in *The Dialectic of Enlightenment*.[3]

To appreciate the scope of their claim, it is necessary to realize that they intended the term "Enlightenment" to have a far broader reference than the eighteenth-century intellectual movement associated with the French philosophies and Kant. They traced the course of Enlightenment back to antiquity and forward to modern science and to the civilization shaped by capitalism and the cultural values of the bourgeoisie.

Today's reader, one with a postmodern sensibility, for instance, would probably be skeptical of an account whose plausibility seemed to depend upon an exaggerated notion of the power of reason to influence events. Admittedly, German scientists and philosophers probably contributed to the atrocities and aggressions associated with Nazi Germany, that reader might say, but those were individual transgressions and therefore individual actors rather than abstract nouns should be held accountable. Wary of reifications, a postmodern intellectual would doubt that any "cause of reason" existed to be betrayed even by time-serving Nazi intellectuals. More than likely she would be impatient with claims to objectivity of the sort which pre-postmodernity had associated with reason and science. The postmodern is inclined, instead, to a deflated view of reason, treating it as a convention of discourse at best and at worst a rhetorical strategy.

That response, while attractive for its modesty, may be using unpretentiousness as a strategy for deflecting some sensitive questions about the role of the philosophical intellectual. At the height of the Cold War all sorts of people worried that the future of the world might be decided by the use or nonuse of atomic weapons. Perhaps more public intellectuals should have been troubled by the fact that both major world powers employed professional reasoners who were able to give coherent and consistent accounts of why one side should or shouldn't drop the bomb, in retaliation or preemptively, upon the other. Perhaps in a world where peace depended upon the logic of mutually assured destruction (MAD), reason had already been transformed by technical/technocratic requirements.

The transformation might be reconstructed as the double institutionalization of reason. In a technocratic society even reason requires credentials. It must first be certified as professionally qualified by an institution of higher learning, preferably a "research university," as, for example, a doctor of rational choice or a game theorist. Next, reason must be adapted to the culture of government bureaucracies and of quasi-governmental, quasi-corporate think tanks and quasi-academic "centers." Reason emerges outfitted with a distinctive praxis: philosophy as the policy science of the new kingdom of means. The form that reason thus acquires, the political and social locations where it is employed, and the masters that it serves are precisely those which Horkheimer and Adorno had anticipated. "Since Descartes bourgeois philosophy has been a single attempt to make knowledge serve the dominant means of production, broken through only by Hegel and his kind."[4]

The postmodern response—if, indeed, that is what I have been describing—tends to evade the problems initially posed by Horkheimer and Adorno and restated later by Herbert Marcuse. Perhaps this is because the postmodern suspicion of meta-narratives disables it from fully comprehending the shock and disillusionment produced among intellectuals by the collapse of the old humanistic cultures of Germany and Italy into totalitarian regimes and by the transformation of Marxism into Stalinism. Or perhaps the events following the dramatic overthrow of communist regimes have so persuaded intellectuals that liberal capitalism is the true embodiment of the Eternal Return that they can say, along with Richard Rorty, that "Western social and political thought may have had the last *conceptual* revolution it needs."[5] Or perhaps it is because postmoderns have tacitly accepted a role that combines powerlessness and complicity and thereby shields the intellectual from any deep feelings of individual or corporate responsibility toward the systems of power shaping their society.

Where Hobbes and Locke, for example, had conceived reason as the attribute of an individual, indeed, all individuals, the postmodern looks for reason in the "guidelines" prescribed by prestigious institutions (for example, corporate and governmental foundations and academic institutes) and experiences individual reason as institutional recognition/reward for "creativity" or "originality."

II

How was it that in enlightened times unenlightened despotism was possible? That modern despotism was able to incorporate the sciences, the arts, and the professoriat? That intellectuals who had once struggled against the premodern tyrannies now mostly served the interests of avowedly anti-intellectual regimes? That people of reason had come to betray civilized values and the promise of modern science and industry to abolish misery?

The fate of reason in the modern world, Horkheimer and Adorno claimed, could be understood as an act of "self-destruction," long in the making, by the bearers of the Enlightenment rather than simply the result of terrorism and regimentation of the sciences and arts by fascism and communism.[6]

Horkheimer and Adorno proposed a genealogy of reason whose effect was, like Nietzsche's *Genealogy of Morals*, to unsettle philosophy by exposing its complicity with the forces of antiphilosophy. Unlike Nietzsche, however, they sought to retain some semblance of the "traditional" meaning of reason and of philosophy. In pursuing that purpose, they would take a most un-Nietzschean turn toward a will to powerlessness. Determined to rescue theory from power and to preserve a critical distance, they would pose the question of whether the disavowal of power might be a necessary precondition for critical theorizing.

The end point of this particular theoretical journey would be registered in Adorno's later formulation, "The moment to realize [philosophy] was missed ... the attempt to change the world miscarried."[7] The political isolation and weakness of the representatives of theoretical reason was a major theme for Adorno and Horkheimer and in pursuing it they would come to reflect it, even consolidate it. The story they would construct was intended to make intelligible the experience of their times—the era of totalitarianism. It told of a deep, and perhaps fatal, diremption within reason itself. In their account, reason comes to confront its other, but that other turns out to be not unreason but reason itself. Although Horkheimer and Adorno would describe that confrontation as primarily a matter of opposing conceptions of philosophy/theory, their analysis was equally concerned with some of the oldest themes in the history of Western political philosophy/theory: how theoretical knowledge is transformed into power by submitting to certain self-imposed operations that enable it to contribute to the generation of power and the exercise of social control; and why theoretical reason is drawn toward total power, that is, toward an ideal society in which all human activities—from sexual to commercial to intellectual intercourse—are prearranged by reason and enforced by power so that they all "contribute" to some postulated end of goodness, well-being, justice, or piety.

Before I discuss the Frankfurt genealogy of reason and the account of reason's diremption, it is useful to recall that, historically, philosophy's self-appointed role as the guardian of reason was accompanied by sweeping political claims that established the nexus for the technical discussions of the grounds of reason in epistemology, logic, and cosmology/theology. What follows is a brief sketch of the early politics of philosophical reason.

III

Throughout most of its history Western philosophy has adopted reason as its principal totem. It was the so-called faculty of reason that was said to distinguish men from beasts, and even from women and children, as well as from other men who happened to be slaves or idiots. Early on, reason was identified as the peculiar province of philosophy and the special property of philosophers. Other men might have wealth, noble lineage, beauty, or great skill at some worldly occupation, such as fighting, governing, painting, or making shoes, but philosophers announced that what distinguished them from other human beings was that they either possessed or practiced reason or were single-mindedly devoted to acquiring it.

At the same time that philosophers were claiming a special relationship to reason and disagreeing among themselves about its right description, they mostly identified reason with truth, or, more precisely, with universal truths, that is, with truths independent of local time and place and powerful enough to bring harmony to the society that ordered its life in accordance with them. Philosophers assigned to themselves the responsibility of interpreting universal truths.

Within that broad economy of norms, political philosophers developed the more specialized claim that philosophical reason entitled them to judge society. The basis of that claim was the philosopher's alleged "knowledge of the whole." A political society was said to consist of "parts" (for example, classes, occupations, and functions such as war-making). The knowledge of how those parts should be interrelated and arranged so as to serve the "good of all" was a special knowledge that rulers needed but only philosophers possessed. "The law is not concerned with the special happiness of any class in the state but is trying to produce this condition in the city as a whole, harmonizing and adapting the citizens to one another by persuasion and compulsion."[8]

Thus it could be said that, historically, there is a standing quarrel between reason and politics. Political philosophers and theorists constructed political and social paradigms, allegedly on the basis of reason, to serve as models. The extreme case was the construction of "utopias," a word that, significantly, is translated as "nowhere" but could more literally be translated "no place" (topos = place), that is, a construction of reason, a complete whole, universally true because it occupies a timeless space disconnected from any historically configured place. But whether engaged in constructing utopias or developing more sober, political sciencelike constitutional typologies, political philosophers were mimicking in thought what rulers were bent upon doing in practice—ordering and regulating society, shaping it to the needs of power and, perhaps, justice, treating it as a whole made up of parts in need of coordination.

Because the theorist enjoyed greater freedom of construction than real rulers, he could use that advantage to judge existing societies and, almost without exception, he indicted them as unjust, unvirtuous, impious, or benighted. Each of these charges was inspired by the belief that insofar as a society was deficient in justice or piety, it was a defective whole and hence must be deficient in reason. Philosophers could not conceive of societies that were unjust or unvirtuous but rational or, conversely, that were just and virtuous though irrational.[9] And they firmly believed that for societies to be just and rational they had to be ordered totally toward those ends. From Plato to Marx, political philosophers identified the just and virtuous totality with the "realization" of philosophy or, in Plato's formulation, with the philosopher achieving full stature. The salvation of society could not be achieved without the fulfillment of philosophy and the ending of its political alienation. That state of affairs can be described as the rationalization of power and the empowerment of theory. Those who ruled would look to reason, and those who reasoned would look to rule, directly or indirectly.

IV

Horkheimer and Adorno engaged a range of questions very different from the ones posed by most ancient and modern theorists. Theorists had asked, What kind of regime would most effectively serve philosophy so that the latter might inscribe its truths upon society? Horkheimer and Adorno were concerned to inquire into the terms that reason/philosophy would have to inscribe upon itself in order to realize its perennial dreams of power. What kind of discipline, what sort of self-denials would it have to observe in order to serve as a decisive element in the structure of power?

Their answer was that reason would have to offer itself in the service of calculation, self-interest, and self-preservation.[10] It would also have to narrow the range of reason, discarding the centuries-old idea that the truths of reason comprehended and determined the validity of moral beliefs and that philosophy was the final arbiter concerning competing claims as to the meaning of the good life for human beings. Reason would disavow the preoccupation with ends or a summum bonum and turn against that enterprise.[11] It would declare that ends were endless, never final, but tentative, experimental, or perhaps simply emotive and subjective. It would focus upon means and techniques of rational inquiry and rational decision. It would become a technology that Horkheimer and Adorno christened "instrumental reason" and, as such, reason and its theoreticians would cease to be powerless. The latter would be enrolled in a structure of power that was peculiarly modern, both in its exploitation of science for the development of technology for the needs of production and for its totalizing power representing the domination of nature and society by those who controlled economic power.[12]

Horkheimer and Adorno set the problem of reason in a context that was richly suggestive of what we might call archetypal themes in the history of political theory, concerning the relationship of reason to society, of philosophy to reason and to the dominant political powers, and of philosophical reason to political context. In their most influential work, *The Dialectic of Enlightenment*, the emergence of reason in the West is described by a complex interpretation of Homer's *Odyssey*.[13]

Odysseus's encounters with various mythic powers are interpreted as reason struggling to disengage itself from myth but, as we shall see, only half succeeding. The encounters occur in the course of Odysseus's wanderings before the gods will permit him to return to his homeland after the Trojan Wars. Homeland, which also has mythical connotations, stands for reason's return from the world of myth.

The relationship between reason and homeland takes on a special poignancy for Horkheimer and Adorno. They, along with most of the other original members of the Frankfurt school, were involuntary exiles from their native Germany, having fled to avoid the fate of millions of other Jews during the Nazi tyranny. The Nazi suppression of philosophy as a free activity was accompanied by official encouragement of various doctrines that pre-postmodernity had no difficulty in designating as irrational myths: of *Blut und Boden*, *Lebensraum*, a pure Aryan *Volk*, and an inspired *Führer*. But, as the Horkheimer-Adorno construction of the myth of Odysseus attempted to show, reason was infected by myth, yet it could coexist with, even make use of it. Nazism may have suppressed genuine philosophy, but it incorporated reason in its modes of organization, its techniques of mass manipulation, and its development of military strategies. Thus philosophy went into exile, but reason remained at home.

The history of political theory is rich in examples of theorists who have been exiled from their homelands. One thinks of Hobbes fleeing the civil war and revolutionary upheavals of his day; of Locke forced to go abroad because of his close ties with the Shaftesbury opposition to the Stuarts; or of Marx journeying to London in the aftermath of 1848 to escape the police of several countries. Unreason, in their eyes, had taken possession of their homelands. Their exile might be interpreted as the forced substitution of reason for homeland—Plato's "city laid up in heaven." All returned in a literal but not necessarily a theoretical sense, for the dream of philosophy had been to make reason and homeland synonymous. Locke may be said to have fully returned, but not Hobbes and Marx. We may want to pose the question, does continued exile, whether actual or not, cause philosophy to adopt mythical elements as it seeks to preserve its dream of being transformed into power? We shall come back to that question later.

It is now possible to see that the diremption of reason into instrumental and critical reason becomes the means of salvaging a rational element for philosophy, that is, of preserving some version of a union of reason and philosophy. But the difficulty is that philosophy has lost its homeland because instrumental reason has been installed there. Philosophy, in the form of critical reason, is then condemned to permanent exile, to wandering as Odysseus had, to engaging mythical powers and becoming infected by myth but doomed to powerlessness. To wander is to have no context. We might think of exile, therefore, as signifying a certain kind of loss, loss of political context. In a later section I show that the crucial and defining element of theoretical context is political and that philosophical reason has had a troubled relationship with political context.

Turning now to a more detailed examination of instrumental reason, I want to explore both the self-inscribed conditions that philosophy/reason adopts in order to become power and, accordingly, the kind of power that philosophy qua instrumental reason thereby becomes.

V

Latter-day instrumental reason appears, in its self-understanding, as a combination of pragmatism and scientific empiricism, of practical applications founded upon verifiable knowledge. The undeniable triumphs of modern science and the dazzling technologies they have made possible encourage a belief that instrumental reason is the discovery of the true nature of reason and of its only legitimate form.

Critical theory attempts to go behind that claim and expose a mixed genealogy. It proposes to reveal how, through various encounters with the powers of society and nature, instrumental reason has acquired elements of antireason. Reason's genealogy is linked to Greek myths and the Book of Genesis to establish that, as soon as it begins to extricate itself from myth, reason reproduces mythic elements. It gains knowledge of how to preserve the self, how to calculate its interests, but it is unaware that it is mutilating the self, making of it a sacrificial object to the cult of power.[14] Accordingly: "If by enlightenment and intellectual progress we mean the freeing of man from superstitious belief in evil forces, demons and fairies, in blind fate—in short, the emancipation from fear—then denunciation of what is currently called reason is the greatest service reason can render."[15]

Throughout its career reason undergoes various transformations yet never completely expels myth, and in the end the two have become inseparable. Reason, in the practice of positivist science and logical positivist philosophy, reverts to an uncritical attitude that renders its own assumptions mythic even as it declaims the more strongly its fidelity to fact and "reality." For the essence of mythology is the acceptance of the status quo: "cycle, fate, and domination of the world reflected as the truth and deprived of hope." Modern positivist science, with its relentless emphasis upon shaping thought so as to enable it to grasp the facts better, its reproduction of the immediacy of existing facts in the guise of mathematical abstractions, confirms the existing state of things. "The world as a gigantic analytic judgment . . . is of the same mold as the cosmic myth which associated the cycle of spring and autumn with the kidnapping of Persephone." The scientific emphasis upon recurrence and regularities reproduces fatefulness and reveals how, in the guise of discovering the "necessary" laws of nature, "enlightenment returns to mythology."[16]

Although historically instrumental reason first appears in antiquity, its full flowering occurs in the modern era when science and industry are constituted by the dynamic needs of capitalism. It operates from within the assumptions of a social order organized by modern capitalism's conception of production and is structured, therefore, according to a logic in which all relationships are commodified and conceived as exchange relationships. It is, however, a special mark of those who practice instrumental reason that they are largely unaware of how it has been socially constituted, especially in its scientific form. Accordingly, critical theory attacked what it conceived to be the myth of the neutral, impartial observer/investigator, the nonreflexive subject who is trained to divest the self of all cultural influences (= "biases") save those of scientific education. In reality, science and empiricism have produced a socially and politically unconscious being, unaware of whom he is serving or of whom she is helping to exploit.

Instrumental reason is a peculiar combination of passivity and aggressiveness. Politically it is deferential, content in its subordination to political and economic powers, but as applied knowledge or practice it displays a different face. It attacks the natural world as a domain to be conquered and a storehouse of utilities to be exploited. The human world is treated as continuous with the natural and hence as a population of manipulable objects fit for social engineering. Reason's instrumental character is expressed in its aspiration to make the most efficient and effective use of what is in the world within the framework and according to goals defined by the ruling authorities.

Instrumental reason is more than a conception of reason as means. It is an antipolitical way of developing power in the handling of objects, animate as well as inanimate, that qualifies as despotic. Objectification is not so much an epistemological category as the expression of a power impulse. If objects are to be used efficiently and effectively, they must be simplified by being represented solely in terms of features or traits that render them manipulable or exploitable. Accordingly, empirical objects, including human beings, whose varied and variable natural or acquired elements of identity resist use and exploitation, must first be stripped of their culturally constituted identities and then reinstated as abstract entities that are now suited to display the regularity, recurrence, and uniformity requisite for classification. Their histories and biographies are irrelevant to their social and political uses.

As reason becomes increasingly methodized and systematized, philosophy becomes mimetic of what it believes to be science. It becomes dismissive of metaphysical claims and views ethical concerns as being expressive of emotions rather than reason. Truth acquires a literalness, and all dialectical notions concerning the contradictory character of reality are ruled out.[17] As reason becomes radically narrower, a more or less technical mode of discourse identified with various specializations, its scope of application grows ever larger. In the twentieth century it is embodied in and supports a system of universal domination, "an administered world," ruled by "state capitalism."[18] Thus the paradox: as reason grows narrower, more dogmatic, its practical applications multiply exponentially as capitalist societies expand their power over their members toward an ideal limit of totalization in which all human relationships are continuously scrutinized, corrected, and coordinated. "The totalitarian order marks the leap from the indirect to direct forms of domination while still maintaining a system of private enterprise."[19] As reason moves inexorably toward its totalization as technical knowledge, in effect, it leaves no room for critical reason. The philosopher is thus doubly exiled, from both real and ideal homeland.

VI

In a famous essay, "Traditional and Critical Theory" (1937), Max Horkheimer expanded the idea of instrumental rationality into a full-fledged theoretical conception, maliciously dubbed "traditional theory" to emphasize its association with the status quo. Modeled primarily after the dominant logical positivist conception of science, it can be summarized as the reconstitution of reason into a technical tool with a consequent shedding of a critical and substantive/legislative role.

In Horkheimer's account, traditional theory proceeds as though there is nothing problematic in its fundamental notions. For example, it recognizes a "fact" as something that is a "datum" or "there" or "empirically proven." This might be described as "the myth of the given." Instrumental reason dismisses as trivial the complaint that its abstractions are created by wrenching some event or phenomenon from its context, that in ignoring, say, the historical forces, social interests, and ideologies that had shaped a particular fact, reason was not only distorting the fact in question but reconstituting it. Reason proceeds this way because of its role within a system of production. Facts need to be smoothed of their peculiarities so that they may be reintroduced as uniform, regular, or homogenous. Thus processed, facts can be more easily assembled to generate lawlike statements that, in turn, present a manipulable world where practical applications and predictions become a matter of course. Thus epistemic modes mimic capitalist modes: just as capitalism subordinates the worker's personal needs to the objective requirements of production, so the scientist applies reductionist methods to facts in order to dissolve their individual peculiarities and force them to conform to, that is, work on behalf of, some hypothesis.

At one time reason had operated as a critical, even a liberating force, opposing ignorance, superstition, and oppression. But it also undermined the grounds on which, historically, human beings had established value and meaning. Religion was condemned as superstition, ethical and political norms were said to be mostly metaphysical and hence without rational warrant, while the idea of nature as a distinctive realm of value was dismissed as sentimentalism and replaced by a notion of nature as an experimental domain of lawlike regularities that served as the basis of scientific predictions and control.

Having demonstrated that competing modes of knowledge are unscientific alternatives and hence powerless, reason becomes the sole oracle to be consulted when choosing among various means. The criterion that governs choice is, What will be the most effective/efficient way to a particular goal? A rational society would be one in which this mode of thinking was extended to all significant areas. In Horkheimer's formulation, "its features can be summarized as the optimum adaptation of means to ends, thinking as an energy-conserving operation. It is a pragmatic instrument oriented to expediency, cold and sober."[20]

By virtue of its association with science, logical positivism shares vicariously in power. In its explication of instrumental reason, in its verification principle, which dismisses as "metaphysical" or "emotive" all statements that are not scientifically verifiable, logical positivism reveals itself to be the theoretical counterpart to fascism. In insisting that philosophy and science rid its language of all traces of subjectivity, metaphysics, and value, logical positivism displays "the need for a purge [*Sauberung*] to which authoritarian states make the most appalling concessions."[21] Logical positivism allegedly "parallel[s] an attitude to culture which now and then finds practical expression in nationalistic uprisings and the bonfires associated with them."[22]

VII

"Critical theory" was the alternative that Horkheimer developed in the hope of retaining links between philosophy and reason while distinguishing critical from instrumental reason. "It is a critique of philosophy, and therefore refuses to abandon philosophy."[23] The crucial link that joined reason and philosophy and separated critical from instrumental reason was a claim that critical reason/philosophy was the true heir to a tradition in which the ideal of theorizing was inseparable from the idea of a social whole. The attack upon positivism, which Horkheimer and Adorno carried on for more than three decades, depended upon the validity of that idea. They defended critical reason as a superior understanding of the world that instrumental reason was helping to create but could not comprehend. The theoretical superiority of critical theory was attributed to a conception of reason as dialectical in character, grounded in historical self-consciousness, and able to grasp the social totality in all of its interconnectedness, including the connection between positive science and the dominant powers in society.

The theoretical power of critical reason is realized in "comprehensive theoretical statements." "In order to understand the significance of facts or of science generally one must possess the key to the historical situation, the right social theory."[24] In its reliance upon general principles and "conceptual wholes," the critical character of theory was inseparable from a conception of theory as privileged knowledge of social totality.[25] Even in Adorno's postwar writings, with their frequent disclaimers that concepts could be adequate to reality, there are assertions that "theory seeks to give a name to what secretly holds the machinery together."[26]

Critical theory's dialectical mode of thinking reinforced its holism. The contradictions exposed by that were significant because they were systemic.[27] "Within dialectical theory such individual facts always appear in a definite connection which enters into every concept and which seeks to reflect reality in its totality."[28] For the prewar Horkheimer and Adorno, dialectical history meant primarily a Marxian view of the evolution of society in terms of the division of labor, commodified exchange relations, and the domination of society by representatives of those who controlled the means of production.[29] Other Marxian categories, such as class struggle, the role of the proletariat, and the necessity of revolution, became, as I explain, steadily more problematic in the Frankfurt reading.

VIII

However superior critical theory might be because of its grasp of totality, there was a troubling quality about the notion itself. If totality was a fact of capitalist and totalitarian societies, and if critical theory claimed to be able to expose the true nature of that totality, could critical theory be critical without setting out its idea of a "true" totality? And what kind of politics was implied by a commitment to theoretical totality? The issue was not whether critical theory had a utopian vision of its own but whether totality was a proper theoretical project or simply the perpetuation of the mimetic of ruling that theorists had reproduced since antiquity, which suddenly had become ominous because totality was political fact rather than fantasy.

Curiously, Adorno had expressed deep reservations about the concept of totality before he and Horkheimer were forced into exile. His inaugural lecture at the University of Frankfurt in 1931 begins: "Whoever chooses philosophy as a profession today must first reject the illusion that earlier philosophical enterprises began with: that the power of thought is sufficient to grasp the totality of the real."[30] Reason, he argued, cannot discover itself in reality because reality has become hostile to reason. Philosophy itself faces "liquidation" as the sciences, logic, and mathematics carve out their respective domains and dismiss as insignificant what cannot pass scientific scrutiny. If philosophy is to be preserved in a fragmented world, it must concentrate upon "interpretation" rather than "research."[31] Philosophy "must give up the great problems, the size of which once hoped to guarantee the totality" and turn instead to historically concrete questions located in a "text" that is "incomplete, contradictory and fragmentary." Adorno likens philosophy to "riddle-solving" that does not seek to get "behind" the riddle but to "negate" it so that the original question "disappears." Thus the riddle of the essence of commodities is exploded once commodities are analyzed in terms of their place within the structure of exchange.

Theory, Adorno seemed to suggest, could dispense with totality yet continue to guide praxis. Interpretations of "given reality" lead to the "abolition" of that reality. A praxis, he insisted, "follows promptly" from "the annihilation of the question."[32]

Was that formulation, however, an example of what Adorno would later call mythical thinking? One question had not been annihilated: Whose praxis? Horkheimer would write, "the methods, categories as well as the transformation of the theory" require the "taking of sides." "Right thinking depends as much on right willing as right willing on right thinking."[33] Taking sides presented no difficulty to orthodox Marxism. The working class was the chosen instrument of revolutionary praxis, of action whose ultimate objective was the overthrow of the capitalist system. In this formula, action and theory were symmetrical. For each the object was a totality. Theory explained the interconnected nature of the whole system from base to superstructure; revolutionary action would seize power and abolish the old values and institutions and completely reorganize social production.

Totalitarianism rendered that whole schema invalid. Not only had it made the idea of totality repugnant by representing itself as the realization of that idea, but it had incorporated and neutralized the working class. Theory seemed without either subject or object.

IX

Despite Adorno's philosophical misgivings about totality, he and Horkheimer clung throughout the 1930s to a Marxist perspective and its version of social totality. That decision enabled critical reason to avoid the possibility that its own distinction between instrumental and critical reason was a contrast between theory as power and theory as powerlessness. Marx had claimed that his theory was not only aligned with the direction of the most powerful forces ever amassed by human beings—forces that were rapidly converting the entire world into one economic totality—but that theory had discovered in the proletariat the power that was destined to reclaim that productive potential in the name of humanity. The inevitability of a proletarian revolution was linked by Marx to his critique of the laws of political economy.

Once Horkheimer and Adorno came to doubt that either capitalist exploitation or totalitarian oppression would provoke the workers to rebel, a wide range of issues opened up. Perhaps political economy was no longer an adequate description of the site of dialectical tensions and the workers no longer the instrument of revolutionary hopes. Where, if anywhere, was the possibility of revolution located, and who, if anyone, was to be its agent? Or were neither agency nor revolution any longer meaningful? Was theory now required to bear the entire burden of opposition? And if so, in what sense, if any, could theory profess to be a representation of power or to be connected in any meaningful way with social forces predisposed to the cause of radical change? "The theoretician . . . can find himself in opposition to views prevailing even among the proletariat."[34]

While Adorno, in order to survive, ironically found himself compelled to learn the language and practice of positivist social science, Horkheimer attempted to formulate a conception of theory in which the theorist seems peculiarly qualified by his isolation to undertake the role of opposition.[35] Opposition, he wrote, begins naturally: "An active individual of sound common sense perceives the sordid state of the world" and decides to change it. That desire not to submit to things as they are causes him to organize facts, to "shape them into a theory," thereby asserting that the subjective interests of the theorist are "an inherent factor of knowledge," not a disqualification.[36]

Those heroic words, while redolent of power images, are mythic in tendency, as is shown by the remarkable fantasy that follows. Horkheimer describes an imaginary society in which logical positivism and scientific empiricism are associated with a ruthless regime. Because of their view of facts, scientists are inhibited from giving any account of the significance of what is happening to them; they can only describe. If the society were then freed by the efforts of "active groups and individuals" who stood "in a different relation to theory," whose "specific action was contained in their very mode of perception," who, "fastening their eyes on a better life . . . saw through it all," only then would science "admit" that its former consciousness had been false.

Horkheimer then proceeds to fashion a tableau of ultimate vindication in which theory squares its accounts with the proletariat. He pictures the masses confessing their errors: "Indeed, the masses themselves would now realize that what they had formerly said and done, and even what they had thought in secret were perverted and untrue."[37] After castigating the masses for their "blindness" and "passivity" under Nazism, he concludes: "When the thoughtless crowd is mad, thoughtless philosophy cannot be sane."[38]

When Horkheimer, in a major essay of 1937, outlined the essential features of critical theory, he deliberately distanced it from the proletariat. There must be tension and conflict, he argued, between the theorist and "the most advanced sectors of the class . . . his thinking is to serve." The critical theorist, rather than the proletariat, assumes the role of a saving remnant: "In the general historical upheaval the truth may reside with numerically small groups of men. History teaches us that such groups, hardly noticed by those opposed to the status quo, outlawed but imperturbable, may at the decisive moment become the leaders because of their deeper insight. . . . The future of humanity depends on the existence today of the critical attitude."[39]

Adorno would supply the epitaph to theory's alliance with the workers. It read simply: "opposition to production."[40] The break with the proletariat also meant the loss of a political context, the context of revolutionary politics as defined by Marx and his successors. Adorno and Horkheimer refused to recontextualize their politics around the fate of democratic politics. They made no effort to develop a theoretical defense of even the troubled form of it in the liberal regime of Weimar or, later, the more robust social democratic politics of New Deal America.[41]

Declaring that "the might of industrial society is lodged in men's minds," Horkheimer and Adorno, especially the latter, began to explore the various ways in which popular culture was being manipulated to serve the ends of domination.[42] Adorno's picture of the masses reflects a mood of betrayal: they are portrayed as passive and, literally, mindless. There is not the trace of a suggestion that some popular cultures exist independent of mass audiences and may even be oppositional. There is, instead, a ressentiment against the masses, as though philosophy were chagrined at having been duped by Marxism into romanticizing the virtue of the oppressed. It was harshly expressed in a pensée by Adorno titled "They, the People": "But the moment simple folk are forced to brawl among themselves for their portion of the social product, their envy and spite surpass anything seen among literati or musical directors."[43]

Cultural critique, whatever its insights into the shaping of mass consciousness, proved a weak replacement for Marx's political economy. Marx's analysis, whatever its shortcomings, gives a plausible motive for the working class to rise up against its oppressors: misery, impoverishment, and the mechanization of labor are credible reasons for revolt. Cultural critique, in contrast, depicts an empty vessel, masses with no culture to lose, no motive for revolt. Critical reason has culminated in a theory about a nonrevolutionary subject.

X

"The truth becomes clearly evident in the person of the theoretician."[44] Horkheimer's brave formula represented an epitaph to philosophy's attempt to retrieve a measure of reason and power, but, in reality, critical theory ends in self-confessed powerlessness, surrendering one purchase point after another. It began by identifying critical theory with a power to grasp wholes; it ended with Adorno renouncing collectivity altogether—"the whole is the untrue"—and seeking to defend what was particular, individual, and, above all, negative against "totalitarian unity" in the postwar world.[45] Once it had declared for the close union of theory and practice, but later it gave up on the idea of developing a social praxis for fear that it would lead to embracing instrumentalism. The more isolated theory became, the more defiant its assertions of superiority over praxis. In Marcuse's words, "Theory will preserve the truth even if revolutionary practice deviates from its proper path. Practice follows the truth, not vice versa."[46]

In the postwar world critical theory would "demand support for the residues of freedom, and for tendencies toward true humanism," but that ultimatum was issued without regard to any political context and in the knowledge that these "residues" and "tendencies seem powerless in regard to the main course of history."[47] Philosophy is declared saved precisely because it has failed to be realized. As Adorno's famous epigram states, "philosophy, which once seemed obsolete, lives on because the moment to realize it was missed."[48] Theory becomes "thought as action," its own homeland, its praxis devoted to eluding dialectical completion.[49]

XI

Horkheimer and Adorno returned in triumph. They were welcomed by the postwar West German government, and their institute was reestablished to general and warm acclaim. Yet there is also a sense in which they, Adorno especially, never fully returned. In *Minima Moralia*, subtitled "Reflections from Damaged Life," Adorno referred to the "intellectual in migration" as if describing a permanent condition.[50] Although Nazi totalitarianism had been defeated, they felt that domination by state capitalism was as strong as ever, if not stronger. The Second World War seemed less a victory of liberal democracy than the repulse of the first primitive reconnaissance of instrumentalist totality. Where Nazism had exploited technology in the interests of propaganda, capitalism was using it to fashion a popular culture that would reinforce the psychology of domination without the rough hand of terror. "The development toward total integration recognized in this book has been interrupted but not abrogated. It threatens to advance beyond dictatorships and wars."[51]

As the influence of technology was clamped more heavily on the culture of mass society and as other intellectual disciplines rushed to imitate natural science and exploit its prestige, the presence of scientific reason seemed ubiquitous in public and private bureaucracies, academic institutions, think tanks, and private life. While reason had thus become more firmly incorporated into the status quo and could rule by police but without a police state, the life of the mind remained in exile. The shape of reason, as Adorno saw it, had to be a "negative dialectics," its task to defend "difference," individuality, and what remained of high culture.[52]

That philosophy should find uncongenial and threatening a world dominated by reason, especially scientific reason, seems ironical and is a reminder of the tense relationship that has existed historically between philosophical reason and politics. In retrospect, *The Dialectic of Enlightenment* and other works by Adorno and Horkheimer appear as an extended meditation on philosophy's experience of exile and inevitably evoke the memory of Socrates, philosophy's martyr to politics. While the condemnation of Socrates by democratic Athens might symbolize the rejection of philosophy by the political, the decision of Socrates to refuse exile from the city and instead to submit to its judgment seems a puzzling choice. Did it signify the submission of the political to philosophy, or was it a statement about the tensions?

XII

Recall that in the *Crito* Socrates has been sentenced to death for subverting the laws of Athens, encouraging atheism, and corrupting the youth of the city.[53] He is entreated by his friends to escape punishment by going abroad, where he could continue to practice philosophy. In his response Socrates does not defend philosophy against the city but rather defends the city, arguing against his friends who regard the judgment of the city as inferior to the value of perpetuating philosophy. Socrates says he will not leave the city, which has nurtured him, nor subvert its laws by evading the judgment of the court. He not only refuses the life of exile but, in a pointed reference to the association of theorizing and traveling or journeying, proudly recalls that he has never left the city, save for military service.[54]

When Socrates defended himself before the Athenian democracy, according to Plato's *Apology*, he defiantly declared that, if given a choice of dying or desisting from philosophizing in public or of going into exile in another city, he would choose death. One reason Socrates advances for his refusal is that the god has "attached me to this city to perform the office of gadfly."[55] What makes Socrates's claim to a public office so striking is that it is accompanied by repeated disclaimers of ever having taken part in the politics of the city. The claim points to a kind of political practice proper to theory that is not the practice of politics but nonetheless explicitly presupposes it.

Socrates's refusal raises the question, If philosophy is identified with the rational pursuit of truth, why cannot the philosopher be anywhere as long as he is not persecuted? If reason is the quest for what is universally true, isn't that pursuit indifferent to context and hence essentially apolitical? Or is political theorizing different from philosophizing precisely because it needs a local politics, a homeland?

Let me interpret Socrates as saying that exile is the worst of fates for a theorist because it decontextualizes theoretical activity, freeing it of political ties and referents. Exile is analogous to the abstract form that theory assumes when it disavows a historically specific context. Because the exile is forced to become an alien in the double sense of being alienated from a "native" land and feeling alienated in a foreign land, she would have to resume theory in a "nonplace," exiled from the civic understandings that supply frames of reference to theoretical expressions. Theorizing requires a civic setting, not just any place but a particular one to which theorizing is attached by deep ties that, in the fundamental sense, are political without being mere politics. As Socrates's formula, it is to care more for "the polis itself" than for "the things of the polis."[56] That is, the ties are those defining and perpetuating a culture of shared understandings and practices that is no one's property and everyone's contribution. It is created by a variety of callings and skills and sustained by an implicit goodwill among the members. At the same time, however, a civic community, if it is to survive, must develop a structure of power and with that comes the likelihood of abuse and misuse of power.

In such a civic context the "office" of theory is, as Socrates claimed, to serve as the gadfly or critic of the dominant structures of power. The objective is not to criticize actors or policies, at least not directly, but to examine the lives of individuals because those lives embody cultural norms that indirectly constitute the politics of the society and contextualize it. The theorist cannot adopt the politics of those establishments without betraying his vocation. And this must not be done because power shares with reason the same temptation of wanting to be rid of the constraints of context: power wants to be omnipotent, reason wants to be omniscient.

On this reading, theory is dependent on a preexisting political context, and it is unnatural for it not to be. The unnatural is the abstract. It is unnatural because it entices thought into a realm where it is beholden to nothing except its own rules. Context is the conceptual trace of civic membership; it is theorizing as citizenship. It means not just objectively taking account of things or practices that have diverse origins and competing rationales but subjectively responding to them. Context works to soften, to tone down, even to exact an element of humility from the self, which recognizes that it is a multiplicity of debts to others, including those it could never have known. The recognition of context is political reason honoring its debts.

Instrumental reason, in the form of technology, is impatient with context and strives to be independent. The extraordinary achievements of technology have elevated one type of reasoning to archetypal status. Technology stands not just as new inventions or processes but for a culture of technical competencies. It is a culture that claims to be both *technē* and *logos*, skill and reason. Contemporary politics, with its reliance upon the mass media, media consultants, and pollsters; contemporary attempts to reduce politics to policy and to make policy the subject of the technical reasoning of economists, philosophers of public policy, and theorists of business management have all contributed to the depreciation and dismissal of more modest, more democratic notions of *technē* and *logos*. The fatal turn was present from the beginning.

One of the most striking passages in the *Apology*, hurried past by many readers, is where Socrates recalls how he had questioned a number of Athenians reputed to be wise or knowledgeable—politicians, sophists, poets, and persons of "great reputation." He concluded that "others who were supposed to be their inferiors were much better qualified in practical intelligence." Socrates then says that finally he turned to "skilled craftsmen" and was not disappointed. They proved to have a genuine kind of wisdom.[57]

In praising the practical intelligence of social inferiors and the wisdom of skilled craftsmen, Socrates was, I am suggesting, paying tribute to the importance of forms of competence that embody reason, not pure reason but reason as culturally embedded: making a shoe in Appalachia is not like making a shoe in Beverly Hills. But he was also saying something as striking in its way as Plato's very un-Socratic formula about philosophers as kings. He was calling attention to the competence of ordinary beings, the praxis that arises from reflection on experience, that is transmitted by a culture, and that represents the power resident in the technologies of everyday life.

However, no sooner had Socrates made this discovery than he limited its importance by saying that, although the skilled craftsmen possessed a form of genuine knowledge, they wrongly insisted upon applying it to other areas where they lacked competence. Clearly Socrates was alluding to the politics of democratic Athens, where, in the public assemblies and law courts, ordinary citizens pronounced on the weightiest of public issues. In Plato's *Republic* we know that such intrusions into the political councils of the city were to be forbidden. That general prohibition against political participation by the demos was not the simple conclusion to a claim about the superiority of expert knowledge over alleged ignorance. It was a political strategy by which philosophy chose to ally itself with kings and aristocrats, the most powerful elements in the community. That choice meant siding with exclusionary forms of politics and using philosophy's claim to know the true foundation of political life to justify an even more exclusive politics, so exclusive that politics disappears from Plato's city. The philosopher had chosen to destroy politics to save philosophy/reason.

As is usually the case, the best critic of Plato is Plato. In the *Protagoras* the sophist Protagoras defends the proposition that the skills needed to run a city are part of a human capability for sharing in justice and a moral sense. These can be acquired, Protagoras claimed, through "deliberate choice, and by practice and teaching." It, too, is a *technē* that can be taught and learned. And when it is, Protagoras insisted, then "your fellow citizens are right to accept the advice of smiths and cobblers on political matters." Without it, he declares, there is no sharing and hence no political association.[58]

Technē, we might say, is thus not the monopoly of technology or other technical applications of reason. The human capability for acquiring skills is not like the philosopher's claim to knowledge, the basis for a claim to power that excludes other claims. It is, instead, a claim that people cannot share in justice unless they share power. In our own day Protagoras's case has, if anything, gained even greater urgency. The growth of state power in advanced technological societies has been accompanied and promoted by the claims of technical reason, as in rational choice theory and its related methodologies and in the bureaucratization of expertise. These developments represent an attempt to make political *technē* the monopoly of governing elites while reducing the possibilities of a more democratized *technē* to the form of hiring its own technical reasoners to oppose governmental and corporate experts.

The danger to the political life of society posed by the dominance of a technological order does not come primarily from the incorporation of reason into the structure of that order, but rather from the incorporation of the philosopher. By "philosopher" I mean anyone whose vocation is the critical nurturing of public values. One of the virtues of democracy is that philosophers haven't liked it. Until late modernity, no defense of democracy was written by any philosopher or political theorist. The reason is apparent: the tradition of philosophy has wanted power to privilege reason. That tradition is now riding high, as philosophers, their protégés, and progeny come to occupy prominent places in public life. It is democratic reason, not philosophical reason, that is in opposition.

CHAPTER 11

HANNAH ARENDT

DEMOCRACY AND THE POLITICAL

THE QUESTION OF DEMOCRACY is not one that has received much attention from those who have written about Hannah Arendt. This omission seems understandable because Arendt herself never systematically addressed the topic in any of her writings. Yet it is not difficult to show that many of the major categories that compose and distinguish her political outlook were either critical of or incompatible with democratic ideas. This I believe to be the case with the distinction on which her political ideals were grounded, the distinction between "the political" and "the social." Her critical attitude toward democracy rested on a correct intuition that the impulse of democracy has been to override that distinction. For historically, democracy has been the means by which the many have sought access to political power in the hope that it could be used to redress their economic and social lot. The "natural" state of society contains important distinctions of wealth, birth, and education that are typically extended into political power. Thus social power is translated into political power which is then used to increase social power. Democracy is the attempt of the many to reverse the natural cycle of power, to translate social weakness into political power in order to alleviate the consequences of what is not so much their condition as their lottery.

Democracy would also obliterate these Arendtian distinctions because it wants to extend the broad egalitarianism of ordinary lives into public life. It is at odds with the emphasis on authority, ambition, glory, and superiority that figured so importantly in Hannah Arendt's conception of authentic political action. It was not accidental that she excluded the sentiments of fellow-feeling—compassion, pity, love—from the political realm, or, more important, that she was silent about "friendship" (so central to her ancient Greeks) and "fellowship" (so basic to Hebraic and Christian conceptions of community). These democratic sentiments and virtues do not accord with the agonistic conception of action she extolled. Democratic action is, perforce, collective; its mode is cooperation; and its presupposition is not a small audience of heroes but shared experience.

In what follows I propose to explore the origins of the antidemocratic strain in Arendt's thought, tracing it from its beginnings in her classic study of totalitarianism to its apogee in her next major work, *The Human Condition*. Then I want to show that in her later writings a change is evident. It appeared first in the last chapter of *On Revolution* (1963) and more strikingly in the collection of essays, *Crises of the Republic* (1969). While on the way to what can fairly be described as a leftward position, she modified some of her most characteristic categories. Within limits, and in her own way, she was in the course of reflecting upon the political events of the 1960s, radicalized.

Hannah Arendt's first major work, *The Origins of Totalitarianism* (1951), was completely silent about democracy. Although *prima facie* there seems to be no necessary reason why an analysis of totalitarianism should discuss democracy, the historical and political context of the subject matter and the book suggest otherwise. The book was written in the immediate aftermath of World War II. During the war years in the United Kingdom, the British Commonwealth, the United States, and in a significant part of Nazi-occupied Europe, the single, most universal theme that set the interpretation of the war in the minds of ordinary people everywhere was of a struggle between "democracy" and "dictatorship." The books, newspapers, magazines, radio, and movies of the time conveyed a pretty unanimous viewpoint that the nature of totalitarianism was to be grasped almost entirely in terms of the political antitheses between democracy and totalitarianism: between democratic freedom of speech and education and totalitarian thought-control and mass manipulation; between democracy's system of free political parties and government by consent and the totalitarian one-party state with its use of terror and intimidation.

While it would be an exaggeration to argue that the *Origins of Totalitarianism* reversed the accepted perspective, it is no overstatement to say that the work adopted a viewpoint that interpreted totalitarianism by means of categories that were drawn from intellectual traditions that were deeply antidemocratic. One tradition was associated with Nietzsche, the other with Tocqueville. A fundamental category of both traditions was the "mass." For Nietzsche democracy was primarily the political expression of the atomistic, unheroic, security-loving culture which had emerged after the defeat of the agonistic, aristocratic political culture of antiquity by the slave morality of Christianity. "The democratic movement," Nietzsche wrote, "is not only the form of the decay of political organization, but a form of the decay, namely, the diminution, of man, making him mediocre and lowering his value."[1]

Tocqueville, whose general influence on Arendt, particularly in her understanding of the founding of the American republic and of the nature of the French Revolution, has not been fully appreciated, not only anticipated Nietzsche's nostalgia for a politics on a heroic scale,[2] but was the first nineteenth-century theorist to revive the ancient notion that certain forms of tyranny might have a popular basis.[3] Tocqueville envisioned "an immense protective power," operating benignly rather than brutally, that "hinders, restrains, enervates, stifles, and stultifies" by "a network of petty complicated rules" that "covers the whole of social life." Democratic "equality," Tocqueville held, "has prepared men for all this," encouraging them to pursue "petty and banal pleasures," to "exist in and for himself," isolated and politically passive.[4]

The echoes of these writers can be heard in the main themes of Arendt's analysis of totalitarianism. "Totalitarian movements," she wrote, "depended less on the structurelessness of a mass society than on the specific conditions of an atomized and individualized mass."[5] "Mass man" was characterized by "isolation and lack of normal social relationships" caused in part by "the breakdown of the class system."[6] Totalitarian movements, she continued, were built on "sheer numbers" of "indifferent people . . . who never before had appeared on the political scene."[7] Totalitarian leaders, such as Hitler and Stalin, "had the confidence of the masses" and enjoyed "indisputable popularity."[8] The triumph of totalitarian movements, she concluded, shattered the "illusion" that the existence of "democracy" had been made possible because the majority had taken an active part and had positively supported democratic government. In reality the majority had been indifferent. This proved that "a democracy could function according to rules which are actively recognized by only a minority." Insofar as democracy rested on the masses at all, it had rested "on the silent approbation and tolerance of the indifferent and inarticulate sections of the people." The moral was that while democratic freedoms might be defined in terms of formal, legal equality, they were viable "only where the citizens belong to or are represented by groups or form a social and political hierarchy," that is, where there was political and social inequality.[9]

The Origins concluded with a warning, that unless human beings resolved to undertake a fresh political start (a "planned beginning of history") that would include the creation of "a new polity," the future was bleak. "There are plenty of indications that the mob . . . will take over and destroy where we were unable to produce."[10]

She undertook that project herself in The Human Condition (1958), and offered her conception of a new beginning that would furnish the ground for withstanding the masses. There was little in the Origins that would have prepared a reader for the archaic vision of "a new polity" that was inspired by the version of pre-Socratic Hellenism associated with Nietzsche and Heidegger. The Human Condition did not present a sketch of a political constitution as Plato had done, but it did offer, in the Platonic sense, an "idea" that embodied an ideal. And like Plato's, her ideal owed virtually nothing to the facts of history and only slightly more to the history of political ideas. "The political" was the ideal. The intention behind it was to combat a different version of the masses than the one which had figured in her analysis of totalitarianism. Although "mass society" remained the danger, the analysis was focused on the phenomenon of "labor" and on the transformation of society and politics effected by the modern emphasis upon productivity and economic growth. These and other notions were assembled under the idea of "the social"; and behind that idea was her main opponent, Karl Marx, who symbolized the destruction of the Western tradition of politics.

Arendt's conception of "the political" had several aspects. It signified not a state or a society but a determinate public space, a forum, an agora, set aside, jealously defended so that those men who wished to test themselves by the highest standards of excellence might compete, by speech and action, in the presence of their peers. It was to be a politics of lofty ambition, glory, and honor, unsullied by private interest of the material concerns in the larger society "outside": a politics of actors rather than citizens, agonistic rather than participatory, encouraging qualities that would enable men to stand out rather than to take part of, share (participation = *pars* [part] + *capio* [seize]). It was a combination of Periclean democracy, idealized so as to expunge the democratic elements of law courts and assemblies, and an Homeric assembly from which the merest suggestion that a Thersites might arise to "quarrel with kings" (*Iliad* 2.211–78) had been removed.

It is difficult to exaggerate either the severity with which she drew boundaries around the political in order to separate it from the banality and low concerns of ordinary life, or the historical distortions which had to be introduced in order to claim for her construct the authority of the Greeks. Among the distortions she ignored the acute class conflicts that were a familiar feature of the Greek city-states and had generated continuous pressure for the broadening of citizenship and for the enlargement of political access so that excluded social elements might enjoy the benefits of political membership. As a result she gave us a politics without the divisive conflicts that have presented the main challenge to politicians, just as she had given us what was said to be a Greek-inspired conception of action but without analyzing the vital place accorded violence and war in Greek conceptions of the *polis* and of noble action.

In the same bowdlerizing vein, she made no mention of the periodic efforts, as early as the Solonic land reforms, to expand the meaning of equality (*isonomia*) so as to include a socioeconomic content and not just an equality of formal legal rights.[11] So insistent was she that political equality had to be confined among the few that she tried to maintain that the "real" meaning of equality as understood by the Greeks had not to do with fair treatment or even with equal rights but with a condition in which the individual was free because he was neither a ruler (or superior) nor a subject (or inferior).[12] In support of this interpretation she claimed that "the whole concept of rule and being ruled . . . was to be prepolitical and to belong to the private rather than the public sphere."[13] The claim is, however, flatly contradicted by Aristotle's familiar definition that "citizens, in the common sense of the term, are all who share in the civic life of ruling and being ruled."[14]

The fragility of her ideal was underlined by the condition which it required. A politics devoted to the production of memorable actions had to be not only exclusive but subsidized. The ancient Athenians had compromised their democracy by excluding slaves, resident aliens, workers, and women, that is, practically the entire work force of the *polis*. Arendt accepted this notion and dressed it out by adopting Aristotle's justification that these human activities were "functions" which embodied the metaphysical principle of "necessity," that is, they were necessary to sustaining human life and, by extension, the collective life of the *polis*. But because these forms of "labor" were bound endlessly to produce and reproduce the means of life, and because the fate of the products and services was to be consumed and thus to pass away without trace, and because the laborer depended on employers or masters, the activities were unfree, without choice or lasting significance. Parenthetically, one might note that this contrast between "freedom" and "necessity" was comparable to the one developed by Marx, but, unlike Marx, Arendt wanted to preserve necessity rather than develop a complex strategy, as Marx did, for exploiting it, overcoming it, and consorting with it. For Arendt freedom resided essentially in the political realm where men could exercise choice. In her eyes, Marx's exaltation of labor, his claim that it should constitute the principle around which society should be reorganized, represented an inversion of the true hierarchy of values. It meant enshrining an activity that was essentially mindless, routinized, and repetitious in place of political action with its drive for the unpredictable and memorable deed. "The art of politics teaches men how to bring forth what is great and radiant. . . . Greatness . . . can only lie in the performance itself and neither in its motivation nor its achievement."[15] Labor, on the other hand, entails a form of sociability that involves "the actual loss of all awareness of individuality and identity." The "*animal laborans*" is marked by "an incapacity for distinction and hence for action and speech."[16]

The distinctive nature of the political or public realm was developed by the contrasts which Arendt drew between it and the concept of "the social." The latter signified all of the activities and relationships which, by nature, were "private." They included work and labor, love, sex, family, and household. These, she contended, were matters that could not withstand the glare of publicity that attends all political actions without being distorted or perverted. Private things, such as labor, "material concerns," and "bodily functions," should remain "hidden."[17]

The crisis of modernity is that the political realm has been invaded by the social realm, especially by private economic interests and private values of consumption and pleasure. The most dangerous invader is the mass whose power has increased with the growth of conformity. The value of equality has been realized in the fact of sameness. Politics has given way to administration as bureaucracies regulate daily life and render it more uniform. The triumph of necessity, and of the labor-principle that embodies it, is realized in the form of a society dedicated to the ignoble ideal of mere life. She described that society in a passage that is pure Nietzsche: "Society is the form in which the fact of mutual dependence for the sake of life and nothing else assumes public significance and where the activities connected with sheer survival are permitted to appear in public."[18]

In retrospect *The Human Condition* seems a work that is highly suggestive at the margins of its chosen problems and irrelevant, even misleading, at its center. There are marvelously perceptive comments about the nature of action and of work, but the main construct, "the political," could not carry the burden assigned to it. This was because two of the most fundamental political problems were either ignored or treated superficially: power and justice. Power, she declared, "exists only in its actualization." It "springs up between men when they act together and vanishes the moment they disperse. . . . Power is to an astonishing degree independent of material factors."[19]

This formulation was fully consistent with her discussion of work, labor, technology, and private property which never succeeded in grasping the basic lesson taught not only by Marx but by the classical economists as well, that an economy is not merely work, property, productivity, and consumption: it is a structure of power, a system of ongoing relationships in which power and dependence tend to become cumulative, and inequalities are reproduced in forms that are ever grosser and ever more sophisticated. It is a system of power whose logic contains no inherent principle of justice, and it is doubtful that, in the absence of the devoted labors of philosophers over the past two decades, it would have ever acquired one. But justice was not discussed by Arendt at all; it simply did not figure for her as it had for Plato and Aristotle, as the main objective of political action.

Arendt's silence about justice was related to another extraordinary omission: the state. That one could claim to have a politics without discussing the state is perhaps the result of her Greek starting point. As is well-known, the concept of the state does not make an appearance until the early sixteenth century. Its absence, both in theory and practice, allowed her attention to be focused on the political actor and action itself to be treated in dramaturgical terms, with not much attention given to institutional constraints, to the difficulties of "action-at-a-distance," and to the dependence of actors upon their own instrumentalities. When the modern state appears and acquires its centralized apparatus of power, the actor anticipates the fate of the contemporary author in a structuralist critique: the text no longer needs him. The presence of the state has even more important consequences for ordinary citizens. It represents not only the greatest concentration of coercive power in history, and it not only demands obedience, but it asks for loyalty, even affection, from its subjects. The conditions which the modern state requires—enormous revenues, a managed economy and labor force, a huge military establishment, ever-more lethal instruments of violence, a vast bureaucracy, and a compliant citizenry that will produce legitimation upon demand—make it increasingly plain that the "democratic state" has become a contradiction in terms.

* * *

On Revolution (1963) saw Arendt exchanging the paradigm of Athens for the early American republic, the agonal actor of Homer for the revolutionary of 1776, and Pericles for John Adams. Many of the categories developed in *The*

Human Condition were retained, particularly the dichotomy between the "political" and the "social" with its antidemocratic and even antipolitical implications. Now, however, the opposition between the political and the social was developed by means of a contrast between the two great eighteenth-century revolutions, the American, which was guided by an authentic political impulse, and the French, which catalyzed the "many" who, since antiquity, had remained outside history, that is, the history of memorable actions. The French Revolution marked the moment when those who had been hidden away in the lower depths of society had suddenly erupted. "This multitude, appearing for the first time in broad daylight, was actually the multitude of the poor and the downtrodden, whom every century before had hidden in darkness and shame."[20] It was as though, she continued, "the slaves and resident aliens [of antiquity], who formed the majority of the population without ever belonging to the people, had risen and demanded an equality of rights."[21] Themselves preoccupied with their "needs," they generated a type of physical "necessity" from their own "misery" and unleashed it upon public space. Thus out of a primal necessity revolution emerged, not as the inspired action of a desperate people unable to secure redress for their grievances, but as an "irresistible process," a necessity so overpowering as to defy human control, and hence signifying—as necessity always does—the denial of freedom.[22]

In the American Revolution, she maintained, "the exact opposite took place."[23] The Americans conducted a genuinely political revolution, one that "concerned not the order of society but the form of government." Among the reasons for the difference, as Tocqueville had argued before her, was nature's bounty rather than colonial virtue. Although there was "poverty," there was little of the "misery" and "want" that would later goad the *sansculottes* to revolt. At the same time there was just the right amount of deprivation to discourage improper political aspirations. The majority of colonists, she noted approvingly, being occupied with "continuous toil," "would [be] automatically exclude[d] . . . from active participation in government."[24] Acknowledging that while misery may not have been the lot of the white majority, it may have been the experience of the black slaves, she insisted that the main point was that "the social question" was absent from revolutionary America "and with it, the most powerful and perhaps the most devastating passion motivating revolutionaries, the passion of compassion."[25] The demands of the miserable that the political order remedy their distress could fall on sympathetic ears in Europe because moderns had come to feel compassion, not because there was any widespread belief that social and economic opportunities ought to be open to all. "The game of status-seeking," she wrote in a passage that is simply historically untrue, "was entirely absent from the society of the eighteenth and nineteenth centuries."[26] And with a fine Nietzschean aside she chided contemporary social scientists for believing that "the lower classes have, as it were, a right to burst with resentment, greed, and envy."[27]

Although Arendt was full of praise for the Framers of the American Constitution for having succeeded in giving lasting institutional form to revolution, something which most modern revolutionists have failed to do, her account of the Constitution displayed again her antipathy toward material questions, in this case, the economic motives of the Founding Fathers, even though many of the founders were not hesitant to argue them openly in public space, as it were. By ignoring these matters her account of the Constitution left uninterpreted the drive for centralization, the determination to curb the power of the colonial legislatures, and the Hamiltonian vision of a national economy presided over by a strong state. Her failure to recognize that the Founders were more concerned to halt the democratic social movement that had captured some of the state legislatures and initiated economic legislation favoring small farmers and that their own plans included a capitalist's version of the social question returns to undercut the proposals for a new conception of the political—or rather, a new embodiment—advanced toward the end of *On Revolution*.

She criticized the Framers for having introduced a system of representative government which meant that "the people are not admitted to the public realm." She charged the Constitution with having caused the withering of the "revolutionary spirit" because it had failed "to incorporate the townships and the town-hall meetings, the original springs of all political activity in the country" into the new political order.[28] Her charge, however, merely accused the Framers of what they openly avowed. The new national government, as its architects made clear, had to break the monopoly which state and local institutions had on the affections of the people.[29] Incorporating local institutions was not something the Founders failed to do; it ran counter to their political vision. They made the Constitution into a triumph of state-sponsored capitalism, an elite version of the "social question" which included the defense of property rights, the encouragement of a national economy through currency reforms, tariffs, taxation, commercial policies, state subsidies, a military power able to extend American commerce, and an enlightened bureaucracy to nurture infant industries. The vision of the Founders was national rather than local, expansive rather than stationary. Consequently, for Arendt to praise the Founders for having kept the rabble and their social concerns from invading public space, and then to tax that same elite for being insensitive to the value of local participatory institutions was to strain at a gnat and swallow the camel.

Arendt's criticism of the Framers was an expression of her unease at the spectacle presented by modern representative government and its system of political parties: they had made politics the monopoly of a professional elite and closed it off to natural elites who are inspired, not by careers, but by genuine love of politics. Her solution was to resurrect an obscure proposal advanced by Jefferson in a private letter written nearly a quarter century after the ratification of the Constitution. Jefferson had envisaged a system of "elementary republics" located in the wards, counties, and states and forming a "graduation of authorities," each with a share of power, that would serve to check and balance each other.[30] Although Jefferson's proposal suffered from some of the same shortcomings as ancient Greek democracy in making no provision for the political admission of women, slaves, and aliens, there were genuinely democratic features to it. "Every man in the State" was to be "an acting member of the Common government, transacting in person" according to "his competence." Each would thus feel himself to be "a participator in the government of affairs, not merely at an election one day in the year, but every day."[31]

Arendt then proceeded to integrate Jefferson's proposal with a tradition of participation which extended back to the likes of the Committees of Correspondence during the American Revolution and forward to the revolutionary councils and committees that had sprung up spontaneously with the outbreak of revolutions. She found them in the French Revolution, the Paris Commune of 1871, the Russian revolutions of 1905 and 1917, and the Hungarian Revolution of 1956. And doubtless she would have included the Solidarity movement in contemporary Poland.

Most of these examples fulfill her exacting criteria of heroic politics and spontaneous appearance. Whether they were purely political and unmarred by social and economic objectives may be more contestable. But granting their importance, it may still be the case that the fact of their existence casts doubt on her entire thesis concerning the corrupting effects of the social question, of material misery upon the capacity of ordinary citizens to act in a genuinely political way. If modern societies were mass societies, how is it possible for ordinary citizens to escape the deadening effects of routinized labor and the corruptions of consumer society and to display an appetite for politics and political action? How is it possible, first, to congratulate the elites for keeping the masses at bay and, then, to welcome these committees and councils as "the political elite of the people"? Arendt did not attempt to answer the question, but it is not difficult to find a plausible explanation, although it involves getting behind the "darkness" which Arendt repeatedly found to be surrounding the lives of laboring people. Thanks to social historians and cultural anthropologists we learn that the poor are not without rich cultures of their own. Once this is appreciated their capacity to act ceases to be inexplicable and the suspicion arises that the concept of the "mass" may be of limited utility. It may even be primarily an intellectual conceit, a displacement of the intellectual's resentment at what capitalist culture does to the status of intellectuals: It restricts "high culture" to the few and then subsidizes the intellectual to protect the few from the cultural banality of capitalism.

Arendt's indifference, to put it blandly, to the culture of ordinary and poor citizens produced a severely impoverished notion of the historical meaning of the political. Here I have in mind what has been one of the most important, perhaps the most important, sources of the popular understanding of a wide range of political notions, such as equality, justice, community, authority, and

power. The historical contribution of Western religions to the political education of ordinary and poor people is almost impossible to exaggerate. Religion
supplied a first hand experience in what it meant to be a member of a community, to sacrifice and share, to be an object of power, to make not just promises
but commitments of long duration, to refuse to conform for conscience's sake,
and, not least, to found new communities.

At the end of *On Revolution* there was an element of pathos to Arendt's project. Beyond extolling the value of these new forms of elitism, nothing is said
about how they might be maintained because institutionalizing them would
destroy the spontaneity which was an essential element of their political au-
thenticity. Their appearance, therefore, is accepted as one would accept the inexplicable workings of Divine Grace. These elites are "chosen by no one," they
constitute themselves. "Politically they are the best and it is the task of good
government and the sign of a well-ordered republic to assure them of their rightful place in the public realm." "To be sure," she added, the recognition of these
elites "would spell the end of general suffrage" for recognition would mean that
the elite had won "the right to be heard in the conduct of the business of the
republic," and that they cared "for more than their private happiness." As for
those who would be excluded, they had not only chosen their fate by remaining
passive, but they had, unconsciously, affirmed "one of the most important negative liberties we have enjoyed since the end of the ancient world, freedom from
politics."[32]

This last remark illustrates Arendt's profound equivocality about politics, an
equivocality that led her to welcome spontaneous political action but to distrust
action when the stakes became so large as to threaten to incorporate the concerns that are located closer to or within "private" life. She wanted a pure form
of politics, one that was consistent with the claim that "power is to an astonishing degree independent of material factors."[33] Political institutions, she declared
flatly, should be made independent of economic forces.[34] It was her vision of
pure politics that led her during the late 1960s to oppose the Viet Nam War, to
defend civil disobedience, to criticize the involvement of universities in the war
business, and, within limits, to welcome some aspects of the student protest
movements. In all of these commitments one can see a common element: a support of actions that were primarily political, or at least could be seen that way,
and without economic motives or broad social aims.

* * *

In closing let me offer some remarks intended as a contribution to an alternative, democratic conception of the political. What would such a conception
look like? How can it escape being merely another arbitrary construction? One
answer is that, historically, the idea of the political and the idea of democracy
have shared so many common meanings as to seem almost synonymous. This
cannot be said of the relationship between the idea of the political and, say, the

idea of a political order that would be controlled by or responsive primarily to the wealthy. Marx expressed this point in one of his early writings: "It is evident that all forms of the state have democracy for their truth, and for that reason are false to the extent that they are not democracy."[35] Marx's point can be rendered like this: It is the nature of the state that, insofar as it claims to be political, it will govern for the good of the entire community and not serve primarily the interests of a particular class or group: this is the democratic "truth." But insofar as the state in question takes a particular form, say, one mainly controlled by the wealthy or by corporations, it will by virtue of its actual nature rule in the interests of a part of the society, that is, be false to the democratic principle of the good of the whole community. It follows that only a democratic state has the possibility of acting as a genuine political state. It might be added that most political theorists, from antiquity to the present, have accepted the premise of this point and resisted the conclusion. They have accepted the principle that the political defines a distinct kind of association that aims at the good of all, depends on the contributions, sacrifices, and loyalties of all, but they have then bent their ingenuity to devising structures that would allow the few (whether kings, aristocrats, representatives, or bureaucratic officials) to use collective power for the good of all while exacting from the population at large the various contributions needed for that task.

These are, however, mainly formal considerations, and while they help to identify correctly the principle that the political means the common well-being is the end and the definition of what is authentic political action, it does not specify what the political has to include so that the common well-being is furthered. Nor does it tell us what the nature of the common well-being is: is it something that is "made" or "created"? And, if so, out of what? Or is it disclosed? Is it a pure good, or equivocal, even ironic? What are the conditions that are needed for the political to come into being so that the common well-being becomes possible and how do these conditions entail democracy?

We can begin not by ignoring the state but by avoiding the error of assuming that the state is identical or coterminous with the political. The state is a modern phenomenon and its raison d'être was to develop, or better, to capitalize the power of society—the power resident in the human activities, relationships, and transactions that sustain life and its changing needs. The state became a coercive agency declaring and enforcing law, punishing miscreants of all descriptions, systematizing taxation, encouraging commerce and manufacture in the direction of national economies, conducting diplomacy, waging war, and seeking empire. Its characteristic form of action is the decision which it "makes" with relentless regularity; its typical expression is the announcement of a "policy," and its mode of governance ranges from inducements to force.

The appearance of the state signifies that surplus power is available, that collective life has succeeded in producing more power than the daily needs of the members require. The existence of surplus power is a sign that the political has come into being in the common life that makes the state possible. Common life resides in the cooperation and reciprocity that human beings develop in order to survive, meet their needs, and begin to explore their capacities and the remarkable world into which they have been cast. The political emerges as the shared concerns of human beings to take care of themselves and the part of their world that they claim as their lot. The political emerges, in the literal sense, as a "culture," that is, a cultivating, a tending, a taking care of beings and things. The common life and the political culture emerge to the accompaniment of power. Shared concerns do not eliminate the need for power; they depend upon it. This was partly glimpsed in a remark by the late Roland Barthes: "One must naturally understand *political* in its deeper meaning, as describing the whole of human relations in their real social structure, in their power of making the world."[36]

There is, of course, an irony here in that the skills of social cooperation, which human beings acquire through experience and apprenticeship, and which enable them to settle their existence, eventually are made to work against them. Their skill produces more power than they need. Surplus power enables them to project: to control more of the future and so to develop plans and expectations, i.e., projects. The dynamics of collectivity then take hold. The search for surplus power then gets institutionalized, which is the organizational language for talking about the routinized manufacture of surplus power. Surplus then becomes the province of administration; it is managed and administered in the form of programs, including programs for the deployment of power converted into weapons and man-power. In all of this the political, which had emerged as shared concerns and involvements, has disappeared.

The loss of the political is a clue to its nature: it is a mode of experience rather than a comprehensive institution such as the state. The thing about experience is that we can lose it and the thing about political experience is that we are always losing it and having to recover it. The nature of the political is that it requires renewal. It is renewed not by unique deeds whose excellence sets some beings apart from others, but by rediscovering the common being of human beings. The political is based on this possibility of commonality: our common capacity to share, to share memories and a common fate. Our common being is the natural foundation of democracy. As beings whose nature displays common elements, we have an equal claim to participate in the cooperative undertakings on which the common life depends. We are not equal to power or ability, and that is precisely why equality is crucial. The development of power upon which the common life depends requires different qualities and it produces different beings, differences which are interpreted as inequalities. At the same time, and stated somewhat differently, our human being is not exhausted by its common being. It is, as Hannah Arendt so often and eloquently reminded us, a being that is capable of expressing the most remarkable and glorious diversity. That diversity has important implications on how power is exercised democratically.

Each of us is a contributor to the generation of power without which human life cannot endure. The problem of the political is not to clear a space from which society is to be kept out but it is rather to ground power in commonality while reverencing diversity—not simply respecting difference. Diversity cannot be reverenced by bureaucratic modes of decision-making. Diversity is the nightmare of bureaucracy. The bureaucrat's response to it is either to invent another classification or, in the corporate world, to manufacture fifty-seven varieties. The mode of action that is consonant with equality and diversity is deliberation. Deliberation means to think carefully. We must think carefully because what is at stake is the exercise of human power. To exercise power democratically, that is, with the fullest possible participation by equals, far from being an exercise of crude mass power, is the most sensitive way of handling power. Democratic deliberation implicates our common being in decisions which are bound, in a complex society, to threaten harm to our diverse beings. It requires not that we come to terms with power—representatives and bureaucrats can do that for us—but that we face it.

CHAPTER 12

HANNAH ARENDT AND THE ORDINANCE OF TIME

HANNAH ARENDT WAS A RARE UNION of passion, nobility, and intellect. Her passion was expressed in affection for public things and public deeds, *res publicae* and *res gestae*, and a determination to preserve them. Her nobility was displayed in her response to these public themes. She elevated politics and political action to the level of epic and tragedy, not in order to exonerate actors from their misdeeds or to glorify a particular nation, but to impose a demand upon those who presumed to decide great public matters and upon those who presumed to theorize about political actors and actions. The power of her intellect was revealed in the subjects she elected to confront. By any reasonable criterion of importance, they were among the fundamental problems of twentieth-century politics: totalitarianism, anti-Semitism, revolution, and the nature of political action. She also created a distinctive language to convey their meaning and urgency. Finally, and above all, she disclosed some important truths about politics; and even when she erred, her errors were instructive in that they compelled the critic to face a problem rather than remain content with scoring a logical point.

The briefest epitaph for Hannah Arendt would be: She lived the theoretical life, the *bios theoretikos*. While brief, the epitaph is not simple. To live the theoretical life is not just to pursue the truth but to tell it. The authentic theorist is, as she put it, a "truth-teller." Telling the truth about politics, not for partisan purposes or for self-dramatization, can be dangerous, as she learned when she wrote *Eichmann in Jerusalem*.

Before discussing some of her theoretical ideas, I want briefly to call attention to a special achievement of Hannah Arendt, one that is apt to be overlooked because it lacked the dramatic importance of her other accomplishments. She occupies a special place in the recent history of political theory in the United States. Prior to the appearance of *The Origins of Totalitarianism* and *The Human Condition*, the study of political theory was essentially a special branch of the history of ideas. It was neither political nor theoretical. As a consequence, political theory was exceedingly vulnerable to the challenge posed shortly after World War II by the proponents of the scientific study of politics who argued for an idea of theory based upon the methods of the natural sciences. The version of theory which political scientists borrowed from their colleagues in the more advanced social sciences was remarkable not only for its tendency to associate theory with "methodology" but for its distinct hostility toward history and philosophy. As a consequence, this new form of theory had nothing very significant or interesting to say about the issues which dominated the politics of the twentieth century: war, totalitarianism, democracy, imperialism, racial oppression, ecological policy, and corporate power.

To those who were trying to restate a conception of political theory relevant to the contemporary world the appearance of *The Human Condition* in 1958 came as a deliverance. It fulfilled the criterion which she was later to invoke in discussing the phenomenon of revolution: that book brought something new into the world. It introduced a distinctive language ("political action," "public realm," "political space") and with it a new political sensibility which invested politics with a high seriousness and dignity that transcended the dreary and trivial categories of academic political science. It retrieved the great political theories of the past from their interment in history texts and showed how they might be used to illuminate the predicaments of the present. It showed, in brief, that to reflect upon political theories of the past was to be drawn toward an engagement on the most exposed of terrains, the one she later located as being *Between Past and Future*.

AUTHENTIC POLITICS

Then and in her later writings she insisted that theory must be relentlessly and ruthlessly concrete. Concreteness was more than a theoretical condition. It was the fundamental ground of political judgment. Political judgment was about events and action which had taken place in fact. There is a vital connection between concreteness and political judgments because of the natural antagonism between politics and factual truth. Politicians, parties, sects, and nations have an unquenchable urge to rewrite reality to accord with their interests. Factual truth is the testimony which enables political judgment to contradict the appearances created by politicians and to say to the atrocities and misdeeds of politics, *J'accuse*.

Truth-telling about concreteness takes on a paradoxical character. Insofar as it defends facticity against political distortions, it is antipolitical in spirit. But insofar as it protests the subordination of factual truth to political considerations, truth-telling acquires the character of a political act fraught with critical, even subversive, potentialities. In an age when deception is claimed as a governmental prerogative and practiced as a systematic art, truth-telling *is* a way of defending the possibility of politics by defining its limits.

In her eyes, factual truth and authentic politics shared a common quality of fragility. They could be destroyed, lost, or forgotten. This happened when men cared more for other things, such as power or economic goods, and were prepared to use politics and truth instrumentally. The corruptibility of politics formed a constant theme in Hannah Arendt's thought and it served as the basis for a vision of politics that was radical and critical. Her radicalism had nothing to do with current ideologies. It was instead the classic radicalism that can be found in any of the great political theorists from Plato to Marx. The distinctive mark of the radicalism of the *theoros* is the claim that what most men most of the time take to be politics is not politics at all.

The radical thrust of her claim lay in its denial that problems of distributive justice or socioeconomic equality are the main objects of political action, the essential stuff of politics, or the test of the quality of political institutions and political leaders. On the contrary, the fact that such questions dominate public debates and that, normally, we expect political men to produce policies for resolving these kinds of questions was, for her, symptomatic of a political malaise. Public preoccupation with the redistribution of wealth and material goods, with the productivity of society, with levels of employment, and with social security was indicative of a state of affairs in which antipolitical forces and values had driven authentic politics from the public realm. To ground politics in the needs and desires of the working masses was to order it by the rhythms, imperatives, and values of two fundamentally antipolitical activities, production and consumption.

What was it about production and consumption, about laboring to produce goods that will satisfy human needs and desires, that was alien to and corruptive of politics? Hannah Arendt's view was that laboring signified activity grounded in necessity; mankind labors in order to support its existence as a species. Existence is governed by an inescapable rhythm of birth, growth, decay, and death. It is always coming into being and passing away. It is eternally transient. Labor is the means of satisfying the demands of existence, but it can do so only by adapting its rhythms to those of necessity: it takes the form of repetition, of the endless performance of acts that are progressively routinized. The fate of labor is monotony. Similarly, the products of labor are overtaken by the cycle of necessity: they are made, exchanged, and consumed. They have no durability; they leave no reminders.

This conception of labor is not restricted in its application to what is ordinarily called "the working class." Repetition and impermanence are characteristic of other activities that have come to dominate modern life: administration, technical work, and the production of culture. Labor is thus a description, not of a class, but of a common *mentalité*. If we ask, what is the meaning of a condition governed by necessity, dedicated to production or fabrication, and defined by activity that is specialized repetition and whose end products are perishable, we might try to answer by following an indirect route. We might try to grasp the meaning of that condition by considering the values and activities which contradict or oppose a society defined by labor. What are the antitheses to necessity, to making, to consuming, to repetition, to impermanence, and, above all, to the private needs and gratifications for which all laborers strive? The antitheses are: freedom instead of necessity; action or performance instead of making; deeds and words instead of products; durability instead of impermanence; remembering instead of consuming; public happiness instead of private satisfactions.

These antitheses formed the rudiments of Hannah Arendt's conception of authentic politics. Freedom, action, speech, duration, memory, and public happiness were the elements which constituted her vision of the political and her judgment of what was at stake in the wars, revolutions, and tyrannies of the twentieth century. The future might hang on how this question was considered and answered: What is the meaning of the political? What does it mean for it to be present, that is, what is political presence? The overtones to these questions are unmistakably from the philosophy of Heidegger and its discussion of the presence of Being. And just as Heidegger's search for the true form and content of philosophy led him back to the ancient Greeks and to the pre-Socratics, Hannah Arendt returned to the same period and sought to discover in Homeric myths, in pre-Socratic philosophy, and in the politics of the Greek *polis* what was authentically political. This personal experience of a return to origins was reproduced in a distinctive Arendtian practice of theory and in a conception of politics quite unlike that of any contemporary theorist in the English-speaking world. Theorizing was conceived as an act of recovery, of reacquiring lost meanings, of remembering. She did not intend theorizing to be archaeology, an excavation of lifeless political remains; but a mode of *re*-flection and *in*-sight which carried the mind back to a privileged moment in the history of politics when the genuinely political—political Being, we might say—was embodied for the first time. In ancient Greece a new species had appeared, *politikon zoon*, the animal who aspired to political being and, fleetingly, realized it. That experience had left traces of its passage in the stories and poems of bards and in the fragments of philosophy. These were of inestimable value to a later age which had come perilously close to losing all understanding of the political. The task of political theory was to rethink the political in the present.

From the deeds and words of this first political people she evoked images which were strange and puzzling, especially to those of us reared in a tradition which instinctively associates politics with "interests" and political action with the rational calculation of consequences. For Hannah Arendt, politics was essentially dramaturgic. It consisted of public performances staged in a clearly defined public realm and witnessed by an audience of equals engrossed in what was taking place and indifferent to calculations of material benefits or consequences. Political men were not, however, actors reading lines; they were men engaged in a contest, an *agon*, a striving for excellence defined in terms of praiseworthy acts which exceeded normal standards and evoked awe and admiration from the spectators.

However, actions do not speak louder than words; they do not speak at all. They require speech, that is, words which will disclose the aims and intentions of the actor while articulating the meaning of the act. Speech is constitutive of action, rescuing it from the void of meaninglessness by which it is forever being threatened and preserving it from the natural rhythms of coming-to-be and passing-away. Speech alone, however, cannot preserve action. Only memory can decide whether an action or actor was "memorable." The political actor desires to be remembered; otherwise his endeavors will have been meaningless. And this is why he comes to be dependent on an audience. Audience is a metaphor for the political community whose nature is to be a community of remembrance. But political communities are not exempt from mortality; they, too, will pass away unless there is someone to memorialize them. Behind, as it were, the political community and the political actors stands the storyteller, the one who preserves the memory of great actions, noble words, and genuine politics. He may be a Thucydides, or she may be a Hannah Arendt.

POLITICS AND LABOR

If this conception of politics seems puzzling to the modern reader, the conditions stipulated by Hannah Arendt for its survival are likely to seem harsh, archaic, and repellent. As she acknowledged, authentic politics in its ancient form depended upon exclusivity, upon sharply demarcating the public from the private realm and narrowly limiting the number and class of citizen-participants. The political life of the Greek *polis* depended upon a leisured class of citizens freed from the activity of labor so that they could devote themselves to politics. Ancient politics was sustained by an economic system in which noncitizens—artisans, craftsmen, slaves, and resident aliens—were engaged in production, business, and commercial transactions. Aristotle stated the matter bluntly: authentic politics depended upon a sharp separation between citizen-equals who engaged in politics and the producer-unequals whose labor, while necessary for securing the conditions of life, did not contribute directly to the good actions that were the essence of politics.

Thus political action and labor signified primordial opposites: freedom versus necessity; extraordinary action versus repetitive activity; life-risking versus life-sustaining; action occurring in the bright light of the public stage versus activity hidden away in private places and private transactions; and finally, action constituted and signified by utterance and preserved in remembrance versus activity that is speechless, that issues in products destined to be consumed and forgotten.

This vision of politics, when directed at the modern world, led toward a radical pessimism. The public realm has become invaded and engulfed by the culture of labor; power and greatness are measured by productivity; governments exist to manage economies; consumption is the purpose of activity; political speech has been replaced by political huckstering and image-peddling; political actors have been transformed into administrators and technical managers, citizens into uncomprehending spectators, storytellers into methodologists.

If we were to reflect on this antithesis between politics and labor, we would, I suggest, be paying the highest tribute to Hannah Arendt, the tribute of caring enough about her theoretical achievements to think about them critically and thereby to prevent them from falling into the same oblivion as articles of consumption. Serious thoughts about serious matters, such as the antithesis between politics and labor, are like some creations of work as she described them: things to be cared for and used with affection, things which may possess a durability denied to the consumer goods fabricated by labor.

In pondering the antitheses of politics and labor, it would be appropriate to begin with a quotation that Hannah Arendt must have reflected upon often. It is a fragment from Anaximander (fl. 617–545 B.C.), the pre-Socratic, and probably the first writing in the history of Western philosophy:

> But that from which things arise also gives rise to their passing away, according to what is necessary; for things render justice and pay penalty (or make reparation) to one another for their injustice, according to the ordinance of time.[1]

The political ideas of Hannah Arendt may be likened to those "things" which "arise," which emerge from some more fundamental substratum. That deeper fundament, as we have observed, was ancient Greece. It signified a privileged moment in Western history when man stood at the beginning of philosophy and politics, when mind first became aware of itself as a communing medium and turned to reflection upon Being without having first to struggle through the later mediations erected by traditions of philosophy. In that first privileged moment, when the philosophical air was fresh and philosophy itself joyfully naive, when thought and language had not yet learned to trick each other, mind briefly gained a unique relationship to *logos*, to ultimate being. Mind responded and corresponded to Being, to that which governed all things as they appeared. The mind, according to the pre-Socratic understanding, did not come away with a program or a project. That would be to misunderstand the relationship. Thinking was not like work, form-creating, but as Heidegger would later phrase it, *Beistimmung*, "attunement," that is, a sensitive responding to or feel for the atmosphere surrounding Being and a glimpse into its essential nature.

In her studies and reflections on ancient Greek philosophy and politics Hannah Arendt acquired that "attunement" and she gave expression to it in a celebration of authentic politics, "the joy and gratification," as she once described it, "that arise out of being in company with our peers, of acting together and appearing in public, of inserting ourselves into the world by word and deed, thus acquiring our personal identity and beginning something entirely new."[2]

Anaximander had also voiced a warning: "But that from which things arise also gives rise to their passing away according to what is necessary." Perhaps it was the attraction and influence of Greek philosophy and politics that drew

Hannah Arendt's thought into the pattern described by Anaximander and gently brushed it with the mortality that is the lot of all things human. Why might this be so? Anaximander's reply was, "for things render justice and pay penalty (or make reparation) to one another for their injustice, according to the ordinance of time." In what sense might Hannah Arendt's achievement fall under the "ordinance of time" and have to submit to the decrees of justice? Would her achievement be the less for it and our indebtedness cancelled?

Now Anaximander's notion of justice was not concerned with simple wrong-doing, with the violation of human *nomoi*. It had to do, instead, with a conception of the world in which the elements (*stoicheia*) stood in opposition to each other (*enantia*) and tended to encroach or transgress upon the preserve of each other. In this connection we might think of labor encroaching upon the preserve of politics, or the reverse. Justice (*diké*) would then require that the violation of limits would be visited by retribution, compensation. Let us attempt an Anaximander-like reinterpretation of the tensions between labor and politics and of Hannah Arendt's claim that in the modern world labor has unjustly invaded the public realm.

THE TRIUMPH OF THE LABORING MENTALITY

We may begin by questioning the ancient premise that unique and extraordinary action is strictly an individual deed. Common, collective action is likewise capable of performing prodigies; it too is capable of public performance, of political action. Marx—that thinker who exercised a profound fascination for Hannah Arendt, part attraction, part repulsion—was the first theorist to compose an epic of collective action, an epic in which action transformed itself from being economic, social, private, and monotony-ridden (or "alienated") into action that was political, public, and extraordinary. That epic had been gathering anonymously for centuries; it was an epic that embodied a quintessential feature of all politics, power. Marx wrote:

> During its rule of scarcely one hundred years the bourgeoisie has created more massive and more colossal productive forces than have all preceding generations together. Subjection of nature's forces to man, machinery, application of chemistry to industry and agriculture, steam navigation, railways, clearing of whole continents for cultivation . . . whole populations conjured out of the ground—what earlier century had even a presentiment of such productive forces slumbering in the lap of social labor?[3]

Before this prodigy, poor Hercules seems but an insignificant stable boy; for the modern epic of social labor has "produced world history for the first time,"[4] that is, a new public stage that required a new form of dramaturgy, production, and a new species of actor, the proletariat. It was an epic "written in the annals of mankind in letters of blood and fire."[5] It recounted how "great masses of men . . . [were] suddenly and forcibly torn from their means of subsistence and hurled . . . on the labor market."[6] The countryside was depopulated, the cities swelled into festering centers of poverty and sickness where crooked streets matched crooked bodies. Within the productive system itself forces swirled and raged: commodities oppressed men; abstract forms of power dominated society as surplus value was squeezed from labor time and familiar tangible things were constantly disappearing and reappearing in new forms, commodities into exchange values; money into machines; machines into processes, and so on.

Although Marx's epic was cast in a language which became progressively more "economic" in its vocabulary, the revolution of labor was depicted by him as a supremely political act. This was in keeping with one of the earliest of Marx's concerns, to endow the proletariat with a political significance which would both challenge the classical conception of the political and preserve its element of truth. Early on he employed one of the most ancient metaphors in political theory to describe the proletariat, the metaphor of the "representative" who is the symbol of the collective unit called society. In earlier centuries the metaphor had been claimed by kings, priests, warriors, philosophers, aristocrats, and the bourgeoisie. But now, Marx declared, it was the proletariat which was the "representative" of "the whole of society."[7] Its gathering strength signified a direct challenge to the modern form of the classical conception of politics. That conception required that the many should labor to furnish the material conditions which would enable the few to engage in political action. That conception saw no contradiction between its view of the political as an association of shared advantages made possible by a variety of contributions and its view that the largest class of contributors had no rightful claim to the civilized advantages, the *paideia*, which political society makes possible. According to Marx's prophecy, the ordinance of historical time, with its workings in necessity, will bring the triumph of the new representative of the political, the revenge of social labor against political action.

Contrary to Marx's hopes, time's ordinance has not been executed, and the revolution of labor has failed to materialize. But has there been, nonetheless, an ironic justice, one that Hannah Arendt described but did not fully identify?

She saw truly that, while the proletariat had not triumphed over the political realm, the laboring mentality had. Was this, then, labor's revenge upon politics, the fulfillment of Anaximander's warning, "for things render justice and pay penalty to one another for their injustice"? Or is this only an illusion created by a mistaken identification of the protagonists? Are political action and labor mere surrogates or, better, puppets controlled by a third activity, the *vita contemplativa*, the activity of the mind which reaches its most sublime expression in contemplation, philosophizing, and scientific theorizing? The *vita contemplativa* was for her a precious theme, and in *The Human Condition* she argued powerfully against the two forms of its corruption. Theorizing must be kept strictly separated from action, and it must not become assimilated to "making," to the mode of activity identified with artisans and laborers.

But what has happened to *theoria* since that time long ago when Aristotle defined theorizing as contemplation of unchanging Being, as activity distinct from that of practical action and from making? To compress the odyssey of the theoretical mind over the centuries, we can say, first, that mind has suffered successive losses in the eternal objects it was supposed to contemplate: first Being was displaced by God; then God by Nature; then Society and Man each enjoyed a brief popularity; and now we find the theoretical mind at play with its own constructs: models, artificial entities postulated, not because *they* exist but because if we pretend they exist we can account for other things. This means, *inter alia*, that contemplation is no longer an adequate description of the highest form of theoretical activity. The contemporary mind is not much given to reflection or contemplation and does not easily give itself over to mental rhythms suggestive of calm and serenity. The true character of the modern theorizer was anticipated in Locke's phrase, "the busy mind of man," a phrase that jars harshly against Aristotle's notion of theory as godlike contemplation. The power of the new theoretical mind is expressed in its steady expansion into new domains of life, while its unique fervor takes the form of a total commitment to perishable truths. Scientific achievement, in Max Weber's heroic conception, "asks to be 'surpassed' and outdated . . . [this] is our common fate, and, more, our common goal." "Why does one engage in doing something," Weber asked admiringly, "that in reality never comes, and never can come, to an end?"[8]

The upshot is a world in which mind is triumphant. Virtually everything that we see, touch, smell, taste, and use is the end product of a theory. Likewise the objects we move among: schools, factories, offices, even cities. Increasingly our personal, familial, social, political, and economic affairs are being ministered by those who claim theoretical knowledge: economists, psychoanalysts, sex therapists, counselors. There is even a theory which prescribes the correct manner of dying. In some curious way, Hegel, not Marx or Freud, was the truer prophet: Absolute Mind reigns supreme, everywhere incarnate and universal. Of one thing we can be certain: mind is not at the end of its tether, for there is no tether.

The encroachments, then, are not those of labor into the political realm. They are instead the encroachments of mind into both realms, the realm of politics and the realm of work. The tyranny of mind may be the cruelest of tyrannies, for it brooks no appeal except to itself. The alternative to mind is not the politics of mindlessness but of reflection grounded in experience. For the modern tyranny is peculiarly the tyranny of abstraction. There are, I would suggest, modes of experience hinted at in the language of political theory, and some of it is very old: the language of participation, sharing, common experience, pooled contributions of diverse competencies, deliberation. If we were to explore this language we would, I think, be both amending Hannah Arendt's thought and preserving it, and by preserving it we would be saying, gratefully, that to talk at all about politics in fitting ways is to talk the language that she both recovered for us and creatively reinterpreted.

CHAPTER 13

THE LIBERAL/DEMOCRATIC DIVIDE

ON RAWLS'S *POLITICAL LIBERALISM*

I

Despite the political setbacks of the last two decades, American liberals could console themselves that liberalism retains intellectual superiority over its critics. During those same decades, analytic philosophers in Britain and America put aside their prejudices and began gingerly to practice "political philosophy." Insofar as it is possible to attribute to one man and one book the principal responsibility for both developments, John Rawls incontestably would be that man and his *A Theory of Justice* (Harvard University Press, 1971) would be that book. His accomplishment is nothing less than to have set the terms of liberal discourse in the English-speaking countries.

Beyond his professional accomplishments, there is much to admire in the man: honesty, lucidity, moral and professional seriousness, and a remarkable receptiveness to criticism and suggestion. Rawls is truly the virtuous philosopher whose great personal achievement is to have rejected celebrity status.

Although *Justice* provided a comprehensive theory of rights and of the moral principles appropriate to a liberal society, its political and constitutional principles were sketched only briefly. Now, in *Political Liberalism* (Columbia University Press, 1993), he has attempted to remedy these and other deficiencies and to connect his proposals with cultural and historical traditions to a far greater degree than was previously the case.

The avowedly political focus of *Liberalism* invites some critical lines of questioning that were closed in *Justice* or were, at best, tangential to that enterprise. One such line is suggested by the remark of a reviewer who congratulated Rawls for putting "the 'political' back into 'political philosophy.'"[1]

Accordingly, in what follows, I explore Rawls's notion of the political by asking what kind of politics it promotes or encourages. I do this by raising what is for Rawls a nonquestion of the status of democracy within his version of liberalism. And because *Liberalism* is a work of political philosophy, I want to say something about its conception of that vocation and its relation to a democratic politics. Although that too may appear to be another non-Rawlsian question, it goes to the difference between liberalism and democracy and to the question of how it is possible to theorize democracy without resorting to anti- or undemocratic impositions; or, if it is possible, whether Rawlsian constructivism and its sovereign theorist are the way to do it.

The idea of democracy that I employ runs roughly like this. Democracy should not depend on elites making a one-time gift to the demos of a prede-signed framework of equal rights. This does not mean that rights do not matter a great deal, but rights in a democracy depend on the demos winning them, extending them substantively, and, in the process, acquiring experience of the political, that is, of participating in power, reflecting on the consequences of its exercise, and struggling to sort out the common well-being amid cultural dif-ferences and socioeconomic disparities. The presence of democracy is not sig-nified by paying deference to a formal principle of popular sovereignty but by ensuring continuing political education, nor is democracy nurtured by stipu-lating that reasonable principles of justice be in place from the beginning. De-mocracy requires that the experiences of justice and injustice serve as moments for the demos to think, to reflect, perchance to construct themselves as actors. Democracy is about the continuing self-fashioning of the demos.

II

Despite frequent reference to "liberal democracy" and "constitutional democ-racy," democracy is not a distinctive presence in *Liberalism*, and one can say that *Liberalism* does less for democracy than it does for liberalism. Its supreme political value is not dispersed power but individual liberty; its pivotal institu-tion is neither popularly elected nor democratically responsible but is the su-preme court; and it locates the true expression of political identity not in the vitality of local institutions but in the constitution.

When democracy is invoked only to be subaltern, what sorts of possibilities, realities, and historical memories are being denied?

Liberalism's reduction of democracy is not by direct attack but results from an understanding of politics that Rawls shares with the contract theorists he cites. The understanding is one in which the meaning and scope of politics is to be "settled" beforehand, that is, before conflict and controversy among social groups and the alignment of classes is recognized. So contract schemes, Rous-seau excepted, settle politics into constitutional arrangements of representative government, periodic elections, a bill of rights, and judicial review. Politics has to be settled lest it unsettle broader social concerns. For Rawls, values such as "stability," "social unity," and "cooperation" are central and are served by his em-phasis on preserving intact the "structure of government," because "frequent controversy" over it "raises the stakes of politics and may lead to distrust and turmoil that undermines constitutional government" (*PL*, p. 228).[2] The settle-ment itself is made to appear to take place in a pure "political" realm outside pol-itics; Rawls, accordingly, excludes from the imaginary deliberations fair equality of opportunity and the principle of redistribution (the "difference principle") on the grounds that they are not "essential" (*PL*, pp. 228, 230).[3]

The crucial question raised by the allegory of contract concerns not only the terms of agreement and how they are arrived at but the state of the socially forceful and the socially forceless on which the terms are to be superimposed. As we know from the history of contract theories, for most of the major exemplars, Rousseau again excepted, the signing of the contract is preceded by an abeyant moment when the author suspends temporarily the actual inequalities of power to establish a predictable narrative, a scenario of abstracted rationality in which each act of consent is equal to every other act of consent even though the actors are not. In that allegory, there are no politics of consent, no negotiation, and no seeing of consent through the eyes of different classes, groups, and sects, only a politics in which reason argues with itself to legitimize the contract, as though the central issue were rationality rather than disparities. Contract theory is Ireton without Rainborough.

The Rawlsian settlement of politics begins by assigning a mechanism, "constructivism," precedence over politics. Constructivism is justified on logical grounds, but the priorities it establishes are temporal and normative. Constructivism is described as the name for "a certain procedure" or moral "structure" designed to induce the "representatives of citizens" to produce the desired "outcome" of "the public principles of justice" that are "to regulate the basic structure of society" (*PL*, p. 90). Constructivism is intended to produce agreement before there is actual consensus; in Rawls's scheme, consensus supports agreement rather than creating it, as in traditional contract theories. Citizens will also be constructed so that they will support and play a certain role in the institutions.

I want to suggest that Rawls adopts the worst feature of contract theory while missing the radical element that connects the device to democratic ideas. By the worst feature, I mean the mystifying role of consent. In describing how society can be founded on the agreement of each member, the impression is created that a political "foundation" is being laid that materializes the equality of the members. From that start, it is then possible to mystify all later elections as ritual reenactments of original equality, later moments that periodically invoke the original agreement, evoking it as a "real" presence, a political transubstantiation.

The radical element inhering in contract theorists was their engagement with revolution—either past, present, or potential. Contract theory had an urgency, a theoretical-political compulsion to work out fundamental principles—even by a champion of order such as Hobbes—because revolution had encouraged the hope that deep grievances concerning arbitrary authority, social inequalities, and political exclusions could be alleviated. Contract theory, perforce, had to be diagnostic of the troubles that had led to the collapse of traditional authorities. The question posed by Rawls's device of the original position is, What are the implications to constituting political society by a contract abstracted from any revolutionary referent and unpersuaded of the urgent need for a deep-running critique? The answer is, An idealization of the status quo.

III

In *Liberalism*, the individuals in the original position are to choose just principles, choosing, that is, as the theorist thinks that they should rather than because they have discovered for themselves the values of equality. Thus a kind of "guardian democracy" is foreshadowed from the start. Guardian democracy privileges constitutional structure over democratic politics and culminates in the exaltation of the supreme court, perennially the favorite institution of those concerned to check the demos. Ever since Plato's *Laws*, political philosophers have been enamored of constitutions as the practical correlative of a complete theory and, equally, of nocturnal councils; the combination ensures the realization of theory through an institutionalized interpreter insulated from politics.

This would hardly be worth mentioning were it not that *Liberalism* insists that the device of an original position, which is designed to screen out temporarily "the contingencies of the social world," "must eliminate the bargaining advantages that inevitably arise within the background institutions of any society from cumulative social, historical, and natural tendencies" (*PL*, p. 23). From that promising diagnosis, Rawls develops the wrong political prescription. The diagnosis amounts to an admission that a society governed by liberal principles is not per se immunized against the "tendencies" toward inequalities. Instead of that knowledge figuring decisively in Rawls's construction, he gives us an original position in which our "trustees" aim at a "fair agreement on the principles of political justice between free and equal persons"—even though, in fact, the persons being represented are neither free nor equal and the agreement itself will "inevitably" be unable to prevent those inequalities (*PL*, pp. 23, 104, 106).

The admission that a liberal society will be divided by significant inequalities should have led Rawls to the question of whether inequality was systemic to a liberal society, that is, whether such a society harbors arrangements, liberal in character, that produce inequalities as a matter of course. If that should be the case, as I believe it is with the economic arrangements of late modern capitalism, then it becomes imperative to consider the need for more continuous political activity on the part of those who historically have been the most politically disadvantaged and for treating that need as urgent rather than perfunctory. Given the structural tendencies toward inequalities, political action on the part of the socially and economically disadvantaged becomes the crucial means of saving themselves.

But Rawls sees the problem not from their perspective but from that of the successful classes for whom the values of *res publica* are what remains after subtracting private concerns and attractions. Accordingly, he assigns a "lesser place" to political participation relative to the satisfactions derived from civil society and its associations and professions (*PL*, p. 330). Rawls admits that there will always be a need for continuous readjustment in the distribution of material resources if political rights are to be accorded their "fair value." That argument fails to appreciate that the rich would agree to such material readjustments only if they have somehow acquired greater political virtue than corporate culture and a fiercely competitive society ordinarily instill, and that assumption requires faith in the autonomy of political culture as a source of virtue.

Instead of addressing the structures that historically have perpetuated inequalities—corporations, elite universities and colleges, centralized governmental bureaucracies, the mass media—Rawls falls back on a remedy of controlling campaign financing as though that were a cause rather than an effect (*PL*, pp. 325–29, 358, 361).

IV

The scope of *Liberalism* is dictated by its purpose: to provide a guide to deliberations about basic "political values"—about "constitutional essentials and questions of basic justice" and how these connect with culture, tradition, and other "background" conditions. These values "alone" are meant "to settle such fundamental questions" as voting, religious toleration, equality of opportunity, and ownership of property. Rawls expects his citizens or, more precisely, their representatives at a constitutional convention to be able to decide these matters, and he wants to ensure that they will be decided properly and openly.

Accordingly, he proposes—an earlier age would have said legislates—a hegemonic mode of discourse, "public reason," which citizens are to accept and employ in their discussions of basics. It applies broadly to "public advocacy in the public forum," to elections, to citizens, to candidates, and even to political groups whenever essentials are at issue (*PL*, p. 215). Otherwise, Rawls warns, citizens will be "hypocritical," saying one thing and doing another (*PL*, pp. 214–15). Thus public reason is to be the discourse of a transparent political society earnestly seeking the public good in public (*PL*, p. 213).

Rawls's assumption throughout is that a politics of reason is a neutral instead of a neutralizing principle, which works against those who have not had the leisure to adopt it as the governing ideal of human conduct. Its model is neither demotic nor pluralistic but a discourse of the authoritative: "To check whether we are following public reason we might ask: how would our argument strike us presented in the form of a supreme court opinion? Reasonable? Outrageous?" (*PL*, p. 254).

Public reason has moral as well as discursive imperatives, for in addition to incorporating a political conception of justice (which includes basic rights and opportunities, the priority of rights over the good, and ensuring all citizens of "adequate all-purpose means" to make use of their liberties), public reason is constrained by "guidelines of inquiry that specify ways of reasoning and criteria for the kinds of information relevant for political questions." Public reason is to conform, therefore, to preestablished rules of evidence, inference, and reason (*PL*, pp. 223–26). Citizens have "a moral, not a legal, duty" to explain to others how the principles and policies they espouse find support in public reason (*PL*, p. 217). The condition that makes possible this lofty level of public discourse is that the topic of "social and economic inequalities" is ruled out of order even though those inequalities are acknowledged to be "political" in nature (*PL*, pp. 229–30).

Rawlsian democracy might be likened to a hermetically sealed condition of deliberation that allows rationality to rule by suppressing certain topics and historical grievances and excluding diverse languages of protest from public councils. Inadvertently, the limitations of Rawlsian reason are exposed: it cannot make sense of, much less function within, a setting of sharp conflicts, whether doctrinal, economic, political, or rhetorical.

V

Public reason, we might say, is the general will in the age of academic liberalism. And like the general will, it is haunted by the specter of differences. Unlike Rousseau, Rawls will not banish certain groups (although he will come perilously close to doing so) but will seek their incorporation, a solution rendered easier because of the politically trivial character of the differences with which Rawls is concerned.

Rawls proposes a "reasonable pluralism." It is not designed to obstruct and mediate State power (the discourse of *Liberalism* is innocent of the idea of the State), nor is it driven, like Madisonian pluralism, by interests, primarily economic. "Reasonable pluralism" converts differences from a threat to an accomplice of stability, co-opting them so that in the end they are eviscerated, absorbed into a consensus that requires smoothing off the rough, possibly irrational edges of differences. The crucial move is where Rawls locates differences and how he represents them.

Rawls introduces *Liberalism* as the remedy for the "unrealistic" aspect of his classic *Justice* and the restatement of its theory in the narrower form of a "political" rather than a "moral" conception (*PL*, pp. xvi–xvii). As a moral theory, *Justice* belonged to the category of "comprehensive doctrines," which *Liberalism* now regards as the source of the political problem rather than the solution. A comprehensive doctrine is defined as covering "all recognized values and virtues within one rather precisely articulated system" (*PL*, pp. xvi, 152, note 17). Although he notes that such doctrines may be philosophical, religious, or moral, the only doctrines he pauses over are the moral philosophies of utilitarianism and Kantianism. There is little or no allusion to the likes of democratic localists, socialists, radical feminists, Christian fundamentalists, Black Muslims, or Jewish Hasidim. Given his narrow representation of comprehensive doctrines, Rawls might have marginalized those doctrines that aim at imposing their

comprehensive beliefs on society as a whole; instead he proceeds, first, by defining the problem as one of finding the proper basis for a "profoundly divided"
liberal political society (*PL*, p. xxv). Liberal freedom is alleged to have spawned
comprehensive belief systems that not only are in "doctrinal conflict" with one
another but have "no prospect of resolution" (*PL*, p. xxviii). Fortunately, they
are also "reasonable." The question then becomes, how to make a pluralism of
comprehensive doctrines work so as to create a consensus that will ensure a
stable cooperative society?

Rawls's solution to a problem whose contours are left vague and whose political importance is underdescribed is to exploit an alleged element of "reasonableness" common to some or most comprehensive doctrines and to declare
that the sum of the parts equals an "overlapping consensus" of the whole. This
is said to solve the problem of "how a well-ordered society can be unified and
stable" (*PL*, pp. 133–34). A consensus that appeals to all reasonable comprehensive doctrines will enable their adherents to share in the common rights and
freedoms of equal citizens and, as we shall see, to become acculturated in the
allegedly noncomprehensive doctrine of political liberalism.

Because it embodies the reasonable, liberalism is recommended as a noncomprehensive doctrine that is uniquely qualified to unify a doctrinally divided
society. However, there appears to be a price exacted of some doctrines. As
Rawls unfolds his conception of a society based on a consensus of reasonable
doctrinaires, it seems less a theory than a strategy for establishing a liberal political hegemony. Citizens may expect "limits [on] their freedom to advance
certain ways of life" (*PL*, p. 209). At the same time, their support of an overlapping consensus composed of reasonable comprehensive doctrines confirms
not only that they have "sustained ways of life fully worthy of citizens' devoted
allegiance" (*PL*, p. 209) but "this fact" should reassure them that the society is
allowing space to worthy ways of life (*PL*, p. 210). Despite that space, however,
those who subscribe to such doctrines are warned that they may have to allow
some "leeway" so as to accommodate their teachings to the conclusions of public reason. A "reasonable and effective public conception" will eventually "bend
comprehensive doctrines toward itself, shaping them if need be from unreasonable to reasonable" (*PL*, pp. 246–47). At the same time that citizens are thus
being pressed toward conformity, they are expected, if incongruously, to strive
always to express "sincerity of opinion" (*PL*, pp. 241–42).

The deeper significance of this formulation is that it reveals how a liberal society creates cultural pressures to restrain the individualism that forms so fundamental a part of *Liberalism*. In *Justice*, Rawls tried to juggle a concern for distributive justice with a severe conception of individual autonomy. "Each person,"
he wrote, "possesses an inviolability founded on justice that even the welfare of
society as a whole cannot override" (*TJ*, p. 3). Although that position is reaffirmed in *Liberalism*, primarily as the priority of liberty and individual rights,
Rawls wants nonetheless to combine that conception of a rights-sensitive, individualistic being with a stronger, more active civic being. This requires that he

temper liberal egoism—"free and rational persons concerned to further their own interests" (*TJ*, p. 11)—which *Justice* used as a departure point. To make civic beings of those who were liberals before they were citizens requires that Rawls relax the inviolability of his individuals to render them permeable to, and malleable by, the influences of "tradition" and "culture."

VI

How should a political theorist distribute his concern between the political and the theoretical? The obvious answer is, of course, to both. But it is not so easy to look inward and contemplate an order one is creating and then, looking outward, ponder not only its relationship to the public world but one's interpretation of that world. What is easy is to follow the "logic" of the inner order to a satisfactory conclusion and then, in ad hoc fashion, point to the contacts it establishes with one's representations of the external world.

Liberalism is described by Rawls as preoccupied with "a few long-standing classical problems" of "the grounds of the basic religious and political liberties and the basic rights of citizens in civil society" (*PL*, p. xxviii). He defends the omission of questions such as "democracy in the firm and the workplace . . . retributive justice and the protection of the environment," gender, or family by asserting that solutions to "the classical problems" can furnish an "outline" for addressing more recent questions (*PL*, pp. xxviii–xxix). It does not turn on its potential for enabling us to see unsuspected connections in the world or to see familiar things in a new light but rather to see new things in a familiar light. The problems that attract Rawls are "internal" to his own theory rather than in the world; his concern is to fill in "the few missing pieces" in the earlier work. "Justice as fairness [uses] a fundamental organizing idea within which all ideas and principles can be systematically related and connected" (*PL*, p. 9). His theory is preoccupied with its own theoreticalness, with looking inward.

But what are the implications of pursuing the ideal of theoretical completeness while looking outward and admitting that a liberal society will be plagued continuously by inequalities—inequalities that are inevitably translated into injustices? How does theory encompass simultaneously the contraries of an ideally just whole and a dirempted reality?

Rawls defends the character of his theory by saying that it "is abstract in the same way that the conception of a perfectly competitive market, or of general economic equilibrium, is abstract, that is, it singles out certain aspects as especially significant from the standpoint of political justice and leaves others aside" (*PL*, pp. 154–55; see also p. 20). The issue is not, however, the uncontroversial point that a theorist may omit matters but whether the "standpoint" justifies omissions so damaging to the theory that they cannot afford to be included. Assuming that abstractness is not dictated solely by theoretical economies, decisions about what is to be excluded might represent a strategy for resolving what

Rawls takes as his fundamental concern, "the conflicts implicit in the fact of reasonable pluralism." Or, it may be that his remark, "I don't think I really know why I took the course I did," is as much a tribute to his honesty as it is a revelation of liberalism unable to comprehend the political world it claims to address (*PL*, p. xxx). Political matters omitted from *Liberalism* include class structures, bureaucracy, military power in a liberal order that is constitutionalist and capitalist, economic institutions and their powers, the great question of how to limit drastically the control over public discourse exercised by corporate and governmental bodies, and the compatibility of the ethics and culture of capitalism with the ethics and culture of Rawlsian citizenship, let alone with democracy.

Given these excluded topics and the genuine divisiveness they imply, it is formulaic and empty to proclaim that "in a democracy political power, which is always coercive power, is the power of the public, that is, of free and equal citizens as a collective body" (*PL*, p. 216). If we ask how citizens actually exercise that awesome power, we are told, anticlimactically, "by voting and in other ways" (*PL*, pp. 217–18). In fact, Rawls is interested not in the exercise of coercive power by the citizens but in the construction of a civics class in which all "should be ready to explain the basis of their actions to one another in terms each could reasonably expect the others might endorse as consistent with their freedom and equality" (*PL*, p. 218).

However, it is not merely contentious political problems that are omitted. Comprehensive doctrines that are deemed "unreasonable" are to be cordoned off. Thus, if there are "unreasonable and irrational doctrines," the recommended response is "to contain them so that they do not undermine the unity and justice of society" (*PL*, p. xvii).

That rationale could justify repressiveness, but the truly repressive elements are in Rawls's positive prescriptions rather than in his negative injunctions. The Rawlsian ideal is of a reasonable person who can accept reasonable disagreements "between persons who have realized their two moral powers to a degree sufficient to be free and equal citizens and who have an enduring desire to know fair terms of cooperation and to be fully cooperating members of society" (*PL*, p. 55). But to modulate such a formulation by saying it is an ideal is either to say that it is politically problematic or to give a shocking response to the "real" pluralism of ghettoized populations, to the escapees who are enraged at being lumped with those they have left behind as well as at the bestowal of liberal "advantages," and to the remnants of the working class who see no place for themselves in a society where the liberal boast is that all are "in." To impose the bland ideal of reasonableness and to posit a "nonhistorical" original position from which to stipulate basic principles is to lobotomize the historical grievances of the desperate.

If that should seem too harsh, consider the following formulation in which Rawls attempts to fill in his principle that not all conceptions of the good should be allowed to be pursued but only those "ways of life worthy of citizens' devoted support." "Strong feelings" and "zealous aspirations," Rawls declares, do not justify a claim to "resources" or reshaping institutions to achieve "certain goals." "Desires and wants, however intense, are not in themselves reasons in matters of constitutional essentials and basic justice" (*PL*, p. 190).

Rawls does not pause over the possibility that "strong feelings" and "zealous aspirations" might be directly related to frustration on the part of those social classes and groups for whom the rhetoric and processes of "reasonable pluralism" have been least responsive. Instead, he seems to look forward to the elimination of the passions generated by oppression and neglect, apparently forgetting his own insight into the intractable existence of significant inequalities. Thus, by guaranteeing "primary goods" (basic rights and liberties, fair equality of opportunity, and minimum economic needs), "reasons of justice" can be detached "not only from the ebb and flow of primary wants and desires but even from sentiments and commitments" (*PL*, p. 190). Rawls would even impose an additional norm on public reason, the "burden of judgment." It emphasizes the difficulties that citizens face "in the ordinary course of political life." It reminds us that evidence is often conflicting and of uncertain weight, that our concepts are often vague and inadequate, and that our experiences are different (*PL*, pp. 55–57).

Clearly, such considerations matter, but they are not neutral. The rhetoric of the desperate is likely to be a simplifying one, reflective of a condition reduced to essentials. A rhetoric of complexity, ever since Burke, has found favor with those whose expectations are secure.

VII

Classical utopias, characteristically, sought to eliminate conflicts that posed a threat to "order" and "stability." Rawls's "well-ordered society" stipulates that "the most divisive issues, serious contention about which must undermine the basis of social cooperation," will be removed from the public agenda (*PL*, p. 157). Admittedly, Rawls is thinking about the agenda of constitutional matters, but the effect of insulating constitutional conflicts is to encourage the somatization of the politics with which real pluralism is concerned. The result is the construction of two realms: an ideal "political" realm in which order, stability, and cooperation result from the congruent reasonableness of comprehensive doctrines, and a politics in which a century of laws, amendments to the constitution, and rhetoric of democratic equality have left the majority of the powerless substantially where they always have been and left unresolved as well the embarrassment of explaining away the anomalous presence of the powerless many in a democracy.

Although Rawls posits a citizenry in which all are free and equal and "have an equal share in the corporate political and coercive power of society" (*PL*, pp. 61–62), that vision is hopelessly at odds with the central fact of political life—power is never freely shared in a free society of individualists and free-wheeling entrepreneurs. Power is wrested in conflict. Rawls avoids the problem by treating conflict as primarily involving doctrines and by using consensus as the solution. He wants a consensus that meets "the urgent political requirement to fix, once and for all, basic rights and liberties, assigning them special priority" so that they will not be affected by "the calculus of special interests" and will be safe from "controversy" (*PL*, p. 161). Religion, which was not a presence in *Justice*, supplies the object lesson for a new age wracked by "profound doctrinal conflict" (*PL*, p. xxv) and "endless and destructive civil strife" (*PL*, pp. 158–59).

Stability, cooperation, duration, and unified system seem but the yearnings of an ideology seeking repose. The expression of that exhaustion is in the resort of extrapolitical beliefs to buttress the foundations of the system of "reasonable pluralism." The guarantee of "stability" is not, say, the citizens' deep affection for a democratic way of life or even simple patriotism (the latter is never mentioned) but in an overlapping consensus. His consensus allegedly rests on a moral conviction that is rooted not in a political or civic ideology but in the comprehensive religious or philosophical doctrines that each brings to political life (*PL*, pp. 147–48). The grounding of the political in extrapolitical beliefs is summarized by the observation that the overlapping consensus goes "deeper" than does consensus about the constitution (*PL*, pp. 149–50).

And yet, Rawls also wants to argue that the fervor of doctrinaires eventually will subside as they become accustomed to living under liberal principles (*PL*, pp. 162–64). They will progress from "mere" acquiescence in liberal principles of justice to supporting a constitutional consensus and from thence to an overlapping consensus. This evolution presupposes, as Rawls acknowledges, that the comprehensive doctrines of "most people are not fully comprehensive," thus enabling them to develop "an independent allegiance to the political conception" (*PL*, pp. 167–68). Rawls believes that pluralist politics would have a sobering effect on doctrinaires. The necessity of appealing to more diverse constituencies "makes it rational for them to move out of the narrow circle of their own views and to develop political conceptions" with an eye toward constructing a majority (*PL*, p. 165).

Thus liberal toleration is as valuable as a dissolvent as it is as a guarantee. According to Rawls's prognosis, because doctrinaires will be in a minority, conflict will shift from less fervently held doctrines to political values; and because political values and those doctrines have become "congruent," the conflicts promise to be less intense. We may note in passing that the fate of "certain kinds of (religious) fundamentalism" is left obscure (*PL*, pp. 169–70).

VIII

In the late twentieth-century United States, while inequalities have increased at a cancerous rate, equality has virtually disappeared from public rhetoric. As a result, liberal/democracy faces a choice between its two parts, giving either near-absolute priority to liberty and individualism or making as its first priority the creation of political democracy. Thus far, liberals have favored the liberal side while relying on the idea of policymaking to hold democracy at bay.

Policy is flexible. When occasion requires inaction, it will declare that gross, large-scale inequalities—say, mass unemployment—are due to temporary disequilibria and hence intervention would be imprudent. But policy is also prepared to intervene into the most intimate corners of human life and prescribe in the most fastidious detail an exact social minimum ("above or below the poverty line"), to fix the number of weeks recipients may receive welfare benefits, or to decide when interest rates should be adjusted to avoid inflation although it may bring unemployment. Policy is also the theater in which rationalization is so successfully disguised as rationality that author and audience alike can be tone deaf to the irony in a script line such as the following: inequalities must be "consistent with equal liberty and fair equality of opportunity" (*PL*, p. 282).

The "consistent" solution is an updated version of philanthropy and no more democratic: "Social and economic inequalities whether great or small" are to be adjusted "to the greatest benefit of the least advantaged members of society" (*PL*, pp. 6–7). Rawls acknowledges that the formula is "hardly clear" and full of "complexities," but one consequence is clear: the less well off will be passive recipients who will have their material lot eased, not because they have won some political advantage but because a redistributive mechanism acceptable to the "haves" is in place. The haves, those who get more, are "justified" in the Calvinist sense because they also "improve the situation of those who have gained less." That improvement is like the Calvinist justification by faith and unlike, say, a quick fortune on the stock market; it can only be known "over time" (*PL*, p. 282).

The "basic structure" of society, Rawls observes, establishes and promotes "significant social and economic inequalities." Inequalities, Rawls maintains, are even-handed; "inevitable or else necessary, or highly advantageous in maintaining effective social cooperation" (*PL*, p. 270). At the same time, the origins of inequality appear as irrational, due mostly to "happenstance" (cf. Calvin's inscrutable god). The "most fundamental" inequalities "arise from social starting positions, natural advantages, and historical contingencies" (*PL*, p. 271).

Even granting that interpretation, the fact that a person is born into a welfare family may be natural happenstance, but the construction itself—"welfare family"—is not. Inequalities seem to belong—although Rawls does not put it this way—to the domain of the given. This means that for the Rawlsian liberal, it is not rational to plot a society in which inequality is continuously attacked and concentrations of power and privilege are actively discouraged. Such a course is declared to be "either irrational or superfluous or socially divisive" because "it does not permit society to meet certain essential requirements of social organization and to take advantage of considerations of efficiency and much else" (*PL*, p. 329).

Rawls does not explain what "essential requirements of social organization" he has in mind (those of Michels? Hayek?) or, more importantly, how the same "culture" that he invokes to promote democratic values and behavior manages to flourish despite being surrounded by antiegalitarian social organizations and values. Here and elsewhere, Rawlsian liberalism needs the idealizing blur supplied by democracy. The fundamental primacy accorded individual rights justifies unequal persons and powers, but because every citizen can claim them formally, the norm of equal right gains priority over the fact of inequality. Thus liberal inequality is democratized and democratic equality is liberalized.

What is not appreciated by the liberal formula, Equal Rights + Freedom = Democracy, is that African Americans, other peoples of color, Jews, and Irish Catholics will fail to resonate to liberal values of toleration, equality, and freedom, because their historical experiences have a different threshold than the optimistic historical sensibility of liberalism allows: a threshold on one side of which were the experiences of nativism, slavery, anti-Semitism, and anti-Catholicism and, on the other, the ready-to-wear categories of equal rights for everyone regardless of historical traumas.

Just how political equality justifies social and political inequality is illustrated when Rawls, apparently without sensing its antidemocratic character, insists on equal opportunity for all to positions of political and social power, that is, to positions in hierarchical organizations where they can exert unequal power and influence while receiving disproportionate compensation and protection from an institution that is often allowed to pay damages for its crimes without having to admit that it had committed any. Rawls tries to ameliorate the realities of unequal power by providing subsidies intended to enable the less affluent to use their rights more effectively. This not only would have the demeaning effect of creating what the neo-cons would quickly stigmatize as "welfare citizenship" but would serve as a lightning rod for resentment whenever widespread economic insecurity occurred.

IX

Rawls emphasizes frequently that political liberty occupies a higher plane than economic rights; the latter are "less significant" (*PL*, pp. 367–68) and not to be included in formulating basic constitutional principles. Similarly excluded are the principles by which social inequalities are to be regulated (*PL*, p. 337). Justice does not require that "the actual distribution [of goods] conform at any given time (or over time) to any observable pattern, say equality," or that "the degree of inequality" fall within a given range. "What is enjoined" is that inequalities "should make a certain functional contribution to the expectations of the least favored," provided that there is a surplus. How this is to come about in a society in which "unpredictable interference" is enjoined is unclear (*PL*, pp. 282–84). Nor is it plausible that in a society of rapidly changing technologies and bitter international competition, a "surplus" would be given to the needy rather than to subsidizing research and development and promising future jobs. The guarantee of equal rights is not so much to promote participation, Rawls explains, as it is to ensure "just legislation," a result that evidently Rawls believes will come about by the political forays of an occasional citizenry (*PL*, p. 330). His hope is that political parties can be kept independent of private power by public financing of elections (*PL*, p. 328). To believe that such reforms would go a considerable distance in ensuring "just legislation" is to be not only oblivious to the political economy of lobbying but innocent of the extent to which corporate power affects educational institutions, shapes popular culture, and limits public discourse.

The political problem for liberals is to prevent the basic causes of deep inequalities from being treated as "fundamental" or as "basic" as the principles that legitimate the inequality-generating structures. Rawlsian "political justice" attempts to adjust liberalism to this problem. It might be described as constitutional equality tempered by *richesse oblige*, by the moral duty of the powerful to ameliorate the condition of "the worst off" while being careful not to jeopardize in any degree the relative power of richesse or increasing that of those Proudhon called "the most miserable classes." The sensibilities of *les riches* are relieved of guilt by making both their good fortune and the bad fortune of *les misérables* seem a matter of which way the fortune cookies crumble.

That outcome is foreshadowed in the practice of systematic exclusion, which, for Rawls, begins at the very beginning, in his "device" of an original position where Rawlsian individuals—whose abstract individualism is never more "perfectly" represented—are to decide on the basic principles of justice, that is, come to the same conclusions that Rawls believes a reasonable and rational person would. The conditions that make for rational choice in the original position are, to a significant extent, essentially principles of exclusion.

Those exclusions are necessary for the very reason that Rawls thinks *Liberalism* represents an advance over *Justice*. It has, in his view, succeeded in answering the critics who charged that the earlier work relied on self-interest to motivate choosers into opting for justice as fairness (*PL*, pp. 370–71). But that theoretical advance is possible because Rawls has suspended self-interest while tacitly acknowledging its power in denying certain knowledge to the choosers. They are ignorant of their own socioeconomic situation as well as of "the present state of society" (*PL*, pp. 372–73). Indeed, *Liberalism* draws a "thicker veil of ignorance" over the original position than was the case in *Justice*. The parties are constructed "solely as moral persons and in abstraction from contingencies"— such as being poor. The theorist-constructor has allowed the choosers "just enough" information to make the agreement rational, although rationality is itself highly abstract because the choosing will be independent of "historical, natural, and social happenstance."

With no suspicion that, under circumstances where the parties have, admittedly, been reduced to personal and social ignorance (*PL*, p. 277), reason might fairly be described as tyrannical, Rawls asserts that the resulting contract is to be based solely on the rational and "nonhistorical" analysis of the content of justice (*PL*, pp. 272–73). Those who are designated as our "representatives" are described as "reasonable and responsible beings apart from society" (*PL*, p. 277). Denied knowledge gained through experience, the choosers will then be free to select "alternatives" from "a list of conceptions of justice to regulate the basic structure" (*PL*, pp. 277–78). As an afterthought, Rawls adds that they will also benefit from "the availability of general social theory" (*PL*, p. 278; we are not told which social theories or who is to select them, but we are informed flatly that "contribution theory" is to be ruled out [p. 280]).

Clearly, such a construction favors those who "represent" social strata accustomed to abstract thinking—insurance executives, accountants, economists, military planners, philosophers—but leaves unrepresented those whose formative experiences have been focused on winning their rights, defending their existence amid squalor, and enduring the consequences of technological innovation and corporate strategies.

X

Although *Justice* was published in 1971, it was very much a book of the sixties, most especially in its assumptions about continuous economic growth, the existence of a shared consensus centered around New Deal social policy, the defeat of racism, and the good nature of the welfare state. It even contained a cautious defense of civil disobedience—a topic on which *Liberalism* is silent except to say that in a well-ordered society it would be superfluous. For a quarter century, *Justice* enabled liberal philosophy to flourish in the academy long after liberal politics had suffered a series of devastating electoral defeats from which it has yet to recover.

One year after the appearance of *Justice*, the sixties ended abruptly with the overwhelming electoral victory of Richard Nixon. In the two decades that followed, the rhetoric and practice of American politics was dominated by conservatism and by the determination to overthrow most of the assumptions of the sixties. The response of Rawlsian liberalism is to restate a very traditional restrictionist view of democracy.

Rawlsian democracy is always "constitutional democracy" except when it is "well-ordered democracy" or "liberal democracy." In Rawls's world, a constitution "fixes once and for all certain constitutional essentials" including the people. The people are the acknowledged constituent power but "only" for approving the constitution. "The idea of a right and just constitution and basic laws is always ascertained by the most reasonable conception of justice and not by the result of an actual political process" (*PL*, p. 233). Absent the procedures established by the constitution, the people "can have no [democratic] will." A "democratic constitution" is described glowingly as the ideal of a people "govern[ing] itself in a certain way," the way of "public reason"—yet public reason is to be modeled after "the reason of its supreme court the exemplar of public reason" (*PL*, pp. 231, 232)—an enviably clear statement of how a constitution is supposed to construct the sovereign people.

Then follows Rawls's alarms about majority rule that, to put it plainly, are not earned by a formulation that otherwise rarely falters in its faith in the ability of citizens to talk reasonably about the most fundamental matters. Rawls echoes the antimajoritarian rhetoric of Hamilton's *Federalist*, with the great difference that Hamilton had emphatically warned against trusting human nature with power, and from this followed his conception of the court as reason without power. Rawls flatly asserts that when a majority attempts to make the constitution conform to its wishes, that act represents "simply a fact about political power as such" and has no claim to right. Rawls is not as fastidious, however, when he finds it necessary to invoke the power of the majority to validate his constitution. The "fact about political power" is smoothly transmuted into right. His constitution, Rawls reassures us, is not "straightforwardly anti-democratic," only "anti-majoritarian with respect to ordinary law" (*PL*, pp. 233–34). That, Rawls hastens to add, does not mean that the constitution is simply what the court says it is. Appealing to what looks suspiciously like "a fact about political power as such," although a mystified one, Rawls says that his constitution "is what the people acting through the other branches eventually allow the Court to say it is" (*PL*, p. 237).

Cutting democracy to the specifications of constitutionalism is only the first Procrustean operation. The second is to fit "democracy" into an antidemocratic social framework. In the introduction to *Liberalism*, the starting point is not democracy but the discovery of the importance of "stability." Rawls is correct in asserting that "the problem of stability is fundamental to political philosophy" (*PL*, p. xvii). But each and every one of the canonical political philosophers, from Plato to Mill, typically has accompanied a paean to order with an indictment of democracy as the most unstable of all the forms of government, save tyranny—although no thinker, post-Aristotle and pre-Tocqueville, had actually experienced democracy. Rawls's formula, "a well-ordered democratic society," is not congenial with the turbulent history of democracy: not with fifth-century Athenian democracy, the Leveller movement, the early American republic, Jacksonian democracy, nineteenth-century America in general, the politics of the sixties, or any number of rowdy local school board or council meetings. Instead, as I shall suggest shortly, Rawls's formula is congenial with Calvin's ideal of a church: *une église bien ordonnée et réglée*.

The "serious problem" that directs Rawls toward stability is the threat of disorder. This he finds imminent in "a modern democratic society." But where the canonical writers had almost unanimously located the potential of democratic disorder in class conflicts or, more simply, in the lusts of the have-nots and know-nothings, Rawls finds it in "a pluralism of incompatible yet reasonable doctrines" (*PL*, p. xvi). If that is *the* problem, then clearly the solution will be to find a formula that will at one and the same time join and contain the doctrines. The formula is as follows: restrict the conflict to doctrines, thereby substituting ideas for actors and classes; hone the rough edges of the doctrines by stipulating that they conform to a standard of reasonableness; and fashion a stable cooperative society around the reasonable principles acceptable to all ("overlapping consensus").

If that formula seems more a prescription for a graduate philosophy seminar than for the deliberations of a political society, the next step reinforces that impression. It defines the boundaries or space within which the conflict is to be resolved. Rawls refers to this as "the 'basic structure' of society." It is defined as "the main political, social, and economic institutions, and how they fit together into one unified system of social cooperation from one generation to the next" (*PL*, p. 11). That conception of a unified system of indeterminate duration is not, Rawls insists unconvincingly, the application of a "comprehensive doctrine." He visualizes it as the product of democratic agreement. That, however, fails to reckon with the coerciveness embedded in the "arguments" that he employs to override or neutralize conflicts. Thus, when he asserts that one feature of a political conception of justice is expressed in terms of "certain fundamental ideas seen as implicit in *the* public political culture of a democratic society" and that "in a democratic society there is *a* tradition of democratic thought" (*PL*, pp. 13–14; emphasis added), the conclusion is, not surprisingly, that "the fundamental idea" of *the* tradition is the ideal of "a fair system of cooperation over time" (*PL*, p. 14).

Ordinarily, the antithesis of cooperation is said to be conflict, and conflict has been considered an invaluable as well as an inevitable accompaniment to free politics. In the age of vast concentrations of corporate and governmental power, the desperate problem of democracy is not to develop better ways of cooperation but to develop a fairer system of contestation over time, especially hard times. In classical terms, that means confronting the crude imbalance between oligarchic and democratic elements.

Whenever the economy is allowed to appear, Rawls invariably makes it anodyne—not the economy of widening class divisions, vast disparities of wealth, ruthless downsizing, union busting, exporting of jobs, and corporate corruption and fraud. Instead an economy of "moderate scarcity" is postulated and allowed to serve as a limitation on any significant scheme for redistribution of wealth.

The near invisibility of the economy, of its power relationships, and of the interconnections between corporate and political powers are as though Rawls has himself been victimized by what might be called the narrow perceptualism of *Liberalism* that encourages those powers and relationships to remain veiled and unseen. That they are unseen by the citizens is a crucial element in the coercive character of the political system Rawls has imagined.

XI

The conceptual setting for Rawls's construction of vision and its liberal vistas is the "original position." Like its archetypal predecessor, the social contract, it is a narrative cast as an argument, a narrative embodying the theorist's fantasy of constitutive power. It constructs a hermetic setting in which the homunculi who are designated representatives of the citizens choose the principles of justice that are to shape the nature of the "political." The choosers are first endowed with "two moral powers" (a capacity for a sense of justice and a conception of the good) and powers of reason, but they are also deprived of their fundamental moral convictions and the knowledge of their own social and economic statuses (*PL*, pp. 23–25). In Rawls's society, although we may have different comprehensive views, "everyone accepts and knows that everyone else accepts the very same principles of justice." Justice thus produces "a shared point of view" (*PL*, p. 35); its principles are "designed to form the social world in which our character and our conception of ourselves as persons are first acquired" (*PL*, p. 41).

The most crucial omission from the original position is any recognition that a political society inevitably carries a historical burden as part of its identity, that it has committed past injustices whose reminders still define many of its members. Rawls, by contrast, gives a picture of an expiated community that has settled its injustices on terms that merely need to be recalled, as in the antislavery amendments to the constitution.

The result is a conception of a transparent political society in which three forms of Puritanism converge: New England, Rousseau, and Kant, ascetics all, united by a joyless politics and featuring a polarity of individualism and a coercive community of virtue. The publicity required of political deliberations is intended to brace citizens, making them "confident" while strengthening the "public understanding." "It means that in their public political life nothing need be hidden" (*PL*, p. 68). This will guarantee no "ideological or false consciousness" (*PL*, p. 69, note 21). The cleansing spotlight of "publicity" thus serves as a secular version of testifying before the congregation.

The recipe is for a civil religion in which the dogmas boil down to "reasonableness." Just as Rousseau banished the atheist, so Rawls reads the unreasonable out of his political society. The "coercive power" that Rawls gives to the corporate body of citizens poses no problem because the real coerciveness, which ensures how "coercive power" will be exercised, lies in the practices that acculturate the citizens. Seeing the same way is a version of dogmatism: what you do not see, in effect, you suppress. When members of pariah groups that historically have been wronged are fully acculturated so that they see through categories such as "reasonable," "free and equal," and "democracy," they are reconfirming the original position as amnesic ritual.

XII

Despite its numerous references to a concept of "the political," what is most wanting in *Liberalism* is an analysis of the current condition of the political and of the political prospects of liberalism itself. *Liberalism* needs a departure point such as the opening question of Emerson's essay *Experience*: "Where do we find ourselves?"

In the context of political philosophy and of a book with the title *Political Liberalism*, it is not tendentious to read Emerson's question as a political question: Where do we find ourselves politically? The question might then induce a philosopher to say whether his undertaking is intended primarily as a contribution to formal philosophy, whether formal philosophy means contextless (except for philosophy itself) and what sense it makes to talk about the contextless political, whether it will help us find who and where we are politically, and why we are where we are and why that is or is not importantly different from where and who we were.

It would not do for the philosopher to excuse himself, as Rawls does, saying that he has set aside questions of "gender and the family" because "the same equality of the Declaration of Independence that Lincoln invoked to condemn slavery can be invoked to condemn the inequality and oppression of women" (*PL*, p. xxix). Rawls might have felt sufficiently prodded by the Emerson protocol to reflect on why his particular formulations are at all responsive to the lapsed political condition of a society that has publicly endorsed those values for a very long time while disregarding or rejecting them in practice. Or, he might wonder what would be analogous to slavery in today's advanced economies of low wages, coerced overtime, and a permanent underclass.

By honoring Emerson's question, the political philosopher might help us to find our political selves or, at least, to find ourselves politically. To be able to do that would mean recognizing that, by itself, philosophy does not equip the philosopher to make his way around politics. Or, stated differently, philosophy does not become "political" simply because it treats political topics in a philosophical way; it becomes political when it gives evidence of grasping what is happening to the political world. Specifically, it would mean that the starting point for even a minimalist democrat should be the recognition that, considered broadly as a political project, democracy is out of synch with or opposed by virtually every dominant tendency in the American economy, cultural life, and politics.

In rebuttal, of course, the political philosopher can reject the Emersonian counsel to present a picture not of where we are politically but of what he wishes us to be politically (e.g., a "constitutional democracy"), and he may do it not by addressing us directly as actors but by constructing us as homunculi in an original position, reprogrammed to respond so that the philosopher may speak formally to other philosophers, seeking their approval of his "device of representation" rather than our gratitude for illuminating our condition.

The philosopher might justify his practice by saying that he is not in the business of empirical analysis or policy prescriptions but seeks instead a theoretical justification of the main principles that constitute the political. As Stuart Hampshire explains defensively in a review of *Liberalism*, the liberal philosopher "is not called upon to propose some general method of resolving casuistical problems of public policy."[4] That objection, perhaps licit under the conventions of philosophy, should be considered an evasion for the same reason that moves Hampshire's mild complaint that "the noise and muddle of actual politics are altogether absent" from *Liberalism*.[5]

To satisfy the Emersonian prerequisite, a political philosopher would be expected to provide not a detailed empirical analysis but rather an informed and thoughtful estimate of a condition. A model is available in Sir Thomas More's *Utopia*, the first part of which consists of a condensed critique of the economic, social, and political practices of England; the second part, "Utopia" proper, details the institutional background and political and moral principles that were offered as remedies for the unjust condition exposed in the first part. Ironically, although Utopia literally means "nowhere" and More playfully locates it in no specific part of the world, it is firmly grounded in a critical analysis.

For his part, Rawls postulates a nowhere that is oxymoronic, a "well-ordered democratic society." His society "is to be viewed as a complete and closed social system . . . [with no] relations with other societies . . . [and] where we will lead a complete life" (*PL*, pp. 40–41). Without a gesture acknowledging the human beings streaming across our southern borders, Rawls adopts a starting point, although imaginary, that is harsh, even claustrophobic: "It is also closed. in that entry into it is only by birth and exit from it is only by death. We have no prior identity before being in society" (*PL*, pp. 40–41).

Although it may serve the purposes of a formal theory to posit a closed society with *a* tradition and a citizenry informed by *the* public political culture, these erasive monochromes are not hospitable to democracy. In Rawls's closed polity, all of politics seems centered in one abstract public space whose vast dimensions are never a problem. The result is a curious asymmetry. For Rawls, those spatial dimensions preclude, without argument, participatory democracy as a serious alternative, but they do not prevent Rawls from levying a series of stringent moral demands and ideals of reasonableness that presuppose closer, more intimate relationships of the kind that localized democracy might well foster but surely a highly bureaucratized, market-driven society would not.

Where Rawls most resembles More is to the credit of neither. His ideal world is the realized yearning for a frictionless polity. If the constitutional guarantees are "secure," Rawls assures us, no basic conflict "is likely to arise" that would justify opposition to his political conception as a whole. Institutions should be framed, he opines, "so that intractable conflicts are unlikely to arise" (*PL*, pp. 154–56). While claiming that his concern is not with the actual world, Rawls repeatedly invokes the practices commonly identified with his own society.

The result is a construction that claims merely to be that of a free-standing society but is, in actuality, a utopia in the pejorative sense, an ideological project whose author is unaware that he has fashioned a disguisement instead of a solution.

PART FOUR

POSTMODERNS

CHAPTER 14

ON THE THEORY AND PRACTICE OF POWER

PERHAPS NO WRITER OF THE LAST HALF of the twentieth century has done more to illuminate the nature of power than Michel Foucault. Almost singlehandedly he moved the discussion of that most elusive and illusive concept from its modern or state-centered understanding to a postmodern or decentered version. Yet for all of its fertility, Foucault's critique left standing some of the bastions of modern power while ignoring its peculiar dynamics. The best that it could produce was an insurrectionary gesture against a corporatized world with no exits. The Foucaldian conception of power remains, therefore, incomplete. This is fortunate because it allows the opportunity to criticize current postmodern conceptions before they settle in as reigning orthodoxies.

For the purposes of the present discussion I shall take the phrase *postmodern politics* to mean:

(a) Politics conducted with minimal dependence on any principle of legitimacy which justifies the exercise of power by appealing to some myth of origins or by deriving it from some *Grundnorm*, for example, popular sovereignty; the authority of a constitution; natural law; or a social contract. For the postmodern the traditional conceptions of legitimacy are tainted by transcendentalism, foundationalism, myths, or meta-narratives.

(b) Accordingly, postmodern politics is content with a minimalist justification for the exercise of power. In this respect it presents a striking historical contrast to modern democratic and liberal conceptions. The modern politics inaugurated by the English revolution of the seventeenth century and the American and French revolutions of the eighteenth century was shaped in important ways by the belief that for power to be legitimate it had to be grounded in a broad public basis. The metaphor of a basis or foundation had concrete and specific referents: to increased popular participation in political processes, to the securing of political rights (voting, rights of association and assembly, and free public communication), and to the establishment of a national forum, a definite focus of attention where political actors would debate matters of public concern. The modern economy of power, especially in its liberal rather than its democratic form, was profoundly if not always self-consciously shaped by revolutionary experiences that were simultaneously wars that attempted to mobilize the energies and resources of entire populations. Consequently, the revolutionary appeals to a broadly public conception of power were the ideological mirroring of a broader, more collectivist actualization of power which would become the hallmark of the modern state.

Postmodern politics preserves the public as an opinion rather than as a set of practices. Postmodern politics solicits approval rather than requires legitimation. Approval is broadly expressed as a rating that registers the opinion of the citizen about the job performance of politicians. It is not tied to periodicity as elections are but can be elicited at whim. This minimalist conception of legitimacy gives to contemporary politics its peculiarly asymmetrical character. The power that modern science has made available to the postmodern state exceeds all previous scales, but the political basis for it has steadily shrunk. We might say that the postmodern attack upon foundationalism has abetted a politics whose simulacrum is a pyramid of power resting on its apex.

(c) That job performance has assumed importance as a principal category of appraisal reflects the elevation of competence to the top rank of political virtues. Postmodern politics fears incompetence more than corruption because it is haunted by fears about the fragile character of postmodern structures. If competence is the first of the virtues for maintaining the system, human error is the cardinal vice that always threatens it.

(d) Competence is one of several entries in the postmodern lexicon which contribute to obliterating the modern distinction between public and private. Others are: management, expert, and cost/benefit. The practices of postmodern politics are illustrated by the revolving door through which executives pass from corporate positions to governmental agencies and vice versa, or by selling governmental functions to private entrepreneurs ("privatization").

Foucault's central preoccupation was with power, and he approached it through a running criticism of some of the distinctive categories of modern political theory. The most important of these were theory, action, and the sovereign state.

Theory and action is a formula as old as Western political theory, but it became the hallmark of modern political thinking, both in Hobbes's conjunction of theory and technology and in Marx's linking of theory to revolution.[1] The differences between the two are, for my purposes, less relevant than that the formula itself represents the kind of conceptual language which Foucault considered suspect: theory signified in his eyes a totalizing system of thought, an all-inclusiveness that was at once authoritarian and ignorant. Theory professed to explain all phenomena when it was merely transposing them to a plane of abstract generality whose terms it controlled. Preoccupied with deep questions of history's meaning, man's fate, and universal truths, theorists, according to Foucault, mostly ignore the relationships and systems of meaning which actually constituted human life. Although Foucault indicated that this conception of theory had its origins in ancient philosophy, the modern representatives, such as Hegel and Marx, were his special targets.

Foucault was equally, if not more, suspicious of the association of theory and action in the formula of theory and praxis made familiar by Marxist writers of this century. "Do not," Foucault urged, "use thought to ground a political practice in Truth; nor political action to discredit, as mere speculation, a line of thought."[2] If the common theme in this injunction is liberation—the liberation of practice from the tyranny of transcendental foundations and of thinking from the leaden and limited horizon of practicality—that theme was produced because Foucault himself had initially theorized a tight and systematic union between thought and action that rivaled anything projected by German idealism or materialism. Foucault identified liberation with resistance rather than revolution, exploiting the interstices that exist because all power formations are incomplete. Action is, however, unable to escape from the formations that constitute, in Foucault's conception, its own necessary and sufficient conditions. There can be no leap from the realm of necessity to the realm of freedom, only an insurrectionary moment before power is reconstituted and action is redomesticated.

Foucault's conception of power seemingly depended on a thoroughgoing rejection of the proudest achievement of modern theory, the conception of the sovereign state as the center of power and authority, the ultimate source of rules, and the final arbiter of social conflicts.

> What we need, however, is a political philosophy that isn't erected around the problem of sovereignty, nor therefore around the problems of law and prohibition. We need to cut off the king's head: in political theory that has still to be done.... To pose the problems in terms of the state means to continue posing it in terms of sovereign and sovereignty, that is to say, in terms of law. If one describes all these phenomena of power (discipline, normalization, surveillance) as dependent on the state apparatus, this means grasping them as essentially repressive.[3]

Foucault was protesting against juridical conceptions of the state, arguing that there were innumerable networks of power which were outside state authority and that the state was not an independent source of power but rather "can only operate on the basis of other, already existing power relations. The state is superstructural" (*P/K*, p. 122).

Foucault's conception is flawed by a narrow construction of state power as essentially negative and preventive ("this meta-power with its prohibitions"), parasitic rather than grounded ("rooted in a whole series of multiple and indefinite power relations that supply the necessary basis for the great negative forms of power") (*P/K*, p. 122). Still trapped by Marxist metaphors of base and superstructure, Foucault failed to grasp the positive role of the modern state in promoting the modernization of society. Although the state repressed (for example, abolishing local standards of weight and measure in favor of nationally uniform standards), it also created (roads, bridges, schools). What it created was the infrastructure of modernity, most strikingly in the form of modern science whose subsidization by the state over the past three centuries has made possible the phenomenal growth of scientific knowledge and its practical applications.

The modernity of modern power in its state-centered form is captured most tellingly in the phrase *industrial democracy*. Less than a decade ago that phrase was widely employed by social scientists to categorize societies that were highly industrialized, were considered dynamic, and were governed by a representative system of government, responsible officials, the rule of law and free elections. The use of the word *democracy* was intended to signal that state power was legitimated by the citizens who voted its governors in or out. Thus state power was distinguishable from most of the other great types of social power, such as wealth, status, knowledge, ownership of property, and (most) religions.

The second feature of the world of advanced modernizing societies is the remarkable degree to which it is the premeditated product of mind. From weaponry to medicine, from social therapies to administrative organizations, we see artifacts that do not merely happen to come into existence but are planned and invented. All of these products are the result of the systematic application of mind. They are also the constraints within which mind must operate. So while mind is demiurge, it is also conscript. Its name is technical knowledge: knowledge that is methodized, administered as a practice.

Third, the imperatives of the modernizing, technical state shape a politics in which policy is the central focus. Politics takes the form of policymaking, policy formulation, and policy implementation. The modes of action characteristic of this politics are negotiation, compromise, adjudication, and litigation. Policy signifies the attempt to create a private space in which decisions can be removed from the unpredictable pressures of mass publics. Private space is established by the cult of technical expertise which envelops policy formulation with the aroma of the sacred. Then everything turns on what powers have access to the various stages of the policy process. The primacy of policy relegates electoral politics to the margins where it functions as a myth of legitimation.

Although much more could be and needs to be said about this version of the political world, it is a world with a central political paradox. The hoariest cliché is that we live in a changing world. The second hoariest cliché associates change with progress toward freedom, democracy, and the alleviation of mass suffering. The significance of Reaganism and Thatcherism is that change has become a conservative category. We live in a constantly changing world because change is institutionalized and manufactured. Its institutionalization imposes narrow limits—intensive rather than extensive—so that rigidity seems to be built into change. As a consequence it reenforces those forms of power which have managed to oligopolize the process of change and are best adapted to a technocratic politics.

Those who consider this system of politics to be unjust, inegalitarian, repressive of human potentialities, and a threat to the health, welfare, and future of mankind must contend with the absence of any point of leverage. For the evils and dangerous tendencies of the system are interwoven with its material inducements.

Foucault attempted to supply a point of entry into this problem by developing a notion of power focused upon the interplay of knowledge and power. He promised entry into the world shaped by technical knowledge and centralized state power. He rejected the ideal of theoretical knowledge and sought a conception that would bridge the gulf between knowledge and its application and thus would eliminate the traditional problem of the proper relationship between theory and practice. His solution was contained in the notion of a discursive formation.

A discursive formation consists of practices and institutions that produce knowledge claims that the system of power finds useful. A specific discourse serves a maieutic function: it brings objects into being by identifying them, delimiting their field, and specifying them, as when psychiatry declares schizophrenics to exist and to be the objects of psychiatric therapies.[4] Objects of knowledge are defined in ways that converging practices can use: the practices of the criminologist, the psychiatrist, the hospital administrator, and the legislator. Thus a discursive formation unites thought and practice in a seamless and circular web: Practices set the conditions for discourse and discourse feeds back statements that will facilitate practice. Discourse appears completely incorporated into practice. It has no autonomous identity or distance.

The concept of a discursive formation represents a sharp break with state-centered conceptions of power and, by extension, with revolutionary or radical politics which defined itself by opposition to, or overthrow of, the state. Foucault proposed a vision that could be called Frondiste: it opposes centralization in favor of localism. It is in these local formations that the element of mind, as I have called it, plays its double role, partly constitutive of power and partly the creature of power. So closely are knowledge and power associated that it is difficult to say whether Foucault's legacy is primarily a politics of discourse rather than a discourse about politics or whether it is a discourse in which each is absorbed into the other and transformed by it: politics becomes discourse and discourse politics.

His notion of genealogy seemed to have been fashioned as a weapon in a political struggle against the dominant form of discourse.[5] But the announced aim of the struggle was to liberate forms of knowledge, not to found a new society. Genealogy, he wrote, is "a kind of attempt to emancipate historical knowledges" from the "hierarchical order of power associated with science" and "to render them capable of opposition and struggle against the coercion of a theoretical, unitary, formal, and scientific discourse"(P/K, p. 85). Although the specific target was Marxism, the criticism reflected Foucault's rejection of any "global systematic theory which holds everything in place" (P/K, p. 145). The critical references scattered throughout his writings to Plato, Hobbes, and Hegel made it clear that his attack was directed at the idea of theory as the representation of political totalities and the idea of the theorist as the creator of political truth, "the sovereign figure of the *oeuvres*" as Foucault called him (*AK*, p. 139). The theoretical project and the theoretical subject are targets for Foucault because they are the carriers of a state-centered, authority-centered politics that is inherently repressive.

Foucault's discourse about politics was thematized in the following: "The set of relations of force in a given society constitutes the domain of the political. . . . To say that 'everything is political' is to affirm this ubiquity of relations of force and their immanence in a political field" (*P/K*, p. 189). Foucault took the idea of force literally, insisting that politics was war conducted by different means and that "the mechanisms of power are those of repression" (*P/K*, pp. 90–91). He also drew certain implications for the relationship between politics and discourse: "Do not use thought to ground a political practice in truth; nor political action to discredit, as mere speculation, a line of thought."[6]

These statements sketch a conception of the political and of the relationship between political theory and political action which sharply challenges received notions. There is a strong sense in which each of the major terms—political, theory, and practice—has been reduced to power. This is not surprising because in all of its manifestations—words, things, beings, institutions, and relationships—Foucault's world is suffused with power. There is no social space undefined by power relationships and no socially significant form of power which is not housed. It is a social world totally dominated by power but not necessarily a totalitarian world.

In a curious way, therefore, Foucault seems to have repeated the same error of totalistic thinking with which he taxed classic theory. Foucault's error may have had its own troubling consequences. Not only does he give us a vision of the world in which humans are caught within imprisoning structures of knowledge and practice, but he offers no hope of escape. Every discourse embodies a power drive and every arrangement is repressive. There is no exit because Foucault has closed off any possibility of a privileged theoretical vantage point that would not be infected by the power/knowledge syndrome and would not itself be the expression of a Nietzschean will-to-power. "It is not possible for us to describe our own archive, since it is from within these rules that we speak" (*AK*, p. 130).

But for that position to be consistently maintained it would have to confront the fact that for three centuries most Western societies have firmly believed that such a privileged body of knowledge is in their actual possession and they have deliberately banked their social and political future on it. They have believed that this mode of knowledge is not class-biased in its nature, that its progress serves the interests of all humanity, and that it is, so to speak, objectively objective despite being highly theoretical.

Since the seventeenth century the modern ideal of knowledge has been identified with scientific theory. As the writings of Bacon, Hobbes, and Descartes illustrate, the modern understanding was perfectly clear about why scientific knowledge was valuable. It was, according to Bacon, for "the enlarging of the bounds of human Empire, to the effecting of all things possible."[7] It was, after all, Bacon who first proposed a design whereby power and knowledge would "meet in one." Despite the quasi-Nietzschean candor of these early proponents of science, subsequent thinkers helped to create a divided vision of science. While urging kings and parliaments to support science for its practical value, they themselves treated it as though it were a body of truths which might offer itself in the service of power without becoming distorted. The political nature of science was thus concealed in an epistemological myth which taught that because scientific knowledge could be rendered into mathematical formulas it must be innocent knowledge.

Although modern science seems to be the perfect example of a discursive formation of power/knowledge, the exact status of scientific knowledge in Foucault's writings is unsure. There is a sense, but a qualified one, in which science occupies a privileged position. It was the standard presupposed in his description of the various stages or "thresholds" a body of knowledge would pass over on the way from "positivity" to "scientificity" and "formalization" (AK, pp. 186–187). Although he acknowledged the possibility that ideological elements might penetrate science, he seemed to resist, as a working hypothesis, the idea that ideological influence could be detected in the theoretical ("ideal") structure of science and in technological applications of science (AK, p. 185). His denial was part of an unargued distinction between "the contents, methods, or concepts of a science," which are placed outside genealogical suspicions, and "the effects of the centralizing powers which are linked to the institution and functioning of an organized scientific discourse within a society" (P/K, p. 84). Nor did he contest the scientific pretensions of the social sciences. Although he located the social sciences among those archaeological territories where scientific aspirations exceeded scientific achievements, Foucault seemed not to have doubted that they were useful and should be accorded a measure of scientific respect. He dismissed as "a secondary matter" the question of the ideological content of the social sciences and of their place in a system of rule (P/K, p. 112).[8]

This impression of ambivalence is not dispelled by Foucault's criticisms of the role of "organized scientific discourse" in sustaining systems of domination. A careful examination of these criticisms shows that they were directed not against the seamless web of involvements between science, governmental bureaucracies, and business corporations, but against "the power of a discourse considered to be scientific," that is, against Marxism (P/K, pp. 84, 85). The problem, he insisted, was not whether Marxism was truly a science but the determination of Marxists to make it one. The problem was "the politics of the scientific statement" (P/K, p. 112). Wanting Marxism to become a science, Marxists were seeking to invest their discourse with "a power which the West since Medieval times has attributed to science and has reserved for those engaged in scientific discourse" (*P/K*, pp. 84–85).

There was, however more at stake than what got articulated in Foucault's attack upon Marxist science. It had to do with the precarious status of science within classical Marxism. Like Bacon, classical Marxists exalted the economic power of scientific knowledge and exempted it from being under the sway of various idols whose influence caused thinking to err. While claiming to be a science and, by definition, immune to social distortions, Marxist theorists were also busy discrediting all other forms of discourse as ideological, that is, their truth-value was historically relative, a product of their function in a power formation grounded in control over the material means of production and expressed through rule by a particular class. Clearly the perpetuation of the myth of epistemological innocence left science poised at the edge of the ideological abyss into which all the other discursive constructions—theology, philosophy, ethics, and classical political economy—had already tumbled.

From the middle of the nineteenth century to the 1960s the vulnerability of science to *Ideologie-Kritik* went unnoticed because most thinkers, from Marxists to conservatives, believed scientific knowledge to be immaculately perceived. Pure theory was the usual name, and the distinction between basic and applied science was the typical way of rephrasing the mythic warning about purity and danger. The modern function of the myth was to make the following question appear silly: How was it conceivable that scientific knowledge was permeated by ideological elements when that knowledge had provided the basis for an endless number of technologies that plainly worked?

Soviet Marxism betrayed the myth not only by openly employing science (psychiatry) to suppress dissent and to buttress the authority of the Stalinist dictatorship (the Lysenko affair in genetics or the linguistics controversy), but by injecting ideological elements into scientific methods and theories. As a consequence of this trauma, the presumption of scientific innocence was shaken. Scientific knowledge became a guilty knowledge. Although Soviet Marxism displayed the crisis of scientific faith in its most brutal form, the crisis ran deeper in the non-Marxist West. Ever since Hobbes bravely declared that human beings could be scientific and at the same time interest-driven and power-obsessed, it had become an article of faith that in scientific method the mind had devised a prophylaxis against interest and bias. Accordingly, in the predominantly bourgeois world of the West where, thanks to the canonical status of political economy, the widespread acceptance of notions of self-interest, class-interest, and national interest testified to the conviction that interest pervaded the entire range of personal, social, and political relationships, the vocation of science alone seemed disinterested. In a corrupt world science seemed the only saving knowledge.

In the non-Marxist West the Vietnam War destroyed the illusion of scientific innocence. Thanks to television, itself a product of applied science, everyone could see that this was a war between a technological power and a prescientific society and that science alone had made possible the terrible devastation loosed upon that society. In addition, the critique of American power developed by American radicals contributed to the end of illusions about science. The attack upon corporate capitalism exposed the role of scientific knowledge, while the rise of the environmental movement and the early opposition of establishment scientists to it helped to deflate the myth of scientific purity. Henceforth the meaning of science included an ineradicable political element.

A postlapsarian science produces a problem for all forms of discourse. In a secular age guilty knowledge suggests ideological taint. The surrender of innocence means that instead of being buoyed by the hope that mankind is about to enter the long-promised era of science triumphant, in which mere modernizing will be succeeded by postmodernity, we find that that hope may be our secret nightmare and that we shall be left with nothing more than scientific man with all of the frailties that a genealogical expose insinuates.

Foucault did not quite face the circularity that his own analysis implied but proceeded as though a permanent residue of strict scientificity remained. The privileged character of science did not mean that it occupied some absolute sanctuary where it was shielded from the relativism that is inscribed in all Foucaldian formations. In Foucault's discourse science enjoyed the sanctuary of equivocation despite its inconsistency with his basic principle that there is a power element that is constitutive of knowledge and a knowledge element that is constitutive of power. While insisting that the institutionalization of science embedded it in structures of power and rendered it complicit in strategies of domination, Foucault wanted nevertheless to limit the contaminating effects of complicity, "the world's slow stain," by denying that they had seeped into the infrastructure of knowledge itself, into its concepts, data, hypotheses, logical or mathematical proofs, and so on.

If Foucault did not challenge the epistemological myth of science directly, he did so indirectly by showing that science did not hold a monopoly over the generation of social power and that social control was exercised through other forms of knowledge which were just as firmly integrated into the knowledge/power circuit. Disciplines with varying claims to scientificity—psychiatry, medicine, sociology, criminology—were deeply implicated in structures that defined while they disciplined the human being. He accomplished this in a novel way. He did not challenge the fact-value dichotomy on which positivist social science continues to rest, albeit less securely than before, nor did he deny the existence of objective knowledge, only its neutrality. "What is at stake in all these genealogies is the nature of this power which has surged into view in all its violence, aggression, and absurdity in . . . the last forty years. . . . My aim [has been] to expose [the fact of domination in] both its latent nature and its brutality" (*P/K*, pp. 87, 95).

Foucault's intention was not, however, to expose a general system of domination but to identify the dispersed nature of power formations. One of the curiosities of Foucault's writings is that, despite his fascination with power, nowhere does he systematically analyze its supreme embodiment in modern totalitarianism. He was not directly concerned with great tyranny but with smaller ones. His choice rested on strategic considerations as well as on theoretical (or perhaps countertheoretical) ones. The focus on dispersed power follows consistently from Foucault's attack on the centralized conception of power in classic theory.

Foucault paid a heavy price for his refusal to engage central power structures, for he virtually ignored those social sciences that were most heavily implicated in them, namely, economics, political science, and law.[9] It is as though his notion of politics oscillated between two extremes: on the one hand, carceral institutions and, on the other, the dispersed forms of control which define sexuality.

Foucault's attack on the classic conception of theory seems motivated by two contradictory beliefs. One is that the structure of such theories forms a homology with structures of domination. Theories display the same "unitary," totalizing tendencies as the centralized apparatus of the modern state.

Yet at the same time Foucault appears to dismiss the great theoretical constructs described in histories because they were and are dissociated from systems of power. Thus theory appears both dangerous and impotent. My concern is not to belabor the apparent contradiction but to try and show the consequences that follows from Foucault's dismissal of classic theory and of his belief that classic theory neglected the problem of practice.

In using the (not altogether happy) term *classic theory*, I want it to designate a certain kind of project rather than to identify myself with the contents of any particular theory from the past. I shall try to conceptualize the classic project of theory and especially its understanding of the relation of theory to practice. I intend this not as a plea to resurrect the classic project but to clarify the stakes in Foucault's disavowal of it.

My starting point is Foucault's rejection of the notion of theoretical truth independent of practices. For Foucault truth is not a knowledge claim that has been validated by procedures or conventions recognized by some appropriate community of inquirers. "Truth," for Foucault, is always accompanied by quotation marks to signify that it is being unmasked as it is being described: " 'Truth' is to be understood," he writes, "as a system of ordered procedures for the production, regulation, distribution, circulation and operation of statements." It is "linked in a circular relation with systems of power which produce and sustain it" (*P/K*, p. 133). Truth, then, is literally and ambiguously a fabrication. Truth is to Foucault's discursive formations as the commodity was to Marx's account of capitalist production. It is a product of the practices that make it possible.

The obvious criticism to be made is that Foucault has overstated the coherence and ambiguities of discursive formations. They never attain the monolithic unity ascribed to them, not even in that perfect combination of precept and practice known as the Catholic church, much less in that rancorous and divisive discourse that goes by the deceptively unified name of psychoanalysis. But this answer, while perhaps telling, is too facile. The more important point is that although theoretical discourse has never achieved that perfect symbiosis with practices implied in Foucault's notion of a formation, a good many political theorists wished it had, as any reader of Plato's *Republic* or Hobbes's *Leviathan* can testify. Does this mean that theory has always longed to be swallowed up into practice? Did Plato, for example, want to disappear into the *Republic* and reappear in the philosopher guardians, or into the *Laws* and reappear in the Nocturnal Council?

The answer is, I think, mostly no. I say "mostly" because, undeniably, the temptation was there. But the main reason for my answer lies in the nature of the theoretical project itself. That project as a practice—that is, the activity of theorizing—declares its autonomy from politics, its separate identity from political practices, even while it is prescribing them. The reason why Moses, who was Israel's founder and lawgiver, does not enter the promised land is why Socrates, who is used by Plato to describe the ideal polis, would have been the first political prisoner in Plato's *Republic*. The reason lies with the necessary tension between the objectives of theorizing and the tendencies of political action.

In *The Republic* Socrates asks, "Is it possible for anything to be realized in deed as it is in spoken Words, or is it the nature of things that action should partake of exact truth less than speech?"[10] Plato's formulation may be interpreted as a double warning that serves to establish the nature of theoretical discourse. The first is the relationship between critical distance and political failure. If theory is absorbed into the discourse of action so as to become inseparable, it will be impossible for it to perceive when action has fallen short of what it should be. It is the nature of action to fall short of theory and it is the role of theory to declare that. Theory can only perform that critical function if it retains a separate identity. Otherwise theory becomes *techne*, and the theorist becomes indistinguishable from the technician of power. Moses does not enter the promised land and because he does not, theory can return as prophecy and criticize the Canaanizing of the desert religion, the "baalizing" of its religious life.[11] Plato is careful to specify that if a state were to come into being it would be only an approximation to the ideal, but the discrepancy would signify that theory would remain distanced from power (*Republic*, 472E, 473A).

The second warning embodies a form of folk wisdom as old as politics and theoretical discourse. Political practice, like its close companion religion, does not simply apply ideal truths but diminishes them. Practice does not merely use theory as it would technical knowledge but uses it calculatingly. The history of religious discourse is a history that testifies to the experience of betrayal through incorporation and to the need for continual rededication and renewal. Collective life reflects the same experience: of justice systematically applied and individually denied, of revolutionary hopes frozen into a new establishment, of virtue smoothed into realism.

For Foucault there is domination but not betrayal or diminution because theory has been denied integrity. In fact, truth only becomes truth when it is integrated with practice and systems of power. The tensions between theory and practice have disappeared. At best any discrepancies appear as mere slippages, technical problems of ironing out applications of thought to practical realities, not as an ontological predicament.

The disappearance of the critical element is signaled by the focus on what Foucault called "political technologies" represented by such institutions as asylums, hospitals, prisons, barracks, and schools. Each of these is treated as a discrete world in which power and the discourse of experts converge upon the body of the individual who, in isolation, is the perfect object of their ministration, not only because he is enclosed but because he is an inmate without choice. These carceral institutions signify the perfect melding of discursiveness and practice into a hermetic whole with no outside. Consequently there is no purchase point for criticism because there is no general plane remaining, either in theory or political practice. In Foucault's political world we are oppressed, yet no one is oppressing us and no single system dominates us. We can agree that we feel oppressed solely because Foucaldian discourse is parasitic. It has resonance because it presupposes the theoretical forms, especially Marxism, that it discredits.

To be sure, in the *History of Sexuality* Foucault appeared to retreat from the emphasis in *Discipline and Punish* on total institutions. "Power," he now declared, "is not an institution, and not a structure . . . it is the name that one attributes to a complex strategical relationship in a particular society."[12] Which is to say that the idea of strategical relationships is a more fitting focus for studying sexuality. Whatever else it may be, however, sexuality is not, like the forms of power previously studied by Foucault, a carceral creation. The power relationships of sexuality are, instead, the most localized and rationalistic. Relations are formed, Foucault declares, that are "intentional and non-subjective." He even insists that there is a general level at which power relations are inscribed upon sexuality and at which the logic and aims are clear. Yet unlike the local practices, the general power relations are the result of no one's intentional thoughts or actions. "No one is there to have invented them, and few can be said to have formulated them" (*Sexuality*, 1:95).

This analysis naturally suggests the question, how does Foucault's discourse stand in relation to the discursive formations it analyzes? His answer to the question has two aspects, a disavowal both of the centered and totalistic approach to discourse identified with classic theory, and of the state-centered politics that has been a notable feature of modern theory beginning with Bodin and Hobbes. "One impoverishes the question of power if one poses it . . . in terms solely of the state and the state apparatus" (*P/K*, p. 158). His answers take him to a conception of discursive activity as decentered and of politics as decentralized. That conception will prove to be remarkably and perhaps fatally faithful to the etymological origins of the word *discursive*: the latter derives from the Latin verb *discurere*, or "to run in different directions."

As we have already noted, Foucault rejects theoretical systems and the idea of a theorist-author. He rejects as well what he characterizes as "the traditional question of political philosophy. . . . How is . . . philosophy as that discourse which par excellence is concerned with truth, able to fix limits to the rights of power?" Foucault insisted that the notion of power could not be usefully investigated independently of discourse because "relations of power cannot themselves be established, consolidated nor implemented without the production, accumulation, circulation and functioning of a discourse" (*P/K*, p. 93). He proposes, therefore, the humbler notion of a theory as "a toolkit." The tool is described as an "instrument" or "logic" for analyzing "the specificity of mechanisms of power," "power relations," and "the struggles around them" (*P/K*, p. 145). Or in the fuller formulation that he gave toward the end of his life. His aim, he announced, "is to move less toward a theory of power than toward an analytics of power: that is, toward a definition of a specific domain formed by power relations and toward a determination of the instruments that will make possible its analysis" (*Sexuality*, 1:82).

Thus society is dissolved into a pluralism of power domains and to these the "analytics of power" will apply appropriate "instruments" of analysis. The political purpose motivating the investigations would be "to build little by little a strategic knowledge [*savoir*]" (*P/K*, p. 145). This strategic knowledge, in turn, will link up with "local criticism." There exists, Foucault contended, "an autonomous, non-centralized kind of theoretical production" (*P/K*, 81). Examples were to be found, he maintained, in prisons and asylums and in the student revolt of May 1968.

Although Foucault did not develop the idea of subjugated knowledges in detail, it clearly formed a piece with his rejection of overarching theoretical systems and state-centered politics. During the heady years of the late sixties and early seventies Foucault testified that "we are witness [to] . . . an insurrection of subjugated knowledges" (*P/K*, p. 81). This sets the stage for Foucault's conception of the political role of those who pursue knowledge without illusions about its purity or, presumably, the purity of their own motives. In his discussion of "subjugated knowledges," Foucault distinguished between the "knowledges of erudition," which refers to the "exact historical knowledge" of those who, like Foucault himself, expose "blocs" of knowledge which have been suppressed and ignored, and a "particular, local, regional knowledge" that is "popular" in character, disorganized but rich in the memory of historical struggles (*P/K*, pp. 81–83). An example of the latter is the knowledge of the psychiatric patient. The two knowledges are combined in genealogies that will unite them as antisciences. The union was in preparation for a struggle against "the claims of a unitary body of theory" which would assign them a place in a hierarchy of knowledge or delegitimate them altogether (*P/K*, p. 83).

In a slightly later formulation Foucault restated the idea. In place of the "knowledges of erudition" he inserted "the specific intellectual." The latter was to replace the "universal intellectual" of the past whom Foucault scornfully described as "the spokesman of the universal . . . the consciousness/conscience of us all" (*P/K*, p. 126). The specific intellectual, who Foucault thought was ideally embodied in the physicist J. Robert Oppenheimer, is the "expert" who possesses a "competence" valued in the truth-domains of society, but who uses that knowledge for "political struggles." The specific intellectual is identified by Foucault as having acquired his importance from "the extension of techno-scientific structures in the economic and strategic domain" (*P/K*, p. 129).

But why should the specific intellectual employ his or her knowledge in political struggle and why should he side with the dominated? Unfortunately Foucault is silent on these questions, unfortunate because, as the work of Richard Rorty suggests, there is nothing inconsistent between combining advanced views on the demise of theoretical hegemony with political views that are, at best, complacent, and at worst reactionary. Foucault has come to a dead end, the consequence of having accepted an unqualified Nietzschean conception of knowledge as generated by power drives that leaves no room for conceptions of theoretic vocation and civic commitment.

A fundamental political and theoretical question that used to be asked of a radical thinker was this: has he identified the crucial point of vulnerability in the system(s) of power he seems to be opposing? One thinks, for example, of Habermas's legitimation crisis, Marx's analysis of the downfall of capitalism, or of Machiavelli's conception of civic corruption. Within the context of vulnerability, the peculiarity of Foucault's discourse is exposed: there is no place allowed for notions of decline or crisis. Discursive formations seem to have acquired the occult qualities that the ancients ascribed to circles: they reproduce themselves to infinity. Even if one discursive formation, say, criminology or penology, were captured by the forces of deconstruction, it would become immediately evident that what was captured was merely one element in a linked system of fairly substantial, though not necessarily total, interconnections. In short, the problem of theory presents itself not only as the need to identify those interconnections but also as a problem of action. For the practical problem is not simply what to do about the discourse that encompasses prisons and asylums, but how to deal with the practical pressures emanating from an apparently nondiscursive formation, such as an elected legislature that annually votes appropriations for asylums.

The futility that emerges as the key characteristic of Foucault's politics is, I would suggest, not the consequence of an endlessly changing world constituted by mind, but its reflection. Foucault insisted that in adopting a genealogical method he was deliberately choosing to remain at the surface of things, a strategy that was universally applauded by sympathetic interpreters fatigued by the traditional talk about essence and logos. But Foucaldian genealogies—unlike, for example, the logical positivist attack on "metaphysics"—do not puncture linguistic illusions; they simply reduce metaphysical chatter to a historical instance of power/knowledge discourse, more feckless than psychiatry perhaps, but not necessarily its intellectual inferior.

Foucault could not, of course, appeal to a privileged form of discourse without reinstating the heresy of a hierarchy of knowledge. As a result all discourse is reduced to the level of positivity at which power and thought reproduce each other. This means that henceforth knowledge lacks the legitimating quality that in earlier centuries had been associated variously with sacred, divine, or ontological origins. In fact its status is virtually indistinguishable from practices because both are rooted in power. Which is to say that interpreters of Foucault who claim that his discourse is ungrounded are wide of the mark. It is grounded in precisely what ancient conceptions of knowledge were always grounded in, namely, power. One need only recall that Yahweh was a god who was not only omnipotent but omniscient.

What is different is the nature of power: for Foucault the emphasis is upon the repressive, dominating quality of power. Even when he tries to suggest the idea that the objects of power come to serve as its bearers, not simply as its focus, he clearly implies their passivity. Ancient understandings, whether, for example, biblical or Aristotelian, conceive of power as a political relationship in which the object must be receptive without being passive, that is, he possesses a being or structure with its own integrity. He responds to power by learning what it exacts of him, but he tries to connect that exaction with practices designed to make power work on his behalf. Thus in the medieval and early modern institution of kingship the coronation rites had the king pledging to promote the true religion. That promise also tried, however, to connect God's blessing with the practices of monarchy. God was supposed to support the king's military ventures, inspire his judges, and quicken his counselors. But Foucaldian power operates in a world where things do not have a nature, only a discursive definition shaped by the needs of power. It is not enough to say, as Foucault does, that in the notion of insurgent discourses he has supplied a conception of a subject who, as it were, fights back and resists discursive formations. The Old Testament shows how a people can resist the discourse of Yahweh but also gain his favor and in the end help to shape the terms of the covenant. Or a more humble, contemporary example: consider the "welfare cheat" (in the language of Ronald Reagan) who chisels a system of power by using it while being used by it.

These options were not open to Foucault because he consistently confused politics with the political. Foucault's identification of politics with power has a genealogy of its own extending back to Thucydides and to Plato's portraits of Thrasymachus and Callicles.

The problem of the political is not to deny the ubiquity of power but to deny power uses that destroy common ends. The political signifies the attempt to constitute the terms of politics so that struggles for power can be contained and so that it is possible to direct it for common ends, such as justice, equality, and cultural values. Commonality is what the political is about. Whatever the pretentiousness and vanities of theorists may have been, it was the recollection of commonality and the restatement of its terms which defined the point of theoretical discourse.

Foucault has posited an untrue antagonism between theory and decentralized politics. The result is to leave us with an unlocated self who is denied the critical vantage point that theory allows. The vantage of theory is interconnected with its proclivity toward superiority and quasi-domination. What follows is not that we should renounce theory to avoid its dominating discourse; rather, we should find forms of theory that will be consistent with a localizing—or better—participatory, community-oriented politics. As a starting point: most people don't live in carceral institutions and are only episodically subject to distinct discursive formations. They are instead, located in a certain place. Place is geography and vocations. (Vocations: what we do in and to the world.) This means that subjectivity and historicity are connected. Our place in the double sense of geography and vocations is known only by its history, so, therefore, is our identity.

Locality is the ground that has to be defended against state-centered politics. Which bring us to the crucial role of theory.

The preferred form, I would argue, was prefigured by those writers whom, ironically, Foucault singled out as the most horrendous examples of totalizing: Plato, Hegel, and Marx. And although each was a totalizer, each also held to a conception of theory in which, as it were, theory self-destructs. Thus Plato's dialogue is always incomplete and the issue is never closed. Hegel and Marx both understood theory dialectically, and it was only an urge toward premature—though not logically demonstrable—closure that undid this element.

Self-consuming theory—to use Stanley Fish's term—preserves the playful, self-derisive mien of theory without surrendering its potential contribution to decentered politics. Theory locates the self and the local grouping in relation to the more encompassing structures of power which are the hallmark of state-centered politics. But theory is valuable not only for being able to locate movements but also for helping to overcome the autistic tendencies of localism and the self-centered preoccupation of the postmodern individual. Theory has been a civic discourse. It has called the self out of the self, beckoned it to a plane of generality which reminds the self in its locality that other beings and other life forms inhabit public space and are bent on establishing their own collective identities.

This conception of theory also liberates action from being haunted by theory and absorbed into the notion of practice. Foucault has no place for action, only for practice. Action is not identical with practice. Practice signifies doing things competently according to the appropriate received canons. Action is often role-breaking or custom-defying, for frequently it seeks to defend the collectivity against evils that are sanctioned by rules and traditions. Action can only play this role if it is free to respond to experience and is guided by theory only to a limited extent. By this formulation discourse is denied the pretensions illicitly gained by its incest with practice.

But this conception of theory makes no claim to the power that discourse enjoys in the discursive formation. The irony of Foucault's attack on the pretensions of totalizing theory is that his own notion of the production of truth represents a power-laden conception of theory which is the equal of the claims made by any theory-intoxicated totalizer of the past. A return to a critical conception of theory, one that can intimate but not prescribe practice, can preserve the means of thinking that can both grasp state-centeredness and point to ways out of it.

CHAPTER 15

DEMOCRACY IN THE DISCOURSE
OF POSTMODERNISM

A SHORT TIME AGO, BEFORE THERE was "postmodernism" and before there was "discourse," there was "philosophy." Now there is postmodern discourse that purports to be postphilosophy. A long time ago, philosophy was invented and, independently of it, the Greeks invented a version of democratic politics. Greek philosophy, especially the philosophers descended from Socrates, invented a conception of politics that represented itself as superior to all forms of existing politics. Even when that conception was later resisted by a Machiavelli or Hobbes, the starting point was the one fashioned by Plato or Aristotle.

Included in that starting point were claims such as these: politics should be grounded in a higher truth to which philosophy alone has access; a basis in truth converted a society into a community, a close or solidaristic grouping; a good political society would be one in which philosophers not only were tolerated but were honored members of the community and, ideally, would have influence over those who ruled or, stated slightly differently, the alienation of the philosopher, as dramatized by the death of Socrates, the political isolation of Plato, and the flight of Aristotle from Athens, would be over; and, finally, the politics of virtually all of the Greek philosophers descended from Socrates was antidemocratic.

The above characterization is essentially a post-Nietzschean one. It interprets ancient philosophy and political theory as an expression and instrument of the philosopher's will-to-power. It discounts another claim of ancient theory, and one repeated by many moderns from Machiavelli to Marx and Tocqueville, that the theoretical vocation meant taking on a public burden, of being a critical conscience before the greatest power of which human beings were capable, the power of a political collectivity. Post-Nietzschean readings would, of course, consider this claim as merely a prettified version of the will-to-power. But that post-Nietzschean reading might, in turn, rest on bad faith: that claim, if plausible, would render the post-Nietzschean criticism suspect of being the expression of its own will-to-power. And since the post-Nietzschean denies him or herself any neutral means of arbitrating, that allows us to pose the questions: Has the discourse of postmodernism, while renouncing philosophy, renounced these claims, or only some of them? And what is the form that, as avowed post-Nietzscheans, its will-to-power takes and what are its disguises?

THE RIGHT QUESTIONS

One of the commonest ways by which a reader tries to understand a theory and figure out what a theorist is up to is to look for a focus, for some point that will foreshadow the text and give a clue to the particular theorist's sensibilities. A focus need not be as startling as the opening lines of the *Communist Manifesto*, "A specter is haunting Europe—the specter of Communism." C. B. Macpherson's classic, *The Political Theory of Possessive Individualism*, opens by noting, "A great deal has been written in recent years about the difficulty of finding a theoretical basis for the liberal-democratic state." A reader will have been clued immediately by the mention of "difficulty" to expect to encounter a serious hindrance to the values associated with the liberal state, and a few sentences further on Macpherson identifies it as "individualism." The situation, Macpherson states, is one in which the liberal principles hammered out during the seventeenth-century struggles in England no longer meet "the needs, aspirations, and capacities of modern man. . . . The foundations have cracked and tilted."[1]

Richard Rorty, perhaps the leading philosopher, or lapsed philosopher, of postmodernism, also considers himself a devotee of liberal democracy. His writings are important for being one of the few, perhaps the only, major attempts to ally postmodernism with liberal democracy rather than with Marxism or social democracy. He has supplied a focus to his writings that is as remarkable in its way, and as revealing, as the opening lines of the *Communist Manifesto*. The right questions, he writes in postmodernese, are "like" "What is it to inhabit a rich twentieth-century democratic society?" and "How can an inhabitant of such a society be more than the enactor of a role in a previously written script?"[2]

The first question would seem to be simply answered by saying, "Enjoy it." But the second question carries a note of dissatisfaction; it is certainly not outrage or even sharply critical.

Rorty's opening is, of course, meant to startle or, as a postmodern might say, "get our attention." But much more is revealed. There is a certain a-civic connotation to the choice of "inhabitant," as though "citizen" or "member" was not a comfortable usage because insufficiently contingent. This suspicion grows with the second question, for if the category of citizen or member means anything, it means playing a prescribed and -described role. It is also clear from Rorty's first question that the foundations are neither tilted nor cracking, not least because the concept of foundations is rejected altogether by most postmoderns.

The remarkable quality of that first question is that it is uttered without any trace of guilt. Just imagine being rich *and* democratic!

Now to be without guilt is to be blameless or, in older language, innocent. What is it that allows the postmodern, without benefit of clergy, to enjoy such a state, to play at innocence when to pick up any newspaper is to be reminded of growing extremes of wealth and poverty, drug-ravaged slums, and the hopeless-ness of a not-insignificant underclass? The answer is, I think, that innocence is regained by reducing existence to language and then reveling in a medium that appears pure, distorted only by "mistakes" or "errors" in usage, not by the influences of class, wealth, or education. Language may, of course, deceive, but it is language which allows us to expose the deception and then to expose the ex-posé itself *ad infinitum* or rather *ad taedium*, until boredom calls a halt. Which brings us to: The sacrament that bestows innocence, that makes us as a child, is, of course, the "language game." *Sacramentum ludi:* bound and obliged by the sacrament of play. And how serendipitous that language games just happen to be what philosophers, ex-philosophers, literary critics, indeed, all manner of aca-demics, are especially good at! Because then one can confidently say that "what matters in the end are changes in the vocabulary rather than changes in belief."[3]

The concept of a language game is innocent only as long as the emphasis falls on "game" and on the presupposition that certain things happen in the world that render game talk inappropriate. But when certain beliefs become widespread among dominant groups that there are material and political advantages to be gained if game talk becomes, in Rorty's phrase, "literalized metaphor," then lan-guage games are talking power and encouraging power motives. As Lyotard has put it, postmodern politics will be about the competition for knowledge.[4]

This brings us back, not to Rorty's question about what it means to live in a rich democracy, but to the question of that question: What is it for *whom* to inhabit a rich twentieth-century society and *where* exactly do they inhabit it, that is, where do they live in it? And does life present itself as role and script to all, or does a society defined as "rich" need, as Hobbes pointed out, its "others," the nonrich, the nonmobile, for whom the idea of life choices is as remote as the career of astronaut and who, in their own language game, know that they have about as much hope of influencing the Great Scriptwriters as Kafka's character had of getting a straight answer from the Castle? Do "we" say to *animal laborans*, as we would to *homo ludens*, "quirky contingency" instead of "tough luck"?

Rorty seems to suggest that the "ironist," who stands for Rorty's postmodern ego ideal, needs the others for precisely the same reason that Nietzsche "needed" the philistine. The others, and the public or "final" vocabulary in which the ironist addresses them, provide the "contrast" which "an ironist cannot get along with-out. . . . Irony is, if not intrinsically resentful, at least reactive. Ironists have to have something to have doubts about, and something from which to be alienated."[5]

THE MINIMALIST CONCEPTION

Once the question of the question is asked, a certain subtly aggressive quality is exposed in the postmodern strategies, as though if you had to ask who is fa-vored by the question you don't belong. Rationality and truth are not renounced but assigned to "the interior of a language game."[6] And as we shall see there is in fact a troubling, offensive (in both senses) clubbiness, certain exclusionary principles at work that are faithful to the traditional liberal strategy of appealing to ecumenical values that work in something less than an ecumenical way and that help to throw into sharp relief the qualifying function of "liberal" in the cant phrase "liberal democracy." By a cant phrase I mean a usage that is invoked but not earned.

Now irony, contingency, and—as we shall see—a strong assertion of the priority of the values of private life over those of public involvement are the major ingredients in the minimalist conception of politics that is one of the most striking qualities of postmodernist thinking. From this one might conclude that the philosophy of postphilosophy conforms to the archetypal pattern of philosophical alienation from the city, that minimalism is alienation in the postmodern epoch.

But what if, unlike the maximalist politics of the polis or the early New England town, contemporary liberal politics of the postmodern epoch is in fact minimalist, with or without the ideology of postmodernism: does that mean that philosophy has finally found a congenial society, one which it can join without serious reservations? And what does joining mean: does it signify that philosophy no longer wants power in order to impose its truth on the society or, alternatively, that in the "rich North Atlantic democracies" the truth, in the nonfoundational form that a postmodernist can accept, is being realized?

This desire to overcome alienation but on minimalist political terms explains, I think, a good deal about Rorty's version of postmodernism. The opening paragraph of one of his essays is the best evidence. It begins by referring to "complaints about the social irresponsibility of the intellectuals." The form of that irresponsibility is "the intellectual's tendency to marginalize herself." Then in what is surely among the more grotesque analogies Rorty compares the intellectual's marginalization to "the early days of the United Mine Workers [whose] members rightly put no faith in the surrounding legal and political institutions and were loyal only to each other." In this respect the UMW "resembled the literary and artistic avant-garde between the wars."[7]

What Rorty wants to claim is that moral responsibility can be owed properly only to "a historically conditioned community," not to some abstract, "higher" ideal. He goes on to assert, without any attempt at evidence, that "in Dewey's day" intellectuals identified "easily" with their country (like Bourne and Beard?) because they believed it to be exemplary. "The largest single reason for their loss of identification," Rorty opines, "was the Vietnam War." Rorty concludes that "some [intellectuals] marginalize[d] themselves entirely" while others, like Chomsky, by arguing the war was "immoral" and a betrayal of "America's hopes and interests and self-image," were engaged in "pointless self-castigation" and personal catharsis whose "long-run effect has been to separate the intellectuals from the moral consensus of the nation rather than to alter that consensus."[8]

Rorty's clear worry about being separated from "the moral consensus of the nation," his wholly uncritical notion of consensus, and his complete indifference to the possibility that consensus is a product of political management, not simply some casual assemblage of "practices" and "traditions," are, despite his trumpeting about ethnocentrism and its values, rather at odds with American political traditions and their dislike of talk about corporate solidarity. It is not, one might note, at odds with the whole disastrous political genealogy of Hegelianism or nineteenth-century German romanticism.

Rorty defends the notion that the set of historical practices that constitute American liberal democracy is an object with which intellectuals can easily identify. What is most striking about that community is, in Rorty's word, its "solidarity." It is a close community, and Rorty celebrates its closeness as a certain we-ness that makes the community the source of moral judgments and the arbiter of morality: "We don't do that" is for Rorty the equivalent of a basic norm. Morality is not a question of rules but of who "we" are and what we might become.[9] This togetherness is, Rorty insists, constructed out of narratives that contrast our group with theirs or with "worse communities."[10]

A GENEALOGY OF POSTMODERNISM

Indeed, Rorty's questions are themselves less surprising than the appearance of the word "democracy" in the writings of an avowed postmodernist. In considering some of the most prominent figures in the construction of postmodernist thinking, it is striking how rarely the word, much less the idea of, democracy figures. Although in the absence of a Pomo Concordance my research cannot claim to be exhaustive, my strong impression is that Foucault, for example, never made any use of the term. His indirect endorsement of values of individuality, local resistance, concern for the language of the oppressed, and the critique of carceral practices are never identified with democratic ends, however much he may have exhorted those values as a way of weakening authority.[11] Lyotard maintains an even sturdier silence than Foucault, and the same for Derrida.

Rorty has devoted a great deal of effort to constructing a genealogy for his liberal democratic version of postmodernism. It includes not only Dewey (although it is Dewey without scientism or methodism), Foucault, and Derrida but also Hegel, Nietzsche, and Heidegger. Each of the last three may flatly be described as radically antidemocratic. This genealogy assumes considerable importance in Rorty's account because it serves as the inspiration and source for a new "language" to replace that of the Enlightenment. The language of the Enlightenment, he believes, "has become an impediment to the preservation and progress of democratic societies."[12]

I shall leave aside for the moment Rorty's Enlightenment, noting only that he identifies it with the version created by Horkheimer and Adorno's *Dialectic of Enlightenment* and then reinterpreted critically by Habermas.[13] This corpus contains a very special reading of the Enlightenment, one that is deeply responsive to, and often only intelligible within, nineteenth-century German cultural traditions. This assumes some importance only because Rorty will insist upon the primacy of national cultures rather than universal value claims. The American Enlightenment was rather different from the French, drawing, for example, from the Scottish Enlightenment rather than Voltaire, Diderot, and the philosophies. One way to characterize a difference represented, on the one hand, by the line of instrumental reason (identified by Horkheimer and Adorno) that leads eventually to the Marquis de Sade and thence through Hegel, Nietzsche, and Heidegger, and on the other by the American experience of Enlightenment, is to say that the former was fascinated by transgressive thought, thought that breached the boundaries traced by established morality and religious orthodoxy, while for the latter, the American Enlightenment, transgression and its propaedeutic of skepticism were the least influential elements.[14]

The obvious question is, of course, how could the Enlightenment be any more of a hindrance to the "progress of democratic societies" than, say, the one-time rector of Freiburg University during the Nazi era? Rorty's response is to divide his genealogy into two parts based on a distinction between public and private. "As public philosophers," he declares, Nietzsche, Heidegger, and Derrida are "at best useless and at worst dangerous."[15] Rorty does not tell us precisely why these writers might be dangerous, or to whom, or whether the Jew Derrida is dangerous in the same sense as Heidegger. Or is it the ascetic, antitechnological Heidegger that Rorty wants to suppress because that Heidegger would be irreconcilable with the rich and technologically based democratic society that Rorty identifies with?[16] Rather he wants to insist on their status as crucial texts in the cause of private identity. For Rorty, private identity is, by definition, severed from public obligations to others.

Rorty does not offer any sustained account, narrative or otherwise, of the public/private distinction. Rather he asserts that it is a "necessary" one, which I take to mean that it is an item in what elsewhere he calls somewhat disparagingly an "ultimate vocabulary," that is, a way of talking that represents bedrock truth for the nonironist and a way station, at best, for the ironist. It is fair to say that throughout the public/private distinction has a hard-and-fast quality that distinguishes it from the tentative character attributed to most beliefs by Rorty. There is no talk about the shifting boundaries of the public/private but of "sectors," and there is little inclination to explore the interdependencies between the two. The two vocabularies are, Rorty insists, incommensurable. Clearly his concern to retain Nietzsche and Heidegger as gurus of the private depends upon the strictness of the distinction, even though neither Nietzsche nor Heidegger proposed that usage and there is considerable textual evidence to suggest that both would have rejected the rigid form in which Rorty casts it.

But if we introduce the Nietzschean question—What powers are shielded or favored by that distinction in its strong form?—then we may get a better purchase on what the political stakes are for the postmodernist.

Historically, few, if any, philosophers have given even two cheers for democracy. Socrates, Plato, Aristotle, Aquinas, Descartes, Hobbes, Spinoza, Leibniz, Hume, Kant, Hegel, and Nietzsche: not a democrat among them. The democratic philosophers, such as Mill, James, and Dewey, are the exceptions, and it should be remembered that Mill had some substantial reservations. This last trio, in an important sense, believed in democracy because they believed in the possibilities of modern science and universal education to raise the quality of the material lot and intellectual level of the ordinary run of human beings. They believed, in other words, in the Enlightenment project.

Rorty, however, intends specifically to demote the scientist and to replace him by the "strong poet," and he seems to have no particular interest in public education. Moreover, literary criticism, which Rorty wants to install in place of philosophy, "has," by his admission, "widened the gap between intellectuals and the public."[17] The skeptical culture of the ironist is also not for the public domain. "I cannot imagine a culture which socialized its young in such a way as to make them continually dubious about their own process of socialization."[18] Why then has Rorty come to be on such good terms with democracy that he can announce that democracy has "priority over philosophy" when that claim runs completely counter to the position historically maintained by most philosophers? And what sort of sex change of redescription would democracy, that turbulent, leveling, populist, egalitarian changeling of the philosophers, have to undergo in order to be so loved by philosophy as to defer to it?

While today no philosopher would dare to repeat Plato's formula about philosophers becoming kings, this may be due less to a newfound humility than to changing circumstances dictating different stratagems.

In the ancient world, where politics was mainly shaped by the relatively small dimensions of the polis, it was not unrealistic for a philosopher to believe that he might gain the ear of a tyrant, as Aristotle did of Hermias and Plato had attempted with Dionysus. In liberal societies, however, there are no political tyrants holding audiences, only corporate media which rate and shape them. There is, however, a veritable army of bureaucratic policymakers. Unhesitatingly, philosophers have pounced on the opportunity presented by policy studies to abandon the austerities of logic and language for the more sybaritic life of policy prescribers. "Philosophy and public policy" is now a large and prosperous field. Philosophy has thus adapted effortlessly to the needs of a corporate-bureaucratic state. It may be, to use Lyotard's conceit, politics as agonistics, but it is also a politics without agonizing and without the ambivalence which had accompanied even the most politically cheerful philosophers.[19]

Rorty is not, however, concerned with this mode of power. Rather he is intent upon pursuing Nietzsche's lead that the abandonment of philosophy means most importantly the abandonment of traditional truth claims. Philosophy's trust in an objective method by which truth could be "discovered" is for Rorty a delusion.[20] Philosophy is declared "irrelevant" to politics, and liberal democracy is said not to "need" deep philosophical justification because it does not need foundational principles.

RORTY'S CRISIS

Does Rorty's contention that philosophy should abandon the quest for "truth" as understood by centuries of philosophical practice and the belief that our notions of right and truth need to be grounded in some basic or ultimate principle, does that mean that the controversy between philosophy and the democratic city is over? If no ground is needed, then will philosophy have disarmed itself and surrendered the form of power which, historically, its claim to political relevance has rested upon? Or would the Nietzschean suspicion persist? For if philosophy no longer needs its *Grundnorm*, to say that political society should follow suit would be to redescribe the priority of philosophy to politics by saying that society, like philosophy, recognizes no need for foundational truths. It may also serve to purchase a nonalienated relationship with power by relieving philosophy of the burden of the public conscience.

What, then, are the unalienated politics of postphilosophy, and of the antitheoretical philosopher? Although some critics, such as Habermas, have charged Rorty with colluding with neoconservativism, he sees himself as a radical responding to a "crisis."[21] His crisis is whether liberal beliefs and practices can survive the collapse of the Enlightenment justification of them.[22]

Given Rorty's belief that such foundations are unnecessary, it is difficult to see why their collapse should be viewed as a crisis rather than as a godsend, or in what sense a crisis, other than too rich a diet of gourmet food, could even exist in a rich democracy. Typically in political theory crisis is serious talk. It is usually followed by a claim that something is deeply wrong in the world, that it affects us all, and that it will not be solved without active intervention. For Rorty, however, there is no wrong to right, but rather a wish for more, to have it all, as the yuppies say, both liberal democracy as it is and more science, technology, and personal freedom. If the nature of the crisis remains unspecified, what can Rorty mean when he pleads for "utopian thinking" and points to the French Revolution as exemplifying the possibility of radical and rapid change? "The French Revolution had shown that the whole vocabulary of social relations, and the whole spectrum of social institutions, could be replaced almost over-night."[23]

Rorty presents himself as a radical promoting the cause of endless experimentation made possible once "we" decide that there is no intrinsic nature to anything. Accordingly, his form of utopianism has to do with cultural innovation and self-change within the structure of a liberal society in which the private sector is extended as far as feasible.

> The sciences are no longer the most interesting or promising or exciting area of culture [due to] the difficulty of mastering the various [scientific languages]. . . . We can cope [with this] by switching attention to the areas which *are* at the forefront of culture, those which excite the imagination of the young, namely art and utopian politics.[24]

But while Rorty may look toward the French Revolution, his rhetoric is a parody of the sixties if for no other reason than the contrast between the strong politicism among the young of that era and the antipolitical, uncommitted, fashion-sensitive, self-absorbed preoccupations of contemporary young adults which Rorty treats as politics. Without quite saying "make love not war," Rorty does caution against adopting a philosophically aggressive style that, for example, might think it a good thing to drive "Nazis" against an "argumentative wall" in order to force them to confess to the superiority of liberal values. The "goal" of a good society, instead, would be "the creation of ever more various and multicolored artifacts."[25] And, one might concede, Sid Vicious was one of those.

Rorty's utopian politics is, like all utopias, without politics, a version of the sixties without the Vietnam War, the struggle for racial equality, the discovery of poverty amid affluence, alarums over ecological dangers, and anger at nuclear brinkmanship. Rorty's is an effortless, painless radicalism that in one breath can declaim that "the heroes of [his] liberal society are the strong poet and the utopian revolutionary" only to fizzle out with a definition of the revolutionary as one who "protests" against "those aspects of the society which are unfaithful to its own self-image."[26] We need not even drop out but merely drop the idea that there is something called "the nature of truth" and then "see how we get on." Or we can substitute a different formula, "do something else."[27] Truth is not so much argued away as abandoned, a game that has become tiresome.

Rorty's pain-free, cost-free formula for change is accompanied by a "backup," in his vocabulary, by a narrative of how the historical changes he likes have come about. The history which Rorty has been urging upon philosophy is user-friendly. There are no traces of bitter religious struggles, civil wars, class conflicts, or ideological polemics. Instead change insinuates itself:

> Europe did not *decide* to accept the idea of Romantic poetry, or of secular politics, or of Galilean mechanics. This sort of shift is no more an act of will than it was a result of argument. Rather, Europe gradually lost the habit of using certain words and gradually acquired the habit of using others.[28]

How "Europe" becomes a subject is never explained, nor is such usage by the avowed nominalist Rorty claims to be ever justified. But "we" receive a conception of history drawn to the needs of the English Department. Thus where a historian would probably describe, say, the Edict of Nantes as the act of a king

desperate for peace among warring religious groups, each intent upon imposing its will and its arguments, Rorty would see it as a change that came about
because two or more vocabularies "interfered" with each other and a new vocabulary was invented to replace them.[29]

A bland outlook such as this makes one long for the old base/superstructure
days, for if there was ever a view of history as an idealist fantasy, this one would
rank high. It is not that shifts in vocabulary do not occur or that they are not
important. When American public rhetoric and jurisprudence no longer accepted the language of slavery, the move was of some significance. But it didn't
just happen, nor was it simply vocabularies that "interfered" with each other;
rather it was two armies. And when changes began slowly to happen, they did
not affect the substance of race relations for several generations. Nor would
the fact that Americans have "lost the habit" of uttering racialist slurs help to
explain the resurgence of racialism, especially among high school and college
students.

What has been created by Rorty's nihilism is a linguistic politics for a linguistically created state of nature: no authority, no neutral rules, only contingent standards. Politics becomes word strategies.

Rorty names the strategy "redescription." It means simply putting the objec-
tions in a vocabulary different from that of the objector but one which favors
Rorty's aims:

> So my strategy will be to try to make the vocabulary in which these objections are
> phrases look bad, thereby changing the subject, rather than granting the objector
> his choice of weapons and terrain by meeting his criticisms head-on.[30]

Lest we conclude that making an opponent look "bad" would be at odds
with Rorty's kinder and gentler society, he reassures us that redescription is better understood as "refurbishing" a house.[31] What Rorty wants to redescribe are
"the hopes of liberal society in a nonrationalist and nonuniversalist way."

SELF-CREATION

The strategy which Rorty devises for his invented crisis reflects the peculiar
character of postmodernism. It declares itself to be an epoch because it is bored
and fatigued by the haggles which have preoccupied thinkers for centuries to
no avail. The real concern should be "self-creation," the vocation of deciding
how we want to be, feel, perceive, experience, think, relate to others and to a
community. The self is not construed by Rorty in heavy terms such as decision
or commitment, much less by obligations or by concern/care; and even less is
it constrained by them. For the utopia Rorty favors would be one of maximum
freedom and minimal public involvements that let "its citizens be as privatis-
tic . . . as they please as long as they do it on their own time—causing no harm
to others and using no resources needed by those less advantaged."[32]

We may leave aside Rorty's remark about resources and the less advantaged because he never follows it up—it is a cost-free remark—and turn instead to his juxtaposition between the two principles of privatism and not harming others. For "the liberal ironist," as Rorty describes himself, "cruelty is the worst thing we do."[33] It never occurs to Rorty that what he regards as painless, namely, switching metaphors, paradigms, and vocabularies, might be highly painful to those whose hopes, as well as identities, are bound up with certain myths or language games that Rorty declares are no longer "needed."

For Rorty is Hegel as appropriated by Dr. Pangloss: "We can tell the story of progress, showing how the literalization of certain metaphors served the purpose of making possible all the good things that have recently happened."[34] The phrase "the literalization of metaphor" is merely what used to be called "the realization of the Idea" or "theory becoming practice." Hegel's philosophy of history, Rorty continues, is exemplary, for it shows how the past, unwittingly, led up to us. What is called for is a historical narrative about the rise of liberal practices—apparently Rorty has not yet discovered the "Whig interpretation of history."[35]

He tells "us" confidingly, "Indeed, my hunch is that Western social and political thought may have had the last *conceptual* revolution it needs." Thus the praise of contingency, experiment, and novelty is turned off so that the hobgoblin of Truth can be resurrected and redescribed:

> John Stuart Mill's suggestion that governments devote themselves to optimizing the balance between leaving people's private lives alone and preventing suffering seems to me pretty much the last word.[36]

Supposing, however, that some groups in the United States, say, black Americans, were to argue that they have wagered their lives on the hope that the foundational belief in racial equality was "true," that the American political system was pledged to realizing it, and yet they find that they are being harmed by private discrimination in employment, in the production of racial stereotypes in the popular media, and in the racist atmosphere of selective private institutions of higher learning—what will Rorty say about the kind of self that finds itself trailed always by a permanent self, call it "blackness"?

He could tell a story about the contingency of the self, "a network of beliefs, desires, and emotions with nothing behind it." The self which may have thought that it had been forcibly transported as an object, then reduced to slave labor and sexual exploitation, and then freed in a racist society, and that there was some sort of fearful consistency of exploitation with malice aforethought can be counseled to think of its lot instead as "the hit-or-miss way in which cells readjust themselves to meet the pressures of the environment."[37]

But, essentially, Rorty does not speak to them at all; he speaks instead to those American liberals dismayed by "the unending hopelessness and misery of the young blacks of American cities." And he tells fellow liberals that it is "much more persuasive, morally as well as politically," if we "describe [blacks] as our fellow Americans" rather than as "our fellow human beings." And what, in the correct rhetoric, do "we" say about them? "That it is outrageous that an American should live without hope."[38] This for Rorty is solidarity, true community, because it brings "them" in. In reality, all it does is make those who are already in feel good without entailing any commitment that would override the more fundamental belief that the lot of the others is a matter of contingency.

The question is not so much whether "democracy" any longer needs foundational beliefs but what kind of "democracy" is it that does not, that is, what kind of tilt does it have? And who tells whom that "they" no longer "need" certain beliefs?

The problem of liberal politics is not only that several different language games with, fortunately, some points of intersection and overlap are going on simultaneously, and hence there is a high level of conflict. Rather Rorty, like Lyotard, pays respects to Wittgenstein but neglects the Wittgensteinian point that language games are life forms, that is, a lot of people's hopes, fears, very existences are implicated in their language and the converse holds also; but their language is often not *the* language, and hence they are inarticulate, which is, of course, one definition of powerlessness in a society where The Thinkers declare certain language skills *de rigueur*. All human beings may be language-users but it is not clear that they are all language-game players.

Further, language games are not like software, where a new program simply replaces an old one. Old language games don't die gracefully or fade away. At the end of the sixties the language of abortion rights appeared to predominate, and no creationist language was around to create dissonance in high-school biology classes. The scene is very different now. This suggests that new language games are piled on top of old ones, not simply superseded as Rorty's stacked narrative suggests but sedimented, as Husserl would have said. The consequence is one that Nietzscheans should adore but postmodern Nietzscheans shun: the eternal recurrence of cultural and political archetypes. If, once again, we have to endure what we have been through before, say, McCarthyism, genocide, racism, and Bhopal, then the fun and games of language begin to pall.

Rorty's defense of privatism is, unwittingly, something that has been described before. A society in which privatization is publicly encouraged and proclaimed to be the highest value, and government treats its members benevolently, is a society where public space is, as a matter of policy, shrunken. The minimalist politics of most postmoderns is virtually the spitting image of Tocqueville's formula for democratic despotism: a kinder, gentler society whose members have forgotten the elementary "truth" that the enjoyment of freedom depends upon vigorous participation, not withdrawal. Freedom doesn't simply happen because government allows it but because government either encounters determined resistance or chooses not to provoke it.

Rorty's exaltation of privatism is an antidemocratic move, not simply because it never raises the question of what language game is played by those with power, but because the distinction of public/private is not what democracy is importantly about. It is about equality (a notion conspicuously absent from postmodern discourse), the virtues of ordinary men and women, their good sense, everyday integrity, and natural cooperativeness with those who share their fate in the same place. Because of where it starts from—equality and the belief that public power should be devoted to common endeavors—democracy is wary of a sharply defined distinction between public and private and its inevitable accompaniment, the corruption of the public domain by private motives that are activated by the magnitudes of money, resources, and legal authority connected with the daily actions of the few who typically are in charge of the modern state. The liberal politics of the public/private comes down to the politics of access to those who operate the public system. The trick, as the scandals of the Reagan years drearily showed in endless reruns, is to make the latter privately accessible and, at the same time, beholden.

What then is the place of the ordinary person in Rorty's liberal democratic, mostly private, conceptually perfect polity? Rorty tells us that Kant has tried to make "the intellectual world safe" for the modest and dull many, "the unselfish, unself-conscious, imaginative, decent, honest, dutiful persons." He did it by providing room for "faith."[39] This left "us" with a choice, according to Rorty's narrative, between the exciting human paradigm (sc. *Übermensch*) of Nietzsche and Kant's decent dull man. Fortunately, Freud came to the rescue by showing that everyone has a rich fantasy life and that genius, like dullness, is simply a form of adjustment.[40]

Since, however, Freud's solace for the many probably never reached them, not even at prewar prices, leaving the possibility that if, in Philip Rieff's silly phrase which Rorty quotes approvingly, "Freud democratized genius by giving everyone a creative unconscious," we are still left with Kant's dullard, Rorty is prepared to admit, unsurprisingly, that maybe "we" are in "need of a more complex, interesting, less simple-minded model of the self."[41] After treating his readers to this picture of ordinary people as fashioned by the language men, Rorty concludes on this gracefully democratic note about what "we" should remember about "such people":

> [that] even if the typical character-types of liberal democracies *are* bland, calculating, petty and unheroic, the prevalence of such people may nevertheless be a reasonable price to pay for political freedom.[42]

DEMOCRACY WITHOUT THE DEMOS

What is the democratic nature of the democracy that we enjoy today? Rorty does not address that question, but one thing is abundantly clear from his writings, that it is democracy without the demos. Another thing is that the historical animosity of intellectuals toward "the people" has been carried over into postmodernist discourse. These attitudes are not in themselves particularly significant. They become so when we inquire, as Rorty does not, into the social and political function of intellectuals in the postmodern rich democracies.

Over the centuries one of the continuing worries of theorists has been about the corruption of mind by those who rule society. A certain degree of distance has been thought to be necessary to the *bios theoretikos* because the powerful who control society's resources can easily flatter and exploit those who possess valued social knowledge and who believe, perhaps naively, that that knowledge should be for the general benefit of society. Far from sharing that apprehensiveness, Rorty not only longs for reunion but sets as the goal of the good society the promotion of the comforts of intellectuals:

> An ideal liberal society . . . has no purpose except to make life easier for poets and revolutionaries while seeing to it that they make life harder for others only by words, and not deeds.[43]

Thus, in exchange for the comfortable leisure of the theory class, the latter will "make life harder for others," although, clearly, not by subversive talk but, presumably, by instruction in liberal ideals or by criticizing society's lapses from its own standards (although that hardly makes sense in an "ideal liberal society") or, better yet, by concentrating political energies in that purest of political actions, defense of the freedom of other intellectuals.

Leaving Rorty's liberal utopia, we need to inquire into the actual political condition and treatment of Rorty's poets and revolutionaries by a rich democracy and inquire, too, into what is expected from those same poets and revolutionaries by the social and political powers that never cease to remind "us" that there are no free lunches. We shall also want to see if there is a stronger implication to making life harder for others, one that bears on the postmodern intellectual in a democracy.

No one with a passing familiarity with the politics of the richest democracy doubts that it is a highly managed democracy with only rhetorical gestures toward egalitarianism, widespread participation in power, or respect for the sensibilities of ordinary people.

By managed democracy I do not mean that people are puppets manipulated by Washington, Wall Street, or Nashville. It is more disturbing than that. Managed democracy is a created world of images, sounds, and scenarios that makes only occasional contact with the everyday reality of most people. The rest of the time that world floats in dissociation, a realm wherein reference has been suspended. This is why, for example, the media express astonishment when they learn that the "stories" on which they have lavished such energy, ingenuity, and resources are mostly ignored by the citizenry. The latter don't much care about

Ollie North, Jim Wright, or HUD scandals for they know that those revelations are meant to show the "system works" and they understand very well that it doesn't work for them: it only imposes surcharges on vital services.

That manufactured world of information about images is the one that governmental and corporate elites have constructed and shaped so as to maximize the modes of power which they command. They proceed to devise a world that has vast international drug cartels which can be fought only by mustering the armed forces and sending them to aid the forces of law and order in some poor third-world country where those same forces have been on the take from the very cartels they are supposed to be eradicating. Meanwhile, the devastated families in the ghettos are told that all they need to do is say no to drugs. It is not simply that some postmodern power holders are racist. Rather it is that postmodern power is literally dumbfounded in the presence of generational cycles of poverty, poor education, and disease. It cannot operate in ways that effectively meet such conditions, and so it retreats, mumbling that all solutions are "like throwing money after problems."

But in the self-defined age of information and communication, where knowledge is said to be power, and new knowledge more power, managed democracies do need intellectuals who are adept with words and images, who realize that words are more important than beliefs, that contingency is at fault, and who are sufficiently infatuated with their own self-importance as to believe that the "founders" of the liberal utopia will be "poets" rather than "the people who had discovered or clearly envisioned the truth about the world or about humanity."[44] Nowhere is the woman or man of language skills more useful than in the democratic elections of a managed democracy. Then true creativity flourishes to fashion a make-believe world of distortion, half-truths, lies, smears, gossip, appeals to fear, patriotism, xenophobia, racial code words, and imaginary foreign monsters (sc. "Libyan hit-squads"). It is the greatest Language Revel ever conceived. But because it is, its appetite for novelty is voracious.

That appetite calls for an endless supply of catchy phrases, slightly bizarre images, and stylish ideas. Technicians of culture are as necessary as legal, managerial, and scientific technicians. The powers that control that world, or act as though they do, are willing to put their money where the intellectual's mouth is. The intellectual, as writer, provides material to cater to that appetite for novelty, to keep that world going; and as professor he reproduces the technicians of culture and of the other domains. Today the prestigious universities mount one mammoth fund-raiser after another, piling up money in order, as one ex-Ivy League president put it, to have more money. The humanities, hitherto Saturday's child when it came to funds, are now awash with money and busy with new institutes. MacArthur grants are awarded to liberal poets and revolutionaries. It is the best possible world for the language game.

How might a postmodern intellectual earn his/her keep? This is a question of the political meaning of breaking the links between truth and politics. One might expect from Rorty's self-proclaimed "anything goes" outlook and his postmodernist adulation of "difference" that his would be the very model of liberal tolerance. In fact, Rorty can fairly be described as militantly antireligious. The great calling, he avers, is to "de-divinize" and "disenchant" the world further.[45] Now if we recall that the dutiful intellectual will make life harder for some, then one might suspect that American believers, especially fundamentalists, would be in for hard times. What disenchantment means, politically, is the erosion of a powerful support that ordinary people find in religion. To be without it is to be vulnerable to the image culture and its daily diet of novelty. The religions which have done most to shape the American moral consciousness have been populist and culturally conservative; and, as commentators beginning with Tocqueville have frequently noted, this folk religion, with its odd, often picturesque and bizarre ways combined with strait-laced and tight-lipped sense of rectitude, has played an important role in preserving a democratic sense of the self-worth of the ordinary individual.

As Nietzsche predicted, philosophy has produced the "last man": unconscious about power, about how his own powers are being used, about how he is using his own powers, and about the power nature of the institutions which house him.

> The earth has become small, and upon it hops the Last Man. He makes everything small. . . . "We have discovered happiness," say the Last Men and blink.[46]

CHAPTER 16

POSTMODERN POLITICS AND THE ABSENCE OF MYTH

TODAY IN THIS MOST MODERN OF ALL modernizing societies it is not uncommon to encounter the claim that myth survives. As proof of the presence of myth it is customary to point to the use of mythic themes by contemporary poets, dramatists, composers, sculptors, painters, and writers of a religious sensibility. Despite their apparent viability, however, these are more in the nature of postmythic strategies than direct expressions of myth. They are evocations of the archaic in the midst of a modernizing society which, by its own self-understanding, is committed to the systematic extirpation of mythical thought. They are mythmaking self-conscious of itself, aware that it is engaged in a premeditated act of fabrication. There is, consequently, an irreducible element of alienation that accompanies contemporary mythologizing.

A contemporary anthropologist has remarked of ancient myth that it was a form of discourse which did not know its name, that is, was not conscious of itself as myth.[1] For the modern who dwells in a culture in which science is universally acknowledged to be the highest and most exemplary form of knowledge, there is no doubt about the proper name for myth or about its location among the modern topoi. It belongs among the fetishistic modes of thinking that represent the theological stage in the development of the human mind identified by Auguste Comte.[2] In the theological state, according to Comte, the human mind "supposes all phenomena to be produced by the immediate action of supernatural beings."[3]

Myth tends to be the consolation of marginal minds who savor its traces precisely because they appear anachronistic in a world that is progressively being shaped by technological reason and interpreted by social-scientific methods and conceptions. Myth occupies the status of a residual category that justifies whatever intuitive, nonrational, poetic, religious, or other fugitive experiences we happen upon in a world orchestrated by postmythic powers. The experiences are fugitive in the very specific sense of being nonscientific and noninstitutionalized, which is to say the mythic is an alien category in the official hermeneutics by which the controlling elites interpret the symbolic system that is largely their creature. Myth is tolerated as one tolerates the artistic: as a confessional sign of powerlessness in a technological society in which the fate of collectivities and their members is decided by newer principalities and powers.

DISCOURSE ABOUT POWER

This separation of myth from power and power from myth represents, as we shall see, the modern inversion of that relationship. For myth was once preeminently discourse about power, about powers immanent and transcendent, and man's relationship to them. In the myths of the Old Testament (especially in Genesis and Exodus), the *Epic of Gilgamesh*, and Hesiod's *Theogony* we have tales of power centering around the theme of chaos held at bay or overcome, of powers in conflict or rebellion. It was the equivalent of an introductory text to the subject of power. Its special feature was not its poetry but its realism. It is exactly that quality that tends to be obscured by modern social science when it replaces myth not by "realism" but by fiction. We can watch it happening when the contemporary social scientist attempts to identify myth as a function and to deal with it not in its own terms but by means of the fiction of a "social system." The result is that myth is moved to a totally different realm of discourse, as we can see by quoting an eminent authority on Old Testament myths: "The myth is a product of human imagination arising out of a definite situation and intended to do something. Hence the right question to ask about myth is not, 'Is it true?' but 'What is it intended to do?'"[4]

Although there is something ironical to the suggestion, offered in the name of science, that the proper way to understand myth is by means of a fiction, the shift in terms, from myth to science, has the double effect of expunging the power motif in myth while concealing its presence in science. As employed by social scientists, fiction is a political category masquerading as a methodological device. It is political in the double sense of being constitutive and power-laden. To represent society as an integrated "system" composed of functionally interrelated parts is to distort empirical reality by reconstituting it in an ideal form. But the idealization that takes place in many of the artificial constructs devised by the social scientist is of a special sort: it euphemizes power and power relationships. Think of "game theory," or "the market," or the idea of "modernization." In these constructions, when power isn't absent, it is sanitized as, for example, "outputs" or "change." At the same time, inequalities of power and powerlessness itself are literally uncomprehended; they make no sense in this discourse.

The contrast with an ancient myth, such as the one set down in Hesiod's *Theogony*, is instructive. The making of the earth and the genealogy of the gods are described in vivid language that serves notice that violence and treachery were woven into the original fabric of the world. Verse after verse insists on the monstrous and wily natures of the progeny spawned by Earth and Heaven. They tell unsparingly of the terrible deed of Cronos who, at the behest of his mother, Earth, takes a sickle and lops off the genitals of his father, Heaven, while the latter is lying atop Earth and attempting to copulate.

In contrast, the social scientist, who in this regard is modernity's representative, deadens rather than enhances our sensibility toward power by protesting that his models and fictions are but the expressions of a naive playfulness. In actuality they represent a propaedeutic being played out at the level of mind in which the uses of power are rehearsed. This cryptopolitics is initiated typically by the introduction of a simplification—for example, that myth is to be understood in terms of its contribution to the maintenance of a social system. That is the necessary first step toward exercising control over the phenomena under investigation: they are subsumed under a construct, the "social system," and reshaped by its logic of functional explanation. Although the social scientist who studies myths in this manner is seemingly engaged in a politically harmless activity, it is mimetic of the way power is actually exercised in advanced societies where state and corporate decisions are based upon, and legitimated by, the so-called policy sciences such as economics and political science. All of the policy sciences make extensive use of fictions and artificial constructs designed to simplify the world as a preliminary to manipulating some portion of it.

Seemingly, then, it is the absence of myth that helps to define the politics of the modern and the postmodern world. The classic text on the subject is Max Weber's "Science as a Vocation." There the tension between modernist deference toward the natural sciences and postmodernist despair at their cultural consequences is drawn with almost brutal insistence. There are two passages in the essay that vividly express the modernist conviction that scientific thinking has routed mythical modes of thought. The form that this triumph takes was described by Weber as an historical process of "rationalization," that is, the reduction of action-oriented thought to calculating the most instrumentally efficient means for the achievement of a specific end:

> The fate of our times is characterized by rationalization and intellectualization, and, above all, by the "disenchantment of the world." Precisely the ultimate and most sublime values have retreated from public life either into the transcendental realm of mystic life or into the brotherliness of direct and personal human relations.[5]

These remarks occurred in a context where Weber was discussing the meaning of a commitment to a scientific vocation at the historical moment when science had undermined the credibility of religious, moral, and metaphysical systems which had previously endowed the world and, by extension, vocations with meaningfulness. The disenchantment of the world clearly implied that a new world, inhospitable to myth, had come into being; that a new conception of mind had been culturally enshrined; and that that conception, while it reduced the meaningful to the meaningless, disqualified itself simultaneously from filling the cultural silence left by the old discredited myths. For one of the basic taboos in the nonmythic culture of social science is that the social scientist is prohibited from directly pronouncing upon questions of value and hence of meaning. As Wittgenstein would say, Whereof we cannot speak we must remain silent.

However, Weber then introduced another theme that renders the first text equivocal:

> We live as did the ancients when their world was not yet disenchanted of its gods and demons, only we live in a different sense. As Hellenic man at times sacrificed to Aphrodite and at other times to Apollo, and, above all, as everybody sacrificed to the gods of his city, so do we still nowadays, only the bearing of man has been disenchanted and denuded of its mystical but inwardly genuine plasticity. Fate, and certainly not "science," holds sway over these gods and their struggles. . . . Many old gods ascend from their graves; they are disenchanted and hence take the form of impersonal forces. They strive to gain power over our lives and again they resume their eternal struggle with one another.[6]

We may interpret these passages to mean that while the gods of ancient myths and religions have been conquered by new powers, such as those represented by modern capitalism and the technologies invented by modern science, the fact of power and its control over us remain. What has changed strikingly, according to Weber, is man's "bearing": it has been "disenchanted and denuded of its mystical but inwardly genuine plasticity." Thus, while the old personifications of power have given way to depersonified conceptions of power, that change is less striking than the change in the internal life of man.

Unfortunately, it is not altogether clear what Weber meant by his "Lutheran" phrase about "mystical but inwardly genuine plasticity." If he meant to imply that the relationship between the ancient, prescientific self and mythical powers was essentially mystical, he was mistaken; if he meant that the relationship between the modern self and the impersonal powers controlling his world is essentially matter-of-fact, he was only partly right.

THE LATE-MODERN UNDERSTANDING

The ancient self lived in awe of the gods, but he/she also participated in ritual relationships in which gods and humans negotiated and exchanged utilities. The modern self, on the other hand, while it exercises extraordinary control over the natural processes which the ancients ascribed to the gods, nonetheless feels sufficiently dominated by these new powers that it is compelled to revert to quasi-mythical language in order to describe how the relationship appears to the modern sensibility. So the modern will complain that he feels "alienated" from, for example, "the political process"; or "threatened" by the power lodged in the hands of political and military leaders; or "worried" by the unsteadiness of "the economy." Instead of monotheism, we have centralization; instead of polytheism, we have polyarchy.[7]

Our nervous chatter reflects the menace of powers that are larger than individual or collective life; powers that dominate us and render us dependent; powers that we can analyze but, for all our brave talk about "fine-tuning" and "cost-benefit analysis," whose future course we are unable to predict, much less control. Our estrangement has to do not only with the enormous potential of modern power but with the internal economy of the late modern self. We have no inner disposition that would imply the possibility of harmony, or even a collaboration, between us and the powers. What seems missing are any genuinely participatory rituals that might incline us toward communion with powers. We seem capable only of dominating powers or of cowering before them.

The peculiarity of life in so-called advanced societies is that, while extraordinary power is lodged in certain institutions and wielded by small numbers of persons, there is a widespread loss of confidence in these societies about their ability to control its uses and a general sense of powerlessness among their citizens. How is power understood such that its modern presence induces these reactions? In particular, what is the late-modern political understanding of power?

To raise these questions is to confront the central topic of modern political theory, the topic of the state. The state is widely supposed to be the main organization for the exercise of power and the main embodiment of the idea of the political. How, then, is the state understood in relation to power and what does that tell us about the late-modern conception of the political?

There can be no better source to consult in these matters than Max Weber. Of all recent definitions, his is the one that has been repeated by later generations of social scientists and political theorists. Weber's discussion begins with a significant move that his later interpreters have ignored. The state should be conceived, he wrote, as the modern successor to the "political association" (*politischer Verband*).[8] This latter phrase is one of the common translations for the ancient Greek polis and for the famous *politikē koinonia* of Aristotle's *Politics*. Now it has long been recognized by students of ancient Greek political theory that the political (*hē politikē*) comprehended all of the significant areas of life in the community: family, religion, education, poetry, drama, and the fine arts as well as the functions usually associated with government in the narrow sense—for example lawmaking, administration of justice, war, diplomacy, etc. The political, accordingly, was not a department of society, or a separate sector, or a synonym for politics. Rather, it was the constitutive notion that circumscribed the varied life-forms and vitalities which nourished public power and formed its ground.

The broad basis or ground which the ancients attributed to the political association was embedded in the double meaning given by Aristotle to the phrase "the political" (*hē politikē*). *Politikē* was at once "the master science" that dealt with the multiple "ends" or goods appropriate to a political association and the highest human good attainable through collective life: the end of *politikē*, Aristotle declared, "is the good for man."[9]

Thus for the ancients the power of the political order was inseparable from what might be called the "end-fulness" of life lived in common with others. This conception, which persisted mostly unchallenged until the mid-seventeenth century, helps in grasping the significance of the starting point which Weber postulated for the social-scientific conception of the state. "The state," Weber asserted, "cannot be defined sociologically in terms of its ends [*als dem Inhalt*], or what it does."[10] This, Weber maintained, was because it was impossible to demonstrate historically that any particular task or function was "peculiar" to the state. It followed, Weber reasoned, that the distinctive character of the state had to be sought in the means which it employed. The means which distinguish the state and define its nature are "the use of physical force." Today, he asserted, "the relation between the state and violence is an especially intimate one."

From this intimate relationship between state and violence Weber developed his definition of the state: "The state is a human community that (successfully) claims the monopoly of the legitimate use of physical force within a given territory. . . . The state is a relation of men dominating men, a relation supported by means of legitimate (i.e., considered to be legitimate) violence."[11]

Weber completed what can be described as the late-modern conception of the political by extending the centrality of violence to "politics." Politics, Weber claimed, was the struggle for power. Its "decisive means" was "violence." The brutal quality of Weber's conception of the state was scarcely softened by his idea of "legitimacy." As he emphasized, it was the successful claim or fact of legitimacy that mattered. Legitimacy was thus merely the rationalization of successful violence. The political stood for a system of domination (*Herrschaft*) secured by monopolization over the instruments of violence.[12]

The pathos of Weber's formulation is that it claimed both too much and too little for the modern state. It has become evident in recent decades that, whatever the "uniqueness" of the modern state may be, it does not consist in a monopoly of the means of violence. The universal phenomenon of terrorism, by which small private groups or even single individuals use violence to blackmail public authorities and often enjoy widespread public support for their acts (e.g., Basque separatism or guerrilla movements in El Salvador), suggests that the state monopoly on violence is highly tenuous. By insisting that that monopoly constituted the *differentia specifica* of the state, the state's claim to represent the political is thrown into doubt. Having abandoned the traditional conception of the state as having its matrix in the numerous associations which crisscross human existence, what emerges is a conception of the state as degrounded, as having to subsist without being sustained by anything save a thin theory of legitimacy provided by periodic elections which have become less an exercise in civic virtue than in high finance.

AUTOLEGITIMIZATION

At the same that Weberian analysis focuses upon the question of a monopoly of violence, it tends to neglect the extent to which the contemporary state seeks to acquire, when it has not already acquired, various monopolies other than violence. Whether it describes itself as capitalist, socialist, or communist, all modern states have asserted greater and greater power over all aspects of the economy, over individual health and family welfare, communication, transportation, education, culture high and popular, scientific and social-scientific research, and much more. In short, what is striking about the modern state is its steady push toward acquiring monopolies of all kinds, not just over the means of violence. Which is to say that, instead of the state being grounded in the associational life of society, the relationship threatens to become inverted so that the state becomes its own ground and enjoys a condition of autolegitimacy.

The degrounding of the state and the autolegitimacy of the political are the expression of power in an age of high technology that has nullified the traditional notion, as old as the tradition of Western political theory itself, that power emanates from the community. Compared to a microchip, a vote represents a negligible quantum of power. Political power no longer needs a community and hence it no longer needs its predicate "political."

So the questions arise: What might it be like for power to be grounded politically and for the self to be *disposed* toward powers instead of exposed and vulnerable? What does ancient myth have to tell us on these matters? Can we identify the moment when myth was replaced by fiction and a new conception was ushered in regarding man and his relationship to power? Was there a political form in which myth was perpetuated into the modern world?

In an attempt to explore these questions I shall return to some earlier notions of myth, notably those associated with ancient Israel and Greco-Roman antiquity. The fact that the myths of these ancient societies have exerted a profound influence over later Western political thinking becomes doubly significant when we attend to a crucial quality of most of these myths, namely, their radical politicalness. Myths embody mankind's first attempt to envision power systematically and on a scale larger, more concentrated, and more efficacious than any possible human experience of power. The most familiar of these power myths are the so-called creation myths which describe the origins of the world. Others are the eschatological myths that foretell a catastrophic end to the present order of things; and the myths of heroic exploits, such as those recounted in the Book of Exodus where Yahweh triumphantly delivers his people from the hands of the pharaoh.

Power struggles and the exploits of power, which are the leitmotifs of many of these myths, remind us of a striking fact about virtually all of the Near Eastern and Western gods: whether it is Yahweh, the god of the Old Testament, or Zeus or Jupiter, they are quintessentially gods of power. It is not simply that they possess greater powers than mortals. Rather it is that they come to exemplify the Western conception of perfect power. They are omniscient as well as omnipotent; they defy time and are exempt from change; and they enjoy the most precious form of knowledge, prevision or the ability to see into the future.

The combination of power, knowledge, and prevision is most perfectly realized in Yahweh. He performs the supreme political act: he doesn't merely create the world; he constitutes it, that is, he orders it, differentiates levels of power and being, assigns jurisdictions and issues rules for their regulation. What is constituted by these actions is nothing less than "the political," that is, the basic terms on which politics can then take place. For in ordering the world and defining relationships among mankind, between mankind and god, between man and woman, mankind and animals, and mankind and nature, Yahweh has set the conditions and reference points against which the politics of rivalry, of comparative advantage, the quest for power, the exercise of cunning or strategy, and the testing of limits all take place.

Politics begins immediately with the rebellion of Adam and Eve against authority and limits. It then describes a course of widening violence. First there is the rivalry between Cain and Abel that ends in fratricidal murder ("the ground . . . has opened its mouth to receive your brother's blood from your hand": Gen. 4:11). Then there soon follows a general power struggle so intense—"Now the earth was corrupt in God's sight, and the earth was filled with violence" (Gen. 6:11)— that God vows to "blot out man" and "make an end of all flesh." God proceeds to purge the world by a deluge that destroys all except Noah and his company of creatures and family.

Following the flood, God forms a covenant with Noah signifying new conditions for politics that recognize the radical nature of human power drives and proceed to give them scope and legitimacy. "Be fruitful . . . and fill the earth. The fear of you and the dread of you shall be upon every beast" and all "that creeps on the ground and all the fish of the sea; into your hand they are delivered . . . I give you everything" (Gen. 9:1–3). God then stipulates the new boundaries to human action: "Whoever sheds the blood of man, by man shall his blood be shed; for God made man in his own image." For his part God promises never again to destroy the earth and all living things.

The Noahitic covenant does not succeed, however, in securing "normal" politics but only in creating the conditions for man to mount his most ambitious quest for power. " 'Come, let us build ourselves a city with its top in the heavens.' And the Lord said, 'Behold, they are one people and they have all one language; and this is only the beginning of what they will do; and nothing that they propose to do will now be impossible for them' " (Gen. 11:4,6). God then intervenes by introducing a variety of languages and thus dissolving a basic element in the social unity that makes for collective power. Henceforth politics will have to be conducted amid cultural diversity.

There is an ironical element in this mythical understanding of the relationship between "politics" and "the political." The perfect power to design an order exactly as the creator wishes is insufficient to prevent human ingenuity/ perversity (i.e., politics) from generating powers within or in defiance of the stipulated terms and pursuing its own ends. The mythic understanding teaches that the establishment of the political brings protection and security that enables human practices to take hold and to nurture life; from these practices—economic, religious, familial—powers are generated that become the object of strategies of appropriation: politics is born.

The myth of world creation has served as the paradigm for one of the most important political myths of ancient and modern societies, the myth of founding or of an original political constitution that brings into being a distinct form of collective life. In antiquity the myth was identified with the labors of a political hero, a Moses, Solon, or Lycurgus. In imitation of the creator-god, the political hero legislates a complete, enclosed world and establishes its primary norms and basic institutions. It is the constituting of the political, the establishment of the conditions which are intended to contain politics. A constitution is not, however, merely an ordering of offices or institutions, a parceling of power, or a declaration of legal norms. It is an ontological claim in a double sense. A constitution announces the appearance of a new collective being whose existence henceforth will depend upon its constancy in observing the fundamental principles decreed in the originating constitution. Thus the constitution provides an ontological "ground" which assures the vitality of the society as long as it remains faithful to its origins.[13] That promise depends upon a further claim of the constitution to be connected to a still more fundamental order of being that sustains the world.

The idea of a constitution has been the most important means for perpetuating mythical notions into the modern world. When the American revolutionaries described their new constitution as a *novus saeculorum ordo*, they were giving expression to the double ontology mentioned above. They believed that the "fundamental law" of the Constitution was a real embodiment of the laws of nature, the eternal decrees by which the Creator had defined the everlasting nature of all things. It followed that the political system established by the Constitution would be sustained by the same divine power that assured the regular movements of the planets.

The eighteenth-century American could also feel that he was reenacting the archetypal theme in all creation myths, the struggle by which order overcomes primeval chaos. For those who were most responsible for the drafting of the Constitution and its subsequent ratification, the Federalists, argued that it was the necessary antidote to the terrible disorders arising from the weak political system established under the Articles of Confederation. The Constitution, with its vision of a centralized political system replacing the decentralized one based upon the sovereignty of the individual states, can be looked upon as a modern mimesis of the ancient triumph of monotheism, or centralized sovereignty, over polytheism, or decentralized authority.[14]

The ontological foundation identified by the Constitution requires not only that the collectivity adhere to its formative principles but that it periodically renew them. This is done through various practices, such as periodic elections, festivals, patriotic holidays, and the observance/hallowing of certain procedures (e.g., the president's annual State of the Union message to Congress). One of the crucial qualities of these practices is their periodicity, as in the biennial or quadrennial election of public officials. It imparts a temporal rhythm to collective life and a reinvigoration of it by participation. An act of participation—for example, voting—signifies individual consent, but it is also a reaffirmation of the archetypal consent of the original contract by which separate individuals agreed to join together to form one community. Hence it evokes a sacramental quality of members sharing in a *corpus mysticum et politicum*.[15]

Thus in the constitution of what is widely recognized to be the most advanced of all modernizing societies we find the ancient combination of myth and ritual. But the problem is that the myth which is the Constitution no longer serves as the primary source of power and authority for the state, while the practices which were supposed to reticulate the values enshrined in the Constitution have become distended (as in the case of presidential power), distorted (as in the subservience of Congress to corporate influence), or corrupted (as in the decline of the system of political parties and the reduction of political elections to media events). Rituals have become ritualistic. The hollowness of the constitutional myth and the self-caricature of its rituals suggest an ontological crisis of a political order which has lost its political ground.

THE CULT OF POWER

To appreciate the crisis, we need to explore further the idea of myth and ritual. As is well known, there has been a vast scholarly literature in recent years dealing with myth and ritual in the Old Testament.[16] The controversy surrounding certain of the claims by the so-called myth and ritual school, especially the denial of uniqueness to the myths of Israel, need not detain us. Rather, our concern is with what was identified by that school as the focal point of myth and ritual. According to one of its leading proponents, the highly systematized actions that constituted a ritual were "designed to secure the well-being of the community by controlling the incalculable forces by which man found himself surrounded." Ritual consisted of two parts, that which was "done" (*dromenon* in the ancient Greek) and that which was "spoken" (*muthos*). "The myth told the story of what was being enacted" by the ritual. "But the story was not told to amuse an audience; it was a word of power" that was believed could recreate the situation being described.[17] Ritual was a performance that publicized the fact of power.

The broader implications of myth and ritual for the grounding of power can be brought out by exploring the political form which religion assumed throughout antiquity and retained until as late as the mid-seventeenth century. The form is the "cult." A cult can be defined as an assemblage of beliefs, formulas, rituals, ceremonies, festivals, and other observances. It was usually maintained at public expense because cultic practices were regarded as the indispensable means for gaining the favor and protection of the god(s). Cultic observances were the means of orienting an entire community toward the greatest powers that premodern mankind could conceive. The practices might be likened to conduits which, depending upon how the god(s) felt, could transmit divine power into the collective life, empowering it with a supra human element and thereby enabling it to survive and to flourish.

These beliefs are preserved in an account by the ancient historian Herodotus. He tells of how the Ephesians responded when their city was attacked and besieged: "The Ephesians ran a rope from their walls to the temple of Artemis, putting the town, by means of this link, under the goddess's protection."[18] The deeper significance of the cultivation of power is suggested by the agricultural meanings surrounding it. "Cult" derives from the Latin *cultus*. It meant "tilling, cultivation, or tending." It also shaded off into closely associated meanings such as "care, culture, education, and reverence." By extension cultic rituals are the means of tending to the welfare of the community, much as a farmer tends his soil or a herdsman his flock. There was clearly implied a metaphorical notion of a "ground" for communal life that had to be cared for in an attitude combining piety and solicitude. When it is recalled how closely cultic practices were interwoven with legal procedure and political institutions,[19] it is appropriate to describe the entire complex as constituting, literally, a political culture. Through repetition of and participation in cultic practices, a political consciousness was created to complement the communalized power which was achieved by the cult.

The crucial question is, How does power appear in this older understanding and how is the individual's relationship to it conceived? To the modern sensibility, power signified coercion or domination and, as the political theory of Hobbes illustrates, the individual's relationship to power is that of the subject who obeys. For the postmodern, as I have already suggested, power disappears into the circuitry of the "social system" and emerges euphemistically as "input/output" or as a "communication" or "feedback."[20] In ancient times power was widely understood as consisting of two essential elements, a capacity to impart direction and, equally important, a capacity to receive it.[21] It was an understanding that was embedded in the agricultural and the educational connotations of the cultus. The things and beings that were tended by these activities had initially to be receptive or trusting of ministrations received from outside. These meanings implicit in the cultus helped to form it into the archetype for the idea of political power as the care and preservation of the shared concerns of a collectivity. The political required cultivation in a way analogous to the ordinary rounds of daily life by which beings and things were cared for and nurtured. One attended to crops, cattle, and persons by observing the annual round of the seasons and the life cycles of birth, growth, maturity, and decay and by applying the powers of skill.

LEVIATHAN

It is possible to date the moment in the history of political theory when the old cultic archetype was destroyed and a new conception of an ungrounded political order was introduced. In 1651 Thomas Hobbes published *Leviathan*, a title which was intended to provoke comparison between the myths of power revealed in the Old Testament and the new fictions of power produced by a self-consciously scientific political theory. *Leviathan* announced the deontologizing of power and the substitution of sheer human artifice as the basis of collective power. The opening words of Hobbes's great work were a deliberate imitation of the book of Genesis and a challenge that its creation myth was about to be surpassed: "Nature (the Art whereby God hath made and governes the World) is by the Art of man . . . imitated."[22] Hobbes went on to assert that the art of man "goes further" than the art by which God created man and nature. "For by" man's "Art is created that great Leviathan," that "Artificiall Man" which is "of greater stature and strength than the Naturall."[23] By a voluntary act of near-total submission of the individual to an authority constituted on the basis of "infallible rules and the true science of equity and justice"[24] man could create what Hobbes variously described as a "mortal god," "the greatest of human powers," and "the greatest dominion that can be granted . . . limited only by the strength and force of the city itself, and by nothing else in the world." Yet the covenant of "every man with every man," which Hobbes admits is "the only way" such a towering power can be created, rests on nothing more than the acceptance of a Fiction: "as if every man should say to every man, I authorize and give up my Right of Governing my selfe to this Man . . . on this condition, that thou give up thy Right to him. . . . This is the generation of that great LEVIATHAN."[25] Despite its fictive nature, the covenant, Hobbes insisted, represented "more than Consent or Concord; it is a real Unitie of them all in one and the same Person" of the sovereign.[26]

But there was a plaintiveness to Hobbes's insistence that the covenant transformed a "multitude of wills" into a "real Unitie." In his formal philosophy Hobbes was a committed nominalist who would have otherwise denied that a "new" entity could be created merely because discrete individuals pledged themselves to accept a fiction. This half-hearted attempt at a political version of transubstantiation is a logical lapse that exposes a moment of uncharacteristic hesitation as Hobbes recognizes that he has grounded an absolute power on nothing more than the fearful promise of a single generation.

It was when Hobbes turned to one of the great questions of his day, the political status of religion, that he punctured the idea of the cultus by a strategy that emptied it of ontological meaning and substituted an anthropology that strikingly anticipated Nietzsche's notion of a subversive genealogy. "The seed of Religion," he announced, is "onely in Man." By adopting a naturalistic starting point rather than the traditional one of revelation, Hobbes could claim that man had certain natural impulses which might take the form of religion. That they had taken that form was not due to a miraculous intervention by God. It was, in Hobbes's cool view, merely an historical contingency reflective of a pre-scientific mentality in which the impulses that produced religion represented scientific stirrings that had become blocked and misdirected. Man has, according to Hobbes, a natural desire to discover the causes of events. Originally, however, he lacked "orderly methods" of inquiry, and so he attributed to unseen powers the power which caused things to be or to change. This produced "anxiety" and "feare," "a perpetual solicitude of the time to come," because men were powerless to control their future. "When there is nothing to be seen, there is nothing to accuse . . . but some Power, or Agent Invisible. . . . Men by their own Meditation, arrive to the acknowledgement of one Infinite, Omnipotent, and Eternall God." This "Naturall seed of Religion . . . hath grown up into ceremonies" and "received culture" toward the end that men might be rendered "more apt to Obedience, Lawes, Peace, Charity, and civill Society."[27]

With these words Hobbes might seem to have fully anticipated Marx's dictum, "To be radical is to grasp matters at the root. But for man the root is man himself."[28] But the dictum reflected Marx's conviction that because the "critique" of religion had been finished, religion, as an important social phenomenon, was finished. Hobbes, on the other hand, while he virtually announced the principle proclaimed by Feuerbach, Marx's contemporary, that "the secret of theology is anthropology,"[29] accepted the reality of religious beliefs and passions and sought to place them under the management of the sovereign, not in order to exploit them as a ground of authority but to control the seditious tendencies which sectarian movements had displayed in abundance during the century. Accordingly, the Hobbesian sovereign could dictate cultic observances, but it was a cultus without an ontology and with its artificial nature clearly visible. Civic rituals were to be administered rather than ministered.

The displacement of myth by fiction and the transformation of ritual into rules not only prepared the way for the unprecedented concentration of power associated with the modern state; it destroyed the myth-ritual conception of power as repair of the world and replaced it by a conception of power as domination over both nature and man. The effects of these changes were registered at the very marrow of human existence. Ritual, as we have noted, introduced a periodicity into human life that linked man to the rhythms of nature and made power depend on observing the limits inherent in those rhythms. That entire understanding was exploded by the Hobbesian notion of "felicity." Felicity signifies the displacement of periodicity by infinity." "Felicity of this life," Hobbes declared,

> consisteth not in the repose of a mind satisfied. . . . Felicity is a continuall progresse
> of the desire from one object to another; the attaining of the former being still but
> the way to the later. . . . I put for a generall inclination of all mankind a perpetuall
> and restlesse desire of Power after power that ceaseth onely in Death. . . . [This

is] because [man] cannot assure the power and means to live well, which he hath present, without the acquisition of more.[30]

The new understanding of power was one that replaced the approach to power as nurture with inquiry into cause-and-effect relationships. Knowledge of causes allows man to reproduce effects at will, that is, to exercise power and to reproduce it endlessly. Power is thus dissociated from natural needs and from what one might call the economy of need which had been implicit in the fertility cults with their seasonal rhythms. The nature of needs now gets defined by the possibility of unlimited power. Needs become end-less, as in Hobbes's conception of felicity.

Endless needs and a prospect of infinite power signify in the starkest possible form the erasure of the cardinal principle in the mythic approach to power, a margin separating human power from omnipotence. But instead of eliminating the dark vision of world destruction which haunted all myths of primeval chaos, the power of science and technology has, of course, darkened it further and left it unrelieved by eschatological hopes.

Man has become his own myth.

CHAPTER 17

THE DESTRUCTIVE SIXTIES AND POSTMODERN CONSERVATISM

> There are profound things that went wrong starting with the Great Soci-
> ety and the counterculture. . . . We simply need to erase the slate and start
> over. . . . I am a genuine revolutionary. They are the genuine reactionaries.
> We are going to change the world. They will do anything to stop us.
> —Speaker Newt Gingrich[1]

> An Unlikely Legacy of the 60's: The Violent Right. The Radical Right Has
> an Unlikely Soulmate in the Leftist Politics of the 60's, Historians Say.
> —*New York Times* (in the aftermath of the Oklahoma City bombing)[2]

I

About a half century ago conservatism was little more than a crotchety defense of what used to be called vested interests, or a distaste for New Deal "leveling," or a fondness for tasteless jokes about Franklin and Eleanor, or the affectation of English cultural ways. A short time ago any suggestion that associated conservatism with a dynamic politics would have been dismissed as a contradiction in terms. No longer a curiosity or an anachronism, conservatism has been made over into the opposite of its former stodgy self. It is in the process of becoming transformed from a status quo, resolutely antimodernist ideology—typified by William Buckley's jejune *God and Man at Yale*—to a futuristic one—Newt Gingrich canonizing the author of *Future Shock*—that is strikingly postmodernist in some of its elements.[3] Old-style conservatism longed to be Burkean; new style has more than a touch of Nietzsche.[4]

There is a certain paradoxical quality to recent conservative attacks upon the sixties and their simultaneous claim that it is contemporary conservatives who are the real radicals with truly revolutionary ideas. Such boasting might have seemed plausible had it emanated from the far side of the left, but coming from the political establishment of the right and at the very moment when the alumni(ae) of the Berkeley free speech movement were gathering for the thirtieth anniversary of events that marked the beginning of the student "movements" of the decade, it seemed more like a tactic for stealing the thunder of the opposition—except that in this case the thunder of the sixties is scarcely audible. Attempting a response, the aging representatives of FSM, in vintage style, detected a whiff of neofascism in the air and insisted that the principles of 1964 were as relevant as ever.

Before we dismiss the attack upon the sixties as the prelude to political repression, or the claim to radicalism by conservatives as so much political hot air, it might be worthwhile exploring a different possibility. The rhetorical formulations of both the defenders of the sixties and the critics may be indicative of a historical transformation occurring in both conservatism and radicalism. At its center is a reversal of historical roles and of historical consciousness and, along with it, of the political identities formed around conceptions of past and future that once distinguished radicalism from conservatism. The complexity of a reversal that finds conservatives professing to be revolutionaries, while in actuality they are more accurately described as counterrevolutionary, may be a product of the strict taboos imposed by the American political tradition on discussion of the idea of counterrevolution. Consequently conservatives are nudged toward a language that encodes that idea while seeming to contradict it. Although "revolutionary conservatism" may in reality be counterrevolutionary, one effect of that rhetoric is to deprive radicals of their distinctive claim. The effect of having revolution snatched from them may leave exposed an important strand of counterrevolution in contemporary radicalism.

One way perhaps to unravel the complexity is to recognize that the conservative fixation upon the sixties is, in large part, driven by *revanchisme*, specifically by the memory of certain searing defeats that have left their marks on conservative psyches and in the long run contributed to the election of conservative presidents during the eighties and a deeply conservative Congress in 1994. During the sixties there were three substantial victories that the left considered emblematic and about which the right remains unforgiving. Those victories constitute an important part of what defines the counterrevolutionary substance of the "revolutionary" right and the democratic substance of the sixties. They are: the civil rights movement and the drive toward equality, the antiwar movement and the rejection of the whole expansionist mentality of the political and corporate establishment, and the politicalization of a substantial number of students and a smaller number of faculty at many major institutions of higher learning.

Conservatives have believed that these victories were tainted by illegitimacy, concessions extracted by pressure and force emanating from outside the usual political processes. It was a short step from the notion of illegitimacy and a narrow conception of the political to constructing a violent, destructive sixties. There were, of course, actions and rhetoric that could be used to illustrate that construction. Yet the charge is, unintentionally, ironic given the general atmosphere of the sixties. The years from, say, 1964–1974 fairly reeked of violence, most of it officially inspired, sanctioned, or encouraged. The Vietnam War, the murders and beatings that were the normal response to the nonviolent tactics of the civil rights movement, the suppression of the Watts uprisings and the urban ghetto riots, the murders of the Kennedy brothers and Martin Luther King, the police action at the Democratic National Convention of 1968, the tear gas sprayed by helicopters upon campuses, the murder of students by police and National Guard at Berkeley, Kent State, Jackson State, and Orangeburg provided a seemingly endless succession of shocks, a shattering firsthand experience in the delegitimizing of the authority of the state for a whole generation of young Americans.

To its defenders the sixties were a time when Americans, especially younger ones and especially students, began a quest to expand the meaning and practice of freedom. It was a time for seeing the world and themselves with fresh eyes, for believing that it was possible to begin things anew. Criticism and protest—in words, actions, song, and dress—were the means for clearing a space by focusing the revulsion of the young against "the system." That term encompassed not only political and corporate power structures but also conventional moral and sexual norms and the work-and-success ethic. The system was condemned roundly, for being racist and repressive at home and imperialist and bellicose abroad. With the deepening of the war what began as a yearning for liberation quickly became an attack upon modern forms of power and their scales: of a state that was grotesquely overextended, of a corporate system that was heedless of the environment, and of technologies that recognized no limits. To their conservative detractors, however, the sixties were a case of subjectivity run amok, of expressions of personal feelings, no matter how bizarre, being treated as deep truths while any plea for common sense or moderation that issued from some authority could expect only hoots of derision. In conservative eyes the sixties were lawlessness bordering on anarchy, antipatriotism courting treason, and drug abuse masquerading as innocent hedonism.

The incommensurability of the two versions of the sixties extends even to disagreements about when they began, when, or if, they ended, and what their defining moments were. Defenders stretch the decade to include the expansion of the Vietnam War into Cambodia (spring 1970), the shootings at Kent State, and, not least, the disgrace of President Nixon. Detractors prefer to mention the deadly bomb planted at the University of Wisconsin, the battles between police and Black Panthers, and the occupation of campus administration buildings by armed students.

In what follows I shall refer to the conservative version of the sixties as the Myth of the Sixties and the conservative version of its own identity as the Countermyth. And I shall call the response by the defenders of the sixties the Myth Manqué and attempt to explain that designation by recounting some personal experiences of Berkeley during that decade. Naming the myths as I have is preliminary to showing that the identities of the Countermyth and the Myth Manqué are bound together not simply as opposites but in an exchange relation that reveals some of the profound changes taking place in American political life.

By employing the idea of myth with reference to contemporary beliefs and commitments, I do not mean to belittle the serious efforts at description and analysis by those who have criticized and/or defended the sixties.[5] Nor do I want to assimilate my formulations to the usages of cultural anthropologists and students of comparative religion or, worse, dismiss them as false or crude ideologies. The concern is with political myths—that is, with myths that are contesting for the true identity of society by means of a narrative heavy with *fatefulness* and constructed to attract support for the political project of those whom the mythmakers represent. Political myths tend to portray peoples, events, and ideas in language that verges on the preternatural. This is because myths are meant to heighten tension; they are fraught with foreboding and promise. The peculiarity of contemporary myths is that they are meant for an age for which, as we shall see, the preternatural has been normalized.

II

Although myths are made, they are not totally made up. Their persuasiveness to late-twentieth-century information-conditioned audiences requires that myth-makers pay some heed to facts. The content of myths tends toward a compound of the factual and the factitious while their structure comes to resemble that of docudramas: There is a "real basis" for the drama, but "liberties" have been taken.

As a political intervention myths do depict not impersonal forces but actors who represent actual or potential forces. Myths present dramatic personifications, charged narratives rather than formal arguments. These are intended to evoke responses by literally characterizing events or states of affairs. The idea of myth is appropriate precisely because of a crucial change taking place in advanced industrial societies, an evolution from a social form in which science was primary, and technology derivative, to one in which technology is the driving force. The primacy of technology is owing to a direct and virtually immediate relationship between the introduction of new technology and the production of supporting cultures. Technology invents its own cultures almost instantaneously; consider the several cultures, from computer hackers to cyberpunks, brought in by the latest electronic revolutions, or the cultures ushered in by changing technologies involving the reproduction of contemporary music. In contrast, modern science required nearly three centuries before it enjoyed broad support, and even then the culture of science could not be described, as technological culture can, as mass-based. Today new cultural forms are technologically driven and postscientific. The culture of a society that once looked to science as exemplifying the highest ideals of truth telling and seeking but that now has, if not dethroned, at least demoted science can truly be described as postmodern.

A society that shapes its life to accord with the pace and competitive requirements of a market economy founded upon technological innovation will, as a matter of course, ceaselessly destroy and create values or, more precisely, beliefs. It is ripe for myths. For as Schumpeter recognized when likening capitalism to "creative destruction," the market is as nihilistic as any full-blooded Nietzschean could desire, and because of its destructiveness, that same society yearns to believe. Its publicists elevate the market into a dogma and urge submission to its "forces" and faith in the priesthood of advertisers and in the speculative strategies of junk bond dealers.

This is not to suggest that science has by any means disappeared, any more than the "triumph of science" led to the disappearance of religion. Nor is it to assert that science will cease to play the main role in the production of knowledge. What is being suggested is that the cultural context over which neoconservatives are seeking to establish hegemony has undergone a significant shift. Certain ascetic ideals that had formed important elements in the culture of science—rigorous demonstration, parsimonious explanation, empirical proof, verification procedures, and a community of practitioners—have lost their aura of authority, and as a result, the urge to emulate scientists has perceptibly weakened.

Dialogue, which for centuries has been regarded as a method distinctive to philosophy and the humanities, seems pointless at a moment when truth claims are regarded either as a matter of discursive conventions that happen to be in place or as the expression of a will to power. Discourse becomes performance rather than persuasion. The content of the materials is a secondary consideration. What is all-important is that discourse has an inexhaustible supply of materials to process by interpretation, and this technology can supply endlessly. "Culture" is to the eighties and nineties what science was from 1930 to 1960. The difference is that between endless interpretation and cumulative knowledge.

Belief is the operational correlate of poststructuralism and perhaps *the* necessary condition of a postmodern society. Contrary to the faith of earlier theorists of modernization, it appears that as societies modernize, there is a resurgence of religion. In the United States commentators are continually surprised at the vitality of organized religions and at the high percentage of citizens who claim to "believe" in God. That phenomenon is not, I would suggest, a matter of the credulous many resisting the sophisticated few and the blandishments of secular humanism. It reflects instead an interplay going on *within* a large number of individuals in this high-tech society. Consider the parallelism between, on the one hand, a dynamic system of technological innovation that is continuously pushing past previous limits of achievement and, on the other, the extent to which *transgression* has been popularized. Recall the recent news story about the young man who participated in a talk show that explored the "problem" of how he might go about losing his virginity. Five young women hidden behind screens egged him on by graphically describing how they would assist and facilitate. One was his sister. The program was sponsored by some of the country's largest corporations, which are, by most reckonings, among the principal agencies of change. This suggests that transgression—the deliciousness of risk symbolically acted out—is a way of legitimating change, of asserting that it is normal to challenge established limits. The talk show mystifies power (corporate sponsorship) into legitimating authority (*vox populi*), We the People, the undisputed sovereign, that fill the media every day with our opinions, unaware that culture is ephemera, its demos a construction of an electronic market and a ghostly impersonation of a lost political sovereignty.

Hence the puzzle: The audiences for talk shows are widely acknowledged to be conservative, religious, and staunchly in favor of "family values," yet significant numbers of that population are apparently avid fans of cultural performances in which those same norms are publicly flouted. Transgression is, however, far from signifying the absence of belief or atheism. Transgression is initially defiance, even a death wish inciting retribution. The symbolic transgressor, however, does not want to die but to change. Transgression thus generates a need for belief that is parasitic off the radical element in transgression but simultaneously contains it and then endlessly recycles it. The transgressor can sin yet be saved in order to sin and be saved, etc. ("Jesus loves sinners.") Contrary to what sophisticated neoconservatives sometimes suggest, the Religious Right, Moral Majority, fundamentalists, and antiabortionists are not an embarrassment to the new change-oriented conservatism but a necessary mythic element in its Countermyth. If rapid technological change means anything, it means social disruption, uprooted populations, and an anxious work force, all the elements that serve to justify increasing the means of social control. Many liberals, it might be noted in passing, could enthusiastically welcome technological change but were unable to face its implications, preferring to euphemize social control as welfare.

Transgression was a cliché in the sixties, but then it signified individual choice. Its inspiration was likely to be Camus, not Rush Limbaugh, and it was typically a protest against the powers and dominations. Today transgression is a form of complicity with the powers. It has become a permanent practice for the new conservativism because the two crucial forms of power with which that ideology identifies most closely, the market and technological innovation, are viewed as beyond control. As denizens of a market society endlessly exposed to fresh "waves" of change, we are fated to transgress just as surely as any heir of Calvin's Adam was fated to sin.

The Myth and Countermyth of our inquiry, then, are post-, not prescientific; hence the premodern responses to myth, such as awe, wonder, and mystery, are inappropriate or, more accurately, impossible. Postmodern myths are *fabricated*, in the double meaning of the word. They are constructed, and they are, like stories, made up. Premodern mythmaking sought to contemporize the past. The self-conscious project of postmodern conservative mythmaking is to futurize the present, whose meaning it wants to determine and whose direction it hopes to control. Premodern myths were created anonymously, invisibly, and atemporally. Their authors were unknown, while the processes by which they were assembled and the moments when they first appeared remain vague, "lost in the mists of time," in the older formula. Contemporary myths, in contrast, are objects of calculation and forethought; hence their origins and modes of production are, for the most part, transparent. This is especially true of the Myth and Countermyth; they are indebted to conservative foundations, certain publishing houses, and business corporations. The highest expression of the process of fabrication is the think tank where everyone seems to think pretty much alike, the lowest being the talk show host who talks back to everyone but brooks no backtalk from anyone.

The persistence of myth in advanced industrial, scientific societies is related to the second or pejorative meaning of fabrication, the manufacture of untruth. Broadly stated, ancient myths were believed because they were thought to have been *revealed*. Revelation was the guarantee that grounded belief in truth. Today's myths are constructed for an era when truth is embarrassed by its name and subverted by the quotation marks that usually accompany most references to it. They are believed because they are believable to an era in which distraction is ubiquitous and belief is transitory. "Credibility" is accordingly a popular item in the current political vocabulary. That it is rarely embarrassed by quotation marks is testimony to both the kinship of *what* is made credible with *who* is being rendered credulous as well as to low expectations that truth will emerge in public discourse or that it can linger without inducing boredom. A similar skepticism surrounds concepts of "reality" that a short time ago had been assumed to be truth's necessary presupposition. Credibility/credulity is a sign of the displacement of reality, first by the normalizing of the fantastic and the fantasizing of the normal. It includes everything from the latest "world" concocted by computer technology for the few to the latest television commercial that dazzles the many by images of magical transformations of familiar objects, such as an automobile that suddenly soars into space or beer bottles that play football. Second, fantasy and reality become interchangeable, as when a television actress who regularly plays the deceived wife in a soap opera thereby acquires credentials to appear as an expert dispensing counsel about "real" love and marriage on a program for teenagers.[6]

This is not to suggest that contemporary myths are the work of confirmed liars. Rather they are the expression of an age in which the will-to-truth, though not the will-to-believe, has been overwhelmed by perspectivism, the belief that no view is privileged, that each view is merely one among many possible interpretations.[7] So pervasive is perspectivism that what passes as insight among political consultants, advertising executives, and academic Nietzscheans is already the stuff of clichés in less exalted quarters. Stanford's football coach recently noted, "Perception is everything." Postmodern myths are for a world where the distinction between "angle of vision" and "spin" is a matter of concern only to the next to last man.

III

The vitality of our Myth Manqué in comparison to the Countermyth provides an index to the relative power of the political and social forces represented *in* and *by* the competing myths. At the present moment conservatism is clearly in the ascendancy, so much so that it is commonplace to remark that the United States is a conservative country. The banality of that observation, however, doesn't lessen the dramatic changes taking place in contemporary conservatism and shaping its Countermyth.

The evolution of conservatism from standpatism to futurism encompasses a dramatic switch in temporal perspectives that underlies our myths. Ever since the eighteenth-century revolutions in America and France and continuing down to the Bolshevik Revolution, the identity formation of what might loosely be called left and right, as well as the dividing line between them, has importantly turned upon their different conceptions of the relationship between past, present, and future.

Historically the myths most closely associated with the modern left—progress, modernization, and revolution—have been oriented toward a conception of the future as ever more expansive and inclusive. The past in turn was condemned as being scarcity-ridden for all but the few. Discontinuity with the past and even with the present was therefore a positive value. The older right, as represented in the title of Buckley's book, affected a nostalgia for a past whose values were held to be superior to the innovations of the present. Often its cultivated tone belied a certain literalness: Conservatives were dedicated to conserving what was best in the past and present, the best invariably being created and appreciated only by the few who were pledged to defending it against change and the *vulgus*.[8]

At the present moment, however, conservative politicians feel no awkwardness in proclaiming themselves to be the "true revolutionaries," an identification no conservative politician would have dared whisper during the years of the Cold War. What enables the contemporary conservative to talk easily about revolution, about reducing the scope of government and decentralizing its powers, about sweeping alterations in social policies is the new conception of change being hatched that shares certain family resemblances with themes of the sixties. As I write these lines, Senator Dole, a traditional conservative politician desperate to seem modish, has announced that his presidential candidacy would emphasize change, and he contrasted it with the position of the liberal incumbent, saying that President Clinton was firmly opposed to all change.

The postmodern sympathies among self-styled revolutionary and radical conservatives do not prevent them from cohabiting with the primarily Protestant Christian Right. Fundamentalist and evangelical Christians have often described themselves as radicals, as movers and shakers, and associated their radicalism with individual rebirth and renewal, with personal change and vigorous patriotism.

The reversal in temporal conceptions has the consequence of exposing the paradoxical character of postmodern conservatism. It is counterrevolutionary because of its postmodernism, the same postmodernism that allows conservatives also to proclaim their radicalism in the language of anti-Enlightenment. Critiques of the Enlightenment, it will be recalled, are nowadays in fashion among the left literati. Since the Enlightenment change has typically been associated with the widest possible extension of certain fundamental values, such as education, economic opportunity, healthful conditions, leisure time, access to aesthetic objects and experience, and improvements in the technologies of daily life. Change meant improvement in the lot of the Many. During the sixties, however, radicals began attacking the idea of "technological society." Liberal assumptions concerning "growth," "development," "modernization," and technological-scientific solutions to social problems were called into question and declared destructive. At the same time, however, the left held fast to the Enlightenment agenda of extending to all the benefits of education, healthy living conditions, economic opportunity, and leisure—in other words, the benefits that modern technology alone seemed able to deliver. The left was thus accepting a vision of the future that was riven by a deep contradiction between an expansive social program and a constricted, small-is-beautiful economy designed according to "appropriate technology."

Today's conservatism has taken on that dilemma, not to resolve but to puncture it. Conservatives have done nothing less than reconceive change in exclusionist terms while embracing wholeheartedly the gospel that technological innovation is necessary to survival under the Darwinian conditions of international economic competition. In the postmodern era change is no longer as promissory as it was in the expansive and inclusive terms of the Enlightenment. Change does mean dazzling opportunities of wealth, prestige, and power for the few, but for the many it delivers widening disparities, less of most of the basic values, and obsolescence. The Enlightenment is thus turned on its head: The redefinition of change spells the paradox of technological advance in support of counterrevolution. Already the advent of the computer is driving a deeper wedge between classes and races, between those who have the resources to stay abreast of a rapidly changing technology, the educational background to grasp symbolic modes of reasoning, and the material means for joining information networks.[9] At the same time, as is well known, these new technologies offer unparalleled means for control of the contents of education and culture by governments and corporations.

IV

Paradoxically, in the right's Myth the sixties are depicted as a dynamic, dangerous force, as destructive now as it was then. While the decade is kept alive and
contemporary in the rhetoric of its foes, the defenders embalm it, conserving
it as a myth about origins, a Genesis recounting epical deeds in the past. It is
Myth Manqué, an exhausted narrative, unable to say why its story is relevant
to the present or the future and fated to shuffle off into nostalgia, a memorial
service at Woodstock for pudgy yuppies. What was there about the sixties that
encouraged this denouement?

While, in fact, there were several simultaneous sixties, there was also an
amazing amount of carryover, especially from politics to culture, personal life
to politics, education to politics, and vice versa. One powerful unifier was the
self and collective dramatization centered on a myth of liberation.[10] At the time
critics described it as sanctioning anarchy and the subversion of values. The notion common to both the experienced myth and the unfriendly reconstruction
of it was/is revolution. To the committed, revolution functioned like a Sore-
lian myth, a unifying image that fortified the will to act and lent coherence to
what were otherwise disconnected, heterogeneous, and random "happenings."
The mass demonstrations, acts of civil disobedience, communal experiments,
aesthetic innovations, Earth Day celebration, educational innovations did not
spring from a desire to "participate" but from a newly discovered passion for
significant action. In later decades revolution dropped out of the myth, and
with it the element that had unified the sixties in the eyes of those who were living it. What remained after the dissolution were a Myth Manqué and a heap of
disaggregated events and tendencies that made it possible to select the sixties of
one's choice: The sixties could be drugs, sexual revolution, or rock 'n' roll, or the
civil rights movement, or the antiwar demonstrations, or the agonizing of SDS.

While the counterculture in its critical cultural forms may be said to have
ended with the decade, the political sixties did not, although they narrowly
missed interment in the McGovern debacle. During the Democratic primaries
of 1972 and the McGovern campaign a substantial effort was made to lure the
sixties' rebels into the processes of mainstream politics. The result was a Nixon
landslide and a rite of passage for a new generation of mainstream cadres. It is
tempting to claim the sixties were finally vindicated by Watergate and its aftermath, but that would reinforce the notion that while Nixon might eventually be
rehabilitated and later generations forced to lick the backside of stamps bearing
his face, the sixties have passed.

The sixties were, in fact, one of the two great political decades of this century. The New Deal thirties were the other. Both left an imprint on subsequent
decades, and both made a permanent contribution to American democratic traditions. Yet in many ways the political sixties and the political thirties
were antagonists. The New Deal constructed a powerful bureaucratic state and

tried to use it for democratic social ends. During the forties and afterward, however, those purposes became entangled with the projection of American military and corporate power abroad and were ultimately overwhelmed by the Vietnam War.

The sixties were the first great attempt, mostly spontaneous and improvised, at a democratic revival of American political life since the Populist revolts of the last quarter of the nineteenth century. The sixties stood in a long line of protests against the monopolization of politics by the electoral system and the consequent confinement of political action to the official processes that by the mid-twentieth century were dominated by imperial presidents, global corporations, bureaucratized institutions, and big money. But where the New Deal had sought to enlarge the scope and scale of the state, the sixties sought to diminish the state and to relocate and intensify politics by reducing its scales. Protest was a way of opening space for new political forms and rhetoric, new actors and agendas. Groups that had hitherto been mostly silent and passive were galvanized: African Americans, Hispanics, Asian Americans, gays and lesbians, women, students. The sixties converted democracy from a rhetorical to a working proposition, not just about equal rights but about new models of action and access to power in workplaces, schools, neighborhoods, and local communities.

In that vein I should like to offer a brief personal memoir of those days by recalling and reflecting upon two episodes that took place on the Berkeley campus, one in 1964, the other in 1970. During that period I was a tenured member of the faculty and an active participant in the events as well as coauthor of several essays dealing with them.[11] A comparison of the two events is instructive in showing, first, the different dynamics at work even though the setting and the actors remained roughly the same and, second, how the development of the events contained a microcosm of why the sixties became a Myth Manqué instead of the starting point for the redemocratization of American politics.

V

In December 1964 the Berkeley faculty voted overwhelmingly for a series of resolutions aimed at protecting freedom of speech, assembly, and political activity on the campus and at setting down conditions meant to ensure that their exercise would not interfere with the ordinary functions of the university.

It was in the best sense of the term a liberal solution. Constitutional guarantees of free political activity were recognized, and the faculty asserted an implicit claim to being a coeval partner with the administration in determining campus policies. The controversy itself had been cast primarily in a liberal idiom as a dispute about "rules": Who had the authority to make rules—the regents who governed the whole statewide system? The local administration?

Representatives of students, faculty, and administration? Who should judge violations?

The idea of rules was seized upon by all sides and argued with unflagging zeal. Proceduralism became the element that could unify most shades of opinion and prevent the fissures among the faculty from deepening further. There was virtually no discussion of topics such as educational reform or of the proper role of faculty members as consultants to corporations or to federal agencies. What made the politics of the time seem radical was that the student–faculty objectives presented a challenge to the Board of Regents. The board's authority extended over all matters on all the campuses. Its members were appointed by the governor, and the vast majority owed their positions to their wealth and influence. In the end the regents accepted the solution because of the awkwardness of arguing against constitutionally guaranteed rights. Their acceptance, however, was tacit and involved no ceding of formal authority.

The liberal-constitutionalist solution, however, only hinted at tendencies harboring a counterpolitics that had assumed two distinct forms. One was democratic, spontaneous, amorphous, suspicious of the cult of individual leadership, skeptical and humorous, and willing to take risks for ideal rather than material values. The other was corporate (in the medieval sense), attentive to formalities, deliberate in action, liberal rather than populist. The first group of tendencies was most evident in the student "movement"; the second in the actions of the faculty. For the two to find common ground, each had separately to challenge the official conception of the university as a nonpolitical institution established to serve "society."[12]

For the faculty the challenge meant defending the notion that it was consistent with, and not demeaning of, the nature of a university to permit political life on campus. The official conception was that the fundamental prerequisite for a university was for it to be "outside" politics and that the role of the regents was to protect the academy from the corrupting pressures of "real life" in order that faculty would pursue truth and students learn.[13] Instead the controversy brought the "outside" in as the entire state began to focus on the Berkeley campus. The necessity for students and faculty to address a broader audience of citizens, alumni/ae, and legislators and to relate local concerns in more general terms transformed both groups. The faculty, habitually riven by departmental rivalries, budgetary disputes, and senior-junior divisions, came to recognize that what was at stake was the idea that a public university not only might stand scholarly comparison with the great private universities and reject the social, economic, and cultural snobbery that seemed an essential element of identity but could go beyond them and attempt the task of nurturing a *political* culture appropriate to a public institution supported by the citizenry.

In submitting passively to a centralized system in which administrators alone had a public responsibility for the institution as a whole, the faculty had settled for the status of a special interest in a division of labor in which its responsibilities were confined to research and teaching. The administration managed the campus, dealt with the regents, and oversaw student conduct.[14] The regents were formally the final authorities in all matters, in those affecting not only the Berkeley campus but the entire statewide university structure of nine campuses.[15] They were the sole representatives of the entire system before the political authorities of the state.

In the course of the controversy the faculty evolved into a political actor claiming a share of responsibility for the order and well-being of the institution. It became the mediator between the administration and students. That new role was possible only because certain influential faculty members were trusted by the students and because in an important sense a significant number of faculty and students had become allies against the administration and regents. Although many faculty members grumbled about the research time lost to political deliberations, in the process they not only discovered a corporate identity but fashioned themselves into an academic citizenry, at least for the moment. The locus of that transformation was the Academic Senate.

From a sleepy, ill-attended assembly that took its marching orders from the administration, it became an independent, vibrant deliberative institution. Its meetings were packed; the debates were charged with the excitement of competing ideas about the future of the university, yet a decent level of civility and collegiality consistently prevailed. Outside the assembly many faculty members spontaneously organized into distinct political groupings, which divided roughly along liberal and conservative lines. The faculty soon extended its reach by electing an executive committee to represent it in negotiations with the administration and the regents.

This was, in sum, the liberal constitution favored by a majority of the faculty. It sought to establish an element of faculty power against the campus administration and the regents. It allowed politics on the campus but conceived that politics essentially as an extension of the Bill of Rights to students, not as a redefinition of the faculty vocation. It legitimated student political activity on campus, but it was not prepared to break new ground and make room for student participation in any of the areas traditionally conceived as the prerogatives of the faculty—e.g., curriculum and faculty appointments. The conservative faculty who opposed the settlement wanted to preserve the old constitution but with provision for a stronger chancellor. Theirs was a vision of a nonpolitical campus, insulated from political pressures and protected by the oligarchy of the regents. They saw nothing political in the close relationships of faculty with business corporations, agribusiness, or federal agencies (a view shared by many liberal faculty members). Their tacit assumption was that their idyllic enclave was the quid pro quo for services rendered to "society."

Although the Berkeley students were widely characterized as "radicals," their radicalism was not in their objectives but in their appetite for politics. Several of them had acquired it from a political apprenticeship served not in Moscow but in Selma and the civil rights movement. What was truly radical about the students—and the faculty—was the transformation from an apolitical to a political mode of being, from what was assumed to be a career-oriented way of life to one that was denigrated as "politicized." Over several months, without flagging, students kept pressure on the faculty and administration while inventing their own organization, tactics, ideology, and rhetoric. Although their tactics, such as sit-ins, demonstrations, and mass rallies, struck many as outrageous in the disrespect for authority, the name the students chose, the Free Speech Movement, was an accurate indicator of the limited and conventional nature of their aims: to have the right to hold political rallies on campus, solicit contributions for political causes, choose speakers for their own events, and not be subjected to academic punishment for illegal actions committed off campus (e.g., sit-ins). The rhetoric of "student power" was never raised. At no time did students deliberately disrupt teaching or research, much less damage university facilities. They did disrupt the habits of administration.

The achievement of the Berkeley students and faculty was constructive and a tribute to good sense and moderation. That critics, then and now, should have seen "radicals" at work not only is an example of the vocabulary of marginalization at work but also as testimony to much else: to the difficulties of moderate liberal-democratic reforms, to the acute sense of fragility that bureaucrats have of their own structures, and to the general incomprehension of otherwise intelligent people that politics might be seriously concerned with matters other than material self-interests or self-promotion. What was illuminating about the troubles at Berkeley in 1964 was how little it took to arouse the wrath of the leaders and dominant powers of the society. The truly dark side of the times was not the temporary victory of sixties radicalism but the active dislike of democracy—couched as a contempt for "politics"—among the powerful.

VI

The events in Berkeley of the spring of 1970 could, with only slight exaggeration, be called a failed revolution. They were generally overlooked by outsiders and, significantly, have been ignored ever since. One reason was that Berkeley was no longer an anomaly but the name for a general condition.

In that so-called Cambodian spring more than 150 campuses were in a state of revolt. The triggering events were the killings at Kent State and the decision of President Nixon to widen the war by invading Cambodia. By 1970 the war had become a national nightmare, polarizing and paralyzing and ratcheting to an excruciating turn the problem of the university's entanglement with corporate structures and its "complicity" in the war. A special element in the Berkeley context was a strong feeling of beleaguerment caused by the continuous tirades against the campus by the newly elected governor, Ronald Reagan: these culminated in 1969, when the governor ordered the occupation of Berkeley by the National Guard. That led to the shooting death of an innocent bystander, a helicopter attack that sprayed tear gas over the campus, and the encirclement of the university by armed guardsmen with fixed bayonets.

The campus responded to the expansion of the war at home as well as in Southeast Asia by holding a gigantic open-air meeting and voting to strike against the university. The moral, legal, and political implications of that decision were temporarily stayed by the individual decision of striking faculty members to continue with their classes but to hold them off campus, most often at local churches and seminaries. The faculty was deeply divided by the strike, and the divisions became more intense when the strike evolved into a movement for the "reconstitution of the university."

Although reconstitution was never spelled out in detail, the basic idea involved nothing less than the attempt to restructure and redirect the university, toward becoming an educational institution, rather than an auxiliary of government and corporations, and replacing the bureaucratic model of university membership and governance with participatory relationships intended to allow students and staff a role in matters affecting their lives and work. Far more than the settlement of 1964, it meant altering the power relationships within the university and reconstituting them around more egalitarian notions of membership. Except for the later inclusion of student representatives on some faculty committees, the movement came to naught, in part because Governor Reagan ordered the campus shut down and in part because the academic calendar decreed the end of the term, causing students and faculty to disperse for the summer. But the larger reason was that among the faculty the will to radical change never took hold.

The faculty had been willing to make considerable sacrifices for liberal principles of free speech and assembly and even to oppose the war by striking, but they had resisted most of the proposals for educational reform suggested by the special committees appointed by the Academic Senate during the years between 1964 and 1970.[16] Above all, however, the vast majority of faculty drew back from the heavy civic commitment involved, not only in rethinking the nature of the university but in reorganizing it as well. Such an involvement seemed incompatible with the idea of a "research university" that had attracted a distinguished faculty in the first place. The crucial turning point had occurred earlier, in 1969, when, acting upon a proposal initiated by conservative and disenchanted liberal faculty, the faculty ignominiously voted to emasculate its power by establishing a representative assembly (based on the election of departmental representatives) that would function as the principal organ of the faculty. The Academic Senate, which was open to all regular faculty members, would be relegated to a subordinate status, meeting at widely spaced intervals and mostly restricted to dealing with matters sent to it by the assembly. The change was designed to neutralize the most democratic faculty institution and to elevate the importance of a body that, by being closely tied to departments and reflecting their hierarchical and gerontic character, could be relied upon to reflect the interests of the more powerful departments (e.g., physics, chemistry, and engineering) and to support the administration and the authority of the regents. The faculty had clearly signaled its disfavor of the democratic tendencies of the times and its desire to return to the "real work" of research and publication.[17]

VII

It is easy to deflate the significance of the abortive "revolution" of 1970 by saying that participatory democracy was inconsistent with the requirements of a high-powered research university whose central role in the production and dissemination of knowledge made it of crucial importance to a technologically advanced society. But the same could be said of democracy's seemingly anachronistic relationship to virtually every major institution in the contemporary United States: to trade unions, corporations, political parties, and governmental structures. Amid the periodic hoopla about Q-groups, worker participation, sensitivity training, and open-neck shirts at IBM, the simple fact is that all of our major institutions are hierarchical in organization and antidemocratic in spirit.

So with every major bastion of power firmly controlled by antidemocratic practices, why the need to stomp on the sixties and to construct an elaborate myth to counter a nonexistent threat?

One obvious answer is that the sixties formed an irresistible target for those whose sensibilities had been honed by decades of subversion sniffing, loyalty mongering, and humorless politics. The sixties offered acres of nuttiness, lots of shocking behavior, impudent language, outrageous costumes, and innocent forms of spirituality competing with brazen sexuality. And of course, civil disobedience and mass opposition, which, to its undying credit, interfered with the prosecution of the war and in all likelihood helped end the killing and destruction. What went mostly unnoticed, however, was a strong undercurrent of despair, largely fed by the simple observation that the chasm between American ideals and reality was bridged by hypocrisy and, as *The Pentagon Papers* revealed, by official lies. The Countermyth hints at disloyalty where it should see idealism, even an innocent patriotism.

The less obvious answer is that the Countermyth reflects a felt need to suppress the tendencies that, when combined, are perceived as truly threatening to a society whose ever-changing economy is a breeding ground of perpetual insecurities and fears. The main question posed during the sixties was: Where amid American imperialism, its culture of war, cult of leadership, and brutal suppression of attempts to establish equal civil rights was democracy to be found? The sixties responded by saying democracy had to be reexperienced through transforming actions that would attempt to alter the ways in which Americans perceived their environments, responded to the claims of authority, considered the hype accompanying the food they ate and the clothes they wore, treated the knowledge claims of experts, and accepted the superpower categories that had defined the culture of American politics for a half century.

Unlike the "threat" of communism, which could be exploited to increase the power of the state and the legitimacy of corporate capitalism, the main ingredients of the sixties—democracy, spontaneity, rebellion, anticonsumerism, environmentalism, and antielitism—were less easily converted into power, and unlike the values of communism, some of them were the staples of public rhetoric. The animus against the sixties has been framed as an indictment of the alleged destructiveness of the sixties, but fundamentally it is directed against a conception of democracy that carries the threat of breaking out of the molds into which it has been cast by electoral politics and plutocratic democracy. The varied forms of action developed to oppose the war and to extend civil rights *were* destructive of a certain simplistic understanding of national unity, of some racist folkways, and of a mindless patriotism, and they also exposed the shallowness of consensus politics and its ideal of a depoliticized citizenry. Both the civil rights movement and the antiwar protests politicized hundreds of thousands of Americans and simultaneously contested the boundaries of the political domain, its forms, and the monopoly on action enjoyed by the elites. Thousands who had never spoken, protested, advised, or criticized in public did so. The prevailing ideal of the passive citizen, who had to be "motivated" to vote, was being challenged. While the transformation was only temporary, it would make it possible in later decades for a strange and sometimes wonderful assortment of beings to venture out of closets, kitchens, and ghettos.

The sixties, then, serve as cover for the antipolitical and antidemocratic impulses that were strikingly evident in the actions by the conservative majority following the 1994 elections. The campaign itself was remarkable for the vituperation that the victors heaped upon politics, politicians, and government. Following their electoral victory, conservatives in the House and Senate proceeded to denounce Congress and offer to surrender powers to the president and to the states. Somehow forgotten were the old conservative concerns for "authority," or possibly exposed for the sham they had always been.[18] Certainly the profligacy displayed toward cluttering the Constitution with amendments on matters over which there existed more dissensus than consensus (balanced budget, outlawing of abortion and flag burning, school prayer) was suggestive of opportunism rather than reverence toward the nation's fundamental law. That cynicism could only be deepened as Republicans gathered in astronomical amounts of money from the few while promising to relieve the rest of us of a system of governmental favors and benefits. Senator Domenici may have said more than he intended when he declared recently that if Americans wished to have certain social programs, they would have to be prepared to pay for them.

Undeniably there have been serious attempts by conservative thinkers at constructing a coherent, historically rich account and defense of authority.[19] There has also been a lot of maundering about "lost" authority. However, when placed in the context of the last four decades, the ideology of authority seems little more than a defensive maneuver, a smoke-screen thrown up to conceal what no amount of Cold War triumphalism or puerile fantasies about the "end of history" can disprove: that American political elites of the postwar era are a sorry excuse for a political class. From JFK to George Bush they have left a tawdry trail of corruption, constitutional violations, incalculable death and destruction visited upon hapless populations abroad, steadily worsening racial relations, deepening class divisions, discreditation of the idea of public service (except for convicted felons) and, not least, a political system that large numbers of Americans wish to disown. That system desperately needs a countermyth to cover a shameful reality of a society in which politics, culture, and economy are merely mechanisms for exploiting resources, people, and values. The sixties may lack their myth, but its ideal of redemocratization is not dead. It forms a part of a recurrent aspiration: to find room in which people can join freely with others to take responsibility for solving their common problems and thereby sharing the modest fate that is the lot of all mortals.

CHAPTER 18

FROM PROGRESS TO MODERNIZATION

THE CONSERVATIVE TURN

FOR NEARLY THREE CENTURIES MOST Western societies have relied upon ideas about "progress," "development," and "modernism" to express what has commonly been seen as the driving force, the defining *Geist* of their cultures. From roughly the beginning of the eighteenth century progress was a shorthand term for a broad aspiration for social change guided by rational analysis and based, wherever possible, upon scientific knowledge. Change was understood not as mere alteration, but as demonstrable improvement over what had been: "I like the dreams of the future better than the history of the past," wrote Jefferson, the perfect embodiment of eighteenth-century progressivism.[1] To the minds of the early champions of progress, improvement was measurable because they had a remarkably clear conception of what they were against and longed to be liberated from. It was summed up in Voltaire's fantasy of hoping to see the last aristocrat strangled in the entrails of the last priest.

The demand to get out from underneath the suffocating weight of the past was the expression not only of a passionate hatred for oppressive institutions but of a new form of time-consciousness. Priests and aristocrats were, in addition to being social evils, also anachronisms that should be relegated to their proper temporal dimension, "the past." This would allow mankind to institute "the future," a temporal dimension hitherto monopolized by theological discussions of salvation and of "the last days" preceding the inauguration of the Kingdom of God. The idea of progress inspired the notion that a whole society, situated in the here-and-now, should organize its collective life toward realizing the future, the that which-was-not-yet.

From the beginning of its modern history the idea of progress functioned as a political critique directed against the power-wielding institutions of monarchy, aristocracy, and church. Progress quickly became the personal property of liberalism, even though there was no necessary connection between the two. Nonetheless, progress remained the property of the left, for even when the early nineteenth-century socialists, followed by Marx and Engels, then the anarchists, challenged liberalism, they presented themselves as the true inheritors of the idea of progress. Just as "left" and "progressive" became virtually interchangeable terms, so "conservative" and "antiprogressive" were widely regarded as synonymous.

These historical identities, there is reason to believe, are now in a process of realignment. The left's historic monopoly on change is being successfully challenged and conservatism is emerging as the party of progress. These shifts signal that a profound change is taking place in the meaning of progress.

The Heritage Foundation, a conservative center for policy studies with close ties to the Reagan administration, recently circulated the conclusions of a study that dealt with the prospects of economic growth in the coming decades. The study was framed as an attack upon an earlier prognosis, *Global 2000 Report*, which had been prepared under the blessing of the Carter administration. This staged confrontation illustrates our thesis. The conservative experts criticized the liberal experts for having embraced certain false data and assumptions that led to pessimistic conclusions about economic growth, world population, food supplies, and levels of nonrenewable resources. They argued the general proposition that life could be expected to improve rather than deteriorate. In effect they were arguing that progress was still written into the nature of modern things and that the limited-growth mentality of the Carter years was a weird aberration. The liberal experts and the ex-president himself were quick to defend the pessimism of their report.

However the prophecies of the conservative experts may turn out, they were correct in associating contemporary liberalism with pessimism. Until recently it was liberals who claimed a vision of uninterrupted economic growth and exhorted everyone to rush toward a beckoning future. During the past two decades, however, faith in progress has dimmed as liberals contemplated deteriorating cities, thickening pollution, increased racial tensions, widening social inequalities, the worsening of the competitive position of the United States in the international economy, and the puzzles of stagflation. The mood of disillusionment pervaded yet another liberal report, this one by President Carter's Commission for a National Agenda for the Eighties. Its membership was an inventory of the liberal consensus, from Daniel Bell to Common Cause, from the NAACP to the Sierra Club. "Today, as we enter the Eighties," the report cautioned, "the world is decidedly different" from the recent and heady past when it was believed "we could simultaneously eradicate poverty, go to the moon, and win a war in Vietnam." The motto of the future was not unqualified abundance but "trade-offs" based on more "realistic expectations." There was much reference to "difficult decisions" and "hard choices," to the prospect of "a nearly permanent urban underclass," and to the grim fact that the older cities of the Northeast would never recover and so "their 'health' [will have to] be redefined at new, and often lower, levels of population and employment."[2]

As liberals became more defensive and hesitant and often broke ranks to join conservatives in dismantling the social programs that had once stood as monuments to liberal ideals of social progress, it was left to a conservative president to declare expansively that America is growing "more healthy and beautiful each year."[3] Two centuries ago the oracle of modern conservatism, Edmund Burke, portrayed the conservative as one who reverenced the ways of the past, looked upon all proposals for reform as initially suspect, and profoundly distrusted theoretical approaches to practical politics. Today it is self-proclaimed conservatives such as Reagan and Thatcher who champion bold initiatives, take pride in innovation, flirt with untested theories, and promise an early return to high levels of economic growth.

Meanwhile, liberals appear stranded in the past, mumbling the litany of New Deal, Fair Deal, New Frontier, and Great Society, but instead of seeking inspiration for a new and bold vision, they adopt unenthusiastically a negative role: they will restore the social programs that assist the casualties and victims of new-style economic recovery. From being the party of progress, liberals have become the party of consolation, ministering to those who have to be sacrificed if the society is to remain competitive, i.e., progressive.

How is it that conservatives have become the heirs of the ideal of progress? What has progress become such that conservatives appear as its carrier? These questions require that we reexamine the idea of progress and try to identify some of its major transformations. We will want to reconsider, too, some of the ideas and institutions that were early on deemed antiprogressive. They may appear in a different light now that we are in a better position historically to appreciate some of the implications of progress.

The idea of progress was first popularized in the eighteenth century as a major theme in the attack mounted by liberal intellectuals against the established social hierarchies and their conservative ideologies of throne, altar, and inherited status. The most famous of these intellectuals, the French *philosophes*, along with their counterparts in Britain, Germany, and America, passionately believed that societies could be radically improved if only certain rational practices and truths were installed. If science, education, human rights, and representative and constitutional government were made into the foundations of society, mankind would enter an epoch of plenty, freedom, and peace without parallel. Knowledge, especially scientific knowledge, would so expand human powers that the reach of man's dreams would be matched at last by his actual grasp. Condorcet, one of the martyred saints of the Enlightenment, prophesied that

> nature has set no limits to the perfection of human faculties; the perfectibility of man is truly indefinite; and the progress of this perfectibility, from now onwards independent of any power that might wish to halt it, has no other limit than the duration of the globe upon which nature has cast us.[4]

Condorcet and the other *philosophes* were virtually unanimous about the identity of the major obstacles to setting mankind on a linear road to progress.

The hindrances then, as now, were precisely the social practices favored by most conservatives: sharp inequalities of wealth, status, and power; law-and-order governments that dealt harshly with the poor as habitually criminal and with free thinkers as instinctively subversive; the favored position of churches and religious dogmas; education for the few and social discipline for the many in schools and penal institutions; a strong and war-prone state; enforcement of traditional moral and sexual codes; censorship; and instinctive, habitual deference to authority.

All of these practices were charged by the apostles of progress with being oppressive, limiting human potentialities, discouraging experimentation, and having no basis save ignorance, superstition, and class or institutional interests. In criticizing the Old Regime's institutions, Enlightenment thinkers struck also at the religiosity that supported the authorities who presided over the official structure of church, state, and society. The antireligious thrust of the Enlightenment was not confined to the claim that, as Laplace put it, men no longer needed the hypothesis of God in order to explain the universe. The challenge was rather in the revolutionary claims that men were making about their own powers. Science and technology were empowering mankind to renounce a worldly existence that Christianity had taught was irretrievably a vale of tears, a passage full of suffering and pain that would only be redeemed at the end of time when God would make known the meaning of the promise given to Christ and reward those who were elected for salvation. Humanity, it was averred, could now make its own world and so order it as to alleviate, if not eradicate, all of the evils afflicting mankind. Thus humanity could give itself what had hitherto been believed only God could grant, a future of hope and happiness.

At bottom, the confidence in this vision of a man-made future of ever-increasing happiness was founded on the unprecedented powers man was beginning to acquire. The results, demonstrable and quantified, could be readily observed in increasing industrial and agricultural productivity, the rise of wages and in the numbers of employed workers, and the growth of world trade. The first Industrial Revolution, which took shape toward the end of the eighteenth century, appeared as a triumph made possible by the practical applications of science and hence founded not on wishes or prayers but on fact. So Joseph Priestley, a chemist and liberal reformer, predicted that nature

> will be more at our command; men will make their situations in this world more abundantly, more long and comfortable; they will probably prolong their existence in it, and will grow daily more happy . . . and more able . . . to communicate happiness to others. Thus whatever was the beginning of this world, the end will be glorious and paradisaical beyond what our imagination can now conceive.[5]

By associating progress with science, progress appeared as a universal truth rather than an ideology. This helped to mask the appropriation of science by modern capitalism and to leave as unproblematic the extent to which the directions for scientific activity were immanent in science itself or rather were dictated by the changing requirements of capitalism. Concurrently with capitalist exploitation of science, the modern state, which had early recognized the military potentiality of science, began the active promotion of scientific research and technical education. As a result of the combined, and sometimes antagonistic, efforts of industrialists, bankers, politicians, and scientists, a breakthrough in the organization of power was achieved. In all previous epochs power had been notoriously in short supply. Rousseau's formulation was typical of the terms in which power was conceived. Writing about how men generate sufficient power to overcome the obstacles to forming a community, he insisted that

> as men cannot engender new forces, but only unite and direct existing ones, they have no other means of preserving themselves than the formation, by aggregation, of a sum of forces great enough to overcome their resistance. . . . This sum of forces can arise only from the conjuncture of many persons.[6]

Rousseau was expressing the common experience: men were acquainted with power either as the application of labor to raw materials, or as the mobilization of populations for war or domestic exigencies. From a later vantage point, these ways would seem inefficient and unreliable. So much energy, ingenuity, and resources had to be expended in coercing, cajoling, and enticing perverse beings into obeying authority that very little surplus power remained for effecting the goals of rulers.

The new form of power being assembled suffered from none of these disabilities and had certain positive features that rendered it superior to the older forms: it seemed to be inexhaustible, readily reproducible, and endlessly improvable. Its secret was shared by both capitalism and science: in the one case it was called "capital accumulation," in the other "cumulative knowledge." Both involved the systematic investment of a store of resources (money, knowledge) where it would produce results that would increase the original store (profits, advances in knowledge). Political power seemed puny in contrast. The only way it could be increased was by conquest and, more often than not, the resulting gains were not dramatic. Nowhere was the contrast more striking than in the case where political power was to be handed on, as when a new king succeeded a deceased one. It was rarely, if ever, the case that power was increased in the transmission. The hope was mainly that power could be handed down uninterruptedly, something that was often complicated when the heir happened to be a minor. But scientific knowledge was handed on and increased in the process because, beginning with scientific academies in the seventeenth century, it became part of the meaning of scientific activity that scientists would not simply strike out on their own but "contribute" to increasing a preexisting stock of knowledge.

The contrasts between traditional power and modern power are important because they point to a crucial turning point that marked the transformation of the idea of *progress* into a *process of modernizing*. Progress was the vision of the eighteenth-century Enlightenment. Roughly speaking, it consisted of two principal ideas, liberation from the mass of inherited restraints and their presiding authorities, and the increase of human powers of all kinds: material, personal, political (the idea of a nation in arms), sexual (Diderot and de Sade), and intellectual. The first of these, liberation, was pretty much realized for the middle classes throughout most of Western Europe and North America by the end of the nineteenth century. It was formalized in new constitutions, bills of rights, and representative parliaments. In effect, progress as liberation was achieved and there remained only to mop up the anomalies, such as the denial of full citizenship to workers, women, and racial minorities.

The project of modernizing was, however, of a different order, although this was not fully appreciated at the time. The potential for power represented by science, technology, and capitalism depended on certain conditions being fulfilled, that is, it meant that society would have to accept certain means as necessary if this particular form of power was to be exploited to its fullest. Thus the introduction, use, and improvement of machinery, which was a crucial element in the new form of power, required a view of the worker as adaptable and expendable. It also presupposed a view of the world that was matter-of-fact, "thingified" as Hegel put it. The mysterious and ineffable, which were fundamental modes of experience for religion, had no place. Further, each fresh advance brought new prerequisites: a high-technology economy would require computer literacy and the reverberations would be registered at all levels of education.

Unlike liberation, this second aspect of progress could not, in principle, ever be fully attained or completed. Each innovation in knowledge/power demanded a new set of conditions for its maximization; each maximization was organized for fertility: it would spawn new powers, new knowledge that called for new conditions. This stage signified that progress had been transformed into a process of modernizing. The dynamical nature of modernization would soon present a marked contrast to the political principles of liberation. The latter would appear "static"—a strong term of disapproval in a modernizing society—and for good reason. Once a society establishes, say, freedom of speech or universal suffrage, there is nothing more to discover. Rather the task is to protect and extend them, to tend them. They become, as it were, established truths, homilies; and these are not the stuff of research at the frontiers of knowledge. Moreover, to the extent the political principles of liberation become deep-rooted, their very rootedness threatens to make them dysfunctional in a modernizing society where, as we have seen, new power is continuously revolutionizing the conditions of its own reproduction. Thus built into the idea of progress-as-modernization is the possibility that the political principles of progress would be viewed as anachronistic and in need of adaptation or elimination. This possibility has now become a reality and it is intimately connected with the new role of conservatism as the party of progress.

To understand the threat of anachronism to the political principles of liberation, as well as the links that have come to connect conservatism and modernization, we need to look more closely at the unique structure of power invented in the name of progress. We shall see that it was profoundly antidemocratic. I shall call that conception of power the New Trinitarianism because it is composed of three elements that resemble those in the creedal formula: capital (the father), state bureaucracy (the son), and science (the holy ghost). Like the old formula, the new one is silent about humanity.

The seventeenth- and eighteenth-century philosophies that had been instrumental in forming the idea of progress, had also done much to popularize the notion of a "social contract" that stipulated power had to be based upon the explicit consent of the members. One of the most striking features common to the elements in the New Trinity, however, is that each depended only minimally, if at all, on the consent of the members of society. The definition of a capitalist, for example, was that he owned certain instruments of production that, according to the principle of private property, entitled him to do virtually what he pleased with them without consulting workers, consumers, or citizens. Similarly the state bureaucracy. Although according to legal forms the bureaucrat was the employee of the state and the "servant" of society, he rapidly became a formidable power-wielder in his own right: he was a decision-maker, a rule adjudicator, and a crucial contributor to policy formulation. He was also deliberately insulated from public pressures and buffered by an elected legislature and executive. Although the bureaucrat was supposed to be controlled by the elected officials, in practice they became more dependent on the bureaucrat's expertise. The shift from servant to silent partner was marked by the eventual recognition of bureaucracies as the "permanent" element that preserved "continuity" in policies despite the fluctuations of electoral politics. Thus an important branch of government had been created that, in principle, was not supposed to be responsive or responsible to the citizenry. This was all the more ominous since bureaucracies were to play the leading political role in the process of modernization.

Science, the third element in modern power, became the perfect incarnation of a conception of power that was to be generated independently of any social contract or democratic agreement. It was an ideal that had its own theological resonance: power as immaculately conceived because born of the purest, most disinterested, and objective form of knowledge ever invented by mankind. For more than two centuries science was depicted mythically, not as a social institution but as the miraculous gift of solitary geniuses—a Copernicus, Galileo, or Newton. The myth of science was crucial to the new form of power for it both etherealized and sanctified the other elements of power, both of which were reducible to wills-to-power, one of the state, the other of the capitalist. As a social myth science came to represent expertise grounded upon "truth," the highest form of knowledge in an age that has mostly forgotten the meaning of "God's omniscience" but remembers its attribute: knowledge that in no way required validation by ordinary beings.

The common feature in these elements of power is that by nature each functioned best under conditions of autonomy: the capitalist was most efficient when least regulated, the bureaucrat most expert when least trammeled by public opinion or self-serving legislators, and the scientist most productive when allowed the maximum freedom of research.

The new ground of power being prepared by modern industrial capitalism, science, and governmental bureaucracies constituted a direct challenge to the political ideals espoused by most of the theorists of progress, and pointed to a political contradiction at the center of their thinking. In America, France, Britain, and Western Europe it was widely assumed that the struggle for more popular, liberal systems of government was as authentically progressive as the advancement of science or industry. What was overlooked at the time was that the movements for the liberalization and democratization of politics took a diametrically opposed view of power from the one being developed by the collaboration between capitalism, science, and state bureaucracies. The battle cry of the revolutionary movements in seventeenth-century England, colonial America, and eighteenth-century France had been stated by John Locke: all legitimate power "has been laid in the Consent of the People." It was reaffirmed in the Preamble to the American Constitution: "We the People . . . do ordain and establish this Constitution." We shall call this the majoritarian formula. Locke had stated its main point: when individuals have agreed to institute a community, "they have thereby made that *Community* one Body, with a Power to Act as one Body, which is only by the will and determination of the *majority*."[7] The underlying notion was that power was generated by and from the people: by their participation, their active involvement in carrying out common tasks, their deliberations over public issues, their contributions of money and labor, and their willingness to risk and sacrifice their lives.

But from the time of the earliest Trinitarians, such as Alexander Hamilton and Saint-Simon, down to the latest neoconservatives and neoliberals such as Samuel Huntington, Daniel Bell, Seymour Lipset, Jeane Kirkpatrick, and Daniel Moynihan, populist politics has been viewed as fickle, subjective, emotional, and ignorant—the very opposite of scientific and social scientific knowledge. Trinitarianism has thus shaped the original idea of progress into an elitist ideology in which progress depends upon preserving the autonomy of political, corporate, and scientific elites and preventing the masses—whose incompetence has been certified by social science—from intruding their inexpert opinions into the rational decision-making processes of corporations (as in the disputes over

public regulation of and representation in corporate decisions), public bureaucracies (as in the efforts to make public utilities commissions publicly responsive), or scientific laboratories (as in the flap over the efforts of elected bodies to
regulate aspects of genetic engineering).

The new conception of progress was given its proper name by its advocates:
modernization. It represents the mature form of the trinitarian vision. There
have been two versions of modernization in America, one adapted to domestic society where the trinitarians have had to contend—mostly successfully—
against an indigenous majoritarian tradition composed of liberal, democratic,
and populist elements. The other version has been sent abroad in accompaniment to the global expansion of American capitalism and military power. The
same tendencies are evident both at home and abroad: the depoliticization of
society, especially to discourage mass participation (except at election time)
and the formulation of mass demands; and the creation of a technocratic structure whose task is to rationalize the conditions that will preserve order, promote
conditions favorable to capitalist enterprise, and strengthen American military
power.

There are, of course, differences between the two forms of modernization. In
the United States a persistent majoritarian tradition has had to be contained but
not repressed. It is not only that the costs of repression would, at this time, be
prohibitive, but also counterproductive. Trinitarianism has learned that nothing
legitimates power like the spectacle of critical groups participating in debates
over policy that, save for minor tactical successes, they rarely win. As a result,
the historical function of the left under conditions of advanced modernization
has been, as the experience of Jews, blacks, women, and Hispanics testifies, to
bring dissidents within the system, or, more accurately, to make them "a part of
the process." Abroad, the modernizing process operates in a rawer form, as an
export that is either forced upon premodern cultures or is attached as a condition of assistance. The difference is between the Federal Reserve Board and
IMF; between defense budgets haggled through Congress and military weapons
and advisers deployed covertly; or between spending corporate millions to buy
elections at home and spending a few millions of taxpayer dollars to buy them
abroad.

If a society conceives of itself as "going forward," then by the same token, it
is going to leave behind some of its people and institutions. Progressives have
tried to justify these consequences by labeling as "anachronistic" or "archaic"
those who have been stranded by the "advances" of civilization. The early champions of progress were clear about which groups or institutions were anachronisms: aristocracy, monarchy, and church. These were "feudal" institutions that
could have no place in a future society based on reason, liberty, equality, and
representative government. During the French Revolution the lines between
liberal revolutionaries and conservative opponents were drawn on the issue of
anachronism. The defense of the archaic, from Burke and de Maistre to Maur-

ras, Eliot, and Waugh, has tended to be politically reactionary, culturally elitist, and socially impossible. It has nurtured an antimodernist bias that sees society threatened by the "masses" who have been deracinated from their natural culture of deference and shaped by modern advertising and technology into consumers of a mass culture that is rapidly engulfing education, literature, and the arts.

The American experience of progress struck foreign observers, like Tocqueville, as completely different. America had no feudal past, no Old Regime, no aristocracy or church. When its Revolution came it was swift, less costly, and less radical because there was no system of inherited privilege and power to uproot. By the nineteenth century America would be heralded as an instant utopia, painlessly realized. "America," the historian Hofstadter would drily remark, "was the only country in the world that began with perfection and aspired to progress."

But because America had no feudal past, it did not follow that archaism would never exist. Archaism had to be created before it could be destroyed. This occurred when progress passed into modernization. Modernization took its bearings from the demands of economic competition, first for domestic markets, then in rivalry with other, more "advanced," industrial societies, for world markets. It meant introduction of laborsaving, productivity-enhancing technologies that rendered anachronistic the experience of meaningful work and would eventually create countless persons who would never be employed. Modernization meant an industrial culture designed to produce anachronisms as a constant by-product of the relentless replacement of the recently new by the latest invention or process. The pressures of modernization cancelled any practical meaning to notions of skill or life-rhythms: the one was replaced by "retooling" or simple demotion to the ranks of the unskilled, while the other disappeared into the murderous tempo of the assembly line. Modernization was equally destructive of the places where people lived, the relationships of family, friends, and neighbors, and the values they lived by. It was as though a social *tabula rasa* had to be recreated daily, because the new form of progress exacted certain conditions. Life had to be antitraditional, secular even when it was religious, urban, pragmatic, noncontemplative. These conditions bred an industrial, urban innocence to succeed the romantic, urban innocence about nature (the latter created by Cooper writing about Natty Bumppo from England and by Whitman who heard America singing in Brooklyn). It was the innocence that one could elude the effects of constant change by introducing more change, that human beings could be so completely caught up in experiencing the new that they would be invulnerable to the universal experience of traditional society, the experience of irremediable loss accompanied by renewal, of what the ancient poet Vergil called *lacrimae rerum*, the tears of things. Who can measure an innocence that remained unshaken despite a bloody civil war? Or who can but marvel at the historical *fortuna* that has confirmed that innocence by arranging two unprecedented world wars in which, save for the nearly hidden cemeteries, not a scratch was registered on the land, its cities, or its civilian populace?

Archaism in America was not, however, remotely similar to the reactionary archaism of Europe; it was not about aristocrats, priests, social hierarchy, or the oppressive bureaucracy described so bitingly by Tocqueville. What modernization came to define as archaic were the first halting, limited but genuine attempts at a participatory politics centered around small towns, villages, cities, and state governments. It had many different and changing forms, not all of them theoretically coherent or even attractive: Regulators, Shays's followers, anti-Federalists, urban mechanics, working men's associations, abolitionists, populists, and suffragettes. That much of the ethos of American archaism derived from rural and small-town America; that it was typically religious in a simple, often fundamentalist sense made its aspirations seem quaint in a society that was on the way to becoming the world's greatest example of a progressive, modern society. But if the archaism of the Old Regime had been defined by contrasting the old monarchy with the new representative government; the old established church with religious pluralism and indifference; and the old aristocratic social hierarchy with bourgeois conceptions of political and legal equality, the archaism of America was being defined by inverting the original contrast. In America, participatory politics is dismissed as "populism" and elitism is openly espoused; the efforts of citizens to take control of the political institutions that stand closest to them or to invent new ones are disparaged as "localism" and politics is located around centralized institutions in which the bureaucracy looms as the major power; and protests against assigning huge amounts of the society's material resources to military purposes and following an economic policy that imposes severe suffering solely on the lower classes are waived aside with Old Regime appeals to "reason of state," only now couched in the language of "national security" and of the objective needs of "the economy."

Majoritarianism has been condemned as archaic, but this has not prevented the president from using archaism to prevent a majority from coalescing. Reagan proved a past master at appealing to archaic virtues, turning them into prejudices and then using the aroused emotions to sow animosity and mistrust among groups who are the natural heirs to "archaic" political traditions of popular revolt and egalitariansim. He has adroitly manipulated conservative religious groups, advocates of prayer in public schools, antiabortion groups, anti-ERA movements, and champions of censorship to discredit and weaken groups that might constitute the basis for resistance to the harsh logic of modernization.

Modernization means the attempt to rationalize an entire society, make it conform to a model designed to impose the most efficient use of available means for the achievement of particular ends, such as reindustrialization, military security, education for international competition, etc. Some groups are natural victims of rationalization: skilled workers and unions; the unskilled youths of black or Hispanic backgrounds; women seeking entry into employment and on equal terms; teachers whose vocation is increasingly viewed as anomalously "labor-intensive"; and young people of all descriptions who find themselves regarded as a resource that must be exposed to intensive technical training so that America can retain its scientific and technological edge. These are some of the groups that can be neutralized politically by mobilizing archaic strata. Archaism thus becomes an instrument to promote progress—and in the process swell the ranks of the archaic. Is a black teenager from an urban ghetto any less archaic in the new world of high technology than the Appalachian coal miner?

For two centuries first progress, then modernization, have stood for steady growth, greater benefits more widely distributed, all classes contributing and receiving more. Now, however, there are increasing signs that the expansive phase of modernization is over. Change will next occur in a context of austerity rather than abundance, of lowered rather than raised expectations. There are numerous causes pointing in that direction: the pressure on scarce resources, the nature of modern technology that allows premodern societies to leap decades and become almost instantly competitive with modernized societies, and, not least, the rising pressures from Third World countries who are not likely to permit a few nations to enjoy extraordinary levels of consumption unto eternity while they contend with worsening conditions of famine, poverty, and miserable living conditions. There is a fair prospect that modernization will have led America and its allies into a state of siege with the rest of the world. It is a prospect for which conservatives have a natural appetite. To make America great again there will have to be sacrifice; agencies of control and surveillance will be needed; a premium will be placed on those few who have the technical skills to keep America competitive; military valor and patriotic submission will be the sum of civic virtues with no nonsense about reverse discrimination, desegregation, and aid to the disadvantaged.

An alternative politics is in bad faith if it pretends that by some substitutions in the Trinitarian formula of power—workers for capitalists, our planners for their bureaucrats, nonscience for their science—the society can be placed on course for the Good Society. The world created by modernization cannot be conjured away. A start can be made on repairing it. But this counsel, too, is guilty of bad faith unless there is a recognition of what is possibly the gravest harm wrought by modernization: it uses the idealism that has been handed down, reworked, and enhanced over the centuries, but it cannot replenish the moral and political resources by which we learn to make our way in the world and care for it. Not from capitalism based on self-interest; not from science which cannot, *qua* science, tell us why we ought to care for anything, not even science; and not bureaucracy which prides itself on serving any formally legitimate master. We need to recur to examples of associations where human beings have found a basis for cooperating and nurturing power without being tempted to surrender their active roles for some impersonal process that promises relief from involvements and greater efficiency; where intelligence, skill, and inventiveness have a digni-fied place but are not reified into omniscience which demands power to match its hubris; and where taking care of people and things, rather than using them up, is the basic stance toward the world.

The question is not where to look but what to remember, to recall, and to use as a beginning.

PART FIVE

REVISIONING DEMOCRACY

CHAPTER 19

EDITORIAL

MOST AMERICANS DO NOT OBSERVE OR EXPERIENCE politics firsthand. Under a system of representative government they depend upon their elected representatives to convey, by words and symbolic gestures, what conditions are like in the political world: how the republic is faring, what we need reasonably fear, and what we may reasonably hope. We expect that politicians will not only act but interpret reality for us, tell us what it is and what it means. Acknowledging that certain circumstances may compel a politician to lie or to be less than candid or that often he or she may lack information or have failed to think carefully, there remains a responsibility for truthfulness in the public realm that transcends the exceptions and is prior to them. Systematic lying and misrepresentation corrupt public discourse, breeding cynicism and apathy among the citizens and uncertainty among those who are responsible for making decisions of the gravest sort.

It is not coincidental that systematic lying by governments is conventionally dated from World War I and that in the decades that followed there emerged totalitarian dictatorships that developed deceit and manipulation into governmental functions and total wars in which both sides competed to construct pictures of the world favorable to their cause. The extraordinary levels of violence, directed first against combatants, then against civilians and cities, and finally against nature as well, could only be justified by reconstituting the common understanding of the world so as to conceal or euphemize the horror and irrationality now woven into the structure of things from Verdun to Auschwitz to Hiroshima to My Lai.

The response of those who sought to preserve some integrity of meaning in the public realm was to confront the lies of politicians and propagandists with the truth of facts. During the Vietnam War notable examples of this were Daniel Ellsberg's Pentagon papers and the courageous writings of Noam Chomsky. Since then the status of facts has become equivocal: experts crop up on all sides of most controversies, each with evidence in support of his or her contentions. Above all, the contemporary sensibility has been shaped to recognize that facts have to be interpreted and that interpretations appeal to criteria that are considerably less conclusive than a syllogistic proof. The problem of public discourse is no longer a matter of "setting the record straight" or of producing "facts" that will refute falsehoods. We live in an interpretative world where demonstrable lies coexist with useful fictions, where each of us depends on others for assistance in deciphering the meaning and value of states of affairs and affairs of state in a world that is constantly fragmenting into ever more specialized areas of knowledge and activity. The first value in an interpretative world, especially in the political part of it where power and violence are everyday realities, is trust.

For nearly two decades Americans have witnessed, experienced, and been shaped by the steady corruption of the public realm and its modes of discourse. The deceptions of Vietnam and Watergate were the climactic moments in this experience but not the sole instances of a condition in which the experiment of a politics without trust is being attempted. This is the context for reflecting upon the most recent episode, the purloined briefing papers made available to the Reagan campaign organizers.

"We're handling this 100 percent different from Watergate," declared a high-ranking administration official. "The Nixon people tried to hide something, but we're sending every scrap of stuff to the Justice Department as soon as we find it." Good faith is thus demonstrated by "handling" matters by bureaucratic procedures, as though these were the natural antithesis to Nixon's evasiveness or as though it had been forgotten that one of the early casualties of Watergate was the integrity of the Justice Department, not least because the long political relationship between the then attorney general and the president created doubts about the department's zeal.

The fact that the two scandals have happened within a decade or that both have involved Republican campaigns may be no more, or less, significant than the fact of the predominance of Californians in both cases. What matters is not so much whether a "third-rate burglary" (as the Nixonites called it) was more heinous than "filched" campaign documents (in David Stockman's description), but that the comparison should force into the open the major question. It is not whether the Reagan campaign was as corrupt as Nixon's, but concerns the different ways in which the Reagan administration is corrupt and what corruption now means.

In the varied strands of evil composing it, Watergate resembled a chapter from the history of the early Roman empire. It included simple venality: high politicos were on the take and bribes passed freely. There were shabby episodes of "dirty tricks" where eager young men tried to curry favor by unfair stratagems designed to mislead the rival party. But there were also versions of what the Romans had called "proscriptions" (dangerous citizens were declared outlaws and their property confiscated) but which came to be known as "enemies lists" and "the Huston Plan" for intimidating and surveilling unfriendly persons and causes. These, too, took place in the context of an interminable war for empire that gradually revealed the cracks and weaknesses in the otherwise imposing facade of world hegemony. The Nixon men attributed their failure to impose their will on events to a disloyal bureaucracy and so they attempted to purge the disloyal and replace them by faithful conservatives. They would then eliminate the shiftless from the welfare rolls, make it clear to blacks and other minorities that the civil rights days as well as riotous urban nights were over, and restore the work ethic. Like the Romans the Nixonites tried to mount a contradiction. They wanted to preserve and strengthen imperial power while corrupting the remains of the republican political tradition, the source of the nation's political vitality.

Lies and rumors of corruption had trailed Nixon ever since his political debut. Twice he was rejected for important office by the citizens: in the presidential election of 1960 and in the California gubernatorial contest shortly thereafter. In the end the Vietnam War and the lies of LBJ debased the public realm sufficiently to elect and then to reelect Nixon president. Jimmy Carter, who promised the nation he would never lie and largely honored that promise, failed as a president, not simply because of inexperience and a talent for selecting small-minded advisers, but because few appreciated the toll that a decade and more of lying, deceitful discourse, and governmental lawlessness had taken on the fabric of civic trust.

How Ronald Reagan has discharged his responsibility toward the public realm and its legacy of meanings was summed up in a wholly truthful, if unconscious, remark he made not long ago. After charging that an enormous campaign existed to misrepresent his administration's environmental policies, he then asked rhetorically, "Now how about five minutes of the truth?" Which is about what the citizenry has gotten. Several months ago the *New York Times* reported that White House aides were relieved because the media were giving less publicity to the President's numerous and now legendary misstatements of fact and misleading accounts. Reagan's men attributed this to "a decline in interest by the general public." They went on to say, with a logic befitting the age of interpretation, that the public recognized the accuracy of the president's "larger points" even if some "nits and nats" were "open to debate." It is an actual fact that the president has systematically misrepresented such nits and nats as: the administration's level of aid to education, previous levels of defense spending, the vulnerability of American defenses, the extent of cuts in social spending and environmental matters by his administration, and the condition of the social security system and his own plans to reform it.

Like the deceptions of the Nixon regime, the untrustworthiness of the president and his men is linked to the tightening of state power, threats to civil liberties, and the encouragement of higher levels of violence. The Reaganites have systematically sought to weed out ideologically disloyal bureaucrats and replace them by what the president calls "a whole new cadre of young conservatives in government." While rejecting the cruder methods of the Nixon years, the Reaganites have not foresworn the old hostilities toward desegregationists, dissenters, environmentalists, and militant ethnics. The tone was conveyed in the lecture that the president recently read to a group of high school students, several of whom favored a nuclear freeze. Rights, he told them, are a "privilege" and "with that privilege goes a responsibility to be right." Where the Nixon administration struck at its enemies mainly out of malice, the Reaganites have sublimated enmity into ideological principles, mainly libertarian, and used the legal powers of the government to roll back desegregation, reduce constitutional safeguards for public employees, and eat away at the Freedom of Information Act.

Nowhere is lying more conspicuous than in the administration's efforts to revitalize imperial power and, in the course of it, to increase the potential and actuality of violence in the world. The president's attempts to deny covert American assistance to the "contras" fighting in Nicaragua and to conceal the amount of American aid flowing into Honduras and El Salvador may not have attained the level of Nixonian grandeur but the same contempt for truth is evident: Somocistas are "freedom fighters"; the recent pastoral letter on world peace by the Catholic bishops has "the same purpose" as the administration; the nuclear freeze movement is "counterproductive" because "we are all talking of a freeze."

Perhaps the most remarkable evidence of the president's cynicism is the attitude that he displays toward conservatism. Although in actual fact he has implemented many of the pledges he made to conservative groups, he persists in denying that he has cut back on environmental protection, social welfare, and education or that he has significantly increased defense spending. It is as though lying has become so congenial that one is forced to mislead supporters and opponents alike.

It was fitting that an administration that places such store upon the manipulation of images, the expert use of television, and the skills of the Great Communicator should have stolen a briefing book for a televised debate. That it should not be laundered-clean money or dirty tricks but a document that has been prepared for the culminating moment of a long public debate is indicative of a more general indifference—except for rhetorical purposes—toward the things that the people as a whole have a stake in, not the least being the conditions that make for public discussion. In a society where political involvement has become dangerously attenuated for many citizens and where that involvement so frequently is vicarious, the open corruption of politics endangers what is already a fragile connection. For it is a corruption of politics, not just old-fashioned give-and-take, when the president suggests that Communists are behind the nuclear freeze movement or that teachers are engaged in deliberately brainwashing students about the nature of nuclear war.

The ideological element that joins the president's indifference toward truth with the convictions and goals of his influential supporters among corporate leadership is a deep conviction that if a wide range of government functions were given over to private enterprise and made to conform to the discipline of the market and to corporate-style authority, then most domestic problems, at least, would become more manageable. In all lying there is an element of contempt. Here it happens to be contempt for political life on any terms other than those embodied in corporate values. There was a small bit of poetic justice recently when the administration had to fire an assistant secretary in HUD because he had improperly used government personnel to complete a book on "Privatizing the Public Sector."

Before long another presidential campaign will be underway. Unless the president disavows all of the signals he has given thus far and chooses not to run, as citizens we can look forward to an experience from which it is difficult to emerge feeling other than unclean and demeaned. The tragedy is that while President Reagan has taken public discourse to a desperately low point, the issues facing the country are profound and to some extent even unprecedented in our history. What makes the discussion of them troubling is that possibly for the first time in American history there is a widespread sense of emptiness at the center of our collective existence. For more than two decades it has become steadily clearer that we do not know what we are about in this world, except as mainly passive instruments of whatever combination of corporate, military, and bureaucratic purposes happen to have jelled at particular moments. And we are largely unable to talk about our common concerns because it is no longer clear how, after decades of the corruption of speech, we should begin political talk: Reagan exploits while he travesties traditional values, while technicians and academic experts can be induced to provide the scientific lyrics to any melody.

There are at least two vital questions that citizens must find ways of forcing into the coming campaigns. They are not the usual stuff of quick policy solutions but they are quite basic to the political revitalization of the society. One concerns the terrible damage done to the character of political life by the pursuit of empire. Empire is, at its essence, domination over other peoples. It exploits their wealth, uses their bodies, and is prepared to sacrifice whole societies to the dictates of military and economic strategies. Empire means being hated by others because exercising tyranny is synonymous with being hated. But empire is also at war with democracy at home. They stand for diametrically opposed notions of power and of social worth. The enemies of democracy have repeatedly stated their case; this election needs to be one where the friends of democracy insist on confronting the issue of imperial power.

The other concerns the restructuring of society. All of the current talk about reindustrialization, reinvestment, free trade, and the like is about big plans in the making for the thorough modernization of America, from education to defense, from industrial plant to social security. Here, too, those who care about democratic values of participation, the uses to which one's body, skills, and resources are put, and rendering power shareable and controllable by popular constituencies must struggle actively and transform democracy from a campaign flourish to a fundamental issue.

CHAPTER 20

WHAT REVOLUTIONARY ACTION MEANS TODAY

ONE OF THE CHAPTERS IN TOCQUEVILLE'S *Democracy in America* is titled "Why Great Revolutions Will Become Rare." His thesis was that once a society becomes democratized in its political system and more egalitarian in its social institutions, it is unlikely that it will ever undergo the type of revolutionary upheavals experienced by France in 1789 and England in the 1640s. The great revolutions had resulted from gross political and social inequalities. Thanks to its system of equal political rights (i.e., for white males), and to the ready availability of land, American democracy had eliminated the causes of revolution. He claimed that the revolutionary impulse would wither because for the first time in Western history the masses of ordinary human beings had a tangible stake in defending the status quo.

Tocqueville's conclusions have been restated in many ways. Democracy, it has been said, is the form of government that has had its revolution. Others claim that for the people to rebel against democracy is for them to rebel against themselves, or that a revolution against democracy in the name of democracy is a contradiction in terms. In each of these formulations the implication is that as long as a political system is democratic, it makes no sense to think of revolutionary activity as an appropriate or obligatory form of action for the democratic citizen. But the real problem is, is it right for the democratic citizen to undertake revolutionary action when the political system retains some of the formal features of democracy but is clearly embarked on a course that is progressively antidemocratic without being crudely repressive? What are the precise ways in which a system that is formally democratic conceals its antidemocratic tendencies? Are pseudo-democratic substitutes introduced that create the illusion of democracy? Was the idea of a democratic citizen partially skewed at the outset so that its development in America was truncated? And, finally, does it make sense even to discuss the possibility of revolution under the circumstances of an advanced, complex society? In what terms would it make sense to talk of revolution today—what would revolutionary action by democratic citizens be?

Our starting point is with a significant silence. Although the United States has been repeatedly described as being in a condition of crisis, no one seems to have suggested that there is a crisis at the center of American democracy, in the idea of citizenship itself. While there are many voices, with varying degrees of good faith, ready to testify for democracy—especially when the purpose is to contrast the United States with the USSR—there is virtually no one who is given to reflecting about the democratic citizen, to asking what it is to be one, or why, if each of us is one and there are so many of us, the society seems to have so many antidemocratic tendencies.

In a speech last June to the British Parliament Ronald Reagan announced that the United States was about to throw its prestige and resources behind a program launched to strengthen "democracy throughout the world," but he made no reference to the idea of democratic citizenship or any suggestion that democracy might need strengthening at home. The silence on the subject is not peculiar to conservatives or reactionaries. The democratic citizen does not appear in any substantial form in the writings of Barry Commoner, the titular leader of the Citizens' Party, or Michael Harrington, the theoretician of Democratic Socialism of America. Most Marxists are interested in the "masses" or the workers, but they dismiss citizenship as a bourgeois conceit, formal and empty, although Marx himself was much preoccupied with the idea in his early writings.

The present silence is a symptom of a crisis that has been in the making since the beginning of the republic. Its origins are in the one-sided conception of citizenship that was reflected in the Constitution. Beginning with the movement for a bill of rights, which was mounted in the midst of the controversy over ratification of the original Constitution (1787–1789), and extending through the era of Jacksonian Democracy, the battle over slavery, and the adoption of Amendments 13, 14, 15, 17 (providing for the direct election of senators), and 19 (prohibiting the denial of suffrage on the basis of sex), a distinct pattern emerged in which each extension of rights was assumed to be an advance toward the realization of democracy. In actuality, the ideal of rights was usurping the place of civic activity. A liberal conception of citizenship was becoming predominant.

A democratic conception of citizenship, if it means anything at all, means that the citizen is supposed to exercise his rights to advance or protect the kind of polity that depends on his being involved in its common concerns. The liberal view was that citizenship is democratic in the United States because every citizen, regardless of cultural, social, economic, and biological differences, can equally claim the right to vote, speak, worship, acquire property and have it protected, and be assured of the elements of a fair trial. Unfortunately, the liberal civic culture never supplied any content to rights. A citizen was no less a citizen for espousing Klan doctrines than he was for joining the NAACP. To possess rights was to be free to do anything or say anything as long as one did not break the law or interfere with the rights of others.

How could a democratic conception of citizenship be said to be fulfilled—as a liberal conception would be—by having rights exercised for antidemocratic ends, as the KKK choice would be? It is not that a liberal view of rights disposes one toward the Klan, only that liberalism is fulfilled by protecting those who are so disposed. The American Civil Liberties Union, with its commitment to defending the entire range of opinion, from the most liberal to the most il-liberal, was, one might say, immanent in the historical failure of liberalism to create a vision of civic commitments and of common action that could furnish both content and guidance to the exercise of rights.

This failure was inevitable, given the nature of the original liberal project, which was to protect rights by limiting governmental power. That project was written into the Constitution. The Constitution was not designed to encourage citizen action but to prevent arbitrary power, especially the form of power rep-resented by the will of the majority. Among several of the states, the majority principle was being actively tested in the period from the outbreak of the Revo-lution in 1776 to the ratification of the Constitution in 1789. The Constitution was intended to shatter the majoritarian experiment at the national level by in-corporating several devices that were supposed to frustrate the natural form of democratic action: separation of powers, checks and balances, federalism, the Supreme Court, indirect election of the president and Senate, and brief tenure for representatives. At the same time, the Constitution made no reference to the right to vote or hold office or to the principle of equality. Save for a somewhat enigmatic clause that was later interpreted to prevent a state from discriminat-ing against citizens of other states, citizenship hardly figured as a basic institu-tion. When the first ten amendments were quickly added to the Constitution, the outline of the citizen began to emerge, but it was primarily as a bearer of rights than as a participant in a collective undertaking. Several rights in the original Bill of Rights were couched in language that was less suggestive of what a citizen might actively do than what government was prohibited from doing. ("Congress shall make no law . . . abridging the freedom of speech." "No person shall . . . be deprived of life, liberty, or property, without due process of law.")

The present silence about democratic citizenship is a sign of the disintegra-tion of the liberal conception of rights and, necessarily, of the idea of citizenship dependent upon it. What happened is that in the twentieth century the liberal practice of politics rapidly undermined the liberal conception of rights. The the-ory of rights enshrined in the Bill of Rights conceived of special forms of free-dom and protection that were to be beyond the ordinary reach of legislative or executive power. Once they had been given constitutional status, rights were not only beyond the scope of positive law, they were assumed to be "above" politics. Whenever an historical controversy arose about rights, the point was made repeatedly that constitutional guarantees were intended to protect rights against "transient majorities" and "temporary gusts of passion."

At almost the exact moment when the liberal theory of rights was about to be given the material form of the first ten amendments to the Constitution, James Madison, who was the prime mover of that effort, also produced what came to be the classical formulation of the liberal theory of politics. In Letter 10 of the *Federalist* papers he argued that one of the sternest tests for the proposed Constitution would be whether it could control "factions," the distinctive form of politics in a society founded on freedom. A faction was a group organized to promote its interests by political means. Inevitably factions would be in continual conflict with each other, not only over property rights but over political and religious beliefs as well. Thus the liberal conception of politics, with its conception of groups as pursuing interests that would conflict with other interests protected by legal rights, carried the presumption that politics was an activity that, by nature, posed a threat to rights. The task, as Madison and later liberals saw it, was to encourage institutional devices that would control the effects of politics, not to reconstitute politics. Citizens would be engrossed in private actions, for when men and women are given freedom they use it to promote their self-interests, and it would be unjust and oppressive to limit that pursuit in the name of encouraging common action for common ends.

There were at least two further respects in which the liberal conception of politics was at odds with liberal rights. First, the protection of rights presupposed that government would be their defender, intervening to prevent interest groups from violating the rights of other groups or individuals. For this presupposition to work, government itself would have to withstand effectively the pressures generated by interest-group politics, pressures that were guaranteed to be unrelenting by the system of elections, campaign contributions, and lobbying. The presupposition collapsed because once politics was reduced to interest groups, there was no general constituency to support government in its role of impartial defender of rights. Instead of playing the role of defender of rights, government assumed a function more consistent with the politics of interest groups, that of "balancing" rights against certain overriding matters of state. Thus when wider latitude was given to the CIA and FBI to conduct surveillance, or when First Amendment rights of the press were limited by the prohibition against disclosing the names of CIA agents, the government's justification was that there had to be a balancing of national security needs with civil liberties, as though the setting were simply another instance of having to weigh the demands of conflicting groups.

Interest politics discourages as well the development of a civic culture favorable to the defense of rights and to the acceptance of integrative action as the activity definitive of citizenship. Interest politics dissolves the idea of the citizen as one for whom it is natural to join together with other citizens to act for purposes related to a general community and substitutes the idea of individuals who are grouped according to conflicting interests. The individual is not first and foremost a civic creature bound by preexisting ties to those who share the same history, the same general association, and the same fate. He or she is instead a business executive, a teamster, a feminist, office worker, farmer, or homosexual whose immediate identity naturally divides him or her from others. As a member of an interest group, the individual is given an essentially anticivic education. He is taught that the first duty is to support the self-interest of the group because politics is nothing but a struggle for advantage. In contrast, the citizen has to decide what to do, not in a setting where each has the same interest as the other, but in one where there are differences that have to be taken into account and, ideally, incorporated into the decision. The citizen, unlike the groupie, has to acquire a perspective of commonality, to think integrally and comprehensively rather than exclusively. The groupie never gets beyond "politics," the stage of unreflective self-interest.

The inability of liberals to develop either a tradition of the state as the consistent defender of rights—save, of course, property rights—or a civic culture that nourished political action rather than politics eventually led to the radical alteration in the status of rights. The underlying philosophy of the Bill of Rights, which drew heavily from the tradition of natural-rights thinking, was that the status of rights could be "settled" on a more or less permanent basis, that once a right was included in the Constitution it was "fixed" or, in the language of the eighteenth-century natural-law writers, "unalterable." But rights proved no less tractable to interest-group politics than did other lofty subjects, such as foreign polity or national defense. Throughout the nineteenth century and down to the New Deal, property rights, rather than civil or political rights, dominated American politics—even the issue of slavery was formulated as a matter of rights of ownership. But in the twentieth century, especially after World War II, it has been the civil rights of citizens that have been contested, not only in the courts and before administrative tribunals, but in the arena of interest-group politics. Some of the most powerful groups are organized for the express purpose of using political and legal means to deprive other citizens of their rights or to restrict the exercise or scope of them. Rights to abortion, sexual freedom, freedom from censorship, public education free of religious influences, rights of privacy against sophisticated surveillance, affirmative action quotas—these and a multitude of other issues are an indication of how profoundly politicized rights have become, how unassured their status is. This is not, as the Founding Fathers or latter-day conservatives would have it, because of the tyranny of the majority. Many of the limitations imposed on rights through legislation or administrative rulings have been inspired by minorities obsessed with single issues. Society is now accustomed to the dangerous notion that rights, like crop subsidies or taxes, are part of the normal give-and-take of politics.

The transvaluation of rights from a quasi-absolute to a contingent status, from being constitutive of politics to being very nearly derivative or reflexive, is vividly illustrated by the recent fate of the system of "economic rights" that liberals had vigorously promoted and touted as the answer to socialism. Beginning with the New Deal, liberals argued that political rights were formal and ineffective if citizens did not have jobs, social security, unemployment compensation, the right to organize unions and bargain collectively, access to higher education, and, in general, a decent standard of living. The claim was frequently made that because material needs were primary, economic rights were more "fundamental" than political rights. This primacy should be given recognition by legislating an "economic Bill of Rights" that would supply a "real" foundation for the exercise of what would otherwise be formal or "legal" rights. Although this proposal was not explicitly adopted, it accurately foreshadowed the extraordinary growth of social benefits and services that evolved into the program of the welfare state. It proved to be a latter-day version of Esau's bargain, a selling of a political birthright for a mess of pottage. Economic rights, or, as they more recently have been called, "entitlements," do empower people. There is a gain in dignity, autonomy, and well-being, and no democrat should believe otherwise. But this must not blind one to the antipolitical consequences resulting from the preoccupation with economic rights. Unlike the situation with political rights, where, for example, my possession of a right to form a voluntary association does not diminish your right to free speech, economic rights are contingent upon finite resources: your right to medical care will necessarily utilize resources that cannot be allocated to satisfy my right to job training. In the context of an expanding economy such as existed from roughly 1945–1970 the political consequences of economic rights were temporarily suppressed, but with the onset of economic recession, stagflation, and unemployment the diverse effects of basing the value of citizenship upon economic benefits became apparent. Given a capitalist economy and an increasingly harsh conception of it by the dominant groups, all of the solutions to the deepening crisis involved cutting back social benefits and thereby creating or exacerbating cleavages among the citizenry: racial, religious, class, ethnic, and regional prejudices moved closer to the surface as groups competed for survival in a declining economy. Interest-group politics became intensified, while concern for shared values and a common fate seemed either incomprehensible or utopian and naïve.

Yet this is not quite a complete description of our political condition because it omits one of the most striking and seemingly puzzling facts. Despite the deepening unemployment, the irrational level of defense expenditures, the utter hopelessness for millions of blacks and many Hispanics, and the brazenly business-oriented bias of the Reagan administration, there is an astonishing passivity among those who have been hurt most by the current economic policies. All of the elements for radical political protest appear to be present. And yet there has been no general mobilization of outrage, only a few parades.

There are, of course, many reasons for the political passivity of the unemployed and the permanently poor, but one of the most important is the depoliticization to which they have been subjected. For more than three decades the thinking behind as well as the substance of public policies dealing with the poor, the unemployed, and racial minorities, have treated them as having a pariah status quite unlike other interests. The tacit assumption of interest-group politics has always been that there was one common element among farmers, workers, employers, and teachers, etc.: they were all productive in one way or another. They might receive subsidies, benefits, or protections from the government, but, after all, it was they who in the last analysis were contributing to what they were receiving. This is why farmers and businessmen have always been outraged whenever the federal government has attempted to use government aid as a justification for government regulation and intervention. Farmers and businessmen have never conceived of themselves as receiving handouts and therefore as being dependents. As a result, they have been able to retain a strong sense of dignity and have been able to act with others who share their interests.

Those who are poor, unemployed, and members of racial minorities can be treated differently, in ways that are divisive, that render them incapable of sustained political action. They are "targeted" by specialized programs that, in effect, fragment their lives. One agency handles medical assistance, another job training, a third food stamps, and so on ad infinitum. If a person's life is first flensed by bureaucrats whose questionnaires probe every detail of it, and that life is reorganized into categories corresponding to public programs that are the means of one's existence, the person becomes totally disabled as a political being, unable to grasp the meaning of common concerns of even so small a totality as a neighborhood. This is because he or she has been deprived of the most elemental totality of all, the self.

Depoliticization is more extreme among the poor and racial minorities because they are the most helpless of all groups in the political economy, the new social form that is replacing the older form of the political order. The political economy has taken the liberal idea of the citizen one apolitical step farther. The conception of the citizen as a bearer of rights, who in principle could exercise his capacities to speak, petition, write, and associate, gave way to a conception of a wholly new kind of being whose existence consisted of indices which told him what his condition was objectively: an index for prices, another for wages, inflation, unemployment, consumer spending, and, most grandly, "a misery index."

However useful indices may be for those who have the power to make decisions, they are simultaneously a symbol of powerlessness and a persuasive force toward further depoliticization for those who cannot. An index, such as one representing inflation rates, does not tell the individual what he is doing, but rather what is happening to him. It registers forces that are beyond his ability to influence or control.

Perhaps there is no more striking indication of the extent of depoliticization than the level of popular awareness concerning how the political system really works. Most people understand that our system makes it relatively easy for wealth and economic power to be translated into political power and influence, which are then retranslated into legislative enactments, Treasury rulings, defense contracts, FCC policies, export licenses, and the like. They also know that money, especially corporate money, buys candidates, finances campaigns, hires lobbyists, and keeps a legion of experts, especially academic ones, on long retainers and short leashes. What is so striking is not that people know these things, but that the dominant groups in the political economy are now so confident of their control that they encourage rather than suppress public knowledge of their enormous power. It becomes the interest of corporate power, not simply that ordinary citizens should perceive how money buys politicians and legislation, but that they should perceive how much money it takes. That knowledge provides an invaluable lesson in powerlessness. Lurid accounts of political scandals are doubly useful in this regard, especially when large sums are involved; they teach how much money it takes to purchase favors and how purchasable public officials are, and how utterly cynical it has all become when government corrupts its own members. One Abscam is worth a thousand Mobil ads.

Corporate politics has perverted the forms of politics that meant to connect the institutions of government with the citizens. These changes have been recognized but not frontally challenged because—at the most obvious level—the political economy developed over the past century has been a spectacular success. The very functioning of a successful economy seems to transform political categories and expectations into economic ones, and thereby creates an illusion of "economic democracy." If we do not participate as citizens we do participate as consumers, exercising our freedom to choose our satisfactions whenever we wish—and as if by magic when new products suddenly materialize on the store shelves, we feel that the economy is responding to our every impulse and desire—which is more than we can say about our elected representatives and nonelected public administrators.

About seventy-five years ago, Elihu Root, a representative public figure of the age, remarked after surveying the state of American politics that "in the whole field of popular government I am convinced that one of the plainest duties of citizenship is hopefulness, and that pessimism is criminal weakness."[1] In a land where optimism is virtually a patriotic duty, pessimism is still taken as a symptom of resignation and despair. But pessimism is, I think, something else: the sign of suppressed revolutionary impulses. Pessimism is the mood inspired by a reasoned conviction that only a revolutionary change can ward off the consequences that are implicit in the tendencies in contemporary American society, but that such a revolution, while politically and morally justified by democratic standards for legitimate authority, is neither possible nor prudent—if by revolution we mean launching a campaign of violent insurrection or civil war. Revolutions of that nature are plainly pathological under contemporary conditions of interdependence.

Democrats need a new conception of revolution. Its text should be John Locke, not Karl Marx, because the problem is not to show that a social class should seize power—no social class in an advanced society can pretend to the universality of right which Marx presupposed in the workers of his day—but to reinvent the forms and practices that will express a democratic conception of collective life.

Locke is best remembered for the argument that when those who rule seem bent on acquiring "Absolute Power over the Lives, Liberties, and Estates of the People," their power, which they hold on trust from the people, reverts, and the people are free to fashion new institutions. The right to revolution is not solely a right to overturn and destroy institutions but to fashion new ones because those who rule have perverted the old ones. The right to revolution is the right to create new forms.

Locke insisted that if that right was to be meaningful, people were not required to wait submissively until absolute power had been established:

> The State of Mankind is not so miserable that they are not capable of using this Remedy till it be too late to look for any. . . . Men can never be secure from Tyranny if there be no means to escape it, till they are perfectly under it . . . they have not only a right to get out of it, but to prevent it.[2]

When the right to revolution is conceived as justifying political creativity rather than violence, it is easy to understand why Locke was so insistent that people should and would not revolt over "every little mismanagement in publick affairs." Establishing new institutions was justified only after the rulers had engaged in "a long train of Abuses, Prevarications, and Artifices, all tending the same way." Elsewhere he alluded to a "general course and tendency of things" and to "a settled Design." Given the complex judgment required, Locke's discussion was remarkable for its democratic implications. At various times he referred to the right to revolt as an option that belonged to the "people," to "the majority," and even to individuals; but he never implied that it was so weighty a matter that only a high-minded elite could be entrusted with it. This last point is crucial, for if the right to revolt is about devising new institutions, citizenship is more than a matter of being able to claim rights. It is about a capacity to generate power, for that is the only way that things get established in the world. And it is about a capacity to share in power, to cooperate in it, for that is how institutions and practices are sustained.

Under contemporary conditions, the Lockean question is: are there signs of rebellion, symptoms of disaffection but also examples of political creativity? For some years now social scientists have uncovered widespread civic apathy and pollsters have reported on the low esteem in which politicians and major political institutions are held. Now in a society where the official rhetoric and the rituals of political socialization are still heavily democratic, *incivisme* of the kind documented by voting studies is a serious matter. It is not alienation but disaffection and rejection. I want to suggest that "rejectionism" pervades our society and that its presence and intensity represents a form of rebellion, a gesture of defiance in the face of a system that is immovable and so interconnected as to be unreform-able as a totality. We see rejectionism in the vast underground economy of illicit transactions; in the chronic insubordination that plagues the armed forces; and even, I would hazard, in the patriotic zeal of the Moral Majority: for if one looks at their rhetoric and actions, one finds a profound loathing for the current condi-tion of the body politic. We see it among professional groups where the obses-sion with money and status seems inspired less by greed than by the inability to find any moral point to serving a society so wholly dominated by the corporate ethos. And it is present in its most exaggerated form among high school achiev-ers and undergraduates who are convinced that if they can transform themselves into technical functions—law, medicine, public administration, and business management—they will be hermetically sealed off from the cynicism and cor-ruption of society.

The origins of rejectionism lie in the 1960s. The turmoil of those years was not solely about the Vietnam War: it was about racism, imperialism, profession-alism, affluence, moral codes, orthodox notions of sexuality and gender, and much more, from junk food to slick culture. It was revolutionary not because it was violent—the violence was exaggerated by the media—but because it was uncivil and yet civil: uncivil in withdrawing from and condemning the bour-geois forms of civility, but civil in inventing new ones, many of them bearing the marks of an obsession with participation and equality as well as an intoxi-cation with the first experience of power, the experience of cooperation, com-mon sacrifice, and common concern. "Sharing" threatened suddenly to lose its sentimental overtones and become a political word.

The truth of rejectionism is that it recognizes that it is naive to expect the ini-tiative for reform of the state to issue from the political process that serves the interests of political capitalism. This structure can only be reduced if citizens withdraw and direct their energies and civic commitment to finding new life forms. Toward these ends, our whole mode of thinking must be turned upside-down. Instead of imitating most other political theories and adopting the state as the primary structure and then adapting the activity of the citizen to the state, democratic thinking should renounce the state paradigm and, along with it, the liberal-legal corruption of the citizen. The old citizenship must be replaced by a fuller and wider notion of being whose politicalness will be expressed not in one or two modes of activity—voting or protesting—but in many.

A political being is not to be defined as the citizen has been, as an abstract, disconnected bearer of rights, privileges, and immunities, but as a person whose existence is located in a particular place and draws its sustenance from cir-cumscribed relationships: family, friends, church, neighborhood, workplace, com-munity, town, city. These relationships are the sources from which political beings draw power—symbolic, material, and psychological—and that enable them to act together. For true political power involves not only acting so as to effect decisive changes; it also means the capacity to receive power, to be acted upon, to change, and be changed. From a democratic perspective, power is not simply force that is generated; it is experience, sensibility, wisdom, even melancholy distilled from the diverse relations and circles we move within. Democratic power, accordingly, bears the marks of its diverse origins—family, school, church, workplace, etc.—and, as a result, everything turns on an ability to establish practices whose form will not distort the manifold origins of power.

The practical task is to nurture existing movements that can provide constructive forms for rejectionism and make it genuinely political. The most important of these are the grassroots movements that have become epidemic throughout the country. Their range and variety are astonishing. They include rent control, utility rates and service, environmental concerns, health care, education, nuclear power, legal aid, workers' ownership of plants, and much more. Their single most important feature is that they have grown up outside the state-corporate structure and have flourished despite repeated efforts to discredit them.

While it is of the utmost importance that democrats support and encourage political activity at the grassroots level, it is equally necessary that the political limitations of such activity be recognized. It is politically incomplete. This is because the localism that is the strength of grassroots organizations is also their limitation. There are major problems in our society that are general in nature and necessitate modes of vision and action that are comprehensive rather than parochial. And there are historical legacies of wrong and unfairness that will never be confronted and may even be exacerbated by exclusive concern with backyard politics.

During the last year hopeful signs of discontent have emerged at this more general level in the antinuclear movement, the opposition to an imperialistic foreign policy, and the defense of human rights. These developments are suggestive because they represent the first steps ever toward systematic popular intervention in the sacrosanct domain of state secrets and national security. This is new terrain for democratic politics and it is genuinely political, for the problems of war, rights, and imperialism concern us all, not only because our survival is at stake but also because our bodies, our labor, and our legitimating name are frequently used for purposes that implicate us in shameful actions.

CHAPTER 21

THE PEOPLE'S TWO BODIES

IN THE SPAN OF A FEW SHORT YEARS, as Americans have watched the visible deterioration of their nation's power at home and abroad, they have experienced something unknown to American history since the early nineteenth century: a sense of collective vulnerability. The several idols of our common cave—unlimited power, growth, and prosperity—have toppled, depriving us of the collective image by which we had come to recognize ourselves, the American colossus astride the American century. A lot of anxious talk has followed: about America's dependence (on foreign oil, capital, etc.); about the conditions that other nations are able to impose on us; about America as victim rather than autonomous power.

That Americans were beginning to perceive their government as powerless was confirmed by the astonishing rapidity with which the "hostage crisis" in Iran was converted from an incident into a general symbol of national impotence. The government's inability to impose its will on a raggle-taggle mob led by a frail fanatic seemed proof that the familiar world had suddenly been inverted: *they* were strong and convinced of their righteousness, *we* were disorganized and morally ambivalent. The nation's sense of weakness was further deepened by the President's response to the Soviet invasion of Afghanistan, by the incongruity between his interpretation of the event and his actions. "The Soviet invasion," he declared, "could pose the most serious threat to the peace since the Second World War." He proposed to meet that danger by a series of gestures: boycotting the Olympic games, imposing an embargo on grain and high technology, and instituting a system of registration for a possible draft.

Perhaps the clearest proof of the widespread perception of powerlessness is in the eagerness with which virtually all segments of the American public have supported the extraordinary increases in defense spending over the past decade. Doubtless these trends have been encouraged and orchestrated by representatives of geographical regions and of specific sectors of the economy, just as they have been enthusiastically hailed by many trade unions. But knowing who is "behind" the escalation of military spending is less important than grasping its meaning. There is broad support for it because of a deep fear about the loss of collective power and a desperate hope that a huge injection of money will arrest the decline in power.

Reliance upon the technology of war to revive American power marks a shift in the theory and practice of power in this country. As everyone knows, today's military weapons are the products of an economy that is remarkable for its integration of scientific knowledge, its technological adaptation of that knowledge, and the translation of technology into mass production. This economy has increasingly become the means of manufacturing state power, rather than goods and services. Its products, whether armaments, high technology, or the food of agribusiness, are essentially counters to be used to gain advantage in the political market of the international economy of power. Thus the domestic economy produces forms of power that, by their nature and design, can only be used by the state—the state whose symbol is the Pentagon, where "public" and "private" representatives mingle identities and rotate jobs. What the domestic economy does not produce is democratic power: the material, cultural, and educational goods that enable ordinary people to gain dignity, understanding, and power. Defense budgets are the quantified form of our domestic subjection and personal powerlessness. Every neutron bomb is the ritual symbol of a thousand or more children destined to remain ignorant, spiritually empty, incompetent, and morally retarded.

The question that this development poses is this: what does it mean for America to ground its collective existence upon the type of power embodied in a highly advanced economy whose destructive effects upon nature, society, and the human body and psyche are documented daily with depressing regularity? The question is about political identity, about who we are as a people.

Political identity is shaped by the ways a society chooses to generate power and to exercise it. Societies must generate power if they are to survive in the world, and they have to be constituted so as to be able to generate it continuously. The particular ways in which a society is constituted to generate power is its political constitution. The historical project of most societies, including our own, is to shape its members so that they do more than obey or submit: they become *disposed*, inclined in such a way that political authorities can count on their active support most of the time. These dispositions have to be cultivated if power is to be generated and continuously available. Power depends importantly on an historical accumulation of dispositions. But dispositions are not something so trite as "learned behavior." They are inscribed demands of the kind that the village laborer had to "learn" in the factories and slums. Power is not, therefore, an exchange or a transaction but an *exaction*. It is had on terms that exact over time and become cumulative. The terms of power take away from the place in which the collectivity is located and from the *time* in which it exists. A place consists of land, resources, and indigenous forms of life; time refers to the tempos and rhythms by which beings live and things exist: societies define time and enforce it (think of the mechanization of animal life). The most fundamental terms of power are those that exact from the members of a collectivity by prescribing and proscribing activity that will enable power to be generated and to be continuously available. The working out of the terms of power *determines* the political identity of the collectivity. Power and identity are never fixed once and for all: they are historical projects being worked out over time and in a claimed space.

The current crisis is widely proclaimed to be a crisis of governmental power, but it may be wider and deeper than that. To ask, what have we become? we must first ask, what kind of people did we conceive ourselves to be?

Our starting point is the eighteenth century, when the sovereign position of monarchs was challenged by revolutionary movements and when, in some countries, the sovereignty of the people was proclaimed and the political theories of the day began to refer to "the body of the people." I want to suggest that in the American political tradition, the people has had two "bodies," with each standing for a different conception of collective identity, of power, and of the terms of power. In one of these bodies the people was conceived to be politically active, while in the other it was essentially, though not entirely, passive. The one collectivity was political and democratic and can be called a body politic; the other was primarily economic and intentionally antidemocratic and it can be called a political economy. Each of these bodies has a long tradition of theory and practice.

The classic statement of the body politic was the Declaration of Independence, its charter, the Articles of Confederation. The conception of political economy is more composite: the Constitution, *The Federalist* papers, and Hamilton's great state papers dealing with finance, manufacturing, and the interpretation of the powers of the national government. The first American body politic was formed by the revolution of 1776, the second by the ratification of the Constitution.

On the first: revolution is the most radical action that a people can undertake collectively. Revolution means rejecting an established mode of authority, withdrawing the power that flows to it, and snapping the continuity between past and future. The gravity of the act requires a people to ask themselves who they are as a collectivity, what justifies the destruction of their prior identity, and who they hope to become by reconstituting themselves.

The greatness of the Declaration of Independence was its sensitivity to these questions and its attempt to capture a new and emergent identity. For about ten years the colonists had been arguing and protesting about their status within the British Empire. The Declaration caught and preserved the moment when Americans renounced their status as colonial dependents who were required to accept and obey a system of political authority over which they exerted little control and in which they did not directly participate. In the words of the Declaration, the revolutionaries had determined "to dissolve the political bands which . . . connected them" with the mother country, and "to assume among the powers of the earth the separate and equal station to which the laws of nature and of nature's God entitle them." The Declaration conceived of a new kind of political being, not the colonial subject of an empire, or even the "citizen," who demanded "the rights of Englishmen" and especially the right not to be taxed by some distant authority. "All men are created equal . . . with certain unalienable rights . . . to secure these rights, governments are instituted among men, deriving their just powers from the consent of the governed." The new conception went beyond even Aristotle's political man, who knew how to rule and be ruled in turn. The Declaration envisaged a being who would not just participate in politics, but would join in actually creating a new political identity, to "institute," "alter," or "abolish" governments, to lay a "foundation" and to organize power. The "self-evident truths" of the Declaration were not, as later generations often assumed, abstract and ideal constructions with no basis in experience, but a recapitulation of nearly one hundred years of practice. Not only had the colonists been practicing something close to self-government for over a century before the revolution, but in the years immediately preceding its outbreak they had telescoped and compressed that experience in novel ways. About two years before the Declaration, the committees of correspondence and the Continental Congress had been invented to coordinate the resistance of the colonies, and in May of 1776, the Congress instructed the colonial assemblies to undertake the one political act that alone compares in significance to the act of revolution: the founding of new governments that would "best conduce to the happiness and safety of their constituents."

The Declaration summarized a political identity in the making, one that stretched back to the Mayflower Compact and to seventeenth-century ideas about political and religious associations as voluntary unions. That identity was perpetuated and strengthened in the eighteenth century by two profound political experiences, those of revolutionary struggle and of the construction of new political orders. Both experiences were experiences of action, of ordinary people acting together to order their common existence. Thus the Declaration had a profoundly political conception of collective identity and a profoundly democratic conception of power; power was grounded in the deliberations of the governed and exercised within a structure that had been democratically organized.

Throughout most of the 1780s, the states operated under the loose system of authority set up by the Articles of Confederation. Save for certain powers relating to war and diplomacy, the Confederation clearly favored a decentralized condition in which the states were the major political entities. It represented a widespread belief that democracy and equality had an appropriate scale. The political discourse of the day was full of references to the affection and loyalty commanded by the states and towns. From reading these documents, it is apparent that the colonists recognized that democracy depended upon making political experience—the true basis of equality—accessible to all.

The conception of the body politic as participatory, democratic, and egalitarian did not mean that economic relations were ignored. The emphasis upon political participation was directly related to the great economic controversies of the 1770s and 1780s concerning debtor laws, paper money, interest rates, and taxes. Those who formed the body politic and opposed the new Constitution tended to be small farmers who suffered from shortages of money and credit, and hence were frequently in debt. They believed that it was natural and desirable for their government to "interfere" in the economy. The economy was not a sacred object, but a set of relationships that might have to be amended when the good of the members required it.

All of the notions of a body politic were challenged throughout the 1780s by a gathering movement among the higher social classes and the more powerful economic interests. It produced the Constitution, with its very different conception of collectivity and power. The framers of the Constitution made no secret of the fact that representative government was designed, as Madison put it, "to preserve the spirit and form of popular government" but to take away its substance, so that an "unjust and interested majority" could not invade the rights and freedom of the propertied classes.[1] The new Constitution aimed to reverse the direction of the country, to set it against the democratic and participatory politics flourishing in the states. This was to be accomplished by two wide-sweeping changes. One was to construct a national government that would be based on the principle of representation instead of on democracy. Except for the House of Representatives, no officer of the new government would be directly elected by the people. "We the people" were acclaimed as "the pure original foundation of all legitimate authority" (Hamilton),[2] but this was a formula to give the Constitution a legitimate basis, not to encourage an active citizenry.

The second change was aimed at breaking the power of the states where the democratic tradition of the body politic had taken hold. The Constitution created a centralized system of government with strong powers to tax, regulate, legislate, and coerce citizens who, hitherto, had been the objects of the state legislatures. Thus the citizen was placed in an entirely new set of relationships—with a government that was almost as remote as the British Parliament. At the same time, the state governments, to which the citizen stood closest, were forced to surrender or share many of the powers they had exercised during the era of the Articles of Confederation—powers over currency, commerce, and taxes.

Hamilton saw that the new Constitution would take hold only if it were able to attract the loyalties of citizens away from their state governments and local institutions and change democratic citizens into beings disposed to render "a due obedience to [the federal government's] authority."[3] The transformation of the citizenry would come about, he reasoned, if the activities of the national government were to penetrate the states and localities so as to become part of "the common occurrences of . . . political life." The role of a strong state would be to promote, regulate, and protect the economic interests crucial to state power-manufacturing, commerce, banking, and agriculture—"those objects which touch the most sensible chords and put into motion the most active springs of the human heart." In appealing to self-interest and economic motives, Hamilton hoped to promote a new set of civic dispositions that would strengthen "the authority of the Union and the affections of the citizens towards it."[4]

The nature of these "dispositions"—Hamilton himself used the word—and their potential for producing power were associated by Hamilton with the division of labor and specialization. "The results of human exertion," he observed,

> may be immensely increased by diversifying its objects. When all the different kinds of industry obtain in a community, each individual can find his proper element, and can call into activity the whole vigor of his nature. And the community is benefitted by the services of its respective members in the manner in which each can serve it with most effect.[5]

These dispositions ran squarely against the ones incorporated into the Declaration's conception of a body politic, for the "community" that he conjured up was not an association of equals or of sharers. By "diversifying" the "objects" set before man, the division of labor encouraged "the diversity of talents and dispositions which discriminate men from each other." While it could be claimed that human potentialities were thus being encouraged, there is no doubt that this was not Hamilton's main aim. "The addition of a new energy to the general stock of effort" had as its end "the wealth of a nation,"[6] that is, the foundation of the material basis of national power. Hamilton's concern with the human dispositions that generate power was part of a larger strategy to make economic activity the basis of political order. "The possession" of the "means of subsistence, habitation, clothing, and defense" is, he wrote,

> necessary to the perfection of the body politic, to the safety as well as to the welfare of the society; the want of either is the want of an important organ of political life and motion.[7]

The strategy was based on two assumptions, that the collectivity was symbolized in the state, not in the citizenry, and that state power was derived from the structure of the economy.[8] A political economy, in which the state would be grounded in economic relationships and act mainly through its administrative branch, was to be promoted by a system of subsidies and incentives. This vision was later incorporated into Hamilton's program for the national government to assume the war debts of the states, to establish a national bank ("a political machine of the greatest importance to the state"),[9] and to encourage "infant" industries. The dynamics of economic growth that would be unleashed by encouraging self-interest was expected to produce "the momentum of civil power necessary to . . . a great empire."[10]

The emphasis upon the capacity of the new national political economy to generate great power was not an incidental consideration, but was central to a bold conception of the Constitution that envisaged a political society that would stretch from the Atlantic coast far into the unexplored westward regions. "Civil power properly organized and exerted is capable of diffusing its force to a very great extent; and can in a manner reproduce itself in every part of a great empire" (Hamilton).[11] The founders clearly understood that a large, expanding state was inconsistent with a participatory body politic, but they knew as well that there had to be concessions to the democratic tradition of "free government," in which, as one of its anti-Federalist defenders put it, "the people is the sovereign and their sense or opinion is the criterion of every public measure."[12] They opted for a representative government because, as a system capable of being extended almost indefinitely, it fitted more snugly with an economy that was conceived in dynamic terms. At the same time, westward expansion was expected to dilute political passions and to frustrate popular political action. Enlarging the scope would increase the number of competing interests and thereby make it difficult for a majority will to form among such a widely scattered people. "Extend the sphere and . . . you make it less probable that a majority of the whole will . . . discover their own strength and act in unison with each other."[13] Thus the aim of the Federalists was not only to found a strong state, but also to depoliticize the people. They posed a choice to Americans between "pure democracy," in which "a small number of citizens . . . assemble and administer the Government in person," and an extended republic, in which there was "the delegation of the Government . . . to a small number of citizens elected by the rest."[14] The choice was between participatory democracy, with its inherent inability to generate sufficient power—a vision of America that Hamilton ridiculed as "an infinity of little, jealous, clashing, tumultuous commonwealths, the wretched nurseries of unceasing discord"[15]—and, on the other hand, a powerful republic, "one great American system, superior to the control of all transatlantic forces or influence, and able to dictate the terms of the connection between the old and the new world."[16]

The two bodies coexisted throughout the nineteenth century. The democratic and participatory body politic found expression at the local levels—in the westward movement that saw Americans founding communities along the way and improvising political forms to meet their needs, and in the great Populist movements of farmers and workers after the Civil War. But it was the political economy that displayed the greater vitality. Its political component, the state, became more centralized and acquired a professional bureaucracy. Under the pressures of the world wars of the twentieth century and the Great Depression, the American state grew in size, power, and functions. Its economic basis radically changed in nature, evolving from a society of small-scale producers and small farmers into an integrated economy dominated by large corporations and monopolies and characterized by the concentration of economic wealth and power in a small number of giant firms. Despite ritual conflicts between "government and business," the union of the polity and the economy became ever tighter, as the antidemocratic, antipolitical implications of the terms of power under this form of collectivity became clearer.

After the victory of World War II, Americans were taught, and they avidly learned, to conceive of themselves in the image of a nation of power, the greatest power in the world, the superpower among superpowers. American power was able to girdle the globe, police the world, claim the moon, and even, if necessary, destroy most life on earth. "Man holds in his mortal hands," John Kennedy declaimed at his inauguration, "the power to abolish all forms of human poverty and all forms of human life."

An incident recorded in Harry Truman's unpublished papers expressed perfectly the nation's self-intoxication with power during the postwar years. During the negotiations for ending the Korean War, Truman grew incensed at what he perceived to be the obstructionist tactics of the Chinese and Russians, and so he vented his rage and frustration by dashing off an imaginary ultimatum to them: "You either accept our fair and just proposal or you will be completely destroyed."[17]

Although Truman never sent the ultimatum, such fantasies of power had begun to obsess Americans far beyond what was needed to sustain and protect collective life. Lyndon Johnson gave them expression for the space age:

> We are, even now, concerned with what some currently regard as the ultimate weapon. . . . There is something more important than any ultimate weapon. That is the ultimate position—the position of total control over earth that lies somewhere out in space.[18]

To support power that was cosmic rather than political, the citizenry would have to acquire civic dispositions corresponding to the new forms of power. What were the new elements being incorporated into the constitution of the collectivity? One was imperialism. The United States accepted almost every opportunity for extending its influence to all parts of the globe, taking responsibility for stabilizing regimes perceived as favorable and destabilizing those deemed hostile, and for developing a world market in which the natural and human resources of the globe were organized mainly for the benefit of America. Accordingly, the American had to adopt the attributes of an imperial citizen. He had not only to support military and economic interventions abroad and to identify his own well-being—his job, his profession, his very identity—with the expansion of American power, but to profess a servile patriotism such that, for example he would submit to having his sons rot in the stinking jungles of remote lands. The imperial citizen could not be a democratic citizen, because imperial power called for dispositions different from those which generate democratic power. Democratic power, as Tom Paine had noted, is possible when people "mutually and naturally support each other."[19] Imperial power is not just more power, but qualitatively different: it is always remote and exercised far from where the citizen lives; he cannot feel immediately involved in it, nor is he required to. The dispositions needed from him were being defined by the code words of the imperial state: "National security" becomes the substitute for the "common good," and "defense spending" the primary means for promoting it. Each of these was a symbol that connected with the terms required for the new magnitudes of power and the dispositions of deference that they would exact. "National security" meant not only unquestioning support for wide discretionary power for the President, but support, too, for invasions of civil liberties and the harassment of dissenters. "Defense spending" meant not only applauding huge defense budgets, but identifying, too, with the corporate and financial institutions that actually produced the weapons and the jobs. The new vision of power was expressed by John Kennedy in his message to Congress of February 1961:

> America has the human and material resources to meet the demands of national security . . . and the obligations of world leadership while at the same time advancing well-being at home. But our nation has been falling further and further short of its economic capabilities.

These enlarged notions of the scope of American power signified the end of the Hamiltonian political economy with its vision of a powerful and autonomous nation-state grounded in a national economy and preoccupied with the development of its own territory. The new age would see the imperial state attempt to derive its power from and to assert its mastery over an international economy. That change would undermine the political settlement established by the original Constitution of the Federalists. The institutions of representative government, including the party system that was developed to lend plausibility to the legitimation process of popular elections, would weaken and decline. The successors to Hamilton would take his case one step further. While careful to continue his tirade against democracy for arousing unrealistic expectations among ordinary people and for encouraging them to question the superior wisdom of elites, the new men would also turn against representative government itself. They had to find a new basis of legitimacy to replace the political compact that had drawn the original colonies and their citizens into "a more perfect union." One was found in a form of agreement, a *social* contract, that would signal the demise of the political citizen and the emergence of the American voter. In return for the surrender of their political power, and along with it the practice of the arts of the citizen, Americans would be rewarded with purchasing power and "consumer sovereignty."

After World War II, Americans traded off or bargained away the vestigial remains of democratic citizenship in exchange for new forms of participation. They wanted to participate in the economy on a guaranteed basis, to share in the rising levels of consumer goods and in the expanding job market. In committing their being, individual and collective, to the economy, Americans did not explicitly reject political values of equality, participation, or popular sovereignty; nor did they specify that greater authority and discretion should be allowed to elected officials and bureaucrats, or that the principle of elitism, thinly disguised as meritocracy, should be the dominant social and political principle.

By a simple kind of action that spoke as eloquently as the provisions of any contract imagined by Locke, Rousseau, or Jefferson, Americans simply abdicated the political realm, allowing their civic involvements to languish to the point that by the 1970s, scarcely one-half of the electorate could stir itself to vote in national elections, while the percentages ran even lower for local elections.

From the 1950s onward political passivity was presented as a civic virtue. The crucial requirement of the society, Americans were told increasingly, was "leadership," and hence they should always seek "strong" Presidents to "provide" leadership. As for the citizen, he should think of himself as playing a "role" in a "system"—a supportive role requiring only that he stir himself on occasion and vote, so that those who ruled could thereby claim "authority" for their actions and exactions.

These civic dispositions, passive and deferential, were a natural complement to the forms of rule that were rapidly taking hold. For this same period also saw the rise of the manager, the counterpart to the apolitical citizen. The new type was remarkable for ruling without the appearance of it. The manager combined professional skill with selflessness, low visibility, and a pronounced aversion to public discourse. His unthreatening, technical mien helped to conceal the authoritarianism inherent in the idea of "strong Presidents." It is an historical fact that the credit for systematically introducing "professional" management into government belongs to the New Deal, the administration that, more than any other in this century, was identified with "social legislation" and with the policies and programs that came to form the provisions of the "social contract." Fittingly, the New Deal poetized the "managers," describing them as men with "a passion for anonymity."[20]

The terms of the new social contract and the depoliticization of the body politic were confirmed at a specific moment when it seemed as though America might take a first step toward reclaiming its political life.

Throughout most of the '60s and the early years of the '70s, a continuous and vocal opposition was mounted against the legitimate rulers of the society and their policies. This resistance originated and remained outside the conventional political institutions. For the most part its forms were local, spontaneous, and improvised. It had started with the civil rights demonstrations of the early '60s, gathered momentum in the campus rebellions of the mid-'60s, and become ominous in the revolts that occurred in the urban ghettos of major cities. It reached a climax in the "Cambodian Spring" of 1970, when the extension of the Vietnam War into Cambodia provoked the greatest expression of antiwar opposition.

There were many ingredients in these events—youthful rebellion, black resentment, provocative cultural forms (such as rock), radically changing sexual mores, etc.—but also the possibility of a repoliticization of America, a revocation of the social contract that was stifling political life. But it never got much beyond the campuses and the ghettos. American working-class families were mostly hostile, as were the overwhelming majority of middle- and lower-middle-class Americans.

The failure of the opposition politics of the 1960s to take hold and to encourage different dispositions toward power and authority was clearly demonstrated by the smashing electoral triumph of Nixon in 1972. He received a larger majority of votes than any previous presidential candidate. It was not only a defeat for the forces of repoliticization loosely gathered around McGovern's candidacy but powerful evidence of how the terms of the social contract had sapped the political will of most Americans. The Watergate revelations, which disclosed a systematic pattern of lying, bribery, corruption, arbitrary exercises of power, and calculated invasion of the rights of private citizens, and the continual intimidation of public officials and private individuals by civilian and military agencies of the federal government, should have shaken the legitimacy of our most basic political institutions. Instead the crisis was contained and then resolved by the resignation of the President.

By focusing upon the "abuses of power" by the President and the misdeeds of his henchmen, those who ran the system managed to avoid the fundamental question of what the political society had become, such that Richard Nixon was being punished for doing what his immediate predecessors had done less crudely; that with a public record of having lied, misrepresented, and offered himself to the major corporate and financial interests of the country, he had been reelected by an unprecedented popular majority of the American voters. The conclusion was not so much that the elites succeeded in containing the legitimation crisis, but that the citizens had dutifully honored their engagement. By the terms of the social contract the average American had agreed not to be actively engaged in the life of the citizen and not to challenge the enlarged authority and discretion of public officials, the increased power of bureaucracy over ordinary life, or the thinly concealed power structure in which public institutions and private corporations were striking daily bargains about the direction of the society and the use of its resources and common wealth.

The depoliticization of America is the necessary precondition for the current demand for "reindustrialization" that has become the slogan of the powerful political and economic forces rallying around the vision of a new, more rationally planned society. Its manifesto was composed by *Business Week*. Calling for a "new social contract" that would replace the politics of conflict by a "collaborative relationship" among labor, management, and academia, this influential voice of corporate America coolly noted that "the drawing of a social contract must take precedence over the aspirations of the poor, the minorities, and the environmentalists." Declaring that "the goal must be nothing less than the reindustrialization of America," it stated clearly the antidemocratic, corporatist vision of the new America:

> The question of whether the U.S. will reindustrialize depends on whether the business, bureaucratic, and political elites can get together to provide the leadership.[21]

The vision, in its silence, adopts the advice recommended ironically by Brecht in *The Solution*:

> Wouldn't it
> be simpler in that case if the government
> Dissolved the people and
> Elected Another?

Today's crisis is centered in the economy, but not in economic problems as such. The crisis is one of collective identity and of power because "the economy" has come to embody the identity of the collectivity and to serve as the ground of its power. According to a 1977 poll, nearly 70 percent of Americans believed that while the economy could stand some improving, it was basically sound. This vote of confidence in "the economy" was in sharp contrast to the findings of a 1979 poll reporting that a majority of Americans (55 percent) believed that the "political system" needed revision or was completely outmoded. The civics lesson contained in the contrast had been delivered in a slightly earlier poll, which had found that 96 percent of those polled believed that Americans must be "ready to sacrifice for the free enterprise system." Clearly some profound displacement of loyalty had occurred in which citizens declared themselves in favor of getting rid of a significant part of their political order and, at the same time, announced that they were prepared to sacrifice for an economic system, even, apparently, for one that existed nowhere except in the prose of the inspired *clercs* of Mobil Oil and Citibank.

Historically the Carter administration has played a pivotal role in expressing the meaning of "the economy," the new and depoliticized form of collectivity. Jimmy Carter correctly perceived that for such a collectivity the search for "energy" would be the moral equivalent of war, that "on the battlefield of energy . . . we can seize control again of our common destiny," and that "every gallon of oil" saved "gives us more freedom . . . that much more control over our own lives so that solutions to our energy crisis can also help us to conquer the crisis of the spirit in our country."[22] The historical mission of Jimmy Carter's pseudo-populism—with its laments about a lost purity and a government grown "distant" from "the people"—was to provide a mass basis for a new state—corporate, bureaucratic, technocratic, and managerial. "We are talking about the United States of America," Jimmy Carter thundered in his speech accepting renomination, "and those who count this country out as an economic superpower are going to find out just how wrong they are."

That speech pays reconsidering, for it was perhaps the most important statement of the nature of the new collectivity. Declaring that his administration had "laid the groundwork for a new economic age," he made it clear that the new ground would represent a reversal of the modestly progressive social policies of the New Deal tradition in the Democratic Party:

> We've slashed government regulation and put free enterprise back into airlines, to trucking and the financial system of our country.

Then he interred the New Deal for good and identified the concerns of the new collectivity:

> This is the greatest change in the relationship between government and business since the New Deal, We've increased our exports dramatically. We've reversed the decline into [sic] basic research and development. And we have created more than eight million new jobs, the biggest increase in the history of our country.

The new collectivity in the new economic age would be devoted to "revitalization"—not of the body politic—but "revitalization of American industry"; the new citizen would be absorbed in the "real work [of] modernizing American industry," not in reclaiming his or her political self or recreating a common life. The President's speech was another expression of the forces that are exploiting the current crisis to accelerate the movement of the society toward a new and undemocratic form. The ideology for this new form starts from the claim that the crisis is located in the economy, whose woes are the result of the fact that American products are no longer competitive in the world market. Our declining competitive position, it is said, is due to lower productivity, inefficiency, lack of "discipline" among the work force, and an "adversary mentality" of trade unionists. But we must not only "reindustrialize" but emulate the proper model—which turns out to be West Germany or Japan. "We have two ways to go," warned an Assistant Secretary of Labor, "the way of the British or the way of the Japanese."[23]

During the last several months something that looks suspiciously like a concerted campaign has been mounted against the "citizens" of the present political economy, contrasting the lazy and contentious American worker with the regimented enthusiasm of Japanese workers, who have appeared at their obliging best on several television shows, hopping up and down to canned music during their "breaks," making constructive suggestions about how to improve further their highly automated production lines, and displaying the serenity of a work force that has been given paternalistic reassurances of cradle-to-grave security. The television cameras did not stray from the factories to explore the political implications of a model citizen who would combine, in equal parts, the values of automation and of feudalism; much less have the media invited their audience to consider the broad implications of "learning" from West Germany and Japan, societies with old, rich authoritarian traditions and fresh totalitarian pasts, while turning away from virtually the only society, Britain, whose political values were once closest to our own.

The current crisis is inherent in the form of state power constituted by, and grounded in, an economy whose "dynamism" and "innovations" exact an awesome price in the destruction of received values, skills, knowledge, and the basic human institutions for transmitting them. Family, school, and city: they have all been damaged and twisted to the point where they produce more despair than happiness. The present constitution of power, and the social contract that legitimates it, has produced the present deepening crisis. The crisis consists of two interrelated parts: the unprecedented magnitudes of power at the disposal of the American state and the peculiarly abstract quality of it. Think of the proposed MX missile system, its tracks winding through the "empty" spaces of western states, its lethal payload disappearing and reappearing, and its power wholly disconnected from any community. It is a symbol of contemporary power. It takes hold by destroying existing human relationships and then expanding its logic in the void it has created.

What is remarkable about these forms of power is that we know perfectly well that they are, at bottom, antihuman. Everyone knows that the two most powerful institutions of our society, the "private" corporation and the "public" bureaucracy, are unaccountable, unresponsive, distended, and inept. It is equally plain that the social evils that they produce are inherent in them, and that no subtlety of cost/benefit analysis can begin to comprehend the genetic and ecological damage done to generations unborn, much less even attempt to come to grips with the terrible demands that are being endlessly pounded into each generation of the permanently poor and the racially excluded. Everyone knows, too, that the dominant position of the corporation and the government bureaucracy means that the most powerful institutions in our society are radically antidemocratic. Both are hierarchical, and hence biased toward authority and elitism. Finally, everyone knows, too, that these institutions have betrayed and continue to betray the American promise: they have shaped a society of ever widening disparities of wealth that translate into increasing inequalities of power, of life chances, and of access to cultural and educational values.

Nothing short of a long revolution, aimed at deconstituting the present structure of power, makes much sense. It is illusory to believe either that the same modes of power that, by their constitution, use up humans, society, and nature at a fearful rate can simply be "turned around" and trained in a more benign direction; or that the same human dispositions toward power—passivity by the many, control by the few—will serve as well for a new social order as for the current one.

The task is an enormous one—difficult, endless, full of unknowns. We need new forms, new scales, new beings. The forms need to be what constitutions truly are: life forms for taking care of a part of the earth and of the beings who are there. That constitution cannot be given; it can only come to be in the concrete actuality of people taking hold of conditions at hand and steadily shaping them to accord with how they think equal beings should live and by what time they should order their lives together.

CHAPTER 22

THE NEW PUBLIC PHILOSOPHY

> Ours are not problems of abstract economic theory. These are problems
> of flesh and blood; problems that cause pain and destroy the moral fiber of
> real people.

THESE WORDS, SPOKEN BY RONALD REAGAN when he accepted his party's nomination for President, mirror the dilemma that faces the powerful groups that, through the medium of the Reagan presidency, now control American politics. They have won power in the name of conservatism but they are intent upon effecting a species of radical change, change that will be harsh, without the promise of progress or of rising expectations. The dilemma is that the program for change rests upon a public philosophy different from, even antithetical to, the one on which he campaigned. The dilemma ran throughout the acceptance speech: he proclaimed the need for "a new beginning" and then proceeded to go backward to the Mayflower Compact for inspiration.

The quotation cited above appears to keep faith with the sentiments that have been Reagan's hallmark—that if elected, he would restore an older, simpler, public philosophy. In that spirit, the speech drew a contrast between two conceptions of politics: one that was sensitive to moral concerns ("flesh and . . . pain . . . moral fiber"), the other a politics guided by "abstract economic theory" and insensitive to human suffering and moral consequences. The distinction was reiterated later in the speech when Reagan promised tax relief and jobs but without resorting to "any new form of monetary tinkering or fiscal sleight-of-hand. We will simply apply the common sense that we all use in our daily lives."

But well before the inauguration of the new President, the Reagan regime had distinguished itself by two qualities: an assertive and dogmatic commitment to "abstract economic theory," and a determination to effect sweeping changes— the word *radical* was welcomed at one point by an administration spokesman— on no other basis except an admittedly untested economic theory. In the weeks that followed the election, the country resembled an economics seminar as politicians, commentators, corporate spokesmen, and academic experts debated the merits of Laffer curves, supply-side economics, monetarism, and reindustrialization. Once the Reaganites were installed in office, they quickly demonstrated that their commitment to theory was not purely theoretical; what seemed "theoretical" was their commitment to conservatism. The new President challenged the society to have the courage to shake off the old ways. "Isn't it time," he asked, "that we tried something new," that we "chart a new course," and that we resist the temptation to cling to "old economic practices"?[1] Within a few short months, the new administration initiated a far-reaching program of spending cuts, tax changes, deregulation, and reduced social services that completely turned on its head the campaign rhetoric quoted earlier. "Problems of flesh and blood" were sacrificed to "abstract economic theory," causing "pain" and destroying "the moral fiber" of real people.

In the context of the problem of establishing the legitimacy of a course of action that is intended to reverse, change, and even destroy a fair number of established rights, institutions, and powers, the important point is not the seeming contradiction between campaign rhetoric and actual practice, but the difficulty of the dominant groups in reconciling two opposing conceptions of legitimacy, one that appeals to traditional moral and religious sentiments, patriotism, and homely wisdom, the other to the authority of economic theory. The former is the basis of the conservatism that Reagan professes. For two decades his rhetoric has attempted to evoke a world of God-fearing friends and neighbors, close-knit families, and self-evident truths about "the work ethic" and the immoral lives of those on welfare. This conservative or, better, traditionalist conception of legitimacy assumed practical importance as an organized political force during the last presidential campaign. Religious fundamentalists, evangelicals, anti-abortionists, anti-ERAers, moral majoritarians, textbook and library censors, and opponents of teenage sex were among Ronald Reagan's earliest and most enthusiastic supporters. Although many of the beliefs and demands of these groups are sharply at odds with democratic values of diversity, freedom, and tolerance, the beliefs themselves, while sometimes twisted almost beyond recognition, are historically grounded in the political culture of the country.

Broadly speaking, until World War I, what there was of an American political culture derived from three main sources: religion (primarily Protestantism), English common-law principles, and seventeenth- and eighteenth-century political theories of natural law, natural right, and social contract. From this stock of notions, Americans fashioned a language of public discourse for discussing and arguing about their common condition and its problems. It gave Americans their basic ideas of "power," "justice," "right and wrong," "equality," "freedom," and "authority." Insofar as Americans were disposed to question the legitimacy either of those who governed or of their policies, they relied upon a language that had an inherent bias toward treating political questions in moral/ religious or legal terms. For example, leaving aside such obvious illustrations as the Mexican War, the slavery controversy, the Spanish-American War, and World Wars I and II, and recalling instead the intense debates over Hamilton's financial plan, the Jacksonian attack upon the National Bank, or the post-Civil War disputes about paper money and silver, one is struck by the moral and religious fervor surrounding the debates over fiscal and monetary policy. In a sense, Americans had no notion of economic policy independent of politics and morality. Bryan's famous "Cross of Gold" speech, with its crucifixion imagery, was the perfect expression of American political culture.

The second form of legitimacy, which is expressed in the Reagan regime's commitment to economic theories, is antitraditional. It symbolizes the forces that have been the carriers of a counterculture that has been in the making since about the seventeenth century. The most important of these are science and technology, the centralized and administratively oriented nation-state, and corporate capitalism. Historically, each of these forms of power has had a devastating impact upon traditional culture. In their beginnings, science, the modern state, and capitalism had a strong religious cast: early scientists avowed that their investigations would demonstrate the true wonders of God's creation; early modern rulers were "God's anointed" and "defenders of the faith"; and, if Weber and his followers are to be believed, early capitalists consecrated their economic activities to the service of God. But in the course of time these religious associations were not only shed, but religious beliefs and institutions were attacked as false and as impediments to progress. Many of those who championed the cause of science, a free capitalist economy, and a rational administrative state tended as well to be strongly critical of customary moral notions and of the political values associated with the natural law-social contact tradition. Customary morality was dismissed as unthinking habit, natural rights as metaphysical speculation or, in Bentham's jeer, "nonsense on stilts." Only later, when science, state, and economy were secured as autonomous spheres, was toleration extended to traditional religious and moral values. It was, however, a limited toleration. Those who developed the orthodox conceptions of science, capitalism, and state insisted that successful activity in each of these spheres depended upon the systematic exclusion of religious and moral values—that the decisions of government officials and private entrepreneurs, like scientific investigation itself, had to aim at "objectivity."

This counterculture may be said to have been groping toward a concept of legitimacy that would be the exact opposite of the one favored by a traditional culture. It needed a concept that would serve to justify and rationalize change. More pointedly, it needed to legitimate the type and tempo of change peculiar to modern science, technology, capitalism, and state: change that is unceasing, rapid, expansive, and deliberately fostered. For this, a different public language had to be found. Its precise form would have to accord with the cultural characteristics of the forces it would be expressing. It would have to be scientific in method and spirit; technological, in the sense of being a science with practical application; completely at home with the spirit and institutions of capitalism; and adaptable to the needs of the modern centralized and bureaucratized state. These were the specifications that economics would have to fulfill if it were to serve as the public philosophy for the society being evolved through the collaborating powers of capitalism, science, and the state.

Following their electoral victory, the leaders of the Reagan administration hoped to pursue a strategy that could exploit both these forms of legitimacy—the traditional one, now narrowed and intensified into the demand that public policies accord with absolute morality and revealed truth, and the scientific one embodied in the administration's "economic philosophy." But early on the administration settled the question of which form had priority and showed that it would not hesitate to sacrifice tradition to change. It drew up a legislative strategy that distinguished "economic" programs (budget, taxation, etc.) from "social and emotional issues" such as abortion, school prayer, and virtually all of the other pet projects of the religious and moral activists. The emotional issues were to be held back until passage of the economic measures was assured. This was merely the first of a series of confrontations in which the administration overrode the wishes of the old believers. The refusal to fight for the LeFever nomination and the insistence upon fighting for the O'Connor appointment in the face of outraged cries of betrayal made clear the administration's preference for technicians—Mrs. O'Connor was touted for her competence, not for her conservatism—over ideologies without redeeming economic significance.

The President's somewhat cavalier treatment of those who had loyally supported him in the belief that his election would mark a return to the old verities and pieties is not to be ascribed to cynicism but to the demands of a program that aims at important substantive changes in the responsibilities of government rather than in its role or even in its powers. Thus while social services are being reduced, the government-controlled defense economy is expanding and, *pari passu*, so are the powers of government. Control over monetary policy, taxation, agriculture, foreign trade, scientific research and development, and education are not being surrendered. The law enforcement, intelligence, and surveillance powers of the government are being increased, not diminished. There is the strong likelihood, therefore, that when the Reagan years are over the country will have a stronger, pared-down state, one that exerts its control over the entire society through a restricted set of instrumentalities, instead of through a vast network of programs that it is beyond the capacity of government to manage efficiently.

The importance of economics in public counsels is not a Reagan innovation. Economists have been a familiar and ever-growing presence in national affairs since the early years of World War II. But it is not their numbers alone that are significant or the use that is made of their knowledge. It is rather that the prominence of economics is both the herald and the agent of a profound transformation in American political culture. "The economy" has emerged in the public consciousness as a sharply outlined, autonomous entity, the theater in which the destiny and meaning of the society will be worked out. Relegated to secondary importance are the main notions through which the society once understood its identity, notions such as "democracy," "republic," "the Constitution," and "the nation" whose meaning was essentially political. As we suggested earlier, American society is fast acquiring a new public philosophy to express its collective nature.

The strongest evidence for the quiet revolution in the public philosophy that has taken place over the past half-century is in the changed terms of public discourse. The state of the nation becomes meaningful only when we are able to talk about it as "rates" of various kinds—rates of "inflation," "interest," "productivity," "money supply," "capital formation," and, last but least, "unemployment." If, as philosophy has taught us, the limits of our language are the limits of our world, and if, as the linguists say, language sets limits to what we can think, then the change in public discourse implies that some of the things the old language was suited to express and emphasize are being lost or downgraded by a new public vocabulary, while some things which may have been devalued by the old vocabulary, or discreetly veiled, are being exalted.

What can hardly be doubted is that economics now dominates public discourse. It is now common practice to rely upon economic categories to supply the terms of discussion in legislatures, bureaucracies, and mass media; to frame the alternatives in virtually every sphere of public activity, from health care, social welfare, and education to weapons systems, environmental protection, and scientific research; and to function as a sort of common currency into which all problems have first to be converted before they are ready for "decision-making." "The methodology of public choice," according to one standard account, "is that of economics."[2] Lester Thurow's way of posing the problem of "environmentalism" is a representative example of the faith that practically any public concern can be reduced to economic categories. "Environmentalism," he asserts, "is not ethical values pitted against economic values. It is thoroughly economic."[3] Economics thus becomes the paradigm of what public reason should be. It prescribes the form that "problems" have to be given before they can be acted upon, the kinds of "choices" that exist, and the meaning of "rationality."

One of the most widely used techniques that have enabled economic thinking to penetrate almost every sphere of public action is "cost-benefit analysis." Its basic principle is that it is rational to prefer one alternative if its benefits are greater than those of the next best alternative. For the technique to work, numerical values have to be assigned to the costs and benefits involved; that is, a price tag has to be put on all the relevant values, otherwise comparison is difficult, and without true comparisons the chooser cannot make "trade-offs," such as accepting lower prices in exchange for dirtier air. The universal application of the technique and the simplicity of its terms—no small recommendation to bureaucrats—were stated by one economist in a letter to the New York Times: "Everything has a cost, and . . . it is not rational to undertake an action unless its benefits are at least as great as its costs."[4]

The political implications of these developments are obscured by the claim of economists that a technique is neutral, and that whatever use is made of the results of a technical analysis is not the responsibility of the analyst. Unfortunately these neat compartments, which attempt to separate technical analysis from political judgment, do not hold. This is because economics considers a judgment "rational" only when it encourages efficient utilization of resources or the maximization of profits—thereby blurring the distinction between analysis and judgment. This is illustrated by the celebrated Roskill Commission Report in which some British economists, applying cost-benefit analysis to a question about the best location for an airport, came to a conclusion that showed not only how analysis and judgment formed a seamless web, but also a way of justifying the imposition of sacrifices on a segment of the community:

> The right answer in the interests of the nation rests in a choice which, however damaging to some, affords on a balanced judgment of advantages and disadvantages the best opportunity of benefiting the nation as a whole.[5]

A revealing glimpse into the role of economics in the struggle to change the public philosophy was provided by the response of the Reagan administration to a recent Supreme Court decision. In 1978, acting under the authority of the Occupational Safety and Health Act, the then Secretary of Labor issued a rule designed to limit workers' exposure to cotton dust. According to the Court, the Secretary had issued "the most protective standard possible." The cotton industry protested the standard, arguing that the Act required that before a standard could be imposed it had first to be justified by a cost-benefit analysis. The Court rejected that reasoning and declared that Congress had chosen "to place preeminent value on assuring employees a safe and healthful working environment."

The Court clearly recognized that the point of the Secretary's ruling was to place the health of the workers outside the profit framework and, in effect, to render the balancing of benefits against costs wholly irrelevant. However, by the time that the Court's ruling came down, the Reagan administration had taken office. Its response was swift and indicative of the decisive role assigned economics in the new public philosophy. Fittingly, the response came from a member of the President's Council of Economic Advisers. He promised that the administration would move to change the law so that henceforth all government regulations would have to meet the standard of a cost-benefit analysis.

As this incident shows, the public role of economics cannot be understood as though economics were simply a scientific body of knowledge that seeks to represent a particular segment of reality in the manner suggested by Nobel laureate Samuelson:

> All sciences have the common task of describing and summarizing reality. Economics is no exception. There are no separate methodological problems that face the social scientist different in kind from those that face any other scientist.[6]

As the language being used to formulate public choices, economics is necessarily engaged both in constituting reality and in legitimating the reality it has helped to bring into being.

The claim that economics is neutral appears plausible primarily because of the illusion that surrounds the existing political system. The usual picture depicts a system that is responsive to a broad array of interests and that sometimes inclines toward one set, other times toward another. Or sometimes the system is run by Democrats, other times by Republicans. Economists are widely perceived as working for the government, that is, developing the technical means to further policies that have emerged from the give-and-take of the political process. In reality, economics works within a system that is dominated by the power of corporations whose wealth and influence economists help to strengthen and promote. When the economist is dealing with the alternative uses of scarce productive resources, he is abetting a system that enables those who possess great power to use the system to reproduce and increase it. The same process, of course, serves also to reproduce and increase the powerlessness of the less powerful.

Until roughly forty years ago, government and business managed without relying much on the services of economists. There are doubtless many reasons for the economists' population explosion. One of them is the transformation of the interrelationships between state power, corporate power, and science. Once relatively informal and occasional, they have developed in the twentieth century into a set of dynamic interactions that are increasingly integrated and rationalized. The total wars of the twentieth century, with their close collaboration between science, industry, and the state, were the fullest expression of this. The role of economies as the public philosophy of this collaboration awaited the development of economics to the point that it could be recognized as authoritative knowledge. The quest for authority was triumphantly vindicated in 1969 when, in the company of mathematics, physicists, chemists, and biologists, an economist was named Nobel laureate, the first in what was to be an annual honor. The ceremony climaxed the efforts of generations of economists to systematize their subject and to develop the formal features of a science, paralleling the course of the national economy and the nation-state, both of which followed a pattern of development toward increasing centralization and rationalization. The interlocking system of state and economy, which had begun in earnest after the Civil War, needed a body of knowledge that would enable the two systems, economy and polity, to be treated as one political economy or as one economic polity; and in the age of extraordinary scientific achievements and universal deference to scientific authority, the body of knowledge that would serve as the basis for a new public philosophy must, of necessity, be seen as scientific.

The question raised by these developments is whether economics can fulfill the requirements of a public philosophy. Most contemporary economic doctrines, whether libertarian, neoclassical, or neo-Keynesian, depend upon certain politically relevant assumptions that have remained virtually intact since the eighteenth-century beginnings of classical economics. These assumptions were antipolitical in their first formulation and they remain so today. It will repay to revisit them in their original.

Adam Smith's *Wealth of Nations* (1776) is generally acknowledged to have provided the first foundation of modern economics. Instead of focusing upon the political nature of society and analyzing it in terms of notions drawn from law, political theory, and political history, Smith looked upon society as a structure of production, as the organization of human activity into a form of power that supplied society "with all of the necessary conveniences of life which it annually consumes."[7] In order to explain how society worked, Smith set aside the notions popularized by political theorists, and instead of picturing society as formed by a free act of consent, as the social contract theorists had, and then working out related notions of obligation, right, equality, and membership, he relied upon nonpolitical concepts such as the division of labor, the market, competition, and exchange. Instead of taking the citizen as the fundamental unit, concentrating on the citizen's relationship to political authority, Smith saw men as either workers, capitalists, or landowners, with their most important relationships arising from the division of labor and the market. Society could thus be described without recourse to a political vocabulary. The depoliticizing effect was reinforced by Smith's conclusion that economic relationships function most effectively and harmoniously when individuals are allowed to pursue their own interests without interference by political authorities.

Smith's reasoning took him from the claim that the economy embodied the essential structure of society to the claim that the self-adjusting mechanism of the free market would efficiently perform the essential coordinating functions that the state had traditionally undertaken but botched. According to early modern political notions, the state was responsible for coordinating and directing human activities toward the common ends of security, justice, peace, prosperity, good morals, and piety. Smith rejected that conception. "The duty of superintending the industry of private people and of directing it towards the employments most suitable to the interest of society" is, he averred, beyond all "human wisdom or knowledge."[8]

Smith's famous alternative to a politically ordered society was a society in which the common good—a traditional political notion for which he would typically substitute an economic concept, such as "the annual revenue of the society"—would materialize without anyone intending it. Or, more accurately, the common good would result from a myriad of individual actions inspired by a goal that was the exact opposite of the common good:

> [The economic actor] neither intends to promote the public interest, nor knows how much he is promoting it. . . . He intends only his own gain. He is in this . . . led by an invisible hand to promote an end which was no part of his intention.[9]

The antipolitical thrust of Smith's outlook extended beyond doubts about the competency of political rulers to skepticism about the likelihood of human beings developing communal ties that placed any significant strain on their limited supply of altruism. Human beings, he thought, need each other because no one can be self-sufficient; but this did not mean that we should expect others to help us: we have to "address ourselves not to their humanity but to their self-love, and never talk to them of our necessities but of their advantages."[10] When economics made the basis of a public philosophy, the image of the economic actor as naturally self-regarding, calculating, and competitive becomes the assumption that public policies and the way citizens are spoken to, dealt with, and treated. The contemporary economist has, if anything, a harsher view of human beings. Thus Thurow dismisses the argument by Schumacher that "small is beautiful" on the grounds that "it does not exist because it does not jibe with human nature. Man is an acquisitive animal whose wants cannot be satiated."[11] The same assumption has been placed at the center of the so-called theory of public choice, one of the academic versions of the new public philosophy: "The basic behavioral postulate of public choice, as for economics, is that man is an egoistic, rational, utility maximizer."[12]

When a notion of human motives and potentialities that was originally conceived to explain private behavior is pressed into public service, its limitations become serious. In the ordinary course of political events—as well as in the extraordinary occasions of war, natural disaster, and even economic crisis—the constant assumption cannot be that most citizens are egoistic and insatiable. The reason for a civic culture is that citizens will have to cooperate, tell the truth, respect each other's rights and sensibilities, observe the law, and pay taxes, if a self-governing and free society is to be possible. Under the conditions of war or emergency, even more is expected of them. Some can expect to die, others who may already suffer from extreme deprivations will be asked to suffer more, to "trade off" Harlem, say, for Vietnam. But because a public philosophy grounded in economics cannot nurture a civic ethic, it is forced to declare it obsolete. In the words of a former chairman of the President's Council of Economic Advisers:

> Market-like arrangements ... reduce the need for compassion, patriotism, brotherly love, and cultural solidarity as motivating forces behind social improvement. ... Harnessing the "base" motive of material self-interest to promote the common good is perhaps *the* most important social invention mankind has achieved.[13]

It was possible to stave off the antipolitical and demoralizing implications of economics as long as the prevailing public philosophy was grounded in strong beliefs about religion, morality, law, and political values, and as long as economic modes of thought remained marginal and Americans retained their historical skepticism about the motives of businessmen. Most of this was clearly understood by some noted economists earlier in this century. "A theory of economic policy, in the sense of a body of precepts for action," one of them wrote, "must take its ultimate criterion from outside economics."[14] This viewpoint assumed, as the great welfare economist A. C. Pigou noted, "a stable general culture" in which "the things outside the economic sphere either remain constant, or, at least, do not vary beyond certain limits."[15]

Since World War II this presupposition about a stable culture has collapsed along with the culture itself, both victims of the incessant and rapid changes in which ever-advancing societies specialize. When the moral and political ground of public philosophy has disintegrated and a new ground is sought in economics, politics reaches the dead end perfectly mirrored in Thurow's widely praised *Zero-Sum Society*.

Thurow is the purest example of the political innocent armed with economic realism. That all public questions can be converted into economic terms has no doubt ("Wilderness areas are to some extent natural resource insurance policies");[16] that there are economic solutions to most of our major domestic problems he is equally convinced. There is really only one problem that prevents America from being the best of all technocratic worlds: every one of the solutions Thurow draws from his bottomless kit requires "that someone must suffer large economic losses."[17] Our society is, through and through, a "zero-sum society," trapped in economic *immobilisme*, because the rational solutions to all our major problems are solutions at some group's expense. In a society where everyone and every group is presumed to be rationally egoistic, deaf to all pleas save self-interest, there are no volunteers ready to offer themselves on the altar of the common good. "Everyone wants inflation in his own prices and wages and deflation in everyone else's prices and wages."[18] Faced with a situation where, as he delicately puts it, society "must make equity decisions" and "decide when losers shall suffer income losses and when losers should be compensated,"[19] Thurow discovers that he is saddled with a theory that cannot provide good reasons why people should act contrary to their interests even though the future of society may depend on it. "Equity decisions," he acknowledges, "cannot be deduced from purely factual or logical statements," which is to say that they cannot be deduced from a science like economics.[20] Adam Smith's good friend David Hume could have saved Thurow considerable trouble: If we think in economic terms, then there is no reason why I should prefer the scratching of my finger to the destruction of the Universe.

Left to his own devices, Thurow wavers between despair and technocracy, only to end in incoherence. Since he has even more trouble than Adam Smith had in conceiving how anyone with an economic stake in a matter could act disinterestedly in it—Smith described disinterestedness as "an affectation not very common among merchants and very few words need be employed to dissuade them of it"[21]—he is forced to embrace the illusion that somehow the society will elevate a Great Technocrat in the Sky and give him their burden: "But somehow there has to be a disinterested judge with the power to decide or tip a political decision in the right way."[22]

"To tip a political decision in the right way": that phrase, with its implication that the "political" element enters at the end—after the technical process of formulating economic alternatives has been completed—shows what the ultimate

function is in the political use of economics. It is to mask power by presenting what are essentially political and moral questions in the form of economic
choices. As the society moves from a condition of surplus to one of scarcity,
economic policies are ways of distributing sacrifices. We choose to fight inflation rather than to increase employment; to introduce a tax policy that favors
the affluent because they already enjoy a sufficient margin so that they can invest
their tax savings; and to increase defense spending and reduce social programs
because the global reach of our corporations needs to be promoted and protected by credible violence. Each of these decisions is a political decision involving increased benefits to some, deprivations to others. But it is prevented from
reaching the impasse depicted by Thurow because the power generated within
the politicized economy and the economized polity is cumulative. Powerful corporations destroy communities and then leave for another region where they
have used their power to extract tax concessions, improvements (roads, sewers,
etc.), and antiunion conditions. Or they bargain to stay and squeeze economic
favors from beleaguered cities, e.g., tax exemptions, relaxation of environmental
protections, and suspended zoning ordinances.

The enormous concentrations of power being generated by the quest for private advantage is essentially antipolitical power, as the measured abandonment
of factories, the extortionist tactics used against cities, and the destruction of
Poletown demonstrate. It is antipolitical because, inherently, it contains no principle for transcending conflict to find common ground. There is no reconcilia-
tion, only winners and losers; there is no basis for common action, only threat,
inducement, or corruption. When the economy becomes the polity, *citizen* and
community become subversive words in the vocabulary of the new political philosophy. The ultimate achievement of this form of politics is that it completely
reverses Lord Acton's dictum. Instead of power corrupting, this politics manages
to corrupt power by divorcing it from its grounding in a political community.
The necessary condition of a political ground to power has been stated and restated for about 2,500 years: power becomes political when it is based; not when
a victor emerges and imposes his will, but when shared and common concerns
are discovered through a process of deliberation among civic equals and effected
through cooperative action. Which is not only why the new public philosophy
cannot rise to a genuinely political plane, but also why it will continue to need
the backing of the moral and religious conservatives. In their fury over welfare,
abortion, sex, women's rights, and school prayers, they furnish a substitute for
politics, replete with solidarity, a sense of community, and a glow of moral superiority. And they leave the entire structure of power, inequality, hopelessness,
and growing repression wholly untouched.

CHAPTER 23

DEMOCRACY, DIFFERENCE, AND RE-COGNITION

I

> To act collectively is according to the spirit of our institutions.
> —Thoreau[1]

From the squabbling sects of colonial America to the regional conflicts, nullification disputes, and secessionist movements of the first half of the nineteenth century; from the abolitionist campaigns, the agitation for women's rights, the controversies over immigration policy of the last half of the nineteenth century to twentieth-century disputes over discrimination, sexual preference, and bilingualism in the public school, a significant amount of American politics has revolved around differences of race, gender, and culture. From Roger Williams's *Bloody Tenent* (1644) to John Calhoun's *Disquisition*, Margaret Fuller's *Woman in the Nineteenth Century*, Booker Washington's *Up from Slavery*, and the *Autobiography of Malcolm X*, discursive representations of difference have appeared but until recently have had little effect on the main conceptual vocabulary or thematic structure of the theoretical literature of American politics. Instead, from Madison's Tenth *Federalist* to the writings of Mary Follett, Charles Beard, Arthur Bentley, David Truman, and Robert Dahl, those modes of difference mostly disappeared or were reduced to the status of interests.[2] The result: on one side, themes of separation, dismemberment, disunion, exploitation, exclusion, and revenge and, on the other, themes extolling American pluralism as the distinctive American political achievement and the main reason for the unrivaled stability of American society and its political system.

If, as Georg Simmel once suggested, "the interest in differentiation in fact is so great that in practice it produces differences where there is no objective basis for them," why then should the acknowledgment of differences be an acute problem for "the world's oldest democracy" and the nation with the oldest written constitution?[3] Conversely, why should some groups in democratic America be determined to make the preservation of their differences a condition of their inclusion—a reserve clause, as it were, in the social contract—while insisting on being recognized as full members? Are these tensions the result of a clash between, on the one hand, the evolving practices of a late modern society in which individualism is being transferred from persons and affixed to group identities (e.g., color, gender, sexual orientation, victims of AIDS) and, on the other, an ideology of national identity that remains hostage to an early modern myth that is tightly communitarian (*e pluribus unum*) rather than hospitably pluralist (*e uno pluribus*)? Is it that a new pluralism is emerging to challenge the old, one not couched in appeals to putatively shared values of patriotism, religion, family, private property, and the Founding Fathers, but that relies on provocation, flaunts fixed differences, and tirelessly exposes past injustices so distant in time as to strain common understandings of justice, responsibility, and remedy?

What appears like a confrontation between sharply opposed conceptions of pluralism is, however, more in the nature of an exaggeration or exacerbation of positions that share certain ideological beliefs. Notions of difference that emphasize ethnic, racial, religious, or gender singularity are radical extensions rather than rejections of pluralism. They share a decentered conception of the political; yet both are compelled to appeal to a center of authority to mediate, even though the idea of central authority cuts against the grain of both. There are, however, divergencies between them that are discussed later by means of a distinction in which "diversity" will stand for conventional pluralism and "difference" for the recent and more exclusivist pluralism.

II

In seeking to extend the established pluralism of interest group diversity, the new pluralism of cultural difference reinforces and promotes a further form of decentering, this one involving an important democratic category: the citizen. In theory, the citizen is metaphorically a political center and this for two principal considerations. First, the citizen should be the main actor in a democratic society, hence the primary importance of political participation to democratic practice and to democratic notions of legitimate power and authority. Second, because of the variety of interests, beliefs, aspirations, and concerns within any political grouping—some of them conflicting—the citizen is confronted with the need to deal with them and, when necessary, to decide between competing claims.

It appears paradoxical, therefore, to claim democracy for a theory that lacks a strong conception of the citizen-as-actor. One way to resolve the paradox would be to say that when the eighteenth-century American Constitution makers founded a national government they did not formulate a conception of the national citizen, much less a democratic conception of the citizen. The citizen-as-actor was a notion primarily expressed in local and sectional accents. At the same time, however, pluralism was present at the Creation in the subtext of *Federalist* No. 10. This suggests a peculiar combination of elements: a national government without a conception of a national citizen; a conception of pluralism from which it is difficult, if not impossible, to develop such a conception. As is well-known, Madison's pluralism was developed as a criticism of participatory democracy. Later theorists of pluralism were more oblique but equally decentered. Arthur Bentley's *Process of Government* (1908), the acknowledged *Ur*-text of the theory of interest- or pressure-group politics, scarcely mentioned democracy and made no attempt to spell out the implications of his analysis for the idea of the citizen. The same is true of his intellectual epigone, David Truman in *The Governmental Process* (1951).[4]

This is not to claim that the pluralism constructed by political scientists is necessarily antidemocratic. Certainly, the writings of Robert Dahl represent a lifetime of devotion to arguing for the democratic character of American pluralism. Yet the criticism that has dogged pluralism from the beginning remains unresolved even though it cuts to the heart of the pluralists' claim to democracy: namely, that pluralist politics favors those groups able to command the larger resources of money, time, organizational skill, and the means of propaganda; that for nearly three centuries the dominant groups have been a relatively narrow representation of the increasing diversity of American society; and that the gap between the privileged and unprivileged is widening. Tocqueville remarked that he could not imagine America becoming an unequalitarian society; today it would be difficult to imagine it becoming equalitarian.

Pluralism and, by extension, the problems presented by differences create serious difficulties for democracy precisely because inclusiveness and equality tend to undercut each other. Inclusiveness necessarily increases social complexity. It welcomes all sorts of differences and allows others to enter through porous borders. But equality relies on some broad measure of similarity if only to support a notion of membership that entails equality of rights, responsibilities, and treatment.

III

By way of preliminary, it is worth noting that although both "difference" and "diversity" refer to dissimilarity and unlikeness, there are some subtle distinctions between them. These may be suggestive in explaining why pluralism is more comfortable with diversity than it is with difference, even though, paradoxically, its politics is more preoccupied with the latter than the former. Because difference is less than an exact synonym for diversity there are tensions, conceptual and practical, between it and "pluralist democracy."[5]

Diversity is blandly democratic; it recognizes mere unlikeness. Its intellectual godfather could be said to be John Locke of the *Letter on Toleration*. Faced with diverse views among religious groups, Locke adopted a tactic that reduced the power of organized religion by treating it as a matter primarily of individual beliefs rather than collective representations. Individuals, he argued, should be allowed to pursue a personal road to salvation, thus implicitly weakening the hold of churches over their members while increasing the power of the State by defusing the actual danger of organized heterodoxy. Lockean toleration did not shield "opinions contrary to human society, or to those moral rules which are necessary to the preservation of civil society." Locke also balked at extending recognition to certain groups whose beliefs allegedly encouraged conduct threatening to the commonwealth. Accordingly, toleration was denied to Catholics and atheists. They were perceived as signifying differences rather than Protestant diversities. Locke's toleration was meant to serve religion, not religions.[6]

Locke's equivocations confirm what early modern religious wars had demonstrated: that difference has acquired an edge to it. One of the *OED*'s definitions defines it as "a diversity of opinion, sentiment, or purpose; hence a dispute, a quarrel." A further implication—and one suggested by Locke's reservations—is that a difference possesses a certain inner coherence that may indicate the presence of a hard core of nonnegotiability, some element that is too intimately connected with identity to allow for easy compromise. Accordingly, as the example of Locke's *Letter* illustrates, a politics that is strongly dependent on the practices of negotiation will be perplexed or alarmed by the presence of stubbornly maintained differences and hesitate to extend recognition or do it grudgingly and only after difference has "proved" itself to be mere diversity. One might say that Lockean toleration characteristically assumes a pluralism of voluntary associations, that is, of identities we are not stuck with. The new pluralism, in contrast, assumes involuntary associations (e.g., of color, gender, sexual preference, etc.) of markings that stick.

IV

> My verse to constancy confined
> one thing expressing, leaves out difference.
> —Shakespeare, *Sonnet* 105.8

It is one of the quirks of language that the word "identity," which figures prominently in many discussions of cultural difference and of recognition, has two contrasting meanings. One appears to favor the recognition of difference, the other to oppose it. "Identity" may mean absolute sameness, as when I say "Jane and Jill have an identity of purpose," or it may mean individuality, as when someone says, "I am determined to defend my own identity." In the first meaning, identity implies a convergence that could be the preliminary to action; the second reflects a population of monads or a condition of extreme pluralism: simple, irreducible entities, each defined by a unique point of view.

The ambivalence of identity reappears among many who consider themselves to be postmodern beings: they assert the value of identity as meaning individuality and—often at the same time—they proclaim the value of identity as a sameness that is simultaneously differentiating and exclusionist, as in those who employ gender, race, ethnicity, or sexual preferences to construct a community of grievance or special qualities. The sameness that is used to establish the community then becomes the "difference" that distinguishes its members from nonmembers. Not infrequently it is accompanied by a demand that "difference" be "recognized." The implication is that somewhere external to the community there exists a "recognizer" whose acceptance is deemed important because behind the recognizer is some collective identity, some association that has resisted extending the sort of recognition that the denied groups want because they feel threatened, diminished, slighted, oppressed, or because of all of the foregoing.

Seemingly, democracy avoids the dilemmas of difference. The theory of democracy, it is often claimed, asserts equality as a constitutive principle and, accordingly, condemns the superiority between giver and receiver as demeaning. In the familiar words of the seventeenth-century English Leveller, "The poorest he has a life to live as much as the greatest he."[7] Democracy appears to stand for inclusiveness that implies that every person qua person is recognized and no one is "the" recognizer. Later experience suggests otherwise. The greater "he"s manage to live better lives and to exercise greater political influence than do the poorer, so much so that it is unclear in what sense the poorest have democratic lives at all. Democracy abolishes "the" recognizer without empowering the unrecognized. Pluralist politics allows for the kind of power that thrives on remaining unrecognized, exercising power and influence incognito, and leaving its signature rather than its name.

Inclusiveness may be a necessary condition of democracy, but it is in the nature of a formal rather than a constitutive principle and hence, at best, a precondition for equality. Certainly, inclusion is no guarantee of re-cognition. The framing of the American Constitution demonstrates how the opportunity for re-cognition was passed over in favor of recognition.[8] Although the language of the preamble seems inclusionary in its reference to "the People" and "a more perfect union," the original provisions of the Constitution contained a number of exclusions, some by silence, as in the case of women, while others were recognized and defined with precision, as in provisions relating to eligibility for office. When it came to the recognition of the existence of slavery, the language of the Constitution turns excruciatingly exact as its authors strained to distinguish between "free persons," "Indians," and "all other persons" while avoiding any explicit mention of slavery. Those in the first category were to qualify as persons for tax purposes; in the second, none would count; in the third, each was to count as three-fifths of a person.

The question of recognition or, more precisely, the situation of recognition, is two-sided. To say that it involves a recognizer and a recognized seems banal at first. However, when those terms are taken as the starting point for a binary conception of the political, as, for example, in Hegel's master/slave paradigm, then the conception is anything but banal. It implies that one party is active, the other passive; that one bestows recognition, the other a supplicant seeking it; that one is the interpreter, the other the interpreted; and that only after humiliating appeals to "shared values" the petitioner learns that social and political recognition has to be won from a granter who has habitually segregated difference from reciprocity. Because the granter denies the theory but not the practice of difference, the petitioner is forced to acknowledge that if he or she wants to settle for recognition rather than demand re-cognition, then some concession must be made in the impregnability of identity.

V

The idiosyncratic sociologist Georg Simmel has written, "It is above all the practical significance of men for one another that is determined by both similarities and differences among them." He went on to say what that "practical significance" is about. Observation of the differences in others leads to a decision whether "we want to use them and adopt the right attitude towards them":

> Our practical interest concentrates on what gives us advantages and disadvantages in our dealings with [others], not on that in which we coincide.[9]

This formulation of difference contains more than a hint of calculation and aggressive intentions. It is reminiscent of the Hobbesian conception of the Others as a collection of usable powers.[10] Differences are recognized for their power potential, for contributing to what I lack. But that is not the preliminary to a theory of mutual needs and dependencies nor to a cognitive shift in my understanding of difference but to a profile of my insecurities/deficiencies. They provoke, accordingly, the question of how I shall act toward the owners of differences so as to cause them to place certain of their attributes at my disposal, thereby diminishing their autonomy while adding to mine. Clearly, I and they are in a realm of otherness where certain paradigms of power become relevant: The Hobbes/Schmitt vision of the political as grounded in enmity; the contractual or bargaining or market relationship; white over black; the bipolarity of gender; and, more sophisticated, the paradigm of toleration.

These paradigms of power can be distinguished by whether they presuppose that differences are really diversities and hence the stuff of negotiation or are irreducible differences requiring concessions, submission, or counterdemands. Bargaining appears to presuppose diversities; master/slave, gender, and race to imply differences; whereas toleration depends on treating differences as private diversities, although when toleration turns politically cynical, what formerly were diversities may be reconceived as, pace Simmel, politically exploitable differences, as when "race is pitted against race."

We might sort these out by referring them to a hypothetical construct that might be called a liberal pluralistic theory of recognition. It is composed, as liberalism itself was historically, of economic as well as political elements. It contrasts with medieval and early modern theories where difference was the starting point for a conception of social order that depended on sharply etched, gradated differences and on human beings of different capacities, skill, genders, origins, beliefs, and statuses.[11] Unlike its predecessors, liberal pluralism grants rights that are supposed to enable differences to be expressed as diversities and defended and hence to be recognized, right down to the smallest and most privileged element, the individual. In principle, liberal theory defines itself by opposition to the master-slave paradigm;[12] it asserts a formal equality of legal and political rights for all citizens that allows others to be used; it promises formal safeguards against "involuntary servitude" but permits forms of exploitation. It recognizes by means of a negative re-cognition that excludes difference by prescribing that persons shall not be discriminated against because of a particular difference, that is, the standard for what counts as nondiscrimination is produced by a process of elimination. In the language of Article XV of the Bill of Rights,

> The right of citizens of the United States to vote shall not be denied or abridged by the United States or by an State on account of race, color, or previous condition of servitude.

Negative re-cognition redeems the promise of the Hobbes-Locke covenant that required each person to suspend all genealogies of difference—class, gender, race, religion, skill—in order for all to register the exact same "bare" consent (Hobbes) and to enter society on the same terms. But once the covenant is sealed, differences are restored, recognized but not re-cognized.[13]

Yet like ancient, medieval, and early modern formulas, liberal pluralism not only recognizes the inequalities of ability, cultural inheritances, life chances, status, and social rewards but is committed to defending them as a matter of right and justice. This requires that differences be treated as diversities and ascribed either to contingency ("X happens to have been born black") or to impersonal "forces" (the market). If toleration of diversities is liberal theory's most generous form of recognition, its sternest is the principle of merit and of unequal rewards. Paradoxically, precisely because liberal writers denied what the ancient or premodern orders assumed to be true regarding some of the most important differences among human beings, liberal societies proved as stubbornly obtuse in disregarding some differences as premodern societies had been in accepting them as ineradicable and permanent.

Liberal writers claimed, and liberal practice endorsed, that certain disabling effects of differences were ameliorable diversities, that a person might be poor, uneducated, of inferior abilities or even moral qualities, but he or she could improve and advance themselves. In T. H. Green's formula, liberal society should remove the "hindrances" to individual "development." The ideal was a society that would no longer take notice of differences; instead, it would be rendered "color blind" and "sex blind" by a structure of recognition constructed from various measures of "development."

Revealingly, the deepest domestic traumas of liberal pluralist society are intimately connected with difference and equality. The Civil War of the nineteenth century and the civil rights movement–Vietnam War race riots of the twentieth both left seemingly permanent scars, testimony to the difficulty of attempting to accommodate difference, equality, and meritocracy—and this despite a concerted effort of the last half of the twentieth century to remedy discriminatory treatment of women, racial minorities, and ethnic groups. The policies and laws that were put in place to equalize opportunities to work, vote, and learn were, in large measure, the result of large protest movements that had attracted the support of many citizens who were not themselves victims of discrimination and often were its beneficiaries. In the 1980s, a reaction set in, and many of the programs were either discontinued, severely limited, or sabotaged bureaucratically. It appeared as though democratic equality could recognize widespread discrimination but was unprepared to re-cognize it as requiring preferential treatment.

VI

> A scholar wrote a book [in which] . . . he tried to prove that the Tower
> of Babel failed to reach its goal, not because of the reasons universally
> advanced, or at least that among those recognized reasons the most
> important of all was not to be found. . . . [He claimed] to have discovered
> that the tower failed and was bound to fail because of the weakness of the
> foundation.
> —Franz Kafka[14]

Simmel also alludes to a possibility for human interaction that is not based on the exploitation of differences. "Similarity," he writes, "provides the indispensable condition for any developing action whatever."[15] Simmel's point might be interpreted as saying not that those who are similar form a distinct class or species but that human beings are capable of recognizing in others certain beliefs, skills, grievances, sympathies, and aspirations that agree with or complement their own so that working or joining together becomes attractive for reasons other than the division of labor. Similarity is a moment when differences have been bracketed and their exploitive impulse suspended, when a commonality is forged. Commonality is, it needs to be emphasized, fugitive and impermanent. It is difference that is stable. How long differences can remain bracketed depends on how skillfully the politics of similarities is conducted and that depends on the most important aspect of similarity. Similarity in this context is not an empirical description but a normative aspiration. It expresses a will to share actively in a common experience rather than in a common life, much less in a monochromatic life of the kind represented in More's *Utopia*, where all citizens wear similar clothes, live in identical houses, and undergo the same education. The experience of commonality has found expression in a rich vocabulary: the "common good," "sharing," "participation," "equality," "universal rights."

However, unless similarity is understood as a necessary but not a sufficient condition of commonality it degenerates, becoming absolutized as totality, collectivism, conformism. Simmel's notion, that common or collective action depends on the recognition of similarities, finds a dissonant echo in one of the earliest texts of the Old Testament to conceive of similarity as the condition of common action and to establish thereby a connection between the possession of a common culture and the generation of power. Significantly, the text used the shorthand Hebraic word for "language" to signify culture in the specific sense of a symbolic system of social communication.[16] According to the Book of Genesis, at one time "All the earth had the same language and the same words" (Genesis 11:1)[17]—thus a condition of absolute similarity. Differences have not yet been bracketed or exploitation suspended; these are, for the moment, simply unregistered in language. Why that is the case becomes apparent when the text reveals how certain connections, between shared culture, political unity, and power, came into being and had to exclude recognition of differences. Another way of putting this: the account in Genesis is remarkable for its abstractness, a quality characteristic of languages of power. Abstraction is the denial of difference, its symbolic annihilation.

According to the biblical story, in that era of one language and one culture, human beings lived in no particular place. It was an era when existence appeared undifferentiated: no "inside" or "outside." Cultural homogeneity and abstractness seem peculiarly related. For no apparent reason, some portion of mankind settled on the plain of Shinar. Then, we are told, they said to one another, "Come let us build a city, and a tower with its top in the sky, to make a name for ourselves, else we shall be scattered all over the world" (Genesis 11:4).[18]

Now we may infer that the prior existence of the men of Shinar was apolitical and that their "same words" did not include a basic political vocabulary. That changed with their decision to found a city. Although we do not know how they acquired a political vocabulary, the important point concerns the kind of political vocabulary they generated. A "name" identifies those gathered under it and announces a oneness that had been achieved/ imposed by separation from a primal, indiscriminate nonbeing. "City" demarcates the boundaries of political inclusiveness. A "tower" is a symbol of the city's power and of its "watchful" determination to protect its collective life and to defend its identity. Finally, the "we" that is being "entowered" and collectivized refers to the "men of Shinar."

The excluded are thus inside the city as well as outside and the watchtower can easily survey the inside of the city as it can the outside. Because similarity facilitates undistorted communication and efficient organization it has expanded the number of "same words" available to its users by adding a vocabulary of power.

In the narrative of the Tower of Babel, the Lord decides to "go down" and inspect what the men of Shinar have accomplished.[19] He discovers an unprecedented achievement, a tower rising into the sky and thus seeming to challenge Him in His domain. He sees the impressive results of cooperative human action made possible by a shared culture and exclaims, "If, as one people with one language for all, this is how they have begun to act, then nothing they may propose to do will be out of their reach" (Genesis 11:6).

According to the text, the Lord then "confounded the speech of the whole earth" and "scattered [mankind] over the face of the whole earth" (Genesis 11:7).[20] The confounding of speech refers to the introduction of several distinct languages/cultures. Cultural diversity forces the reconstruction of recognition by undermining the undistorted communication founded on homogeneity. Power is re-cognized and restored but on a smaller scale. That result is laconically described in the text: the men of Shinar "stopped building the city" (Genesis 11:9).

Thus diversity challenges the type of power made possible by similars. The limitations of the language of homogeneity prove to be the limits of its power. Cultural diversity was created not by a revolt of dissimilars, for common action is difficult for them, but through the intervention by an outside power, a god who perceived that his hegemony was threatened by the mode of power based on homogeneity of culture. God's power, evidently, thrived in a condition where human beings were "scattered," that is, were weakened by cultural divisions.

Now up to this point, a striking feature of the biblical account is that God's power is acquired by defeating rival gods without the assistance of a "people." However, soon afterward, as the Torah relates, the god "chooses" a people and proceeds to shape them into "His people" and His alone. What is described in the various books of the Torah is a new form of power: monotheistic power. It demands not only absolute obedience but absolute uniformity of belief. Thus it imitates the men of Shinar in basing power on one culture, that of the Chosen People, with the "same words," those of the Decalogue or Ten Commandments. Although this power promises its "citizens" that someday it will triumph over all rival powers and rule the world, for the present it must deal with the "scattered" peoples who came into existence as the result of the Lord's destruction of the Tower of Babel. The language of power must now take account of differences. This will mean acknowledging not only the presence of "other" peoples and their cultures but differences within each culture—of class, status, wealth, gender, race—and their translation into differentials of knowledge and other resources of power.

Monotheistic power, with its language of similarity and its few "words" about differences, served as a model for the development of State power, first in the form of absolute monarchy and then in the form of the centralized administrative State.[21] For some purposes, the State recognized cultural diversity but restricted it to "society" where those "scattered" powers could be played off against each another (*divide et impera*) so that their rivalries and conflicts furnished justifications for State intervention and, at the same time, for State repression of attempts by civil society to discover the similarities of a common plight as a basis for common action.

VII

My second text is from *The Histories* of Herodotus. It is only slightly less ancient than the story of Babel, although far more sympathetic to cultural diversity. It contains the first recorded defense of democracy and reveals the latent tension between democracy and diversity.[22] Its title, *The Histories*, is intimative of the author's tacit rejection of "a" privileged narrative and his reliance on diverse cultural sources for his account of the war between Persia and the Greek city-states. Although Herodotus was concerned to preserve for posterity the "astonishing" triumph of the Greeks over the huge Persian empire, he also declares his intention to record the achievements of other peoples as well, including the enemies of Greece. His breadth of sympathies leads him to indicate the numerous cultural debts of the Greeks to the Chaldeans and especially the Egyptians.[23] The Greek *historie*, as several commentators have suggested, implies "researches" or "inquiries" rather than the tightly integrated narrative favored in later ages.[24]

If Herodotus enlarges the language of recognition by undermining the traditional distinction between "Greek" and "barbarian," he understands that he has been able to do it because Athenian democracy alone promoted the intellectual freedom that allowed him to praise the contributions of alien cultures. But by his own account the moving principle of democracy, equality, was opposed to the forms of human difference that other political systems treated as foundational. In the famous passage of Book III, Herodotus presents three Persians, each of whom defends, in turn, one of the three forms of political constitutions: democracy, aristocracy, and monarchy. Democracy is praised by its spokesman as the rule of equality. It deliberately excludes rule by the best man or by the few best or by the wealthiest (III.80). Thus it refuses political recognition to certain obvious human differences and denies that such differences constitute a valid claim to exercise power over the society. In part, it does this because of prior experience at the hands of oppressors who have used their wealth, their military skill, and their leisure to create relations of nonreciprocity, systems by which the labor, property, and bodies of those who are weaker and less skillful in the ways of organized power are made to serve the purposes of those who rule. "The time has passed," according to democracy's spokesman, when one man can be trusted with absolute power. A king "breaks up the structure of ancient tradition and law, forces women to serve his pleasure, and puts men to death without trial."

Now in Herodotus's *Histories*, as in all of ancient and medieval political thinking, the "people" do not speak for themselves. Herodotus has a Persian speak for democracy; among later writers it is always the writers themselves who tell us what democracy "is." It is they who construct "the people" and then describe its attributes. Invariably—Aristotle's *Politics* was an exception—the people is a truly "collective" noun, as though their crafts, trades, genealogies, and other social differentiae did not exist. Although this practice might be chalked up to class bias, it might also reflect a strategy on the part of those represented as "the people."

Democracy's animus against difference expresses a discovery about power. The principle means by which those who are less wealthy, less skillful, less experienced in ruling can redress their grievances is by bracketing actual differences, even though the dullest is aware that in no literal sense are human beings created equal or made equal by law or command. Like the men of Shinar, democracy knows that the weak can gain power only by discovering a commonality that is artificial, *isonomia* rather than *physis*.

Herodotus's defender of democracy declares that it has "the loveliest of all names to describe it, equality." But the speaker takes pains to deny that isonomia stands for leveling, that is, eradicating differences. Nor does he say that the people will rule by forming a single mass assembly. So the question is, what kind of sameness is being assumed?

The answer is, I think, suggested by the speaker's opening remarks when he describes how other regimes end in arbitrary rule. The sameness is a common condition of oppression, of injustice, which is to say that sameness is created not by democracy when it is installed as a construction, as a politeia, but by a predemocratic experience. It is nondemocratic rulers, the men who justify their rule by appealing to differences—heredity, divinity, merit, knowledge—who reduce populations to a common condition. Misery creates the basis for an opposing conception of the political based on community.

VIII

> I'll teach you differences.
> —Shakespeare, *King Lear*, 1.4.100

According to some contemporary authorities, democracy is uniquely inclusive.[25] In practice, however, inclusiveness has not always brought recognition and recognition has not always sought inclusion. The American Indian nations have long been recognized, but recognition has meant genocide, neglect, and exclusion. Women and blacks have been included, but for a long time they were excluded from political life, from most professions and employments, from the full protection of the laws, and from many social relations. Even with the passage of the fourteenth, fifteenth, and nineteenth amendments, when legal recognition brought formal inclusion, the forms of nonrecognition and exclusion persisted along most dimensions of social, political, economic, and cultural life.

In America the language of recognition and inclusion has promised more than formal inclusion while the society has accepted far less. This is because insofar as inclusion is expanded to legitimate new differences common action is rendered more difficult. A pluralist ideology that teaches that every group, of necessity, must organize its difference and exert "pressure" if it is to gain "its share of the American dream" at once minimizes the possibilities of common action and maximizes the opportunities for certain kinds of uncommon action that are elitist in spirit, hierarchical in structure, bureaucratic in their modus operandi, and in control of formidable social resources. It is not so much the need for legitimation that makes democracy useful to social organizations that are corporationist, meritocratic, and inegalitarian; rather, it is the "democratic" state-of-nature politics among sharply defined, though materially disadvantaged, differences and the illusion of internal unity within each difference—which culturalism fosters—that make possible the political domination of pluralist democracy by antidemocracy.

Not surprising, the contemporary quest for recognition tends to seek inclusion not for its own sake but because it has given up on integral notions of membership or what I shall call incorporation.

Incorporation has behind it a rich history of terms, such as body politic, *corpus mysticism*, *koinonia*, sodality, and community. Each of these metaphors suggests that to be incorporated is to be become an integral part of some stable grouping and to accept it as the principal identity of individuals and the primary object of their loyalty.[26]

The most important modern attempt to appropriate the tradition of incorporation and to put its conception of corporate community in the service of equality and democratization was made by Rousseau. In radical anticipation of Simmel's thesis, Rousseau conceived a polity whose character was defined by a citizenry compressed to similarity. He argued that significant differences of wealth and status must be canceled out if the community is to be capable of doing what all political sovereigns have to do: express a clear will. According to his classic statement of incorporation, to be a member I must cede all of my rights to the political community, receiving in return such rights as the community chooses to grant every citizen and acquiring in the process a new identity, that of citizen-member, and incorporation into a body composed of similars, a *moi commun*.[27]

A Rousseauist conception of incorporation not only refuses to recognize my differences, it suppresses them from my new identity, as though the notion of commonality, which citizenship claims to embody, can exist only if differences do not. Thus Rousseau returned democracy to the Tower of Babel, and it is not difficult to see why many modern interpreters have denounced Rousseau as a totalitarian democrat.

Political modernity might be defined as the reaction against Rousseau that rejects incorporation and opts, instead, for inclusion. It wants legal equality but distrusts community. Its conception of equality is formal—the guarantee of equal civil and political rights to all citizens—and deeply compromised. The political exponents of modernity, notably the social contract theorists, insisted on protecting substantive inequalities relating to the self, its property, and its social status. The theorist of this version of modernity was Hobbes who imagined a political society that, in principle, would be open to anyone who accepted its terms: the total surrender of all rights to a sovereign authority and a promise to obey it. The similarity that brings each into society is fear for one's life and possessions and the humbling knowledge that any person is capable of killing any other person.

The power of the Hobbesian myth lies in its depiction of the primal act of recognition as enmity. We are all enemies because our nature and our condition force us into furious competition over scarce goods. Our individual differences of strength, cunning, wealth, knowledge, and so forth are differences of power. Enmity and differences are not eliminated by the covenant that establishes a sovereign but—like receiving back one's loose change after passing through an airport security check—are resumed afterward and played out according to legal rules decreed by that authority. Recognition develops along two lines: each recognizes the other as a rival while recognizing the sovereign as a protector. The overall image that Hobbes projects is of a contained chaos, a competitive society with a necessary, if indeterminate, potential for authoritarianism.

Hobbes's kind of similarity was not meant to produce common action but a serendipitous result. By different routes individuals arrive at the same conclusion: the need for peace. Although the individual is made aware that his decision to enter political society entails an obligation to obey the sovereign, he is not told that he will enter a fiercely competitive society in which war has been sublimated into economic activity and into the struggle for social status and power. The competitive pursuit of individual happiness effectively destroys the premodern idyll of an organic community in which everyone was protected by and obligated to some specific social grouping. Now the individual is unequal and unaffiliated, free to develop differences in wealth, status, learning, and power so long as he does not challenge the sovereign authority. The crucial role of sovereignty is to define public language, that is, to use the law to prescribe the meaning of key public words, such as rights, property, promises, duties, and where necessary, true beliefs. The necessary condition of Hobbes's all-inclusive society is political passivity. In Tocqueville's comment on modern democracy, "The taste for well-being distracts men from becoming involved in government, and the love of well-being puts them in ever closer dependence upon government."[28]

IX

> Each [entrepreneur with a new project] freely admits the general prin-
> ciple that public power ought not to intervene in private affairs, but as an
> exception each wants the state to assist in his particular project.... One
> can say that a democratic society becomes more centralized as it grows
> older.
> —Tocqueville[29]

Perhaps the United States was once a liberal society tempered by nostalgia about "traditional values." Now it is ultramodern and often belligerently illiberal, ultraconservative without being traditionalist, increasingly inegalitarian, vocally more different than similar. It is not surprising that many who have chosen to live within its boundaries accept only a limited sort of inclusion. They want not only public recognition of differences but positive public support that will enable them to nurture an irreducible core of exclusivity.

For example, suppose that I am a poor refugee from Southeast Asia. I want to be included as though I am a citizen when it comes to welfare eligibility because, initially, it is difficult for me to establish my economic independence. At the same time, however, I want to preserve my distinctive cultural heritage, and therefore I want the public school to offer my children instruction in our native language. In short, I want public recognition of a certain cultural exclusiveness validated and maintained, and by that demand I have announced my intention of resisting incorporation and accepting only a minimalist inclusion that may or may not lead to a rich and complex notion of membership.

That example presupposes a different understanding of recognition, one that is more in accord with contemporary experience. Recognition had been the response of a society blessed with limitless space and opportunities. This allowed the immigrant to be absorbed rather than engaged. Today, however, the recognition of differences is an upsetting encounter, akin to what Edmund Wilson called "the shock of recognition." When the system of representations that guides recognition is upset, re-cognition is possible. We might think of re-cognition as a radical revision in the culturally produced representations of a familiar being as when once current images of "Negro," "Indian," "woman," or "sexual deviant" were shattered during the last half of the twentieth century. What was and is unique about that experience is that the iconoclasm was principally the work of those being represented.

There is, however, a political paradox in the re-cognition of difference. I want to be bound only by a weak and attenuated bond of inclusion, yet my demands presuppose a strong State, one capable of protecting me in an increasingly racist and violent society and assisting me amidst increasingly uncertain economic prospects. A society with a multitude of organized, vigorous, and self-conscious differences produces not a strong State but an erratic one that is capable of reckless military adventures abroad and partisan, arbitrary actions at home—oscillating as it were between Watergate and Desert Storm—yet is reduced to impotence when attempting to remedy structural injustices or to engage in long-range planning in matters such as education, environmental protection, racial relations, and economic strategies.

This impasse is one to which the politics of difference and the ideology of multiculturalism have contributed by rendering suspect the language and possibilities of collectivity, common action, and shared purposes. And yet the politics of difference is compelled to appeal, either tacitly or explicitly, to presupposition of commonality: to judges who will equitably enforce the laws; to teachers who will sympathetically portray cultures other than their own; to social workers who will continue to assist the poor, the people of color, the addicted, and the abused; and to politicians who still work to reform deep-seated, structural injustices. Those appeals presuppose some culture of commonality, democratic in its practice, capable of respecting differences and responding to their grievances and needs, and, above all, a notion of membership that is centered without monopolizing loyalties.

Tocqueville remarked that the special advantage of Americans was to have been born equal rather than having to gain it by revolution.[30] Today, one might say that Americans are born unequal and that what once appeared to Tocqueville as a fact of American life is now largely ignored in the rhetoric of public occasions and tactically invoked mainly by those who aim to undo certain protections and guarantees extended to blacks, homosexuals, and women. Because Americans are born unequal they must now learn equality. For some, it will mean rejecting dependence and inferiority; for others, it will mean rejecting superiority.

CHAPTER 24

CONSTITUTIONAL ORDER, REVOLUTIONARY VIOLENCE, AND MODERN POWER

AN ESSAY OF JUXTAPOSITIONS

I

During 1988 and 1989 centenary celebrations were held in the United States, Great Britain, and France that linked together constitutions and revolutions. Americans observed the two hundredth anniversary of the ratification of their constitution; Britons the tercentenary of the Glorious Revolution of 1688 and of the constitutional settlement that followed; and the French the bicentennial of their revolution of 1789. What was being celebrated, even by conservatives, was the liberal idea of revolution and constitution.

We begin with some questions in search of the affiliations between revolution and constitution. Is it an accident of centennial celebrations, themselves an accident of calendars, that found 1988–1989 a moment for celebrating the anniversaries of two conceptual opposites, the ratification of the American Constitution and the outbreak of the French Revolution? Is it less of an accident of calendars than a conditioned reflex that in the United States, the bicentennial of the Constitution should have been observed with hardly any reference connecting the Constitution to the revolution of 1776 that had made it possible? In France there was the reverse situation: because of the numerous breaks in modern French constitutional history, the present constitution lacks direct continuity with the Revolution. Consequently, the French were in the awkward position of having to salute a pure revolution disconnected from any existing constitution and to do it at a political moment when all "advanced" Western societies considered themselves to have progressed to the point where revolution had become an obsolete category. As the resident political theorist of the *New York Times* observed, "the worth of revolution was never more in question."[1]

The uncertainty of the French citizenry—as reported by American newspapers—about how it was supposed to celebrate its revolution, a revolution marked by considerable violence, slaughter, and terror, tends to substantiate the axiom most emblematic of the mood of 1989: that unless revolutions produce "genuine" constitutions there is no reason to celebrate them and perhaps good reasons not to.

The same columnist approvingly noted that French citizens "wisely are emphasizing the Declaration of the Rights of Man . . . and to the murderous passions of the time." In attempting to identify with a constitution—the Declaration was made part of the Constitution of 1791—today's French citizens were reacting much as their American counterparts who, in the 1976 commemoration of their revolution, seemed to want to remember it less as a revolution than as the prelude to the Constitution.

II

These mildly antirevolutionary celebrations were latterly overshadowed but also uplifted by the extraordinary events occurring in the Soviet Union and Eastern Europe. Something like a revolution was taking place and something like constitutions were being installed in Poland, the Soviet Union, Hungary, and, perhaps most astonishing, in East Germany and Czechoslovakia. In particular the developments associated with *glasnost* and *perestroika* in the Soviet Union and the triumph of Solidarity in Poland have included the incorporation of important gestures toward liberal constitutionalism: freer political activity and expression, including elections, protection of individual rights, autonomy for religious and ethnic groups, and considerable rhetoric about expanding participation and decentralization. Official interest has been expressed about introducing the market mechanism and allowing more opportunities for private entrepreneurship. With these liberal tendencies in mind, Western observers have announced that the Soviet bloc (to invoke a term that is rapidly becoming an anachronism) has resolved "to enter history," that is, the particular history which was memorialized by centenary observances.[2]

These dramatic developments have been instantly seized by many American and British intellectuals and interpreted as the demise of totalitarianisms and/or revolutionary Marxism. "The end of modern times," according to one pronouncement. "The Cold War is over," according to another, "and we have won!" "An opportunity to redesign the world," exulted a third. Thus *glasnost*, *perestroika*, and Solidarity are taken as proof negative of the Marxian promise and, at the same time, as proof positive of the universal truth of liberal values. The developments are not only cause for rejoicing but for self-congratulations: we have been right all along and they have been wrong from the beginning.

While everyone, save possibly the disoriented, unrepentant, but budget-conscious Pentagon Cold Warriors, welcomes the events, the events themselves are not without ambiguities. For example, there is the astonishing spectacle of a Great Leap backward from Communism to Liberalism. In all of its theorizing about the "stages" of historical evolution toward communism, the regime-Marxists had never contemplated a situation in which a communist state would reverse itself and establish the political and economic system of its great historical enemy.

Lenin's temporary reintroduction of capitalist elements (NEP) had not been accompanied by the rehabilitation of Kerensky or the restoration of the Duma.

At the same time, the liberalization that appears to be taking place in the USSR has not primarily been a revolution from below. The initiative has come from above and appears to depend heavily on the galvanic energies of Mikhail Gorbachev who, as Andrei Sakharov has reminded us, has managed in the process of liberalization to concentrate more personal power than any Soviet leader since Stalin. (Marx's maxim, that no ruling class voluntarily surrenders power, applies as well to Marxist ruling classes.) Nonetheless, the apparent fact is that a dictatorship is turning itself into a presidential and quasi-parliamentary system and struggling to contain a revolution from below while warding off the new version of counterrevolution, disgruntled diehard Communists!

To see these events as simply an inexplicable reversal by which a tyranny transforms itself into a liberal constitutional regime may not be the best description of what those societies are becoming or of what we, whose image they are allegedly copying, have become.

Perhaps instead, the turnabout is related to "blocked postmodernization," the belated recognition of certain necessary conditions not only for exercising power in the modern world but for generating power in its successor, the postmodern world. One of the striking features of the Great Leap Backward is that many of the discontents being voiced have to do with economic dissatisfactions, not with grinding poverty but with frustrated consumerism, and with administrative incompetence, not just arbitrary rule. As Poland's last communist prime minister put it:

> Not only Poland but most socialist countries are threatened with relegation to the position of countries incapable of keeping up with the revolution of technological development in capitalism.[3]

III

Such considerations seem rather different from those that ignited the liberal revolutions of 1688, 1776, and 1789. They have more to do with the special transformations and discontents associated with "high-tech societies." For in addition to certain historical associations, the common bond among the three celebrants is that they represent and aspire to be postmodern, that is, to be a social organization geared to technological innovation and to becoming an affluent society for the elite and a consumer society for the many. This brings me closer to my main concern which is the kind of power peculiar to, or characteristic of, high-tech or postmodern societies.

Another way to approach these concerns is to recall the ironic fact that while American public officials and the media are currently praising the Russians and

East Europeans for finally embracing liberal values, during the most recent American presidential campaign liberalism was likened to an obscenity. A significant number of American politicians currently believe that the price of political survival is to avoid identification with the infamous "L-word." If the legacies of Reaganism and Thatcherism prove to be enduring, the East may well have chosen a model that the West is relinquishing. As the one liberalizes, the other seeks for stronger social controls.

This suggests that postmodern politics may, in part, be identified as a post-liberal politics and, in part, as a postmodern liberalism. Certain major elements of modern liberalism are still widely endorsed, e.g., individual rights, interest-group politics, and free-wheeling economic entrepreneurship. What is it, however, that is being sloughed off and how recent is this development? These questions are, at bottom, questions about postmodern power and specifically about the conditions for the exercise of power when mind rather than body has evolved into power's constituent element, when Locke's "the labor of my body and the work of my hands" seems more modernity's epigraph while Hegel's *Phänomenologie des Geistes* more the epigraph to postmodernity.

We might approach the question through the opening provided by bicentennialism. After all, revolutions and constitutions are about the same phenomenon, power.

IV

Revolutions and constitutions are events that seem to presuppose and to oppose each other. Each represents an extraordinary concentration of pure political power. Between the two they account for political power in its two primal forms. The one is the power to overthrow a political order, the other the authority to empower a new one. Each causes the other to disappear; each disappears into the other.

According to the liberal reading of the modern experience, however, the contradictions between revolutions and constitutions are a relatively recent development. Once upon a time they were complementary and a "proper" revolution would ultimately be consummated by a constitution embodying the ideals of the revolution. As Locke's *Second Treatise* and Jefferson's Declaration of Independence sought to demonstrate, revolutions signified a breaking point at which constitutional power had been so abused that its operatives could no longer count on their commands being obeyed. Revolutions had, however, a limited utility: they could arouse "the people" to overthrow arbitrary political authority, even destroy oppressive political institutions, but they had an inherent limitation. While revolutions were good at mobilizing mass power they could not stabilize it for long. Hence revolutions had to disintegrate or be transfigured into a new constitution, a new stabilization of power.*

The liberal experience was properly solemnized when Prime Minister Thatcher attended the extravaganza staged by President Mitterand in celebration of 1789. When (reportedly) she sniffed that the British had recently celebrated the tricentennial of their great revolution, but had done it with far less ostentation, she was not only contrasting French glitziness with British reserve but also putting down their revolutions with the reminder that the Revolution of 1688 was called "glorious" for the very good reason that, because it was bloodless, it produced a lasting settlement to the series of crises provoked during the seventeenth century by the high-handedness of kings, prelates, and aristocrats.

Between the so-called Settlement of 1688–89 and the revolutions of 1848, something intervened to upset the liberal faith that constitutions were the means of settling power or that modern power was sufficiently tractable as to be settled by a constitution capping off a revolution. Tocqueville's reaction to 1848 was the discovery that the revolution of 1789 had not ended:

> 1830 seemed to have closed the first period of our revolutions, for there has only been one which has remained always the same through varying vicissitudes and different passions. Our fathers witnessed its beginning and we, in all likelihood, will not see its end.[4]

V

Perhaps Tocqueville was only partly correct. While the Revolution was still continuing, another revolution was pressing its claims, "the revolution of modern power." Modern power might initially be described as a type of power that can be produced and handled, reproduced and transported. Modern power's greatest achievement is the production and reproduction of change. The achievement carries within it, so to speak, the eventual transfiguration of modern into postmodern power.

One of the most vivid descriptions of it was by Marx and Engels in the *Communist Manifesto*: "The bourgeoisie cannot exist without constantly revolutionizing the instruments of production, and thereby the relations of production, and with them the whole relations of society . . . Constant revolutionizing of society . . . Constant revolutionizing of production, un-interrupted disturbance of all social conditions, everlasting uncertainty and agitation distinguish the bourgeois epoch from all earlier ones . . . The bourgeoisie during its rule of scarce one hundred years has created more massive and colossal productive forces than have all preceding generations together. Subjection of nature's forces to man, machinery, application of chemistry to industry and agriculture, steam navigation, railways, electric telegraphs, clearing of whole continents for cultivation, canalization of rivers, whole populations conjured out of the ground."[5]

Thus modernity marked not simply another stage in the history of power, but an unprecedented one.[6]

The genealogy of modern power is intertwined with the version of science developed in the West beginning in the seventeenth century. Its main elements were:

1. Scientific knowledge was worth cultivating because of its practical utility. Technology was not a byproduct but the foreplanned end product of science.
2. The state had to play the leading role in materially supporting scientific research, technological invention, economic innovation, and technical education and training.
3. The kind of power identified with science and technology was different from traditional, political, military or economic power. It was, in principle, capable of continuous reproduction and hence had no obvious limits. It was noncoercive, directed at nature, and benign because it would improve the material lot of all of humanity.

The consequences that followed the cultivation of modern power have been, of course, profound. One result was to fashion an image of society whose condition would be one of permanent revolution. Another was to introduce a deep and continuing tension between the modern state and the modern conception of constitutionalism, between, on the one hand, the centralized authority which was to supervise the continuous increase of power that modern knowledge and techniques would make possible and, on the other, the constraints upon power, represented by the law, bill of rights, independent judiciary, and elected legislatures, all of whose authority required a relatively fixed element that was captured in the familiar constitutional rhetoric about "foundations" and "fundamental law." Finally, modern power is distinctively the creature of the closest possible union between theory and practice: between the theoretical knowledge of science and mathematics and the praxis of modern technology. Because of its inaccessibility to the common understanding, that union permanently constitutionalizes, that is, gives structural enforcement to, the priority of elites over democracy.

VI

The major theoretical apologists of modern power were: Bacon, Hobbes, Descartes, and Leibniz. Each of them understood that a revolution was in the making, a revolution different from the cycle of constitutional change depicted in classical political theories. It was, of course, a revolution in beliefs about man's relationship to the universe, about the kind of god who could coexist with the new universe and its discourse. It was, above all else, a revolution demanded by the new vision of power. While the revolution in scientific knowledge was at the center of that vision, the instrument of the revolution was to be the State.

The peculiarity shared by the three great liberal revolutions of 1688, 1776, and 1789 is that none actually destroyed the state structures at which they were ostensibly aimed. The Glorious Revolution altered the succession to the throne and established Parliament's right to determine it, but it did not revamp the political system. The American revolution left the British state intact and the eventual fate of the revolution was to pave the way to the erection of a state where there had been none before. In France, as readers of Tocqueville's *Ancien Regime* will recall, the irony of the Revolution was to preserve the centralized state created by the French monarchy and to strengthen it by supplying a new legitimating myth.

One reason for the survival of the state through all of these revolutionary vicissitudes was that the legitimating myth for the new postrevolutionary states had been accompanied by a theory which gave to the postrevolutionary constitutions a veneer of democracy while furnishing, at the same time, some basic conditions for the exploitation of modern power. In the equation of modern power, democracy signified the overcoming of the exclusivist character of classical conceptions of the polity. Each of the favored ancient models, monarchy, aristocracy, and oligarchy was based on restricting the civic community to a relatively small number of citizens. Democracy was the only type of polity that was, comparatively speaking, all-inclusive. It was also, next to tyranny, the least liked by classical theorists.

Social contract theory broke down that exclusivity while, at the same time, none of the social contract theorists, with the exception of Rousseau and Paine, used the contract to promote a participatory conception of membership.

Contract theory installs democracy as the "primitive" principle that supports all political systems, but the democracy envisaged was a modification of its classical associations with freedom. Contract theorists associated democracy with a primal act of consent to power.

The crucial point about that metaphorical depiction of political origins is that, in principle, no one is involuntarily excluded from joining the basic agreement.** The agreement creates an interdependency of two terms, authority and membership, political power and rights. In the ideology of contractualism rights are declared to be claims guaranteed to the individual signatory against other signatories and against the government. What is little noticed is that the contract also made the powers of the individual available to the state.

Thus, to say that all are "in" is to imply that all are under the authority and power of the constituted rulers. In Locke's words,

> Every single person became subject, equally with the meanest Men, to those Laws, which he himself, as part of the Legislative had established: nor could any

one, by his own Authority, avoid the force of Law . . . nor by any pretense of Superiority, plead exemption.[7]

Stated differently, there is a certain aspiration toward totality represented by a constitutional system, even or, perhaps, especially when it professes to rest on some form of democratic principles. As Locke put it, "the Majority having . . . the whole power of the Community, naturally in them, may imply all that power."[8]

"Democracy," as signifying the consent of equal individuals in a state of nature, thus becomes a formula that works a certain alchemy. From the minuscule sign of a promise on the part of discrete individuals there emerges a system which claims a monopoly of political power as well as a monopoly of political rights and obligations. In Locke's words, "all the Obedience, which by the most solemn Ties any one can be obliged to pay, ultimately terminates in the Supreme Power (of the Legislative)."[9] The "legislative" power, which had been the symbol of freedom throughout much of the seventeenth-century parliamentary struggles against the monarchy, would also be, as Locke's metaphorical language suggests, the means of tying the individual to the state.

Later commentators, in their zeal to confirm how constitutions establish individual rights, guarantee security and protection, and provide limits on the exercise of state power, have tended to overlook the extent to which modern constitutions and constitutional thinking have been concerned with establishing conditions that will facilitate the exploitation and maximization of what I have called "modern power"; first, through the mobilization and direction of human energies and skills for productive work and, second, through state subsidies for scientific research and technological development.

On the matter of mobilization Hobbes provides a glimpse of how the logic of total organization of power was beginning to extend its reach. After arguing that those who were physically unable to work, the "impotent," should be cared for by "the Lawes of the Commonwealth," rather than left to the vagaries of private charities, Hobbes then deals with "such as have strong bodies." With them "the case is otherwise: they are to be forced to work." To prevent any excuses, there should be public encouragement of "Navigation, Agriculture, Fishing, and all manner of Manufacture that requires labour." If the healthy poor continue nonetheless to increase, they would be "transplanted into Countries not sufficiently inhabited." The natives are not, however, to be "exterminated" but carefully "constrained . . . to inhabit closer together . . . [and] to court each little Plot with art and labour," but "when all the world is overcharged with Inhabitants, then the last remedy of all is Warre; which provideth for every man, by Victory or Death."[10]

Less dramatically, Locke was also concerned to integrate political and economic arrangements. His thinking on these matters was evident in the note on trade cited earlier. In those same notes Locke lists two headings in schematic fashion, "Promoters of Traders" and "Hindrance of Trade." Under the former he entered items such as "freedoms of traders," easy naturalization, "freedom of religion," "Register of certainty of property," "publique workhouses," day labor, coins difficult to counterfeit, low customs, and "new manufactures at home." Under "Hindrances": "intricacy of law," "*Arests*," "Arbitrary power," and "Vices tending to prodigality."[11]

VII

Both Hobbes and Locke were enthusiasts for the promotion of the practical application of scientific knowledge and both recognized some of its implications for state power, "the increase of lands and the right imploying of them is the great art of government."[12] More importantly, they both saw the need for certain conditions of security to be met that would encourage the population to concentrate on improving their lot with some reasonable assurances of possessing what they had labored to produce:

> And that Prince who shall be so wise and godlike as by established laws of liberty to secure protection and incouragement to the honest industry of Mankind against the oppression of power and narrowness of Party will quickly be too hard for his neighbours.[13]

As is well-known, Locke closely tied the right to property to God's injunction to improve the earth and emphasized repeatedly the importance of cultivating unused land. In his account, the earth had been deeded to the "Industrious and Rational" and the Lockean constitution lays down the assurances that need to be tendered to them if they are to apply their labor in accordance with God's command. Indeed, one of the striking features of Locke's defense of property rights was the close ties he established between secure property and high productivity. This emphasis is, I believe, more significant and striking than any alleged concern on Locke's part to lower the inhibitions on acquisitiveness through accumulation. Once the emphasis on productivity is appreciated, then the more comprehensive conception of property that Locke introduces—life and liberty as well as estate—serves, not as many commentators have argued, as some kind of humanistic mollification of the harsh edges of what would otherwise be a crudely materialistic formula, but rather as allowing for the full mobilization of the self—its life, liberty, and labor—for productivity. What Hobbes had conscripted through directed labor, Locke accomplished through property rights.

VIII

The route taken by these attempts to organize and maximize labor emphasized the values of privatization while simultaneously eroding public ones. Public values were not discarded by the theorists of modern power. Rather they were shifted from the citizen to the state. *Salus populi suprema lex est*, the Roman maxim which had become a shibboleth in the antimonarchical ideology of the civil wars and used to justify resistance to rulers, was preserved by Locke but also constitutionalized into a justification for the expansion of executive power.[14] Those who governed were exhorted and pressed to promote the common good as the *suprema lex*, and the legitimacy of their power was declared to depend upon it.

In contrast to this reinvigoration of the state, the modern citizen was encouraged to see himself as politically protected rather than politically engaged, "the Governours, whom the Society hath set over it self," Locke wrote, have a "Trust" which is to use the power that each individual surrenders for "the preservation of their Property"—"property" meaning here "lives, Liberties and Possessions."[15] The crucial point about property that Locke kept coming back to was that it is one's "own." "Every Man," Locke declares "is born with a double Right": a right of disposing of his own person as he sees fit and a right to inherit his father's goods.[16] The strongest expression of privatization and symbolically its most telling moment is when private property is established by the act of labor. For that act destroys the "one Community of Nature" where the earth belonged to each in common.[17]

The right of property which each has "in his own Person," when it is exercised as labor, "excludes the common right of other Men" from the objects with which that labor has become intermixed.[18]

Locke's formulation reveals the dual nature of property as power. As the means of producing objects of consumption and exchange, private property serves a broad public end of meeting the needs of individuals while increasing the power of society against foreign nations. At the same time its private character becomes an incitement to the individual to define his political concerns as centered around what is his "own." He will have an "interest" in its protection and encouragement and hence once these basic conditions are met and the terms of the original contract secured, henceforth he can be stirred to becoming "political" primarily if is a proposal to "regulate" or to tax his property. Property becomes the means for the production not only of economic goods and national power but of the privatization of politics.

Why should modern power require privatization as a condition of its development? What are the modes of politics that accompany it and how are they related constitutionally to the revolutionary origins of modern constitutionalism?

IX

In the late modern understanding revolutions are not visualized as a chain of events that culminates in a "settlement." In a similar vein, the political processes of modern constitutions are not primarily viewed as the means for promoting broad social values such as freedom, justice, property rights, and security. As the modern begins to elide into the postmodern, the emphasis is shifted and the principal task is to render change orderly. Revolutions are categorized as protests about blocked change, the absence or the slow rate of it. Revolutionaries began to be typecast as opportunists who succeeded in arousing the masses only because the existing system is perceived as unresponsive, or because it is in fact reluctant to introduce needed changes. The problem becomes one of technique in the management of change.

Once more the moral is supplied by our *New York Times* columnist:

> Radicals can come as reactionaries or revolutionaries, but they do come, and find their audiences. So the task of rationalists and responsible people is to guide change step by step, to prevent the accumulation of frustration and despair, which lead to revolutionary disaster.[19]

The framers of the American constitution, who were embarking upon the greatest political change in American history up to that point, made no secret of their intention to erect barriers that would block majorities form tampering with property rights, contracts, and currency. They associated democracy with excessive change: democracies were "turbulent" and "fickle." But nowadays democracy has apparently acquired sufficient manners to win the praise of the *New York Times* theorist for a "modest and generous nature" that allows it "to correct mistakes without a new revolution." How is it that democracy has become synonymous with those "rationalists and responsible people" who are exhorted to "guide change step by step?"

Change appears as an objective sociological category but it is more than that. Modern power has brought a politics of change and a rhetorical strategy that obscures what was once thought to be the driving force behind revolutions, namely, protest against oppression and injustice. The strategy requires that revolution be assimilated as a species of change, and then treated as its deviant version, fickle and quixotic, much as democracy itself has been treated by political theorists from Plato to *The Federalist Papers*. As a result, the political character of revolutionary action is tacitly suppressed.

Change implies by its very nature the presence of power, of some force that is expelling or substantively modifying that which had been defining of some demarcated set of relationships.

The paradoxical task that so-called industrial democracies have undertaken is to stabilize change. That quest subtly alters the way such societies want to perceive change. Change is transformed from being a standard historical experience, and hence widely accessible, to being a technical category. Its technical character is derived from modern power and its technologies. These institutionalize change in the form of new products, processes, and instruments whose way is smoothed by the image-industry. But since they depend upon technical knowledge, the changes which they produce are themselves technical matters. They are not subjects of civic participation and its deliberative modes but objects of consumption.

The effort to stabilize change and to obviate its adverse effects as much as possible is represented as the practice of "normal politics." Its antithesis is represented as a form of destabilization that is typically regarded as emanating from some populist surge.

The shift is registered in the changing rationale for elections. In the older myth of legitimation the emphasis was distributed so as to include the "expression of the will of the people" or the "choice" among candidates or enforcing "accountability." Now, however, elections are principally a means for a gross simplification in which "campaign issues" are divorced from policies and candidates from their images while the idea of an "opposition party," that which steadily and consistently opposes, exists only in the idealized "two-party systems" with which political scientists once consoled themselves. The so-called disappearance of substance from elections, while important, tends to conceal the main point: elections are merely the first step in the selection, exclusion, or nonrecognition of the vast number of social differences so as to render difference manageable and to identify the ones that count politically.

Manageability, rather than difference, is the important consideration because it makes compromise possible. Compromise signifies a distinctive way of handling power, namely, through bargaining and negotiation that permit changes in the pace and course of change. These so-called modes of conflict resolution are simply the legislative *bureaucratic* counterparts to technical knowledge. Bargaining occurs, however, only when some party has acquired sufficient power to extract a change in the terms of change. Constitutional provisions serve as counters that can be used to check or favor particular forms of power and the changes they portend. The struggle that centers around the establishment of a constitution and, later, around the interpretation of its provisions, is for control over the authority to check certain forms of change/power.

X

Constitutions stabilize power by legitimating it, most typically through elections and representation. What is legitimated is the articulation of the powers prescribed by a constitution, e.g., the distinction between legislative, judicial, and executive powers. The separation of powers, which modern liberal constitutionalism hailed as the main safeguard for preventing a dangerous concentration of power in one branch of government, has evolved into a stage where the contrary tugs between the modern and the postmodern are most evident.

The form of that struggle is between, on the one side, lawmaking and representation, as symbolized by the legislature, and on the other side, interpretation/rationalization, as symbolized by the executive and the judiciary. The stages can be gauged by recalling that the Glorious Revolution was an important landmark in modern constitutionalism for it proclaimed the principle of legislative supremacy. According to John Locke's manifesto,

> [the] legislative is not only the supream power of the Commonwealth, but sacred and unalterable in the hands where the Community have once placed it. [It] is the Soul that gives Form, Life, and Unity to the Commonwealth: From hence the several Members have their mutual Influence, Sympathy, and Connexion. And therefore when the Legislative is broken or dissolved, Dissolution and Death follows.[20]

Although the idea of representation owed much to medieval constitutionalism, the proliferation of numerous forms of difference—religious, aesthetic, cultural, ethnic, racial, and ideological—that are the distinctive mark of modernizing societies lent that idea a special salience. According to the theory of modern constitutionalism, the special function of legislatures was to represent the many varieties of difference: regional and municipal, economic, religious, etc. Since legislatures were, at the same time, the supreme lawmaking body the practical problem was discerned to be, how to formulate uniform rules for a highly differentiated society? Threatened with being overwhelmed by the very subjectivity modernity had encouraged modern constitutionalism responded by reducing difference to the common denominator of interest.

That discernment was, however, being shaped by the impulse toward rationalization that had already been evident in Hobbes's case for absolute authority. A government in which authority was parceled out among several interpreting authorities, he argued, had sown the seeds of future conflict, especially when the new age was one in which each individual thought that he had a right to his own political and religious opinions. There had, therefore, to be a single, final interpreting authority, "publique Reason," as he called it. Implicitly Hobbes associated rationality with efficiency/effectiveness and, conversely, believed that these values were hampered by diversity and anomaly. The discordances introduced by difference (the representative legislature) and encouraged by the modern doctrine of toleration could be handled by interpretation rather than suppression.

The institutions that best embodied and led the drive for rationalization were the "interpretive agencies" of courts and administrative bodies, especially ones with quasi-judicial and quasi-lawmaking functions. These agencies of rationalization have traditionally distanced themselves from the processes of representation on the grounds that they were "outside" politics. In this respect they were striving to imitate the nature of the very powers for which their interpretations were smoothing the way. Modern power, in its scientific and capitalist form, has represented itself as objective knowledge and, therefore, dissociated from politics, even though both modern science and modern industry have been represented explicitly as "revolutions" and implicitly as revolutions without politics. Like administrative and judicial interpreters, modern science and modern economics (which Marx defined as the "mouthpiece of capitalism") have denied being subjective interpreters.

XI

The drift of modern constitutionalism away from legislative supremacy became a marked trend during the twentieth century. It meant the attenuation of popular participation which modern revolutions had encouraged and had aimed to perpetuate through the legislative. That dampening effect had appeared most strikingly in the framing of the American Constitution. The American *Federalist*, writing in the aftermath of the American Revolution, had noted that the citizenry felt more attached to legislatures than to the other branches.[21] It was not by coincidence that the Framers of the American Constitution were resolved to check the ascendancy which the legislatures of the several colonies had attained during the Revolution.

The power of the state legislatures would be limited by preemptive provisions of the national constitution while the national legislature would be divided, with the senate not subject to popular elections and designed to check the popularly elected house of representatives. Through the innovations of a president and a supreme court, neither of which was directly chosen by the sovereign people, the Framers deliberately struck at the principal medium for perpetuating revolutionary popular participation, namely, majority rule.

The rhetorical strategy adopted to reverse the participatory tendencies encouraged by the Revolution was ingenious to sublimate democracy into representative government. The classic example of this stratagem was the argument of James Madison in *The Federalist*, No. 10. For the purpose of legitimating the new constitution by giving it a revolutionary genealogy, Madison associated the revolution of 1776 with the "principles" of republicanism. Republicanism, he argued, was superior to democracy. It checked the excesses of democracy and overcame the inconveniences of attempting to assemble a citizenry scattered over great distances. Yet it did so without renouncing democracy's main principle, the sovereignty of the people. Popular sovereignty was preserved by the great achievement of the modern "science of politics," representative government. Madison had created a conception of representation that honors the principle of popular rule while attenuating popular participation.[22]

XII

The strategy of redescribing revolutionary action as predestined to pass into representative government eliminated a crucial feature of most modern revolutions since the seventeenth century, namely that they have importantly involved the "people" as actors. Modern revolutions, by their nature, involved the vast masses of human beings in action, not just fictionally as in the myth of popular sovereignty. More precisely, modern revolutions created the idea of collective action thereby contesting the monopoly on action previously enjoyed by kings, military leaders, aristocrats, and prelates. While constitutions constitute governments, revolutions had constituted a different entity, a new political subject, "the people." A constitution institutes a shift toward popular passivity and away from collective action, toward identifying the constitution with governmental power while distancing the constitution from the people. In this specific sense, modern constitutions are counterrevolutionary.

When in 1791 the French revolutionaries turned to establishing a constitution they introduced a law that erected a famous/infamous distinction between "active" and "passive" citizens. Only the actives could vote and serve in the National Guard. The distinction was based upon differences in wealth; it was also applied to the qualifications of deputies eligible for election to the national assembly.[23]

Modern constitutions aimed at eliminating or radically reducing the significance of that demotic intrusion by redescribing the people in fictional terms, such as "the sovereign people." The category of citizen was then constructed from the materials of privatism and occasionalism, the citizen as bearer of rights and as voter. The collective category of revolutionary actor lingers on as a ghostly, residual existence, as "We, the People," "the badge of lost innocence," as Tom Paine would say, or, as we might want to say, the sign of a suppressed narrative about lost politicalness.

The American Constitution marked an important modification of liberal constitutionalism. Although that document can be read as continuing the early liberal commitment to devising constitutions that would prevent tyranny, the identity of the tyrant had significantly changed. What was now feared was the majority of those very same "people" who are installed as the ultimate sovereign. It was not without a certain maliciousness that Madison, in defending the constraints on the majority in the proposed constitution, quoted the arch-democrat, Jefferson, to the effect that a legislature of "173 despots would surely be as oppressive as one . . . An elective despotism was not the government we fought for."[24]

The dethronement of legislative supremacy, the basic principle of Lockean constitutionalism, concerns the new location of crisis in the liberal conception of the relationship between revolution and constitution. Crisis no longer precedes revolution but is incorporated within it. The problem was how to prevent, not popular sovereignty which, like the British monarchy, was supposed to reign passively rather than rule actively, but how to depoliticize a populace which had been politically aroused. This latter problem was not simply the result of one class wanting to keep another from power but of the emerging modes of power that were perceived in terms that seemed to require a different view of the people than as individuals who were equal partners in a social contract and citizens with a right to a share in their own governance. This conception and the modes of power it was anticipating can be glimpsed, appropriately, in some rough notes made by John Locke, one of the great modern founders of social contract theory and majority rule:

> Power consists in numbers of men, and ability to maintain them. Trade conduces to both these by increasing your stock and your people. And they each other.[25]

XIII

Thus two different careers for the individual were being constructed side-by-side by modern constitutionalism: producer and citizen, a producer of power and a producer of legitimacy. We have already seen the producer being prepared in the Lockean conception of property. In the passage just cited the producer has become the primary category through which the person is treated by the state. For the producer is the terminus ad quem of modern power: he applies the technology of modern power to making goods and furnishing services that society will consume. Modern power dictates a system that rewards those who contribute to the development of modern power. Because of its theoretical origins in modern science, modern power assigns greater rewards to those who organize, apply, invent, or discover it.

Modern power has not been shaped and defined as the stuff from which citizen participation and deliberation are made. What, then, is the role assigned to the citizen in the constitution of modern power?

The answer to that question is best represented by the nature of contemporary electoral politics. There the citizen has become the political equivalent of Marx's industrial reserve army. Thanks to the skillful organization of images, the packaging of candidates, the targeting of constituencies, and the manipulation of prejudice and ignorance, elections have become events in which politics is adjusted to what is designated to be the level of voter understanding. In between elections voters are exposed to the banalities and innocuities of the media, especially television, that set that level. Consequently, when the voter is mobilized for election turnouts, a preconditioned being appears who depresses the level of politics in a way that corresponds to the effects which the industrial reserve army has upon wages. Since the latter has either lost skills or never had them, its recruits will gladly accept low wages for jobs from which mechanization has eliminated the skilled worker. Similarly, the voter has also been deprived of political skills: by the apathy induced through the natural operation of representative government; by the ever increasing role of interpretive agencies; and by the deprivation of skills caused by the passivity induced by popular culture. Sections become the political counterpart to the lower reaches of the service sector of the economy where service carries a significant component of servility. Politics, like work, has been de-skilled for the many.

This does not mean that modern power has discovered a steady state that will go on indefinitely. Already there are strong signs that the core of modern power, the concept of truth created by science, is eroding rapidly. Science was originally conceived and retailed in the terms of a strongly foundationalist ideology that emphasized the objectivity of scientific truth and the disinterestedness of scientific truth-seekers. Neither proposition commands wide support today. It may be, therefore, that the near future will see a reconstitution of the terms of power. What is more problematic is whether those terms will reinstate the citizen or, instead, disguise them as the consumer.

ENDNOTES

* These differences were subtly described in a famous passage by Madison that has frequently been cited by later political writers as capturing the essential principle that a government must have sufficient power to meet any and all contingencies. What is usually overlooked is that the context in which Madison set down his principle concerned the criticism that the proposed constitution should provide for popular referenda when issues of grave constitutional importance arose due to the encroachment of one branch of government upon the legitimate sphere of another. Madison resisted the idea, even though, as he noted, Jefferson had broached it. He argued that it posed "the danger of disturbing the public tranquility by interesting too strongly the public passions." He also rejected the strong argument on behalf of such a provision that recalled how similar provisions had been invoked among several of the colonies in the course of the revolution when they had revised their charters to make them more in accord with revolutionary principles. Despite the importance of that experience for showing that revolutionary action did not just mean the people at the barricades or serving in revolutionary armies but as engaged in that most delicate of all political tasks, defining a constitution, Madison turned it aside by pointing out that revolutionary enthusiasm had been operating to stifle "the passions most unfriendly to order and concord."[26]

** Note: It is worth noting the contrast with the republican anticontractualism of Harrington. In *Oceana* he remarks that it would have made better economic sense if Ireland had been turned over to the Jews for cultivation and England had enjoyed the rents. But, he went on, "To receive the Jews after any other manner into a commonwealth were to maim it; for they of nation never incorporate . . . while they suck the nourishment which would sustain a natural and useful member."[27]

CHAPTER 25

AGITATED TIMES

I

Ever since the 1960s mass rallies, protests, and street demonstrations have been a persistent, if not universally welcomed, phenomenon in Britain, many western European countries, and, to a lesser extent, the United States. Although the rights to assemble peacefully and to protest have long been guaranteed in these societies, attention to their status as forms of politics has been, like the phenomena themselves, fitful and episodic. In the United States mass protests have been associated primarily with liberalism, despite the fact that many recent demonstrations have been directed against liberal policies, for example globalization and NAFTA. In western Europe it is not uncommon for mass rallies to be organized against "leftist" policies, as in the recent protests in Spain against same-sex marriage or as in the anti-immigrant demonstrations in France and Germany.

Characteristically demonstrations take place "outside" the official institutions prescribed by constitutions and legislation and thus form a parallel politics. In official politics, the aim is to confine politics to constitutionally sanctioned locations and processes and thereby to reserve legitimacy for those outcomes. Official politics comprehends not only the actions of legislators, executives, bureaucrats, and judges but of interest groups, lobbyists, and the news media. The major mechanism for coordinating official politics is the party system. Political parties supply a form of intelligibility to the actions of elected officials and a focal point of attention for what in official circles is assumed to be a fitful electorate.

A demonstration might be defined as unincorporated politics or uninstitutionalized politics. It does not follow a calendar or hold prescribed sessions. By definition its actions are inconclusive, and intentionally so. The aim is to disrupt the ordinary tempos of the political process either by demanding a halt or a change in direction or a redoubled effort. Unlike the deliberative mode of institutionalized politics, demonstrations are incitements, agitations that have an inescapably populist quality even when the particular cause does not.

II

A tried and true method for turning off potential readers is to begin with dictionary definitions. The case of "agitation" might be pleaded as an exception on grounds that the standard definitions embody, if not contradictions, then an element of dissonance that reappears when we explore the place of agitation in democratic politics.

According to the *Oxford English Dictionary* "to agitate" can mean to "perturb, excite, or stir up." According to the same entry "agitate" can also mean to "discuss." Clearly there is some tension between the first meaning, with its provocative and frenetic connotations, and the second which implies a sedate, perhaps even a leisurely conversation. In exploring the second definition one might propose that discussion is typically accompanied by a certain assumption about temporality. Discussion implies an openness due to the presence of differences and a consequent need to persuade or reconcile. Accordingly discussion "takes" time: participants normally expect an opportunity to present their ideas or case. Moreover, and not uncommonly, it often presupposes time for preparation, for organizing one's thoughts, evidence, or arguments and for anticipating what other discussants might assert or claim.[1]

Extrapolating, one might say that the two meanings and their implications of temporality suggest two rather different notions of politics. The first might be associated with a style of critical radicalism, perhaps a noncommunist left of the benign types in the United States that attempted a nonviolent disruption of the Republican Party's political convention in 2004. The agitators were not appealing to viewers in immediate proximity, the unsympathetic Republican loyalists at the convention; rather they were attempting to arouse an invisible, passive audience of television viewers and to convert it into a national public.

The frenetic, disruptive tempos of these democratic agitators contrast with, say, Fascism, with its regimented movements ideally represented in Leni Riefenstahl's film, *Triumph of the Will*, and its precise, densely packed rows of uniformed soldiers marching in unison (i.e., in the same time), with no space for differences. If we add footage from other Nazi documentaries we see regimented parades that are framed by enthusiastic crowds whose passion, even frenzy, are stimulated by the spectacle of uniformity and, at the same "time," are firmly restrained by police from spilling into the street (controlled agitation).

The second meaning of "agitate" with its reference to discussion might be associated with the deliberative politics of representative legislatures. Representation presupposes the presence and legitimacy of differences and guarantees that some of these will be heard and considered. In contrast to the first meaning, the second could easily apply to action in slow motion, its tempos governed by procedures that protect the expression of differences. It also assumes a temporal hiatus, time that elapses to allow communication between the representative and constituents.

The *OED* defines the noun "agitation" in a way that might be said to straddle the two definitions of its verb while introducing its own political implication. Agitation is defined as "the keeping of an object before public attention by appeals." In referring to "public attention" that definition introduces what we might call an embryonic political note. It is embryonic in the sense that it refers to "public attention" rather than, say, to the "attention of the public." It is possible that agitators might aspire to turn mere attention-getting into a constitutive act that brings a public into existence, temporarily uniting otherwise disconnected singulars who might then proceed to discuss the concerns of the agitators and, whether intentional or not, help to disseminate them and thereby expand the original audience.[2] However, by linking agitation to "appeals" a note of equivocation enters. Ordinarily we do not associate appeals with discussion, or, more precisely, while discussion implies a difference of opinion, appeal seems more univocal, perhaps because of its association with accusation.

III

Here is an historical example that contains both the theme of discussion and of "agitation" and its public consequences. During the seventeenth-century English Civil War, in the course of negotiations between the army's soldiers and their officers and between the soldiers and Parliament, there emerged representatives of the soldiers. These "agitators," as they were called, were elected by each regiment. They pressed the grievances, demands, and aspirations of the ordinary soldiers to higher authorities and even established their own organization.[3] The agitators were the expression of a parallel, more demotic politics emerging to challenge the official established politics monopolized by Royal Court and Parliament.

A remarkable political context made the activities of agitators possible. Civil war and revolution, and the heightened political consciousness they brought, inspired an unprecedented frenzy of pamphleteering, much of it by ordinary citizens; intense debates within the army and Parliament; and a canvassing of a wide range of possibilities concerning the future, not only of political and legal institutions, but of property relations, marriage and women's status, and the proper role of religion in society. The striking features common to all of these forms of agitation were, first, the combination of popular discussion and a speeded-up tempo for action and, second, the contrast with the slower tempo of tradition-bound society.

Although the agitator represented forms of oppositional power crystallized by the war, his power was derivative rather than autonomous. Whatever creativity he might inject into protesting, appealing and negotiating, his work was confined and limited by the intense discussions that preceded and governed his actions. He was a representative rather than an independent, a conveyer of the energies, hopes, and grievances of others. Those impulses had been given focus by institutional forms, such as the army, and by the events of civil war and revolution. The existence of Parliament and the presses helped further to create a genuine public space, accessible to many as readers and spectators. But it is worth noting that the army's agitators represented a parallel institution to

Parliament in the precise sense that they represented the rank-and-file of the soldiers who, by virtue of a narrow franchise empowering propertied classes, were precluded from voting for parliamentary representatives. They could be said to represent the unrepresented who, nonetheless, provided the bulk of a highly politicized army.

In reviewing the events of the 1640s one is struck by the contrast between, on the one hand, the grievances which had been accumulating for a long time, and, on the other, the relative rapidity with which ordinary people responded to the quickly changing events and developments of the period. Printers were able to produce pamphlets while events were still fresh; soldiers were able to react and proceed to assemble, debate, and decide upon strategies. Politics was changed in important ways: it was speeded up and yet democratized, two characteristics which, in later eras, would be viewed as in tension.

Time can be of the essence of political events. Revolutions in which a substantial part of the population participates represent an effort to hurry events, and make things happen more rapidly than the resistance to change—the slow pace associated with the regime representative of the past—allows. Revolutions are also notorious for breeding their own agitators, individuals who often seem to come from nowhere but who, by oratory or example, "fire up" a crowd. Perhaps unconsciously these understandings are reflected in the phrase "revolutionary times." Revolutions change and disrupt the established tempos as well as their direction. Events that might ordinarily "unfold" over a long stretch of time are typically described as suddenly "erupting." Yet in describing the genesis of such revolutionary events as the seventeenth-century "Puritan revolution" (as it used to be called) or the eighteenth-century revolutions in America and France, historians tend to emphasize the long build-up that preceded the actual revolutionary outbreaks.[4] In contrast, when measuring the radicalism of revolutionary changes rather than their gradual formation, the dramatic character of the changes tends to create the impression of rapid movement. Thus in the American colonies some of the soldiers were called "Minute Men," the implication being that they were able to respond quickly to a call to arms, and that revolutionary times demanded it. Such impressions have tended to encourage the belief that revolutions are the work of "firebrands" whose fiery rhetoric and tireless organizational energies serve to "make things happen," stirring the masses to a "boiling point" whereupon revolutions "break out" of the old tempos and the arrangements which set them. Clearly, when we attempt to describe the genesis of revolutions the tendency is to introduce a notion of popular action as initially resistant, hesitant, as "slow motion" that gradually gathers momentum until finally it succeeds in fighting free of the old constraints and imparting a faster tempo to events, changing time, as it were.

Yet we learn from the English Civil Wars that at crucial moments communication could appear painfully slow and that often the reactions of various contestants corresponded to situations that no longer prevailed. Indeed, it is not uncommon for events to be described as "outrunning," that is, moving faster than either the revolutionaries or their opponents were able to comprehend or control.

When we assert that "events moved slowly" or they moved "quickly" and ascribe a certain tempo to them, then the obvious question is: "Slow or fast according to what measure or to whom?" Possible answers are: events moved too quickly for some person or persons to grasp their import or too quickly for them to respond appropriately or effectively. Such answers raise yet another question: is the tempo of the events being set by some person who, if he or she wished, could have set a different tempo; or was there some "process," some equivalent of Dickens's *Jarndyce v. Jarndyce* that was dictating the pace independently of the desires of the parties involved? Or are we assuming some convergence of elements (say, workers and intellectuals) whose disparate character does not prevent them from falling into or following the same tempo? And does tempo govern direction?

The mention of Dickens's famous lawsuit raises yet another question: whether slowness implies inexorability or procrastination, the one downplaying human agency, the other suggesting it. There are different tempos and degrees of procrastination represented in the three main institutions of liberal constitutional systems. That legislatures are described as "deliberative bodies" suggests a slow-moving process while the judiciary is associated with an even slower one with endless possibilities of delays (for example, appeals from one level to a "higher" one). The executive, in contrast, is expected to be able to act quickly in response to events that are often unexpected. The Clinton presidency established a "war room," not to respond to sudden threats from abroad but to improvise quick rejoinders to attacks from domestic political foes.

I have introduced the example of the agitators and the notion of tempo as preliminary to the idea of "agitation." Agitation suggests a politics of premeditated spontaneity and of varying but controlled tempos. That, however, represents an older understanding, one that is preciously close to the cooptation and normalization of agitation, agitation as the contrived outrage of orthodoxy. A contemporary conception might evade cooptation by adopting an understanding of agitation as inspired intervention, sudden, short-lived, dramatic, disruptive, unco-optable. But does this last conception, in its concern to avoid entrapment in institutional processes, deprive action of any staying-power and of democratic legitimacy?

IV

I want to attempt to clarify what is at stake by setting up a contrast between two ideal-types of politics and their tempos. One conception represents agitation as disruptive, energetic intervention whose results include a large element of the unpredictable and perhaps some element of the anarchic; the other is represented by an ideal of action as orderly, stylized, shaped, and limited by prescribed processes, procedures, even time-tables, that are designed to produce predictable (i.e., consistent) decisions or results. This latter conception is most famously represented in Max Weber's ideal-type of bureaucratic rationality.[5] There tempo is written into institutional practices, or, better, engraven into them.

Weber's notion of rationalization was built around the idea that some circumscribed portion of the world could be subjected to procedures or practices that would render it orderly and hence predictable. In modern times that premeditated construct was best represented by the bureaucratic institutions that had become the predominant institutional form, not only of the modern state but of industrial and financial capital. For Weber "rationalization" was the key to understanding bureaucracies. Their modus operandi attempts to structure beforehand, to establish a series of steps that "processes" a prescribed range of phenomena by assigning them to predesigned categories and then compelling them to conform to settled procedures, including ever "higher stages" of review. Eventually a "final" decision is arrived at.[6] In this conception one could properly speak of a decision as an end product of ritualized "decision-making."

The bureaucratic tempo is deliberate, the opposite of agitation. Legend and the literature of Kafka depict bureaucracies as enigmatic, that is, they are difficult to fathom, obtuse, and, above all, maddeningly slow. Yet Weber believed that bureaucracy was emblematic of modern times, at least to the extent that modernity signified the displacement of mystery and obscurantism by rationality, especially the type of rationality associated with late-modern science. According to Weber and many other students of bureaucracy, the bureaucrat, unlike the politician, strives for objectivity and that requires bureaucracy to be privileged, to be "outside" partisan politics, even "above" it, and, crucially, protected from it. The bureaucratic ideal asserts, somewhat paradoxically, that the bureaucrat can be both "neutral" and a staunch believer that the common good is realizable through objective thinking based on expert knowledge. Like the scientist the bureaucrat strove for objectivity, adhered to a prescribed method, was guided by the facts, and, as Weber put it, acted "without scorn or bias."[7] No more than for the scientist, speediness was not a bureaucratic virtue. In contrast, politics is depicted as passionate partisanship, the opposite of rational decision-making and its ideal of objectivity.

Weber also believed that modern politics, too, was becoming bureaucratized. Parties were developing bureaucracies staffed with permanent officials whose principal tasks were to maintain party orthodoxy and to win elections by methodically organizing the newly enfranchised, politically inexperienced masses.[8] Bureaucratic organization, with its arcane ways, hierarchy of experts, most of whom were university trained and examination qualified, was often extolled as a corrective to democracy. Precisely because of its depersonalizing and impersonal ways, bureaucracy operated as a salutary brake upon the supposed tempo of impatience and fitfulness of democracy's mood swings, of its susceptibility to agitation.

There was, however, one crucial characteristic of bureaucracy that Weber overlooked, namely, the hidden character of its decision-making that excluded, or rendered difficult, "outside" public scrutiny. That characteristic became all the more significant if avowedly political institutions, such as elections, parties, and legislatures were increasingly becoming bureaucratized. A further oddity, if the bureaucratization of political institutions and processes represented the growth of a species of rationality ("instrumental rationality"), then the anti-democrat's description of democratic politics as prone to irrationalism acquired even more salience.

Allegedly, so irresistible was the impulse to rationalize and bureaucratize that even popular revolutionary movements which might once have originated in spontaneous uprisings by the "masses" would eventually succumb—or their leaders would—to the allure of organization and hierarchical leadership, in short, to Leninism. Eventually, after the revolution had won power and "settled down," the agitated dynamics of popular revolution would be proscribed and the tempos of organization would take over and institute Stalinism and the bureaucratization of violence: the Weberian ideal turned on its head.

V

When Weber likened "politics" to "the slow boring of hard boards," he was acknowledging, albeit reluctantly, that the tempos of politics had come to emulate those of bureaucracy.[9] Yet at the same time that Weber was imposing a cage of bureaucratic rationality upon politics and economic organization, he was struggling to resist it and find a preserve for creative individual action. Sometimes he alluded to the role of religion as providing an emotional sanctuary from a cold, increasingly rationalized world, a haven where human beings could gain fulfillment without reference to economic calculations or bureaucratic requirements. More strikingly, he depicted an ideal scientist and an ideal politician who struggled to preserve integrity, passionate commitment, and a sense of calling or true vocation amidst an all-too-rationalized world.[10] Passion stood for the inspired, the unmethodical, the charismatic, resistance to rationalization. Yet Weber was forced to acknowledge that even charisma could be routinized. A miraculous deed could be translated into ritual and reenacted endlessly and mechanically. So Weber, who took an active part in the reconstruction of politics in the Weimar Republic, made one last attempt to escape, without renouncing, the tempos of bureaucracy and its ideal of rational action.

Although he favored a parliamentary system, he also regarded parliament itself as dominated by bureaucratized parties. His concern to preserve a space for passionate commitment led him to speculate about the possibility of an extraparliamentary relationship based on "leadership." The *Führerprinzip* was intended to connect a passionate, charismatic, antibureaucratic leader with a mass following.[11] This would inject a healthy element of human feeling, emotion, even unpredictability into a process otherwise dominated by the cold calculations of impersonal decision-makers. The *Führerprinzip* thus held the potential for stirring up, enlivening the measured tempos of parliamentary politics and the dispassion of bureaucratic antipolitics. The agitation-idea thus pointed to an attribute of leadership rather than a demotic tendency. Weber was not envisioning a politics powered by a mass movement of which the leader was the expression and on which he depended. The mass was instrumental not constitutive.

The *Führerprinzip* may have been approximated in Hitler's dictatorial regime, where it destroyed the tempos of parliamentary (i.e., deliberative) politics and corrupted those of bureaucratic neutrality. In that form of agitational politics, while the "masses" were kept in a controlled state of excitement and periodically mobilized for fervent displays of national unity, Nazism pursued a dynamic policy of expansionism and aggression that Weber never imagined. While that form of politics has pretty much disappeared, at least in western Europe, agitation has not vanished: its tempos have simply switched locations.

Specifically, the tempos of revolution have been appropriated by corporate capital but not simply by capital as an economic form of organization. The full import of Joseph Schumpeter's formula of capitalism as "creative destruction" is best appreciated by taking into account not only the dynamics of the market and of the globalizing reach of capital, but of the "troika effect" issuing from the union of capital, technology, and science. That combination of powers has made possible a unique revolutionary tempo. By enlisting technological innovation and scientific discovery and joining them with its own impulses, capital has produced an unprecedented form of power. The combination has quickened the rate of change throughout the world, hurrying premodern societies into postmodernity, shaking up social structures, undermining traditional authorities. It is heralded as revolution without violence, or rather, violence is presented as modernization, as "new times" when innovation quickly scrubs out memory.

VI

The troika has set the tempo of our times; in the process it has rendered obsolete the modern conception of revolution as aimed at a culminating moment when democratic and egalitarian forces would have triumphed and the frenzied time of revolution would give way to the new and measured tempo of consolidation. In place of modern political and social revolution the troika promotes a conception of permanent revolution, of revolution as continuous, not pausing for consolidation, awaiting only the latest scientific breakthrough, the next technological innovation to incite investors. In contrast to the settled, virtually permanent structure of Weber's bureaucracy, the contemporary globalizing corporation appears as highly adaptable, poised to adjust to changing conditions, prepared to dismantle its current organization and "reinvent" itself with a flexible structure adapted to the tempos of revolution, whether of "information," stem cell research, or robotics.

Globalized capital is no stranger to frenzies of speculation, rapid technological change, and radical reorganization, thus no stranger to agitation, albeit orchestrated. Indeed, it may be said to monopolize agitation.[12] The corporate economy encourages change, elevates fashion to a norm, and, while using the media to manufacture excitement and dazzle, instructs an agitated populace that virtually every job and habitat are temporary. Thus corporate capital is the agitator, the exemplar of permanent revolution, of normalized agitation. Its hegemony is secured by control over the manufacture of popular and elite culture. That control is so nearly total that the popular demonstrations against the Iraq war in 2003 and the agitation at the conventions of the major American political parties in 2004 either went unreported or were treated as freak shows. The public at large remained unperturbed, unagitated.

Thus the new model agitator serves as pacifier, exploiting change so that its rapid tempo prevents critical thought from gaining a purchase—hence no need to muzzle critics—and structural injustices go unremedied. Like revolution, agitation has been incorporated, its tempo co-opted.

Can agitation find its bearings, become an accomplice to democratization?

VII

"Stop and think," Hannah Arendt once counseled. We might rephrase this advice as "take stock" in order to assess democracy's prospects. Doubtless that could, and perhaps should, entail exploring the outlook for democracy in a variety of settings, from the Ukraine to Northern Ireland, for example. Rather than attempt a task beyond my abilities I should like to apply Arendt's counsel to a context I am more familiar with, that of the United States.

The United States considers itself the world's oldest and most successful democracy and is now busily exporting its recipe to other parts of the world, particularly those with petroleum resources. Official claims to the contrary, the fact is that in the United States itself, substantive democracy is on the defensive. The actual system is best described as managed electoral democracy. Political power is organized to deflect popular determination of the uses of power and to direct it instead into a controlled form of legitimation serving primarily the aims and needs of corporate interests. Two wars—one cold, against the USSR, the other hot, against terrorism—have transformed a liberal and predominantly secular society into a conservative and chiliastic one. Where US power was once preoccupied with "containment," now its leaders dream of remaking the world. Moreover, unlike traditional conservatism, which identified with the slow tempo of habit, custom, and prejudice, the new conservatism is aggressive and proselytizing, in short, agitative.

Accordingly, the challenge is to expose managed democracy and point the way to "redemocratization." What sort of role, if any, might agitation play in that cause? The Bush administration associates democratization with free elections (one person, one vote), equal political rights, and a free market.[13] The unstated presumption underlying all three principles is that freedom and equality are conditions that, far from preventing concentrations of power, can be exploited to enable the more powerful to dominate or control. A well-financed lobbying group has the same right to influence the legislature as the unemployed laborer, just as the corporation can appeal to the same right of free speech as the ordinary citizen. Democracy, or rather democracy-in-bad-faith, is reshaped to serve as accessory to inequalities.

If the idea of democracy is to be disentangled from corporate power and its political *imperium*, its defenders must take a stand on two basic principles: that there must be meaningful opportunities for power to be shared and that a democratic society is committed to an ongoing and unending effort to challenge, reduce and ameliorate the effects of social, economic, cultural, and political inequalities.

How to identify the tempo appropriate to redemocratization and to the scale of a country as large, diverse, and populous as the United States—and as dangerous? Stated schematically, democracy's best hopes lie at the local level of state, county, and municipality. In those locations the tempo of politics is slower, the opportunities to stop and think more numerous, and the possibilities for meaningful participation greater. Participation takes time because, unlike bureaucratic decisions, democratic decisions are "arrived at" rather than "made." Moreover, because the consequences are immediate rather than abstract, decisions depend upon eliciting cooperation and agreement among familiars who are not necessarily similars, but who are individuals and groups living together and sharing familiar though not necessarily similar circumstances. While participation slows time, it does not annihilate it. Time is preserved in civic memory—of achievements and failures, disasters and triumphs, pride and shame.

Because of its different character, sensibilities, and tempos—"set in its ways"—local democracy is not a locus hospitable to agitation and yet is seriously in need of it. Local democracy's communal virtues are inseparable from the vices of parochialism. Enter agitation as mass protest, raucous demonstration, street theater with jarring rhythms, cacophonies that contrast yet complement the slower tempos of parochial politics, directing local attention to broader, more transcending issues of war, peace, environment, and social justice—issues that are beyond the competence of local powers yet demand the attention of citizens who, by definition, are simultaneously local and national.

The best illustration of that complementarity was in the run-up to the invasion of Iraq. At the same time that there were mass rallies in many major American cities, over one hundred city councils passed resolutions opposing the invasion. To be sure, there was no immediate effect upon the decision-makers in Washington. And yet at the present writing there can be little doubt that the majority of Americans regret the administration's actions and their own complicity. Arguably, agitation had contributed to changing the national mood. Agitation, often ignored by the political center, its immediacy, rather than merely dissipating, can be instead a means of educating particularism, energizing it to challenge the center. Democratic agitation takes time.

NOTES

FOREWORD

1. *The Federalist*, ed. Jacob E. Cooke (Middletown, Conn.: Wesleyan University Press, Conn. 1961), No. 62, p. 421.

EDITOR'S INTRODUCTION

1. Sheldon S. Wolin, *Politics and Vision: Continuity and Innovation in Western Political Thought*, rev. and expanded ed. (Princeton, NJ: Princeton University Press, 2004).

2. The most recent contribution to the encyclopedic genre represented by Sabine is Alan Ryan, *On Politics: A History of Political Thought, From Herodotus to the Present* (New York and London: Liveright, 2012). Ryan recounts that a friend suggested to him some thirty years earlier that he write a successor to Sabine (xi).

3. George H. Sabine, *A History of Political Theory* (New York: Holt, Rinehart and Winston, 1937; 3rd ed. 1961), v.

4. Wolin, *Politics and Vision*, xxiii. In his 1960 text, Wolin uses the terms "political theory," "political philosophy," and "political thought" interchangeably.

5. Wolin, *Politics and Vision*, 5.

6. Sheldon S. Wolin, "History and Theory: Methodism *Redivivus*," in John S. Nelson, ed., *Tradition, Interpretation, and Science: Political Theory in the American Academy* (Albany: SUNY Press, 1986), 54–55.

7. Ibid., 50.

8. See, for example, Quentin Skinner, *Liberty before Liberalism* (Cambridge: Cambridge University Press, 1998) for a mapping of a lost "neo-Roman" tradition within Anglophone political theory. Insofar as Skinner articulates a contemporary political purpose to resurrecting this tradition, it is to offer it as an alternative to the current "liberal hegemony" (x). Compare also J.G.A. Pocock, *The Machiavellian Moment: Florentine Political Thought and the Atlantic Republican Tradition* (Princeton, NJ: Princeton University Press, 1975). For an insightful account of Wolin's approach to the history of political theory, see Antonio Vazquez-Arroyo, "Sheldon S. Wolin and the Historicity of Political Theory," *The Good Society* vol. 24, no. 2 (2016)

9. Sheldon S. Wolin and John H. Schaar, *The Berkeley Rebellion and Beyond: Essays on Politics and Education in the Technological Society* (New York: New York Review Books, 1970).

10. Sheldon S. Wolin, "Political Theory and Political Commentary," in Marvin Richter, ed., *Political Theory and Political Education* (Princeton, NJ: Princeton University Press, 1980), 190.

11. Ibid., 199, 203.

12. Sheldon S. Wolin, *The Presence of the Past: Essays on the State and the Constitution* (Baltimore and London: Johns Hopkins University Press, 1990), 1.

13. Sheldon S. Wolin, *Democracy Incorporated: Managed Democracy and the Specter of Inverted Totalitarianism* (Princeton, NJ: Princeton University Press, 2008).

14. Ibid., x.

15. Sheldon S. Wolin, "Political Theory: Trends and Goals," in David L. Sills, ed., *International Encyclopedia of the Social Sciences*, vol. 12 (New York: Macmillan, 1968); "Paradigms and Political Theories," in Preston King and B. C. Parekh, eds., *Politics and Experience: Essays Presented to Professor Michael Oakeshott on the Occasion of His Retirement* (Cambridge: Cambridge University Press, 1968); "Political Theory as a Vocation," *American Political Science Review*, 63 (1969): 1062–1082.

16. Wolin, "Paradigms and Political Theories," 319.

17. Wolin, "History and Theory," 64.

18. See below, p. 43.

19. Sheldon S. Wolin, *Tocqueville between Two Worlds: The Making of a Political and Theoretical Life* (Princeton, NJ: Princeton University Press, 2001), 9.

CHAPTER 1
Political Theory as a Vocation

This is a revised version of a paper delivered September 1968, before the Conference for the Study of Political Thought.

1. "*Methodist*. One who is skilled in, or attaches great importance to, method; one who follows a (specified) method." *Oxford Universal Dictionary*.

Although most social scientists would contend that actual research rarely conforms to a step-by-step procedure, it remains the case that such procedure stands as a model for what they aim at. Thus, in a section of a textbook on research methods titled *Major Steps in Research*, the authors insert the qualification above but acknowledge that "published research strongly suggests the existence of a prescribed sequence of procedures, each step presupposing the completion of the preceding one." Claire Selltiz et al., *Research Methods in Social Relations*, rev. ed. (New York: Holt, Rinehart & Winston, 1963), pp. 8–9.

2. I have discussed Kuhn's interpretation and its relevance to political science in "Paradigms and Political Theories," *Politics and Experience: Essays Presented to Michael Oakeshott*, ed. P. King and B. C. Parekh (Cambridge: Cambridge University Press, 1968), pp. 125–152.

3. G. A. Almond and S. Verba, *The Civic Culture* (Princeton, NJ: Princeton University Press, 1963), p. 43.

4. Ibid., p. 43.

5. Selltiz, et al., *Research Methods*, pp. 6–7.

6. D. Easton, *A Framework for Political Analysis* (Englewood Cliffs, NJ: Prentice-Hall, 1965), p. 7.

7. As a recent work on political socialization (which is described as "a universal feature of political life") admits: "The reader is forewarned that the treatment is heavily biased in favor of a model appropriate to western democracies, particularly in the United States."

8. See, for example, H. Eulau's language in *Contemporary Political Science*, ed. I. de Sola Pool (New York: McGraw-Hill, 1967), pp. 58–59; and the more cautious remarks in A. Somit and J. Tanenhaus, *The Development of American Political Science* (Boston: Allyn & Bacon, 1967), pp. 174ff.

9. This may appear contentious, but, in reality, it is only a restatement of what appears in G. A. Almond, "Political Theory and Political Science," *American Political Science Review*, LX (1966), 873–875.

10. A. Campbell, "Surge and Decline: A Study of Electoral Change," in A. Campbell et al., *Elections and the Political Order* (New York: Wiley, 1966), p. 45.

11. I. de Sola Pool, "The Public and Polity," in *Contemporary Political Science*, ed. Pool, p. 26 (emphasis added).

12. Easton, *Framework*, p.50.

13. Ibid., p. 48.

14. D. Easton, *A Systems Analysis of Political Life* (New York: Wiley, 1965), p. 475.

15. *Works*, ed. J. Bowring, 11 vols. (Edinburgh, 1843), Vol. II, p. 493.

16. Heraclitus, frags. 203, 235; Parmenides, frags. 342, 344–347. G. S. Kirk and J. E. Raven, *The Presocratic Philosophers* (Cambridge: Cambridge University Press, 1957). The idea reappears in Machiavelli, *Discorsi*, Bk. I, Preface; Tocqueville, *Oeuvres complètes*, ed. J.-P. Mayer (Paris: Gallimard, 1961–), Vol. I, p. 293.

17. *Discourse on Method*, tr. J. Veitch, *The Method, Meditations, and Philosophy of Descartes* (New York: Tudor Publishing Co., n.d.), Pt. I, p.149.

18. See W. Ong, *Ramus: Method and Decay of Dialogue* (Cambridge, Mass.: Harvard University Press, 1958), p. 53ff.; N. W. Gilbert, *Renaissance Concepts of Method* (New York: Columbia University Press, 1960), p. 3ff.

19. All quotations are from W. S. Howell, *Logic and Rhetoric in England, 1500–1700* (New York: Russell and Russell, 1961), pp. 21, 23–24. The Ramist influence upon the American Puritans has been discussed by Perry Miller, *The New England Mind: The Seventeenth Century* (Boston: Beacon Press, 1939, 1961), p. 154ff. and Appendix A.

20. Howell, *Logic and Rhetoric in England*, p. 152.

21. *Of the Laws of Ecclesiastical Polity*, 2 vols. (Oxford: Clarendon Press, 1885), I.vi.4.

22. *Discourse on Method* (Veitch trans.), Pt. VI, p. 192.

23. *Works of Francis Bacon*, ed. R. L. Ellis, J. Spedding, and D. D. Heath, 7 vols. (London: 1887–92), Vol. VI, pp. 268–269.

24. Ibid., p. 289. "We know that the founders [of New England] studied Francis Bacon." Miller, *The New England Mind*, p. 12.

25. *Meditations*, II in *Descartes: Philosophical Writings*, tr. N. K. Smith (New York: Random House, 1956), p. 189.

26. Rules X–XI (tr. N. K. Smith), pp. 43–44, 47.

27. Cited in P. Rossi, *Francis Bacon: From Magic to Science*, tr. S. Rabinovitch (London: Routledge, 1968), p. 141.

28. "Preface to the Principles of Philosophy" (tr. Veitch), p. 288.

29. *Francis Bacon: Selected Writings*, ed. H. G. Dick (New York: Random House, 1955), pp. 435, 533. See also Descartes, *Discourse on Method* in *Descartes: Philosophical Writings*, ed. N. K. Smith, Pt. IV, p. 118.

30. *Philosophical Writings* (ed. Smith), *Discourse on Method*, III, p. 111.

31. Ibid., II, pp. 103–104, 112.

32. Ibid., Pt. II, p. 103.

33. Easton, *A Framework*, p. 30.

34. *Discourse on Method*, tr. Smith, Pt. III, pp. 111–113.

35. "It is the very essence of the theoretical enterprise that, if and when it seems appropriate, it should feel free to sever itself from the bonds of traditional ways of looking at political life." Easton, *A Framework*, p. viii.

There is no doubt that breaking with the past has been a feature of all great theoretical innovations, including those in the history of political theory. Yet the matter is not that simple, as witness Plato's respect for tradition, Aristotle's deference to his predecessors, Augustine's retrieval of major aspects of classicism, and Machiavelli's insistence on restoring certain forms of classical political knowledge. Hobbes was probably the first writer to advocate a break in the modern sense. Some aspects of his attempt will be discussed in my forthcoming essay, *Hobbes: Political Theory as Epic* (Berkeley: University of California Press).

36. *Discourse on Method*, tr. Veitch, Pt. II, p. 158.

37. Edward C. Banrield, "In Defense of the American Party System," *Voting, Interest Groups, and Parties*, ed. B. Seasholes (Glenview, Ill.: Scott, Foresman, 1960), p. 130.

38. D. Braybrooke and E. Lindblom, *A Strategy of Decision* (New York: Free Press, 1963), p. 73.

39. *Democracy in America* (ed. P. Bradley), 2 vols. (New York: Knopf, 1945), Vol. II, pp. 42, 99.

40. Ibid., Vol. II, p. 3.

41. W. Riker, *The Theory of Political Coalitions* (New Haven, Conn.: Yale University Press, 1962), p. viii, emphasis in the original.

42. M. Polanyi, *Personal Knowledge* (New York: Harper and Row, 1964), *passim*.

43. Pool, *Contemporary Political Science*, pp. 23–24 (emphasis added).

44. C. H. Backstron and G. D. Hursh, *Survey Research* (Evanston, Ill.: Northwestern University Press, 1963), ed. J. Robinson, pp. xi–xv, 4, 13.

45. T. Kuhn, *The Structure of Scientific Revolutions* (Chicago: University of Chicago Press, 1962), p. 165.

46. R. Taton, *Reason and Chance in Scientific Discovery*, tr. A. J. Pomerans (New York: Science Editions, 1962), p. 64ff.

47. A. Downs, *An Economic Theory of Democracy* (New York: Harper & Row, 1957), p. 21.

48. N. R. Hanson, *Patterns of Discovery* (Cambridge: Cambridge University Press, 1965), p. 5ff.

49. The remarks from Tocqueville are to be found in *Oeuvres complètes*, Vol. I, pp. 12, 14, 222.

50. R. Dahl, *Modern Political Analysis* (Englewood Cliffs, N. J.: Prentice-Hall, 1963), p. 8.

51. Hanson, *Patterns of Discovery*, p. 36.

52. Ibid., p. 30.

53. E.g., K. Popper, *The Logic of Scientific Discovery* (New York: Science Editions, 1961), pp. 19, 38.

54. An exception would be S. Huntington, "Political Development and Political Decay," *World Politics*, Vol. 17 (April, 1965), 386–430. As an illustration of a contemporary way of dealing with the problems the reader is referred to A. A. Rogow and H. D. Lasswell, *Power, Corruption, and Rectitude* (Englewood Cliffs, N. J.: Prentice-Hall, 1963). This work criticizes Acton's epigram, points out how a like animus against power led to the separation of powers doctrine, how the latter frustrates the majority, and how the problem can be handled by organizational and bureaucratic sanctions.

55. H. D. Lasswell and A. Kaplan, *Power and Society. A Framework for Political Inquiry* (New Haven, Conn.: Yale University Press, 1950), p. 145.

56. *Representative Government*, Ch. II (Everyman edition, p. 193). My point would not be affected if political socialization were defined in some other contemporary mode,

e.g., learning "roles," or as "a readiness to tolerate outputs that are perceived to run contrary to one's wants and demands.": Easton, *A Systems Analysis of Political Science*, p. 272.

57. *Political Science*. Newsletter of the American Political Science Association, Vol. I, No. 1 (Winter, 1968), p. 25 (col. 1).

58. *De Cive*, Pref. *ad finem*.

59. D. Apter, *The Politics of Modernization* (Chicago: University of Chicago Press, 1965), p. x.

60. *The Nerves of Government* (Glencoe, Ill.: Free Press, 1963), pp. 94, 98.

61. Ibid., pp. 91–92.

62. *Politicus*, 262 b–c.

63. *Politicus*, pp. 162–1G8.

64. B. Berelson and G. Steiner, *Human Behavior* (New York: Harcourt, Brace & World, 1964), p. 13.

65. Eulau, *Contemporary Political Science*, p. 7. See also G. Almond and B. Powell, *Comparative Politics: A Developmental Approach* (Boston: Little, Brown, 1966), p. 214; H. Alker, *Mathematics and Politics* (New York: Macmillan, 1965), pp. 6–8.

66. Here it is only necessary to recall Plato's long discussion of cognition or Hobbes's effort to place political philosophy upon a new and more scientific basis.

67. Letter to Vettori, April 16, 1527.

68. *Utopia*, Bk. I, tr. E. Surtz (New Haven, Conn.: Yale University Press, 1964), p. 49.

69. *De Cive*, Preface to the Reader, ed. S. P. Lamprecht (New York: Appleton, 1949), p. 18.

70. Selltiz, *Research Methods*, p. 31.

71. Dahl, *Political Analysis*, p. viii.

72. Eulau in *Contemporary Political Science*, ed. Pool, p. 55.

73. If the Seventh Letter is to be believed, Plato also condemned the government of the Thirty, which included some of his kinsmen, for their threats against Socrates (324 d–e).

74. *Republic* 473 (Conford tr.)

75. H. Gerth and C. W. Mills, *From Max Weber: Essays in Sociology* (New York: Oxford University Press, 1946), p. 128.

76. Pool (ed.), *Contemporary Political Science*, p. vii. The essays by Eckstine and Dahl are excepted.

77. *Personal Knowledge*, p. 138.

78. Cited by A. Wilkausky, *The Politics of the Budgetary Process* (Boston: Little, Brown, 1964), p. 178.

79. *Civic Culture*, p. 475.

CHAPTER 2

Political Theory: From Vocation to Invocation

1. *Minima Moralia: Reflections from Damaged Life*, trans. E. F. Jephcott (New York: Verso Books, 1996), 151.

2. For the controversy about whether or not book 8 of Thucydides's *History* is unfinished, see *A Historical Commentary on Thucydides*, ed. A. W. Gomme, A. Andrewes, and K. J. Dover, vol. 5 (Oxford: Clarendon Press, 1981), Introduction and Appendix 1.

3. "What I am attentive to is the fact that every human *relation* is to some degree a power relation. We move in a world of perpetual strategic relations." Michel Foucault in *Michel Foucault: Politics, Philosophy, Culture*, ed. Lawrence D. Kritzman (New York: Routledge, 1988), 168.

4. Melinda Henneberger, "Seeing Politics, and Mirrors, in the Coverage of Capitol Hill," *New York Times*, October 6, 1997, C-1.

5. To be sure, Kuhn's classic account of paradigms emphasized that scientific revolutions were accompanied by alterations in scientific conventions. In its strong version that claim seemed to make insufficient allowance for continuities in scientific conventions. When pressed by critics Kuhn conceded that his original formulation was overstated—thus supplying a personal example of continuity. Lakatos's criticisms and Kuhn's response can be found in *Criticism and the Growth of Knowledge*, ed. Imre Lakatos and Alan Musgrave (Cambridge: Cambridge University Press, 1970), 91–195, 231–278. See also Kuhn's preface.

6. Barbara Crossette, "A New Credo: Make Money, Not War," *New York Times*, August 24, 1997, section 4, p. 1.

7. *Selections from the Prison Notebooks*, trans. Q. Hoare and G. N. Smith (New York: International Publishers, 1971), 275–276.

CHAPTER 3
Transgression, Equality, and Voice

1. John Rawls, *Political Liberalism* (New York: Columbia University Press, 1993), 217.

2. See the discussion of the role of rhetors in fourth-century Athenian democracy in Josiah Ober, *Mass and Elite in Democratic Athens: Rhetoric, Ideology, and the Power of the People* (Princeton, NJ: Princeton University Press, 1989), especially chapter 3. For a more detailed discussion of democracy and constitutionalism, see my "Norm and Form."

3. See Paul Cartledge, "Comparatively Equal," in Josiah Ober and Charles Hedrick, eds., *Demokratia: A Conversation on Democracies, Ancient and Modern* (Princeton, NJ: Princeton University Press, 1996), especially the section "Use in Argument 1: Reference."

4. See Jane Mansbridge, *Why We Lost the ERA* (Chicago: University of Chicago Press, 1983).

5. For an application of this notion to recent events, see my "Democracy without the Citizen," in Sheldon S. Wolin, *The Presence of the Past* (Baltimore: Johns Hopkins University Press, 1989).

6. The tensions between an inclusive view of the polis and an exclusive view of the political community are evident in Aristotle's efforts to justify slavery as being according to nature while admitting that that account does not always fit (*Pol.* 1255a21–b4). See the discussion in Mary P. Nichols, *Citizens and Statesmen: A Study of Aristotle's "Politics"* (Savage, MD: Rowman and Littlefield, 1992), 19–24. On the general topic with some attention to Aristotle, see M. I. Finley, *Ancient Slavery and Modern Ideology* (London: Chatto and Windus, 1977), especially 119–120.

7. *Pol.* I281a40–I281b20.

8. "This is why the theater is the political art par excellence; only there is the political sphere of human life transposed into art." Hannah Arendt, *The Human Condition* (Chicago: University of Chicago Press, 1958), 188.

9. Plato *Rep.* 1, which has sometimes been called "The Book of Thrasymachus," and his *Gorgias* and *Alcibiades* I all give portraits of the actor frustrated by the politics of democracy.

10. Relevant here are the opening passages of Thuc. 1.1–3.

11. An influential example of this formulation is in Arendt, *The Human Condition*, 17–26, 188–194.

12. See Ober, *Mass and Elite*, 104ff.

13. Arendt, *The Human Condition*, 178–179.

14. Cited in Kenneth J. Dover, *Greek Popular Morality in the Time of Plato and Aristotle* (Oxford: Blackwell, 1974), 289.

15. Max Weber, *Economy and Society*, ed. Guenther Roth and Claus Wittich, vol. 3 (New York: Bedminster, 1968), 984–987.

16. See the discussion in Gordon S. Wood, *The Radicalism of the American Revolution* (New York: Alfred A. Knopf, 1992), 229ff.; Pauline Maier, *From Resistance to Revolution* (New York: Random House, 1972); and the survey by Andrew Lintott, *Violence, Civil Strife, and Revolution in the Classical City* (London: Croom Helm, 1982).

17. The classic discussion is by Weber, "Parliament and Government in a Reconstructed Germany," in his *Economy and Society*, vol. 3, 1381–1461.

18. For the Periclean echoes in Cleon's speeches, see Jacqueline de Romilly, *Thucydides and Athenian Imperialism*, trans. Philip Thody (Oxford: Blackwell, 1963), 163ff. Also W. Robert Connor, *Thucydides* (Princeton, NJ: Princeton University Press, 1984), 79n. 1 and references cited there.

19. Connor, *Thucydides*, 87–88, charges Diodotus with "serious" misrepresentation of the facts. In support of his proposal of leniency, Diodotus had claimed that the common people of Mytilene had had no part in the revolt and had willingly turned the city over to the Athenians. Connor assumes that Thucydides provides the truthful representation of the facts (3.27). Although Thucydides's account does not squarely support Diodotus's claim, neither does it support the charge of serious misrepresentation. The commoners had been armed by the wealthy class for the sole purpose of launching an attack on the Athenians. Once armed, the common people "refused any longer to obey their officers" and proceeded to concert their own aims by insisting that the authorities "divide the provisions among all or they themselves would come to terms with the Athenians and deliver up the city." According to Thucydides, the authorities, knowing that they could not resist that demand and fearing they would be "left out of the capitulation," agreed to surrender to the Athenians (3.28). It seems clear that the Mytilinean authorities would not have surrendered in the absence of pressure from the commons. Connor also accuses Diodotus of having misrepresented the favorable disposition of subject people toward Athens. Again, his proof is what Thucydides said. But Thucydides also has Diodotus begin his speech with the broad assertion that any city would rebel because in such circumstances human nature invariably exaggerates possibilities (3.45).

20. Connor has described Diodotus's speech as functioning at two levels, practical decision and "more general political discourse" (*Thucydides*, 83). I would describe that generality as a "nonphilosophical theory." For further background on the Mytilinean

incident, see G.E.M. de Ste. Croix, *The Class Struggle in the Ancient Greek World* (Ithaca, NY: Cornell University Press, 1983), 603–604, n. 26.

21. For a discussion of the different oratory of the courtrooms, see Connor, *Thucydides*, 84.

22. Connor, *Thucydides*, 90. That Thucydides engaged an opaque world and tried to reinterpret it without however wholly emancipating himself from "prehistoric" or mythic modes was suggested nearly a century ago by Francis Macdonald Cornford, *Thucydides Mythistoricus* (London: Routledge and Kegan Paul, 1965), especially viii.

23. Ar. *Pol.* 1278a13–26; Karl Marx, *Capital*, vol. 3 (London: Penguin, 1991), pt. 4, ch. 20; pt. 7, ch. 48; Arendt, *The Human Condition*, 81ff.

24. Here and in all subsequent translated citations from Thucydides, I have followed John H. Finley's translation in *Thucydides* (Ann Arbor: University of Michigan Press, 1963), 59.

25. Connor, *Thucydides*, 89, 90.

26. Marcel Detienne, *Dionysus Slain* (Baltimore: Johns Hopkins University Press, 1979), ix. See also the essays in Michel Izard and Pierre Smith, eds., *Between Belief and Transgression: Essays in Religion, History, and Myth* (Chicago: University of Chicago Press, 1979).

27. Jean-Jacques Rousseau, *The Social Contract* (New York: J. M. Dent, Everyman edition, n.d.), bk. 2, ch. 7, "One who dares to undertake to found a people should feel capable, so to speak, of changing human nature, of transforming each individual, who by himself is a perfect and solitary whole, into a part of a greater whole from which the individual, in a sense, receives—his life and being."

28. Ibid., bk. 3, ch. 4, 73.

29. I have found much that was suggestive in Yirmiyahu Yovel, *Spinoza and Other Heretics*, 2 vols. (Princeton, NJ: Princeton University Press, 1989), esp. vol. 1, 128–137.

30. On the *conatus* see Spinoza, *Ethics* 2.6 (tr. R.H.M. Elwes, Dover). As James Madison wrote to Jefferson in 1787, "In a popular Government, the political and physical power may be considered as vested in the same hands, that is in a majority of the people." James Madison, *The Complete Madison*, ed. Saul Padover (New York: Harper, 1953), 254.

31. *Ethics* III, vii, tr. Elwes.

32. See especially Spinoza's Preface to his *Theologico-Political Tractatus*.

33. Friedrich Nietzsche, *The Gay Science*, trans. Walter Kaufmann (New York: Random House, 1974), section 349. On Spinoza and Nietzsche, see Yovel, *Spinoza*, vol. 2, ch. 5.

34. Friedrich Nietzsche, *Beyond Good and Evil* (New York: Random House, 1966), sections 259–260; Friedrich Nietzsche, *On the Genealogy of Morals* (New York: Random House, 1969), section S.

35. Nietzsche, *The Gay Science*, section 354.

36. Later commentators have described Callicles as a Nietzschean figure. See E. R. Dodds's introduction to his edition of *Gorgias* (Oxford: Clarendon Press, 1959); I. M. Crombie, *An Examination of Plato's Doctrines*, 2 vols. (London: Routledge, 1962), vol. 1, p. 302.

37. Terence Irwin, *Plato, Gorgias* (Oxford: Clarendon Press, 1990). Also *Gorg.* 488c–489c. All subsequent translated citations from the *Gorgias* are Irwin's.

38. *Rep.* 492b–c (tr. Cornford, Oxford). See also *Gorg.* 483e–484a.

39. Here I have borrowed freely from Lintott, *Violence, Civil Strife, and Revolution,* 15–16, 18, 19–23, 25, 28, 126.

40. *Ath. Pol.,* 2.2–3, 5.1–2. Here and elsewhere I have used the translation of J. M. Moore, ed., *Aristotle and Xenophon on Democracy and Oligarchy* (Berkeley: University of California Press, 1975), 183 (41.2). See also the discussion by Ellen Meiksins Wood, *Peasant-Citizen and Slave: The Foundations of Athenian Democracy* (New York: Verso, 1988), 94ff.

41. See Pierre Vidal-Naquet, *The Black Hunter* (Baltimore: Johns Hopkins University Press, 1986), 85–105. And see Plato's remark about how "the lean and sunburned" common men will notice that the pleasure-loving oligarch cannot endure the rigors of battle and will proceed to plot against him. *Rep.* 556 c–d.

42. Thuc. 1.70 (tr. R. Crawley, Random House).

43. The growing confidence of the demos is emphasized by W. G. Forrest, *The Emergence of Greek Democracy 800–400 B.C.* (New York: McGraw Hill, 1966).

44. See the discussion in de Ste. Croix, *Class Struggle,* 281.

45. Ibid., 288.

46. Thomas Hobbes, *Leviathan,* ed. Michael Oakeshott (Oxford: Blackwell, n.d.), ch. 8, 42.

47. *Pol.* 3.4.1277b8–13.

48. I have used Forrest's translation, *The Emergence of Greek Democracy,* 232. Aristophanes (*The Frogs,* 952) has "Euripides" claiming that it was democratic for him to have inserted parts for women and slaves in his rendition of tragic legends.

49. *Demos* might stand for the majority; or it might mean the poor; or it might signify those who supported democracy, including both the common people and the leaders from the upper classes: or it could stand for "the people as a whole." Lintott, *Violence, Civil Strife, and Revolution,* 93–94; Charles W. Fornara and Loren J. Samons II, *Athens from Cleisthenes to Pericles* (Berkeley: University of California Press, 1991), 48–49.

50. Plato, of course, provides an exception. *Gorg.* 515a–516d.

51. Thuc., 2.65.

52. In our own day the Democratic Leadership Conference was formed by "centrist" Democrats to change the "populist" image of the Party. They pledged to limit social programs favored by the working class and poor, to hold down taxes, and to encourage high-technology corporations.

53. I have used the Loeb edition and translation by W.R.M. Lamb (Cambridge, MA: Harvard University Press, 1955).

54. Although this formulation is used earlier by a speaker identified only as the "Athenian," the implication is that abandonment of the city was abnormal, a measure of desperation (Thuc. 1.74). On this point it seems to me that in her splendid *The Invention of Athens: The Funeral Oration in the Classical City* (Cambridge, MA: Harvard University Press, 1986), esp. 53, 55, 57, 60, Nicole Loraux has treated "Athens" and democracy as virtually a single entity. My position would be that in the funeral oration the city tended to absorb democracy and then usurp its position.

55. Victor Ehrenberg, *The Greek State,* 2nd ed. (London: Methuen, 1969), 28.

56. See Connor, *Thucydides,* 24–25; Thuc. 1.8, 143.

57. Plato *Rep.* 557b: Arist. *Pol.* 5.1310a.30–34:6.1317a40–b16.

58. See Barry S. Strauss, "On Aristotle's Critique of Athenian Democracy," in *Essays on the Foundations of Aristotelian Political Science*, ed. Carnes Lord and David K. O'Connor (Berkeley: University of California Press, 1991).

59. *Ath. Pol.* 8–9 (tr. Moore).

60. *Ath. Pol.* 2 (tr. Moore).

61. *Rh.* 1.8.1–3 (tr. J. H. Feese, Loeb).

62. *Rh.* 1.8.6.

63. In *Pol.* 2.12, 1273b26, Aristotle refers to those who have only written about politics and those who have both written and taken part: there is no hint of incompatibility between the two groups. On the notion of manipulation, see Aristotle's discussion of how election requirements may be reshaped to produce desired outcomes (*Pol.* 4.13.1297a14).

64. *Pol.* 4.12.1296b15 and the discussion of quantity and quality.

65. *Pol.* 4.9.1294a30–1294b14.

66. Gregory Vlastos, "Isonomia Politike," in *Isonomia: Studien zur Gleichheitsvorstellung im griechischen Denken*, ed. Jürgen Mau and Ernst Günther Schmidt (Berlin: Akademie-Verlag, 1964), 175. See also Gregory Vlastos, "Solonian Justice," *Classical Philology* 41 (1946).

67. *Pol.* 5.l.1301a39–b1. An argument could be made that democracy found in the rhetoricians of the fourth century (B.C.) its functional equivalents to the philosopher. I have criticized this view in my "Norm and Form."

68. Sheldon S. Wolin, "Democracy: Electoral and Athenian," *PS: Political Science and Politics* 26, no. 3 (Sept. 1993), 475–477.

69. George Boas, *Vox Populi: Essays in the History of an Idea* (Baltimore: Johns Hopkins University Press, 1968).

70. The locus classicus is the Thomason Collection in the British Museum. There are also the Clarke Papers containing the Army debates during the English civil wars. Useful editions: *Puritanism and Liberty*, ed. A.S.P. Woodhouse (London: Dent, 1938); G. E. Aylmer, *The Levellers in the English Revolutions* (Ithaca, NY: Cornell University Press, 1975); Christopher Hill and Edmund Dell, *The Good Old Cause: The English Revolution of 1640–1660* (New York: Kelly, 1969). For a survey of recent scholarship, see F. D. Dow, *Radicalism in the English Revolution 1640–1660* (Oxford: Blackwell, 1985). On the American Revolution see *Pamphlets of the American Revolution*, ed. Bernard Bailyn (Cambridge, MA: Harvard University Press, 1965–); Gordon S. Wood, *The Creation of the American Republic, 1776–1787* (New York: Norton, 1972). On France see Lynn Hunt, *Politics, Culture and Class in the French Revolution* (Berkeley: University of California Press, 1984), especially Part I: and Roger Chartier, *The Cultural Origins of the French Revolution* (Durham, NC: Duke University Press, 1993).

CHAPTER 4

Norm and Form: The Constitutionalizing of Democracy

The quotation from Aristotle's *Politics* that opens this essay is from the translation by Barker (see below, n. 46), and that at the head of Section I from that by Sinclair and Saunders (see n. 40).

1. For a more extended discussion, see my *Constitutional Order, Revolutionary Violence, and Modern Power*, Politics: Occasional Papers (North York: York University, Department of Political Science, 1990), 1–21.

2. Cited in Jean-Clause Lamberti, *Tocqueville et les deux démocraties* (Paris: Presses Universitaires de France, 1983), 180.

3. For a further discussion of constitutionalism, see my "Tending and Intending a Constitution: Bicentennial Misgivings," in *The Presence of the Past: Essays on the Slate and the Constitution* (Baltimore: Johns Hopkins University Press, 1989), 82–99.

4. Quoted in *San Francisco Chronicle*, September 15, 1992, A7.

5. Spinoza was an exception; see *Traclaius Politicus* 11. See also Alexandre Matheron, *Individu et communauté chez Spinoza* (Paris: Minuit, 1988), 420–424, 493–494.

6. Polybius *The Histories*, trans. W. R. Paton, Loeb ed. (Cambridge, Mass.: Harvard University Press, 1923), 6.10.4–5. See also Thucydides's description of the popular leader, Cleon, as "the most violent man at Athens," *History of the Peloponnesian War* 3.36.

7. Alexis de Tocqueville, *Démocratic en Amérique*, in *Oeuvres complètes*, ed. J.-P. Mayer et al. (Paris: Gallimard, 1961–), 1(1):34. "The great advantage of Americans is to have arrived at democracy without the ordeal of democratic revolutions and to have been born equal instead of becoming equal" (1[2]: 108).

8. Alexander Hamilton, John Jay, and James Madison, *The Federalist*, ed. Jacob E. Cooke (Middletown, Conn.: Wesleyan University Press, 1961), no. 55, 374.

9. Robert A. Dahl, *Democracy and Its Critics* (New Haven, Conn.: Yale University Press, 1989), 23.

10. Sheldon S. Wolin, "Political Theory," *International Encyclopedia of the Social Sciences* (New York: Collier-Macmillan, 1968); Moses I. Finley, *Politics in the Ancient World* (Cambridge: Cambridge University Press, 1983), 53; Cynthia Farrar, *The Origins of Democratic Thinking: The Invention of Politics in Classical Athens* (Cambridge: Cambridge University Press, 1988), 1.

11. Still useful as a general discussion: Charles H. McIlwain, *Constitutionalism Ancient and Modern* (Ithaca, NY: Cornell University Press, 1940).

12. Aristotle *Politics* 1313a34ff.

13. The relationship between democracy and constitutionalism is discussed in my forthcoming "Equality, Transgression, and Voice," in the forthcoming *Democracy, Ancient and Modern*, edited by Charles Hedrick and Josiah Ober.

14. Plutarch *Solon* 25; see also *Constitution of Athens* [= *Athēnaiōn Politeia*] 11.

15. Thuc. *History* 1.70.

16. On organization theory, see my discussion in *Politics and Vision: Continuity and Innovation in Western Political Thought* (Boston: Little, Brown, 1960), chap. 10.

17. Josiah Ober, *Mass and Elite in Democratic Athens: Rhetoric, Ideology, and the Power of the People* (Princeton, NJ: Princeton University Press, 1989); Barry S. Strauss, "On Aristotle's Critique of Athenian Democracy," in *Essays on the Foundations of Aristotelian Political Science*, ed. Carnes Lord and David K. O'Connor (Berkeley: University of California Press, 1991), 212–233.

18. Ober, *Mass and Elite*, 52.

19. B. Strauss, "On Aristotle's Critique," 220, 221. See also Peter J. Rhodes, "Athenian Democracy after 403 B.C.," *Classical Journal* 75 (1980): 305–323.

20. "Old Oligarch" [Pseudo-Xenophon] *Constitution of the Athenians*, trans. J. M. Moore, ed., *Aristotle and Xenophon on Democracy and Oligarchy* (Berkeley: University of California Press, 1975), 7–8.

21. See in particular Martin Ostwald, *From Popular Sovereignty to the Sovereignty of Law: Law, Society, and Politics in Fifth-Century Athens* (Berkeley: University of California Press, 1986), and Christian Meier, *The Greek Discovery of Politics*, trans. David

McLintock (Cambridge, Mass.: Harvard University Press, 1990), esp. chap. 4, "Cleisthenes and Institutionalizing the Civic Presence." See also Bruce Ackerman, *The Future of Liberal Revolution* (New Haven, Conn.: Yale University Press, 1992), and *Constitutionalism and Democracy: Studies in Rationality and Social Change*, ed. Jon Elster and Rune Slagstad (Cambridge: Cambridge University Press, 1988).

22. Ostwald, *Sovereignty*, xx.

23. Ibid., xi

24. *Constitution of Athens* 61.1–2.

25. Charles Hignett, *A History of the Athenian Constitution to the End of the Fifth Century B.C.* (Oxford: Oxford University Press, Clarendon, 1952), chap. 9; B. Strauss, "On Aristotle's Critique," 229.

26. For general background and still useful: Antony Andrewes, *The Greek Tyrants* (London: Hutchinson University Library, 1956).

27. I have borrowed Ober's summary, *Mass and Elite*, 54–55. For estimates of how many Athenian citizens participated during the fourth century and how often, see Mogens H. Hansen, *The Athenian Democracy in the Age of Demosthenes: Structure, Principles, and Ideology* (Oxford: Blackwell, 1991).

28. For details, see R. K. Sinclair, *Democracy and Participation in Athens* (Cambridge: Cambridge University Press, 1988), 65–134, and David Stockton, *The Classical Athenian Democracy* (Oxford: Oxford University Press, 1990), 65–116.

29. Stockton, *Classical Athenian Democracy*, 57–67; David Whitehead, *The Demes of Attica: 508/7–ca. 250 B.C.* (Princeton, NJ: Princeton University Press, 1986), esp. pt. 3.

30. Ober, *Mass and Elite*, 97.

31. B. Strauss, "On Aristotle's Critique," 228, 229; see also Hansen, *Athenian Democracy*, 65, 94–95.

32. Ober, *Mass and Elite*, 111.

33. R. Sinclair, *Democracy and Participation in Athens*, 52–60; Stockton, *Classical Athenian Democracy*, 45–46, 78–82, 101–102.

34. See B. Strauss, "On Aristotle's Critique," 213–214.

35. Ober, *Mass and Elite*, 112.

36. Ibid., 99–100.

37. Examples would be Plato's *Republic* where the political arrangement turns entirely on the governing class and his *Laws* with its Nocturnal Council; Aristotle's definition of the citizen in terms of ruling and being ruled and his emphasis on the ruling group (*politeuma*) as defining the nature of a politeia.

38. Old Oligarch *Constitution of the Athenians* 5 (trans. slightly altered).

39. Plato *Republic* 3.416d–e; Aristotle. *Pol.* 1313a18–1315b10.

40. Aristot. *Pol.*, trans. T. A. Sinclair, rev. Trevor J. Saunders (Harmondsworth, UK: Penguin, 1981), 1328a28–30.

41. Ibid., 1277a13–15.

42. Aristot. *Pol.*, trans. Carnes Lord (Chicago: University of Chicago Press, 1984), 1277b29–30. See also 1279a33–35.

43. See Kurt A. Raaflaub, "Democracy, Oligarchy, and the Concept of the 'Free Citizen' in Late Fifth-Century Athens," *Political Theory* 11(1983): 517–544.

44. Gregory Vlastos, "Isonomia," *American Journal of Philology* 74 (1953): 337–366, and "Isonomia Politikë," in *Platonic Studies* (Princeton, NJ: Princeton University Press,

1973), 164–203. And see W. Robert Connor's note in *The New Politicians of Fifth-Century Athens* (Princeton, NJ: Princeton University Press, 1971), 202–206.

45. Old Oligarch *Constitution of the Athenians*, 2.

46. Aristot. *Pol.*, trans. Ernest Barker (Oxford: Oxford University Press, Clarendon Press, 1946), 1287a28–32.

47. Ibid., 1292a15–24.

48. Ibid., 1268a14–28. On Aristotle's association of "extreme democracy" with the superiority of decrees over the established laws, see B. Strauss, "On Aristotle's Critique," 215–219.

49. On the idea of form, especially in its uses by Plato, see William K. C. Guthrie, *A History of Greek Philosophy* (Cambridge: Cambridge University Press, 1978), 5: 147–154, (1981), 6:100–105, 243–246.

50. Aristot. *Pol.* 1292a5–35.

51. On the various usages connected with democracy, see R. Sinclair, *Democracy and Participation*, 13–17; Raphael Sealey, "The Origins of Demokratia," *California Studies in Classical Antiquity* 6 (1973): 253–295; and particularly helpful, Charles W. Fornara and Loren J. Samons II, *Athens from Cleisthenes to Pericles* (Berkeley: University of California Press, 1991), chap. 2.

52. Plato *Rep.* 8.557A.

53. In *Politicus*, Plato still treats democracy at arm's length. He concedes that it is a kind of constitution but only barely. Unlike monarchy and aristocracy, which can be perverted into tyranny and oligarchy, democracy remains democracy, whether it is lawless or law abiding (291e–292a). Only toward the end of that dialogue does he concede that if the choice were between the three lawless types—tyranny, oligarchy, and democracy—it is better to live under democracy (303a–b). Thus Plato could be summarized: Democracy is the worst of the best forms and the best of the worst.

54. For details, see Glenn Morrow, *Plato's Cretan City: A Historical Interpretation of "The Laws"* (Princeton, NJ: Princeton University Press, 1960), esp. 229–233.

55. Leo Strauss asserted, with scant evidence, that Plato's account of rule by the strongest was an allusion to democracy; see his *Argument and Action of Plato's "Laws"* (Chicago: University of Chicago Press, 1975), 47. See also R. F. Stalley, *An Introduction to Plato's "Laws"* (Indianapolis: Hackett, 1983), 73.

56. See Plato *Rep.* 4.420b–c, where Socrates insists that the aim of a politeia is not the happiness of one class but of the whole.

57. Aristot. *Pol.* 1295a25–33, 1277b33–1278a12.

58. Thus in the course of Aristotle's several stipulations about what a constitution is, he remarks that in every constitution the citizen body (*politeuma*) is sovereign and that the politeuma is the politeia; then he applies those formulas to oligarchies and democracies while silently passing over monarchy, even though monarchy is included among the rightly ordered constitutions. Obviously it is awkward to find a place for an Aristotelian politeuma in a monarchy.

59. Aristot. *Pol.* 1278a1–13, 1280b32–1281a8.

60. Old Oligarch *Constitution of the Athenians* 9.

61. Aristot. *Pol.* 1278b10–11.

62. T. Sinclair trans.

63. Herodotus *Histories* 3.80.

64. Thuc. *History* 6.39.

65. One of the best formulations of this point is in Cicero, *De re publica* 1.31–32.

66. Aristot. *Pol.* 1252a17–24.

67. John Locke, *Two Treatises of Government*, 2.107, 110, 111.

68. Polybius *Histories* 6.9.4–5.

69. See G. W. Trompf, *The Idea of Historical Recurrence in Western Thought* (Berkeley: University of California Press, 1979).

70. Poly. *Histories* 6.9.1–4, trans. Kurt von Fritz, *The Theory of the Mixed Constitution in Antiquity* (New York: Columbia University Press, 1954), 363.

71. Locke, *Two Treatises of Government*, 2, 110.

CHAPTER 5

Fugitive Democracy

1. I have discussed this topic at greater length in an essay, "Norm and Form," to appear in a volume on Athenian democracy edited by Ober, Euben, and Wallach.

2. Hobbes, *Leviathan*, ed. Oakeshott, 83.

3. Mary Douglas, *Purity and Danger: An Analysis of Concepts of Pollution and Taboo* (Harmondsworth, UK: Penguin, 1966, 1970), especially p. 137 ff.

4. For a fuller discussion, see my "Democracy, Difference, and Re-Cognition," *Political Theory* 21 1993): 464–483.

5. The concept of *techne* will be treated at full length in John Wallach's forthcoming *The Platonic Political Art*.

6. The classic discussion of this contradiction remains Marx's "On the Jewish Question."

7. See William E. Connolly, *Identity/Difference. Democratic Negotiations of Political Paradox* (Ithaca, NY: Cornell University Press, 1991).

8. Jean Bodin, *Six Books of the Commonwealth*, trans. M. J. Tooley, (Oxford: Blackwell, n.d.). Bk. 6, ch. 4, pp. 192–193.

9. *The Federalist*, ed. Jabob Cooke (Middletown, Conn.: Wesleyan University Press, 1961), no. 10, p. 61.

10. For Tocqueville's complaint, see Jean-Claude Lamberti, *Tocqueville et les Deux Democraties* (Paris, 1983), 180. For Tocqueville's dissociation of American democracy from revolution see *Oeuvres Completès*, ed. J.-P. Mayer, 1:14.

11. I have discussed Plato and Aristotle's treatment of democracy more fully in my essay "Norm and Form." The quotation from Plato's *Republic* follows the Shorey translation in the Loeb series.

12. Aristotle, *Politics* III.vi. 1278b6–1278bl5: "Now in every case the citizen body of a state is sovereign; the citizen body is the constitution. Thus in democracies the people are sovereign, in oligarchies the few" (Sinclair translation, revised by Saunders, Penguin ed.).

13. "Democracy is the generic constitution . . . [It] is the resolved mystery of all constitutions." Karl Marx, *A Critique of Hegel's "Philosophy of Right,"* ed. Joseph O'Malley (Cambridge: Cambridge University Press, 1970), 29–30.

14. On this topic in the ancient world see G.E.M. de Ste. Croix, *The Class Struggle in the Ancient World* (London, 1981), 278–300.

15. Locke, *Two Treatises of Government* 11: 124–126. The enlarged political reemerges when Locke discusses the right of revolution in terms of "the Majority of the People" (11.209).

16. Athenian democracy of the fifth century resorted to heroic measures—lot, rotation, ostracism—to preserve direct democracy, but in the next century it, too, began to exhibit symptoms of Michels's Iron Law of Oligarchy. See Josiah Ober, *Mass and Elite in Democratic Athens* (Princeton, NJ: Princeton University Press, 1989).

17. See, e.g., Plato, *Republic* 7.563e–564a; *Laws* 701a; Polybius, *The Histories* 7.9; Philo, *De Confusione Linguaram* 23.108; *De Fuga et Inventione* 2.10; John Calvin, *Institutes of the Christian Religion* 4.20.8; Sir Thomas Elyot, *The Book named The Governor* 1.1; Claude de Seyssel, *The Monorchy of France* 1.1; David Hume, "Of the Populousness of Ancient Nations," in *Essays, Moral, Political and Literary* (Oxford: Oxford University Press, 1963), p. 374; and *The Federalist*, no 10, p. 61, and no. 14, p. 84.

18. Plato, *Republic*, VIII:557E–558A; and see *Laws*, III693D.

19. Tocqueville. *Journey to America*, ed. J. P. Mayer (New Haven, Conn.: Yale University Press, 1959), 51, 156.

20. Editor's note: the last three paragraphs of this essay mirror those of "Norm and Form." The repetition has been allowed to stand.

21. *Oxford English Dictionary*, entry 2 under "solidarity."

CHAPTER 6
Hobbes and the Epic Tradition of Political Theory

Note: This essay is a revision of a lecture delivered at the William Andrews Clark Memorial Library. I wish to express my thanks to the staff of the Library, especially to Mr. William E. Conway, and the faculty of the University of California, Los Angeles, for making the occasion a pleasant and memorable one for me.

1. H. Warrender, *The Political Philosophy of Hobbes* (Oxford, 1957); F. C. Hood, *The Divine Politics of Thomas Hobbes* (Oxford, 1964); J.W.N. Watkins, *Hobbes's System of Ideas* (London, 1965); *Hobbes Studies*, ed. K. C. Brown (Oxford 1965); M. M. Goldsmith, *Hobbes's Science of Politics* (New York and London, 1966); F. S. McNeilly, *The Anatomy of Leviathan* (New York, 1968); H. Pitkin, *The Concept of Representation* (Berkeley, 1967).

2. Thomas Hobbes, *Leviathan*, ed. M. Oakeshott (Blackwell, Oxford, n.d.) pp. 29–30, 396.

3. L. Strauss, *The Political Philosophy of Hobbes* (Oxford, 1936); R. Polin, *Politique et philosophic chez Thomas Hobbes* (Paris, 1953); M. Oakeshott, *supra*, and "The Moral Life in the Writings of Thomas Hobbes," *Rationalism in Politics and other Essays* (London, 1962); C. B. Macpherson, *The Theory of Possessive Individualism* (Oxford, 1962), ch. ii.

4. *History of the Peloponnesian Wars* I. 23.5.

5. *The Republic of Plato*, trans. F. M. Cornford (New York and London, 1945), 496D–497A.

6. Ibid., 591A–592B.

7. Ibid., 473A.

8. *Laws*, 702E.

9. *Discorsi sopra la prima deca di Tito Livio*, Lib. I (pref.).

10. *Works*, ed. Bowring (11 vols., Edinburgh, 1838–1843), I, 193.

11. Cited in G. W. Pierson, *Tocqueville in America*, ed. D. C. Lunt (New York, 1959), p. 18; Letter to Kergolay, July 6, 1835, *Memoirs, Letters, and Remains* (2 vols., Boston, 1862), I, 303.

12. R. Dahl, *Modern Political Analysis* (New York, 1963), p. 8.

13. The dispute is discussed in W. Jaeger, *Paideia*, 2nd ed., trans. G. Highet (3 vols., New York, 1944), I, 77 ff, 99 ff, 208 ff; II, 214 ff; 348 ff; E. Havelock, *Preface to Plato* (Cambridge, Mass., 1963), *passim*.

14. *Rep.*, 599E–600A; *Ion* 537A ff.

15. *Statesman*, trans. Skemp (New Haven, Conn., 1952), 259b–c, 292e–293a.

16. Ibid., 259d.

17. See my discussion of "Paradigms and Political Theories," *Politics and Experience*, ed. P. King and B. C. Parekh (Cambridge, 1968), pp. 125–152.

18. "It is the function of science to understand and interpret the world, not to change it. A science of politics which deserves its name must build from the bottom up by asking simple questions that can, in principle, be answered: it cannot be built from the top down by asking questions that, one has reason to suspect, cannot be answered at all, at least not by the methods of science. An empirical discipline is built by the slow, modest, and piecemeal cumulation of relevant theories and data." H. Eulau, *The Behavioral Persuasion in Politics* (New York, 1963), p. 9; see also R. Dahl, *Preface to Democratic Theory* (Chicago, 1956), p. 2.

19. G. S. Kirk and J. E. Raven, *The Presocratic Philosophies* (Cambridge, 1960), p. 103 (fr. 100).

20. *Rep.*, 473C–474A.

21. Ibid., 599D–E.

22. Bacon, *Works*, ed. Spedding, Ellis, and Heath. (14 vols., London, 1857–74), III, 475.

23. *Tractatus Politicus*, cap. in *Benedict Spinoza: The Political Worlds*, trans. A. G. Wernham (Oxford, 1958), p. 261.

24. D. G. James, *The Life of Reason: Hobbes, Locke, Bolingbroke* (London, 1949), pp. 2–11; L. Strauss, *The Political Philosophy of Hobbes* (Oxford, 1936), pp. 44 ff; F. Tönnies, *Thomas Hobbes: Leben und Lehre*, 3rd ed. (Stuttgart, 1925), pp. 4–8.

25. *Aubrey's Brief Lives*, ed. O. L. Dick (London, 1949), p. 150.

26. See E.M.W. Tillyard, *The English Epic and Its Background* (London, 1966, first publ. 1954), p. 40.

27. F. M. Cornford, *Thucydides Mythistoricus* (London 1907), pp. 129 ff; J. H. Finley, Jr., *Thucydides* (Cambridge, Mass., 1942), p. 322.

28. *English Works*, ed. Sir William Molesworth (London, 1839–45), VIII, v–vii.

29. *A Briefe of the Art of Rhetorique*, based on Aristotle, was entered in the Stationer's Register in 1636.

30. R. L. Brett, "Thomas Hobbes," *The English Mind: Studies in the English Moralists presented to Basil Willey* (Cambridge, 1964), p. 35.

31. *E.W.*, X, x.

32. I have relied on the translation of B. Farrington which appeared in the *Rationalist Annual* for 1958 (London, 1957), pp. 22 ff.

33. C. M. Bowra, *Heroic Poetry* (London, 1952), p. 13. A slightly different emphasis is given in J. de Vries, *Heroic Song and Heroic Legend*, trans. B. J. Timmer (London, 1963), pp. 186–191.

34. Farrington, *Rationalist Annual*, p. 26.

35. *E.W.* IV, 415.

36. *Leviathan*, pp. 36, 42.

37. Ibid., pp. 214, 218, 398; *De Cive*, Preface to Reader, pp. 7–8.

38. *Lev.*, p. 442.

39. *Lev.*, p. 424; *Cive*, Ep. Ded., p. 3; *Elements of Law*, I, xiii, 3–4; *E.W.*, 1, 7–9.

40. *Thomas Hobbes: Body, Man, and Citizen*, ed. R. S. Peters (New York, 1962), p. 24.

41. Ibid., pp. 27–28.

42. *Lev.*, p. 424.

43. *E.W.*, 1, 7.

44. *From Max Weber*, ed. H. H. Gerth and C. W. Mills (New York, 1946), p. 139.

45. Farrington, *Rationalist Annual*, pp. 26–27.

46. *Lev.*, pp. 215–216.

47. Ibid., p. 397.

48. Ibid.

49. Bowra, *Heroic Poetry*, p. 154. See also de Vries, *Heroic Song and Heroic Legend*, pp. 210 ff, for a discussion of "the pattern of an heroic life."

50. *Cive*, p. 7. There is a great deal of interesting and important material on the relationship between logic, method, and rhetoric in W. S. Howell, *Logic and Rhetoric in England, 1500–1700* (Princeton, NJ, 1956), especially pp. 364–391.

51. *Lev.*, p. 436.

52. Ibid.

53. Ibid., p. 6.

54. Ibid., p. 220.

55. Ibid., p. 30.

56. Ibid., p. 5.

57. Ibid., p. 209.

58. Ibid., pp. 209–210.

59. Ibid., p. 82.

60. Ibid., pp. 104, 110.

61. Ibid., pp. 15–17.

62. Ibid., p. 136.

63. Ibid., p. 100.

64. Ibid., p. 210.

65. Ibid., p. 63.

66. Ibid., p. 104.

67. Ibid., p. 99.

68. Ibid., p. 46.

69. Ibid., p. 104.

70. Ibid., p. 119.

71. Ibid., p. 2.

72. Ibid., pp. 39, 63–64.

73. Ibid., p. 30.

74. Ibid., p. 29.

75. Ibid., pp. 42–43.

76. Ibid., pp. 30, 43, 46.

77. Ibid., p. 46.

78. Ibid., p. 46.

79. Ibid., pp. 14–15.

80. *El. of Law*, p. 51.

81. Ibid., Ep. Ded., p. xvii, and pp. 1, 50–51.

82. Ibid., pp. 50–51.

83. *Lev.*, p. 25.

84. Ibid., pp. 21, 29.

85. Ibid., pp. 35, 57.

86. Among the several helpful discussions of "imagination" the following are particularly relevant to Hobbes: C. D. Thorpe, *The Aesthetic Theory of Thomas Hobbes* (Ann Arbor, 1940), especially ch. III; C. M. Dowlin, *Sir William Davenant's "Gondibert," Its Preface, and Hobbes's Answer* (Philadelphia, 1934). Also suggestive are Addison's essay 409 in *The Spectator* and the recent comments by C. D. Thorpe, "Addison's Contribution to Criticism," *The Seventeenth Century*, R. F. Jones et al. (London and Stanford, 1951, 1969), pp. 316–329. Finally, J. E. Spingarn, *Critical Essays of the 17th Century* (3 vols., London, 1908–09), I, ix–xxxvi, lviii–lxiii.

87. *El. of Law*, pp. 6–7, 11.

88. Ibid., p. 38 (I, X, 4).

89. *E.W.*, IV, 449–452; see also Ibid., X, v.

90. Ibid., IV, 452–454.

91. *Lev.*, pp. 43–46.

92. Ibid., p. 44.

93. Farrington, *Rationalist Annual*, p. 24.

94. Peters, *Thomas Hobbes*, p. 28.

95. Ibid., pp. 27–28.

96. *Lev.*, p. 129.

97. Ibid., p. 241.

98. *Rep.*, 521A–B.

99. *Lev.*, p. 241.

100. See H. R. Trevor-Roper, "Clarendon and the Practice of History" (William Andrews Clark Memorial Library, University of California, Los Angeles, 1965); B.H.G. Wormald, *Clarendon, Politics, History and Religion 1640–1660* (Cambridge, 1951), pp. 165–166, 221–222; John Bowle, *Hobbes and His Critics: A Study in Seventeenth Century Constitutionalism* (London, 1951), pp. 157 ff.

101. *Lev.*, p. 229.

102. Ibid., pp. 43–45, 169–170.

103. Ibid., p. 169.

104. Ibid., pp. 169–170.

105. Ibid., p. 170.

106. Ibid., p. 230.

107. Ibid., p. 170.

108. Ibid., pp. 172, 220.

109. Ibid., p. 241.

110. Ibid., pp. 219–222.

111. Ibid., pp. 224, 437–439.

112. Ibid., pp. 224–225.

113. Ibid., p. 225.

114. Bowra, *Heroic Poetry*, p. 94.

115. Farrington, *Rationalist Annual*, pp. 23–24.

116. Ibid., p. 26.

CHAPTER 7

Hobbes and the Culture of Despotism

1. Karl Popper, *The Open Society and Its Enemies*, 2 vols. (London: Routledge, 1945), 2: 210.

2. Karl Popper, *Logic of Discovery* (New York: Basic Books, 1959), p. 80.

3. Popper, *Open Society*, 1:139, 143.

4. Ibid., 2:209, 210.

5. Ibid., 2:205, 206.

6. Ibid., 2:207, 208.

7. Popper, *Logic of Discovery*, p. 16 (italics in original).

8. Popper, *Open Society*, 1:147.

9. This is the type of argument to be found in Niklas Luhmann, *Soziale Systeme* (Frankfurt: Suhrkamp, 1984). See the critique by Jürgen Habermas, *The Philosophical Discourse of Modernity: Twelve Lectures*, trans. Frederick Lawrence (Cambridge, Mass.: MIT Press, 1987).

10. Gary B. Deason, "Reformation Theology and the Mechanistic Conception of Nature," in *God and Nature: Historical Essays on the Encounter between Christianity and Science*, ed. David C. Lindberg and Ronald L. Numbers (Berkeley: University of California Press, 1986), pp. 168–169.

11. For a recent example see Daniel J. Kevles, *The Physicists: The History of a Scientific Community in Modern America* (Cambridge, Mass.: Harvard University Press, 1971). Kevles says of his book, "It addresses how physicists overcame the difficulties of pure science in the American democratic culture to win world leadership in their discipline and recognition as assets to the modern American state. It is occupied with how they acquired power" (p. ix). For an earlier period see the studies by Margaret C. Jacob, *The Newtonians and the English Revolution, 1689–1720* (Ithaca, NY: Cornell University Press, 1976); and by J. R. Jacob, *Robert Boyle and the English Revolution: A Study in Social and Intellectual Change* (New York: Burt Franklin, 1977).

12. Plato, *Republic* 414b–e. Plato does suggest, though haltingly, that "if possible" the rulers were to be persuaded of the falsehood "but failing that the rest of the city."

13. Montesquieu, *Esprit des Lois* III, 8–10; IV. 12–16; VI. 2.

14. See Leonard Krieger, *An Essay on the Theory of Enlightened Despotism* (Chicago: University of Chicago Press, 1975). See also Melvin Richter, "Despotism," *Dictionary of the History of Ideas*, 5 vols. (New York: Scribner, 1974), 2:1–18. Richter argues (p. 12) unpersuasively that "it is now generally agreed that there is no body of political ideas in the eighteenth century that can accurately be described as 'enlightened despotism,' a term invented by nineteenth century German historians."

15. See Charles F. Bahmueller, *The National Charity Company: Jeremy Bentham's Silent Revolution* (Berkeley: University of California Press, 1981).

16. Locke denied that despotic rule was a form of government and he associated it with tyranny. He recognized a legitimate moment in despotism in the case of a conqueror involved in a just war. Locke insisted, however, that justifiable conquest created rights only over those who had instigated or actively waged the unjust war. *Two Treatises of Government*, "Second Treatise," secs. 174–176, 196, 199. Compare Hobbes, *Leviathan*,

ed. C. B. Macpherson (Harmondsworth, UK: Penguin, 1968). All references to *Leviathan* will be to this edition.

Mario A. Cattaneo has attempted to relate Hobbes's thinking to eighteenth-century currents of enlightened despotism, but he has argued that both should be interpreted as promoting the rule of law. See his article, "Hobbes Théoricien de l'Absolutisme Éclairé," in *Hobbes-Forschungen*, ed. R. Koselleck and R. Schnu (Berlin: Duncker & Humblot, 1969), pp. 199–210. For a recent discussion of the meaning of absolutism in Hobbes's writings see Raymond Polin, *Hobbes, Dieu, et les Hommes* (Paris: Presses Universitaires de France, 1981), p. 105ff. Michel Malherbe's chapter on "La Science de la Nature" in his *Thomas Hobbes ou l'Œuvre de la Raison* (Paris: J. Vrin, 1984), p. 89ff, is also useful. Judging from the absence of entries on the scientific aspects of Hobbes's thought as reported by Bernard Willms, "Der Weg des Leviathan: Die Hobbes-Forschung von 1968–1978," *Der Staat: Zeitschrift für Staatslehre Öffentliches Recht und Verfassungsgeschichte*, Beiheft 3 (1979), there has been a decline of interest in the political implications of Hobbesian science. However, students of the history of science have recently become concerned with Hobbes's critique of the experimental method. See especially Steven Shapin and Simon Schaffer, *Leviathan and the Air-Pump: Hobbes, Boyle, and the Experimental Life* (Princeton, NJ: Princeton University Press, 1985).

17. I owe a great deal indirectly to the work of Francis Oakley. See his *Omnipotence, Covenant, and Order: An Excursion in the History of Ideas from Abelard to Leibnitz* (Ithaca, NY: Cornell University Press, 1984), and "Christian Theology and the Newtonian Science: The Rise of the Concept of the Laws of Nature," *Church History* 30 (1961): 433–455.

18. Jean le Rond d'Alembert, *Preliminary Discourse to the Encyclopedia of Diderot*, trans. Richard N. Schwab and Walter E. Rex (Indianapolis: Bobbs-Merrill, 1963), pp. 22, 29.

19. On Condorcet see Keith M. Baker's fine study, *Condorcet: From Natural Philosophy to Social Mathematics* (Chicago: University of Chicago Press, 1975).

20. "Six Lessons to the Professors of the Mathematics," in *The English Works of Thomas Hobbes*, ed. Sir William Molesworth, 11 vol. (London: John Bohm, 1839–1845), 7: 183–84; *De Cive* in *Philosophical Works of Thomas Hobbes*, ed. Howard Warrender (Oxford: Clarendon Press, 1983–), 3:44.

21. *De Cive*, 3:31–32.

22. *Leviathan*, Introduction, p. 81.

23. Ibid., ch. 17, p. 227.

24. R. Koebner, "Despot and Despotism," *Journal of the Warburg and Courtauld Institute* 14 (1951):288.

25. *De Corpore*, in *Body, Mind, and Citizen*, ed. Richard S. Peters (New York: Collier, 1962), ch. I.6., p. 27.

26. *De Cive* II. x. 8.

27. *Leviathan*, ch. 5, pp. 116–117.

28. Ibid., ch. 5, p. 114.

29. Ibid., ch. 15, p. 216.

30. Ibid., ch. 21, pp. 263–264.

31. Ibid, ch. 18, p. 233.

32. Ibid., ch. 5, p. 115.

33. "Six Lessons to the Professors of the Mathematics," in *English Works*, 7: 183–184.

34. Thomas Hobbes, *De Homine*, in *Man and Citizen*, ed. Bernard Gert (Garden City, N.Y.: Doubleday, 1972), 10, secs. 4–5, pp. 41–43.

35. The quotation is attributed to Nietzsche by Georges Bataille, *Visions of Excess, 1927–1939*, ed. Allan Stoekl (Minneapolis: University of Minnesota Press, 1985), p. 197, but the reference given does not confirm the quotation literally.

36. See the famous comparison made by the fifteenth-century jurist Sir John Fortescue between the impoverished condition of French society under absolute monarchy and the prosperity of England under a constrained monarchy in *De Laudibus Legum Anglie*, ed. S. B. Chrimes (Cambridge: Cambridge University Press, 1949), ch. 29, pp. 35–36.

37. For Hobbes's discussion of "systems" see *Leviathan*, ch. 22, p. 274.

38. *Leviathan*, Introduction, pp. 81–82. Compare Thomas Starkey, *A Dialogue Between Reginald Pole and Thomas Lupset*, ed. Kathleen M. Burton (London: Chatto and Windus, 1948), pp. 61–62, 95–97.

39. *Leviathan*, ch. 29, p. 363.

40. See ibid., ch. 30, titled "Of the Office of the Sovereign Representative."

41. Ibid., Epistle Dedicatory, p. 75.

42. Ibid., ch. 20, p. 256.

43. Ibid., ch. 19, p. 240.

44. Ibid.

45. Ibid., Introduction, p. 82; *De Corpore*, ch. I.I., pp. 277–278.

46. *De Corpore*, ch. I.I., pp. 277–278.

47. *De Cive*, 3:138.

48. *Leviathan*, ch. 20, p. 260.

49. Ibid., ch. 21, p. 264.

50. *De Corpore*, ch. 10.5, p. 122.

51. *Leviathan*, ch. 4, p. 104.

52. *De Homine*, ch. 10, sec. 5, p. 41.

53. *Leviathan*, ch. 21, p. 263.

54. Ibid., ch. 18, p. 237 (marginal note).

55. Ibid., ch. 21, p. 264.

56. Ibid.

57. Ibid, ch. 21, p. 262.

58. Thomas Hobbes, *The Elements of Law, Natural and Politic*, ed. Ferdinand Tönnies (Cambridge: Cambridge University Press, 1928), pt. 1, ch. 1, secs. 6–8, pp. 1–11.

59. *Elements of Law*, pt. 1, ch. 9, sec. 21, p. 36.

60. *Leviathan*, ch. 6, p. 130.

61. Ibid., ch. 21, p. 263.

62. Ibid., ch. 14, p. 189; ch. 21, p. 261.

63. Ibid., ch. 21, p. 261.

64. *De Homine*, ch. 11, sec. 15, p. 54.

65. *Leviathan*, ch. 30, p. 388.

66. Ibid., ch. 30, p. 376.

67. *Elements of Law*, pt. 1, ch. 7, sec. 7, p. 23.

68. *Leviathan*, ch. 26, p. 315.

69. *De Corpore*, ch. 10.1–4, pp. 121–122.

70. *Leviathan*, ch. 14, pp. 189, 190.

71. Ibid., ch. 8, p. 139.

72. Ibid., ch. 11, pp. 160–161.

73. Ibid., ch. 11, pp. 160, 161.

74. Ibid., ch. 12, p. 183.

75. Ibid., ch. 6, p. 120.

76. Ibid., Introduction, p. 81.

77. *De Cive*, 3:44.

78. *Leviathan*, ch. 14, pp. 189ff.

79. Ibid., ch. 15, p. 209.

80. Ibid., ch. 30, pp. 384–385.

81. Ibid., ch. 30, p. 379.

82. *Elements of Law*, pt. 2, ch. 9, sec. 8.

83. *Leviathan*, ch. 15, p. 211.

84. Ibid.

85. Ibid.

CHAPTER 8

On Reading Marx Politically

1. *Capital: A Critique of Political Economy*, ed. F. Engels, tr. S. Moore and E. Aveling, 3 vols. (New York: International Publishers, 1967), Vol. I, p. 11.

2. *A Contribution to the Critique of Political Economy*, ed. M. Dobb, tr. S. W. Rayzan-skaya (New York: International Publishers, 1970), p. 23. Hereafter this will be cited as *CCPE*.

3. Karl Marx and Frederick Engels, *Collected Works* (New York: International Publish-ers, 1975–), Vol. I, pp. 84–86, 492.

4. Note the analogy Marx drew with Themistocles, who urged the Athenians to aban-don their city and "found a new Athens at sea, in another element." Ibid., p. 492.

5. Marx-Engels, *Collected Works*, Vol. I, p. 85.

6. *First Thesis on Feuerbach*.

7. *Second Thesis on Feuerbach*.

8. *Nicomachean Ethics*, Bk. X, chs. 7–9. For a close discussion see B. Eriksen, *Bios The-oretikos* (Oslo: Oxford University Press, 1976); W.F.R. Hardie, *Aristotle's Ethical Theory*, 2nd ed. (Oxford: Oxford University Press, 1980), pp. 345 ff.

9. *Hegel's Philosophy of Right*, tr. T. M. Knox. (Oxford: Oxford University Press, 1942), pp. 12–13.

10. See, among countless early examples, the Pythagorean fragment in *The Presocratic Philosophers*, ed. G. S. Kirk and J. E. Raven (Cambridge, Cambridge University Press, 1957), p. 228 (fr. 278).

11. "The Leading Article in No. 179 of the *Kölnische Zeitung*," Marx and Engels, *Col-lected Works*, Vol. I, p. 195.

12. Ibid.

13. Marx, "Feelings," *Collected Works*, Vol. I, p. 526 (from a poem of 1836).

14. Ibid., p. 195.

15. Ibid., pp. 191–192.

16. For various views on the importance of these works see the following: Louis Al-thusser, *For Marx*, tr. Ben Brewster (London: Allen Lane, 1969), Chs. 2, 5, 7; B. Ollman, *Alienation* (Cambridge: Cambridge University Press, 1971), pp. x ff.; Istvan Meszaros, *Marx's Theory of Alienation* (London: Merlin Press, 1970), especially Pt. III; Erich Fromm,

Marx's Concept of Man (New York: McGraw Hill, 1961), pp. v ff.; David McLellan, *Marx's "Grundrisse"* (New York: Harper, 1971), pp. 12–15.

17. *The German Ideology*, tr. S. Rayzanskaya (Moscow: International Publishers, 1964), p. 50. Hereafter cited as *GI*. The concept of the "whole" in Marx has been suggestively developed by George Lukacs, *History and Class Consciousness*, tr. Rodney Livingstone (London: Merlin Press, 1971) in the essay, "Reification and the Consciousness of the Proletariat."

18. *Capital*, Vol. I, p. 21. The citation is from Marx's Preface to the French edition of *Capital*.

19. *CCPE*, p. 19.

20. Cited in McLellan, *Grundrisse*, p. 6.

21. *Karl Marx, Early Writings*, ed. T. B. Bottomore (New York: McGraw Hill, 1964), p. 63. Hereafter this will be cited as *Early Writings*.

22. Cited in Franz Mehring, *Karl Marx: The Story of His Life*, tr. E. Fitzgerald (Ann Arbor: University of Michigan Press, 1962), p. 341.

23. "Manifesto of the Communist Party," *Marx and Engels: Basic Writings on Politics and Philosophy*, ed. Lewis Feuer (Garden City, NY: Doubleday, 1959), p. 12.

24. Ibid., p. 13

25. Letter of Feb. 22, 1858, Karl Marx and Frederick Engels, *Selected Correspondence* (Moscow: International Publishers, n.d.), p. 124. Hereafter this will be cited as *Sel. Corr.*

26. As is well known, only the publication of the first volume of *Capital* was supervised by Marx; the other two volumes were edited by Engels. *Theories of Surplus Value* is considered to be "the first and only draft of the fourth, concluding volume of 'Capital.'" See the edition translated by Emile Burns and edited by S. Ryazanskaya (London: International Publishers, 1963), Vol. I, p. 14.

27. *GI*, p. 255.

28. Karl Marx and Friedrich Engels, *Werke*, 39 vols. (Berlin, 1956), Vol. 27, p. 228. Hereafter this will be cited as *MEW*.

29. *Capital*, Vol. III, p. 266.

30. *Early Writings*, p. 151.

31. "Political economy . . . can be considered as both a product of the real *dynamism* and *development* of private property, a product of modern *industry*, and a force which has accelerated and extolled the dynamism and development of industry and has made it a power in the domain of *consciousness* . . . it is always empirical businessmen we refer to when we speak of economists, who are their *scientific* self-revelation and existence." *Early Writings*, pp. 147, 170.

32. The concept of the "civilization" of capitalism appeared most prominently in Marx's *Grundrisse*. See *Grundrisse der Kritik der Politischen Ökonomie* (Berlin: Deitz, 1953, and Europäische Verlagsanstalt Frankfurt), pp. 312 ff.

33. "Bourgeois society is the most advanced and complex historical organization of production. The categories which express its relations, and an understanding of its structure, therefore, provide an insight into the structure and the relations of production of all formerly existing social formations, the ruins and component elements of which were used in the creation of bourgeois society. Some of these unassimilated remains are still carried on within bourgeois society, others, however, which previously existed only in rudimentary form, have been further developed and have attained their full significance, etc." *CCPE*, pp. 210–211.

34. *The Eighteenth Brumaire of Louis Bonaparte* in *Karl Marx: Selected Works*, ed. V. Adoratsky, 2 vols. (Moscow: International Publishers, n.d.), Vol. II, p. 315. Hereafter these volumes will be cited as *SW*.

35. "Critique of the Gotha Program," *SW*, Vol. II, p. 563.

36. *The Poverty of Philosophy*, ed. C. P. Dutt and V. Chattopadhyaya (New York: International Publishers, n.d.), pp. 90, 93.

37. These characteristics were exhibited very early. See his protests against the Hegelian Left for its superficial use of socialist and communist ideas in Lloyd P. Easton and Kurt H. Goddat, *Writings of the Young Marx on Philosophy and Society* (Garden City, NY: Doubleday, 1967), pp. 134–135; David McLellan, *Karl Marx: His Life and Thought* (London and Basingstoke: Macmillan, 1973), p. 58.

38. The most awesome example of this is Marx's *Theories of Surplus Value*. It should also be noted that at one time Marx contemplated writing a history of economic theories.

39. See *The Holy Family* (Moscow: International Publishers, 1956), pp. 168–205.

40. See Marx's "Communism and the Augsburg *Allgemeine Zeitung*," *Collected Works*, Vol. I, pp. 220–221.

41. *MEW*, Vol. 27, pp. 233 ff.

42. *CCPE*, pp. 22, 23.

43. *Grundrisse: Foundations of the Critique of Political Economy (Rough Draft)*, tr. Martin Nicolaus (London: Allen Lane, 1973), p. 159. Emphasis added.

44. *Grundrisse*, tr. David McLellan, p. 67. The Nicolaus translation (p. 162) is nearly unintelligible.

45. Ibid., pp. 334, 341 (Nicolaus trans.).

46. Ibid., p. 488 (Nicolaus trans.). Emphasis in original.

47. *Critique of Hegel's "Philosophy of Right,"* ed. Joseph O'Malley (Cambridge: Cambridge University Press, 1970), Introduction, pp. 140–142. Hereafter cited as *CHPR*.

48. *The Cologne Communist Trial*, tr. Rodney Livingston (New York: International Publishers, 1971), p. 62. This is part of some remarks made by Marx before the London central committee of the German Communist society in 1850.

49. *Early Writings*, p. 59.

50. *CHPR*. Introduction, pp. 132, 135, 139, 142.

51. *Pov. of Phil.*, p. 146.

52. *GI*, pp. 46, 50; *Birth of the Communist Manifesto*, ed. Dirk J. Struik (New York, 1971), p. 19 (hereafter cited as *Man.*). *Pov. of Phil.*, p. 147.

53. *GI*, pp. 46–47.

54. Ibid., p. 46.

55. Ibid., p. 47; *Man.*, pp. 12–13; *Pov. of Phil.*, pp. 146–147.

56. *Pov. of Phil*, p. 93.

57. *Man.*, pp. 15, 17, 19.

58. *The Holy Family*, in Karl Marx and Frederick Engels, *Collected Works*, Vol. 4, p. 35.

59. My translation. The Moscow translation renders "darum sich selbst aufhebende Entmenschung" as "therefore self-abolishing" and thus creates a gratuitous determinism.

60. *Holy Family*, p. 37.

61. Ibid. Emphasis in the original.

62. *GI*, pp. 43, 45, 81, 91; *Theses on Feuerbach*, IV.

63. *GI*, p. 76.

64. Ibid., p. 83.

65. Ibid., pp. 82–83.

66. Ibid., p. 83.

67. Ibid., pp. 83–84.

68. Ibid., p. 84.

69. Ibid., p. 86

70. *Selected Writings*, pp. 69, 85.

71. *SW*, Vol. I, p. 254.

72. Ibid., p. 257.

73. "Instructions for Delegates to the Geneva Conference," *The First International and After*, ed. David Fernbach (New York: Vintage, 1974), p. 91.

74. Ibid., p. 81.

75. *Capital*, Vol. I, p. 228.

76. Ibid., pp. 416–417.

77. Ibid., pp. 419, 420, 421.

78. *Grundrisse*, pp. 410, 228.

79. Ibid., p. 410.

80. Ibid.

81. *Capital*, Vol. I, p. 763.

82. Ibid., p. 8 (preface to first German edition).

83. Ibid., p. 763.

84. Ibid., Vol. III, p. 819.

85. Ibid., Vol. I, p. 85.

86. Ibid., pp. 189–190, 232–233.

87. *Grundrisse*, pp. 704, 705.

88. Ibid., p. 278.

89. Ibid., p. 415.

90. *Capital*, Vol. I, p. 421.

91. Ibid., p. 486.

92. Ibid., p. 605.

93. Maximilien Rubel, *Karl Marx: Essai de biographie intellectuelle* (Paris: Marcel Riviere, 1957), p. 435.

CHAPTER 9

Max Weber: Legitimation, Method, and the Politics of Theory

1. "Science as a Vocation," *From Max Weber Essays in Sociology*, trans. H. H. Gerth and C. Wright Mills (New York, 1946), p. 145. Hereafter this volume will be referred to as *FMW*.

2. *Sophists* 225 A–B. trans. A. E. Taylor (London, 1971).

3. *Nicomachean Ethics*, 1177b.25 ff., trans. M. Ostwald (Indianapolis, 1962).

4. "Heraclitus," frag. 253, *The Presocralic Philosophers*, ed. G. S. Kirk and J. E. Raven (Cambridge, 1957). p. 213.

5. *FMW*, p. 151.

6. "The Great Instauration," Preface in *Selected Writings of Francis Bacon*, ed. H. G. Dick (New York: Modern Library, 1955), p. 429.

7. Wolfgang Mommsen, *Max Weber und die deutsche Politik, 1890–1920* (Tübingen, 1959), p. 279. See also the fine study by David Beetham, *Max Weber and the Theory of*

Modern Politics (London, 1974); and Anthony Giddens, *Politics and Sociology in the Thought of Max Weber* (London, 1972).

8. *Economy and Society*, ed. Guenther Roth and Claus Wiltich, 2 vols. (New York, 1968), Vol. 1, p. 3. Hereafter this will be cited as *E & S*.

9. Ibid., p. 215.

10. Ibid.

11. Ibid., p. 3.

12. Max Weber, *The Theory of Social and Economic Organization* (New York, 1947), p. 152 (n. 83).

13. See the comments of the editors. *E & S*, Vol. 1, pp. lxxxviii–ix.

14. "Politics as a Vocation," *FMW*, pp. 121, 123.

15. Max Weber, *The Methodology of the Social Sciences*, trans. E. A. Shils and H. A. Finch (Glencoe, IL, 1949), p. 27. Hereafter referred to as *Methodology*.

16. *Methodology*, p. 17.

17. *E & S*, Vol. III, p. 1381.

18. *Methodology*, p. 74 ff.

19. Ibid., p. 76 (emphasis in original).

20. *Methodology*, p. 90 (emphasis in original).

21. Ibid., p. 18.

22. *FMW*, p. 128.

23. *Methodology*, p. 110 (emphasis in original).

24. Ibid., p. 81.

25. *Republic* 440 B, E, 442 B-D. See also Aristotle, *Nicomachean Ethics* 1.2. I094a27–I094b5.

26. *Gesammelte Politische Schriften*, 2nd ed., ed. J. Winckelmann (Tübingen, 1958), p. 1. Hereafter referred to as *GPS*.

27. Ibid., p. 20.

28. Ibid., p. 14 (emphasis in original).

29. Ibid., p. 12.

30. Ibid., pp. 12, 14.

31. *GPS*, p. 13.

32. Ibid., p. 14.

33. "Elbow-room in earthly existence will be won only by a hard struggle of man with man." Ibid., p. 12.

34. Examples of this genre are: W. G. Runciman, *A Critique of Max Weber's Philosophy of Social Science* (Cambridge, 1972); R. S. Rudner. *Philosophy of Social Science* (Englewood Cliffs, NJ, 1966), p. 68 ff; Dieter Hennch, *Die Einheit der Wissenschaftslehre* (Tübingen, 1952); and the introductory essays of Guy Okes to his translations of Weber's *Roscher and Knies* (New York, 1975) and *Critique of Stammler* (New York, 1977).

35. *The Protestant Ethic and the Spirit of Capitalism*, trans. Talcott Parsons (London, 1930). p. 78. Hereafter referred to as *PE*.

36. *PE*, p. 37.

37. See the translator's note, ibid., p. ix.

38. Ibid., pp. 117, 153.

39. *PE*, p. 180.

40. *Methodology*, p. 52.

41. *Methodology*, p. 57.

42. Ibid., p. 19.

43. *PE*, p. 154.

44. *FMW*, pp. 137, 138.

45. *PE*, pp. 56, 63, 13.

46. Ibid., p. 37.

47. *PE*, pp. 181–182.

48. *PE*, p. 182

49. *FMW*, pp. 137, 138.

50. *E & S*, Vol. I, p. 215.

51. Ibid. Note the personal remark in "Science as a Vocation" where Weber notes that in promoting young scholars he followed the practice that "a scholar promoted by me must legitimize and habilitate himself with *somebody else* at another university." *FMW*, p. 130.

52. *E & S*, Vol. 1, p. 215.

53. *FMW*, pp. 148, 153, 155.

54. Ibid., p. 134.

55. Ibid., p. 135.

56. Ibid., p. 136; *GAW*, p. 591.

57. Ibid. The scriptural passage that seems closest is Romans 3:24.

58. Fr. 345 in G. S. Kirk and J. E. Raven, *The Pre-socratic Philosophers* (Cambridge, 1957). p. 271.

59. Fr. 344 in Kirk and Raven, p. 269.

60. *Roscher and Knies*, p. 58.

61. *Methodology*, p. 116 (emphasis in original).

62. Ibid., p. 111.

63. Ibid., p. 112.

64. *Methodology*, p. 81 (emphasis in original).

65. *Methodology*, p. 105.

66. Ibid.

67. Ibid., p. 110.

68. *E & S*, Vol. I, p. 223.

69. *FMW*, p. 128; *E & S*, Vol. III, p. 1402.

70. *FMW*, pp. 139, 148.

71. Ibid., p.141

72. Ibid., p. 152.

73. *FMW*, p. 155.

74. *Ancient Judaism*, trans. H. H. Gerth and Don Martindale (Glencoe, 1L, 1952), p. 299. I have slightly revised the translation.

75. Ibid., pp. 301, 319.

76. *The Protestant Ethic*, pp. 28, 29.

77. Ibid., p. 29.

CHAPTER 10

Reason in Exile: Critical Theory and Technological Society

1. Max Horkheimer and Theodor Adorno, *The Dialectic of Enlightenment*, trans. John Cumming (1947; London: Allen Lane, 1973), p. 121. In this essay I do not attempt to

treat Horkheimer and Adorno as representatives of the Frankfurt School. I make occasional reference to Herbert Marcuse, who, although a longtime participant in the work of the Institute for Social Research, the School's formal organization, later developed a distinctive political and theoretical orientation that, in crucial respects, departed from Horkheimer and Adorno and took a more radical turn than Jürgen Habermas. Obviously space does not permit me to refine the numerous distinctions or to enter the necessary qualifications regarding a group of thinkers who were as individualistic as they were sophisticated. The various differences are recounted in detail in Martin Jay's standard work, *The Dialectical Imagination: A History of the Frankfurt School and the Institute of Social Research, 1923–1950* (Boston: Little, Brown, 1973).

2. Horkheimer, "Traditional and Critical Theory," in *Critical Theory: Selected Essays*, trans. Matthew J. O'Connell et al. (New York: Herder and Herder, 1972), p. 241.

3. *Dialectic*, p. 6. The work was written in 1944 but not published until 1947. It is critically but sympathetically considered by Jürgen Habermas in "The Entwinement of Myth and Enlightenment: Max Horkheimer and Theodor Adorno," in *The Philosophical Discourse of Modernity: Twelve Lectures*, trans. Frederick Lawrence (Cambridge, Mass.: MIT Press, 1987), pp. 106–130.

4. Cited in Jay, *Dialectical Imagination*, p. 8.

5. Richard Rorty, *Contingency, Irony, Solidarity* (Cambridge: Cambridge University Press, 1989), p. 63.

6. *Dialectic*, p. xiii.

7. Adorno, *Negative Dialectics*, trans. E. B. Ashton (1966; New York: Seabury Press, 1973), p. 3.

8. Plato, *The Republic*, trans. Paul Shorey (Cambridge, Mass.: Harvard University Press, 1935), 7:519e

9. There have been exceptions, of course, e.g., Mandeville and Montesquieu.

10. *Dialectic*, pp. 86, 88, 91.

11. Ibid., pp. 92–93.

12. Ibid., p. 121. The theorist who more than anyone else developed the concept of instrumental rationality was Max Weber, who was also one of its first critics. Although Weber expressed ambivalence about the progressive elimination of different modes of relating to the world—religious, mystical, metaphysical, and heroic—he could no more renounce instrumentalism than he could capitalism, though he might denounce them. Both were extraordinary forms of power, and modernity, whatever else it might mean, was committed to the project of developing power, not abdicating it. See his two classic essays, "Science as Vocation" and "Politics as a Vocation," in *From Max Weber: Essays in Sociology*, ed. Hans Gerth and C. Wright Mills (New York: Oxford University Press, 1946), pp. 77–156; and my essay "Max Weber: Legitimation, Method, and the Politics of Theory," *Political Theory* 9 (1981), 401–424.

13. Parenthetically, although Horkheimer and Adorno did not make the point, it was common for Odysseus to be treated as a symbol of philosophy. See, for example, Thomas More, *Utopia*, bk. i, 11, p. 49; *Complete Works*, vol. 4, ed. Edward Surtz and J. H. Hexter (New Haven, Conn.: Yale University Press, 1965).

14. *Dialectic*, pp. 54, 86, 88, 91.

15. Horkheimer, cited in Jay, *Dialectical Imagination*, p. 253.

16. *Dialectic*, pp. 26–27.

17. For a later restatement of the position see Adorno's Introduction in Theodor W. Adorno et al., *The Positivist Dispute in German Sociology*, ed. Glyn Adey and David Frisby (1969; New York: Harper & Row, 1976), pp. 34–36.

18. *Dialectic*, p. x. The seminal essay on that concept was Friedrich Pollock's "State Capitalism: Its Possibilities and Limitations," in *The Essential Frankfurt School Reader*, ed. Andrew Arato and Eike Gebhardt (New York: Urizen Books, 1978), pp. 71–94.

19. Horkheimer, "The End of Reason," in *Frankfurt School Reader*, p. 34.

20. Ibid., p. 28.

21. Horkheimer, "The Latest Attack on Metaphysics" (1937), in *Critical Theory*, p. 179.

22. Ibid., p. 174.

23. *Dialectic*, p. x.

24. "The Latest Attack on Metaphysics," p. 159.

25. Horkheimer, "Traditional and Critical Theory," pp. 191, 218, and *Eclipse of Reason* (1947; New York: Seabury Press, 1974), p. 8. Substantially the same position was taken later by Adorno, "Sociology and Empirical Research," p. 69. See also Martin Jay, *Marxism and Totality: The Positivist Dispute in German Sociology* (Berkeley: University of California Press, 1984), chap. 8.

26. "Sociology and Empirical Research," p. 68.

27. See Herbert Marcuse, "A Note on Dialectic," in *Frankfurt School Reader*, pp. 444–451.

28. "The Latest Attack on Metaphysics," p. 161.

29. Horkheimer, "On the Problem of Truth" (1935), in *Frankfurt School Reader*, pp. 433–434.

30. Adorno, "The Actuality of Philosophy," *Telos* 31 (1977), 120.

31. Ibid., p. 126.

32. Ibid., p. 129.

33. "The Latest Attack on Metaphysics," p. 162.

34. "Traditional and Critical Theory," p. 221.

35. Adorno's involvement in the Princeton Radio Project headed by Paul Lazarsfeld is described by Martin Jay, *Adorno* (Cambridge, Mass.: Harvard University Press, 1984), p. 34, and by Gillian Rose, *The Melancholy Science: An Introduction to the Thought of Theodor W. Adorno* (New York: Columbia University Press, 1978), pp. 97–98.

36. Horkheimer, "The Latest Attack on Metaphysics," pp. 161–163.

37. Ibid., p. 161.

38. Ibid., pp. 167–168.

39. "Traditional and Critical Theory," p. 215. See Horkheimer's 1968 preface to *Critical Theory*, pp. v–viii, for his rejection of both the proletariat and the student left. In the writings of Marcuse and Habermas the proletariat would have all but disappeared without a trace.

40. "Traditional and Critical Theory," pp. 241, 242.

41. Adorno, *Minima Moralia: Reflections from Damaged Life*, trans. E.F.M. Jephcott (London: New Left Books, 1951), p. 15.

42. For an example of Adorno's lukewarm attitude toward the "political facade" of "late capitalism," see *Minima Moralia*, pp. 112–113.

43. *Minima Moralia*, p. 28.

44. "Traditional and Critical Theory," p. 216.

45. *Minima Moralia*, p. 18; Jay, *Dialectical Imagination*, p. 277.

46. Cited by Jay, *Dialectical Imagination*, p. 79. See also *Negative Dialectics*, p. 144.

47. *Dialectic*, xi–xii.

48. *Negative Dialectics*, p. 3.

49. Ibid., 406–408.

50. *Minima Moralia*, pp. 33–34.

51. *Dialectic*, pp. xi–xii (from the 1969 preface).

52. *Minima Moralia*, pp. 148–151.

53. See John Wallach's fine essay "Socratic Citizenship," *History of Political Thought* 9 (1988), 393–413.

54. *Crito*, 51cff.

55. Plato, *Apology*, 31a.

56. Ibid., 36c.

57. Ibid., 216–22e.

58. *Protagoras*, 324c–d.

CHAPTER 11
Hannah Arendt: Democracy and the Political

1. Cited in Tracy B. Strong, *Friedrich Nietzsche and the Politics of Transfiguration* (Berkeley, 1975), p. 201.

2. See, for example, *Democracy in America*, trans. George Lawrence (Garden City, NY, 1969), p. 15.

3. A. Andrewes, *The Greek Tyrants* (London, 1956).

4. *Democracy in America*, p. 692.

5. *The Origins of Totalitarianism* (New York, 1951), p. 312.

6. Ibid., pp. 310, 308.

7. Ibid., p. 305.

8. *The Origins of Totalitarianism* (New York, 1951), p. 301.

9. Ibid., p. 306.

10. Ibid., pp. 438, 439.

11. See G. Vlastos, "Isonomia," *Classical Philology* 41 (1946), pp. 65–83; J. W. Jones, *The Law and Legal Theory of the Greeks* (Oxford, 1956), pp. 16–23, 84–90; M. M. Austin and P. Vidal-Naquet, *Economic and Social History of Ancient Greece: An Introduction* (Berkeley, 1977), pp. 24–26.

12. *The Human Condition* (Chicago, 1958), pp. 32–33.

13. Ibid., p. 32.

14. *Politics* III.xiii. 1283 b 45.

15. *The Human Condition*, p. 206.

16. Ibid., pp. 213, 215.

17. *The Human Condition*, p. 77.

18. Ibid., p. 46.

19. Ibid., p. 200.

20. *On Revolution*, p. 41.

21. Ibid., p. 33.

22. Ibid., pp. 33, 41–44.

23. Ibid., p. 44.

24. Ibid., p. 63.

25. Ibid., pp. 66, 90.

26. Ibid., pp. 66–67.

27. Ibid., p. 67.

28. *On Revolution*, pp. 241–242.

29. See Hamilton's remarks in *Federalist* 27 *ad finem*.

30. *On Revolution*, p. 258.

31. Cited in ibid., p. 257.

32. Ibid., p. 284. See also *Crises of the Republic*, pp. 231–233.

33. *The Human Condition*, p. 200.

34. *Crises of the Republic*, pp. 212–213.

35. *Critique of Hegel's "Philosophy of Right,"* trans. Joseph O'Malley (Cambridge, 1970), p. 31.

36. *Mythologies*, trans. Annette Lavers (New York, 1972), p. 143.

CHAPTER 12
Hannah Arendt and the Ordinance of Time

1. For a slightly different version, see G. S. Kirk and J. E. Raven, *The Presocratic Philosophers* (Cambridge: Cambridge University Press, 1957), p. 117 (no. 112).

2. Hannah Arendt, "Truth and Politics," in *Philosophy, Politics, and Society*, ed. Peter Laslett and W. G. Runciman, 3rd series (Oxford: Blackwell, 1967), p. 133.

3. Karl Marx and Friedrich Engels, *Manifesto of the Communist Party*, pt. 1.

4. Karl Marx and Friedrich Engels, *The German Ideology*, translated by S. Ryazanskaya (Moscow, 1964), p. 75.

5. Karl Marx, *Capital*, translated by S. Moore and E. Aveling, edited by F. Engels, 3 vols. (New York: International Publishers, 1967), 1: 715.

6. Ibid., 716.

7. Karl Marx, *Critique of Hegel's "Philosophy of Right,"* translated by Annette Jolin and Joseph O'Malley (Cambridge: Cambridge University Press, 1970), p. 140.

8. Max Weber, "Science as a Vocation," in *From Max Weber: Essays in Sociology*, translated by H. H. Gerth and C. Wright Mills (New York: Oxford University Press, 1946), p. 138.

CHAPTER 13
The Liberal/Democratic Divide: On Rawls's *Political Liberalism*

1. Jeremy Waldron, "Justice Revisited: Rawls Turns Towards Political Philosophy," *Times Literary Supplement* (No. 4707), June 18, 1983, 5–6, at 5.

2. I have omitted from the quotation this qualification entered by Rawls: controversy over governmental changes is acceptable when "required by political justice" but not if the changes "tend to favor some parties over others" (*PL*, p. 228).

3. "The higher expectations of those better situated are just if and only if they work as part of a scheme which improves the expectations of the least advantaged members of society" (*TJ*, p. 75).

4. Stuart Hampshire, "Liberalism: The New Twist," *New York Review of Books*, August 12, 1993, 43–47, at 44–45.

5. Ibid., 46.

CHAPTER 14
On the Theory and Practice of Power

1. For a general survey see Nicholas Lobkowicz, *Theory and Practice: History of a Concept from Aristotle to Marx* (Notre Dame: University of Notre Dame Press, 1967).

2. Michel Foucault, Preface to Gilles Deleuze and Felix Guattari, *Anti-Oedipus: Capitalism and Schizophrenia*, trans. Robert Hurley, Mark Seem, and Helen R. Lane (Minneapolis: University of Minnesota Press, 1983), p. xiv.

3. Michel Foucault, *Power/Knowledge: Selected Interviews and Other Writings, 1972–1977*, ed. Colin Gordon, trans. Colin Gordon et al. (New York: Pantheon, 1980), pp. 121, 122. Hereafter cited as *P/K*.

4. Michel Foucault, *The Archaeology of Knowledge*, trans. A. M. Sheridan Smith (New York: Pantheon, 1972), pp. 41–48. Hereafter cited as *AK*.

5. Michel Foucault, *Language, Counter-Memory, Practice: Selected Essays and Interviews*, ed. Donald F. Bouchard, trans. Donald F. Bouchard and Sherry Simon (Ithaca, NY: Cornell University Press, 1977). See especially the essay "Nietzsche, Genealogy, History," pp. 139–164.

6. "Preface" to *Anti-Oedipus*, p. xiv.

7. *Francis Bacon, Selected Writings*, ed. H. G. Dick (New York: Random House, 1955), p. 574.

8. See the discussion in Hubert L. Dreyfus and Paul Rabinow, *Michel Foucault: Beyond Structuralism and Hermeneutics* (Chicago: University of Chicago Press, 1982), pp. 197ff. See also Foucault's ambiguous remarks about the relationship between the Panopticon formation and the emergence of social science in *Discipline and Punish: The Birth of the Prison*, trans. A. M. Sheridan Smith (New York: Pantheon, 1977), p. 305.

9. Although Foucault attended to economics in *The Archaeology of Knowledge*, he was wholly concerned with the emergence of political economy as a mode of discourse, not as an element in a power/knowledge formation. In the *Archaeology* there is a glaring gap between genealogy and power.

10. Plato, *Republic*, trans. Paul Shorey (London: Heinemann, 1930–1935), 473A. Hereafter cited as *Republic*.

11. On this point see F. W. Albright, *Yahweh and the Gods of Canaan* (London: Athlone, 1968).

12. Michel Foucault, *History of Sexuality*, trans. Robert Hurley (New York: Pantheon, 1978), 1:93. Hereafter cited as *Sexuality*.

CHAPTER 15
Democracy in the Discourse of Postmodernism

1. C. B. Macpherson, *The Political Theory of Possessive Individualism: Hobbes to Locke* (Oxford: Oxford University Press, 1962), pp. 1, 2.

2. Richard Rorty, *Contingency, Irony, Solidarity* (Cambridge: Cambridge University Press, 1989), p. xiii.

3. Ibid., p. 47.

4. Jean-François Lyotard, *The Post-Modern Condition: A Report on Knowledge*, tr. G. Bennington and B. Massumi (Minneapolis: University of Minnesota Press, 1984), p. 5.

5. Rorty, *Contingency*, pp. 87–88.

6. Ibid., p. 47.

7. Richard Rorty, "Postmodernist Bourgeois Liberalism," in *Hermeneutics and Praxis*, ed. Robert Hollinger (Notre Dame: University of Notre Dame Press, 1985), p. 214.

8. Ibid., p. 219.

9. Rorty, *Contingency*, pp. 59–60.

10. It is not clear how this squares with Rorty's peroration to an always more inclusive witness. See *Contingency*, pp. 192 ff.

11. Sheldon Wolin, "On the Theory and Practice of Power," in *After Foucault*, ed. Jonathan Arac (New Brunswick, NJ: Rutgers University Press, 1988), pp. 179–201.

12. Rorty, *Contingency*, p. 44.

13. Jürgen Habermas, *The Philosophical Discourse of Modernity*, tr. Frederick Lawrence (Cambridge, Mass.: MIT Press, 1987), pp. 108–130.

14. Henry F. May, *The Enlightenment in America* (Oxford: Oxford University Press, 1976), pp. 358–360.

15. Rorty, *Contingency*, p. 68.

16. For Rorty's comments on technology and his plea for a genealogy that goes back to Bacon rather than to Descartes, see "Habermas and Lyotard on Postmodernity," in *Habermas and Modernity*, ed. Richard J. Bernstein (Cambridge, Mass.: MIT Press, 1985), pp. 170–171.

17. Rorty, *Contingency*, p. 82.

18. Ibid., p. 87.

19. Lyotard, *Post-Modern Condition*, p. 16.

20. Rorty gives the impression that until Hegel and Nietzsche showed that truth was a human creation, most theorists believed that truth was found rather than made. But that interpretation relies too heavily on the German canon, which mostly ignored the *verum factum* tradition represented by Hobbes and Vico.

21. See further Jürgen Habermas, "Modernity versus Post-Modernity," *New German Critique* 22 (1981): 3–22.

22. Richard Rorty, "Priority of Democracy to Philosophy," in *The Virginia Statute of Religious Freedom: Its Evaluation and Consequences in American History*, ed. Merrill D. Peterson and Robert C. Vaughan (Cambridge: Cambridge University Press, 1988), p. 259.

23. Rorty, *Contingency*, p. 3.

24. Ibid., p. 52.

25. Ibid., pp. 53–54.

26. Ibid., p. 60.

27. Ibid., p. 8.

28. Ibid., p. 6.

29. Ibid., p. 12.

30. Ibid., p. 44, 31.

31. Ibid., p. 45.

32. Ibid., p. xiv.

33. Ibid., p. xv.

34. Ibid., p. 55.

35. Ibid., p. 68.

36. Ibid., p. 63.

37. Rorty, "Postmodernist Bourgeois Liberalism," p. 217.

38. Rorty, *Contingency*, p. 191.

39. Ibid., pp. 34–35.

40. Ibid., pp. 35–39.

41. Rorty, "Priority of Democracy," p. 270. Rorty's reference to Rieff is in *Contingency*, p. 36.

42. Rorty, "Priority of Democracy," p. 269; italics in original.

43. Rorty, *Contingency*, pp. 60–61.

44. Ibid., p. 61.

45. Ibid., pp. 21, 41.

46. *Thus Spoke Zarathustra*, tr. R. J. Hollingdale (Baltimore: Penguin Books, 1961, Prologue 5, p. 46. I have altered Hollingdale's translation of *der letzte Mensch*. There are several suggestive similarities between Rorty's ideas and those of Allan Bloom. Both identify with "high culture," both understand the world almost entirely in terms of books (and Great Ones, above all); both are much concerned with constructing their own intellectual genealogies; both are indebted to Nietzsche and Heidegger; both believe that society owes intellectuals a living; both are critical of modern science and enamored of "literature"; and while both offer "criticisms" of contemporary politics, both are fundamentally complacent and accepting. For a more extended treatment of Bloom, see my *The Presence of the Past* (Baltimore: Johns Hopkins University Press, 1989), pp. 47–65.

CHAPTER 16

Postmodern Politics and the Absence of Myth

1. Marcel Detienne, "Rethinking Mythology," in *Between Belief and Transgression*, ed. Michel Izard and Pierre Smith, tr. J. Leavitt (Chicago: University of Chicago Press, 1982), pp. 43 ff.

2. D. G. Charlton, *Positivist Thought in France During the Second Empire, 1852–1870* (Oxford: Clarendon Press, 1959,), ch. 3. John Stuart Mill's *Auguste Comte and Positivism* is still worth reading. See also the thoughtful discussion by Leszek Kolakowski, *Positivist Philosophy from Hume to the Vienna Circle* (Harmondsworth, UK: Penguin, n.d.), pp. 60 ff.

3. Auguste Comte, *Cours de philosophic positive*, in *Auguste Comte and Positivism: The Essential Writings*, ed. Gertrud Lenzer (New York: Harper & Row, 1975), p. 72.

4. S. H. Hooke, *Middle Eastern Mythology* (Harmondsworth, UK: Penguin, 1963), p. 11.

5. Max Weber, "Science as a Vocation," in *From Max Weber*, ed. Hans Gerth and C. Wright Mills (New York: Oxford University Press, 1946), p. 155.

6. Ibid., pp. 148, 149.

7. "Polyarchy" is a technical term used in contemporary political science to describe a pluralistic political society. See R. Dahl, *Polyarchy: Participation and Opposition* (New Haven, Conn.: Yale University Press, 1971).

8. Max Weber, "Politik als Beruf," in *Gesammelte politische Schriften*, ed. J. Winckelmann, 2d ed. (Tübingen: Mohr, 1958), p. 493.

9. Aristotle, *Politics* 1252 a 3–6, *Nicomachean Ethics* 1094 a27–1094 b8.

10. Weber, *Gesammelte politische Schriften*, pp. 493–494; Max Weber, *The Theory of Social and Economic Organizations*, tr. A. M. Henderson and Talcott Parsons (New York: Oxford University Press, 1947), p. 155.

11. Max Weber, "Politics as a Vocation," in *From Max Weber*, p. 78. The parentheses are Weber's.

12. Ibid., pp. 78, 121.

13. The basic text of modern republicanism in this connection is Machiavelli's *Discorsi*, bk. 3, ch. 1, where he writes of the importance of republics returning to their original animating principle.

14. The crucial text here is *The Federalist*, no. 15, where Jay contrasts the "wise, systematic and judicious" national government with the parochial, vain, and excitable state governments. See the edition by Jacob E. Cooke (Middletown, Conn.: Wesleyan University Press, 1961), pp. 16 ff.

15. The fundamental text is that of the fifteenth-century English jurist, Sir John Fortescue, *De Laudibus Legum Anglie*, ed. S. B. Chrimes (Cambridge: Cambridge University Press, 1949), chap. 13. See also Ernst H. Kantorowicz, *The King's Two Bodies* (Princeton, NJ: Princeton University Press, 1957), pp. 223 ff.

16. For a general review of the subject, see the article by O. Eissfeldt in *The Old Testament and Modern Study*, ed. H. H. Rowley (Oxford: Oxford University Press, 1951), pp. 115–161.

17. Hooke, *Middle Eastern Mythology*, p. 12.

18. Herodotus, *The Histories*, tr. Aubrey de Selincourt, rev. A. R. Burn (Harmondsworth, UK: Penguin, 1972), p. 50.

19. The classic starting point remains Fustel de Coulanges's *La Cité antique* (1864).

20. A representative example of this mode of theory is Karl Deutsch, *The Nerves of Government* (London: Free Press, 1963).

21. A formal account can be found in Aristotle's *Metaphysics* IX.1.1046a 7. See also Thomas Aquinas, *Summa Theologiae*, 1A, Qu 25 art 1.

22. Thomas Hobbes, *Leviathan*, ed. C. B. Macpherson (Harmondsworth, UK: Penguin, 1968), p. 81.

23. Ibid.

24. Thomas Hobbes, *English Works*, ed. Sir William Molesworth, 11 vols. (London: Bohn, 1839–45), 6: 251.

25. Hobbes, *Leviathan*, p. 227.

26. Ibid.

27. Ibid., pp. 170, 172, 173.

28. Karl Marx, *A Contribution to the Critique of Hegel's Philosophy of Right*, tr. Joseph O'Malley (Cambridge: Cambridge University Press, 1970), p. 124.

29. Ludwig Feuerbach, *Kleine Schriften*, ed. K. Löwith (Frankfurt: Suhrkamp, 1966), p. 124.

30. Hobbes, *Leviathan*, pp. 160, 161.

CHAPTER 17

The Destructive Sixties and Postmodern Conservatism

1. *New York Times*, November 10, 1994, pp. A1, B3; January 21, 1995, p. 8.

2. Headlines from story by Peter Applebome, *New York Times*, May 7, 1995. pp. A1, 18.

3. " 'New is always better?,' plaintively asked Representative Henry Hyde, a traditional conservative Republican. 'What in the world is conservative about that? Have we nothing to learn from the past? Tradition, history, institutional memory—don't they count anymore?' " *New York Times*, April 11, 1995. p. C22.

4. For examples of this earlier conservatism see Russell Kirk, *The Conservative Mind* (1953); William F. Buckley, Jr., *God and Man at Yale* (1951). There were of course other conservative intellectuals, including self-consciously tough-minded theorists, such as Wilmoore Kendall and James Burnham. But note the terms used by the self-styled neo-Machiavellian Burnham in his criticism of Arthur Schlesinger Jr.'s liberalism: the "liberal emphasis on continuous change, on methods rather than results, on striving and doing rather than sitting and enjoying." Cited in John R. Diggins, *Up from Communism: Conservative Odysseys in American Intellectual History* (1975), p. 419. For a recent thoughtful account of changing emphases in liberal and conservative thinking, see Wilson Carey McWilliams, "Ambiguities and Ironies: Conservatism and Liberalism in the American Political Tradition," in *Moral Values in Liberalism and Conservatism*, ed. W. Lawson Taitte (1995).

5. Such as Todd Gitlin, *Years of Hope, Days of Rage* (1987); Kirkpatrick Sale, *SDS* (1974).

6. Linda Gray, who played the long-suffering wife of J. R. Ewing on "Dallas," also appeared on the program described above.

7. For a discussion of the problem in Nietzsche, the modern father of perspectivism, see Alexander Nehamas, *Nietzsche: Life as Literature* (1985) and Arthur Danto, *Nietzsche as Philosopher* (1965), p. 68ff.

8. Curiously, one bridge between the older conservatism and the new is the Nietzschean element in the Straussian persuasion. It is best represented by Harvey Mansfield, Jr., *Taming the Prince: The Ambivalence of Modern Executive Power* (1989).

9. This is described, with malice toward many, by Richard Sennett, "Back to Class Warfare," *New York Times*, December 27, 1994, p. A15.

10. See Herbert Marcuse, *An Essay on Liberation* (1969).

11. Sheldon S. Wolin and John H. Schaar, *The Berkeley Rebellion and Beyond: Essays on Politics and Education in the Technological Society* (1970).

12. For documents illustrative of these positions in their early stages see *The Berkeley Student Rebellion*, ed. Sheldon S. Wolin and S. Martin Lipset (1965).

13. In the background were the events of the early fifties, when a loyalty oath was imposed on the faculty and several nonsigners were fired.

14. "Administration" here and elsewhere refers to the local or campus administration as distinct from the overall university-wide administration that governed all nine campuses.

15. The regents were political appointees chosen for their wealth and/or political connections. The state constitution provided that the governor, lieutenant governor, and speaker of the assembly would automatically serve as regents.

16. Muscatine Report, *Education at Berkeley*, March 1966; *The Culture of the University Governance and Education*, 1968.

17. The structure of faculty governance was altered again in the late eighties. The reforms further diminished the role of the senate and essentially converted faculty governance into an administrative function rather than a collective deliberation. See

University of California Manual: Berkeley Division of the Academic Senate, November 1992.

18. A good example is *The Radical Right*, ed. Daniel Bell (rev. ed. *The New American Right*) (1971 [1963]).

19. For example, Robert A. Nisbet, *The Quest for Community* (1953); John H. Schaar, *Escape from Authority* (1961); Richard Sennett, *Authority* (1980).

CHAPTER 18
From Progress to Modernization: The Conservative Turn

1. Letter from Jefferson to John Adams, *Works of John Adams*, ed. C. F. Adams (Boston: Little, Brown, 1851) 10:223.

2. *A National Agenda for the Eighties* (Washington, DC: Government Printing Office, 1980), pp. 1, 5, 66, 69.

3. *New York Times*, June 12, 1983.

4. Antoine-Nicolas de Condorcet, *Sketch for a Historical Picture of the Progress of the Human Mind*, tr. Jane Barraclough (London: Weidenfeld, 1955), p. 4.

5. "An Essay on the First Principles of Government," *Writings on Philosophy, Science, and Politics*, ed. J. Passmore (New York: Collier Books, 1965), p. 198.

6. *Du control social*, ed. C. E. Vaughan (Manchester: University of Manchester Press, 1947), pp. 12–13.

7. *Two Treatises of Government*, 2nd ed., ed. Peter Laslett (Cambridge: Cambridge University Press, 1967), p. 349.

CHAPTER 20
What Revolutionary Action Means Today

1. Elihu Root, *Addresses on Government and Citizenship* (Cambridge, Mass.: Harvard University Press, 1916), p. 59.

2. John Locke, *Two Treatises of Government*, II.220.

CHAPTER 21
The People's Two Bodies

1. *The Federalist*, ed. Jacob E. Cooke (Middletown, Conn.: Wesleyan University Press, 1961), no. 22, p. 64.

2. Ibid., p. 146.

3. Ibid., no. 27, p. 174.

4. Ibid., p. 173.

5. "Report on Manufactures," in *Papers on Public Credit, Commerce and Finance by Alexander Hamilton*, ed. Samuel McKee, Jr. (New York: Columbia University Press, 1934), p. 195.

6. Ibid., p. 196.

7. *The Papers of Alexander Hamilton*, ed. H. S. Syrett, 26 vols. (New York: Columbia University Press, 1961–1979), vol. 10, p. 291.

8. See Hamilton's discussion in *Papers on Public Credit*, ed. McKee, pp. 227, 231.

9. "Report on a National Bank," in *Papers of Alexander Hamilton*, ed. Syrett, vol. 7, pp. 305 ff.

10. *The Federalist*, no. 13, p. 81.

11. Ibid.

12. *The Anti-Federalists*, ed. Cecilia M. Kenyon (Indianapolis: Bobbs-Merrill, 1966), p. 7.

13. *The Federalist*, no. 10, p. 64.

14. Ibid., pp. 61–62.

15. Ibid., no. 9, pp. 52–53.

16. Ibid., no. 12, p. 73.

17. Reported in *New York Times*, August 3, 1980, L–22.

18. Lyndon B. Johnson, *The Vantage Point* (New York: Popular Library, 1971), p. 276.

19. *The Complete Writings of Thomas Paine*, ed. Philip Foner (New York: The Citadel Press, 1945), vol. 1, p. 6.

20. *President's Report on Administrative Management*, Washington, DC, 1937.

21. *Business Week*, June 30, 1980, pp. 4, 5, 27.

22. Speech of July 15, 1979.

23. *New York Times*, August 18, 1980.

CHAPTER 22

The New Public Philosophy

1. Speech to joint session of Congress, April 28, 1981.

2. Dennis C. Mueller, *Public Choice* (New York: Cambridge University Press, 1979), p. 1.

3. Lester Thurow, *The Zero-Sum Society* (New York: Basic Books, 1980), p. 105.

4. *New York Times*, March 16, 1979.

5. For a discussion see *Cost-Benefit Analysis*, ed. R. Layard (Harmondsworth, UK: Penguin Books, 1976), p. 429 ff.

6. Paul Samuelson, *Collected Scientific Papers*, ed. J. E. Stiglitz (Cambridge, Mass.: MIT Press, 1966), vol. 2, p. 1752.

7. Adam Smith, *An Inquiry into the Nature and Causes of the Wealth of Nations*, ed. W. B. Todd (Oxford: Oxford University Press, 1976), vol. 1, p. 10.

8. Ibid., vol. 2, p. 687.

9. Ibid., p. 456.

10. Ibid., vol. 1, p. 27.

11. Thurow, *Zero-Sum Society*, p. 120.

12. Mueller, *Public Choice*, p. 1.

13. Charles L. Schultze, *The Public Use of Private Interest* (Washington, DC: Brookings Institution, 1977), p. 18.

14. Lionel Robbins, *The Theory of Economic Policy in Classical Economics* (London: Macmillan, 1952), p. 177.

15. *Economics of Welfare*, 3rd ed. (London: Macmillan, 1929), p. 21.

16. Thurow, *Zero-Sum Society*, p. 115.

17. Ibid., p. 11.

18. Ibid., p. 66.

19. Ibid., p. 195.

20. Ibid., p. 200.

21. Smith, *Wealth of Nations*, vol. 2, p. 456.

22. Thurow, *Zero-Sum Society*, p. 16.

CHAPTER 23
Democracy, Difference, and Re-Cognition

1. Henry Thoreau, *Walden* (New York, Modern Library ed.), 99.

2. I have discussed the theory of pluralism in greater detail in "The American Pluralist Conception of Politics," in *Ethics in Hard Times*, edited by Arthur L. Caplan and Daniel Callahan (New York: Plenum, 1981), 217–259.

3. *The Sociology of Georg Simmel*, edited and translated by Kurt Wolff (New York: Free Press, 1950), 31.

4. See "E Pluribus Unum: The Representation of Difference and the Reconstitution of Collectivity," in my *The Presence of the Past: Essays on the State and the Constitution* (Baltimore: Johns Hopkins University Press, 1989), chap. 7. Bentley's attitude toward democracy is represented in *The Process of Government* (Evanston, IL: Principia Press, 1908, 1949), 454–455.

5. I adopt the phrase from Robert Dahl, *Dilemmas of Pluralist Democracy* (New Haven, Conn.: Yale University Press, 1982). See also his *Democracy in the United States*, 4th ed. (New York: Houghton Mifflin, 1981).

6. *A Letter Concerning Toleration*, 154–155; this version is appended to J. W. Gough's edition of Locke's *Second Treatise of Civil Government* (Oxford: Blackwell, 1948).

7. *Puritanism and Liberty*, edited by A.S.P. Woodhouse (London: Dent, 1938), 53.

8. This was starkly evident in the debates over taxation and how slaves and workers were to be counted when the Articles of Confederation were being drafted. See the arguments preserved in *Jefferson's Autobiography*, in *Jefferson: Writings*, edited by Merrill D. Peterson (New York: Library of America, 1984), 25–31.

9. *The Sociology of Georg Simmel*, 30.

10. *Leviathan*, chap. 10.

11. Exemplary of premodern understandings of difference are Sir Thomas Elyot, *The Book Named the Governor*, edited by S. E. Lehmberg (New York: Dutton, 1962, Everyman ed.), bk. I, 1:1–2; Sir Thomas Smith, *De Republica Anglorum*, edited by L. Alston (Cambridge: Cambridge University Press, 1906), lib. I, chaps. 15–24. For a wealth of further illustrations, sec E.M.W. Tillyard, *The Elizabethan World Picture* (New York: Random House, 1961).

12. In Locke's formula, "no man can, by agreement, pass over to another that which he hath not himself, a Power over his own life." *Two Treatises of Government* II.24, edited by Peter Laslett (Cambridge: Cambridge University Press, 1963).

13. See "Contract and Birthright," in my *Presence of the Past*, 137–150.

14. "The Great Wall and the Tower of Babel," in *Parables and Paradoxes* (New York: Schocken, 1961), 25. My thanks to Judith Butler for suggesting that I look at this volume.

15. Simmel, 30.

16. See the commentaries collected in *Bereishis/Genesis*, translated by Meir Zlotowitz (Brooklyn, NY: Mesorah Publications, 1980), 332–333.

17. I have used the translation issued by the Jewish Publication Society of America, *The Torah: The Five Books of Moses*, 2d ed. (Philadelphia, 1962).

18. Recall how Adam's dominion was expressed in the act of giving "names" to the various creatures and to Eve (Genesis 2:19–20, 3:20).

19. A commentator from an older generation has quaintly explained, "Yahweh must draw near, not because he is nearsighted, but because he dwells at such tremendous height and their work is so tiny" (Otto Proksch, *Die Genesis*, cited in Gerhard von Rad, *Genesis: A Commentary*, translated by John Marks [Philadelphia, 1961], 145).

20. Locke's use of the Babel story is striking. He identifies the institution of absolute monarchy with God's rule so that the apologists for absolutism are accused of advocating an institution that can only sow "confusion" in society. This negative interpretation is then complemented by a positive account of the work of the men of Shinar. Most commentators view their actions as exemplifying human pride, but Locke claimed that the construction of the Tower "was not by the Command of one Monarch, but by the Consultation of many, a Free People" (I.143, 146).

21. See James I's *The Trew Law of Free Monarchies*, in *The Political Works of James I*, edited by Charles H. McIlwain (New York: Russell & Russell, 1965, 1918), 53–70; John Neville Figgis, *The Divine Right of Kings*, 2d ed. (Cambridge: Cambridge University Press, 1934), chap. 7; and more recently, Stephen L. Collins, *From Divine Cosmos to Sovereign State* (New York: Oxford University Press, 1989).

22. It has been pointed out that Herodotus does not actually use the word *demokratia* but rather *isonomia* or equality. The passage in question makes it clear, however, that Herodotus had democracy in mind. See T. S. Sinclair, *A History of Greek Political Thought* (London, 1951), 37.

23. The latter he declares to be the most learned people in the world and the source not only of Greek mathematics but also of many elements of Greek religion. He announces on numerous occasions that he has chosen to rely on the accounts of Egyptians, deeming them more trustworthy than traditional Greek sources. *The Histories*, 1.1; 11.50–52, 77, 99.

24. See Virginia Hunter, *Past and Process in Herodotus and Thucydides* (Princeton, NJ: Princeton University Press, 1982), 50ff.

25. Judith Shklar, *American Citizenship: The Quest for Inclusion*, (Cambridge, Mass.: Harvard University Press, 1991).

26. The metaphor figured prominently in medieval and early modern theories of church membership, of guilds, of the family, and of corporate bodies. The theoretical language employed by theologians, jurists, and political theorists of those eras was highly responsive to diversities, but it was equally concerned to emphasize that hierarchies of authority and social inequalities were inherent in organized social life. The recognition of difference was dependent on and qualified by a mandatory system of religious beliefs and membership in the Church Universal. The classic work is Otto von Gierke's *Das Deutsche Genossenschaftsrecht*, 3 vols., 1868–1881. For a recent survey, see Anthony Black, *Guilds and Civil Society* (Methuen, 1984). Black has also edited much of the first volume of Gierke's work: Otto von Gierke, *Community in Historical Perspective*, translated by Mary Fischer (Cambridge: Cambridge University Press, 1990).

27. Jean-Jacques Rousseau, *Le control social*, I.vi:33 in *Political Writings*, edited by C. E. Vaughan, 2 vols. (Oxford: Blackwell, 1915, 1962).

28. *De la démocratie en Amérique: Oeuvres complétes*, edited by J.-P Mayer, 1961–, vol. 1(2), 314 n. 3.

29. Ibid., 1(2), 301 n. 1.

30. Ibid., 1(2), 108.

CHAPTER 24
Constitutional Order, Revolutionary Violence, and Modern Power: An Essay of Juxtapositions

1. Flora Lewis, "The Legacy of Revolution," *New York Times*, January 29, 1989, E-23.

2. Flora Lewis, "The Return of History," *New York Times*, November 11, 1989, A-23.

3. Mieczyslaw Rakowski, as cited by Timothy Garton Ash, "Reform or Revolution?" *New York Review of Books*, October 27, 1988, pp. 47–56, at p. 47.

4. *Souvenirs, Oeuvres Completes*, Vol. XII, ed. Luc Monnier, p. 30.

5. *Birth of the Communist Manifesto*, ed. Dirk J. Struik (New York: International Publishing Co., 1971), pp. 92, 94.

6. See in this connection my "On Reading Marx Politically," *Nomos*, Vol. XXVI (1983), pp. 79–112.

7. John Locke, *Two Treatises of Government*, ed. Peter Laslett (Cambridge: Cambridge University Press, 1960).

8. *Two Treatises*, II. 132, p. 399.

9. *Two Treatises*, II. 134, p. 402.

10. "Thomas Hobbes, *Leviathan*, ed. C. B. MacPherson (Harmondsworth, UK: Penguin, 1968), Ch. 30, p. 387.

11. Cited in Karen I. Vaughn, *John Locke, Economist and Social Scientist* (Chicago: University of Chicago Press, 1980), p. 160, n. 68.

12. *Two Treatises*, II.42, pp. 339–340. See Vaughn, *John Locke, Economist and Social Scientist*, p. 46 ff. Also the references to Locke's *De Arte Medica* in *The Educational Writings of John Locke*, ed. James L. Axtell (Cambridge: Cambridge University Press, 1968), pp. 72–73; and also Axtell's discussion of "Locke and Scientific Education," p. 69 ff.

13. *Two Treatises of Government*, II. 42, p. 340.

14. *Two Treatises*, II. 158. See my discussion in *Presence of the Past*, p. 166 ff. For examples of its use during the civil wars see *Puritanism and Liberty*, ed. A.S.P. Woodhouse (London: Dent, 1938), pp. 24, 108–109, 121–122, 202, 211, 329.

15. *Two Treatises*, II. 171, pp. 428–429.

16. *Two Treatises*, II. 190, p. 441.

17. *Two Treatises*, II. 6, p. 311.

18. *Two Treatises*, II. 27, pp. 328–329.

19. Lewis, "The Return of History," January 29, 1989.

20. *Two Treatises*, II, 134, p. 401. II. 212, p. 455.

21. *The Federalist*, ed. Jacob Cooke (Middletown, Conn.: Wesleyan University Press, 1961), No. 17, pp. 106–107.

22. *Federalist*, No. 10, pp 51ff. For a sympathetic treatment of Madison that emphasizes the consistency of his thinking, especially on the issue of centralization, see Lance Banning, "The Practicable Sphere of a Republic: James Madison, the Constitutional Convention and the Emergence of Federalism," *Beyond Confederation: Origins of Constitution and American National Identity*, ed. Boeman S. Sotem and E. C. Carter (Chapel Hill: University of North Carolina Press, 1987), pp. 162–187.

23. Leo Gershoy, *The French Revolution and Napoleon* (New York: Crofts, 1946), pp. 146–147.

24. *Federalist*, No. 48, p. 335 quoting from Jefferson's *Notes on Virginia*.

25. Cited in C. B. Macpherson, *The Political Theory of Possessive Individualism* (Oxford: Clarendon Press, 1962), p. 207. The notes date from 1674.

26. *Federalist*, No. 49, pp. 340–341. The reference to Jefferson is on p. 338.

27. *The Political Works of James Harrington*, ed. J.G.A. Pocock (Cambridge: Cambridge University Press, 1977), p. 159.

CHAPTER 25
Agitated Times

1. In recent years the concept of time and its relationship to politics has received increasing attention. See William E. Connolly, *Neuropolitics: Thinking, Culture, Speed* (Minneapolis: University of Minnesota Press, 2002); William E. Scheuerman, *Liberal Democracy and the Social Acceleration of Time* (Baltimore: Johns Hopkins University Press, 2004); and my article, "What Time Is It?," *Theory and Event* 1:1 (1997), http://muse.jhu.edu/journals/theory_and_event/toc/archive.html#1.1.

2. This notion of "public" is indebted to John Dewey's *The Public and Its Problems: An Essay in Political Inquiry* [1927] (New York: Holt, 1946). See my discussion of Dewey in *Politics and Vision: Continuity and Innovation in Western Political Thought*, rev. edn. (Princeton, NJ: Princeton University Press, 2004), p.503ff.

3. See Christopher Hill, *The World Turned Upside Down: Radical Ideas During the English Revolution* (Harmondsworth, UK: Penguin, 1972), Chapter 4; Joseph Frank, *The Levellers* (Cambridge, Mass.: Harvard University Press, 1955), pp. 119–120.

4. Alexis de Tocqueville's *The Old Regime and the French Revolution* is the classic account of a revolution with a long past. See my *Tocqueville between Two Worlds* (Princeton, NJ: Princeton University Press, 2001), Chapters XXIV–XXV.

5. See Max Weber, *Economy and Society*, ed. Guenther Roth and Claus Wittich, 3 vols. (New York: Bedminster Press, 1968), pp. 217–226, 125–130, and 956–958; H. H. Gerth and C. Wright Mills, eds., *From Max Weber: Essays in Sociology* (New York: Oxford University Press, 1946), p.196ff.

6. See Weber's discussion in *From Max Weber*, pp. 204–209, 214–216, 241–246.

7. Max Weber, "Politics as a Vocation," *From Max Weber*, p.95.

8. Max Weber, *From Max Weber*, pp. 83–89, 102–103, and 209ff. During the 1930s in the United States when trade unions sought to organize strikes—only to find Communists attempting to inject a "revolutionary" element—union leaders described the Communists as "outside agitators."

9. Max Weber, "Politics as a Vocation," p. 128.

10. Max Weber, "Science as a Vocation," pp.137 and 125–128.

11. See the discussion in Wolfgang J. Mommsen, *Max Weber and German Politics, 1890–1920*, trans. Michael S. Steinberg (Chicago: University of Chicago Press, 1984), pp.184ff and 397.

12. What could be more agitated than what takes place on the floor of a stock exchange?

13. One of the most revealing statements of the Bush administration's global ideology is to be found in an official document, *The National Security Strategy of the United States* (2002), http://www.whitehouse.gov/nsc/nss.html.

SOURCES

PART ONE: THE POLITICAL AND THEORETICAL

Chapter 1 "Political Theory as a Vocation." *American Political Science Review* 63, no. 4 (Dec. 1969).

Chapter 2 "Political Theory: From Vocation to Invocation." In Jason Frank and John Tambornino, eds., *Vocations of Political Theory* (Minneapolis: University of Minnesota Press, 2000).

PART TWO: HISTORICAL

Ancient and Modern Democracy

Chapter 3 "Transgression, Equality, and Voice." In Josiah Ober and Charles Hedrick, eds., *Dēmokratia: A Conversation on Democracies, Ancient and Modern* (Princeton, NJ: Princeton University Press, 1996).

Chapter 4 "Norm and Form: The Constitutionalizing of Democracy." In J. Peter Euben, John R. Wallach, and Josiah Ober, eds., *Athenian Political Thought and the Reconstruction of American Democracy* (Ithaca, NY: Cornell University Press, 1994).

Chapter 5 "Fugitive Democracy." *Constellations* 1, no. 1 (1994).

Hobbes

Chapter 6 "Hobbes and the Epic Tradition of Political Theory." William Andrews Clark Memorial Library, University of California, Los Angeles, 1970.

Chapter 7 "Hobbes and the Culture of Despotism." In Mary G. Dietz, ed., *Thomas Hobbes and Political Theory* (Lawrence: University Press of Kansas, 1990). Used with permission of University Press of Kansas.

Modern Theorists

Chapter 8 "On Reading Marx Politically." In J. Roland Pennock and John W. Chapman, eds., *Marxism: Nomos XXVI* (New York: New York University Press, 1983). © NYU Press.

Chapter 9 "Max Weber: Legitimation, Method, and the Politics of Theory." *Political Theory* 9, no. 3 (Aug. 1991).

PART THREE: RECENT THEORISTS

Chapter 10 "Reason in Exile: Critical Theory and Technological Society." In Arthur M. Melzer, Jerry Weinberger, and M. Richard Zinman, eds., *Technology in the Western Political Tradition* (Ithaca, NY: Cornell University Press, 1993).

Chapter 11 "Hannah Arendt: Democracy and the Political." In Lewis P. Hinchman and Sandra K. Hinchman, eds., *Hannah Arendt: Critical Essays* (Albany: State University of New York Press, 1994). Originally published in *Salmagundi*.

Chapter 12 "Hannah Arendt and the Ordinance of Time." *Social Research* 44, no. 1 (Spring 1977).

Chapter 13 "The Liberal/Democratic Divide: On Rawls's Political Liberalism." *Political Theory* 24, no. 1 (Feb. 1996).

PART FOUR: POSTMODERNS

Chapter 14 "On the Theory and Practice of Power." In Jonathan Arac, ed., *After Foucault: Humanistic Knowledge, Postmodern Challenges* (New Brunswick, NJ: Rutgers University Press, 1988). Copyright © 1988 by Rutgers, the State University. Reprinted by permission of Rutgers University Press.

Chapter 15 "Democracy in the Discourse of Postmodernism." *Social Research* 57, no. 1 (Spring 1990).

Chapter 16 "Postmodern Politics and the Absence of Myth." *Social Research* 52, no. 2 (Summer 1985).

Chapter 17 "The Destructive Sixties and Postmodern Conservatism." In Stephen Macedo, ed., *Reassessing the Sixties: Debating the Political and Cultural Legacy* (New York: Norton, 1997).

Chapter 18 "From Progress to Modernization: The Conservative Turn." *democracy* 3, no. 4 (Fall 1983).

PART FIVE: REVISIONING DEMOCRACY

Chapter 19 "Editorial." *democracy* 3, no. 4 (Fall 1983).

Chapter 20 "What Revolutionary Action Means Today." *democracy* 2, no. 4 (Fall 1982).

Chapter 21 "The People's Two Bodies." *democracy* 1, no. 1 (Jan. 1980).

Chapter 22 "The New Public Philosophy." *democracy* 1, no. 4 (Oct. 1981).

Chapter 23 "Democracy, Difference, and Re-Cognition." *Political Theory* 21, no. 3 (Aug. 1993).

Chapter 24 "Constitutional Order, Revolutionary Violence and Modern Power: An Essay of Juxtapositions." Department of Political Science, York University, Occasional Papers 1 (1990).

Chapter 25 "Agitated Times." *parallax* 11, no. 4 (2005). http://www.tandfonline.com/doi/abs/10.1080/13534640500331633.

INDEX